David Horner, AM, FASSA, is an emeritus professor in the Strategic and Defence Studies Centre, Australian National University, where he was Professor of Australia Defence History for fifteen years. A graduate of the Royal Military College, Duntroon, he served as an infantry platoon commander in the Vietnam War and later, as a colonel, was head of the Australian Army's Land Warfare Studies Centre.

He is the author or editor of 37 books on Australian military history, defence and intelligence. As the Official Historian of Australian Peacekeeping, Humanitarian and Post-Cold War Operations, he was General Editor of the six-volume series. He was also the Official Historian of the Australian Security Intelligence Organisation, the first volume of which, *The Spy Catchers*, was joint winner of the Prime Minister's Literary Award for history, and the UK Intelligence Book of the Year.

*

'Australia's premier historian of war politics and strategy explains how Australia has found itself at war so often in its first century as a nation. Drawing on a lifetime's understanding of the inside story of decisions made behind closed doors, David Horner expertly reveals how decisions for war have been made. This is essential reading for anyone who wants to understand why Australia has made that decision—over and over again.'

Professor Peter Stanley, UNSW Canberra

'To take the nation to war, apply lethal force in the name of the national interest, values, alliances and security is the hardest, most painful decision of all. Advice is offered by many, but the burden of responsibility is carried by one—the Prime Minister. The price of that judgement is borne in the quiet suffering and inconsolable grief of family homes. *The War Game* is compelling. This is not a game.'

Dr Brendan Nelson AO, President Boeing Australia, New Zealand and South Pacific, and a former Minister for Defence

'This is a book of lessons for Australian political leaders on managing wars. An analysis of actual performance against those lessons is humbling. The book's value lies in its being readily accessible with cautious recommendations.'

The Honourable Kim Beazley AC, Governor of Western Australia, and a former Minister for Defence

'A masterful study of Australian war leadership, by Australia's preeminent military historian.'

Professor Emerita Joan Beaumont, author of *Broken Nation*

Other books by David Horner

Crisis of Command (1978)
New Directions in Strategic Thinking (co-edited) (1981)
Australian Defence Policy for the 1980s (co-edited) (1982)
High Command (1982)
The Commanders (1984)
Australian Higher Command in the Vietnam War (1986)
SAS: Phantoms of the Jungle (1989)
Duty First (1990)
Reshaping the Australian Army (1991)
General Vasey's War (1992)
Strategic Studies in a Changing World (co-edited) (1992)
When the War Came to Australia (co-authored) (1992)
The Gulf Commitment (1992)
The Army and the Future (1993)
The Battles that Shaped Australia (1994)
The Gunners (1995)
Armies and Nation-Building (1995)
Inside the War Cabinet (1996)
Breaking the Codes (co-authored) (1998)
Blamey (1998)
Defence Supremo (2000)
Making the Australian Defence Force (2001)
The Second World War: The Pacific (2002)
SAS: Phantoms of War (2002)
Strategic Command (2005)
Australian Peacekeeping (co-edited) (2009)
In Action with the SAS (co-authored) (2009)
Australia's Military History for Dummies (2010)
Australia and the 'New World Order' (2011)
The Good International Citizen (co-authored) (2014)

The Spy Catchers (2014)
Gallipoli 100 (consultant editor) (2014)
The Limits of Peacekeeping (co-authored) (2019)
The Long Search for Peace (co-authored) (2020)
Strategy and Command (2021)

DAVID

HORNER

The War Game

AUSTRALIAN WAR LEADERSHIP
FROM GALLIPOLI TO IRAQ

ALLEN&UNWIN
SYDNEY • MELBOURNE • AUCKLAND • LONDON

First published in 2022

Allen & Unwin
83 Alexander Street
Crows Nest NSW 2065
Australia
Phone:(61 2) 8425 0100
Email:info@allenandunwin.com
Web:www.allenandunwin.com

NATIONAL LIBRARY OF AUSTRALIA

A catalogue record for this book is available from the National Library of Australia

ISBN 978 1 76106 595 8

Index by Puddingburn
Internal design by Julian Mole, Post Pre-press Group, Australia
Set in 12/16 pt Adobe Garamond Pro by Post Pre-press Group, Australia
Printed in Singapore by C.O.S. Printers Pte Ltd

10 9 8 7 6 5 4 3 2 1

FSC www.fsc.org MIX Paper from responsible sources FSC® C016973

The paper in this book is FSC® certified. FSC® promotes environmentally responsible, socially beneficial and economically viable management of the world's forests.

Contents

Abbreviations x
Introduction 1

1 'To our last man and our last shilling': Cook and Fisher, First World War 1914–15 9
The Decision-makers 10
Preliminary Measures 15
The Imperative to Support Britain 16
Offering an Expeditionary Force 20
The New Guinea Expedition 24
The Cook Government's Final Decisions 25
The Fisher Government 26
Controlling and Supporting the AIF 30
Gallipoli Landing 32
Appointment of General Legge 32
Fisher's Concerns 35

2 'I'm an Attorney-General not a Major General': Hughes, First World War, 1915–17 39
Invitation to Visit London 40
Expanding the AIF 42
Hughes and the AIF Command 45
The Conscription Referendum 50
Outcome of the Conscription Referendum 52
Higher Command Problems 55

3 'We shall have to humour them': Hughes, First World War, 1917–19 59
Forming an Australian Corps 60
Second Conscription Referendum 65
The Command Conspiracy 66
The Imperial War Cabinet 71
Resolving the Command Problem 73

Hughes Takes Firmer Control 76
Armistice 78
War Leadership of a New Nation 80

4 'A disposition to treat Australia as a colony': Menzies, Second World War, 1939–40 84
Robert Menzies 84
The War Cabinet 86
Assessing the Threat 89
Key Decisions 91
Sending the 2nd AIF Overseas 93
End of the 'Phoney War' 99
The Looming Japanese Threat 102
The Advisory War Council 106
Reacting to the Japanese Threat 108

5 'Australia's very existence is at stake': Menzies and Fadden, Second World War, 1941 112
Maintaining the Integrity of the AIF 113
Committing to the Greek Campaign 115
Concern about Japan 123
Menzies in London 129
Menzies' Last Months 132
The Relief of Tobruk 134
Change of Government 137

6 'This is a new war': Curtin, Second World War, 1941–42 140
Outbreak of the Pacific War 141
Reacting to the Japanese Thrust 144
Return of the 1st Australian Corps 148
MacArthur Takes Charge 153
MacArthur and the Defence of Australia 156
Kokoda Campaign 162
Conscription for Overseas Service 171

7 'The decisions are matters for the Australian government': Curtin, Second World War, 1943–45 **174**
The SWPA's Mission for 1943 175
Resources for the 1943 Campaigns 178
Balancing the War Effort 180
Securing Allied Agreement 185
Australians for the Philippines 189
Reallocating Manpower 192
Command Appointments 194
A Role for the AIF 197
Unnecessary Operations 199

8 'We have not a minute more than three years': Menzies, Korean War and Malayan Emergency, 1950–55 **206**
The Menzies Government 207
Deploying Forces to Malaya 210
The Middle East 213
Outbreak of the Korean War 215
Threat of War 220
Further Commitments 223
Higher Command in Korea 226
Influencing the Conduct of the War 227
Focus on South-East Asia 230
SEATO 234
Far East Strategic Reserve 236

9 'Looking for a way in and not a way out': Menzies, Confrontation and Vietnam, 1962–65 **240**
The Decision-makers 241
Crisis in Laos 245
Committing Forces 247
Strategic Policymaking 249
Confrontation 251
Expanding the Training Team 254

Towards Conscription 256
Defence Build-up 261
Proposing a Battalion for Vietnam 262
Committing Troops to Borneo 264
Committing a Battalion to Vietnam 265
Announcement 270

10 'All the way with LBJ': Holt, Vietnam War, 1965–67 274
Restrictions on 1 RAR's Role 274
Expanding Australia's Commitment 277
The Holt Government 279
A Two-battalion Task Force 281
Selecting Phuoc Tuy Province 283
Military Advisers 286
Holt Visits the Troops 289
All the Way 291

11 'I'm certainly no trained strategist': Gorton and McMahon, Vietnam War, 1968–72 299
The Gorton Government 300
Viet Cong Offensive 301
Rethinking Policy 304
Towards Withdrawal 307
Planning the Withdrawal 310
Fraser as Defence Minister 314
The Civic Action Affair 319
Final Withdrawal 322

12 'Australia had vital interests at stake': Hawke, Gulf War, 1990–91 326
The Hawke Government 327
Military Advisers 328
Invasion of Kuwait 330
Security Council Resolutions 331

Multinational Naval Force 332
A Labor Government's Dilemma 333
Committing Naval Forces 335
Despatching the Ships 339
Managing the Commitment 340
Prospect of Hostilities 341
The Government's Decision 343
Preparing for War 347
Managing Information 351
End of the War 353

13 'It is right, it is lawful and it's in Australia's national interest': Howard, Afghanistan and Iraq Commitments, 2001–03 356
Continuing Gulf Commitment 357
The Howard Government 359
Military Advisers 361
Deploying Forces to Afghanistan 362
Planning for the Iraq War 366
The Australian Government's Preparations 373
Countdown to War 379
War Begins 382
Modern War Leadership 385

Conclusion 390
Endnotes 397
Bibliography 437
Index 453

Abbreviations

AAFV	Australian Army Force Vietnam
AATTV	Australian Army Training Team Vietnam
ABC	Australian Broadcasting Commission (later Corporation)
ABDA	American, British, Dutch, Australian (Command)
ACOPS	Assistant Chief of Defence Force (Operations)
ADB	*Australian Dictionary of Biography*
ADF	Australian Defence Force
AIF	Australian Imperial Force
ALP	Australian Labor Party
AMF	Australian Military Forces
ANZAC	Australian and New Zealand Army Corps
ANZAM	Australia, New Zealand and Malaya (area)
ANZUS	Australia, New Zealand and United States (Security Treaty)
ARVN	Army of the Republic of Vietnam
ATF	Australian Task Force
AWM	Australian War Memorial
BCOF	British Commonwealth Occupation Force
CAB	Cabinet Office records (UK)
CAS	Chief of the Air Staff
COSC	Chiefs of Staff Committee
CCOSC	Chairman, Chiefs of Staff Committee
CDF	Chief of the Defence Force
CENTCOM	Central Command (United States)
CGS	Chief of the General Staff
CMF	Citizen Military Forces
C-in-C	Commander-in-Chief
CIGS	Chief of the Imperial General Staff
CMF	Citizen Military Forces
CNS	Chief of Naval Staff

COMAFV	Commander Australian Force Vietnam
CPD	*Commonwealth Parliamentary Debates*
DAFP	*Documents on Australian Foreign Policy*
DEFE	Ministry of Defence records (UK)
DFAT	Department of Foreign Affairs and Trade
DIO	Defence Intelligence Organisation
DMO&P	Director of Military Operations and Plans
FAD	Foreign Affairs and Defence Committee (of Cabinet)
FRUMEL	Fleet Radio Unit Melbourne
GHQ	General Headquarters
GOC	General Officer Commanding
H of R	House of Representatives
HMAS	His (or Her) Majesty's Australian Ship
HMS	His (or Her) Majesty's Ship
INTERFET	International Force East Timor
JCPML	John Curtin Prime Ministerial Library
JPC	Joint Planning Committee
LBJ	President Lyndon Bird Johnson
MACV	Military Assistance Command Vietnam
MIF	Maritime Interception Force
MMMA	MacArthur Memorial Military Archives
NAA	National Archives of Australia
NARA	National Archives and Records Administration, Washington, DC
NATO	North Atlantic Treaty Organization
NCO	Non-commissioned officer
NLA	National Library of Australia
ONA	Office of National Assessments
PREM	Prime Minister's Office records (UK)
RAAF	Royal Australian Air Force
RAF	Royal Air Force
RAN	Royal Australian Navy
RAR	Royal Australian Regiment
RN	Royal Navy
SAS	Special Air Service

SEATO	South-East Asia Treaty Organisation
SPC-A	Sea Power Centre—Australia
SS	Steam ship
SWPA	Southwest Pacific Area
TNA	The National Archives (UK)
UAP	United Australia Party
UKUSA	United Kingdom, United States of America (Agreement)
UN	United Nations
UNSCOM	United Nations Commission (on Iraq)
UNSCR	United Nations Security Council Resolution
US	United States (of America)
VC	Victoria Cross
VCDF	Vice Chief of the Defence Force
VCGS	Vice Chief of the General Staff
WMD	Weapons of Mass Destruction
WO	War Office records (UK)

Introduction

'War! That mad game the world so loves to play'

Jonathan Swift: 1667–1745[1]

War is a deadly serious business—so serious that during the First World War French prime minister and war minister Georges Clemenceau famously declared that it was too important to be left to the generals. It might seem quixotic then, perhaps even disrespectful of the human suffering caused by war, to give this book the title of *The War Game*. In ordinary public discourse a game is more likely to be associated with an amusing pastime, often played by children, or a sport. But warfare certainly has elements of a game: there are two, sometimes several opponents; there are rules, although these are sometimes broken; there are winners and losers; and it becomes addictive. Other writers have also recognised the paradox of comparing war to a game. Writing in 1788, the English politician and man of letters Horace Walpole avowed that 'War is a game, but unfortunately, the cards, counters and fishes [that is, the pieces] suffer by an ill run more than the gamesters.'[2]

If war is so serious, it is startling to note the frequency with which Australia has engaged in it. In a span of just under 90 years—from August 1914 to March 2003—Australia went to war nine times. Further, between 1914 and 2013, Australian military personnel were on active service during 47 years of that century. This from a nation—an island continent—that is largely remote from countries that might pose a major threat. Why then did Australia go to war on these nine occasions? And why have Australian military personnel been on operations for almost half that time?

In a broad sense, the answers to these questions might be found in Australia's history as a British colony, in the nation's insecurity as a sparsely populated country on a vast continent on the edge of Asia, and in the desire of a small country to seek security as part of a protective alliance. But to understand why Australia became involved in specific wars we need to focus on the decisions of the political leaders, and in particular the prime ministers. The gravest decision a government can make is to commit the nation to war. Other crucial decisions then follow, including determining what forces should be committed and where they should be deployed, and when they should be withdrawn. This book therefore focuses on the key players (a term also used for games), but to a lesser extent it is also about the command and organisational structures that support those players.

In calling the book *The War Game*, I wanted to draw attention not just to the frequency of Australia's wars, but to the constant features of how Australia has gone to war.[3] In each war the players have been the same—the prime ministers, their senior ministers, their military (and sometimes civilian) advisers and, because Australia has always fought as part of an allied coalition, the political and military leaders of Great Britain and the United States. The issues have also been constant—primarily the need to respond to the imperatives of being a member of an alliance, be it the British Empire or the US alliance. Further, all Australia's wars have involved commitments far from home, except in the case of the Pacific War during the Second World War, which began at some distance from Australia but was soon on the nation's doorstep.

In a democracy, war leadership involves the interaction between the political leaders and their top military advisers. Despite the arguments presented in books such as Samuel Huntington's 1957 classic

The Soldier and the State, there is no perfect model for the civil–military relationship. During the US Civil War, President Abraham Lincoln famously wrote to the Union Army's General Ulysses Grant: 'The particulars of your plans I neither know nor seek to know. You are vigilant and self-reliant; and, pleased with this, I wish not to obtrude any constraints or restraints upon you . . . If there is anything wanting which is within my power to give, do not fail to let me know it.'[4] Similarly, in the Second World War, Prime Minister Winston Churchill, often praised as an outstanding war leader, drove his military advisers to distraction, but in the end was loath to overrule them. As an activist, hands-on leader, he was keen to visit his troops on the battlefield.

Much insight into war leadership is provided by the biographies of the famous leaders. By one count, there are more than 60 biographies of Churchill (including Carlo D'Este's *Warlord*), and at least fifteen books on Australia's Second World War prime minister John Curtin. Another insight into war leadership can be found in the memoirs of key players, such as those of Maurice Hankey, secretary of the British War Cabinet in the First World War, called *The Supreme Command.*

There are, however, few general histories of war leadership, most books instead taking a case-study approach. In his book *Leadership in War* British historian Andrew Roberts examines the cases of Napoleon Bonaparte, Horatio Nelson, Churchill, Adolf Hitler, Joseph Stalin, General George C. Marshall, Charles de Gaulle, General Dwight Eisenhower and Margaret Thatcher. American historian Eliot Cohen, in his book *Supreme Command: Soldiers, Statesmen, and Leadership in Wartime*, focuses on Abraham Lincoln, Georges Clemenceau, Churchill, and Israeli prime minister David Ben-Gurion. Cohen also discusses the relationship between President Lyndon Johnson and his chiefs of staff during the Vietnam War, and comes to some thoughtful and instructive conclusions about the nature of war leadership.

In a book edited by Gary Sheffield and Geoffrey Till, called *The Challenges of High Command: The British Experience*, Professor Sheffield explains that high command is 'characterised by interaction between military commanders and their political superiors', noting that while 'A divisional commander on the Somme in 1916 was not a high commander; his equivalent in Bosnia in 1997 most definitely would be.' The book is actually about senior military commanders, not political leaders. Indeed, there is quite a large number of books about the challenges of military high command, and numerous biographies of such commanders. Considering the problems at the civil–military interface, Sheffield wrote that 'Politicians and military commanders often have different agendas', a fact that Winston Churchill observed, commenting in 1916 that 'You cannot combine [parliamentary] politics and war. Politics requires popularity, and the direction of war means inevitable unpopularity.'[5]

The leaders mentioned earlier were principal players in their country's wars. Often they were larger-than-life figures—people with big egos—or at least a strong belief in their own judgement and destiny. They were required to make momentous decisions that might decide the survival of their country. By contrast, Australia's war leaders have been on a different level to these historical examples. Australia has always gone to war as a junior partner in an allied coalition. Its leaders have had little scope to influence allied strategy and their decisions have been unlikely to affect the outcome of the war. The main decisions of Australia's war leaders have been whether Australia should go to war, and the level of commitment to the war. But in the cases of both the major world figures and Australia's less Olympian war leaders, the issues of civil–military relations remain the same. One of them is the imperative for political leaders to select military commanders in whom they have confidence, and to dismiss commanders if they feel it necessary.

The prime ministers discussed in this book were all civilians, and indeed only one of them, John Gorton, had even seen active service, in his case as a fighter pilot in the Second World War. Prime ministers do not naturally have any great expertise in military matters. Only one prime minister had previously been a defence minister when first taking up office. Joseph Cook, prime minister on the outbreak of the First World War, had been defence minister in 1909–10, but is 'best remembered for his opposition to the purchase of the River Class destroyers—so-called because the ships bore the names of inland waterways—because he mistakenly thought they could be used only in rivers'.[6] Gorton was the first to admit that he was 'no trained strategist nor a trained tactician'. Australia's third First World War prime minister, William Morris (Billy) Hughes, a lawyer, declared that he was 'an Attorney-General not a Major-General'.

The prime ministers and their defence ministers therefore needed to rely on the chiefs of the armed forces for advice about the availability and capabilities of military forces. Service chiefs fulfil two roles: they are the government's principal military advisers; and they implement the government's decisions. It falls to them to deploy the forces efficiently, to ensure that they are trained to the best possible level, and to make sure they are employed properly to achieve the government's goals. The military chiefs achieve their second role through the command structure. When forces are deployed overseas, they generally have a commander who reports back to the Australian government and ensures that its policies are followed. Hence, political leaders have a critical role in selecting their principal military advisers and commanders.

War leadership therefore involves tension between the two parties—the civil and the military—who often come from different backgrounds. One is based on compromise, consensus and public acceptance; the other is based on discipline, obedience and clear orders. In a democracy there is no question about who is in charge; it is the civilian political leaders. But the military leaders have the professional military expertise. At times military leaders might find themselves being ordered to carry out directions that they believe to be against the national interest. It is often argued that in those circumstances military leaders are left with two alternatives: to obey the government or to resign. There is, however, a contrary argument: as long as the government's direction is lawful, a military chief should not resign, because in so doing they would enter into the political sphere, which the military is not permitted to do. Lieutenant General Sir Sydney Rowell, Australian Chief of the General Staff from 1950 to 1954, wrote that when faced with an unpalatable decision, a chief might consider threatening to resign. But he concluded that 'loose talk of threatening to resign is twaddle; to take the issue to the point of no return merely leads to the protester being replaced by someone more pliable'.[7]

This book examines Australian war leadership in nine wars: the First and Second World Wars, the Korean War, the Malayan Emergency, the Indonesian Confrontation (when Indonesia sought to prevent the formation of the new nation of Malaysia), the Vietnam War, the Gulf War, the Afghanistan War and the Iraq War. In fact, for the purposes of understanding Australian war leadership, the Second World War can be seen as two wars—the European War, which began in 1939, and the Pacific War, which began in December 1941. I examined Australia's war leadership in the Second World War in my 1982 book *High Command*, and inevitably in my discussion here of that war I cover much the same ground, although I try to take account of more recent scholarship. For reasons that I explain at the beginning of the final chapter, in this book I deal merely with the decisions to commit Australia to the Afghanistan War in 2001 and to the Iraq invasion in 2003, rather than the continuation of those wars over the next two decades. Australian war leadership in these recent wars warrants a detailed study. In this book, however, I have tried to provide a more focused account of each war in order to bring out the constant themes that appear over a century of conflict.

Few countries celebrate their military history with as much enthusiasm as Australia. Most Australians possess at least a vague knowledge of the landing at Gallipoli in 1915 and the fighting on the Kokoda Trail in 1942. The personal experience of war continues to hold a fascination. But the really big challenge is to understand why Australia was involved in its wars, and how the Australian government went about managing them. Ultimately these decisions are about war strategy. This might seem to be an esoteric matter, but if governments get the strategy wrong, the cost is borne by soldiers on the battlefield, their families, the nation's treasury and its reputation. War leadership continues to be the crucial factor in considering

Australia's experience of war. As Horace Walpole reminds us, in the game of war the lives of the nation's sailors, soldiers and air men and women are in the hands of 'the gamesters'—that is, the political leaders and their advisers.

1

'To our last man and our last shilling'

Cook and Fisher, First World War, 1914–15

Committing the nation to war is the most fateful decision its leaders can make. But Australia's government did not commit Australia to the First World War. Rather, when Britain declared war on 5 August 1914, Australia was automatically also at war. Australia in 1914 was not a fully independent nation. Federation in 1901 had brought together the six Australian colonies, but in many respects, the Commonwealth of Australia was still a self-governing colony. While the Commonwealth had responsibility for most government functions, including trade, finance and defence, its foreign policy was still in the hands of the British government. The key element in strategic decision-making is timely and relevant information, but Australia's only source of information on international affairs was the British government. Australia's sole overseas representative was the high commissioner in London, and communications with the British government went between the governor-general in Melbourne (Australia's capital until 1913 and seat of government until 1927) and the colonial secretary in London. The new nation remained an integral part of the British Empire, and if people thought of themselves as Australian, at the same time they considered themselves British citizens—members of the Empire.[1]

The crucial decision was not whether to join the war, but the nature and extent of Australia's contribution, and to a large degree even this was preordained. By the end of July 1914, war in Europe had been brewing for a month. Following the assassination of Archduke Franz Ferdinand of Austria in Sarajevo on 28 June, the patchwork of European alliances and commitments was leading towards a major European war. A month later, on 28 July, Austria–Hungary declared war on Serbia. Then Russia mobilised to support Serbia, and Germany declared war on Russia; Germany's declaration of war on France would follow shortly. When on 29 July the British Admiralty despatched a cable to the dominions and colonies advising them to adopt the 'precautionary stage' as set out in the Imperial Defence Scheme, the British government was still debating whether to be involved.[2] The cable arrived in Australia on 30 July.

The Decision-makers

With the prospect of war arising unexpectedly, the Liberal Party government led by Joseph Cook had no preconceived idea about how to manage it. In any case, strategy and war policy would be decided by the imperial government in London. Nonetheless, the Australian government needed to decide the extent of Australia's involvement. At least, as will be discussed shortly, Australia had a small but capable navy, was forming a citizen military force, and its leading politicians were familiar with Australia's broad strategic and defence issues. In determining Australia's initial response, the key decision-makers would be Cook; his defence minister, Senator Edward Millen; their military and naval advisers; and, unusual to modern sensibilities, the governor-general. Most of them had been born in Britain or other parts of the Empire, and they were imbued with the ideals of the Empire.

By July 1914, Joseph Cook had been prime minister for a little over a year, but he was an experienced politician. Born in Staffordshire, England, in 1860, he had followed his father into the coalmines at the age of nine, writing later: 'I never saw daylight except on Saturday afternoons and Sunday, which became a blessed day for me.' He educated himself by studying borrowed books by the light of his lamp during lunch breaks in the mine.[3] In 1885, Cook and his new wife migrated to New South Wales, where he again worked as a coal-miner. A founding member of the Labor Party, he was elected to the NSW Legislative Assembly, but later left the party and joined the Free Traders, becoming an ardent anti-socialist. Elected to the federal parliament in 1901, he was defence minister in the 1909–10 Deakin government.

When Labor defeated Deakin's Liberal government in 1910, Cook became leader of the Liberal Party, and thus when it returned to power following the defeat of the Fisher Labor government in the federal election of May 1913, Cook became prime minister. By this time, in speech, manner and political philosophy, Cook had moved well away from his humble origins. The Cook government had a slim majority and a hostile Senate, and after just a year in government, when, as expected, the Senate rejected a bill, Cook called a double-dissolution election to be held on 5 September 1914, hoping to secure a majority in both houses.

In late July, Cook was electioneering in western Victoria and out of touch with his office, while the defence minister, Edward Millen, was in his home town of Sydney. Aged 53, Millen was a former journalist who was born in England and had migrated to New South Wales at the age of twenty. The official historian of the First World War, Charles Bean, described Millen as 'one of the most experienced and astute Australian politicians', but the governor-general, Sir Ronald Munro Ferguson, 'doubted' whether Millen 'had the confidence of the Services'. Since becoming defence minister in May 1913, Millen had been vigorously reducing the defence budget, and he dismissed the Second Naval Member of the Naval Board for disrupting its work. In April 1914 he refused a suggestion from the British First Lord of the Admiralty, Winston Churchill, that Australia need not maintain a fleet in its own territorial waters, and he expressed 'the sharpest criticism of the British' in a memorandum tabled in the Senate.[4]

Millen's three principal advisers were the secretary of his department, the First Naval Member of the Naval Board, and the First Military Member of the Military Board. At that time, the secretary of the Department of Defence, Samuel Pethebridge, was overseas; and the chief clerk of the department, 42-year-old Thomas Trumble, was acting secretary. Born in Victoria, Trumble had started work in the Victorian public service and in 1901 transferred to the Commonwealth Department of Defence. Trumble would be acting secretary for most of the war and would continue as secretary until 1927. The wartime defence minister Senator George Pearce, who succeeded Millen, observed of Trumble: 'Invariably courteous and patient, self-sacrificing and zealous, he has perhaps borne more of the heat and burden of the day than any other officer, civil or military, with credit to himself and Australia.'[5]

Millen's principal naval adviser, Rear Admiral Sir William Creswell, had been born in the British naval base of Gibraltar in 1852 and had served in the Royal Navy (RN) before migrating to Australia in 1879 to become a pastoralist. Finding he was ill-suited to this new vocation, he took an appointment in South Australia's tiny naval force, and then in 1900 became commandant of Queensland's small maritime force. Creswell was a vocal advocate for an Australian Navy, and in 1904 was appointed to head the newly formed Commonwealth Naval Forces. When the Royal Australian Navy (RAN) was formed in 1911, Creswell became the First Naval Member of the Naval Board of Administration, with the rank of rear admiral. 'Unfortunately,' as the naval historian David Stevens has commented, 'despite his force of character, Creswell's recent naval experience had ill-equipped him for wartime high command'. The businessman Robert Anderson, who conducted a review of the Defence Department in March–April 1915, advised the minister that Creswell had 'only the foggiest idea of modern management . . . An exceedingly pleasant old gentleman, but an expensive luxury in his present position.'[6] Creswell would continue in his post until 1919. Because the Australian ships served under Admiralty control, Creswell's limitations as a naval commander were not critical.

Creswell was supported by the secretary of the Naval Board, 37-year-old George Macandie, a Queensland public servant who had served in the Navy Office with Creswell since 1903. With 'varying titles and status he was Secretary of the Naval Board from 1914 until 1946'.[7] The defence minister chaired the board, which also included the Second Naval Member (responsible for personnel matters and stores), the Third Naval Member (an engineer) and the Finance and Civil Member.

Millen's principal military adviser was the Chief of the General Staff (CGS), who was also the First Military Member of the Military Board, but there was a hiatus in this position. Brigadier General Joseph Gordon had ended his appointment as CGS on 21 July 1914, and had already departed by ship for a holiday in Britain. He was to be succeeded by Colonel Gordon Legge, but Legge was still sailing back to Australia from London after serving as Australia's representative on the Imperial General Staff; he was not due to arrive in Australia until 8 August.

The Military Board had been established in 1904 when Major General Edward Hutton, a British officer commanding the Commonwealth Military Forces, came to the end of his appointment.[8] Hutton had clashed with the government over his determination to structure the new Australian Army in order to provide expeditionary forces to assist the Empire in time of war. The government had resisted this, and the *Defence Act 1904* mandated that members of the army were not to serve overseas. When the Military Board was formed, another position was created, namely Inspector-General of the Commonwealth Military Forces, who in time of war would become commander-in-chief of the home army. Major General George Kirkpatrick, a Canadian-born British Army officer, had concluded his term as inspector-general on 10 December 1913, and his successor, Brigadier General William Bridges, did not take up his appointment until 1 June 1914. In July he was in Queensland on his first tour of inspection.

The defence minister chaired the Military Board, which by 1914 consisted of the CGS, the adjutant-general, the chief of ordnance, the quartermaster-general and the finance member. Each member had his own staff branch in Army Headquarters and was responsible for his specific area of military activity. The 'General Staff' branch, headed by the CGS, was responsible for operations, training, intelligence and censorship. In the absence of Brigadier General Gordon, the Director of Military Operations, Major Brudenell White, aged 37, became acting CGS, even though he was junior in rank to the other Military Board members. Another key officer was the adjutant-general, Colonel Victor Sellheim, who was responsible for personnel, manning and recruitment, and would be tasked with raising any new forces. Sellheim had only just been appointed adjutant-general, but as quartermaster-general he had been a member of the Military Board since 1912.

White was an outstanding and experienced staff officer. Originally a Queensland militia officer, he served briefly in the Boer War and then joined the permanent army as a garrison artillery officer and became aide-de-camp to General Hutton.[9] He absorbed Hutton's ideas about the Australian Army providing an expeditionary force for service overseas as part of an imperial army. In 1906 he became the first Australian officer to attend the British staff college at Camberley, and served with the British Army from 1908 to 1911.

Above the Naval and Military boards was yet another body, the Council of Defence, set up in 1905 to coordinate navy and army policies, and to consider measures for the defence of the Commonwealth in time of war. Chaired by the defence minister, the council included the Commonwealth treasurer, the Inspector-General of the Commonwealth Military Forces, the CGS, the First and Second Naval Members, and a consulting military engineer.[10] The council did not meet between 1905 and 1911, when it met twice; it met three times in 1912, once in 1913 and did not meet during the 1914 crisis.

The other key figure, the governor-general, Sir Ronald Munro Ferguson, was also visiting Sydney at this time. A Scottish laird, Munro Ferguson had been educated at the Royal Military College, Sandhurst, but had pursued a political career as a member of the British Liberal Party, holding a series of junior government positions.[11] Although he became his party's whip, when his career hit a roadblock, he was pleased to accept the vice-regal job, and took up his appointment in Melbourne in May 1914, aged 54. Munro Ferguson became the main channel for communications between the British and Australian governments, and with his political experience and imperialist views he would play a more activist role in the Australian government than any of his successors.

Preliminary Measures

On 28 July, after receiving a precautionary message from the Admiralty, Admiral Creswell, who was on leave in Brisbane, wrote to the secretary of the Naval Board, Macandie, to recommend the implementation of some preliminary steps. These included warning Rear Admiral Sir George Patey, the RN officer commanding the Australian fleet, then off the coast of Queensland, to move his ships to their war stations. Macandie was in Sydney, advising Senator Millen on these developments. After some delay, caused by confusion over the decoding of the Admiralty cable, in the evening of 30 July, Millen agreed that the Australian ships should take up their stations according to the prearranged plan.[12]

The governor-general's activist role was soon evident. Late on 30 July, he pressed Millen for a private assurance that the Australian fleet would be transferred to Admiralty control as soon as war was declared; Australia had previously agreed to do this, but had reserved the right to make the final decision. Munro Ferguson urged Millen to now make the commitment, and when Millen did so the governor-general cabled this 'unofficial' news to London. The following evening, in an extraordinary intervention in Australian politics, the governor-general sent a telegram to Prime Minister Cook, in Ballarat, suggesting that he call a Cabinet meeting so that the 'Imperial government may know the attitude of Australia in case of war'.[13] Munro Ferguson had acted on his own initiative; there is no evidence that the British government had actually sought this advice.

That same day Millen telegrammed Victoria Barracks, Melbourne, directing Major White to hurry to Sydney by train, bringing with him the Defence Scheme. When White arrived in Sydney on Saturday 1 August, he explained to Millen that the cable from London meant that Australia needed to adopt a range of measures, including guarding key points, manning coast guns, and preparing ships for operations. The governor-general pressed Millen to issue the orders to initiate the precautionary stage, but the minister still hesitated to act without approval from the prime minister.

Millen was soon joined by the federal attorney-general, Sir William Irvine, who arrived in Sydney from electioneering in Brisbane. Born in Northern Ireland, 'Iceberg' Irvine (so named because of his cool manner) was a former premier of Victoria and an ardent imperialist. In an election speech on 1 August, he declared that 'When England is at war we are at war. There is no half-way home . . . The statesmen of England are now charged with the terrible responsibility of determining the issue of peace and war for the whole people, and we are not only bound to abide by their decisions but to give them every assistance that lies in our power.' According to Bean, White sought out Irvine to explain 'the call for military precautions'. As a result, Irvine persuaded Millen to act, and hence in the afternoon of 2 August Millen telegrammed the prime minister, advising him that he had directed White to issue the necessary orders for the precautionary stage. Millen found White's 'clear judgment and his intimate knowledge of the several steps, then due to be taken, of the greatest possible assistance'. Keen to ensure that he would be present when the Cabinet considered the situation, that night Munro Ferguson took the express train to Melbourne, accompanied in his vice-regal railway car by Millen, Irvine, Creswell (who had travelled down from Brisbane), Macandie and White.[14]

The Imperative to Support Britain

Millen had issued orders for the precautionary stage without the prime minister's approval, but Joseph Cook was already starting, if belatedly, to take charge. During the election campaign, Cook had concentrated on domestic issues; but as the likelihood of war increased, on 30 July he told a meeting in the western Victorian town of Horsham: 'Whatever happens, Australia is part of the Empire to the full. Remember that when the Empire is at war, so is Australia at war . . . I want to make it quite clear that all our resources in Australia are in the Empire and for the Empire, and for the preservation and security of the Empire.' Although Cook had an 'atavistic attachment to the British Empire', he 'knew that Australian and British strategic interests were not identical'. But as the historian Neville Meaney has observed, Cook 'was most comfortable when he could believe that Australia and the Empire shared one world view which would provide for the security of the whole British race'.[15]

Cook's statement that when the Empire was at war Australia was also at war was not, therefore, just some spur-of-the-moment comment made for political advantage. For at least five years Australia's political leaders of both Labor and the conservative parties had concluded that if the Empire went to war Australia should be involved, not just because it was part of the Empire, but because it was necessary to assist Britain to ensure the security of Australia. Since Federation, the chief imperative for Australia's defence policymakers was preserving the new nation for its white settlers. Under the White Australia policy, Asians, particularly Chinese and Japanese migrants, were banned from entry. After Japan defeated China in 1895, and especially after Japan defeated Russia in the 1904–05 war, fears were raised of a possible attack by Japan as a response to Australia's racial exclusion policies.[16]

Alfred Deakin's Protectionist government, which came to power in July 1905, reacted quickly to these developments, advocating for both an Australian navy and a large militia to be formed through compulsory service. Deakin's government lasted until November 1908, and he returned to power in June 1909, heading the so-called 'Fusion' government, which included both the liberal Protectionists and the conservative Free Traders. Deakin helped engender enthusiasm for a navy when, without consulting Britain, he arranged for the American Great White Fleet of sixteen battleships and auxiliary vessels to visit Melbourne and Sydney during their tour of the Pacific in 1908.[17]

Initially the British government opposed the idea of Australia forming its own navy, preferring to retain existing arrangements whereby Australia contributed to a squadron of the RN, but it eventually conceded to Australia's desire to purchase destroyers. Worried about the expansion of the German Navy, Britain agreed in 1909 to help Australia obtain and man a fleet unit consisting of a battle cruiser, three light cruisers, six destroyers and three submarines. In return, Britain ensured that Australia's ships would be suitable to serve as part of the RN; that is, they were designed for operations around the world rather than for the coastal defence of Australia alone.

The Deakin government's other defence initiative was to raise a large militia through compulsory service. This proposal was supported by the Labor Party Opposition, its leading advocate being William Morris (Billy) Hughes. Like many of his contemporaries, Hughes was born in Britain, in his case in 1862 in London, to Welsh parents.[18] After working as a student teacher, in 1884 he migrated to Queensland, and sought work as a casual labourer in the outback for eighteen months. He then moved to Sydney, where he married and set up shop mending umbrellas, among other activities. He became involved in the Labour movement, was secretary of the Wharf Labourers' Union, and was elected to the NSW Legislative Assembly and then to the new federal parliament in 1901. After studying law part-time he was called to the bar in 1903. He would later become Australia's main wartime prime minister, serving from 1915 to 1923.

The establishment of the Royal Australian Navy (RAN) and the initiation of the universal training scheme took place not under the Deakin government, which had begun the process, but under Andrew Fisher's Labor government, in power firstly and briefly between November 1908 and June 1909, and then for a longer period from April 1910 to June 1913. Born in Ayrshire, Scotland, in 1862, from the age of twelve Fisher had worked as a coalminer before migrating to Queensland in 1885, where he continued working as a miner, becoming leader of the Amalgamated Miners' Union.[19] After serving in the Queensland state parliament, he was elected to federal parliament in 1901.

The Deakin government sought advice from an eminent British soldier, Field Marshal Lord Kitchener, who visited Australia in 1909–10. Acting on this advice, on 1 January 1911 the Fisher government introduced the universal training scheme. Under this scheme, twelve-year-old boys were required to serve in the cadets until, at the age of seventeen, they transferred to the Citizen Forces, where they served through to the age of 26. After seven years, that is, by 1919, the Citizen Forces would number 80,000 men. Also under the Fisher government, Australia's first destroyers were commissioned, and in July 1911 the Commonwealth Naval Forces became the RAN.

The universal training scheme and the formation of the RAN were pushed through parliament by Fisher's energetic Minister for Defence, Senator George Pearce, who would also serve in that role throughout the First World War. Pearce was born in Mount Barker, South Australia, in 1870, left school at the age of eleven, trained as a carpenter, and moved to Western Australia in 1893.[20] He became involved in the labour movement and, self-educated in politics, economics and history, was elected to the first Commonwealth parliament as a senator. With a long interest in defence matters, Pearce was Minister for Defence in both the first and second Fisher governments, establishing good working relationships with his principal military advisers: Captain Creswell, head of the navy; and Colonel William Bridges, Chief of Military Intelligence and then CGS.

Although the RAN and Citizen Forces had been created for home defence because of concern about Japan, these developments displeased the British government, which wanted Australia to provide an expeditionary force in time of war, with Germany looming as a possible enemy. The most important event in preparing Fisher, and particularly Pearce, for their roles in the First World War was their attendance at the Imperial Conference in London in May and June 1911. At the conference, Pearce agreed that in time of war the RAN's ships would come under the control of the Admiralty, but since publication of this statement would provide ammunition for his political opponents in Australia, the statement was 'unwritten'.[21] Nonetheless, the final decision to assign the ships to the Admiralty would still rest with the Australian government.

At meetings at the War Office, Pearce also agreed, at the request of Britain, that Australia would prepare plans to send an expeditionary force overseas in case of war. Pearce explained that Australia's forces were raised for local defence and under the Defence Act they could not be sent overseas. However, in the case of a 'serious war . . . there would be a considerable number of those forces who would volunteer for oversea [*sic*] service'. Therefore, Australian military staff should prepare schemes of mobilisation, although Pearce made clear that the decision to begin planning in peacetime 'would not commit us to take that action' in wartime.[22]

Pearce might have accepted the need to plan for an expeditionary force, but back in Australia he refused requests from Major White (who had attended the War Office conference) to be allowed to develop such plans.[23] Pearce changed his mind in November 1912, when, at a meeting in Melbourne, Brigadier General Gordon and the New Zealand Army chief, Major General Alexander Godley, agreed to prepare plans to form a composite expeditionary force, enlisted on a voluntary basis. Prime Minister Fisher approved the preparation of such a plan, although he emphasised that this would not be a binding commitment for the Australian government to deploy the expeditionary force. Pearce formally approved planning for the expeditionary force on 30 December 1912. The task fell to Major White, but it was overseen by Gordon who later boasted that when 'war was declared the details of mobilising the first division were all cut and dried'.[24]

Offering an Expeditionary Force

Although Fisher, Hughes and Pearce had played major roles in preparing the Australian forces for war, and would later become the key figures in managing Australia's war effort, as noted earlier, they were not in power on the outbreak of the war. Around midday on Sunday 2 August, Prime Minister Cook met with the senior officers of Army Headquarters at the bluestone Victoria Barracks on St Kilda Road,

Melbourne. The officers, after waiting until Cook (a Methodist lay preacher and a teetotaller) had attended church, explained what was required by the precautionary stage, and orders were issued to man the coast batteries, to move the Kennedy Regiment (a Citizen Forces unit) from Townsville to Thursday Island, and to mount guards on the vulnerable points.[25]

The following afternoon, Cook presided over a meeting of the Cabinet in the government offices in Melbourne. Only four of the ten members of the Cabinet were present: Cook, Millen, Irvine and Senator James McColl, vice president of the Executive Council—all had been born in the United Kingdom.[26] The Cabinet asked to be joined by Colonel Sellheim (adjutant-general), Major White and George Macandie (secretary of the Naval Board), and for a while Admiral Creswell and other naval officers. The ministers had seen a report—that later turned out to be erroneous—that Canada had offered to raise a force of 30,000 troops and that New Zealand was considering raising an expeditionary force. They were keen for Australia to match this commitment, but White explained that he had prepared plans for an Australian expeditionary force of only 12,000. When the ministers demanded 20,000 troops, White agreed that this could be achieved in six weeks, or 'near it'.[27]

Late that afternoon the governor-general presided over a meeting of the Executive Council, and then White drafted a cable, which, after amendment, Munro Ferguson despatched to the colonial secretary. In it, the government said that 'in the event of war', it was 'prepared to place the vessels of the Australian Navy under the control of the Admiralty', and was also 'prepared to despatch an expeditionary force of 20,000 men . . . to any destination desired by the Home government'. The force would be at the 'complete disposal' of the British government.[28]

In what he described as 'this extraordinary Cabinet decision', the historian Douglas Newton has argued that the government 'forfeited the chance to weigh up costs and benefits, to assess objectives, or to preserve Australian manhood and treasure for genuinely defensive war aims in the future'. He noted that the decision was made

40 hours before Great Britain declared war, and by acting precipitately, 'Australian politicians were setting the nation up to be taken for granted.'[29] Certainly the Australian offer surprised the British government. Yet it is important not to judge events in the past through modern-day eyes. The self-governing Commonwealth was still in the early stages of its journey towards full sovereign independence. Newton might well have described the decision as 'reckless', but if Australia's political leaders thought the nation's security depended on Britain and its Empire (and they did), then the best way to ensure this was to support the Empire to the fullest extent. Not only were the ministers concerned about Japan, but they knew that Australia's trade depended on protection by the RN. Most of the major newspapers agreed with the government's decision.

And so Australia was committed to providing soldiers to what was to become the nation's greatest tragedy. In some quarters there was enthusiasm for the war, but as historian Eric Andrews later wrote, 'Australia's reaction to the war was more divided, and more hesitant, than most historians have been willing to admit.' Nevertheless, while the extent of Australia's commitment can be argued, it is difficult to see how the nation could have avoided involvement. Australia had a vital stake in the war and could not stand aloof from it. In hindsight, we also know that Germany planned to bring Britain to its knees, with potentially disastrous consequences for Australia.[30]

Britain declared war at 9 a.m. on 5 August (Melbourne time) and next day the British government asked Australia to seize German New Guinea, including its radio transmitters. At the same time, the British government accepted Australia's offer of 20,000 troops, and Millen asked the army's inspector-general, Brigadier General William Bridges, who had arrived back in Melbourne, and Major White to raise this force.

Bridges was another key decision-maker born in the United Kingdom, in his case in Scotland in 1861. When his parents migrated to Canada, Bridges entered the Canadian military college, but he did not complete the course as he wanted to follow his parents, who had moved on to Australia.[31] He received a commission in the NSW permanent artillery and served in the Boer War. Identified by Hutton as a promising officer, he became the army's Chief of Intelligence, and for five months in 1909 was the army's first CGS. Following his mentor, Hutton, Bridges saw the Australian Army as an integral part of the Empire's forces. After serving in London as the Australian representative on the Imperial General Staff, Bridges returned as the first commandant of the Royal Military College, when it opened at Duntroon, Canberra, in June 1911. As noted earlier, he became inspector-general in June 1914, just before the beginning of the war.

Responding to Australia's offer, on 7 August the British government suggested that the Australian contingent consist of two infantry brigades, one light horse brigade and a field artillery brigade (regiment). As Bridges had observed with the Australian colonial contingents in South Africa, this force could be easily fragmented and distributed among larger British formations. According to Bridges' biographer, Chris Coulthard-Clark, Bridges was resolved not to allow this to occur again. On his recommendation, the Australian government proposed sending a complete infantry division with three brigades of infantry and a light horse brigade, and Britain accepted this proposal. As Charles Bean put it: 'The stand thus taken by the far-sighted sardonic soldier-statesman was the first and greatest step towards settling the character . . . of a national Australian army . . . In the stand which he had made General Bridges was actuated by pure Australian nationalism.'[32] As noted earlier, one of the first tasks for a nation's political leaders is to select a commander to lead its forces in war. Bridges was appointed commander of the new division, with White as his chief of staff.

Later, on 15 August, at Bridges' insistence, the force was given the title Australian Imperial Force (AIF), and Bridges was appointed to command the AIF as well as the division. Bridges and White devoted their energies to raising and organising the AIF, which was being formed from volunteers. Although Bean suggested that Bridges already had some vision of a national army, historian Coulthard-Clark has observed that 'he was probably the officer with the least inclination to place Australian national interests above those of the imperial authorities whenever areas of conflict might arise'. Indeed, when Bridges was asked to command the Australian division, his first reaction was to suggest the appointment of Lieutenant General Hutton, who had commanded the Commonwealth Military Forces a dozen years earlier, but the Australian government wanted the force to be commanded by an Australian.[33]

The New Guinea Expedition

On 9 August the Australian government agreed to Britain's request to capture German New Guinea, and the task of raising the expeditionary force fell to the new CGS, Colonel Gordon Legge, who had just arrived back in Melbourne. Legge was another key figure born in Britain—in London in 1863.[34] He migrated to Sydney with his family in 1878, obtained bachelor and master's degrees in arts and a law degree from Sydney University and, after service in the part-time NSW militia, joined the permanent NSW forces in 1884. He served in the Boer War for almost three years as a company commander, adjutant and brigade intelligence officer, but his service was not particularly distinguished.

Back in Australia, Legge became a prominent member of the group of army officers known as Australianists, who believed that Australia should prepare an army for the defence of the continent, and should be wary of sending forces overseas on British imperial adventures. The Australianists were in competition with the imperialists, which included Hutton's disciples, Bridges and White, who believed that Australia was best protected by contributing to the broader defence of the British Empire. In 1909, Legge drafted the universal training scheme. He then served as the Australian representative at the War Office in London from mid-1912 to mid-1914. He was, therefore, an experienced staff officer and organiser with an appreciation of the thinking in London.

Legge's organisational skills were soon to be exercised, raising what became known as the Australian Naval and Military Expeditionary Force. Legge offered command of the force to Colonel William Holmes, a Sydney militia officer with distinguished service in the

Boer War. The force, which was to be ready in six days, consisted of two battalions, and a small number of support troops. An army battalion was quickly raised from volunteers in Sydney, and a navy battalion was formed from the RAN Reserve. Holmes's force departed Sydney in a hastily chartered passenger liner on 19 August. Raising, equipping and embarking such a force in a little over a week was an extraordinary achievement.[35]

While the government was planning to seize German New Guinea, the Australian naval squadron under Rear Admiral Patey was hunting the German East Asia Squadron. The latter, commanded by Admiral Maximilian von Spee and based at Tsingtao (Qingdao) in China, consisted of two armoured cruisers, three light cruisers and various support vessels. The German ships posed a threat to Australian trade—indeed the Germans had prepared plans for such an attack.[36] But the RAN's battle cruiser, HMAS *Australia*, was more powerful than any of the German ships, and von Spee avoided contact with the Australian squadron. After finding that the German ships were not at Rabaul harbour in New Britain, Patey was inclined to head north to seek the German squadron, but he was diverted east to support a New Zealand force landing in Western Samoa. Some critics have suggested that Patey would have been better off chasing the Germans; ultimately, however, the decision rested with the Admiralty, which was now running the naval war across the globe.[37]

By 9 September, Patey and his squadron were back off the coast of Papua where they met up with Holmes's force. Patey would command the combined naval–army expedition. Escorted by the Australian squadron, the force landed near Rabaul on 11 September and, after a short fight, the Germans surrendered.[38] Although conducted at the request of Britain, it was the first campaign planned and executed by the Australian services—all within six weeks of the outbreak of the war.

The Cook Government's Final Decisions

The caretaker arrangements under which a government makes no new decisions during an election campaign did not apply in the first decades of the Australian parliament. Hence, on 30 August Cook announced that Australia would need to provide a larger force than the original 20,000-strong AIF, and he called for volunteers for further contingents. As he explained: 'The struggle in which we are involved together with the rest of the Empire promises to be of considerable duration. Our national existence is at stake, and we must be prepared to take up our share of the burden, without flinching from the sacrifice that may be involved.' Cook explained that the British Secretary of State for War, Lord Kitchener, was 'enrolling volunteers', and: 'We shall fail in our duty unless we follow in the same lines.' On 3 September the government announced that it would be sending a second contingent overseas, and on 11 September, Millen announced that the new infantry brigade, the 4th, would be commanded by a Melbourne militia officer, Colonel John Monash.[39]

By this time, it was clear that Australia would have a new government. In the federal election held on 5 September the Labor Party won an absolute majority in both houses, and Andrew Fisher formed his third government on 17 September. Joseph Cook had led Australia for only six weeks of the war, but it was a crucial time, and his government had made significant decisions. In support of the Empire, it had offered an expeditionary force to Britain and had placed the navy under Admiralty control. It had then raised two expeditionary forces, and the smaller one had seized German New Guinea. In appointing Bridges to command the larger AIF, the government set the conditions for Australia's contribution for the future. In expanding the AIF and appointing Monash, it had given command to an officer who would go on to become Australia's pre-eminent commander of the war.

The Fisher Government

It was unlikely that there would be any change in broad war policy under the Fisher government. During the election campaign Fisher had famously pledged: 'Australians will stand beside our own to help and defend her to our last man and our last shilling,' and he made similar comments on several occasions.[40] Fisher seemed well equipped to be a war leader. Aged 52, he had previously been prime minister for more than three and a half years, and he was familiar with defence issues. But, as a 'pragmatic utopian socialist', Fisher was 'repelled by the brutality and carnage of war', and could not approach his role as war leader with any enthusiasm. With regard to defence policy, he was pulled between a desire to assist Britain and his concerns about a possible Japanese threat in the Pacific.[41] While he favoured conscription for home defence, he opposed it for the AIF.

As noted earlier, during their previous time in government Fisher and his defence minister, Pearce, had played a major role in introducing the universal training scheme and forming the RAN. In September 1914, Pearce returned to his old post as defence minister, and Hughes, the vigorous advocate of stronger defences, became attorney-general. The governor-general, Munro Ferguson, thought himself 'very fortunate in having to deal in these times of crisis with two men of such high character as Mr Fisher and Senator Pearce'.[42]

Munro Ferguson was less enamoured of the attorney-general, Billy Hughes, who was soon displaying his characteristic energy and determination in driving the war effort to the maximum extent. But Munro Ferguson would soon change his mind about Hughes, coming to believe that because of his support for the Empire he was an outstanding war leader. Hughes quickly ushered through parliament two bills—Trading with the Enemy, and War Precautions. The latter, passed on 28 October, gave the government enormous powers to prosecute anyone 'who contravenes or fails to comply with any regulation or order made in pursuance of this Act'. The official historian, Ernest Scott, summed it up:

> scores of the most far-reaching regulations were made under that act and its later amendments; it legalised the censorship; it gave control over newspapers; it penalised the spreading of reports likely to cause disaffection or public alarm; substantially it established military control; and it was, according to legal opinion, wide enough to have enabled the government to inaugurate conscription by regulation if it had been politically expedient to do so.[43]

By instinct, Fisher would have been reluctant to accept such measures, but as Fisher's biographer, David Day, commented, Fisher 'could not allow Hughes to outflank him on the issue of winning the war . . . Nothing could be left unsacrificed to the aim of winning the war, except the principle of volunteerism for overseas service. For Fisher that was sacrosanct.'[44] At this stage Hughes was not closely involved with the military conduct of the war, but that would come soon.

The first decision by Fisher and Pearce on the conduct of the war concerned the despatch of the AIF from Australian ports to a concentration point at Albany, Western Australia, and then across the Indian Ocean and on to Britain. At first, the British Admiralty wanted to delay the departures until the intentions of the German East Asia Squadron became clearer. Bridges, commander of the AIF, advised Pearce that delay was more dangerous than sailing. But Fisher, Munro Ferguson and the New Zealand prime minister, Bill Massey (whose Expeditionary Force was sailing to join the AIF), were still concerned about the risk of the transports being attacked and sunk by German warships, and refused to allow the ships to proceed. When Bridges again sought approval for the transports to sail, the New Zealanders delayed until they received more powerful escorts to cross the Tasman Sea. The combined AIF–New Zealand convoy finally sailed from Albany on 1 November, escorted by two Australian light cruisers (*Sydney* and *Melbourne*), a British cruiser and a Japanese cruiser (Japan had joined the Allies two weeks after the outbreak of the war). Pearce believed the delay was justified when the *Sydney* destroyed the German light cruiser *Emden* at the Cocos Islands in the Indian Ocean on 9 November. Bridges refused to concede that he had been wrong.[45]

The next decision concerned a request on 14 October from the British government for Australian troops to be sent to Yap (1700 kilometres north-west of Rabaul) to relieve Japanese marines who had taken the island from the Germans. Australia formed a third small expeditionary force, known as Tropical Force, and Pearce appointed Samuel Pethebridge, secretary of the Department of Defence, who had arrived back in Australia, to command it. As it turned out, Tropical Force was not required to go to Yap , and Petherbridge would go on to become the administrator of German New Guinea. Trumble would remain acting secretary of the department.

The decision not to send Tropical Force to Yap eventuated because Britain had agreed that Japan could occupy all the former German islands north of the equator. Japan indicated that it intended to keep the islands after the war, thus bringing their territory closer to Australia and heightening the Australian government's concern about Japan. Advised by Britain of this arrangement on 3 December, Australia accepted it; as Meaney commented: 'The Australians were frustrated but knew that they had no other option. The Japanese had had their way and won the day.'[46]

While these problems were being sorted out in Melbourne, Admiral Patey, still patrolling the South Pacific, was anxious to pursue the German East Asia Squadron, now heading across the Pacific, bound for South America and ultimately Germany. Winston Churchill, First Lord of the Admiralty, decided that HMAS *Sydney* needed to be sent to the Indian Ocean to protect the AIF convoy and that Patey should remain near Fiji in case the Germans turned back towards Australia. The Germans had no intention of doing this. On 1 November, von Spee's ships sank two elderly British cruisers in the Battle of Coronel off the Chilean coast, raising questions as to whether Patey, had he chased von Spee, could have prevented the disaster. In truth, however, *Australia* could not have reached South America in time to apprehend von Spee's squadron, and further, the Admiralty was under political pressure to protect the AIF convoy and would not have approved such a mission.[47] As the RAN's ships were under control of the Admiralty, Creswell and the Australian Naval Board could take little action. Effectively, for the remainder of the war, the Australian government had no role in the direction of its naval ships except those in close proximity to the Australian coast.

Fisher was irritated by Britain's lack of consultation on strategic issues in the Pacific. Earlier, in July 1914, Britain had agreed to hold an imperial conference to consider naval defence in the Pacific, but with the outbreak of the war had postponed it 'indefinitely'. Fisher was not happy, believing that the war made 'the holding of a conference more urgent and valuable'. The Colonial Office sought the views of all the dominions (except Australia) on Australia's desire for a conference, telling them it would be 'impossible' to convene a conference before the 'conclusion of the war'. When the other dominions 'fell into line', the Colonial Office then advised Australia that the conference could not be held, and Fisher reluctantly had to agree, even though he continued to believe that a conference was 'desirable, even essential'.[48] Fisher and his government had continued Cook's support for Britain, but he had detected problems of consultation that were likely to continue.

Controlling and Supporting the AIF

At the same time, Pearce was struggling to determine how much control he should continue to exert over the AIF once it had left Australia, heading for Egypt, rather than Britain as originally planned. On 26 November, Pearce learned that Kitchener had appointed an Indian Army officer, Major General William Birdwood, to command the Australian and New Zealand forces, which would be brought together to form an army corps (subsequently known as the Australian and New Zealand Army Corps—ANZAC) in Egypt. The Australian government approved this appointment as 'very satisfactory'.[49] The corps would consist of Bridges' 1st Australian Division, and the New Zealand and Australian Division commanded by Major General Alexander Godley, the British officer who had commanded the New Zealand forces before the war and was commanding its contingent. Once Monash's 4th Brigade arrived in Egypt it would become part of Godley's division.

Pearce and the Australian government believed that once the AIF went overseas it was automatically under the control 'of the British Government and under it, the Army Council'. Pearce's biographer has observed that Pearce was timid in asserting Australian authority over the AIF, but he was not helped by Bridges, who was anxious to command the 1st Division in its first battle and 'deliberately downplayed his [Bridges'] responsibilities' as commander of the AIF. Bridges told Pearce that 'responsibility for maintenance and supply of the Australian Imperial Force should rest with the War Office'.[50] In an abrogation of his national responsibilities, Bridges was content to leave these matters to the imperial authorities.

The one matter that remained in the hands of the Australian government was the raising of forces, and Munro Ferguson was doing all he could to encourage the government to raise and despatch additional troops. The attorney-general, Hughes, was also agitating for more troops. On 23 December an exhausted Fisher departed for New Zealand, ostensibly for discussions with the New Zealand government, but in reality to recuperate from the stresses of the year. In his absence, Hughes became acting prime minister, and he was soon conspiring with Munro Ferguson to despatch more troops. On 16 January 1915, Hughes cabled Fisher in New Zealand that Pearce was recommending sending additional troops, and that unless Fisher vetoed it, he would offer Britain a further 10,000. Placed in a difficult position, Fisher agreed.[51] This would allow Australia to form two new infantry brigades.

Fisher arrived back in Melbourne from New Zealand on 3 February, in time for a meeting of the Council of Defence on 9 February—its first since 1913. Chaired by Pearce, with Fisher attending as treasurer, the council, which included Legge and Creswell, agreed unanimously that new units raised for the war should be retained in Australia 'at all events for the present'. Nonetheless, men continued to volunteer and, encouraged by this response, on 1 April the government decided to raise a third new brigade, and to despatch overseas three infantry brigades (5th, 6th and 7th), a light horse brigade (the 4th) and reinforcements, bringing the total to 17,183 officers and soldiers. The council met again on 26 February and did not meet again until 1918.[52] With no further council meetings and no War Cabinet, Australia's war-policy decisions would be made by the prime minister, the defence minister, and their naval and military advisers, or if particularly important, by the federal Cabinet.

Gallipoli Landing

Although Bridges warned the defence minister in January 1915 that 'the AIF would be taking part in a major operation against the Ottoman Empire', Pearce did not expect to be consulted about the deployment of the AIF. Fisher, however, was becoming concerned about the lack of consultation, evidenced by Britain's refusal to arrange an imperial conference. Further, newspapers carried reports of the RN's ineffective and costly efforts to force their way through the Dardanelles and there was speculation about the AIF's likely role. When Fisher learned that Chris Watson, the former Labor prime minister, was about to visit London on business, he asked Watson to find out what he could about British policies and to raise the matter of an imperial conference. Once he arrived in London, Watson tried but received little encouragement.[53]

Britain's lack of consultation was underlined after Australian and New Zealand troops landed at Gallipoli on 25 April 1915. The first the Australian government knew of it was four days later, on 29 April, when Fisher made a brief statement in the House of Representatives: 'Some days ago the Australian War Expeditionary Forces were transferred from Egypt to the Dardanelles. They have since landed and have been in action on the Gallipoli Peninsula. News reaches us that the action is proceeding satisfactorily.' Next day a cable arrived from King George V congratulating Australia 'upon the splendid conduct and bravery displayed by the Australian troops in the operations at the Dardanelles'. Even then, Fisher knew little of the details or purpose of the landing. The government and indeed the Australian public had to wait until 8 May for a more detailed description of the performance of their troops, when a colourful despatch from the British war correspondent Ellis Ashmead-Bartlett was published in Australian newspapers.[54]

Appointment of General Legge

The Australian government was not required to make any decisions about the Gallipoli campaign until 18 May, when news arrived that

Major General Bridges had been seriously wounded four days earlier. The Cabinet immediately appointed Legge to take over from Bridges as commander of the 1st Division and the AIF, and Legge embarked for overseas that day. Although Pearce was aware of some criticism of Legge, he put much of it down to jealousy, noting that as a result of Legge's 'brilliant administrative work' on the introduction of the Defence Act and universal training, Pearce himself had picked him out for advancement, giving 'great annoyance to those who were senior to him but who, having had the same chances had not displayed the same ability'. Considering Legge's strong views on Australian nationalism, no doubt the minister believed he was the man to preserve Australian interests. On 20 May the British government approved Legge's appointment. That same day Bridges died on a hospital ship.[55]

Although Legge had departed for overseas, he remained CGS, and in his place the minister appointed Colonel Godfrey Irving, aged 46, as temporary CGS. Originally a militia officer from Melbourne, Irving transferred to the permanent forces in 1891 at the age of 24 and served briefly in South Africa at the end of the Boer War. He underwent training in England in 1905 and then in India. He was military commandant in Western Australia from 1909 until he became commandant in South Australia in July 1914, by which time he had been promoted to colonel. Irving was 'a popular officer respected for his military capacity as well as his personal qualities'. Munro Ferguson thought that Irving was 'not at all equal to Legge . . . although he is as much liked as Legge is disliked'.[56]

In the absence of Legge, the strongest member of the Military Board was Lieutenant Colonel Thomas Dodds, who at the age of 40 had succeeded Sellheim as adjutant-general when the latter had joined Bridges' staff. After migrating from England to Queensland in 1883, Dodds became a teacher and militia officer. For his service in the Boer War he was mentioned in despatches and awarded the Distinguished Service Order. In 1906 he transferred to the permanent forces, where his administrative ability when planning the compulsory training scheme was noticed by Legge. As the military historian Alec Hill remarked, Dodds was 'known as a bluff, outspoken and formidable officer. Given the range of his responsibilities for the personnel of the army, including the recruitment of the A.I.F. until 1916, it was fortunate that a man of such strength of character and energy was available. Dodds . . . was one of the earliest and strongest proponents of the "Australianisation" of the commands and staffs of the A.I.F., strongly pressing this policy on the minister for defence.'[57]

Munro Ferguson considered that Legge was unpopular because of his 'disregard for the feelings of others', and this unpopularity soon came back to bite him at Gallipoli. Colonels James McCay and John Monash, both militia officers, and Harry Chauvel, an experienced regular officer, each commanding brigades at Gallipoli, were incensed at the appointment, claiming that Legge was junior to them and had no experience of the campaign underway. Munro Ferguson tried to get Fisher and Pearce to change their minds, but they were adamant that the appointment stood. Further, when Birdwood complained to Pearce about Legge's appointment, the minister left it to Birdwood to sort it out, adding that 'I know you will always give due weight to our very keen desire that, where suitable, our Australian Officers should receive command of Australian units.'[58] It was a sentiment that would be repeated many times over the following years. Legge arrived at Gallipoli on 24 June to assume command of the 1st Division.

Before long, Birdwood found a way out of the dilemma of Legge's unpopularity. The 5th, 6th and 7th Infantry Brigades, then arriving in Egypt, needed to be trained, and Birdwood saw an opportunity to bring them together as the 2nd Australian Division, with McCay in command. Unfortunately, within days McCay broke his leg, and was invalided home to Australia. Since Legge had raised the brigades in Australia, Birdwood therefore proposed appointing Legge to the position. Pearce agreed, and also agreed that a British officer, Major General Harold Walker, resume command of the 1st Division, an appointment he had held after the death of Bridges. Against his wishes, Legge relinquished command of the 1st Division and left Gallipoli for Egypt on 23 July. Seeing his opportunity, Birdwood then suggested that because Legge would now be absent from Gallipoli, Birdwood himself should command the AIF. The government approved this, and Birdwood was appointed on 14 September.[59] Birdwood now wrote frequently to Pearce to keep him abreast of staffing issues. Administrative command of the AIF would therefore remain with an officer of the British Indian Army, rather than an Australian officer, for the remainder of the war. One of a wartime government's most important tasks is to select its army's commander; by force of circumstance this task was taken out of George Pearce's hands.

Fisher's Concerns

By June 1915 it was clear that the Gallipoli campaign to open the way to the Ottoman capital, Constantinople (now Istanbul), was a failure. The Anzacs were clinging under fire to a small perimeter along the rugged west coast of the Gallipoli Peninsula, while British and French troops were confined to a small enclave at the tip of the peninsula. Casualties were mounting for no apparent purpose, with soldiers living in abysmal conditions. Fretting at the lack of reliable information, Fisher saw an opportunity to gain an accurate view of the situation. Before the war he had developed a friendship with a 29-year-old journalist from the parliamentary press gallery, Keith Murdoch. In June 1915 Murdoch was offered the job as managing editor of a cable service in London providing news to Australian newspapers. Torn between accepting the appointment and volunteering for the army, Murdoch sought the advice of his friend, Fisher. The prime minister thought Murdoch would be of better service reporting on the war, and providing him with information from London. Furthermore, on the way to London he could visit Gallipoli and give Fisher a first-hand account of the campaign. So, in mid-July, armed with letters from Pearce instructing him to investigate mail deliveries and medical support for the AIF, about which there had been many complaints, Murdoch departed for overseas.[60]

The big question concerning Australia's war policy remained the raising of additional troops. After a successful recruiting campaign in June, Pearce approved a suggestion from the adjutant-general, Dodds, that Australia offer to double its reinforcements for October and November. The British government accepted this offer, but as casualties at Gallipoli increased, even more troops were required, with pressure growing for the introduction of conscription. Instead, on 23 July, at Fisher's request, the government passed the War Census Act, which required every male between the ages of 18 and 60 to answer certain questions about their readiness to enlist. Held between 6 and 15 September, the census revealed that there were 307,150 men between the ages of 18 and 45. With thousands of men obviously not volunteering, the recently formed Universal Service League (whose members included Chris Watson and the Labor premier of New South Wales, William Holman) started to call for conscription. Both Fisher and Hughes publicly emphasised their opposition to it.[61]

By the time Murdoch arrived at Gallipoli in early September, the situation there had deteriorated. On 8 August, the reinforced Mediterranean Expeditionary Force had mounted a major offensive to break out of the perimeter and to drive the Ottoman forces from the Gallipoli Peninsula, but through faulty planning and incompetent command it had failed, with heavy casualties.[62] After British forces landed at Suvla Bay, north of Anzac Cove, the Anzac–British perimeter had been extended; but British and Anzac troops had been unable to seize the heights of the ridge running along the peninsula. Murdoch spoke to casualties in hospital in Egypt, and then at Gallipoli discussed the campaign with senior commanders, the British war correspondent Ellis Ashmead-Bartlett, and the Australian official correspondent, Charles Bean. The correspondents were dismayed at the conduct of the campaign, and Murdoch could see the appalling conditions at Gallipoli for himself.

When Murdoch arrived in London he wrote a devastating and heartfelt letter to Fisher; it has been described as 'an amazing document—a mixture of error, fact, exaggeration, prejudice and the most sentimental passion'. He explained to Fisher that Gallipoli 'is undoubtedly one of the most terrible chapters in our history. Your fears have been justified.'[63] Murdoch also gave a copy of the letter to David Lloyd George, the British Minister for Munitions, who in turn gave a copy to the prime minister, Herbert Asquith. Asquith thought the letter so important that he had it printed as a state paper. Soon Ashmead-Bartlett was also in London, lending his voice to the criticism. The British government had to act, and on 16 October the commander of the Mediterranean Expeditionary Force General Sir Ian Hamilton was relieved of his command; but at this stage it looked as though the Gallipoli campaign would drag on into 1916.

There was strong criticism of the campaign in Britain, but not in Australia, which preferred to take pride in the efforts of its soldiers. There was no reporting of Murdoch's letter in the Australian newspapers. This was despite other evidence that the campaign was a blunder. On 15 September, the Secretary of State for Colonies, Andrew Bonar Law, wrote to Munro Ferguson that there was 'no immediate prospect of success' in the Dardanelles, and in October Pearce received an assessment from Legge that 'I cannot see that we shall do anything here, except to hang on till the spring.' Pearce was still content to leave the conduct of the campaign in British hands, even if Fisher was having doubts about it. At this time Munro Ferguson assessed Pearce as 'the kind of man for whom Soldiers at Home have prayed for in vain. He gives his military officers a free hand and takes responsibility for all they have done himself!'[64] This included supporting the imperial direction of the war.

Australia's war leadership was, however, about to change. On 27 October 1915, Fisher resigned as prime minister. He had been struggling with ill health for the previous year and was perhaps detecting the first glimpses of the dementia with which he would eventually be afflicted. He would take up the appointment as high commissioner in London, succeeding George Reid, whose term had already been extended. Maybe Fisher felt that as high commissioner and a former prime minister he could gain access to the British government's decision-making. In this respect, he was to be disappointed. Had he remained prime minister, he would probably have continued to oppose conscription, and it is doubtful that his health could have stood the strain of resisting Hughes and Pearce on this issue. While the decision to raise the AIF had been made before he became prime minister, he continued to support it, although he had identified the need for greater consultation with the British government. Pearce remained as defence minister. Hughes, the ablest and most energetic of Fisher's ministers, succeeded him as prime minister, while retaining his portfolio of attorney-general. He would bring a different, more activist and ruthless approach to Australia's war leadership.

2

'I'm an Attorney-General not a Major General'

Hughes, First World War, 1915–17

As prime minister for the last three years of the First World War, Billy Hughes was Australia's first real war leader, actively seeking to control and shape the nation's war effort. His wartime prime ministership was marked by the two divisive conscription referenda in October 1916 and December 1917. The first conscription campaign split the Australian Labor Party, with Hughes and some of his colleagues being expelled from the party, and earning themselves the label of Labor Party 'rats'. During these campaigns, Hughes, in a ruthless exercise of political power, used the War Precautions Act, which he himself had pushed through parliament in 1914, to censor and at times jail his political opponents. The use of military intelligence, the newly formed security bureau and the police to conduct surveillance set a precedent that was to bedevil Australian society for decades. Hughes acted like a dictator, but through gritted teeth he respected the outcomes of the referenda. At the same time, Hughes won support from a majority of the population in federal elections in 1917 and 1919, the first fought on the need to prosecute the war fully.

In governing wartime Australia, the Hughes government needed to deal with a multitude of issues, including trade, finance and industrial relations. For the first time the government became involved in important diplomatic matters, particularly trying to ensure that Japan's power would be curtailed in the post-war world. These issues helped shape the nation in the decades to follow and are important to Australian history. They are not, however, within the scope of this book, which is focused more narrowly on war leadership with regard to military operations. It is concerned with the strategy of the war, the size of Australia's military commitment and how it was to be maintained, how and where the Australian forces were to be employed, and how they were to be commanded. These decisions needed to be considered in an imperial context. Having passed the Australian forces to British control, how much was Australia to be consulted about their use? The extent to which the Australian government was willing or able to control or decide these matters was a measure of the extent of Australia's sovereignty as an independent country. The outcome was at least a step along the road to exercising that sovereignty.

Invitation to Visit London

As Australia's war leader, Hughes came to grips with these imperatives slowly. Within days of becoming prime minister he made two decisions that were to have a fundamental impact on Australia's war effort. The first decision was to visit London to consult with the British government about the conduct of the war. In fact, shortly before he had resigned, Fisher had been told that Britain would 'welcome full and confidential discussions with dominion prime ministers if they visited London'. Hughes received the same invitation on 5 November 1915 and he readily accepted this opportunity for a 'frank interchange of views'.[1]

There is nothing, however, to suggest that Hughes's decision was influenced by Keith Murdoch's inflammatory letter of 23 September in which he had criticised the conduct of the Gallipoli campaign. Rather, Hughes's attitude was displayed on 29 October when he responded to a question in parliament as to whether, in view of the criticism from Murdoch and the British war correspondent Ellis Ashmead-Bartlett, the time had arrived to discuss the failed Dardanelles campaign, and to examine why Australians had been sent 'to useless slaughter'. Hughes replied that the government had no responsibility for 'directing the campaign. Our business is to carry out the instructions of the Imperial government and to give that government our hearty and enthusiastic support.' Australia's duty was 'to refrain from criticising the actions of men who are placed in a situation of frightful responsibility'. Australia's duty was 'to mind its own business, to provide that quota of men which the Imperial government think necessary in the circumstances, and to see that those men are efficiently led, fed and equipped'. Pearce agreed with his prime minister, commenting that he and Hughes were 'content to entrust the conduct of such affairs to our military advisers'. These views certainly won approval from the governor-general, Sir Ronald Munro Ferguson, who 'was greatly pleased to see this response by Hughes'. He thought Hughes would 'make one of the best War Ministers in the Empire'.[2]

The historian Eric Andrews described Hughes's 'refusal to concern himself with strategy' as 'a fatal weakness', but despite the prime minister's soothing words in parliament, it would have been uncharacteristic of such a fierce nationalist not to look more closely at the questions of command of the Australian forces and the strategic direction of their operations. Indeed, referring to the Gallipoli and Suvla Bay landings and to the subsequent Salonika campaign, he wrote later that 'Australia had not been consulted about any of these inchoate plans before they were put into operation, nor told a word about them after they had been set in motion.' He was 'determined to rectify' this situation when he visited England. These comments were written with the advantage of hindsight; there is not much evidence that Hughes was expressing these views at the time. Nonetheless, Hughes also believed that Britain was ignoring Australia's concerns about security in the Pacific, and that this issue needed to be pursued in London. As Douglas Newton has argued, Hughes never lost sight of the need to maintain White Australia against a possible Japanese threat, and in that regard, 'the only war aim that Australia pressed was the need to keep captured German colonies'.[3]

Expanding the AIF

The Hughes government's second decision was to expand the AIF to five infantry divisions. On 23 November 1915 the government advised London that it had decided to raise an additional 50,000 men for active service, which would bring Australia's contribution by June 1916 to about 300,000 men. This would allow Australia to form three new infantry divisions, bringing the total to five. New Zealand military historian Christopher Pugsley has argued that Australia had thus 'embarked on an unchecked and unplanned expansion of formations and units to meet the number of volunteers, with little or no thought as to how these new units would be sustained with reinforcements'. This is undoubtedly right. Although there was a burst of recruitment at the end of 1915, already the government was finding it difficult to sustain the required level of voluntary recruitment, and if casualties were to mount, the force could only be sustained by conscription.[4] The decision to form five infantry divisions would ultimately have unhappy consequences, leading to the divisive and unsuccessful conscription referenda in 1916 and 1917, and, through lack of reinforcements, an almost disastrous strain on the AIF in 1918. But the proposal to form three new divisions in Australia did not by itself result in their formation—the imperative also came from the British commanders of the AIF.

With reinforcements arriving in Egypt, one burning issue was the administration of the AIF, and in November Pearce decided to send the CGS, Brigadier General Irving, to Egypt to command all the AIF troops there. However, Irving's appointment was overtaken by events. On 9 November, Lord Kitchener visited Gallipoli and on 17 November he ordered an evacuation to begin the following month. By this stage Birdwood had assumed command of the newly formed Dardanelles Army, and Major General Godley had taken over the Anzac Corps. Ably assisted by his chief of staff, Brigadier General White, Godley commanded the brilliantly conceived evacuation from Anzac Cove in December. About 50,000 Australians had served at Gallipoli and about half, more than 26,000, became casualties, of whom about 8100 died. When the troops arrived back in Egypt,

Godley took over all the Anzac troops there. Thus, by the time Irving arrived in Cairo on 27 January 1916, there was no obvious job for him, and Birdwood, who had also returned to Egypt, asked Irving to take no further action until he (Birdwood) had received a reply from Australia about a proposal to form further Australian divisions in the Middle East.[5]

The proposal had arisen because there was already a large number of reinforcements in Egypt who were no longer needed for the Gallipoli campaign. If two more Australian divisions, plus a New Zealand division and an Anzac mounted division, were to be formed in Egypt, it would be possible to form a second Anzac Corps (one under Birdwood and the other under Godley). In that case, the ambitious Birdwood saw an opportunity to form an Australasian army with himself in command. Hence, towards the end of January 1916 he wrote to Pearce outlining his plans to expand the AIF, adding that he proposed to appoint British officers to command the two new infantry divisions formed from this expansion. Birdwood also proposed promoting Colonel Sellheim to brigadier general to command the AIF administrative headquarters and that Irving be given command of an infantry brigade.[6]

When these proposals reached Melbourne, the adjutant-general, Dodds, criticised the appointment of the British officers, noting that it 'can only have a heartbreaking effect on Australian officers in being debarred from attaining high distinction . . . I feel sure that, were this matter known at this present time, the result would be an expression of public indignation.' Pearce agreed, and on 4 February he cabled Birdwood his 'general disappointment' with the command arrangements, inquiring whether Brigadier Generals Chauvel, Monash, White and Holmes might be considered for command of the new infantry divisions.[7]

Birdwood replied that most of the Australian officers lacked the experience and capability for higher command appointments, but agreed to appoint McCay, who was recovering from his injury, to command the newly formed 5th Division, and Chauvel to command the Anzac Mounted Division. Legge would retain command of the

2nd Division, the 1st and 4th Divisions would be commanded by British officers, while a commander of the 3rd Division, which was being formed in Australia, was yet to be appointed.[8]

In considering these issues, Pearce had relied on advice from Dodds, and the new CGS, Colonel Hubert Foster, who had replaced Irving. Foster was a retired British army officer who had been director of military science at the University of Sydney since 1906; but by 1915 he had no students. Foster's appointment at the age of 60 was evidence that Australia's most capable soldiers were now serving overseas, but in fact his was a fortuitous choice. According to one of his contemporaries, Foster, soon promoted to brigadier general, brought to the task 'wide knowledge, long experience, and assiduous training', along with 'unwearying patience and a gentleman's charm of manner'. Munro Ferguson thought that Foster was 'the best man we have here, for in addition to his military and administrative capacity he is a man of the world and commands general confidence and regard. He is a great improvement on Irving and Legge so that confidence in the General Staff which suffered with the loss of General Bridges is once more restored.' Munro Ferguson's priority, however, was to support the imperial war effort, even if certain decisions might not be the best for Australia, and Foster, a British officer, was inclined to do all he could to provide the troops sought by Britain.[9]

As 1916 progressed, Munro Ferguson thought that Pearce, as defence minister, was 'a model of right conduct', acting on the advice of the Military Board in which each member was responsible for his own area of activity. As the governor-general put it, the 'Board acts in watertight compartments and each head has considerable power'. Foster 'understood' this and observed it, but at times the adjutant-general, Dodds—a 'strong character'—had much influence with Pearce. Munro Ferguson saw Dodds as one 'of the rough and ready school . . . hard working and capable but ill-mannered, violent and prejudiced . . . tho' to me personally his demeanour is irreproachable and he is helpful'.[10]

On 20 January 1916, well before the command issues in Egypt had been resolved, Hughes had set sail for New Zealand and Canada, heading for England, leaving Pearce as acting prime minister, and by the time Hughes arrived in England on 7 March the situation of the AIF command had changed. Since his return to Egypt in mid-January, Birdwood had commanded both the Australian and New Zealand forces, but on 29 February he was warned that the 1st Anzac Corps, then commanded by Godley and consisting of the 1st and 2nd Australian Divisions and the New Zealand Division, was shortly to begin moving to France. With Birdwood left behind in Egypt commanding the 2nd Anzac Corps (4th and 5th Divisions), the matter of command of the AIF had to be resolved.[11] Was it to be Godley in France or Birdwood in Egypt?

Hughes and the AIF Command

Once he arrived in London, Hughes turned his mind to this issue, even though when reporters asked him about the disposition of the Australian forces he replied that he had no claim to military knowledge: 'You'll have to ask Lord Kitchener that. I'm an Attorney-General not a Major General.' Nonetheless, when on 11 March he learned from the Chief of the Imperial General Staff (CIGS), General Sir William Robertson, about the problem of appointing a commander of the AIF, he cabled urgently for Pearce's advice. Pearce replied that while Godley was fit for the position, 'we sincerely trust that Birdwood will continue to command the Australians as soon as circumstances permit'.[12] Through numerous letters, Birdwood had assiduously cultivated his relationship with Pearce, who had come to trust the British general unreservedly.

Robertson had anticipated Hughes's concerns and had already sought advice from General Archibald Murray, the British commander in Egypt. Murray strongly supported Godley, adding that he would have 'greater confidence in Godley' than Birdwood for operations in France. On 13 March, Robertson 'had a bad morning with Hughes who . . . insisted that Birdwood should command the Australian Corps coming to France'. Hughes thought that Robertson 'was as unresponsive as a stone image'. Murray still preferred to send Godley, but after further discussion with Hughes and Kitchener, Robertson ordered Murray to send Birdwood. The designation of the corps headquarters was changed, and on 29 March Birdwood and the 1st Anzac Corps embarked for France. Pearce cabled the War Office, welcoming the plan and adding that he hoped that it would be possible to form all the troops into an 'Australasian Army'; the War Office advised that every effort would be made to meet this wish when circumstances permitted. Through Hughes's advocacy, Australia was at last taking a role in the control of its forces.[13]

Meanwhile, advised by Foster, Pearce had suggested that Australia form a 6th Division, but early in April the British War Office rejected this proposal. Hughes still doubted the intentions of General Sir Douglas Haig, the British commander-in-chief in France, and on 12 April he asked Robertson whether it was true that the Australian Corps was to be broken up. Haig advised Robertson that he had no intention of breaking up the 'Australian Corps', but that six Australian divisions 'may be too small to form an army'. There was an element of aggrandisement and delusion in Australia wanting to form an army of six divisions. Already it was becoming obvious that voluntary enlistment was not providing sufficient troops to sustain five divisions if they suffered heavy casualties. Excusing the decision to form five divisions, Bean observed that 'the new divisions had in fact been provided not from the 50,000 men (or three divisions) promised by the Hughes government after considering the War Census, but from the flood of recruits who had come forward during the previous months'.[14] This is true, but when Birdwood proposed to form two new divisions in Egypt, Australia could have put the formation of the third division (the one to be formed in Australia) on hold until the requirement for reinforcements became clearer after the first battles in France. Australia, however, was still keen to form five divisions.

With the deployment of the Australian divisions to France, the first priority was to establish an Australian base organisation in England, but this question was linked directly to Birdwood's status as commander of the AIF, and it was late April before Birdwood was permitted to go to England. By this time Hughes had become ill and the negotiations were conducted by the new Australian high commissioner, the former prime minister Andrew Fisher. On 21 and 28 April, Birdwood, Fisher and New Zealand representatives met British officials at the War Office, and they agreed that dominion bases would be established in England.[15]

This was the first opportunity for Birdwood to meet the mercurial Australian prime minister, and he wrote to the governor-general that he was 'delighted' to meet Hughes who had 'certainly taken a tremendous grip on the people at home and I fancy that a very large majority would like to see him succeed Asquith as Prime Minister tomorrow'. It seems that Birdwood had no views on the strategy being employed on the Western Front, although admittedly at this stage Haig was still developing his strategy, and he had not yet begun his Somme offensive. Birdwood was more concerned with lobbying Hughes to ensure that he retained command of the AIF, and he and Hughes decided to bring Brigadier General Sellheim from Egypt to command the AIF administrative headquarters in London.[16]

On 6 May, Pearce informed the War Office that Birdwood would continue to command the AIF from France with Sellheim acting as his representative in London. The War Office objected that Birdwood 'could not possibly perform all the administrative duties' in addition to his command in the field.[17] Not to be put off, Hughes was convinced that Birdwood had to retain command to enable him to form an Australian Army, and he set out to persuade Haig that it was practicable for Birdwood to combine both the administrative and field commands.

Hughes and Fisher arrived at Haig's headquarters in France in the evening of 31 May. Haig wrote in his diary that Hughes was 'very deaf, but quick and most intelligent. He suffers from nerves, sleeps badly and did not come down for breakfast at 8.30 am. I saw him about 9.30 am before he went.' Hughes began by asking Haig to regard the Anzacs as an army and saying that Birdwood should command it. Haig replied that he had no intention of breaking up the 'Australian Corps', but even if Australia put six divisions into the field, it would not be a large enough force to be called an Australian Army.

Hughes 'regretted very much' this view, and asked that Birdwood be given command of all the Australian troops in France. Haig agreed, 'subject of course to the fundamental principle that nothing must be done that would hamper the Imperial Forces in attaining the object for which the Empire is fighting . . . if at any future time I can see my way to employing all the Australian forces together under his command for some special operations, I will do so'. Haig told Hughes of the coming Somme offensive, and Hughes concluded the conversation by assuring Haig that 'he had the most thorough confidence' in him and that he would do all he could to help him. Fisher, who struck Haig 'as inferior to Mr Hughes in many respects, also said he would do his best to help'.[18]

Subsequent negotiations between Haig and Birdwood resulted in Haig retaining control over the transfer of sick and wounded soldiers from France to England and the despatch of drafts from England to France. Thus not only had Haig retained freedom in the operational use of the Australian troops, but Hughes's efforts to ensure Birdwood would have administrative control over the Australian forces had been watered down. Hughes wrote later: 'The Dominions could only place their armed forces at the disposal of the leaders Britain chose to appoint . . . the Dominion governments were not in a position to judge the ability of the British High Command.'[19] At this stage, Hughes was not concerning himself with the broader strategy of the war, but only with command of the AIF.

Dressed in grey tweeds, new brown riding gaiters and a grey felt hat, Hughes visited various Australian units and headquarters. He was keen to see the soldiers, and he spoke to Legge, the senior Australian officer in the force. There is no strict requirement that a war leader visit his troops, but it certainly helps if he has some understanding of the conditions that they are enduring. In this respect, Hughes grasped the importance of his visit, even if the troops were not impressed with having to wait several hours for him to arrive. No doubt the meeting with the soldiers reminded Hughes of the need to secure greater control over their use, and Andrew Fisher's letter to Pearce describing the visit emphasised this aspect. He had learned that the British 'staff were a little exercised' at Birdwood communicating directly with Pearce. 'I am strongly of the opinion,' wrote Fisher, that 'Australia should exercise greater control than formerly. Though British officers mean well they do not understand our conditions. I regret to say that some of them (few) hardly know of our existence nor the fact that we are paying as well as supplying fighting men on land and sea.'[20]

On returning to England, Hughes redoubled his efforts to increase Australian influence, stimulated in this endeavour by the Australian journalist Keith Murdoch, the 30-year-old managing editor of United Cable Service, who became Hughes's 'publicist, fixer and runner'. Winston Churchill, out of office after the Gallipoli fiasco, wrote to his brother Jack serving at Birdwood's headquarters: 'I have made friends with Mr Hughes. We are all trying to secure command of the Australian Army for' Birdwood.[21]

By now Hughes, encouraged by Murdoch, had begun to doubt whether Sellheim was 'capable of battling' with the War Office. Meanwhile, Colonel Robert (Mac) Anderson, a successful Sydney businessman whom Pearce had sent to Egypt to improve the AIF's logistics, had moved with the AIF headquarters from Cairo to London. Probably because Hughes knew and trusted Anderson from his pre-war Sydney days, he decided to replace Sellheim with Anderson, who, he said, would run the AIF base on 'strict business principles'. On 1 August, Anderson took over from Sellheim, who returned to Australia and subsequently became adjutant-general.[22] Thus, after almost four months of effort, Hughes had settled the command and administrative organisation of the AIF. There was one other command appointment at this time, which was decided by Birdwood, namely the appointment in early July of Brigadier General Monash to command the 3rd Division on the Salisbury Plain. It was an appointment that was to have far-reaching importance.

Command of the AIF was only one of many issues worrying Hughes when he was in London. Through his speeches, attendance at the British War Cabinet, and consultations with British leaders, 'Hughes reached the pinnacle of his career; he had become an international celebrity overnight.'[23] At this stage, however, he had not concerned himself deeply with war strategy. Rather, he was fighting for Australia's case on the management of the AIF and recognition of Australia's contribution. Much of Hughes's time was taken up with non-military issues such as trade and shipping.

While Hughes was in London, the British government began to consider setting up a parliamentary inquiry into the Gallipoli campaign. But by 20 July, when the government announced what would become the Dardanelles Commission, Hughes was at sea, heading home, having left London on 29 June. The Australian high commissioner, Andrew Fisher, was given a seat on the commission, but took little part in it. The Australian government did not approve of the inquiry; as Pearce, the acting prime minister, told Fisher: 'I think it is a foolish blunder and displaying great weakness on the part of Govt.'[24] As always, Pearce was putting imperial interests first. The commission presented an interim report in February 1917 and the final report, critical of the conduct of the campaign, was not released until November 1919. Clearly, during 1916 and 1917, Australia's war leaders were reluctant to take any action that might criticise the British government or its conduct of the war.

The Conscription Referendum

By the time Hughes arrived back in Melbourne on 8 August 1916, Australia's military position had changed dramatically. Haig's offensive on the Somme had begun on 1 July, a day that became notorious as the bloodiest day in the history of the British Army, when 52,470 men became casualties, of which 19,240 were killed or later died of wounds. The Australians were soon in action; at Fromelles on 19 July, McCay's 5th Australian Division lost 5533 men, of whom 1917 were dead and a further 470 were prisoners. On the Somme, beginning on 23 July, the 1st, 2nd and 4th Australian Divisions followed each other in bloody attacks at Pozières. Each division then returned to the line, and by the time it was withdrawn on 5 September, the Australian Corps had suffered 24,139 casualties. Recruiting was producing insufficient reinforcements to replace these losses, and already Pearce had concluded that the only solution was to introduce conscription.

On 14 August, in the midst of the Somme campaign, Haig suggested to Birdwood that reinforcements could be drawn from the 3rd Division, still training on the Salisbury Plain. Based on advice from Birdwood and Anderson, the British Army Council cabled Australia stating that if the 3rd Division were not to be broken up, a special draft of 20,000 men should be sent straight away, with a further 16,500 men to be despatched every month. This was the critical cable that pushed Hughes towards conscription and, having no way of questioning it, he accepted it in good faith. Hughes did not know that the figures were about double what was needed. The CGS, Foster, advised Pearce that these demands could not be met. But after consultation with Foster, Pearce approved a cable to Britain that stated that apart from the 15,000 men of the 3rd Division, the AIF had 25,000 men in England and a further 15,000 were in ships on the way. Australia hoped to embark a further 20,000 men in November, with the requested 16,500 reinforcements available in each of January, February and March 1917. Thus Australia was committed to meeting the British demand; but it was not clear how these ambitious numbers were to be achieved, and in parliament in the next few days both Hughes and Pearce said that the voluntary recruiting system could not be relied upon.[25]

Hughes and Pearce were now convinced that the only option was to introduce conscription, and on 14 September Hughes announced in parliament that a referendum would be held on 28 October to decide whether Australia would introduce conscription. As well as the problem of meeting the shortfall in voluntary enlistments, Hughes was driven by two other concerns—news that the United Kingdom and New Zealand had already introduced conscription, and concern about Japan. The best way to prevent Japan becoming a threat was to ensure that Britain won the war in Europe. As Hughes explained: 'At present, the white races are engaged in destroying their manpower, leaving the coloured race untouched. This makes it all the more necessary that the war be brought to an end as quickly as possible, in order that our nation, at any rate, may not be absolutely exhausted when peace comes about.'[26]

The conscription campaign was bitter and divisive, with many in the Labor Party opposed to it. Following the Easter uprising in Dublin in April 1916, and considering Australia's large Irish Catholic population, the campaign caused sectarian strife. Hughes used the War Precautions Act to harass and arrest members of the Industrial Workers of the World who were actively opposing conscription. The result was a narrow overall majority for the 'No' campaign, with three states, New South Wales, Queensland and South Australia, voting no. The effect of the campaign on Australian society, which was to last for decades, is beyond the scope of this book, which is concerned primarily with the conduct of the military side of the war. But the way the campaign split the Labor Party was to affect directly Hughes's ability to manage the war effort.

Outcome of the Conscription Referendum

When the Labor Party caucus met on 14 November 1916, it was certain that a majority would vote to oust Hughes as leader. Instead, before a vote could be taken, Hughes and 23 MPs and senators walked out of the Labor Party, calling themselves the National Labor Party. Hughes then led a minority government, in which he was protected from a Labor Party no-confidence vote by the support of Joseph Cook's Liberal Party. Hughes's biographer noted that 'Hughes was walking a political tightrope. On one side yawned the abyss of "undying hostility" separating him from the party he had helped to create and in which he had spent his whole political life; on the other was the host of those who had been his adversaries since Federation . . . Only his wholehearted dedication to winning the war and the confidence in him of the Governor-General stood between him and destruction.'[27] It was a reminder that in a democracy war leadership can never be separated from politics. Decisions about the conduct of the war need to take their political impact into account.

On 17 February 1917, after intense negotiation over the summer months, the National Labor and Liberal parties formed a coalition government with Hughes as prime minister and Cook as his deputy. George Pearce retained his portfolio as defence minister, and Cook became navy minister. The Liberal Party had demanded that Cook receive the Defence portfolio, but Hughes fought successfully to retain it for his old colleague and friend. Eighteen months earlier, in July 1915, Pearce had split the Defence portfolio to form a separate Navy Department in an effort to ease his administrative load. This had little real effect, however, because the first navy minister, Jens Jensen of the Labor Party, and his successor, Cook, had little to do, given the RAN's ships were serving overseas under Admiralty control.

In the midst of these discussions, the new British prime minister, David Lloyd George, who had succeeded Asquith, suggested a special imperial conference in London to discuss 'the War including strategy, possible terms of peace in view of overtures by the Central Powers; Ireland; the German colonies'. Hughes had frequently complained about the lack of consultation with Britain, but the political situation made it difficult for him to leave Australia and he had to decline to attend. Hughes did not ask the high commissioner, Fisher, to represent him, as he did not think Fisher would do it adequately. Hughes's absence was unfortunate, because if he had attended he would have gained some insight into how Britain was running the war. As Eric Andrews has argued, a decision that after the war the former German colonies in the Pacific north of the equator should be retained by Japan 'would not have passed so easily if Hughes had been present'. The historian Peter Spartalis thought it 'rather tragic, or at least deplorable, that the political situation in Australia' did not allow Hughes to attend. When the Imperial Cabinet met in March 1917, its first item of business was to express 'great regret' that no Australian was present.[28]

As well as the political fallout from the failed referendum, on the military side, the AIF would continue to be supported by voluntary enlistments, but recruiting still declined sharply. On 11 November 1916 the Australian government advised Britain that it would not be possible to provide the 20,000 troops as promised, and suggested that the 3rd Division be retained in England for the present. The British government was adamant that the division had to go to France as already arranged, and urged Australia to spare no effort in providing adequate reinforcements for five divisions. It seemed that Foster was unwilling to worry the minister with unpopular advice. The governor-general wrote later that he received a shock 'before the New Year', when Foster 'blandly informed me that he had "reinforcements for everything except infantry". I suggested that if he had them for infantry, the rest didn't matter. He knew this as well as I did but, as I have said, his fault is that of the politician who always seeks to circumvent difficulties and is satisfied with a plausible case.'[29]

Contrary to the Army Council's threat in August 1916 that the 3rd Division would be broken up if Australia did not provide more reinforcements, by December the division was in action, although admittedly it was in a quiet area. Furthermore, although it seemed that Australia could not increase its rate of recruitment, on 1 February 1917 the British government asked Australia to raise a 6th Division. The CIGS, General Robertson, followed this with a direct appeal to Hughes, stating that the operations later in the year would 'be of supreme importance to [the] ultimate issue of [the] war'. Pearce's departmental staff provided him with calculations that showed it would be possible to raise the troops, and on 15 February Hughes approved the creation of the 6th Division.[30] The division would be formed in England from men recovering from sickness or wounds.

Meanwhile, the British commander in Egypt, General Murray, had decided to reorganise the light horse brigades in the Middle East so that in addition to the Anzac Mounted Division, an Imperial Mounted Division would be formed with two Australian light horse brigades, commanded by a British officer. Major General Harry Chauvel, commander of the Anzac Mounted Division, failed to tell Pearce about this new formation—evidence that many Australian commanders, such as Chauvel, still continued to think of themselves as agents of the Empire rather than Australia. It was 26 April 1917 before 'Pearce received an apology from the War Office for not consulting him before reorganising the mounted divisions'.[31]

Higher Command Problems

Between the beginning of Hughes's minority government on 14 November 1916 and the formation of the coalition government on 17 February 1917, Pearce had to deal with a number of command issues. The first one was relatively easy. The British officer, Major General Herbert Vaughan Cox, commanding the 4th Division, was transferred to India, and Birdwood replaced him with a Sydney militia officer Brigadier General William Holmes. Another Australian officer was now in a higher command appointment.

At the end of November 1916, Major General James McCay, commander of the 5th Australian Division, who was being troubled by his injured leg, was invalided to England with influenza. In truth, Birdwood thought that McCay had 'not been an entire success as a divisional commander', and when doctors confirmed that McCay was unfit to return, Birdwood, mindful of the exhortation from Pearce to fill vacancies with Australians, offered the division to Brigadier General Talbot Hobbs, commander of the 1st Division artillery.[32]

Towards the end of December, Birdwood was presented with a dilemma when Legge came down with influenza while his division was in the line. The British Army rule required that once a general officer was evacuated to England he had to be replaced, and when he recovered take his chance on being employed when a suitable vacancy occurred. Birdwood believed that none of the brigadiers in the division were suitable to take even temporary command, and he wired Pearce seeking permission to appoint a British officer, Nevill Smyth, then commanding the 1st Brigade, to the 2nd Division. Pearce cabled back what Birdwood called 'a rather ungracious approval' of this appointment.[33]

Recuperating in England in January 1917, Legge began to consider the prospects of employment for both himself and McCay. After discussions with Anderson, commandant of the AIF headquarters and now a brigadier general, Legge cabled various recommendations to Pearce. McCay also cabled Pearce, suggesting that he be made General Officer Commanding (GOC) all the troops in Australia. Advised by Dodds, Pearce responded to Birdwood suggesting that

McCay take over from Major General Sir Newton Moore, GOC of the AIF training depots on the Salisbury Plain in England, and that Legge return to his previous post as CGS in Australia. Moore, a former premier of Western Australia, was the agent-general for Western Australia in London, a position he continued to hold while also GOC of the AIF depots. He had previously served in the militia, reaching the rank of lieutenant colonel. At this stage, however, Legge preferred to remain overseas and made further representations to Pearce. Legge also wrote to Trumble, secretary of the Department of Defence, to express his concerns about the administration of the AIF. He believed that the British authorities had detached various Australian divisions with the intention of making it impossible to command the AIF in the field. He thought that Birdwood was 'not altogether Australian in sympathy', and had failed to fill sufficient vacancies with Australian officers.[34]

Birdwood was furious at this interference by Legge and McCay. In forthright letters to Pearce and the governor-general, Birdwood made his case. While he admired McCay's courage and determination, he thought that his injury would make it impossible for him to supervise training well, and his temperament would not allow him to be more of a success in the training job than Moore, who had stood up to the British authorities effectively. As for Legge, Birdwood stated frankly that if he had not been evacuated he was doubtful 'how long he would otherwise have lasted'. In the struggle to find a job in England, McCay, a former defence minister, was able to pull more political strings than Moore. Thus when Pearce responded to Birdwood, 'he approved the recommendation that Legge should return to Australia, but directed that if either Moore or McCay should return to civil life, it should be the former'.[35]

Legge continued fighting to remain overseas, arguing that he had only lost his command because of illness, and he told Birdwood that he intended to appeal to Haig's General Headquarters (GHQ). Birdwood now had two challenges to his authority—from the minister and from Legge. Brudenell White, chief of staff of Birdwood's corps and Birdwood's chief staff officer in his role as commander of the AIF, claimed that if he had been in Birdwood's position he would have resigned immediately, but Birdwood had partly caused his own difficulties by his failure to be frank with Legge, even giving him two letters saying that he was 'perfectly satisfactory in his division'. Birdwood now sent White, who had been promoted to major general, to London to tell Legge that 'he was not competent in the field'. White's advice to Legge was blunt: 'You can make a fuss if you like. But I would not. A man [Birdwood] may be driven to say what he doesn't want to, if you insist on driving him far enough.' Legge backed down. Indeed he soon rationalised his return to an Australia that in the previous months had been racked by the conscription referendum and the witch-hunt against members of the Industrial Workers of the World. As Murdoch explained: 'Legge goes back fairly contentedly convinced that he has been called back because Australia is on the verge of civil war and requires a strong man.'[36]

Birdwood did not give up in his efforts to retain Moore, but the government was determined to recall Moore, probably because Anderson had told the prime minister that Moore was responsible for failing to distribute Hughes's electioneering manifesto to the troops before the conscription referendum. As Bean noted, Anderson was 'far too underhand for the old politician [Moore] who is, despite his bluff, an overground man'. Pearce's instructions were clear, and Birdwood had no option but to direct that McCay take over from Moore on 1 May, but he left the minister in no doubt about his views. Birdwood praised Moore's shrewdness and his strength in dealing with a very serious riot at the AIF's No 4 Command Depot at Wareham in Dorset, and he reiterated his view that McCay did not have the 'exact temperament required'.[37] Birdwood and Moore loyally accepted the minister's decision, but as White observed, 'a great mistake had been made'.[38] Moore was not completely cast aside. He returned to his post as agent-general in London until September 1918, when he was elected to the British House of Commons.

So by March 1917, new commanders of the Australian divisions in France had been appointed, McCay was to become GOC of the AIF in England, Anderson was commandant of the AIF headquarters in London, and Legge was to return to Australia. On the political side, Hughes was leading a fractious coalition government, faced by an opposition Labor Party majority in the Senate. Unable to visit London, Hughes had little knowledge of British military plans for the northern spring of 1917. It would be the hardest year of the war, with a damaging railway strike in New South Wales, little success on the battlefields of France and Flanders, and a revolution in Russia. The Germans would begin an unrestricted submarine campaign that would bring the United States into the war in April, but the United States would make no impact on the war until the following year. For Australia's political and military leaders, the main focus would be on bringing the Australian divisions in France together as one corps under one commander, so that Australia could at last gain greater control over the employment of its troops.

3

'We shall have to humour them'

Hughes, First World War, 1917–19

Without a Senate majority the Hughes coalition government was in a precarious position, and having failed to wangle a majority through political tricks, on 5 March 1917 Hughes called an election for 5 May. After a bitter campaign, fought on a 'Win the War' ticket, the government won a resounding victory, indicating that the failure of the conscription referendum did not mean that the majority of Australians opposed the war commitment. The National Labor and Liberal parties merged to create the Nationalist Party and formed a new government with Hughes as prime minister and Cook as deputy prime minister. Pearce continued as defence minister, although with a lower rank in the Cabinet.[1]

Hughes and Pearce would still lead the war effort, but events in London were to cause further changes to their key advisers in Melbourne. Although Brigadier General Anderson had been confirmed as commandant of the AIF headquarters, fortunately for harmonious relations in London, he decided to return to Australia. In April, Colonel Thomas Griffiths, deputy adjutant-general on Birdwood's staff, took over from Anderson in London. Colonel Dodds, the adjutant-general in Melbourne, was to succeed Griffiths on Birdwood's staff, but Pearce was reluctant to let him go. According to the governor-general, while Dodds was 'not a tactful man', he alone was 'really in touch with the Minister', and his influence was 'all pervading'.[2] It was not until Legge arrived back in Australia that Pearce decided that he could spare Dodds, who could now provide Birdwood with first-hand advice on the minister's views and directly influence appointments within the AIF.

When Legge arrived back in Melbourne on 15 April 1917, Foster was unwilling to step aside as CGS, so Pearce made Legge inspector-general, in which capacity he toured AIF training camps, schools and hospitals to report to the minister. By early 1917 Pearce had developed a good working relationship with Foster, whom Munro Ferguson held in high regard for 'his tact, zeal and knowledge of the world' and wanted to retain as CGS. But as the year progressed, Munro Ferguson became less enthusiastic about the relationship between Pearce and Foster, noting that the Military Board was 'not strong', and while Foster was 'sound in knowledge' and 'did some things very well', he did not even preside when the minister was absent. Munro Ferguson thought that although Pearce was a 'charming personality', he was 'unstable in purpose and guided by some one individual instead of by the Board as a whole'. As Foster continued to hang on as chief, the governor-general became disillusioned with his performance, believing him to be 'so anxious to continue as CGS that he yields to political considerations and never puts effective pressure on the Minister'.[3] Legge eventually took over as CGS on 1 October 1917 and Foster became commandant of the Royal Military College.

Forming an Australian Corps

While these administrative issues were being resolved, the fighting had continued in France, with the Australians following up the unexpected German withdrawal to the Hindenburg Line. In April and May 1917, the 4th and 2nd Divisions lost heavily in poorly conceived and unsuccessful attacks at Bullecourt. In June, the 3rd and 4th Divisions were more successful in an attack at Messines, further north, just across the border in Flanders (Belgium). With the casualties at Bullecourt and Messines, Birdwood abandoned the plans to form the 6th Australian Division. The decision did not please Munro Ferguson, who advised Pearce that he 'entirely' disagreed, claiming that Birdwood was 'so wrapped up in his command that he is liable to lose his sense of proportion between the interest of his 6th Division and that of the Army and the Empire as a whole'. He thought that Foster was 'absolutely right' to press for retention of the 6th Division.[4] As casualties mounted, however, Birdwood was proved right. And Bullecourt did more than kill the 6th Division. The exchange between British general Hubert Gough, Birdwood and White before First Bullecourt, in which the Australians complained rightly about Gough's plans, emphasised the need for Australian commanders to have direct access to the commander-in-chief, and also to the Australian government when they thought that the safety of their men was at stake.

But how was the Australian government to obtain some say over the operational use of its forces? Birdwood was commanding the 1st Anzac Corps (now the 1st, 2nd and 4th Divisions) and Godley the 2nd Anzac Corps (3rd, 5th and New Zealand Divisions). Birdwood was also administrative commander of the AIF, but this gave him no standing when dealing with Haig. Although Hughes had not taken up the invitation to go to London, and Australia took no part in the deliberations of the Imperial War Cabinet, the journalist Keith Murdoch would not let the matter of control of the AIF slip. With high-level contacts in London, he would have been aware that at the Imperial Cabinet on 2 May the Canadian prime minister, Sir Robert Borden, had requested increased Canadian staff representation. Distressed by the Australian casualties in the Bullecourt battles, on 11 July Murdoch sent a cable to Hughes. He explained that the Australians prized their identity and that decisions were being made about Australia's 'government, public and national future' by people who were 'responsible to quite another public'. Murdoch recommended that all Australian units in France be brought together under Birdwood's command; that Birdwood provide a list of British officers attached to the AIF, and state which were 'irreplaceable'; and consider appointing a liaison officer at the War Office. The cable had been sent though the office of the high commissioner, Fisher, but indicates that it was Murdoch, rather than Fisher, who was actively pressing Australia's case in London and advising the prime minister. Eventually, at the end of July and in early August, the Australian government sent several proposals to Britain similar to those stated by Murdoch, and Birdwood was requested to prepare a list of British officers to be replaced.[5]

In response, the British Army Council strongly deprecated Australia's desire that only Australian officers should serve on the staff of Australian formations, describing it as 'retrograde and contrary to the whole spirit of Imperial policy'. The Australian requests now became sharper in tone, and on 25 August Hughes cabled that he was 'disappointed' at the British reply, 'from which it is evident that the Army Council is not in sympathy with the desire of this Government that Australian divisions should be grouped in one or more Australian corps with Australian staff officers'.[6] The Army Council replied that a corps of five Australian divisions would be 'unwieldy' while two smaller corps would be 'uneconomical'. It was 'essential' to the 'Imperial character of [the] staff that British officers should serve on [the] staff of Dominions formations and vice versa'. Hughes, however, was determined to have his way.[7]

It was with this outlook in mind that Murdoch visited Haig in France on 29 August and expressed the 'wish of Australia to have their five divisions organised as "an Army"'. As he had to Hughes more than a year earlier, Haig pointed out the 'impossibility of complying with this wish'. He promised to do all he could to keep the Australians together, but he noted in his diary: 'I could not help feeling that at the back of this fellow's mind there is a desire to be independent of the old country.' Haig thought the time had come for Birdwood to give up his corps command and to devote himself to the administration of the AIF.[8]

News of these discussions provided Hughes with further ammunition, and on 25 September he cabled the colonial secretary to emphasise the government's strong desire to place its divisions under one commander. He would 'be glad if this matter could be referred to my colleagues in the Imperial Cabinet'. However, the colonial secretary, Walter Long, and his permanent under-secretary, Sir George Fiddes, sat on this telegram for a whole month, and Lloyd George heard nothing about it. Nonetheless, the Army Council considered the telegram and asked Haig whether the proposal was 'practicable'.[9]

At this stage Haig, in the midst of the Ypres fighting in Flanders, was too busy to reply. But on 17 September he had visited the headquarters of the 1st Anzac Corps and was impressed by the Australian division and brigade commanders he met there. The Canadian Lieutenant General Arthur Currie had recently been put in charge of the Canadian Corps, and during this visit Haig told White that an Australian should be commanding their corps and he [White] was the most suitable candidate. White replied that Birdwood's reputation was too valuable for Australia to lose. Haig is reported to have 'turned away impatiently', and after that was 'very short with White'.[10]

When Haig visited the 1st Anzac Corps it was about to begin a series of well-planned attacks: at Menin Road on 20 September, at Polygon Wood on 26 September and at Broodseinde on 4 October, when two divisions from each of the 1st Anzac and 2nd Anzac Corps assaulted in line together. These strikes were a resounding success, driving the Germans back by relentless hammer blows, although AIF casualties were heavy, numbering more than 17,000. Then the rain came. In the last battle on 12 October, Monash's 3rd Division tried to take Passchendaele. The division lost more than 3000 men and the 4th Division in support another 1000. By the time Haig called a halt on 14 November he had lost 250,000 men, 38,000 of them from the five Australian divisions, thus creating a further problem with reinforcements. The attack at Passchendaele gave added impetus to Australia's efforts to gain control of its forces, as illustrated by a letter Monash wrote to his wife on 18 October:

> Our men are being put into the hottest fighting and are being sacrificed in hare-brained ventures, like Bullecourt and Passchendaele, and there is no-one in the War Cabinet to lift a voice in protest.
>
> It all arises from the fact that Australia is not represented in the War Cabinet, owing to Hughes, for political reasons having been unable to come to England. So Australian interests are suffering badly, and Australia is not getting anything like the recognition it deserves.[11]

Eventually, on 19 October Haig replied to the War Office. Reiterating the argument that a corps of five divisions would be 'unwise and impracticable', he said that he would discuss the matter with Birdwood at the earliest opportunity. In the meantime, Birdwood was faced with two threats to the integrity of the Australian force. First, his army commander, General Sir Herbert Plumer, had informed him that he was to lose the 4th Division to the 2nd Anzac Corps and that it might not be returned after the winter. Second, the severe shortage of reinforcements threatened the disbandment of the weakest division, the 4th. Birdwood and White now had to consider alternative arrangements, and on 27 October Birdwood proposed to Haig that all five divisions be brought together, but that the 4th Division be withdrawn from the line to become a depot division. If another division incurred heavy casualties it could be rotated with the 4th to become the depot division.[12]

That same day, Hughes asked Murdoch to find out if there was any reply to his cable of 25 September. Murdoch reported that Haig had hinted he was considering appointing Monash as a corps commander. Birdwood might remain as GOC AIF, but without a corps command. Eventually it came to light that Hughes's cable had been delayed in reaching the Cabinet until the influential politician and assistant Cabinet secretary Leo Amery 'accidentally got upon the traces of it', as he put it, 'through an enquiry addressed to me by Murdoch'.[13]

It was not until 31 October that Lloyd George brought Hughes's unanswered cable to the War Cabinet. Lloyd George was angry at the failure of the colonial secretary, Long, to bring the matter to the

War Cabinet as Hughes had requested: it was 'discourteous' to the Australian government and might 'cause some trouble'. Long replied that since the Australian government was having difficulty obtaining men for the AIF, their efforts would be assisted if it were known that the Australian troops would all be 'under a general officer in whom the Australians had unbounded confidence'. By now Haig had already gone a considerable way towards meeting Australia's wishes, and all the War Cabinet had to do was endorse a telegram outlining the changes and ensure that it expressed regret for the delay in answering Hughes's original request.[14]

The War Cabinet felt that it had no other option. As the Secretary of State for War, Lord Derby, explained to Haig, the 'Colonial Forces' were causing a 'great deal of trouble'. The Australians were beginning to see themselves as a foreign army like the Portuguese, and with regard to Birdwood, 'the Australians have got an implicit belief' in him, 'and are quite determined that he shall be their Chief in the Field . . . I am afraid in this respect we shall have to humour them.' He was proposing to inform Hughes, as he 'wants all the assistance he can get at the present moment as he is again going very pluckily for conscription'. At last, on 13 November, the British government replied to Hughes's cable, informing him that all the Australian divisions would be grouped as the Australian Corps. The British still wanted an interchange of British and Australian staff officers, but Hughes refused to budge.[15] Thus, in his efforts to bring the Australian divisions together and staff the Australian Corps with Australian officers, Hughes had got his way. The 1st Anzac Corps became the Australian Corps, the Australian divisions in the 2nd Anzac Corps were transferred to the new Australian Corps, and the remaining 2nd Anzac Corps, which included the New Zealand Division, became the British 22nd Corps.

Second Conscription Referendum

As Lord Derby had intimated, Hughes was indeed seeking to introduce conscription, with another referendum to be held on

20 December. While the voluntary recruitment rate was 2500 per month at the end of 1917, Hughes claimed that 7000 recruits were needed each month.[16] As with the first conscription campaign, the issue was divisive and bitter. Whereas in the first campaign Hughes's main target had been the Industrial Workers of the World, now it was the alleged treasonous activity of Irish nationalist organisations, such as Sinn Fein. The result of the referendum was a slight, if marginally larger, majority against the introduction of conscription, with four states—New South Wales, Victoria, Queensland and South Australia—voting no.

Hughes had undertaken not to govern unless the referendum was passed, but no one else was able to form a government, and although he formally resigned, the governor-general asked him to form a government again. On 10 January 1918 the governor-general swore in the new government with Hughes as prime minister. After a short interregnum while the ailing Sir John Forrest held on as treasurer, William Watt took over the portfolio. Watt was a former premier of Victoria who had been elected to the federal parliament as a Liberal Party member in 1914. Pearce continued on as defence minister and Cook, the deputy prime minister, continued as Minister for the Navy. Pearce's administration of the Defence Department had come under scrutiny from a royal commission, and Liberal members of the government 'wanted him replaced'. Pearce had also 'fallen out with Hughes, his most important political ally.'[17] Although Pearce had lost some influence, Hughes was about to take a stronger hand in the higher command issues of the AIF.

The Command Conspiracy

It was not long before Hughes was preparing to travel to London again for a meeting of the Imperial War Cabinet, which was likely to be faced with some crucial decisions. The German offensive on the Western Front began on 21 March 1918 and continued through to July, and during at least part of that time Hughes was in transit. On 25 April, Hughes, accompanied by his deputy, Joseph Cook, departed

Australia, travelling via New Zealand and North America, leaving the treasurer, Watt, as acting prime minister. Frustrated by his inability to attend the Imperial War Cabinet in 1917, Hughes was determined to pursue the questions concerning Australian command that had been on his mind during his earlier visit in 1916. An example of his attitude is shown by a cable he sent to Murdoch on 31 March. Complaining that the Colonial Office telegrams about the German offensive were 'meagre and hopelessly belated', Hughes asked Murdoch to arrange for the Colonial Office to send him 'full facts and prospects', and if they could or would not, to do so himself.[18]

Murdoch, however, needed no prompting from Hughes. On 1 April he cabled Hughes that GHQ 'did not credit the Germans as capable [of] such an effort'. The next day he reported that the 'possibility of decisive defeat' was 'haunting high quarters'. It was 'imperative' that Australia be strongly represented at the Imperial War Cabinet. On 7 April he responded to Hughes's cable with the news that Lloyd George was sympathetic to the need for up-to-date reports, but even he was 'frequently without battle information'. The Colonial Office, he said, was 'hopeless'. In Murdoch's view, the Australian government was 'dangerously isolated from real news especially concerning Battle Fronts, diplomatic tendencies, policies and Australian Army. Full information [is] vital for shaping policy, and moreover you must some day face responsibility for immense things you do not even hear about.'[19]

Each day, Murdoch sent cables to Hughes with his summary of the battle situation, raising the question as to why Birdwood could not have done likewise. On 15 April, Murdoch reported that the position was serious but not desperate: 'Australians have justifiable complaint of bad British Generalship. We have suffered frequently in the cruellest way through mistakes of high Commanders.' Three days later he told Hughes that he had arranged for the War Office to send through the Colonial Office the same information that it was forwarding to British ministers. On 8 May he cabled that the Australians were 'fighting splendidly but a feeling of disappointment and bitterness at present prevails'.[20]

In pressing these views, Murdoch would have been aware of the contrast between the Australian and Canadian divisions. Haig was frustrated by the demand of the Canadian Corps commander, Lieutenant General Currie, supported by his government's representative in London, that his divisions fight only as a corps.[21] By contrast, at one stage the Australians had divisions operating in three separate British corps.

Although the German offensive delayed the consolidation of the Australian Corps, it also provided the opportunity to complete the task, for on 12 May Haig summoned Birdwood to GHQ and instructed him to assume command of the newly reformed Fifth Army, which had been shattered by the German offensive. Birdwood was to take White with him as his chief of staff and to appoint Monash to command the Australian Corps. Despite the fact that Haig had already decided to appoint Monash, Birdwood went through the formality of immediately cabling Pearce his recommendation that Monash succeed him as corps commander. Birdwood added that he intended retaining command of the AIF. On receipt of this news, Pearce commented to the governor-general: 'I am not sure that the proposal that he should retain our Corps and the AIF generally under his control is sound as a permanent measure but have no doubt as to its advisableness [sic] temporarily.' In notes he prepared at the time, Murdoch commented: 'The damage will be wilful and lasting if an Indian Army officer remains supreme commander to the end.'[22]

On 20 May, Murdoch reported to Hughes in America that Birdwood's prestige among the men had 'sunk very low, he is not Australian and as army commander he will be absorbed' with wider issues. In an effort to give the corps command to White, who he thought would be better than Monash, Murdoch recommended that Monash be given administrative command of the AIF, based in London, and that White become the corps commander. Murdoch added that Bean and the AIF's chief medical officer, Major General Sir Neville Howse, VC, had asked him to indicate that they supported his proposal. In a similar cable to the acting prime minister, Watt, Murdoch added that as an inducement Monash could be promoted to full general. The

Cabinet in Melbourne preferred to accept Birdwood's proposal that he command both the AIF and the Fifth Army, and Watt then cabled this view to Hughes, although suggesting that he examine it carefully once he reached England. Hughes did not believe that one man could do justice to both the command of an army and to the administrative command, and urged that Birdwood's appointment be considered temporary until he himself arrived in London. In fact, Birdwood's command of the Fifth Army had already been made temporary.[23]

In his book *The Great War*, Les Carlyon neatly summed up the relationship between Hughes and Murdoch:

> The Drama had now lurched towards farce. Consider first, the behaviour of Hughes. He had twice divided Australia with campaigns for conscription. In doing so he had said, in effect: 'Trust me. I know what is going on in the war'. Yet he knew so little about what was going on that he relied on Murdoch to tell him who was fit to command the AIF. One might have expected the Prime Minister to have thoughts of his own on who should command his army.

Carlyon added that Murdoch, 'elected by no-one, apparently accountable to no-one', was 'as powerful as anyone in the Cabinet in Melbourne. He had just managed, with one cable to Hughes and a word here and there around London, to have Birdwood's new command changed to "temporary".'[24] As a war leader, Hughes was struggling to take charge.

Although his own appointment remained to be finalised, Birdwood went ahead with his plans to place Australian officers in the senior command positions in the corps. Major Generals Walker and Smyth, the British officers commanding the 1st and 2nd Divisions, were moved to British divisions, to be replaced by Brigadier Generals William Glasgow and Charles Rosenthal. On 31 May, the day Monash took over the corps, command of the 3rd Division passed to Brigadier General John Gellibrand. Major General Ewen Sinclair-MacLagan, who had led the 4th Division since Holmes was killed in July 1917, and Major General Hobbs of the 5th Division retained their commands.

In what Monash's biographer Geoffrey Serle called 'perhaps the outstanding case of sheer irresponsibility by pressmen in Australian history', Murdoch continued to work for his own scheme. For example, on 3 June he wrote to Birdwood, urging him to give way, and on 6 June he wrote to Monash, suggesting that he become commander of the AIF and also controller of repatriation: 'You as a full General with supreme authority in all matters, would be the solution of many of our country's difficulties.' Monash described the offer as 'a palpable bribe'. Birdwood thought the 'intrigues of Murdoch and Co' were 'a bit annoying and doing harm for such things can so easily upset a force. [Murdoch] is a very zealous Australian but with a very limited horizon.' General Sir Henry Rawlinson, GOC of the Fourth Army, of which the Australian Corps was part, thought Murdoch was a 'persistent villain', and Monash wrote that he profoundly mistrusted him. Bean supported Murdoch by sending a ten-page memorandum to Hughes on the 'work to be done for the AIF', arguing for White to be given the corps and Monash command of the AIF with the rank of general.[25] Bean's desire to keep Monash away from the corps command was partly driven by anti-Semitic prejudices, as Monash was Jewish.

It was not just Murdoch and Bean who were involved in the intrigue. On 14 June, Major General McCay, GOC of the AIF depots in England with his headquarters on the Salisbury Plain, told Talbot Hobbs of the 5th Division, on leave in London, that he wanted to be appointed GOC of the AIF. The next day, 15 June, McCay was waiting on the station platform when Hughes and Cook arrived in London, 'quite confident that he is going to out Birdwood as GOC AIF and get the job himself'. Hobbs said he would resign if this happened. On his return to France, Hobbs wrote to Birdwood to tell him what had occurred, and to Pearce to plead for Birdwood's retention; if Monash were not to command the corps, it 'would mean the loss to the AIF of a Commander [Monash] of very great ability and exceptional energy and experience, who enjoys absolutely the complete confidence and respect of the AIF as a fighting leader'. Monash had also advised Pearce that Birdwood should continue to command the AIF: 'He has been the chief factor in creating and maintaining its prestige and its spirit of unity.' Pearce consulted the Cabinet and cabled Hughes in the same vein.[26]

Meanwhile, in the afternoon of 16 June, Murdoch and Bean called on Hughes to press their case, and Bean noted in his diary 'that Hughes is really doing what he thinks is best for Australia. In talking to Murdoch and myself he said: "The chief thing to consider is not the political effects so much—the question is what is best for the force and for the men in it".' Countering Murdoch and Bean's views, Major General Rosenthal, in London on 20 June, spoke to Sir Joseph Cook to argue for no change.[27]

Hughes received other views. Early in June, Monash had urged him to make no changes before he visited him in France, and Birdwood advised him that since his command of the Fifth Army was temporary and he might have to revert to command of the corps, there should be no alteration at this stage. On 21 June, Birdwood told Hughes that he, along with Generals Haig, Plumer and Rawlinson, were 'absolutely confident' in Monash's suitability for the corps command. On top of this, when Hughes spoke to White on 19 June, the latter refused to accept the appointment of corps commander in these circumstances. Hughes therefore decided to wait until he had visited France and discussed the proposals with the Australian generals.[28]

The Imperial War Cabinet

While Hughes was considering these views, he was also getting down to work on the main purpose of his visit, the Imperial War Cabinet. On 13 June, before Hughes had arrived, the Canadian prime minister, Sir Robert Borden, had delivered a withering attack on the high command's conduct of the war, and also on the approach of the professional soldier in contrast to that of the civilian soldier such as Canada's Lieutenant General Currie. Borden had earlier told

Lloyd George: 'Mr Prime Minister, I want to tell you that, if ever there is a repetition of the battle of Passchendaele, not a Canadian soldier will leave the shores of Canada as long as the Canadian people entrust the government of their country to my hands.' At that time, the Germans were at the peak of their success on the Western Front. Although held by the British and Australian forces on the Somme, the Germans had turned on the French and were advancing towards the Marne River and Paris.[29]

Hughes joined the Imperial War Cabinet for the first time on 18 June, and on 20 June he supported the other dominion prime ministers in their criticism of British strategic direction. 'Australia had poured its men out into the machine and had had heavy losses,' he said, 'but had never had a scratch of a pen to explain what had really happened. He wished to feel sure that the sacrifices that were being made were not wasted for want of proper leadership and strategy.' Hughes was 'gently reminded by Borden that if he had no voice it was because he had neglected to attend the Imperial Cabinet' the previous year. Hughes wrote later that the 'professional soldiers were more concerned with their careers than with the welfare of the nation', and he complained that the Australian government 'was never consulted about any plans; it was sometimes, though rarely, notified that this or that project was contemplated; usually it was told this or that had been done or was on the point of being done'. The following day Hughes commented forcefully on the disastrous waste of manpower, and encouraged greater use of aircraft and tanks.[30]

Belatedly, Hughes was trying to come to grips with strategic issues and the role of the Australian forces within the wider Allied strategy. The problem was that while Borden was advised by Currie, Hughes did not receive similar advice from Birdwood, who as a regular British officer, was hesitant to criticise British methods. Referring to Passchendaele, Currie had told Borden that 'the British staff, even after three years of war, was guilty of gross bungling'. The Imperial War Cabinet in April and May 1917 had not been informed of the Flanders offensive planned for mid-1917 that ended in the Passchendaele battles. Hughes realised that strategic policy had been at fault, but he lacked an experienced, qualified and informed military adviser.[31]

Attendance at the Imperial War Cabinet gave the dominion prime ministers an opportunity to consider some of the issues concerning war policy, and possible peace terms. However, the key decisions about war strategy and military policy were made when Lloyd George, the Secretary of State for War Lord Milner, and the CIGS General Sir Henry Wilson, met informally before they attended the Imperial War Cabinet. In one of these meetings, Lloyd George admitted that British reports of the operations on the Western Front confirmed that the 'whole organisation was unsatisfactory and wasteful'.[32] Nonetheless, Lloyd George could not avoid dealing with the dominion prime ministers' concerns in the larger meeting.

In response, Lloyd George set up a Committee of Prime Ministers to investigate the failure of the 1917 Flanders offensive and the reasons for the success of the German counteroffensive in early to mid-1918. That Lloyd George was sensitive to criticism of British generalship was shown towards the end of August 1918, when Haig proposed sending two American divisions to assist the Canadians in their offensive against the Hindenburg Line. Lloyd George reminded Wilson 'that last year we had lost about 150,000 men at Bullecourt. To allow the Canadians to be sacrificed as the Australians had been last year in attacking this difficult region would be sheer folly.' He did not want a repetition of that experience.[33] Informed in the Imperial War Cabinet that the war was likely to continue until 1919 or even 1920, by which time the AIF was likely to be reduced to two or three divisions, Hughes insisted that he was to be consulted before the AIF 'was involved in operations likely to involve heavy casualties'.[34]

Resolving the Command Problem

These discussions emphasised for Hughes the need to resolve the command of the AIF, and early in July he visited France to meet the senior Australian generals. The view of Hobbs, the most senior Australian after Monash, would be crucial. But first, on 2 July 1918,

Hughes and Cook visited the brigades that were to take part in the attack on Hamel two days later, telling the soldiers that the future nation would be built on their deeds and that they would be looked after once they returned home. At each brigade, Hughes spoke to its divisional commander, and all except Gellibrand (who probably did not see Hughes) were adamant that Monash was the best man to lead the corps. Hughes, Cook, Birdwood and Monash lunched with Hobbs at the 5th Division headquarters, and after lunch Hughes and Hobbs spoke privately. Colonel Julius Bruche, Hobbs's chief administrative staff officer, recalled that Hobbs said to him: '"Bruche, I can't tell you what we discussed but I think it will be all right". I knew then that Monash was to be appointed.' Monash, Sinclair-MacLagan (4th Division) and Rosenthal (2nd Division) all urged Hughes not to make any changes to the arrangements. As Bean commented in his diary: 'The result was that Hughes was seriously shaken. He said to Murdoch just before he left: "Well—I haven't met a single one of them that thinks as you do. They all say the same thing. You tell me there are men who think the other way. Where are they?"'[35]

As a canny politician, Hughes was non-committal, telling Monash, 'You may thoroughly rely upon your wishes in this matter receiving the greatest possible weight,' but two days later Monash's corps won a brilliant victory at Hamel, confirming in Hughes's eyes his fitness for command. At that time Hughes was at Versailles attending the Supreme War Council, along with the political and military leaders of Britain, France and Italy; the US military commander in France; and the prime ministers of Canada, New Zealand and Newfoundland. Hughes basked in their congratulations for the 'most thoroughly successful' attack 'undertaken by the Allies since the German offensive'.[36]

Murdoch, however, did not give up his campaign to have White appointed to the corps and Monash to the command of the AIF. On the night of 11 July he had a 'raging conversation' with White, who charged him 'with impropriety in interfering as a pressman or as a publicist, in a decision made by the government of our country on the advice of responsible authorities'. Murdoch argued strongly that

Australia needed to have complete control of its forces, and when he was unsuccessful in persuading White he concluded that White 'has still in him a lot of the old feeling of subservience to England'.[37]

Despite Murdoch's efforts, there was no change in the command arrangements until 27 July, when General Wilson advised Hughes that Birdwood's appointment to the Fifth Army had been confirmed. On 1 August, Hughes cabled Watt that he was concerned Birdwood could not 'serve two masters . . . he looks to the War Office for his orders for preferment for maintenance of his position. Where interests of Australia and Britain clash—and that they do clash and have clashed in military matters is certain and that interests of Australia have suffered—for which will he stand?' Hughes pointed out that the Canadians had reaped the benefit of having separate administrative and operational commands, and he proposed offering Birdwood the choice of remaining GOC AIF or commander of the Fifth Army. If Birdwood selected the latter appointment, then Monash could be GOC AIF with White receiving the corps, although if Monash preferred, he could retain the corps. Hughes told Pearce and Watt that they would have to choose 'between accepting advice given by Cook and me . . . or [a] union of generals at front who feel bound to stick to Birdwood although they know that this is not the best thing for Australia'. The Cabinet gave way and agreed to Hughes's proposals, and on 12 August Hughes gave Birdwood the choice, stating emphatically: 'The two offices cannot be held by one man.'[38]

Birdwood replied unexpectedly that he was willing to accept the command of the AIF and to give up the Fifth Army, but he believed that the decision was for Field Marshal Haig, not him, to make. The commander-in-chief agreed that Birdwood should accept, but 'in the general interest of the Allied cause', he hoped that Mr Hughes would 'see his way clear to lending' Birdwood's services to the British Army until 30 November. With the continuing success of the Allied offensive, which had begun on 8 August, Hughes felt that he had no option but to accept. When he saw how neatly Birdwood and Haig had outmanoeuvred Hughes, Pearce commented to Munro Ferguson, 'No wonder our Generals beat the Germans.'[39]

Hughes Takes Firmer Control

Despite Hughes's demand that he be consulted about the use of the Australian Corps in a major offensive, the first he heard about its involvement in that of 8 August was in the Imperial War Cabinet, when General Wilson started describing its success. Hughes was about to question why the corps had been used without his permission when it became clear that the offensive had been the 'greatest Allied victory of the war, and any protest died away'.[40]

Hughes might have savoured this success, but he was now determined to take an even more direct hand in the management of the AIF. He had been very much impressed by Australian soldiers on leave in London telling him: 'There'll be no AIF if they don't rest us soon.' As Hughes wrote to the governor-general, 'the Australians have been fighting continuously—always on the aggressive for over six months this year—[and] they were in the line all the year'. To ensure that the troops would be available for operations in 1919, Hughes was determined to give them some rest, to be achieved in three steps. First, the original 'Anzacs' should be granted two months' leave in Australia. Second, the rest of the corps should be given a rest to begin in October. And third, all the Australian infantry should be sent to the south of France or Italy during the coming winter. As Hughes wrote later, 'if these splendid men, who had been fighting incessantly for months, and for who there was no hope of rest and relief for many months more, were to have any chance to fight, and not merely stumble, utterly worn out, into the arms of death, it was imperative that the whole Australian Army should go into decent winter quartering'.[41]

General Wilson responded to these requests with what Hughes called 'chilling disapproval', stating that there would be 'insuperable difficulty' in finding the ships to send the men home on leave. Eventually, on 30 August, Wilson agreed that 7000 Australians and New Zealanders, in appropriate proportions, could be sent home, probably in October. As Hughes described it: 'After a pitched battle with the War Office I managed to get the Authorities to agree to home leave for the 1914 men.' Then there was the battle to obtain the ships, which eventually Hughes won. As for the request to withdraw the corps from operations in mid-October, Wilson said that it was a matter for Field Marshal Haig. Hughes's reply was telling: 'I shall not see Haig or anyone else. If the Belgian government wants its troops withdrawn from the line it does not ask any one's leave. It simply says they are to be withdrawn.'[42]

The Allied offensive, of which the Australian Corps was part, continued its successes. The Australian units were understrength, but the troops were experienced and confident, and the battalions now had a higher allocation of Lewis machine-guns. On 1 September, in an outstanding feat of arms, the Australians crossed the Somme River and captured Mont St Quentin. The Australians pushed on towards the German Hindenburg Line. Concerned that Australia was not receiving sufficient credit for these achievements, between 12 and 16 September Hughes visited the Australian Corps accompanied by journalists and newspaper proprietors.

The same day that Hughes arrived at Monash's headquarters, the corps commander received an order from Birdwood to release immediately 800 original Anzacs so that they could return home on two months' furlough. In issuing this order, biographer Geoffrey Serle described Hughes as springing 'a most embarrassing coup'. Monash objected, especially as the men would come from the 1st and 4th Divisions preparing for an attack on the Hindenburg Outpost Lines (the outer edge of the Hindenburg Line). Birdwood, who was following Hughes's direction, insisted that Monash comply. The men departed on 14 September after they had been addressed by Hughes. Monash and his senior commanders also objected to the plan to release a further 6000 men. Hughes was adamant that the furlough plan should proceed.[43]

Ignoring Wilson's suggestion that he consult Haig, Hughes directed Monash that his corps was to be withdrawn from action by 15 October. Monash had reached the same conclusion that his men needed a rest, and indeed his superior, General Rawlinson, GOC of the Fourth Army, had agreed, but when he submitted that the needs of the campaign might render it impossible to meet the date, Hughes told Monash that his position as corps commander would depend on it. In his official history, Bean has suggested that Hughes was taking a risk because the Australian government might not have supported his direct methods, and that Monash might have cabled Australia to overrule him. As Bean wrote, Hughes 'accepted that chance'.[44]

After successfully breaking the Hindenburg Line, the Australian Corps was withdrawn from action on 5 October, expecting to receive the long period of rest promised by Hughes. However, on 21 October, Rawlinson warned Hobbs, who was commanding the corps while Monash was on leave in England, to prepare for operations again. Hobbs explained that Hughes had promised the soldiers would be given a rest, and that none of them would be fit for action for three weeks. Rawlinson agreed to a two-week delay. Hearing of this, Monash in England wrote to Hughes, who summoned him for an interview. Hughes's first reaction was to insist 'that the troops should have a long and unbroken rest before being called upon to go into the line'. But eventually he gave way; as Monash explained, 'in the question of the employment of the Corps, Hughes stood alone on one side and all the authorities on the other—Wilson, Lloyd George and all of them. They urged that for Australia herself it was important that the Australian divisions should be put in again.' Haig thought that the Australians had the least claim for any considerations 'on account of losses'. This decision was overtaken by events, as the Australian divisions did not go into action before the Armistice came into effect on 11 November. The question of who was responsible for withdrawing the Australian troops from action in early October later became a point of dispute between Hughes and Monash. Monash claimed the credit, but Hughes was adamant that it was 'his own work really', and that Monash could not have done it without his support.[45]

Armistice

The discussions over the terms of the Armistice reveal the limits on Australia's capacity to influence events, or even to be consulted. On 1 October, Hughes attended a meeting of the Imperial War Cabinet to hear news that Bulgaria had surrendered and to discuss terms for an armistice with the Ottoman Empire. Lloyd George then went to Paris for a meeting of the Supreme War Council, which was considering an armistice with Germany. The Australian Cabinet agreed that Hughes should remain in London while these issues were discussed. In the meantime, Hughes was kept in the dark about the talks in Paris, and it was not until 5 November, when he attended a meeting of the Imperial War Cabinet, that he learned the Armistice would be based on President Woodrow Wilson's Fourteen Points. The Imperial War Cabinet had not discussed these, and Hughes was furious, telling Watt that 'Australia has not been consulted nor had any opportunity to state its views'. Hughes and Cook agreed that they had 'been treated very badly.'[46] Lloyd George tried to argue that the peace terms had been discussed at the Imperial War Cabinet in 1917, which Hughes had not attended. But Hughes would not accept this. He averred that 'We who have fought for four years as equals are treated as lackeys.'[47]

When Hughes made his complaint public with an address that was printed in *The Times*, the Australian Cabinet thought he had gone too far. Although they agreed with the substance of Hughes's complaint about not being consulted, the Cabinet members did not share all Hughes's concerns about Wilson's Fourteen Points and they were more accepting of Lloyd George's explanation, which he had sent them. They were also concerned about Hughes's attack on Lloyd George. The historian Neville Meaney thought that the difference between Hughes and his Cabinet 'was not primarily one between an egotistical nationalist and his more conservative imperialist colleagues'. Rather, it was the difference between those who had seen the workings of the Empire at close quarters in London, and the members of the Nationalist Cabinet in Melbourne. The ministers in Melbourne 'had defined Australia's Britishness as an unquestioning loyalty to the Empire and justified their very existence in those terms, [and] could not tolerate the notion that the British government had been disloyal to Australia'.[48] Rebuffed in London, Hughes visited Paris to speak to the French government and won the concession that he could attend the Paris Peace Conference, to begin in January. Seeing the way the wind was blowing, in this respect Lloyd George supported Hughes.

In the meantime, Hughes set in train arrangements for the repatriation of the Australian troops. This should have been the responsibility of the Minister for Repatriation, Edward Millen, or perhaps the Minister for Defence, Pearce, but Hughes was on the spot and took on the job himself.[49] On 21 November, Monash was appointed Director-General of Repatriation and Demobilisation, and Hobbs took over the Australian Corps in France. Birdwood continued as GOC AIF. Pearce eventually went to England to provide ministerial supervision of the repatriation of the Australian troops, but the main work was done, and with great expertise, by Monash.

The role and performance of Hughes at the Paris Peace Conference are beyond the scope of this book. There he fought for issues he considered vital for the defence of Australia, insisting on retaining control of German New Guinea. Woodrow Wilson asked Hughes whether he was defying the opinion of the whole civilised world. Hughes replied, 'That's about the size of it, Mr President.' Wilson again asked Hughes whether he would set Australia's 5 million people against the 1200 million represented at the conference. Hughes replied: 'I represent sixty thousand dead.'[50] Ultimately, Australia received control of New Guinea through a Class-C Mandate from the League of Nations, which, while less than what Hughes wanted, allowed Australia to control immigration and trade. When the Japanese wished to insert in the covenant of the League of Nations a guarantee of the 'equality of nations and of equal treatment of their nationals', Hughes saw this as a threat to Australia's White Australia policy, and against much opposition ensured that the Japanese statement was not accepted. Historian W.J. Hudson has argued that Hughes's effort at the Peace Conference was the 'birth of Australian diplomacy'.[51]

War Leadership of a New Nation

As has been emphasised in this and the previous chapters, Australia's war leaders had been constrained by the fact that the new nation had not yet reached full sovereignty and was still operating as a deferential part of the British Empire. The Australian government lacked the mechanisms or relevant information to manage its war effort. In particular, the Australian Army did not yet have experienced, well-trained senior officers who could provide the government with wise counsel on matters of war policy. As for the navy, its major warships had been handed over to the British Admiralty.

From October 1915 to the end of the war, Australian war leadership was in the hands of Prime Minister Hughes and his defence minister, Pearce, who had held the portfolio since September 1914. In managing Australia's military effort, they had been concerned with four issues.

The first was the raising and maintenance of five infantry divisions in France and one and a half mounted divisions in Egypt and Palestine. In the face of heavy casualties in France and Belgium, Australia had not provided sufficient volunteers to maintain the five divisions at full strength, leading to the conscription referenda in 1916 and 1917. Driven by their concerns about a future threat from Japan, Hughes and Pearce had been determined to support the imperial war effort to the maximum extent.

The war incurred a tremendous cost in terms of deaths and injury. At the outbreak of the First World War Australia had a population of 4.875 million, and 416,800 served in the armed forces. Most of these, 331,781, served overseas; more than 60,000 were killed or died of wounds and more than 150,000 were wounded. The high proportion of casualties can be attributed partly to the fact that most Australian soldiers were in combat rather than logistic units. The numbers of casualties do not include the men who had not sought treatment after being gassed but then endured breathing difficulties for the rest of their lives. Nor do they include the thousands of ex-servicemen who suffered from what is now called post-traumatic stress disorder. Having joined the war, the only way that Australia could have lessened its losses would have been by reducing the level of its commitment.

The second issue was the effort to place Australians in command of divisions and brigades. While laudable from a national point of view, Australia faced the real problem that at the beginning of the war the army lacked sufficient officers with the necessary experience and training for these command appointments.

The third issue was the effort to bring the Australian divisions together as one corps under one Australian commander. As described earlier in this chapter, this aim was achieved in mid-1918.

The fourth issue was the matter of consultation about the use of the Australian forces. The Australian government was slow to tackle this issue. Initially Hughes and Pearce were content to leave matters of war policy in the hands of the imperial authorities, and Pearce never wavered from this view. It was only by the time of his second visit to London in 1918, just six months before the end of the war, that Hughes tried to exercise some control over the Australian Corps, but he lacked an experienced and qualified adviser. The journalist Keith Murdoch, with no military or diplomatic training, tried to step into this role, and the one man who was better qualified, Birdwood, the GOC AIF, had no inclination to advise Hughes on high policy matters, owing his allegiance to the British commander-in-chief.

Pearce's biographer John Connor concluded that 'Pearce was a great Defence Minister, but his failure to administer his department adequately during the First World War cannot be ignored.'[52] Connor based his conclusions on a favourable comparison with the administration of other dominion defence departments. Connor acknowledged that the Defence Department expanded beyond the ability of one man to administer it, but believed that Pearce retained two important virtues as minister: he listened to his advisers, and he was honest.[53] But these judgements do not consider that Pearce was too willing to accept British strategic direction of the war uncritically. While he corresponded regularly with Birdwood, he never sought Birdwood's advice on issues of strategy or war policy. As noted above, however, as a loyal servant of the Imperial Army, Birdwood would have been unwilling to comment on these issues, and he was probably ill-equipped to do so any way. Pearce could have sought advice elsewhere, but his advisers in Melbourne were no more in touch with events in the war theatres than he was. The problem went back to the appointment of Birdwood as GOC AIF in the first place. We saw how Birdwood manoeuvred Legge out of that position and took it for himself. Ultimately the problem rested with the failure of the Australian Army to develop higher commanders before the First World War. John Robertson was damning in his assessment of Pearce: 'Although hard-working, effective in a quasi-administrative role, and active in promoting Australian command of its own troops, he was an unimaginative minister and lacked a grasp of many wider issues.'[54]

Certainly Hughes can be criticised for his broader role as prime minister, particularly for the way he tried to stifle debate in Australia, suppress his opponents and set up rifts in Australian society that were to last for decades. However, considering Australia's subservient place within the British Empire, perhaps Hughes did as well as could be expected on the issue of managing Australia's military commitment. Nevertheless, as Australia continued on its journey towards full sovereignty, its future war leaders would need to do better.

4

'A disposition to treat Australia as a colony'

Menzies, Second World War, 1939–40

At 9.15 p.m. on Sunday 3 September 1939, Prime Minister Robert Menzies addressed the nation by radio. 'Fellow Australians,' he said, 'it is my melancholy duty to inform you officially that, in consequence of the persistence by Germany in her invasion of Poland, Great Britain has declared war upon her, and that, as a result, Australia is also at war.' Menzies went on to add: 'No harder task can fall to the lot of a democratic leader than to make such an announcement'; but as in the First World War, the decision to go to war appeared to be out of Australia's hands. In fact, Australia could have made a separate declaration of war, but as Australia was a member of the British Empire, Menzies considered that when Britain was at war, so too was Australia. Percy Spender, one of Menzies' cabinet ministers, wrote in 1972 that at the time he agreed with Menzies, but added: 'It is not a view I now hold—or one which I have held for many years.'[1]

Robert Menzies

Responsibility for leading Australia for the first two years of the war would rest on the shoulders of Menzies, who, while just 44 at the outbreak of war, brought considerable experience to the task.[2] After graduating in law from Melbourne University he became a successful barrister and by 1928 was a member of the Victorian Legislative Council. By 1932 he was attorney-general and Minister for Railways. In 1934 he moved to the federal parliament and was immediately appointed attorney-general and Minister for Industry in the United Australia Party (UAP) government led by Joseph Lyons.

During visits to England and Europe in 1935, 1936 and 1938, Menzies made valuable contacts and took a keen interest in international affairs, but some of his views, especially after his visit to Germany in 1938, seem misinformed at best. He did not think Germany wanted war and, along with other members of the Lyons government, as well as the Chamberlain government in Britain, he supported the policy of appeasement. He thought that the Sudeten Germans in Czechoslovakia had legitimate grievances, and that once this problem had been resolved, Hitler would have reached the limits of his ambitions. Menzies had deeply misjudged Hitler and his intentions.[3] He also lacked knowledge of military matters, and his failure to serve overseas in the First World War had drawn criticism. His great strength in Cabinet was his lawyer's ability to grasp the essentials of an issue and bring the argument to a logical outcome. His apparent weakness was his failure to appreciate the sensitivities of his colleagues.

By September 1939, Menzies had been prime minister for less than five months, having ascended to the position on the death of Lyons in April. Sir Earle Page, leader of the Country Party—the junior party in the coalition government during the 1930s—had been prime minister briefly, but he had bitterly and rashly claimed that Menzies did not have the courage, judgement or loyalty to be prime minister, and refused to serve under Menzies. The Country Party therefore did not join Menzies' government, although without a majority of his own, Menzies depended on the Country Party for its support. The official Second World War historian, Paul Hasluck, who served as a minister under Menzies, thought that the new prime minister 'had the disadvantage of his own brilliance. A man of fine presence, ease of manner, poise and style, he incurred the suspicion of being vain, of lacking sincerity, and of being aloof. A man of keen intellect, he inevitably had often made lesser men seem foolish.'[4]

The War Cabinet

Menzies would lead Australia's war effort with the assistance and advice of a small committee of Cabinet called the War Cabinet. The government had not established a War Cabinet during the First World War, but between the wars Defence officials had sought to prepare the government for the next war. The central figure in these efforts was the secretary of the Department of Defence, Frederick Shedden, who took up his appointment in 1937 at the age of 44. He would hold the position until 1956.[5] Shedden had the most thorough preparation of any Defence secretary. After joining the department in 1910 as a 16-year-old junior clerk, he studied accountancy, served with the 1st AIF in France and England as a divisional paymaster, gained a Bachelor of Commerce degree at Melbourne University, and in 1928 attended the Imperial Defence College in London. He was then attached to the War Office, where he made valuable contacts with senior British Defence officials, including Sir Maurice Hankey, secretary of the Committee of Imperial Defence. Later Shedden would be described as the 'Australian Hankey', or sometimes the 'pocket Hankey'.

Influenced by Hankey and by what he had learned in England, in 1935 Shedden helped reconstitute the Council of Defence to consist of several ministers and the service chiefs of staff. Shedden saw that the council could be turned into a War Cabinet, and on 18 March 1938 the Cabinet agreed to form a War Cabinet on the outbreak of war. Australia's war leadership would therefore be centred on the War Cabinet.

On 15 September 1939, Menzies announced the formation of the War Cabinet. In addition to himself as prime minister and treasurer, it included the attorney-general, William Morris (Billy) Hughes, who was also deputy leader of the UAP; the Minister for Supply, Richard

Casey; the Minister for Defence, Geoffrey Street; the Minister for Commerce, Senator George McLeay; and the Minister for Information, Sir Henry Gullett. The War Cabinet was to deal 'with all matters in relation to the conduct of the war other than matters of major policy', which were to be determined by the full Cabinet. War Cabinet meetings would generally be held in Melbourne to maintain contact with the Department of Defence, which was located there.[6]

Membership of the War Cabinet was to change over the years, but certain features introduced in 1939 persisted. The first was that the chiefs of staff were invited collectively to attend the War Cabinet to advise on military aspects. The second was the appointment of Shedden as secretary of the War Cabinet. He attended almost all its meetings, prepared the minutes confirming the outcome of the discussions and then, as secretary of the Department of Defence, ensured that the decisions were implemented. Shedden was a confidential adviser to a succession of ministers and prime ministers, and was the soul of discretion. While the members of the War Cabinet made the final decisions, usually it was Shedden who provided his minister with the well-argued propositions for discussion.

There is no suggestion, however, that Shedden dominated his ministers. In November 1939, the Department of Defence was separated into four departments—Defence Coordination, Navy, Army, and Air. Menzies took the Defence Coordination portfolio, and the War Cabinet was reconstituted. In addition to Casey, Hughes, Gullett, Street (now Minister for the Army) and McLeay, it also included the Minister for the Navy, Sir Frederick Stewart; the Minister for Air, James Fairbairn; and the Minister for the Interior, Senator Hattil (Harry) Foll. There was a blend of experience and youthful energy. Hughes was a former prime minister who had led Australia in the First World War, and Casey, Gullett and Stewart had served a number of years as ministers. Casey, Street, Gullett and Fairbairn had all given distinguished service in the First World War. As Minister for Defence Coordination as well as prime minister, Menzies controlled the conduct of the war, and the Department of Defence Coordination, with Shedden at is helm, became the most important government department.

As noted, the War Cabinet was advised by the chiefs of staff. The Chief of Naval Staff (CNS) was Admiral Sir Ragnar Colvin, RN, who had taken up his appointment in 1937, aged 55. To his Australian deputy, Captain John Collins, he was a 'magnificent man', quiet, thoughtful and cooperative. Colvin had been well indoctrinated into promoting the Admiralty point of view. During the interwar period, Australian defence policy had been centred on the Singapore Strategy, whereby, in the event of a Japanese threat arising in the Pacific, Britain would undertake to send its main fleet to Singapore, where a naval base had been constructed. Successive governments had accepted the Singapore Strategy, which was supported by both Shedden and the navy chiefs—generally officers from the RN. Senior Australian-born naval officers were given little encouragement to concern themselves with matters of higher strategy. Collins, for example, doubted Britain's ability to hold Singapore in time of war, but was neither senior enough nor confident enough to speak out.[7]

The CGS, Major General John Lavarack, had held the position since 1935, but was nearing the end of his five-year appointment and had lost the government's confidence.[8] A capable Australian officer with a good record from the First World War, Lavarack had challenged successive defence ministers over the government's reliance on the Singapore Strategy and its insistence that army funds be spent on coastal defences rather than the field force. In 1938 the government appointed a 55-year-old British officer, Lieutenant General Ernest Squires, as Inspector-General of the Australian Military Forces, and he prepared plans for reorganising the army so that it would be more suitable for war. In May 1939, Lavarack departed for a tour of Britain. When war broke out Squires, who had been acting CGS since May, was confirmed in the post.

The acting Chief of the Air Staff (CAS) was 48-year-old Air Vice-Marshal Stanley (Jimmy) Goble, an Australian airman who had served in the Royal Naval Air Service in the First World War. In February 1939 the government had removed the long-serving CAS, Air Vice-Marshal Richard Williams, from his post after adverse reports on flying training, and Goble, who had acted for Williams on several occasions, was again acting CAS. Williams and Goble had been more concerned with trying to preserve the small Royal Australian Air Force (RAAF) with its obsolescent aircraft than examining matters of strategy.[9]

Assessing the Threat

Although Menzies, Shedden and the chiefs of staff were all disciples of imperial defence, it should not be assumed that at the outbreak of war they gave no consideration to home defence and the Japanese threat. Indeed, soon after he became prime minister in April 1939, Menzies had sought further assurances from Britain that, in the event of war with Japan, a fleet would be sent to Singapore.[10] On 5 September, two days after the outbreak of war, Menzies cabled Stanley Bruce, the Australian high commissioner in London, that until Japan's position was established it would 'be useless even to discuss the sending of [an] expeditionary force'.[11] The Australian government also hesitated to release its warships for service outside Australian waters.

The Australian government had only limited capacity to assess the strategic situation. Australia's only overseas diplomatic representative was the high commissioner in London, and the nation had no strategic intelligence gathering agency. The Australian government therefore relied on the assessments of the British government, which provided its views in a cable received in Australia on 9 September. Assuming that Japan remained neutral, Britain suggested that Australia release a second cruiser and five RAN destroyers for service outside the Australia Station (i.e. waters around the Australian continent). The first cruiser, HMAS *Perth*, was already serving under Admiralty orders in the Atlantic. With regard to the army, the British government based its recommendations on two hypotheses. First, if Japan was neutral but friendly, Australia might prefer to relieve British formations in places such as Singapore, Burma (now Myanmar) and India. Second, if Japan was neutral, but reserved its attitude towards democratic countries, then it might be unwise for Australia to despatch an expeditionary force overseas. However,

Australia could assist by holding formations ready to move at short notice. The British government also suggested that complete units of the RAAF be sent to Britain.[12]

The service chiefs responded in different ways. With Admiral Colvin on leave in England, Commodore Maitland Boucher, RN, was acting CNS, and unsurprisingly he advised the government to concur with the British suggestion of releasing a further cruiser and five destroyers. Air Vice-Marshal Goble agreed with the British recommendation that complete RAAF units should be sent overseas, although he thought they should be equipped by Britain.[13]

Lieutenant General Squires was more cautious, arguing that there was a third possibility—a hostile Japan. 'It would be unwise,' wrote Squires, 'to assume that Japan would not, at some future date when democratic Powers are deeply committed in other theatres, take advantage of their difficulties to further her designs in the Pacific.' Australia should not despatch a large expeditionary force at present. However, when the situation allowed troops to be sent, they should participate actively in the war, rather than be employed on garrison duties. The chiefs were therefore reluctant to accept the British recommendations.[14]

Menzies agreed with these sentiments, explaining to Bruce that 'As to Japan—I have had a growing feeling for some time that though the Far East is a major problem for us, it is a relatively minor one to Whitehall.' Menzies thought that Japanese neutrality for an 'indefinite period' was 'open to extreme doubt', and he hesitated to announce the formation of an expeditionary force. Perhaps Menzies' reluctance was also linked to his hope that after Hitler invaded Poland he might be persuaded to reach a settlement. Menzies told Bruce that 'nobody really cares a damn about Poland . . . I feel quite confident that Hitler has no desire for a first class war, and until the Polish debacle is complete he will not be disposed to assume the offensive against either France or Great Britain.' It is not clear how Menzies arrived at this unrealistic assessment, and for years he sought to keep these embarrassing views hidden from researchers. Whatever happened in Europe, however, the Department of Defence warned that the possibility of Japanese hostility had to 'be seriously reckoned with for some time'.[15]

Key Decisions

In the first month of the war, the Menzies government made four key decisions that were to affect Australia's military commitments for the remainder of the war. The first concerned an expeditionary force. It was only after pressure in the press following New Zealand's announcement that it was raising an expeditionary force that Menzies announced, on 15 September, that Australia would raise a force of one division for service at home or abroad depending on the circumstances at the time. It was to be known as the 6th Division, and in its second major decision the government selected 55-year-old Lieutenant General Sir Thomas Blamey as its commander.[16] Blamey was a former regular officer who had been General Monash's outstanding chief of staff in the First World War. In 1925 he had transferred to the militia when he became chief commissioner of the Victoria Police, a position he had held until 1936. For the previous year, Blamey had been chairman of the Manpower Committee in the Department of Defence. His appointment as commander of the 6th Division would prove to be one of Menzies' more important decisions, for Blamey was to become Australia's senior military officer for the remainder of the war.

The third decision concerned the navy, as the British government continued to press Australia to release more warships. The British Admiralty was communicating directly with the Australian Naval Board urging the release of Australian ships, and at a War Cabinet meeting on 6 October Admiral Colvin, who had arrived back in Australia, succeeded in persuading the government to release the destroyers to go to Singapore and the cruiser to leave the Australia Station provided it did not proceed west of Suez. When in mid-October the destroyers sailed for Singapore, Britain then asked that they be allowed to proceed to the Mediterranean. The Australian government approved this 'with some misgiving'. In return, Britain promised to send two old cruisers to the Australia Station, but never did so.[17] It was not until 7 November, more than two months after the outbreak of war, that Australia placed its naval ships at the disposal of the Admiralty.

The fourth decision concerned the RAAF. On 20 September, Menzies announced that the government would offer Britain an expeditionary air force of six squadrons—four of bombers and two of fighters. The Air Board was confident that it could provide the men for such a force, and at the same time urged that the strength of the RAAF be built up for home defence.[18] Yet unbeknown to the Air Board, the government was already considering a proposal from Britain whereby the dominions would train airmen for the Royal Air Force (RAF). On 5 October, without consulting the Air Board, the Cabinet agreed in principle to the establishment of what became the Empire Air Training Scheme. On 20 October, the War Cabinet decided 'for the present' not to proceed with plans for the air expeditionary force.[19] By then, the Minister for Air, James Fairbairn, had departed for Ottawa to negotiate the scheme, and the completed document was signed in London on 5 December 1939.

Joining the Empire Air Training Scheme was the most far-reaching decision affecting the air force made by the government during the war and, as historian John McCarthy has argued, it 'seriously prejudiced the possibility of providing for local defences in 1941–42'.[20] The RAAF squadrons in Britain operated as part of British air formations, and generally senior Australian airmen did not receive the experience of higher command appointments. Vast resources were spent on operations over which Australia had no control or say.

With the government bypassing the Air Board, Goble asked to be relieved of his duties. Meanwhile, the government had been negotiating to appoint a British officer as the new CAS, and in February 1940 Air Chief Marshal Sir Charles Burnett, aged 58 and nearing retirement from the RAF, was appointed. This was to have unfortunate consequences, for Burnett, a strong advocate of imperial defence with a forceful personality, considered that his main purpose was to train aircrew for the RAF, and he was little interested in the home defence of Australia. In his view, the defence of Australia rested on the existence of the Singapore base.[21] The three Australian chiefs of staff were now British officers.

Although the pendulum had now swung strongly towards an active role in imperial defence, the Menzies government did not completely overlook home defence. On 5 September, two days after the beginning of the war, the militia was called out for war service in successive drafts of 10,000 to serve for sixteen days' continuous training, and to provide guards on 'vulnerable points'. On 19 October the Cabinet decided to introduce compulsory training for a month at a time to maintain the militia at a strength of 75,000. This was opposed by the Labor Opposition, but compulsory training began on 1 January 1940.

Sending the 2nd AIF Overseas

Having decided to raise the 6th Division, the government's most important decision concerned its employment. Worried about Japan's intentions, the government still hesitated to despatch the special force, soon to be known as the 2nd AIF, overseas. The War Cabinet did not begin to face this issue seriously until early November, by which time Richard Casey, the Minister for Supply and Development, had gone to London to discuss the purchase of British aircraft engines and the sale of Australian wheat and other primary products. The War Cabinet asked Casey to obtain an up-to-date appreciation from the Committee of Imperial Defence as to the potential threat to Australia, to help it determine the appropriate destination for the 2nd AIF.

At home, Menzies was in considerable political trouble. Leading a minority government, he was under pressure from the Country Party over the price to be offered to wheat farmers after their record harvest. Unlike the Country Party, the opposition Labor Party, led by John Curtin, was opposed to sending the 2nd AIF overseas, and both parties were critical of the government over the allegedly excessive pay for the soldiers of the 2nd AIF.

On 3 November Casey, accompanied by Major General John

Northcott, the Australian deputy CGS, met the British prime minister, Neville Chamberlain, and the dominions secretary, Anthony Eden, to seek assurances that Australia would be safe from Japanese attack if it were to send forces to Europe. Casey reported that the British government thought that the immediate danger to Australia from Japan was 'remote', and was pressing for the Australian division to go overseas, preferably to the Middle East. Northcott cabled Squires that the Germans would be likely to have a numerical superiority of two to one on the 'Western Front'. Australia should send troops as a 'counter to enemy propaganda regarding half-hearted dominions cooperation'.[22]

On 13 November the Defence Committee (usually the service chiefs and a representative of the secretary of the Department of Defence) met to consider these cables. The three service members at this meeting were Lieutenant General Squires, Air Vice-Marshal Goble and Commodore Boucher. Presented with Northcott's strong recommendation, the Defence Committee recommended that the 6th Division complete its training in Egypt or Palestine and that a second division be despatched as soon as it could be raised and organised, to complete an Australian corps of two divisions.[23]

Menzies was still not persuaded, and reminded Casey that they had not yet received an 'up-to-date appreciation' of the Japanese position. The War Cabinet considered the Defence Committee's recommendation on 15 and 16 November, and Squires was present for the first part of the discussion. Billy Hughes, now aged 77, attended as attorney-general and Minister for Industry. For almost 40 years he had warned against the Japanese threat, and he recommended waiting to see what Japan would do. Menzies agreed with the need to wait for the review from Britain, and the War Cabinet deferred the decision for consideration by the full Cabinet.[24]

Clearly, Menzies had strong reservations as to whether the British government was being completely honest. On 17 November, Casey cabled the British appreciation of the Far East situation. This stated that Japan would 'sit on the fence as far as the European war' was concerned. A Japanese attack on Singapore would require at least

50,000 troops and would take some four or five months to complete. (In fact, in February 1942 Japanese forces numbering 36,000 would seize Singapore in a little over two months after landing in Malaya.) It was not considered likely that Japan would embark on such an enterprise, and in any case the British advised that 'the duty of defending Australia against serious attack would take precedence over British interests in the Mediterranean'. When the full Cabinet considered this advice on 20 November, again it made no decision.[25]

Perhaps one reason for the delay was that Menzies was trying to use the lever of the despatch of the 6th Division to persuade Britain to buy Australian wheat. On 21 November, Menzies came under heavy attack in parliament from both the Country and Labor parties over the price to be offered for wheat. That same day Menzies cabled Casey that he was puzzled to learn that whereas the British had found great difficulty in obtaining even a fraction of the shipping needed for the export of wheat, it appeared that there was no difficulty in securing ships and a naval convoy for a military force. Menzies conveniently overlooked the point that passenger ships were not suitable for the transport of wheat.[26]

Beyond its concerns about wheat sales, the Australian government was worried about other issues, and on 23 November Menzies explained them to the British high commissioner, Sir Geoffrey Whiskard: it was not apparent that additional men were needed on the Western Front; the Labor Party was opposed to the despatch of forces; there was difficulty in obtaining shipping for wheat and mineral concentrates, and it was more important to send commodities than men at this stage of the war; if Germany invaded the Netherlands then the Indies would be a tempting prize for Japan; and priority should be given to the Air Training Scheme rather than to the 6th Division. Menzies had just heard that New Zealand had decided to send a force overseas, which was 'embarrassing' to the Australian government and he personally was 'highly incensed'. He thought that the New Zealand announcement would give rise to a demand in Australia, which could not be resisted, and that therefore the government would have to agree to send the 6th Division overseas.[27]

Before making the decision, the government received more encouraging news from Casey that Winston Churchill, the First Lord of the Admiralty, had given a qualified promise: 'We would undertake to send adequate naval force to prevent any serious catastrophe but we would not make pledges to give a hundred percent security against dangers which would probably never eventuate.' Casey reported to Menzies that the British government had promised that in the event of war with Japan, 'the Admiralty would make such dispositions as would enable them to offer timely resistance either to serious attack upon Singapore or to the invasion of Australia and New Zealand'. Casey thought that 'the greatest menace to Australia' was the 'possibility of Britain being beaten in Europe', and he therefore recommended that 'the wisest conclusion' was to despatch the expeditionary force as soon as possible.[28]

On 28 November the full Cabinet decided to send the force abroad, and Menzies announced the decision in parliament the following day: 'we regard the protection of Australia itself as of primary importance; indeed, it is naturally the first aim of any Australian defence policy. But our second aim must be and is to make the best possible contribution to the victory of the Empire and allied cause wherever and whenever that contribution is needed.' He added that 'adequate assurances have been given . . . with respect to the capacity and availability of the Royal Navy . . . to give us protection against any major aggression. Under these circumstances, the government is of [the] opinion that it is possible, and that being possible it is most desirable, to send the special Division abroad.'[29]

Despite this confident statement Menzies was not satisfied. He had been hurried into the decision by the British government and New Zealand's announcement. When he learned on 29 November that, to free British units in the Middle East, Britain proposed that the first Australian brigade leave Sydney for the Middle East on about 2 January 1940, Menzies replied tartly that the Australian government agreed, but 'we do so under protest as we feel that in this matter we have been in effect forced into a course of action which we would not otherwise have adopted'. He resented not being consulted before ships were already despatched to collect the troops. 'It is the general feeling of Cabinet that there has been in this matter a quite perceptible disposition to treat Australia as a colony and to make insufficient allowance for the fact that it is for the government of Australia to determine whether and when Australian Forces shall go out of Australia.'[30]

The decision to send the 6th Division overseas reveals several problems with the decision-making process in Australia. The War Cabinet was trying to make decisions about the conduct of the war without access to the higher-level thinking in London. The Australian chiefs did not have information on which to make reasoned judgements about the course of the war in Europe, nor did they have independent intelligence about Japanese capabilities and likely intentions.[31] Australia had no representative in the British War Cabinet, and had to accept the advice from Britain at face value. And the Japanese threat looked more menacing when viewed from Victoria Barracks in Melbourne than from Whitehall.

The Australian ministers could not ignore the political dimension. Despite the outbreak of war, party politics continued. Menzies considered the decision to send the 6th Division overseas of such importance that it had to be made by the full Cabinet. There were also financial implications. For example, on 22 December the War Cabinet learned that 'Any large increase in the amount of our annual external commitment may have the most serious effects upon this country's economy.' The expeditionary force was expected to cost about £5 million a year, which would have to be borrowed in Britain. In deciding to deploy the AIF, Menzies had cautiously tried to balance political, economic and strategic issues. The diplomatic historian Peter Edwards thought the decision was 'surely right, albeit risky'.[32]

On 1 January 1940 Squires recommended the formation of a second division (the 7th) which, with ancillary troops, would allow the formation of a corps for overseas service, and on 28 February the War Cabinet accepted this recommendation. The first troops of the 6th Division had departed for the Middle East in January, with a second convoy to depart in mid-April. The experience of the First

World War had shown that an Australian corps would give the nation more control of its force than the deployment of a single division.

Already by early 1940, Squires was seriously ill, and when he died on 2 March, the government, at the suggestion of General Blamey, called General Sir Brudenell White, aged 63, out of retirement to take over as CGS. One of Australia's most distinguished soldiers, White had been chief of staff under General Sir William Birdwood in the First World War and had been CGS from 1920 to 1923. Nonetheless, as he put it, he felt 'like Cincinnatus called from his farm'.[33]

Before his appointment as CGS, White had worked to ensure that the government had learned some important lessons from the First World War. When Blamey was appointed to command the AIF, he was determined that the government provide him with a charter that clearly spelled out his powers, and White showed him some of his correspondence about the problems experienced by the 1st AIF. Meanwhile, Charles Bean, the First World War official historian, advised Menzies and the army minister, Geoffrey Street, of the need to ensure that the AIF retained its distinct Australian identity.[34]

Menzies agreed, and on 28 February the War Cabinet approved a charter to be issued to Blamey that stated he would have the right to communicate directly with the government, and that no part of the force was to be detached or employed without his consent. Although the force would be under the operational control of the commander-in-chief of the theatre in which it was serving, policy regarding its employment was to be decided by consultation between the Australian and British governments. The British government agreed with these principles, and Blamey was formally issued with his charter on 19 April 1940.[35] By this time the AIF had expanded to a corps, with Blamey in command.

The decisions taken during the first uneventful seven months of the war—the so-called 'Phoney War'—shaped Australian strategy for the remainder of the war. The government had placed its ships under Admiralty control, had committed to the Empire Air Training Scheme, and had raised the 2nd AIF. The decision to deploy the 2nd AIF overseas was important. Eventually four divisions were sent overseas, three to the Middle East where they took part in major campaigns that determined the outcome of the war in that area. Whether these deployments denuded Australian defences—making Australia more vulnerable to attack—or whether they helped save the British position in the Middle East and provided valuable battle-trained units for the later defence of Australia, is one of the great questions in Australian military history.

John Dedman, a later Labor Party minister and one of Menzies' political opponents, has sympathised with the problems facing the prime minister, observing that 'the first six or seven months of the war constituted a period of great difficulty for whoever happened to be leader of the Australian government'. Dedman doubted whether

> anyone else could have given a better leadership to the people than did Mr Menzies during those early months of war . . . the people were not then ready to submit to that high degree of direction by the government, which is the *sine qua non* of an all-in war effort . . . No leader in a democracy can pursue a policy very far in advance of public opinion: if he does he will soon be displaced and in Australia an election was due towards the end of 1940.[36]

End of the 'Phoney War'

It was not until Germany attacked Denmark and Norway in April 1940, followed by its lightning war, or 'blitzkrieg', beginning against France and the Low Countries on 10 May, that Australia's perceptions changed. Whereas previously the government had rather unfortunately spoken of 'business as usual', it now called for an 'all-in' war effort. With the German Army advancing rapidly through France, on 15 May the dominions secretary advised that in view of the danger of Italy joining the war, the third AIF convoy, then heading for the Middle East, should be diverted via Cape Town to the United Kingdom. After initially doubting the wisdom of the diversion 'which would mean splitting' the Australian forces, the War Cabinet agreed, even though some members still suspected that the British aimed to split the AIF into units that would then be integrated into British formations under British command.[37] At that time, almost half of the members of the War Cabinet had seen active service alongside British forces in the First World War. In response to the deteriorating situation, on 22 May the War Cabinet announced further war measures, including the formation of a third division of the AIF (the 8th), even though at this stage there were still insufficient volunteers to fill the 7th Division.

On 11 June, the day after Italy entered the war on Germany's side, the War Cabinet met the chiefs of staff to assess the strategic position. Asked about the naval situation should France be defeated, Admiral Colvin replied that in such an event, Britain would have to withdraw from the Mediterranean. Requested to assess the likely impact of the changed strategic situation, the next day the chiefs recommended that an armed merchant cruiser and a sloop be made available for use in the Indian Ocean and Red Sea area, and three extra RAAF squadrons be sent to Singapore to release RAF units for employment elsewhere.[38] One squadron of Hudson bombers had been sent earlier in the year.

With France collapsing 'like a house of cards', many in the Cabinet could not get their minds around the consequences. Percy Spender recalled Henry Gullett repeating: 'I just can't believe it. I just can't believe it.' In the end, the full Cabinet accepted the recommendations from the chiefs, but the government urgently needed more information from Britain on the alternatives likely to confront the Empire, and whether Australia could 'continue to rely on the pre-war undertaking that a British squadron of capital ships would proceed to Singapore immediately on hostile action in the Pacific'. The dominions secretary swiftly replied that Japan might take the opportunity to alter the status quo, and it was 'most improbable that we would send adequate reinforcements to the Far East'. Australia and Britain would 'have to rely on the United States of America to safeguard our interest there'.[39]

This startling and disturbing statement called into question the whole pre-war strategy of relying on the Singapore base to defend

Australia; but there is no evidence that Menzies challenged Britain on this issue. The quandary facing the government was revealed on 12 June when Menzies, accompanied by Shedden, General White and other officials met the now influential publisher Sir Keith Murdoch, who had been appointed Director-General of Information. White explained that if the Japanese defeated the RN in the Pacific they would not need to invade Australia because it would be cut off from assistance. But if the Japanese did invade Australia, the army could only fight for a month before it ran out of ammunition.[40] Four days later the government decided to raise and equip a militia force of 250,000 men for home defence, but this would be a slow process. Initially there was to be a call-up of 40,000 men for eighteen days, and then two successive groups for three months. At any time there would be 30,000–40,000 AIF personnel in training in Australia and these were included in the 250,000 figure. The limitations would be the lack of facilities and equipment.

The situation was made worse on 17 June when France surrendered, leaving Britain and the dominions alone fighting against Germany and Italy. Meeting on 18 June, the chiefs told the War Cabinet that Japan might occupy the French colonies of the New Hebrides and New Caledonia, and little could be done to prevent it. Turning to the defence of Australia, Admiral Colvin said that the situation in northern Australia 'hinged on a battle fleet based at Singapore. If such was not possible, the situation became radically changed.' General White agreed, observing that with its naval superiority, Japan could bring Australia to terms without the need for invasion. That is, Australia would be forced to surrender. Two days later Britain advised that there was 'no hope of being able to despatch a fleet to Singapore'.[41]

This was a critical point for Australia's decision-makers. Should Australia continue with its plans to send forces to the Middle East, or hold them back for the defence of Australia or perhaps Singapore? The Minister for the Navy, Billy Hughes, recalled that at the meeting on 18 June he stated that Australia had to prepare for invasion, but all White could say was: 'Our strategy is based on the navy being here to help us when it is needed. Our strategy is based on us holding

Singapore; on Japan not coming into the war.' Hughes was upset at this reply and remembered saying to the man beside him: 'Look at that man's profile. Did you see it? He may have many things, but he has not got guts.'[42]

This comment was grossly unfair to one of Australia's most distinguished soldiers. At Gallipoli, White had shrugged off being struck by shrapnel. For his part, White thought that the meeting had been 'a shocking waste of time'. Hughes's comment, however, highlights White's continued faith in imperial defence. Like Menzies, he believed that while Australia should be concerned for its own defence, true security could only come from imperial cooperation, and that it was an illusion for Australia to hope to stand alone. Nevertheless, it is surprising that White did not treat the threat of invasion with more urgency. White still seemed to be thinking in terms of the First World War. Earlier, on 4 June, he had told the ministers that he was confident the Germans could not stage another offensive like the recent one without six to nine months' preparation. The next day the Germans crossed the Somme and, as Charles Bean noted, 'the confidence of ministers in his judgment was very sharply shaken'. White himself admitted that he 'was not what he had once been'.[43]

The Looming Japanese Threat

The defeat of France and the Netherlands had repercussions in the Far East, where Japan, already at war in China, took the opportunity of moving into the northern part of the French colony of Indochina (now Cambodia, Laos, Vietnam and parts of China). Japan demanded that the British garrison in Shanghai be withdrawn, the Hong Kong frontier closed and supplies to China along the Burma Road halted. If the Australian government had not yet fully accepted that Britain might not be able to send a fleet to restrain the Japanese, it was forced to consider the question on 29 June with the receipt of a frank cable from London stating that since a fleet could not be sent, the land and air defence of Malaya (now Malaysia) would have to be improved. As

Curtin's biographer John Edwards commented, troops needed to be sent not to defend the naval base, because no fleet was coming, but 'to defend a British colony, its tin and rubber and its United States dollar contributions to the Exchequer'. Britain requested that the three air force squadrons offered by Australia be sent to Malaya, that Australia also send a division, and if that was not immediately available, send brigades as they became available.[44]

The War Cabinet, which met with its advisers in July to consider this request, had changed its composition. In February, Casey had resigned to take up the appointment as first Australian Minister in Washington. It was the first step in an effort to establish an independent source of information and influence. Then, in March, the Country Party agreed to enter a coalition with the UAP. Several Country Party members joined the ministry, and the War Cabinet was restructured. Menzies remained as prime minister and Minister for Defence Coordination. The second most important position went to Archie Cameron, leader of the Country Party, who became Minister for Commerce and Minister for the Navy. The chiefs of staff advised the re-formed War Cabinet that their 'first obligation was to equip the AIF forces already in the Middle East and were reluctant to overthrow their reliance upon imperial strategy', a view the War Cabinet accepted. In the meantime, General Blamey, commander of the 1st Australian Corps, and now in the Middle East awaiting the arrival of the 7th Division, had asked for reinforcements. The War Cabinet therefore decided to await an appreciation from the British chiefs of staff before making a decision.[45]

When it arrived on 12 August, the British appreciation revealed the full extent of the British Empire's weakness in the Far East and urgently requested the early despatch of Australian troops to Singapore. The British prime minister, Winston Churchill, who had succeeded Chamberlain in May, added that if 'Japan set about invading Australia or New Zealand on a large scale' then Britain would cut its losses in the Mediterranean and proceed to Australia's aid.[46] Churchill was determined that Australia not be diverted from supporting the imperial defence effort by concerns over a Japanese threat.

Churchill's promise was militarily worthless. Japan was unlikely to begin an invasion on a 'large scale' until it had secured naval domination and bases in the area, including the capture or neutralisation of Singapore. In those circumstances, Britain would be in little position to assist Australia. Rather than reassure the Australian chiefs, Churchill's promise made them look even more closely at the defence of Singapore and the Netherlands East Indies, and they concluded that strategically the area was of greater importance to Australia than was the Middle East. The most effective contribution towards the defence of Australia would be to despatch the 7th Division to Malaya, and they recommended the first two brigades be sent as soon as practicable.[47] This was to be decided at a War Cabinet meeting on 13 August.

Before it could consider this issue the War Cabinet suffered a devastating blow. Menzies recalled that he was sitting in his office at Parliament House in Canberra on the morning of 13 August:

> A knock came on my door, and somebody walked in. There had been a dreadful air crash, almost within sight of my windows. Gullett was dead; Street was dead; Fairbairn was dead; the most scholarly and technically talented soldier in Australian history, Sir Brudenell White . . . was dead . . . I shall never forget that terrible hour.[48]

The crash had occurred near Canberra airport. All three ministers were experienced men with war service, and Hasluck observed that 'the loss of any of these men alone would have weakened the Ministry and the Parliament. The loss of the three together tore a great hole in the fabric of the government.'[49] Senator Philip McBride, who took over as Minister for the Army, and Arthur Fadden of the Country Party, who became Minister for Air and Civil Aviation, joined the War Cabinet. Major General Northcott became acting CGS until Lieutenant General Vernon Sturdee was appointed at the end of August.

Sturdee would hold the position for the next two years—a period of critical decision-making in which his advice would be crucial.

Born in 1890, he was a regular officer from the Royal Australian Engineers who had fought at Gallipoli and on the Western Front, and had ended the war as a staff officer on the headquarters of Sir Douglas Haig. After attending the British Staff College at Quetta and the Imperial Defence College in London, he became Director of Military Operations and Intelligence in Army Headquarters and a keen critic of the Singapore Strategy. Soon after the outbreak of war he had been appointed GOC of Eastern Command, and in July 1940 was given command of the newly formed 8th Division, before the death of White saw him promoted to CGS. Lieutenant General Sir Sydney Rowell, who served with him for part of this time, wrote that Sturdee 'had a very precise mind—he had a great sense of the need for priorities—he saw the problem very clearly—he was able to give orders which left no doubt as to what was wanted and he then left people to get on with the job'.[50]

Since both Northcott and Sturdee doubted the wisdom of the Singapore Strategy, they were keen to reinforce the Middle East. Furthermore, by this stage Churchill, in an about turn, was now arguing strongly for the Australians to be sent to the Middle East. The chiefs were not unanimous about whether to reinforce Singapore, and it seems that the newly formed War Cabinet, unlike the chiefs, put particular value on Churchill's promise, and were already convinced of the importance of the Middle East. At the War Cabinet meeting on 23 September, the ministers agreed that the 7th Division would go to the Middle East.[51] In hindsight, this major decision can be justified, for it is unlikely that three more Australian brigades in Malaya would have been able to balance the lack of air support in early 1942. With little capacity for self-defence, Australia had no choice other than to try to make imperial defence work. Nonetheless, in agreeing to the British government's request to send the 7th Division to the Middle East, the War Cabinet and the chiefs had accepted too readily the advice from London without testing it against the situation as viewed from Australia. Both the War Cabinet and the chiefs would soon change their attitudes about British strategic leadership, and a new decision-making body was soon to appear.

The Advisory War Council

At the general election held at the end of September the government lost several seats and retained power only through the support of two independents. The War Cabinet, sworn in on 28 October, consisted of Menzies; Arthur Fadden, leader of the Country Party and treasurer; Billy Hughes, attorney-general and Minister for the Navy; Percy Spender, Minister for the Army; John McEwen, Minister for Air and Civil Aviation; and Senator Philip McBride, Minister for Supply and Development.

It was a much less experienced War Cabinet than earlier, but included a number of figures who were later to make their mark. Arthur Fadden, who would succeed Menzies as prime minister a year later, had only just taken over from Cameron as leader of the Country Party—officially he was only the acting leader as the party had not been able to agree on a leader. A 45-year-old accountant from Queensland, he was, as Hasluck wrote, an 'affable, astute, story-telling man, untroubled by the deeper significance of problems . . . He was not the cleverest, the most experienced, or the wisest man in the Country Party, but he was the best colleague and probably the staunchest character.' Spender found him to be 'a hail-fellow-well-met associate of everyone, but he was as astute a politician as one could meet'.[52]

Spender, aged 43, who became Minister for the Army, was seen as a possible leadership contender. A successful Sydney barrister, he had entered the House of Representatives in 1937. By 1940 he was treasurer. He approached his new portfolio with great energy, determined to improve the army's administration and to prepare it for the home defence of Australia

The election also brought another change of great significance. With the parties finely balanced in the House of Representatives, Menzies tried to persuade the Labor leader, John Curtin, to join a national government. Curtin declined, but as an alternative proposed an Australian War Council. Menzies accepted and agreed to look favourably on such Labor social policies as child endowment. In turn, the Labor Party agreed to 'place the services of individual members of the party at the disposal of the government to assist Ministers occupied on war and defence efforts. It will not take political advantage, as an Opposition, of its numerical strength to embarrass the government in its war efforts.'[53] After an exhaustive Caucus ballot, the Labor Party selected Curtin, Frank Forde and Norman Makin to join the council, to be known as the Advisory War Council, and made a position available to John (Jack) Beasley of the splinter Non-Communist Labor Party, based in New South Wales. By this time Curtin had persuaded the Labor Party to drop its isolationist policies and to support conscription for home defence.

Set up on 28 October, the Advisory War Council's functions were to 'consider and advise the government with respect to such matters relating to the defence of the Commonwealth or the prosecution of the war' as referred to it by the prime minister. The initial government members were Menzies, Fadden, Spender and Hughes. Shedden was appointed secretary of the council—a position he held in addition to being secretary of both the War Cabinet and of the Department of Defence Coordination. The formation of the Advisory War Council was a considerable achievement by both Menzies and Curtin. On the one hand, Menzies was able to involve the Opposition and, in effect, ensure that it would not hamper him as his government went about the conduct of the war. On the other hand, without forming a national government, Curtin had managed to involve senior members of the Opposition in the war effort.

Curtin's role in helping form the Advisory War Council was typical of his approach during the 1930s, in which he had rebuilt the party, changed many of its policies to those more acceptable to a large number of Australians, and increased his own stature and reputation for acting responsibly.[54] By October 1940, the 55-year-old Curtin had been Opposition leader for five years. A former journalist and trade union organiser, he had been jailed briefly for anti-conscription activity in the First World War. Elected to parliament in 1928, he was disappointed at not being elevated to the ministry in the Scullin government in 1929 and began to drink heavily. He was elected leader of his party on the death of Scullin in 1935 only after he vowed to abstain from alcohol. During the late 1930s he had taken an interest in international affairs but could claim no real expertise in military matters. Experience on the Advisory War Council would be invaluable to him.

Reacting to the Japanese Threat

In the meantime, before the Advisory War Council was inaugurated, the government was coming to the conclusion that Churchill could not be trusted. At the very time he was requesting the 7th Division be sent to the Middle East, unknown to the Australian government, the RAN flagship, HMAS *Australia*, was taking part in the ill-fated expedition to seize Dakar in West Africa from the Vichy French (the French state collaborating with Nazi Germany). The first information Menzies received was on the first day of the operation, 23 September, and there was little subsequent information. Menzies complained vigorously to Churchill that the lack of information had 'frequently proved humiliating'. Churchill strongly resented this criticism and sent back a stinging reply. But the incident should have warned the Australians of Churchill's methods.[55]

At the same time, with the agreement of the Australian government, the old cruiser HMAS *Adelaide* had assisted in the overthrow of the Vichy authorities in New Caledonia, thus easing the threat of a Japanese occupation. But Japanese intentions were becoming more ominous. During September they moved into northern Indochina, and at the end of the month signed a pact of mutual cooperation with Germany and Italy, recognising their leadership in Europe in return for their recognition of Japan's leadership in 'Greater East Asia'. Australia's blinkered approach is evidenced by the War Cabinet deciding that this Tripartite Pact should not influence the decision to send the 7th Division to the Middle East.[56]

Once it started work, the Advisory War Council focused on the Japanese threat. By September the British government was in discussion with the United States about a joint approach to a possible war with Japan and, as a result, between 22 and 31 October a conference was held in Singapore to consider defence problems in the area. Australia was represented by Captain Joseph Burnett, assistant CNS; Major General John Northcott, deputy CGS; and Air Commodore William Bostock, deputy CAS. The conference proposed that in the event of war, Australian, British, Dutch and New Zealand naval forces operating in the Far East and Pacific Ocean should be placed under US command. With the reservation that local Australian forces remain under Australian control, the War Cabinet agreed.[57]

On 16 November the Australian chiefs of staff presented their report on the Singapore conference, which emphasised that 'in the absence of a Main Fleet in the Far East, the forces and equipment at present available in this area for the defence of Malaya are totally inadequate to meet a major attack by Japan'. Therefore, 'The first and immediate consideration must be to ensure the security of Malaya against direct attack.' They recommended that a brigade of the 8th Division be located in Malaya as a temporary measure until the division could be concentrated in the Middle East, when it should be relieved by Indian troops. They pointed out that the Far Eastern situation had deteriorated since 7 September, when the Australian government had informed Britain that the major threat to the Empire outside Britain was in the Middle East. In the event of war with Japan, Australian naval forces serving overseas would need to be returned to Australia.[58]

At the Advisory War Council on 25 November Menzies referred to the 'alarming position in regard to the defence of Singapore, as revealed by the report', and that he would probably need to go to London to urge reinforcements for the Far East. The following day the War Cabinet expressed 'grave concern' at 'the most serious position revealed in regard to the defence of Malaya and Singapore'. In the event of war it would be necessary for two 8-inch cruisers, three 6-inch cruisers and five destroyers to be located in Australian waters, and these could be provided by the return of RAN ships serving overseas. The War Cabinet decided to ask Britain whether it needed an Australian brigade to go to Malaya. The Australian cable to Britain, sent on 1 December, was hard-hitting, reminding the British government that the 'discussions in London in 1937, regarding the defence of Singapore, had led us to believe that the situation would have been much better'. Churchill gratefully accepted the offer of a brigade for Malaya, assuring Menzies that if Australia were to be 'seriously threatened by invasion we should not hesitate to compromise or sacrifice the Mediterranean position for the sake of our kith and kin'.[59] In early February 1941 the 22nd Brigade Group sailed for Malaya.

On 8 January 1941 Menzies advised the Advisory War Council that during his visit to London he would be discussing the Empire's policies towards Japan and the Netherlands East Indies, the Singapore base, the position in the Middle East, the policy towards France, aircraft construction and ship building.[60] Nevertheless, the main issue would be defence in the Far East. Finally, accompanied by Shedden and John Storey of the Aircraft Production Commission, Menzies left Sydney on 24 January. He was to be absent for four months.

The deliberations of the War Cabinet and later of the Advisory War Council in the second half of 1940 over the Japanese threat and the destination of the AIF divisions were unsatisfactory in many respects. The government and its military advisers were pulled between the need to reinforce Singapore and the desire to make a contribution to the imperial war effort in the Middle East. As Paul Hasluck, the official historian, put it, 'although the Singapore conference had revealed the weakness of Singapore and hence, in the reasoning of the Australian defence advisers, of the home defences of Australia, it did not lead to any substantial action to repair the weakness'.[61] The Labor members of the Advisory War Council went along with the decisions about the employment of the AIF, but they were more insistent about the immediate naval reinforcement of the Far East.

In hindsight it might be easy to criticise the decision to reinforce Singapore when it was already unlikely that Britain would send a substantial naval force there. But it must be remembered that for the past six months Britain had been under heavy air attack. The Italians had not yet been pushed out of Egypt, and the 6th Australian Division was soon to enter battle in the Western Desert. Having thrown its lot in with Britain, Australia had little option but to support Britain as much as it could.

5

'Australia's very existence is at stake'

Menzies and Fadden, Second World War, 1941

Australian forces were involved in few combat operations during 1940. The RAN's old destroyers and the light cruiser HMAS *Sydney* did valuable work in the Mediterranean, the most notable engagement being in July, when *Sydney* sank the Italian cruiser *Bartolomeo Colleoni*. But the big question was when and where the 2nd AIF, then training in Palestine, would go into action. In deciding these issues Menzies was the key figure, but Australia's war leadership also included his deputy, Arthur Fadden; the Minister for the Army, Percy Spender; their key advisers, Shedden and the chiefs of staff; the commander in the field, General Blamey; and, through his membership of the Advisory War Council, the leader of the Opposition, John Curtin. During 1941 these leaders and advisers were to face an increasingly complex strategic situation, in which they would need to balance the growing threat from Japan against new demands and challenges in the Middle East.

Appointed Minister for the Army after the death of Geoffrey Street in August 1940, Percy Spender was determined to get a grip on his portfolio. Although, as army minister, he was responsible only for the administration of the army, as a member of the War Cabinet and the Advisory War Council, Spender also had a role in policy formulation. So in November 1940 he suggested to Menzies that he and the CGS, General Sturdee, visit the Middle East, to 'consult with Blamey and some of his officers in the field', and also 'to see our Australian troops'. Menzies strongly disapproved of Spender's desire to visit the Middle East, but Spender insisted and on 20 December 1940 he and Sturdee headed off.[1]

Maintaining the Integrity of the AIF

By December 1940, Blamey had been in the Middle East for six months, where he was mainly concerned with the administration and training of his force. But he never lost sight of his responsibility to ensure that his force was not broken up or dispersed by his British superiors. Requests for assistance from the British commander-in-chief, General Sir Archibald Wavell, had already come thick and fast. Blamey handled most of these without reference to Australia, but in letters to both Menzies and Spender he assured them that he had kept in mind 'the principles of retaining the AIF to fight as a single force'.[2]

It was soon clear that the British generals did not understand that Australia was an independent nation, albeit within the Empire. At the end of October 1940, Italy declared war on Greece and immediately began an invasion from its recently acquired territory in Albania. At Churchill's request, Wavell sent British troops to help garrison Crete, but could not meet all Churchill's demands without calling on dominion troops. Churchill then asked Menzies for permission to use Australian troops. Menzies approved their use, as long as they were fully equipped.[3] Blamey advised Menzies that while his force was not fully equipped, Wavell 'was faced with a most difficult situation should he be compelled to accept battle before all his units are fully equipped. He cannot avoid battle since the enemy for the time being have the initiative.' There was, however, 'no reason to anticipate a serious Italian offensive against Egypt in the immediate future'. This appeared to satisfy the government, and Menzies told Spender: 'We have General Blamey in Egypt, and there could be nobody better qualified to advise us on problems of equipment and disposition.'[4]

Blamey was, however, deeply worried over this incident. He had not been shown Menzies' cable to Churchill, and when he learned that Churchill had authorised the use of the troops he was placed in a difficult position. As he explained to Sturdee, 'the authorization in this way removes all control over the matter from me, and gives the C-in-C Middle East carte blanche for any action that he thinks desirable'. He thought Middle East Command had a 'penchant for breaking up organizations, and I have hitherto been able to resist this in regard to the AIF, but the position that has arisen over Crete has defeated me temporarily'.[5] As it happened, Wavell concluded that the Crete garrison was adequate for the defence of the island and no further troops were sent.

By December 1940, Blamey had succeeded in having Australian policy recognised at GHQ in Cairo. Blamey's chief of staff, Brigadier Sydney Rowell, commented that 'anybody with less force of character and sense of responsibility both to the AIF here and his Government at home, would probably have split the show'. Blamey had been adamant 'that he owed this duty to his Government' and 'that the British could not simply order Australian units about as they liked'.[6]

Blamey had agreed that the 6th Division, commanded by Major General Iven Mackay, could be deployed to the Western Desert, and on 31 December the division began a major attack on the Italian stronghold of Bardia across the Libyan border. Next day, as the Australian infantry thrust into the Italian defences, Blamey was at Lake Tiberias in Palestine to meet Spender and Sturdee as they arrived by flying boat. Blamey accompanied them on inspections of the Australian units in Palestine and Egypt, and for discussions with Wavell and other senior British commanders. According to Spender, 'The talks ranged over many subjects—the general strategy upon which plans had been based, enemy strength, air cover and sea support for our troops, the attitude of the Egyptian Government', and subjects concerning supply and equipment. As Spender acknowledged, the discussions were more in the nature of a briefing, but he considered they were 'of critical value to me in the discharge of my Ministerial duties'.[7]

Spender and Sturdee were back in Sydney by 15 January, as operations continued in the Western Desert. On 21 January the Australians captured the port of Tobruk, and then continued on to take Derna, before entering Benghazi on 6 February. Before this, on 2 February, Blamey had returned to Lake Tiberias to meet Menzies and Shedden. Menzies had come to see Blamey and the Australian troops before he continued on to London to seek reinforcements for the Far East. It was not long before he became involved in one of the most contentious issues in Australian military history: the decision to send troops to Greece.

Committing to the Greek Campaign

The War Cabinet's decision to approve the employment of Australian troops in the Greek campaign illustrates the problem of operating as part of the wider British Commonwealth military effort. Essentially, the decision was made by the British War Cabinet, advised by its own military leaders, and although the Australian government could veto the use of its forces, it could not do so lightly if the war were to be conducted with any cohesion. By the same token, Australia had to be given sufficient information, and in enough time to make a balanced decision.

In the three weeks before the Australian government finally approved the Greek expedition on 26 February, the main issue was how much General Wavell discussed it with Menzies during the latter's visit to the Middle East. Although the British government had not yet decided definitely to send a force to Greece, Blamey was aware that Wavell's staff were privately working on plans and, according to Shedden, in Cairo he told Menzies that the question was whether there were sufficient forces in the Middle East to ensure the success of the expedition, because withdrawing forces from Cyrenaica in Libya 'might render it vulnerable to renewed attack'.[8]

Like Hughes in the First World War, Menzies wanted to see the conditions under which the troops were serving, so he flew out to visit the Australian units in the desert. Menzies then returned to Cairo where, on 10 February, he discussed with Wavell the necessity of keeping the AIF together. Wavell replied that the 'aggregation' principle for the AIF was good, but should not be applied too rigidly as it was not always possible to find a front that would occupy an entire corps. Obviously with Greece in mind, Wavell raised the matter of needing a 'certain latitude' with Australian troops, and he reported to Churchill that he found Menzies 'very ready to agree' to what he suggested. There is no evidence that the secretive Wavell told Menzies of his plans for the Greek expedition, and Menzies made no mention of it in his diary.[9] However, since Blamey had already warned Menzies of the possibility, it is odd that he did not raise it with Wavell.

Next day, Menzies flew to Tobruk, collected Blamey and Rowell, and flew on to Barce, near Benghazi, where the corps headquarters had recently arrived. Menzies inspected the troops, attended a victory dinner and recounted to Blamey his recent interview with Wavell. Blamey said: 'Australian forces must be regarded as national, under national command. This does not exclude the use of smaller units in special places, but all must be subject to consent of GOC AIF. "If you give these English Generals an inch, they'll take an ell."' Apparently there was no discussion of the possible expedition to Greece. In the afternoon of 12 February, Menzies returned to Cairo, 'confirmed in my belief that we had the right man in the right place'.[10]

Menzies saw Wavell again in the evening of 13 February. By this time Churchill had advised Wavell that the British foreign secretary, Anthony Eden, and the CIGS, General Sir John Dill, were on the way from London and that it was hoped to send a force to Greece. It is not known exactly what transpired in this meeting. Menzies wrote in his diary that Wavell was 'clearly contemplating the possibility of a Salonika [Thessaloniki] expedition', and in his memoirs he recalled that he expressed concern about a possible German offensive in Libya, which Wavell had dismissed. It appears that Wavell had not been definite about the Greek expedition. The following morning Menzies set out for London without having had another chance to speak to Blamey.[11]

It was not until 18 February that Blamey learned from Wavell that he planned to send the 6th and 7th Australian Divisions to Greece. Blamey informed Wavell that he would need to refer the proposal to Australia but, according to Blamey's account, Wavell 'stated that he had discussed the possibility of such an operation with the Prime Minister of Australia'. After the conference Blamey told Rowell that 'he didn't like the prospect', but at this stage he took no action to inform the Australian government. The previous day Wavell had told Major General Bernard Freyberg, commander of the New Zealand Division, that his force was to go to Greece and that the New Zealand government had agreed. No evidence has been discovered that the New Zealand government had in fact agreed.[12]

Menzies arrived in England on 20 February, having flown via West Africa, and on Sunday the 23rd at the British prime minister's country house, Chequers, Churchill outlined the Greek proposal and Menzies reported that 'as usual, Winston went at it at a hand gallop'. Churchill explained that Britain could not let the Greeks down and he hoped to persuade Yugoslavia and Turkey to come in on the Allied side. In what he later called a 'momentous discussion', Menzies replied that he 'wanted to know more about the military prospects before he committed himself'.[13]

The next day Menzies attended the British War Cabinet. Before the ministers lay the copies of the optimistic signals from Wavell and Dill, together with a gloomy assessment from the British chiefs of staff. Encouraged by cables from Eden in Athens, Churchill declared himself in favour of the expedition and invited comments. Menzies was the first to reply, pointing out that he would have to communicate with his colleagues in Canberra. He wanted reassurance on two points. 'How long, for instance, would it take to put our troops into Greece in order to take up defensive positions? Could our shipping maintain the strain of the operation?' Menzies was also 'a little uneasy' over the equipment for the 7th Division. The vice CIGS, Lieutenant

General Sir Robert Haining, then told Menzies that he 'could rest assured that no Australian force would be put into the line without the full establishment of the necessary weapons'.[14]

Menzies realised that the ability to support the force in Greece hinged on the defence of Egypt, but was told that Wavell believed there was little chance of the Axis forces making a comeback in the Western Desert. Menzies replied that he 'had just come from the Western Desert and that the opinion there [obviously at Blamey's headquarters] was not so sanguine about the dangers of a German counter stroke, and [he] felt that the danger was underestimated'. He continued that 'the justification for the enterprise rested upon the prospect of our being able to put up a good fight. If the enterprise was only a forlorn hope, it had better not be undertaken.' He concluded by asking whether he could tell his colleagues in Canberra that 'the venture had a substantial chance of success'. Churchill replied unhelpfully that the Australian Cabinet had to assess this in the light of advice from Menzies. In his opinion, however, the enterprise was a risk worth taking.[15]

As the meeting drew to a close, Churchill asked each minister to state whether he agreed to the operation; all were in favour. All that remained was to secure the approval of the dominions. The following day, 25 February, Churchill cabled the Australian and New Zealand governments and explained the situation. He pointed out that Dill and Wavell, who represented 'the most prudent and experienced military opinion at our disposal', recommended immediate action. Churchill also stressed the effect on world opinion.[16]

Menzies had already despatched a private cable to the acting prime minister, Arthur Fadden, outlining the arguments in favour of the expedition. This was the critical cable. In it Menzies said Churchill had told him that 'if Japan goes to war against us America will unquestionably come in', and 'that should Australia be attacked and America be not in it, adequate naval reinforcements would at once be despatched to Australian waters'. Menzies thought, however, this 'view might be a little discounted'. He concluded: 'With some anxiety, my own recommendation to my colleagues is that we should concur.' Curtin's biographer John Edwards has argued that Menzies had implied Australia's agreement to the Greek campaign was in return for an assurance of 'adequate naval reinforcements' if Japan entered the war and America did not. But in his cable Menzies acknowledged that the substantial naval forces involved in the Greek campaign would affect Britain's ability to divert naval forces from the Mediterranean.[17]

On the afternoon of 26 February the Australian War Cabinet met in Sydney to consider Churchill's cable. Fadden began by asking whether they should obtain the views of the chiefs of staff, but in view of Menzies' recommendation, the ministers agreed that they needed to decide. Essentially, it was a political rather than a military decision. Part of the problem was the composition of the War Cabinet. With Menzies absent, the inexperienced Fadden was acting prime minister. Hughes, with his vast experience, was too old at 78 and after the meeting became ill. Spender, clever and energetic, was under attack in the press and parliament for a premature statement that the Australians had captured Tobruk. As he put it, 'in parliamentary circles I was held up to ridicule'.[18] John McEwen and Senator Foll had both been ministers for four years. The able secretary, Shedden, was overseas with Menzies.

Eventually consensus was reached, and afterwards Fadden cabled Menzies that 'despite risky nature of adventure we have been impressed with necessity for an immediate decision. Had more time been available we would have sought your further advice.' Fadden requested further assurance that the force was of sufficient size and suggested that it be augmented as additional numbers became available. He insisted that 'under no circumstances are our troops [to be] allotted this task unless equipped on maximum establishment scale'. He also requested that evacuation plans be prepared.[19]

When the British War Cabinet met on 27 February, Menzies reported the concurrence of his government, and Churchill asked the War Cabinet to put on record their high appreciation of the attitude of Australia and New Zealand, which had also concurred. The decision of 24 February was therefore confirmed.[20]

The following evening the British War Cabinet met again, and in the light of news that Turkey had declined to join the Allies and that German mechanised units were arriving in Libya, Menzies subjected the proposal to intense scrutiny. He complained that the War Cabinet had not been kept well informed and 'the action of the Foreign Secretary regarding the military agreement between General Dill and General Papagos [the Greek commander-in-chief] was embarrassing'. After reminding the War Cabinet that the dominions were providing three-fifths of the force, he explained that 'If they were told that they were now committed to the use of their forces in a situation which had definitely worsened, without further effective consultation . . . there would be a great deal of resentment.' Menzies' realistic assessment shook the War Cabinet, which decided to defer its decision pending a reply from Eden.[21]

Churchill had already warned Eden of the grave issue of committing Australian and New Zealand troops to a hazardous enterprise. He now sent Eden a further cable reminding him of the responsibility towards the dominions, which needed to be told that the decision was made because Dill, Wavell and the other commanders-in-chief were 'convinced that there is a reasonable fighting chance'.[22] Churchill was distancing himself from responsibility.

The receipt of Menzies' account of these latest developments caused intense concern in the Australian War Cabinet. The ministers agreed that 'Greece should be assisted', but they suggested to Menzies that he 'personally evaluate the situation, particularly in regard to the possibilities of a successful thrust by a German armoured force in North Africa'. At the British War Cabinet meeting on 7 March, Churchill declared that he was convinced the operation should go ahead. Menzies agreed, but as one secretary noted, he 'made some caustic comments'. He thought it curious that 'while a decision was being taken in virtue of the trust which we reposed in the judgment of our advisers in the Middle East . . . the argument with which they had supplied us told against rather than in favour of their advice'.[23]

With Menzies' agreement, the Australian War Cabinet authorised the operation to proceed, but Menzies said later that he had had an anxious time over the decision. On 8 March he told Fadden that the British military advisers discounted the possibility of a successful German thrust in North Africa, and that although the Greek expedition was hazardous it was 'by no means hopeless'.[24]

Until this time the Australian government had still not received an assessment from Blamey. In fact, a few days earlier, on 5 March, Blamey had written to Menzies to express his misgivings about the enterprise, but the letter did not arrive until 18 April. In the meantime, after pondering the matter further, and after he gained more idea of the military forces available for the expedition, on 8 March Blamey cabled Spender seeking permission to submit his views. Spender agreed and Blamey forwarded a detailed cable in which he said that the military operation was 'extremely hazardous in view of the disparity between [the] opposing forces in numbers and training'.[25]

On 12 March, Blamey wrote to Spender that despite the fact that Wavell and Dill 'hold very firmly that the operation should be put in hand . . . I regret that I still feel very strongly that without a definite plan for building up the strength of the force adequately within the next few months, the operation is most hazardous'. He explained that Wavell and Dill considered that in the mountainous terrain of Greece 'the operation, although risky', had 'a reasonable chance of success'. Blamey thought they had not given sufficient weight to the Germans' ability to improve their mobility in the area, and their likely air superiority. As it appeared that the operation was going ahead, however, he urged 'most strongly that vigorous action be taken to ensure that adequate forces for the task are provided at the most rapid rate possible'.[26] Writing to Sturdee on 14 March he said he was 'greatly concerned' at the 'sending of a boy to do a man's job'.[27]

Blamey's cables worried the Australian War Cabinet, but it was nonetheless 'undivided in its view that if the military advisers, having properly evaluated the risks', thought that the expedition should proceed, then it should agree to make Australian troops available.[28] In fact, five days earlier, on 5 March, the first Australian troops had started embarking for Greece.

Menzies, in London, could now do little more than watch the

situation closely. On 14 March, Menzies informed Fadden that Churchill had stated the venture was not based on a commitment by Eden, but on 'the estimate on the spot by our military advisers and the overwhelming moral and political repercussions of abandoning Greece'. It is hard to believe that Churchill was being candid. When at the end of the month there was a coup in Yugoslavia, which belatedly joined the Allies, he sent a confident message to Fadden: 'When a month ago we decided upon sending an army to Greece it looked rather a bleak military adventure dictated by *noblesse oblige*. Thursday's events in Belgrade show the far reaching effects of this and other measures we have taken on [the] whole Balkan situation.'[29] In other words, before the illusory optimism engendered by the Yugoslav coup, the venture had indeed been dictated by *noblesse oblige*.

The government received further despatches from Blamey on 27 March, including his letter written on 5 March. Fadden immediately pointed out to Menzies that Blamey's reports indicated he had not been consulted, and that he disagreed with the operation. This had placed Menzies and Fadden 'in an embarrassing situation with the Advisory War Council and with Cabinet, particularly as I have there stressed that General Blamey has agreed to the operation'. Menzies replied that Blamey knew his powers as GOC AIF and should not have hesitated to offer his views. Later Menzies said that 'quite frankly . . . some pains had been taken to suppress the critical views of General Blamey'.[30] Blamey learned a lesson, and never again failed to give his views on the wisdom of a proposed operation.

It was now too late, however, to act on Blamey's concerns. By the time the Germans attacked on 6 April, Blamey was in Greece commanding the newly formed Anzac Corps consisting of the 6th Australian Division and the New Zealand Division. By the end of the month the Germans had driven the Allies out of the Greek mainland. More than 300 Australians were killed and more than 2000 became prisoners of war.

The War Cabinet's decision to approve the commitment to the Greek campaign demonstrated the problems of a small country in coalition with a larger ally. The War Cabinet had to rely on advice from the British War Cabinet and chiefs of staff without having the capacity to make an independent assessment, and the ministers had not yet gained the experience or capacity to think ahead about strategic issues. Blamey had failed to provide the government with advice early enough, although there is the lingering question as to whether Wavell deliberately misled him into believing that Menzies had already approved the operation. For his part, Menzies might have made more effort to discuss the matter with Blamey or to seek his advice by cable. For all that, if the full information had been made available to the War Cabinet, it might still have approved the operation for the same reason that inspired Churchill—the effect on American public opinion. For the first time the War Cabinet had had to make a decision about the commitment of troops to battle—it would not be the last such decision.

Concern about Japan

In the 21st century the concept of political warfare has received more attention in the face of activities by China and Russia. But the concept is not new, and became evident to Australia's war leaders in the lead-up to the Pacific War. Thus, while Menzies and the War Cabinet were considering the British request to support the Greek campaign, they were also attempting to deal with an ever-growing threat in the Pacific. In fact, this had been the main reason Menzies had gone overseas in January.

The United States had already decided that in the event of war its main effort would be in the Atlantic and in Europe, while it remained on a 'strict defensive' in the Pacific. When in November 1940 Churchill heard of the American plan (known as Plan Dog) he described it as 'strategically sound and . . . highly adapted to our interests'. The Americans then invited the British to staff conversations in Washington, DC, and on 29 December the dominions secretary, Lord Cranborne, warned Menzies that the general policy to be discussed would 'be to defeat Germany and Italy first and then deal with Japan'. It seems that the Australian government did not fully appreciate the importance of this proposed policy. Australia had not been invited to take part in the Washington conversations, due to begin at the end of January 1941, but the Australian Minister in Washington, Richard Casey, and the newly appointed naval attaché, Commander Henry Burrell, tried to keep abreast of the discussions through the good offices of the British Embassy.[31]

Unaware of the outcome of the Washington conversations, on 5 February 1941 Arthur Fadden chaired a meeting of the Advisory War Council at Victoria Barracks in Melbourne.[32] The non-government members requested a discussion about Japan's relationship to the Axis and Allied powers, and Percy Spender, just back from Singapore and the Middle East, began by reporting that, from advice being received, Japan was now veering towards intervention in the war against the Allies. Although Japan was uncertain about what action to take, 'there was every possibility of Japan making a move against us in the next three months'. The leader of the Opposition, John Curtin, thought that Japan was 'opportunistic' and would make war when it thought the situation favourable. The greatest threat appeared to be from the Japanese Navy, which could 'demobilise Australia, with disastrous effect on our commercial and economic life'. Considering events in the Mediterranean and the Atlantic, in his opinion, the next six months would 'be fatal to one side or the other', and actions needed to be taken to inform the population and to improve the defences of Australia.

At this stage, the chiefs of staff were invited to join the meeting, and Curtin asked Admiral Colvin to what extent the Australian naval squadron could be reinforced. Colvin replied that the British Navy was 'at present extended to the utmost'. The maximum effort was being taken to build up the naval defences of Australia, but 'the Naval effort was being set back by continuous strikes and labour problems in shipyards and docks'. Air Chief Marshal Burnett added that labour problems were also causing problems for the Air Force. As a result, the council agreed that Fadden would release a press statement that Australia 'was now entering upon a period in which its very existence is at stake'.

During the following week advice came from London, probably based on deciphered cable intercepts, that 'the Japanese may already have decided to push southward even if this means war'. The Australian Minister in Tokyo, Sir John Latham (who had taken up this new appointment in August 1940), forwarded the same opinion. His appointment was another step in the government's efforts to widen it sources of information. Although not yet understood by government ministers, a new element had now entered strategic decision-making, namely signals intelligence—information gained by deciphering an opponent's diplomatic cables. In this respect the Australian government had to rely on Britain, as Australia had not yet developed a strategic signals intelligence capability.[33]

On 12 February the War Cabinet met in Sydney to consider the British reply to the report of the Singapore conference of October 1940. The New Zealand prime minister, Peter Fraser, was also present. The British had decided that the 582 aircraft recommended for the defence of Malaya should be reduced to 336, which 'should give a very fair degree of security . . . Capacity of the Japanese should not be over-estimated.' The British glossed over the request for the return of Australian ships promised in the event of Japan entering the war. Both the Australian and New Zealand governments were adamant that their ships should return, stressing that the main naval threat to their countries would be through the Pacific towards the Tasman Sea. In that case, British ships in the Indian Ocean would be no help. This view was cabled to the British government later that day.[34]

The next day at the Advisory War Council, Curtin spoke of the danger of America concentrating its efforts in the Atlantic, and suggested strengthening the naval force at Singapore, if possible. The council agreed to release a statement that the war 'had moved to a new stage of urgency'. This statement, issued jointly by Fadden, Curtin and the Non-Communist Labor Party's Jack Beasley, had an immediate impact on the public. For example, the headline of the *Canberra Times* in the morning of 14 February read: 'Japanese Battle Fleet Moves Southward to Indo-china'. The heading of one of the stories immediately below the main headline was: 'Utmost gravity for

Australia: War Council Warning: Defence Chiefs Summoned to War Cabinet'.[35]

Hasluck was right in claiming that one reason for the release of the statement was an attempt to alleviate the industrial disputes holding up war production.[36] Nevertheless, the Advisory War Council meetings on 5 and 13 February mark a significant turning point in Australian strategic decision-making, for Curtin managed to persuade the government leaders to put their names to statements emphasising the danger to Australia. Furthermore, although there might have been slender evidence to warrant the statements, it was obvious that Britain was paying insufficient attention to the Far East.

While the discussions had been underway in Sydney the Australian chiefs had been meeting in Melbourne with the British commander-in-chief in the Far East, Air Chief Marshal Sir Robert Brooke-Popham. Following these discussions they had prepared an appreciation, based on the threat if Japan entered the war and American intervention was uncertain. The chiefs concluded that it was unlikely Japan would undertake an invasion of Australia until it had secured Malaya and the Netherlands East Indies and had, in some way, dealt with 'the possibility of American intervention from Hawaii'. It was necessary, therefore, to reinforce Malaya and strengthen the East Indies. But only the AIF could be used to reinforce Malaya, as the militia could not be sent out of Australian territory. It was not possible to increase the AIF as there was insufficient equipment for further units, and even the 22nd Brigade Group of the 8th Division, then arriving in Malaya, was not yet fully equipped. The solution was to withhold the remainder of the 8th Division from the Middle East and retain it for the defence of Australia, one battalion being sent to Rabaul to secure a forward airfield. Other forces were to be held in readiness to go to Timor and Ambon.[37]

The War Cabinet and the Advisory War Council discussed this appreciation in Sydney on 14 February, with Brooke-Popham and the Australian chiefs present on both occasions. Brooke-Popham presented a more optimistic view than the chiefs, claiming that Singapore could defend itself for six months until a fleet arrived, and that he was not pressing for the rest of the 8th Division to be despatched to Singapore. In his opinion, 'Japanese planes were not highly efficient' and the 'Malayan Air Force would put up a good show against them'. He did not mention his private doubts about the security of Singapore, and gave the Australians what one historian called 'a less than comprehensive survey of his view of the situation'.[38]

The proposals of the chiefs—that naval forces be returned to Australia, that the 8th Division not be despatched to the Middle East, and that air bases be established so that aircraft could operate in the area between Burma and Australia—were accepted by the War Cabinet. The limits of Australian responsibility were delineated and were to include Timor. The bipartisan approach was confirmed when the Advisory War Council recommended that the proposals be adopted.

The government's confidence in Allied commitments to defend the Far East was shaken by the further receipt on 13 and 14 February of a batch of important cables from Washington.[39] Burrell reported that the British government was advocating a policy of defeating Germany and Italy first and only then dealing with Japan. While Australia and New Zealand were essential to the security of the Far East, retention of Singapore was a key to the defence of the area. Nevertheless, the Americans had no intention of sending a fleet to Singapore, and the British government was pressing the Americans to move ships from the Pacific to the Atlantic. Burrell reported that, as a last resort, the Americans would abandon the Far East in order to ensure the maximum concentration in the Atlantic and Mediterranean. Furthermore, the US president had reportedly stated that if Japan attacked only the Netherlands East Indies or British possessions, America would be unlikely to declare war.[40]

The receipt of this information shocked the Australian ministers, although the crucial cable was not shown to the council. Fadden wrote later: 'If Australia were to be abandoned by these two great powers until the war in Europe was decided, we and our countrymen might well be pulling rickshaws before long.' The next day, 15 February, the Australian government despatched a cable to London advising that the 8th Division would be retained for use in Australia and the Far East and that arrangements for it to proceed to the Middle East had been cancelled.[41]

On 22 February another cable was received from Burrell that indicated Britain intended to do no more in the Far East than wait to see what action America would take in the event of war. 'Such grave and most disturbing information', as Fadden described this news, could not be released to the public, but he called parliament together for a special secret session on 12 March. Whether or not Fadden had shown Burrell's cable to Curtin, the Opposition would have gathered the same point when Fadden said that 'even if the United States were to be involved in war with Japan, it was felt that to fight an active war in the Pacific would make a dangerous diversion of forces and material from the main theatre of operations which, in American opinion, was the Atlantic and Great Britain'.[42]

These deliberations had important outcomes. At another conference in Singapore at the end of February, the Australian representatives agreed to provide troops and an air striking force at Darwin to reinforce Ambon and Koepang (i.e. Kupang) if required, and this commitment was accepted by the War Cabinet on 22 March.[43] Army Headquarters then issued instructions that there was a possibility of war with Japan. A special battalion was to be raised for service at Port Moresby, the force at Darwin was to be brought up to brigade strength, and militia training was to be stepped up.[44] Thus twelve months before the surrender of Singapore, Australia's pre-war defence policy of relying on a British fleet stationed at Singapore had been revealed as totally inadequate. In accepting these recommendations, the Cabinet endorsed a major change in Australia's strategic focus. Australia's defence was now linked closely with the region.

February 1941 had been a testing time for Fadden, and as a result the Country Party at last appointed him leader. He had been only acting leader since the previous October. The British high commissioner described Fadden as the 'arch-mixer', claiming that 'you couldn't meet a better chap in a bar . . . Good-natured, shrewd, likeable, has hardly any real thoughts of his own, means well.'[45] These qualities had enabled him to work well with the Opposition and had contributed to the work of the Advisory War Council. On 17 March Fadden reflected that recent events had caused him 'to utter a warning more grave than has ever been heard in this country. I had to say that within a brief time our country might be attacked. A few scoffed at that warning as exaggerated, but they did not know the facts. I spoke with every care, and every word I said was justified. We were, and we remain, in the greatest danger.'[46]

On 27 March the British and American representatives in Washington signed their report (known as ABC-1). A copy was flown to Australia, and another copy was given to Menzies in London. The report was explicit: 'Since Germany is the predominate member of the axis powers, the Atlantic and European area is considered to be the decisive theatre . . . If Japan does enter the war, the military strategy in the Far East will be defensive.' Nothing could have been clearer! The War Cabinet had little option but to agree to the report, but it did so on the understanding that Britain would make every possible effort to move the 'main fleet' to Singapore.[47]

Menzies in London

Throughout this period, in London, Menzies had been discussing reinforcements for the Far East. On 26 February he visited the Foreign Office, but was disappointed by the permanent under-secretary, Sir Alexander Cadogan, whose attitude he described as 'one of remoteness and almost indifference'. Menzies reported to Fadden that the Foreign Office had adopted a 'fatalistic attitude' towards Japan.[48]

Eventually, on 1 April, Menzies forwarded to the British chiefs a memorandum setting out the questions he felt still needed to be answered. He referred to the inadequacy of the defences in Malaya and asked for a statement of the forces necessary for its defence. The British chiefs replied on 11 April, claiming that, with the exception of certain artillery units, land forces in Malaya would reach their full strength by the end of April 1941. They accepted that air strength was 'below that necessary for reasonable security in the absence of the Fleet', but considered the risk no more serious than that being accepted elsewhere. Britain's ability to send a battle cruiser and a carrier to the Far East had to 'be judged entirely on the situation at the time'.[49]

Shedden advised Menzies that while the British chiefs' paper 'may not be very encouraging in certain respects, we certainly know where we stand, the degree to which we must rely on our own efforts, and the necessity for expanding them to the utmost extent'. The British comments indicated 'a degree of complacency which we have come to expect about the defence of the Pacific region. It is now evident that, for too long, we readily accepted the general assurances about the defence of this area.' The relief of Singapore did 'not look very reassuring'.[50]

By mid-April the course of the war had changed dramatically. On 31 March, German and Italian forces in North Africa, under a newly arrived commander, General Erwin Rommel, had begun an offensive, and by 4 April had entered Benghazi. Two days later the 9th Australian Division near Benghazi was ordered to withdraw to Tobruk, and by 11 April the siege of Tobruk had begun. Under the command of Major General Leslie Morshead, the 9th Division plus a brigade of the 7th Division would form the majority of the Tobruk garrison. Meanwhile, on 6 April, German forces had begun an invasion of Greece and Yugoslavia. A week later the British force had been forced back to the Aliakmon (i.e. Haliacmon) line and, on 15 April, the Anzac Corps withdrew south to the Thermopylae line, just 150 kilometres north-west of Athens.

Problems in the Middle East dominated the British War Cabinet discussions and diverted attention from Menzies' concern about the Far East. After the successful offensive that had besieged Tobruk, Rommel's forces were on the Egyptian border, while the British forces in Greece were beginning their evacuation. On 28 April, Churchill said that Japan would be unlikely to enter the war unless Germany successfully invaded Britain, and that a major disaster in the Middle East would not tempt Japan. No reinforcements were planned for Malaya. The question of what would happen if Egypt fell was discussed at a War Cabinet meeting on 29 April, attended by both Menzies and Shedden. Menzies noted that the answer was 'a lemon'.[51]

Menzies eventually discussed his concerns about the Far East with the British chiefs on 1 May, but achieved little. He learned that the previous night the British Defence Committee had cabled Washington to concur with American plans to transfer part of their Pacific Fleet to the Atlantic. As Sir Alexander Cadogan described it at the War Cabinet meeting later that day, 'Menzies, quite rightly, made a stink about the telegram.' In response, on the advice of Menzies, Fadden asked Britain to propose that America's Pacific Fleet not be reduced below six capital ships and, as a concession to Australia and New Zealand, America agreed to move fewer ships to the Atlantic than had been planned. Fadden also asked that Britain consider releasing 'adequate British capital units to at once reinforce Singapore'.[52]

Menzies' visit to London, which ended on 3 May when he and his party headed for Canada, marked a turning point in Australian strategic decision-making. Before the visit, Menzies had believed in imperial defence—that there should be integrated armed forces controlled by one directing body. His visit to London did not alter his belief in the value of such a concept, but he found that Churchill's understanding of it was quite different.[53] It was not just that Churchill's strategic view did not reach to the Far East, or that he still thought of the dominions as colonies, but also that he was surrounded in the Cabinet by 'yes men' who were unwilling to oppose him

Some historians, most notably David Day, have argued that Menzies hoped to overthrow Churchill and take over running the imperial war effort. Menzies' biographer Allan Martin has persuasively rejected this radical proposition, pointing out that Hankey and the former British prime minister Lloyd George merely wanted to limit Churchill's power and hoped that Menzies' presence in the War Cabinet might do so.[54] There is no evidence that Menzies actually pursued this ambition, but the fantasy affected his actions and probably contributed to his subsequent downfall. On a more practical level, Menzies and Shedden were brought face to face with the reality of

Churchill's war leadership, and the fact that however cogently they might argue for reinforcements for the Far East, they had no leverage to back their arguments.

Menzies' Last Months

Menzies arrived back in Australia on 24 May to face not only considerable political difficulties, but further decisions about the role of the 2nd AIF in the Middle East, as well as a deteriorating strategic situation in the Pacific. While he had been travelling, on 20 May the Germans had invaded the island of Crete, where an Australian force, cobbled together after their evacuation from Greece, comprised part of the garrison. Under intense air attack, the RN evacuated a good proportion of the British Commonwealth troops, the last leaving on 31 May. The Australians lost 274 killed, 507 wounded and 3102 captured.

Meanwhile, Menzies was considering a British proposal to invade Vichy-controlled Syria, where it was feared the Germans might establish an air base. Advised by Casey in Washington and Bruce in London, on 29 May Menzies urged Churchill to occupy Syria. The British were indeed planning an invasion, and two brigades of the 7th Australian Division were to be involved. Shortly before it began on 7 June, Blamey told Menzies that the invasion was 'largely a gamble'.[55] Although not a great consideration at the time, Australia had been party to an invasion of a territory of Vichy France, an entity not at war with the Commonwealth.

On 10 June, Menzies reported to the War Cabinet on the prime purpose of his overseas visit, namely securing reinforcements for the Far East. The War Cabinet seemed to accept, as Menzies had in London, that little more could be done to persuade Britain of the danger in the Far East. Next day the War Cabinet decided to send a second AIF brigade to Malaya. This was in response to a British request after an Indian brigade was diverted to Iraq, and not specifically as a result of Menzies' report.

With the decision to send the 27th Brigade to Malaya, the

Australian government had used its only uncommitted trained force. Yet the strategic situation in the Middle East was precarious; the only Australian brigades not actually in action were those recovering from their ordeals in Greece and Crete, and even several of their battalions were soon involved in bitter fighting in Syria. As Curtin pointed out in the Advisory War Council on 12 June, 'defeat in the Middle East would be an open invitation to Japan to attack the Netherlands East Indies'. Menzies reorganised his Cabinet and called for 'an unlimited war effort'. Belatedly, the Defence Committee was ordered to prepare joint operational plans to meet attacks on specific areas of Australia.[56]

The situation in the Far East changed completely on 22 June, when Germany attacked Russia. Knowing that Russia would be too preoccupied to attack in Manchuria, which Japan had occupied since 1931, Japan decided to strike south on 2 July. American cryptanalysts had broken the Japanese diplomatic ciphers and this decision was soon known in London, Washington and Canberra.[57] President Roosevelt froze Japanese assets and imposed an oil embargo. It was another example of the way signals intelligence affected strategic decision-making. The Australian government could do little about these developments except prepare home defences.

The ministers believed that, as they had limited capacity to influence events, Australia should be represented in the British War Cabinet, and to Menzies it seemed that the only way Australia could be sure of representation in the British War Cabinet was for him to return to London. However, Menzies came under increasing criticism from senior members of his party and eventually, at a joint meeting of the UAP and Country Party parliamentary members, on 29 August he resigned as prime minister. Fadden was elected as his successor, but all the other ministries remained unchanged, with Menzies continuing as Minister for Defence Coordination.

By this time there had been a change to the government's military advisers. In February 1941 Admiral Colvin had resigned as CNS because of ill health, to be replaced by Vice-Admiral Sir Guy Royle, then British Fifth Sea Lord and Chief of Naval Air Services. Colvin was relieved by his deputy, Commodore John Durnford, RN, until

Royle arrived in Australia in July. Royle had been naval attaché in Japan in the 1920s, so had some appreciation of strategic issues in the Pacific, but as George Hermon Gill, the official naval historian, wrote, when he arrived in Australia he was 'a sick man, temporarily mentally exhausted from a period of considerable strain overseas'.[58]

The Relief of Tobruk

One of the most important issues dealt with by the short-lived Fadden government was the relief of the Australian garrison of Tobruk, which had been besieged by German and Italian troops since April. The matter had been simmering since the failure of General Wavell's 'Battleaxe' offensive in June. On 21 June Menzies had asked Blamey, who in April had been appointed deputy C-in-C Middle East, whether the garrison could hold out, or whether Australia should press for an evacuation. As he explained to Blamey, a 'disaster at Tobruk, coming on top of those in Greece and Crete, might have far-reaching effect on public opinion in Australia'. Blamey replied that he was satisfied Tobruk could be held 'for the present'.[59]

Blamey had established amicable relations with Wavell and he felt sure that Wavell understood his special responsibilities as GOC of the AIF. But when on 5 July General Sir Claude Auchinleck replaced Wavell as C-in-C Middle East, Blamey had to begin the process of education once again. Meanwhile, Blamey had received reports from his chief medical officer and also from Major General Morshead, commander of the Tobruk garrison, that its capacity to resist a sustained assault was diminishing. On 18 July he formally asked Auchinleck to evacuate the 9th Division from Tobruk so that he could bring all the Australian troops together under his command, and he advised Menzies of his action, explaining that the troops now needed 'respite to refresh, restore discipline and re-equip'.[60]

Auchinleck was initially sympathetic, and Menzies then asked Churchill to relieve the 9th Division. Churchill thought that this was a 'needless relief', and after Auchinleck visited London and discussed it with Churchill, Auchinleck was less inclined to order the relief. The

British naval and air commanders in the Middle East were also afraid of losses to their forces if the relief continued. Churchill had still not replied to Menzies' request, and the army minister, Spender, advised Menzies that it seemed Blamey was 'not carrying the weight to which his position entitles him'. Menzies then recommended that Blamey be promoted to the rank of general.[61]

On 7 August, Menzies cabled London again to urge the relief of the 9th Division. Spender described the reply from the dominions secretary, Lord Cranborne, as a 'put off'. Cranborne tried to reassure the Australians that the British government agreed in principle to the concentration of the AIF, but that there might be difficulties with the Tobruk garrison.[62] The British arranged the relief of the 18th Brigade (from the 7th Division) but the 9th Division remained in Tobruk.

By the beginning of September it was clear that Auchinleck no longer intended to relieve the remainder of the Tobruk garrison, and Blamey reported this to Australia, urging the government to insist on the relief: 'Unless you take firmest stand feel convinced that 9 Div will be left in Tobruk indefinitely in spite of my concerns. Position causes me grave concern.' Fadden, who was now prime minister, immediately cabled Churchill to demand the relief, stating that there would be 'grave repercussions' in Australia if there should be any catastrophe caused by the troops not being fit enough to repel an attack. Churchill passed this cable to Auchinleck and left it up to him to decide.[63]

A fierce dispute was now raging between Blamey and Auchinleck. Blamey wrote to Spender that 'once any Australian unit gets into the command of a UK formation, it's like prising open the jaws of an alligator to get them back again'. In a final showdown with Auchinleck, Blamey demanded the relief of the troops 'in the name of my Government'. Auchinleck shrugged and said: 'Well, if that is the way you put it, we have no alternative.'[64]

Churchill tried to remind Fadden that if the troops were relieved he would have deprived 'Australia of the glory of holding Tobruk till victory was won'. Fadden did not fall for this rhetoric and again demanded the relief, giving a point by point rebuttal of Auchinleck's arguments (which he had received from Blamey). Churchill now directed Auchinleck to issue orders for the relief, but when he received this order Auchinleck took it as a personal affront and wanted to resign. As a compromise, the British government's minister in the Middle East, Oliver Lyttelton, suggested that Churchill ask the Australian government to replace Blamey. Churchill demurred, as he thought such a request would 'injure the foundations of the Empire'. Instead, on 24 September the Australian government promoted Blamey to full general. The British air commander in the Middle East later criticised Blamey as 'really a rather unpleasant political soldier'.[65] But in fact the commander of a national force operating as part of an allied force needs to be attuned to the political considerations affecting his force.

A few days later the first brigade of the 9th Division was relieved. By this time Auchinleck had begun planning for the 9th Division's training and employment after it was withdrawn from Tobruk. Blamey was not consulted, and when he heard of these plans he wrote sharply to Auchinleck that it appeared he had 'not been fully informed of the conditions of employment of the Australian Imperial Force, nor of the direction of the Australian Government for its command'. Earlier Auchinleck had said he would have Blamey removed from his command. Blamey told him strongly that it was for the Australian government to 'determine any question of Command of the Australian Imperial Force'.[66]

By 29 September the 24th Brigade had been relieved, but two brigades remained, and Churchill again asked the Australian government to reconsider its decision. Fadden reaffirmed the original decision, but within days, Fadden's government was defeated in the House of Representatives. Churchill thought the change of government might offer one last hope and on 13 October he asked John Curtin, the new Australian prime minister, to reconsider the previous government's decision. Curtin replied that the War Cabinet would not vary the decision. Churchill immediately informed Auchinleck that the Australians had 'sent an obdurate reply' and the relief had to proceed. By the end of October only one Australian battalion remained in Tobruk. Between 1 March and 15 December 1941 the

9th Division lost 832 killed, 2177 wounded and 941 prisoners, which was more killed and wounded than suffered by the other Australian divisions in either Libya in early 1941, Greece, Crete or Syria.[67]

Change of Government

Another matter dealt with by the Fadden government was securing Australian representation in the British War Cabinet. Churchill was against this idea, but as he told Lord Cranborne on 6 September: 'We have got to treat these people, who are politically embarrassed but are sending a splendid army into the field, with the utmost consideration.'[68] On 14 September the British government invited the dominions to send a cabinet minister to Britain for discussions and soon afterwards Fadden selected Sir Earle Page, a former prime minister, to represent Australia. Page was instructed to seek the reinforcement of Singapore, but there was no guarantee that he would be able to achieve any significant influence.

This was the last major decision by Fadden's government. On 3 October two independent members of parliament, who held the balance of power, voted against the government. Fadden resigned and the Labor Party formed a new government with John Curtin as prime minister. The government had just two months to get organised before the outbreak of the Pacific War.

The Australian government had made only a few independent decisions about the defence of Australia during 1941: in March to send troops to Ambon and Dutch Timor in the event of war with Japan; in June to send an additional brigade to Malaya; and just before the outbreak of war to send forces to Portuguese Timor. Australian representatives also took part in the Singapore conference with the aim of increasing cooperation and coordination in the Far East. Australian decision-makers, however, had little room for manoeuvre, for they found themselves locked into a strategic policy that had been decided the previous year. Once troops had been committed to the Middle East it was not politically acceptable to recall them to Australia. Perhaps the only option would have been to renegotiate the Empire

Air Training Scheme to ensure greater autonomy for RAAF units in Britain and therefore make it easier for Australia to have a say in their deployment, but this was unlikely to be suggested by the CAS, Sir Charles Burnett, who was an RAF officer and a fierce proponent of imperial defence.

In terms of organising the country for war, the achievement of the Menzies government was significant. Most of the government departments and many of the directors-general—departmental heads with exceptional powers of direction, control and expenditure—remained unchanged during the Curtin government. Nonetheless, the organisation of the Home Army showed the danger of trying to maintain forces beyond the capability of the country. The militia was seriously depleted in men and equipment in order to maintain the AIF. Clearly, the military chiefs did not envisage the rapid successes achieved by the Japanese between December 1941 and February 1942, and they assumed that when Japan decided to strike there would be many months for the militia to mobilise.

Australia's efforts to influence Allied strategy were singularly unsuccessful. Menzies did not persuade Churchill or his chiefs of staff to increase the defence of Malaya, nor even to promise to defend the Netherlands East Indies. Fadden later claimed that his and New Zealand's representations ensured that fewer American capital ships were transferred from the Pacific to the Atlantic than had been planned, but some American senior officers held similar views and may have had greater influence in this issue. There is no evidence that Page's overseas mission influenced Churchill's decision in November to send the battleship *Prince of Wales* and the battle cruiser *Repulse* to Singapore. Perhaps the constant pressure from Australia made Churchill aware of the need to send ships, but probably the Americans influenced him just as much.

In his unpublished history of Australian defence policy, Shedden observed that some politicians claimed that the main cause of Menzies' resignation had been his government's lack of vigour in prosecuting the war, and that this had also led to Fadden's downfall. Shedden thought, however, that 'to any fair-minded person nothing could be wider of the mark'. He thought it was 'to the redounding credit of the Menzies Government that Australia had played a significant part in Empire defence and in producing a notable war effort, which could readily be adapted to regional defence of Australia, and as such, was passed on to the Curtin Government for use by it when Japan came into the war'.[69] Shedden had played a key role in driving this war effort, so it is not surprising that he was full of praise for it. Nonetheless, there is much truth in his claim, and many of the Menzies government's shortcomings could be attributed to political problems. Ultimately, a war leader in a democracy must be master of the political side, and in this respect Menzies failed.

6

'This is a new war'

Curtin, Second World War, 1941–42

The outbreak of the Pacific War tested and tormented the prime minister, John Curtin, and his War Cabinet, as for the first time since white settlement Australia trembled under the threat of foreign invasion. The Labor government that had come to power on 7 October 1941 was poorly prepared for the ordeal. Only two members of the War Cabinet had previous ministerial experience: Frank Forde, deputy prime minister and Minister for the Army, had been an assistant minister in the Scullin government a decade earlier; and J.B. (Ben) Chifley, the treasurer, had briefly been Minister for Defence. The others—Curtin, who was also Minister for Defence Coordination; H.V. (Bert) Evatt, attorney-general and Minister for External Affairs; Jack Beasley, Minister for Supply and Development; Norman Makin, Minister for the Navy and Minister for Munitions; and Arthur Drakeford, Minister for Air and Civil Aviation—had no ministerial or military experience.

Curtin had resisted pressure to force the previous government out of power and had seemed reluctant to take on the responsibility of prime minister. He was respected by members of both sides of politics. Fadden, from whom he had taken over as prime minister, thought that 'there was no greater figure in Australian public life in my lifetime . . . clear in mind and expression, firm in principle . . . he was a man of unusual political courage'. Sir Percy Spender believed that Curtin 'stood above' all of his ministers: 'a kindly, warm-hearted man, despite a rather prim and somewhat cold appearance; he was an outstanding wartime leader'. Menzies wrote that 'confronted by a practical and difficult world, [Curtin] grafted a pragmatic approach on to the historic dogmas of his party, and so made a fine place in Australian history'.[1] Yet Curtin had some unattractive features: shy, tense, unforgiving of criticism; one of his ministers, Arthur Calwell, observed that one of Curtin's 'weaknesses was his habit of spurning his colleagues'. Some members of his Cabinet remained implacable enemies.

Soon after the outbreak of war with Japan, John Dedman, Minister for War Organisation of Industry, joined the War Cabinet. Of the eight War Cabinet members, five had been members of the Advisory War Council, and, significantly, Curtin decided to retain the council, whose membership remained little changed from that under the previous government. The government members were now Curtin, Forde, Beasley, Makin and Evatt, while the non-government members were Fadden, leader of the Opposition; Hughes, who had taken over from Menzies as leader of the UAP; Menzies; Spender; and McEwen. The War Council experience had been invaluable in helping to prepare Curtin and his senior ministers for government. Nonetheless, like them, Curtin lacked expertise in defence policy matters. He would depend on the counsel of his professional advisers, particularly Shedden, who quickly established himself as Curtin's main consultant on strategy and defence.

Outbreak of the Pacific War

As the likelihood of war with Japan had grown, in the first week of December the War Cabinet had met frequently, with the last on Friday 5 December. Curtin remained in Melbourne over the weekend while incoming cables warned of war. Then, soon after 5.45 a.m. on Monday 8 December, Curtin was awoken at his hotel with the news that Japanese aircraft had attacked the US naval base at Pearl Harbor in Hawaii and a US air base near Manila in the Philippines. Within the hour, the Navy Office advised Shedden that the British Admiralty had ordered: 'Commence hostilities against Japan at once.'[2]

A War Cabinet meeting was called for that morning with the acting CNS, Commodore John Durnford, the CGS, Lieutenant General Sturdee, and the CAS, Air Chief Marshal Burnett, also present. Durnford was acting for Admiral Royle, who was in Singapore for a conference on naval cooperation. After summarising what they knew about the Japanese attacks, the chiefs then outlined the emergency measures being taken, including the despatch of troops to Koepang in western Timor. Shedden, who thought the chiefs' efforts were disappointing, advised Curtin that 'The information they had to present as to preparedness for this emergency was, I thought, scrappy and meagre, and I almost gathered the impression that this new and nearby threat to Australia was merely another incident in the present war.' The government needed to 'press it right home that this is a new war'. He suggested that the chiefs produce a new appreciation covering the defence of Australia, while a broad review was sought from the British chiefs of staff. Curtin agreed and the chiefs were so ordered.[3]

That evening, in a broadcast to the nation, Curtin stated that Australia was 'at war with Japan', and would soon be fighting for its life in the 'gravest hour in our history'. He spoke of 'a complete revision of the whole economic, domestic and industrial life' of the country.[4] Over the following months, his government would introduce a large range of measures, but in examining Australian war leadership this chapter will focus on military and strategic issues.

After a meeting on 9 December, which decided not to recall two RAAF squadrons from Britain, the War Cabinet reassembled on 11 December with the devastating news that the British battleship HMS *Prince of Wales* and the battle cruiser HMS *Repulse* had been sunk by Japanese aircraft off the Malayan coast. Faced with mounting reports requiring decisions, Curtin sought to streamline procedures. Since the War Cabinet and the Advisory War Council dealt with similar issues, he proposed that, as the council included five of the eight War Cabinet ministers, if they agreed to a proposal at the council it could be accepted automatically as a War Cabinet decision. This would give the council a key role in managing the war during the next twelve months.[5]

These changes were agreed, and the ministers were then joined by the chiefs, who presented their appreciation. Shedden was now pleased with the chiefs, whom he said later 'showed extremely sound judgment in anticipating that the Japanese would first attack the vital links in the South and Southwest Pacific Area, of the island line of communications from the United States to Australia'. The chiefs assessed that the attack on Malaya 'might well be a first step in the Japanese plan for a major attack on Australia', and 'the possibility of a direct move on Australia via the islands to the north and north east must now be considered'. The Japanese might attempt to occupy Rabaul, Port Moresby and New Caledonia, from which they could launch an attack on Australia. The chiefs recommended stationing brigade groups with anti-aircraft and coastal defences in all three localities, as well as on Timor. If the Japanese occupied Singapore, the Netherlands East Indies and the bases in the north, then they would be able to invade Australia. All these situations were possible and the chiefs advised that it was 'necessary to establish and train now the forces that would be required to prevent and to meet an invasion'.[6] One would have thought that this would have been an admirable aim a year earlier. With these considerations in mind, the War Cabinet approved the calling up of an additional 114,000 army personnel, on top of the 132,000 already on full-time duty.

On 15 December, in a further appreciation, the chiefs recommended that Darwin be retained as a fleet operational base, that the Port Moresby garrison be increased to one brigade group, that Rabaul be left with its existing garrison of one battalion group, and that an independent company be sent to New Caledonia 'to enhance the morale of the [French] . . . and for demolition purposes'. Although the Rabaul garrison was too small to resist an invasion successfully, 'it was essential to maintain a forward observation line as long as possible and to make the enemy fight for this line rather than abandon it at the first threat'.[7] In view of the almost non-existent navy and air force available in Australia, and the untrained and ill-equipped militia, which was the only available military force, the decision not to reinforce the north-eastern approaches seems unchallengeable.

Over the following year, Curtin, his ministers and their advisers would seek to bring the nation to a total war footing, deal with the Japanese threat, determine what forces should be raised and how they were to be employed, and attempt to influence Allied strategy to give the defence of Australia higher priority. Rather than trying to cover all these issues, this chapter will examine six key aspects that give an insight into the performance of Australia's war leaders. The first of these was their reaction to the Japanese attack in Malaya.

Reacting to the Japanese Thrust

The events in Malaya focused the early attention of the government and its advisers. There, the Japanese were already advancing down the peninsula towards Singapore, the naval base on which Australian defence policy had been centred for the previous twenty years. It was not long before Curtin was cabling London, reminding the British government that they had promised to reinforce Singapore and Malaya. Meanwhile, Major General Henry Gordon Bennett, commander of the 8th Australian Division, whose two brigades had not yet been in action in Malaya, was requesting reinforcements.[8] The government decided to despatch to Malaya a machine-gun battalion, the last of the trained AIF battalions in Australia, plus almost 2000 largely untrained troops. This was an unwise decision, as these latter, unprepared troops would become a burden on Bennett's command.

By this stage the locus of Allied decision-making had moved to Washington, where Churchill had arrived with his military advisers for talks with President Roosevelt and his advisers. Richard Casey in Washington tried to keep his government in Canberra informed of the discussions. Meeting on 23 December, the Advisory War Council agreed that Australia's future was bound up with the conversations in Washington, and that day Curtin cabled Roosevelt and Churchill appealing for reinforcements for Singapore. At the same time, Curtin told Roosevelt that if the US government wished, Australia would gladly accept an American commander in the Pacific area.[9]

On 24 December, the Minister for External Affairs, Bert Evatt, received a cable from Australia's trade commissioner at Singapore, Vivian Bowden, stating that the deteriorating situation in Malaya was 'assuming landslide proportions'.[10] Bowden had been appointed Australia's representative on the newly formed War Council in Singapore. Evatt immediately forwarded the cable to Casey in Washington. Next day, Churchill replied to the Australian requests for reinforcements, advising that some were on the way to the Far East.[11]

Despite this news, by now the Australian government was becoming intensely frustrated by the apparent lack of a sympathetic response from Churchill. This frustration was given vent in Curtin's article in the Melbourne *Herald* of 27 December, in which he stated that Australia looked to America 'free of any pangs' of kinship with the United Kingdom. Churchill responded with a bitter cable in which he spoke of Australia's 'mood of panic', and offered to broadcast to the Australian people.[12]

Earlier, on 23 December, the British chiefs of staff had sent Australia an appreciation in which they stated that the position in Malaya was 'very serious', and neither the United States nor Britain would be able to send a fleet. Admiral Royle, who barely six months earlier had been the British Fifth Sea Lord, had no hesitation in vigorously attacking this appreciation. On 29 December the Australian chiefs commented that the situation disclosed was 'most unsatisfactory . . . In other words, the United States Pacific Fleet on which we had based great hopes is unable or unwilling to assist.'[13]

The Australian troops first went into action on 14 January with a successful ambush in the southern Malay state of Johore, but on 20 January, Bennett told Sturdee that two of his battalions had been cut off. Next day, Curtin cabled Churchill: 'Just as you foresaw in Europe so we feel that we saw the trend in the Pacific situation more clearly than was realised in London. Events have unfortunately justified our views regarding Malaya.' On 23 January Bowden reported that the position was 'desperate and possibly irretrievable'.[14]

Remarkably, in the midst of these reports, in the evening of 21 January, Curtin boarded a train in Melbourne, beginning a slow three-day journey to Perth. Tense and exhausted after dealing with the constantly changing military situation, Curtin was bowing to demands from his doctor to take a rest.[15] Curtin hoped to keep in touch with his deputy, Forde, and Shedden by telephone and telegrams, but this would be difficult, and much would happen in those three days. Meanwhile, two Australian battalions were trapped, fighting desperately at Muar in Malaya, and the Japanese had started to bomb Rabaul in New Britain. Curtin would not arrive back in Melbourne until the evening of 1 February.

In Melbourne on 23 January, Forde presided over a meeting of the War Cabinet, with the chiefs present. The ministers decided to make a strong representation to Churchill about the lack of support for the AIF in Malaya. The meeting also learned that the Japanese had landed at Rabaul that morning, although it was not yet certain that the town had been captured—Australian territory had now been invaded.[16]

Before the cable could be sent, a telegram arrived from Earle Page, the Australian representative in the London-based Pacific War Council, advising that Churchill and his Cabinet were considering the evacuation of Singapore. The Pacific War Council had been set up to give countries such as Australia a voice in strategic policymaking, but it was to prove ineffective. Page said this evacuation would cause 'irreparable loss of prestige and I think irreparable damage to the allied cause'. He told the Australian government that the British had decided to wait for a couple of days to see if the Australian and Indian soldiers could fight their way back to the main army. In Curtin's absence, Evatt now amended the cable to Churchill to say that 'After all the assurances we have been given, the evacuation of Singapore would be regarded here as an inexcusable betrayal.'[17]

Churchill took immediate exception to the cable and informed Curtin that the 18th British Division and some Hurricane fighter aircraft, then on ships crossing the Indian Ocean, were on the way to Singapore. He continued: 'In such circumstances I really cannot pass without comment such language to me as "inexcusable betrayal". I make all allowances for your anxiety and will not allow such discourtesy to cloud my judgment or lessen my efforts on your behalf.' Subsequently, Churchill wrote that the 'inexcusable betrayal' message did not decide the issue of sending the 18th Division to Singapore. He realised the effect that a British 'scuttle' would have had on American opinion; nonetheless, he acknowledged that there was 'no doubt what a purely military decision should have been'. In retrospect, the CIGS, General Sir Alan Brooke, thought they were wrong to send the 18th Division to Singapore.[18] On the fall of Singapore the division went into captivity.

Whatever the views about the wisdom of the decision, Churchill felt that the Australians could not escape some responsibility for it, and he emphasised this to Curtin a month later when Singapore had been lost and he (Churchill) was trying to persuade Curtin to allow the 7th Australian Division to reinforce Burma. Churchill wrote in his memoirs that 'it was not for Mr Curtin, after taking a strong part in the discussions, to feel that he had no more share in it'.[19] Churchill was aware of the paradox that in January 1942 Australia had urged the reinforcement of a threatened area without considering whether it could achieve anything, while a month later, when the reinforcements consisted of an Australian corps, every consideration was given as to whether their arrival could be justified.

There is much strength in Churchill's arguments. The Australian chiefs did not seem to take into account that if Singapore became a beleaguered fortress, Britain would not have the ships or planes to relieve it, and thus Japan would not be prevented from operating elsewhere at will. Certainly, Britain had deceived Australia over the security of Singapore, and there was justification in calling it an 'inexcusable betrayal'; but this was a time for clearly considered decisions, not for scoring points off the British government. The episode highlights the role of Dr Evatt, whom Menzies described as 'a seething mass of frustrated ambitions'.[20] Curtin's biographer John Edwards concluded:

> It was an inglorious episode. Curtin was in the wrong place, Evatt was foolish, and the Australian chiefs and Shedden should certainly have informed a sensible discussion of evacuation options. In London, Page should not have rejected Churchill's view without consultation and reflection . . . No participant came out of the episode well, except perhaps Churchill, who had the force of mind to suggest withdrawal.[21]

On 29 January the chiefs argued that it could no longer be assumed that Malaya and the Netherlands East Indies would hold, nor that the American Pacific Fleet would achieve supremacy in the Pacific, and they advised that Australia should plan on trying to counter the maximum scale of attack. In fact, in the next three weeks the Japanese were to attack Ambon (30 January), capture Singapore (15 February), attack Darwin (19 February) and land on Timor (19–20 February). During this time the government was to have its most notable disagreement with the direction of Allied strategy.

Return of the 1st Australian Corps

The decision of the Australian government in February 1942 to defy a request from Churchill and Roosevelt that the troops of the 1st Australian Corps be diverted to Burma, and to demand that they return to Australia, was one of the most important made by Curtin and his War Cabinet. Contrary to some popular accounts, the initiative for redeploying Australian troops from the Middle East to the Far East was not opposed by Churchill. Rather, when in mid-December 1941 he suggested that one of the Australian divisions in the Middle East be despatched to India or even to Singapore, initially the Australian government was loath to allow this transfer. It was not until 5 January that the War Cabinet approved the despatch of the 1st Australian Corps, comprising mainly the 6th and 7th Australian Divisions, from the Middle East to the Netherlands East Indies.[22]

By early February the convoys carrying the Australian Corps were heading towards the Far East, but the strategic situation had deteriorated rapidly. The Commonwealth forces, including Australia's 8th Division, had been driven out of the Malay Peninsula and were preparing to face a final Japanese attack on Singapore Island. General Sir Archibald Wavell had been appointed supreme commander of ABDA (American, British, Dutch, Australian) Command, which was responsible for the Burma–Malaya–Philippines–Netherlands East Indies Area. He had his headquarters on Java in the Netherlands East Indies, where he had been joined by Lieutenant General Sir John Lavarack, GOC of the 1st Australian Corps. An attack on the Netherlands East Indies was expected any day.

On 6 February Lavarack wrote to Sturdee to warn him that the defences of the Netherlands East Indies were not adequate and that the decision to land the Australian Corps might need to be reviewed. Before Sturdee received this warning, on the night of 8 February the Japanese landed on Singapore Island, and by 12 February they were closing in on the city. Meanwhile, as a fast personnel-carrying ship, the *Orcades*, with 3400 Australian troops, had gone ahead of the main convoy and was approaching Java, Lavarack prepared an appreciation recommending that the AIF not be landed in the Netherlands East Indies.[23]

It was now obvious that Singapore was about to fall, and in Australia senior officials were making their own assessments. Relying mainly on Lavarack's letter and cabled appreciation, on Sunday 15 February Sturdee prepared his own appreciation. In it, Sturdee pointed out that the troops in Java would probably be lost, and even if they were not lost, Java did not provide a suitable base for a counter-offensive. Meanwhile, late in the afternoon of 15 February a cable arrived from Wavell, stating that the odds against a successful defence of the Netherlands East Indies were mounting: 'From [a] purely strategical aspect there are advantages in diverting one or both divisions to Burma or Australia.'[24]

Next day, with news that Singapore had surrendered the previous day, the chiefs reviewed Wavell's appreciation and Sturdee's paper. The burden was squarely on Sturdee, for the other two chiefs, Burnett and Royle, were British officers. They felt that any advice they might offer could be biased, and they told Sturdee that they would unreservedly support him. Sturdee's deputy, Major General Sydney Rowell, considered that this was 'the most fateful recommendation [Sturdee] had to make in his service'. The chiefs recommended that, if possible, all the Australian forces 'under orders to transfer from the Middle East to the Far East should be diverted to Australia'.[25]

That night Curtin agonised over the decision. As he told reporter E. Harold Cox: 'Before tomorrow morning I must take the biggest and most important decision I have had to make since Japan entered the war.' Next morning, the cable went off to Churchill, requesting that urgent arrangements be made for the diversion of the AIF to Australia. The cable also went to Wavell, the prime minister of New Zealand and Page, who was expected to press the Australian government's view.[26]

On 17 February Curtin, senior government ministers, and Opposition leaders travelled to Sydney, where Curtin opened the £35,000,000 Liberty War Loan at a rally in Martin Place. According to one newspaper report, before the rally Curtin 'was in acute agony, but insisted on fulfilling his engagement'. He was suffering from 'gastritis resulting from prolonged nervous strain', and within three-quarters of an hour of finishing his speech he was taken to St Vincent's Hospital.[27]

The following day Forde chaired a meeting of the War Cabinet to consider the future employment of the AIF. According to one account, Sturdee informed the ministers that he would tender his resignation if the AIF was not returned to Australia. Dedman, who was present, wrote that Curtin's cable was approved, 'but only after discussion had made clear the gravity of the situation we were facing'. At the Advisory War Council that afternoon, Sturdee explained that 'for all practical purposes' the 8th Division had been lost. Evatt then said that 18,000 men of the AIF were due to arrive in Batavia (Java) in seven or eight days. The choice was whether they should go to Burma or to Australia. The meeting agreed to wait on the answer from Wavell about the troops that had already arrived in Java, and to consider whether they should go to Burma the next morning.[28]

That evening two cables arrived from Page, reporting that the Pacific War Council in London had recommended that the 7th Australian Division go to Burma. Page had misread Curtin's cable of 17 February and had supported sending the division to Burma. Curtin immediately cabled Page that it was unlikely that the government would change its mind and that the convoy should not be committed to Burma.[29]

At the War Council in Sydney on 19 February, the non-government members, Spender, Hughes, Fadden, Menzies and McEwen, immediately seized on Page's recommendation that the Australian troops go to Burma. Beasley and Spender became involved in a bitter argument. Earlier that morning, Japanese planes had bombed Darwin, but the council did not know it at the time. According to Spender, Beasley left the room briefly. 'Suddenly he returned, bursting into the room in a very agitated state. Loudly he proclaimed, as I recall his words: "The Japs have bombed Darwin! That settles it!" It was an odd performance.'[30]

The War Cabinet, which met later that day, agreed that there should be no change in the government's position. With Curtin in hospital, it was left to Evatt to draft the answering cables to Page, emphasising that the decision was unchanged. After a secret session of parliament on 20 February, Curtin again confirmed the decision.[31]

Before receiving Curtin's final confirmation, Churchill had seemed willing to accept the Australian decision, but perhaps encouraged by Page, at 9 p.m. on 20 February he ordered the Admiralty to tell the convoy to steam northwards, and ten minutes later he cabled an appeal to Curtin. He did not mention that the convoy was heading towards Burma, but emphasised that the Australian force was the only one which could reach Rangoon in time to prevent its loss. At the same time, Churchill urged Roosevelt to appeal to Australia, which he did in cables directly to Curtin, and through Churchill and Casey to Curtin.[32]

These latest cables were considered by a special meeting of the War Cabinet in Canberra, with Curtin back in the chair, on the morning of 21 February. Curtin said that if they went against their better judgement and approved the diversion of the troops they would be exposing Australia to greater danger. In the early hours of 22 February, Curtin despatched his reply: 'our wishes in regard to the disposition of the AIF in the Pacific theatre have long been known to you'. The decision remained.[33]

Meanwhile, the British high commissioner to Australia, Sir Ronald Cross, had reported to London that the Opposition was 'hotly in support of the United Kingdom government request and some leading government supporters are said to be wavering'. He suggested that Churchill try again to persuade Curtin, and Churchill replied to Curtin: 'We could not contemplate that you would refuse our request, and that of the President.' He continued that the convoy was already proceeding to Burma, and was now too far north to proceed to Australia without refuelling. The Australian government therefore had a few days to review the position.[34]

According to Evatt, Curtin was 'greatly shocked' by Churchill's action. Curtin went for a long walk around the lower slopes of Mount Majura in Canberra, returning to his office in East Block in time to despatch his cable to Churchill. This reply was to the point: 'We feel a primary obligation to save Australia not only for itself but to preserve it as a base for the development of the war against Japan . . . it is quite impossible to reverse a decision which we made in the utmost care and which we have affirmed and re-affirmed.'[35]

Churchill, of course, had no option but to comply. Australia made good use of the Australian Corps when it returned. Troops of the 7th Division fought in Papua in August 1942 and the first troops of the 6th Division, which spent some months in Ceylon (Sri Lanka), were in action in Papua by October 1942. Undoubtedly the 7th Division would have been lost if it had landed at Rangoon. Wavell's biographer thought that it was 'a hard but surely a just decision'.[36]

A further matter needed to be resolved, namely the fate of the men from the *Orcades*, then arriving on Java. On the order of the British government, the *Orcades* troops remained on Java, and were eventually captured by the Japanese, who landed on 28 February.[37] By leaving the matter in Wavell's hands, the War Cabinet had missed the opportunity to demand their recall to Australia, but the incident demonstrated the difficulty faced by the War Cabinet in dealing with operational issues in the midst of a fast-moving Allied campaign.

During the battle for Java, the light cruiser HMAS *Perth* was sunk in Sunda Strait, and as part of this battle, on 3 March Japanese aircraft raided Broome in Western Australia. Five days later Japanese forces landed at Lae and Salamaua in New Guinea. On 15 March, Japanese Imperial GHQ debated whether to attack Australia and decided instead to capture Port Moresby and the southern Solomon Islands, and then 'to isolate Australia' by seizing Fiji, Samoa and New Caledonia.[38] The Japanese high command never really agreed to invade Australia, but this was not known in Australia; the government and the public were therefore fully justified in planning to repel an invasion. Towards the end of March, however, several events caused a revival in confidence. The first of these was the return to Australia of the 7th Division and one brigade of the 6th Division. The second was the arrival of General Douglas MacArthur.

MacArthur Takes Charge

When MacArthur arrived in Darwin from the Philippines on 17 March, he was aged 62 and had had a long and distinguished military career. At the end of the First World War he had been a divisional commander on the Western Front, and by 1930 he was chief of staff of the US Army. Later he became military adviser to the Philippines government and then commander of the US Army there, until his force was overpowered by the Japanese invasion. Roosevelt ordered MacArthur to depart the Philippines and take up a command in Australia, even though there were only about 25,000 US troops in Australia. American troops had started to arrive in Australia in December 1941, on the way to reinforcing the Philippines, but as the Philippines became isolated the troops had remained in Australia and additional forces had arrived as the Americans built up a base for a later offensive. Aloof, highly intelligent, widely hated and also loved throughout the American Army,

MacArthur believed that it was his destiny to lead an Allied force to victory in the Pacific.

For all his faults, MacArthur gained the confidence of Australia and of the government. On 18 March it was announced that he would probably take over a command to be known as the Southwest Pacific Area (SWPA), which would include all the Australian and American forces in and around Australia. From the first day of his arrival in Melbourne on 21 March, MacArthur had a major impact on the government. For example, the deputy prime minister, Forde, who met MacArthur at the railway station in Melbourne, was tremendously impressed. He recalled that faced by 'the greatest catastrophe that could have happened, the country looked to America . . . MacArthur was the man who would influence his government along the right lines.'[39]

MacArthur's arrival heralded a complete change to the Allied military command structure and its relationship to the Australian government. There would also be changes in the Australian Army: General Blamey had been recalled from the Middle East to become commander-in-chief of the Australian Military Forces, the Military Board would be abolished, and its former members would become senior staff officers working under Blamey's command.

By the time Blamey arrived in Melbourne on 26 March, MacArthur had already departed to attend a meeting of the Advisory War Council in Canberra later that day. There MacArthur explained that many in Britain and the United States believed that the European theatre was the predominant one; but others, including himself, thought that the Allies had to concentrate sufficient forces in the Pacific to strike a decisive blow. He urged Australia to 'stand firmly by its view that the Pacific is the predominant theatre'. The first step would be to make Australia secure as the base from which a counter-offensive could be mounted towards the Philippines, but that would depend on the speed with which men and equipment could be moved to Australia. He doubted whether the Japanese would undertake an invasion of Australia, but they could conduct raids and attempt to secure air bases in Australia. This was the first time that MacArthur had met Curtin, and despite their different backgrounds and experience, they established a warm relationship. 'Mr Prime Minister,' said MacArthur, putting his hand on Curtin's shoulder, 'we two, you and I, will see this thing through together . . . You take care of the rear and I will handle the front.'[40]

MacArthur started to organise his command, and changed his title to Commander-in-Chief SWPA. His headquarters was located in Melbourne, and despite the fact that it was supposed to be an Allied headquarters, it was staffed almost completely by American officers. MacArthur's Allied Naval and Air Forces were commanded by US officers, but since Australia provided most of the land forces, command of the Allied Land Forces went to Blamey. In mid-1942 the Australian Army consisted of ten infantry divisions, two motor divisions and one armoured division. The 9th Division was still in the Middle East and part of the 6th was in Ceylon (Sri Lanka), but the remainder were in Australia with some units in New Guinea. Admittedly some divisions were poorly trained, as the eight divisions of the militia had only recently been called up for full-time service, but the 6th and 7th Divisions had fought in the Middle East. By contrast there were only two under-trained US divisions in Australia. There were 38,000 Americans in Australia, while the AIF troops under MacArthur's command totalled 104,000 and the militia 265,000.

While these command arrangements were being initiated, Curtin, advised by Shedden, produced a plan for the higher direction of the war.[41] The Department of Defence Coordination would revert to its earlier title of Department of Defence; it would deal with defence policy, joint-service matters and provide the secretariats for the War Cabinet, the Advisory War Council and various senior defence committees. Curtin would become the link between the government and MacArthur, who would have operational control of the Australian forces. There would be no link between the government and the commanders of the Allied naval, land and air forces, as this would be in MacArthur's hands, but Blamey would have contact with Curtin through his position as commander-in-chief of the Australian Military Forces.

The senior strategic decision-making body would be the Prime Minister's War Conference, which would consist of MacArthur, Curtin and any ministers or officers who might be summoned by the prime minister. In practice, Shedden would also be present at all meetings—not as secretary, as he was for the War Cabinet and the Advisory War Council, but as full participant. Thus Shedden gained increased influence, for Blamey had been excluded, and MacArthur became Curtin's chief adviser on military matters. Furthermore, as Curtin wrote to MacArthur on 10 April, 'if I should not be readily available, Mr Shedden has my full confidence in regard to all questions of War Policy'.[42]

Thus the whole structure of strategic decision-making was revised. Whereas previously the chiefs of staff had been the government's principal advisers on strategy, they were now replaced by a foreign general who was responsible for operations in the defence of Australia. Curtin could still receive advice from the Australian chiefs, particularly Blamey, but supported by Shedden, Curtin looked to MacArthur as the main source of advice.

MacArthur and the Defence of Australia

When MacArthur arrived from the Philippines, he brought with him his army radio intercept unit, and it soon joined with newly formed Australian Army and RAAF signals intelligence units to form an Allied unit known as the Central Bureau. At the same time, the US Navy signals intelligence unit from the Philippines also moved to Australia, where it became the US Navy's Fleet Radio Unit Melbourne (FRUMEL). These units became part of a worldwide Allied signals intelligence network. Signals intelligence (known later as Ultra) was not a perfect source, as enemy enciphered cables and radio messages could not always be broken, but when they were they provided priceless information. The intelligence gained by breaking Japanese diplomatic communications was known as Magic.[43]

Signals intelligence was closely protected, because if the enemy became aware that their communications were being intercepted and deciphered they would have changed their codes, thus cutting off this valuable source. Only top-level commanders were given access to this information, and it is not certain that even Curtin (let alone members of the War Cabinet) was given full access. Nonetheless, information was provided to him in the Combined Operational Intelligence Centre summaries, even though the source was disguised.

In deploying his forces, MacArthur was able to draw on the valuable intelligence provided by FRUMEL, which was beginning to reveal that the Japanese would soon attempt an invasion of Port Moresby. On 24 April, MacArthur issued a warning that a Japanese force of three aircraft carriers and five cruisers might strike the north-east coast of Australia between 28 April and 3 May.[44]

In view of these warnings, the Allied high command in Australia believed that the Japanese thrust towards Port Moresby posed a definite threat to the Australian mainland. Some historians have suggested that decrypted Japanese radio intercepts should have revealed that Australia was not under threat of invasion, and that the government was not justified in raising that possibility. However, since the Japanese did not decide to invade Australia until mid-March, the charge that the government manufactured an invasion threat in February and March is false. It did not, however, take long for Japanese intentions to be detected. As early as 11 April, Allied intelligence concluded that it was not practical for Japan to launch a major offensive against Australia at that time. Furthermore, on 18 April the Magic intelligence summaries reported that discussions between the Japanese foreign minister and the German ambassador to Tokyo revealed that there was no plan to invade Australia. The same day, the US Pacific Fleet intelligence staff concluded that there was no evidence Japan intended to invade Australia. On 23 April MacArthur told the Prime Minister's War Conference that 'a large-scale attack on Australia was possible but not probable. There might be predatory raids but he did not think a major attack was likely.' Nonetheless, on 29 April Curtin stated in parliament that a Japanese attack was 'a constant and undiminished danger. As part of this purpose . . . the Japanese may seek to isolate Australia by cutting the sea routes whereby essential supplies reach this country.'[45] This last sentence was, in fact, a clear statement of what the Japanese were actually trying to do.

At the next meeting of the War Conference, held at Victoria Barracks, Melbourne, on 20 April, and attended by Shedden, Blamey and MacArthur's chief of staff, Major General Richard Sutherland, MacArthur began with a review of the military position, before the meeting turned to its task of hammering out 'the fundamental basis of the strategical appreciation', which they hoped would be approved by the authorities in Washington and London. In Curtin's view this would be 'the essential starting point from which to build up the flow of reinforcements and equipment'.[46] The conference decided that MacArthur and the Australian chiefs would work out the requirements, and that these would be sent simultaneously by the prime minister through Evatt (who was travelling overseas) to the Pacific War Council in Washington, and by MacArthur to the chief of staff of the US Army, General George C. Marshall.

By the beginning of May the Japanese had already begun a major offensive in which they landed in the southern Solomons Islands, while a convoy set out from Rabaul to seize Port Moresby. An Allied naval force countered the Japanese force, and on 8 May, in the Battle of the Coral Sea, aircraft from American and Japanese aircraft carriers attacked each other's fleets. Both sides lost an aircraft carrier and had another damaged, but the invasion convoy was forced to return to Rabaul.

The full details of this battle were not available when MacArthur and Sutherland met Curtin and Shedden for another meeting of the War Conference on 11 May. However, MacArthur reported that the Japanese had 'suffered a repulse and [had] probably abandoned for the time being any attempt to occupy Port Moresby, or getting a footing on the mainland of Australia'. The next day the Advisory War Council expressed disappointment that heavy losses were not inflicted on the enemy during the Coral Sea battle. It was felt that not enough land-based aircraft had been concentrated in the north-east. When he heard of this criticism, MacArthur told Curtin that he felt 'a sense of disappointment' with the council. He thought that the battle had been 'a very brilliant effort . . . which undoubtedly saved Australia from a definite and immediate threat'.[47]

The next meeting of the War Conference was in Melbourne on 1 June. Again Shedden and Sutherland were present. The previous night Japanese midget submarines had entered Sydney Harbour and had sunk an Australian depot ship. MacArthur advised the release of a communiqué. Discussion then turned to cables from overseas that indicated that Britain and the United States were only able to provide Australia with limited support. MacArthur therefore urged Curtin to seek the return of the 9th Division from the Middle East and the allocation of aircraft carriers to the SWPA.[48]

Historian Peter Edwards has argued that perhaps the most important part of MacArthur's statement was his comment that 'Australia was part of the British Empire and it was related to Britain and the other dominions by ties of blood, sentiment and allegiance to the Crown.' By contrast, the United States 'had no sovereign interest in the integrity of Australia. Its interest in Australia was from the strategical aspect of the utility of Australia as a base from which to attack and defeat the Japanese.' MacArthur added that 'though the American people were animated by a warm friendship for Australia, their purpose in building up forces was not so much from an interest in Australia but rather from its utility as a base from which to hit Japan'. This was a salutary reminder to Curtin that MacArthur and the United States would put their own interests first; Australia could expect no special favours.[49]

While MacArthur was discussing these issues with Curtin, the Australian chiefs, Vice-Admiral Royle, General Blamey and the new CAS, Air Vice-Marshal George Jones, were preparing a report on the same issues. After Air Chief Marshal Burnett returned to England in May 1942, the Minister for Air, Arthur Drakeford, had promoted the RAAF's director of training, Air Commodore George Jones, to Air Vice-Marshal and appointed him CAS. According to RAAF historian Alan Stephens, Jones, who was ninth on the RAAF officer seniority list, was probably 'chosen by mistake'. The uninspiring Jones was junior to Burnett's deputy, Air Vice-Marshal William Bostock, and when Bostock became commander of RAAF Command under MacArthur's air commander, Major General George Kenney, a long and bitter feud was initiated between the two Australian air officers. Part of the problem was that Jones was responsible for the administration of the RAAF, but operational matters came under MacArthur. The chiefs' report recommended an offensive against Japan and Blamey urged the return of the 9th Division.[50]

In the meantime, news was received that the US Navy had achieved a great victory over the Japanese fleet in the Battle of Midway. Curtin and MacArthur discussed the outcome by encrypted secraphone on 6 June and met again for the War Conference in Melbourne on 11 June. MacArthur began by advising Curtin that 'the security of Australia had now been assured. It would now be merely interpreted as a timid cry for help, if we were to persist in demands for assistance for the defence of Australia.'[51]

MacArthur reaffirmed his views at the War Council on 17 June. In his opinion, the Battle of the Coral Sea had been 'the most crucial incident of the war insofar as Australia was concerned . . . Australia was in grave danger up to the time of the Coral Sea action. The results of that action and the successes gained at Midway Island had assured the defensive position of Australia.' In a remarkable disclosure of Allied signal intelligence capabilities, he added that in both the Coral Sea and Midway battles 'we had the great advantage in each action of knowing the Japanese plans beforehand'.[52]

It was one thing for MacArthur to disclose Allied signals intelligence successes to ministers who had been sworn to secrecy, even if it was unwise of him to do so. It was another thing for the prime minister to pass on this information to select members of the press gallery, but this is what he did. On 11 May, soon after the Battle of the Coral Sea, the *Canberra Times* reported that 'No secret is made of the fact that the Japanese invasion preparations have been known to the Allied High Command and the action by Allied forces is hailed as a well-timed and perfectly executed intervention.' Such reports raised the ire of Rear Admiral Edwin Layton, head of US naval intelligence in Hawaii, while Admiral Chester Nimitz, commander-in-chief of

Pacific Command 'was increasingly disturbed about how' Layton's intelligence bulletins 'were being used by Australia's prime minister'. The influential *Herald* journalist Joe Alexander wrote in his diary that after the Battle of Midway, Curtin told journalists: 'The NIP Naval concentration was discovered ten days ago by means of an intercepted signal.' It has been claimed that journalists who attended Curtin's background briefings abided by his request that the information be kept confidential, but inevitably some information crept out.[53]

Building on the success at Midway, on 2 July the US Joint Chiefs of Staff issued MacArthur with a directive ordering offensive operations with the ultimate object of seizing the New Britain–New Ireland–New Guinea area. MacArthur discussed these plans with Curtin in Canberra on 17 July, explaining that he was preparing to advance to the north coast of Papua and would be moving his headquarters to Brisbane to take charge of the offensive. Journalist Erle Cox recalled Curtin then revealing to journalists that MacArthur had told him the first counterattack of the war would be launched against Guadalcanal in the Solomon Islands. Curtin's sympathetic biographer John Edwards described this as 'Curtin's most amazingly indiscreet disclosure'.[54]

In preparation for his offensive, MacArthur opened his headquarters in Brisbane on 20 July, but the Japanese beat him to the punch. The next day Japanese forces landed on the north coast of Papua and all plans for an Allied offensive dissolved. Once MacArthur left Melbourne, the Prime Minister's War Conference met less frequently. Furthermore, the general strategic framework for operations in the SWPA had been established. Curtin would continue to seek advice from MacArthur until the last year of the war, but the War Conference became less important.

Curtin's relationship with MacArthur has become a key point of contention over his performance as war leader. The Second World War official historian, Gavin Long, claimed that by accepting MacArthur's appointment, the government 'made a notable surrender of sovereignty'. In other words, Curtin gave MacArthur almost a free rein in deciding when and where Australian forces would be deployed. In the view of John Edwards, 'In Curtin's mind he was subject to MacArthur's authority, in the sense that MacArthur, who reported to the US Joint Chiefs of Staff, had authority over Australian armed forces and the defence of Australia.' Edwards argues that MacArthur's 'presence enabled Curtin to seek resources from the United States, and that MacArthur never asked the Australians to do something they did not want to do'. That is, Curtin consciously used MacArthur to Australia's advantage. Handing command to MacArthur 'was both a clever and obvious decision'.[55]

Given Curtin's lack of military experience, Australia's limited military capability and the magnitude of the Japanese threat at that time, there was little alternative but to place Australia's forces under the command of a foreign general. Curtin maintained good relations with MacArthur, whose strategic concepts in 1942 were not at variance with those of the Australian government. But having handed strategic direction to MacArthur, Curtin failed to monitor MacArthur's intentions as thoroughly as the situation required, and this was to have some less advantageous consequences for Australia later in the war. In April 1942, Curtin had stated that military matters were 'for military men and neither the Government nor the Parliament [would] override their decisions'.[56] In mid-1942 he put that policy into practice, and would do so during the fighting on the Kokoda Trail.

Kokoda Campaign

When on the night of 21 July 1942 a Japanese force landed at Buna on the north coast of Papua, the Allied commanders in the SWPA were faced with a new and unexpected threat. Soon the Japanese pushed inland, against light resistance from a small Australian militia force, and by 29 July they had secured the important airfield at Kokoda. But initially MacArthur remained unconvinced that the Japanese would try to march over the forbidding Owen Stanley Range to seize Port Moresby. And when American forces from the nearby South Pacific Command landed at Guadalcanal in the southern Solomon Islands on 7 August, it seemed that the Japanese would be occupied elsewhere.

In the ensuing campaign, the War Cabinet and particularly the Advisory War Council were kept closely informed and became keenly involved with some aspects of the campaign, appreciating that defeat in Papua would have grave consequences for Australian security. For example, on 5 August Billy Hughes, leader of the UAP and a member of the War Council, stated publicly that Australia would suffer the same fate as Malaya unless an offensive strategy were adopted and Buna and Gona on the north coast of Papua were retaken without delay. Curtin replied publicly, pointing out that the council had had numerous consultations with MacArthur, Blamey and the service chiefs, and that Hughes had had many opportunities to indicate his proposals in the council.[57]

The government's military advisers continued to be optimistic about the fighting in Papua. For example, at the War Council on 13 August, the CGS, Lieutenant General John Northcott, advised that 'operations were continuing on a small scale in the Kokoda area'.[58] The 7th Division was being deployed to Papua and Lieutenant General Sydney Rowell was assuming command of New Guinea Force. Northcott had succeeded Sturdee when the latter had been sent to Washington as the Australian military representative. He had been deputy CGS from 1939 to 1941, and had recently been commander of the 2nd Corps. Although Blamey was commander-in-chief of the Australian Military Forces, Northcott represented him on the Chiefs of Staff Committee.

It was a considerable trial for these busy senior military officers to appear regularly before the War Council. Rowell, then deputy CGS, attended a meeting earlier in the year when Sturdee was ill. He recalled 'that I had to contend with three King's Counsels in Menzies, Spender and Hughes, and it wasn't roses all the way by any means'. Air Vice-Marshal Jones had a similar experience: 'I found Hughes a very sharp-tongued individual, and at first I was no match for his overbearing attitude.' When Blamey attended he was more aggressive; on one occasion Curtin was critical of a minor administrative matter and Blamey thumped the table: 'Prime Minister, I want you to know that I have no ambitions in this war. If you don't like the way that I've been running things, you can damn well get somebody else.' When Hughes spoke sharply to Blamey 'he would get a barked reply, and Hughes would recoil in his shell. "I was only asking, General," he would mutter.'[59]

Curtin met MacArthur in Brisbane on 17 August and was again given optimistic advice about New Guinea. MacArthur assured the prime minister that the Japanese 'could not attack Port Moresby with any strength of land forces over the mountain range'. MacArthur said that he was planning an offensive in New Guinea with two US divisions and the 7th Australian Division.[60]

Soon after, on 26 August a force of Japanese marines landed at Milne Bay, while another force began a major offensive at Isurava on the Kokoda Trail—the narrow footpath that wound its way over the rugged Owen Stanley Range from Kokoda in the north to Port Moresby on the south Papuan coast. It was some days before the seriousness of the attack on the Kokoda Trail became apparent, and in the meantime there was intense concern at MacArthur's headquarters in Brisbane about the landing at Milne Bay. In the midst of this fighting, the Advisory War Council met in Canberra on 27 August. The three service chiefs were present, and General Northcott described the fighting at Milne Bay, adding that 'General Blamey was confident that we would be able to defeat the Japanese'. Curtin replied that the government had confidence in MacArthur and his senior commanders and that there was a good relationship between MacArthur and Blamey. The non-government members criticised some aspects of the operations. Hughes, for example, was concerned about the problem of driving the Japanese out of the Buna–Gona area, claiming that the situation was a result of a 'defensive strategy'.[61]

With the Japanese continuing their advance, Curtin decided to hold a secret session of parliament on 3 September to review the war situation. In his speech-notes, Curtin quoted MacArthur as saying that Japanese intentions were to attack the lines of communication between Australia and the United States. In his own handwriting Curtin added the words: 'and ultimately the mainland of Australia', although he had no evidence of this. During what was generally an optimistic speech, Curtin appealed to members to control their criticism, because, 'unless public criticism is well based on vital factors it can only place a distinguished American soldier, who has come here to help us, in a most invidious position. If this is carried out to any great lengths on unsubstantial grounds, I forecast a grave reaction on American co-operation in this theatre.'[62]

In a broadcast that evening, Curtin developed the same theme: 'Our fate is in the balance as I speak to you. The Battle of the Solomons is not only vital in itself, but, as part of a continuing action which will go on, it represents a phase of the Japanese drive in which is wrapped up invasion of Australia.' He said that if Port Moresby and Darwin fell then inevitably Australia would be faced 'with a bloody struggle on our soil, a struggle in which we would be forced to fight grimly, city by city, village by village, until our fair land might become a blackened ruin'.[63] In fact, the Magic summaries had informed MacArthur and Curtin in June that the Japanese had no plan to invade Australia; but if the Japanese had succeeded in their offensives, they might have reconsidered their broad strategy.

Just as the forces at Milne Bay began to gain ascendancy over the Japanese, it became evident that the Australian troops on the Kokoda Trail were facing an even more dangerous threat. Despite the arrival of leading elements of the AIF 21st Brigade, the Australians began to withdraw over the crest of the mountains towards Port Moresby. By 5 September they had withdrawn through the so-called 'Gap' and by 8 September the headquarters of the 21st Brigade had become isolated. MacArthur and his staff again sent urgent messages to Port Moresby and additional troops were ordered to New Guinea.

This was the situation when the War Council met in Canberra on 9 September. The three chiefs were present and General Northcott reported that Australian forces had cleared the enemy from the northern shores of Milne Bay. However, according to Northcott, the 'Japanese had penetrated as far as Efogi, 6 miles [10 kilometres] on the Port Moresby side of the gap in the Owen Stanley Ranges'. The non-government members immediately began an aggressive cross-examination, with Spender referring to the failure to appreciate what the Japanese might do. Hughes questioned the military leadership in New Guinea. The chiefs argued that these questions were unfounded. The Minister for the Army, Forde, said that he was arranging for Blamey to go to New Guinea, although this 'did not infer [sic] that he had any criticism to make of the Commanders in this area'.[64]

The next day in parliament, Labor member Arthur Calwell suggested that Curtin should visit New Guinea to gain 'first-hand knowledge' of the operations, but Curtin replied that he was 'fully acquainted with New Guinea operations and there was nothing he could do by being on the spot'. When Forde told Blamey that he should visit New Guinea he discovered that Blamey had already resolved on this course, and Blamey arrived in Port Moresby on 12 September. By this time the newly arrived 25th Brigade was about to go into action at Ioribaiwa, and Blamey arranged for the headquarters of the 6th Division to be flown to Port Moresby. On the evening of 15 September, after his two-day visit to Port Moresby, Blamey said in a broadcast that he was fully confident of the outcome in New Guinea, and the following morning newspapers quoted him as saying that he 'had been impressed with the confidence of the troops in their leader, Lt-Gen Rowell'.[65]

While Blamey had been absent in New Guinea the confidence of the politicians and of MacArthur had continued to decline. At a confidential briefing for newspaper editors on 11 September, Curtin revealed that General Sutherland had visited New Guinea and there was 'now official worry about the position there. MacArthur told Curtin the Allied forces had been out-generalled and out-manoeuvred . . . However the position is not yet serious and the Allies have started a movement which they are confident will out-flank the enemy.' A few days later MacArthur's air commander, Major General Kenney, visited Port Moresby, and, although he did not speak to Rowell, returned to Brisbane to inform MacArthur that Moresby would be lost 'if something drastic did not happen soon'.[66]

An atmosphere of criticism was growing. For example, in parliament on 16 September, Eric Harrison of the UAP asked the government whether it had considered sending Lieutenant General

Gordon Bennett to New Guinea. Forde replied: 'We have a corps commander in New Guinea who is one of the outstanding military officers in Australia.'[67]

Against this backdrop of criticism, on 17 September Blamey addressed the War Council in Canberra. He described the supply difficulties on the Kokoda Trail, the fighting withdrawal of the 21st Brigade, and the arrival of the 25th Brigade. He said that it was 'imperative to hold Port Moresby', because while it was held 'it was improbable that an attack would be made on Australia'. He shared with Rowell and the commander of the 7th Division, Major General Arthur Allen, their confidence that the Japanese would 'not be able to take Port Moresby from the land'.[68]

There was then a heated discussion led by Hughes and Beasley. Eventually, at the end of a lengthy exchange, Curtin said that he did not wish Blamey to have the impression that responsibility for the mistakes and miscalculations of past commanders was being placed on present commanders. Blamey again assured the council 'that all that could be done was being done and the military leaders and men were confident of success'. The crucial issue was whether the members still retained confidence in Blamey and the other commanders. Blamey's address did not allay anxiety for the safety of Port Moresby, and Forde was one minister who still felt that Moresby might yet fall. In a confidential briefing for senior newspapermen that evening, Curtin said that there had been 'a bit of a row' at the War Council, but there had been no criticism of MacArthur.[69]

After Blamey's optimistic statement about the situation in New Guinea, it must have come as a shock when that night MacArthur spoke to Curtin by secraphone. He told Curtin that he was worried about the situation in New Guinea where, despite superior numbers, the Australians were still withdrawing.

MacArthur admitted that this was a different picture from that presented by Blamey, and acknowledged that 'the Australian command may be right', but he had 'a feeling of uneasiness'. He therefore recommended that Curtin direct Blamey to go to Port Moresby to 'take personal command, not only to energise the situation, but to save himself, because, in the event of the situation in New Guinea becoming really serious, it would be difficult for General Blamey to meet his responsibility to the Australian public'.[70]

Curtin accepted this advice, telephoned Blamey, and ordered him to New Guinea. John Edwards has argued that Curtin made the 'right decision', given the apparent failure to prevent the Japanese advance. By advising Curtin to send Blamey, MacArthur had 'forced Curtin to assume responsibility for a military command decision'. In truth, having placed his confidence in MacArthur, Curtin could not easily have refused to accept his advice. Later Curtin confessed that, 'in my ignorance (of military matters), I thought that the Commander-in-Chief should be in New Guinea', but he would have been supported by some of his colleagues. For example, Beasley was reported to have said in the hearing of other ministers, 'Moresby is going to fall. Send Blamey up there and let him fall with it!' Blamey's comment was more to the point. He was not worried about the situation in New Guinea, but as he told one of his senior staff officers, 'Canberra's lost it.' Later he wrote to Rowell about the 'very inexperienced politicians who are inclined to panic on every possible occasion'.[71]

In fact, after the fighting withdrawal by the Australian battalions the Japanese were never likely to take Port Moresby, and indeed they were ordered to withdraw to the north coast. MacArthur's telephone call to Curtin had resulted from his own lack of confidence and concern for his own position. He told one of his senior commanders that he did not think the Australians would fight. He accepted the views of his own air commander, Kenney, over those of the Australian Army commanders, and for the sake of his reputation in Washington he was already ensuring that the Australians would be blamed for any possible disaster. Yet by the time Blamey arrived in Port Moresby on 23 September, the Japanese had advanced no further and the Australians were patrolling forward. At a confidential briefing for senior newspapermen on 21 September, Curtin said that the supply problem 'had just about tricked the bloody Japs', and he did not think that the Japanese could now take Port Moresby.[72]

When the War Council met in Canberra on 24 September it

heard a more encouraging story from the service chiefs. The remnants of the Japanese force at Milne Bay were being mopped up, patrols were advancing from Imita Ridge towards Ioribaiwa, and another infantry brigade was moving up to join the 25th. Curtin informed the council that after discussions with MacArthur, and in view of the critical importance of the defence of Port Moresby, he had requested Blamey 'to proceed there in order to take personal command of the operations'. Blamey was already there, but strict censorship had been imposed on this development. Hughes then suggested that since Blamey had been sent, a minister should go to New Guinea to investigate the situation on the spot.[73]

At the end of September the Minister for Air, Arthur Drakeford, visited Port Moresby, accompanied by Arthur Coles, one of the two independent MPs on whom Curtin relied to maintain his government. On 1 October the Minister for the Army, Frank Forde, arrived, and the next day he went forward with MacArthur and Blamey to the beginning of the Kokoda Trail, where they spoke to troops of the 16th Brigade as they were about to begin the offensive back along the Trail. Despite the fact that some of these troops had already fought in Libya, Greece, Crete and Syria, Forde, wearing a pith helmet, told them that they were about to have their baptism of fire. At a press conference on 3 October, Curtin said that 'the Ministers had been forced there through reflections on their courage. He did not like having so many eggs in one basket.'[74]

By that time there had been another meeting of the War Council—on 1 October. As usual, the chiefs reviewed the recent operations, and General Northcott said that the Australian troops were continuing their advance along the Kokoda Trail. Spender then said that he understood General Rowell and his chief of staff, Brigadier Henry Rourke, had returned to Australia, and that this was an indication that things had not been satisfactory. Curtin replied that he did not have full information and 'was not in a position to go into the reasons for it', but 'he did not believe, however, that Lieut-General Rowell had been transferred because of any lack of confidence by General Blamey in General Rowell's decisions on operational matters'.[75]

Blamey's relief of Rowell as Commander New Guinea Force related directly to Rowell's belief that in coming to New Guinea, Blamey had shown lack of confidence in his ability to handle the situation. There was a longstanding antipathy between the two commanders going back to the Greek campaign in April 1941, and Rowell believed that Blamey had not shown sufficient moral courage to resist the government directive to travel to New Guinea.[76] But Rowell did not appreciate the pressure on Blamey from MacArthur and the government. Ultimately, responsibility for the clash between Blamey and Rowell in Port Moresby relates to the fact that the government preferred to accept MacArthur's advice over Blamey's, and that both MacArthur and the government had lost confidence in the Australian forces and commanders in New Guinea.

The government's continuing concern over the outcome in New Guinea was demonstrated early in October. On the 4th, Curtin said in a radio speech: 'The enemy strikes now at Moresby. We are staging a holding fight.' This extravagant statement did not accord with the optimistic description of the operations he had received at the War Council on 1 October, and on 3 October he had confidentially told senior newspapermen that the situation in New Guinea 'at present is favourable'. On 4 October, Blamey wrote to Curtin that the Australian offensive was progressing more rapidly than expected.[77] Thus by early October the government could be in no doubt that the tide of battle had turned in New Guinea.

A week later, on 8 October, with the Australians on the offensive, Blamey suggested that Curtin visit him in Port Moresby to get a first-hand understanding of the conditions in New Guinea. Curtin referred the idea to MacArthur, who was 'utterly opposed to' such 'a foolish and reckless adventure', claiming that 'the situation does not warrant in any way the entirely unnecessary strain and hazard of such a trip'.[78] MacArthur knew that Curtin was desperately afraid of flying, and the flight would indeed have been a great stress, but a visit would have enabled Blamey to confer with Curtin on important command issues. It is hard to imagine Churchill deciding to visit Cairo (as he did in August 1942) and then bowing to the wishes of the theatre commander not to proceed with the visit. In truth, Curtin did not see that his role as war leader required him to visit Australian troops on operations.

It would be almost four more months of hard fighting before the Japanese were pushed into the sea on the north coast of Papua, but essentially the Japanese threat to Port Moresby, and thus the threat to Australia, had been countered successfully. It had been a trying experience for the government and the members of the War Council, and at times there had been some keen cross-examination of the service chiefs. The fighting in the Owen Stanley Range during the withdrawal from Kokoda had been of crucial importance to the security of Australia. The reaction of the members of the council shows that they were fully aware of this fact at the time.

Conscription for Overseas Service

In the First World War, Curtin had been jailed briefly for his opposition to the introduction of conscription for service overseas. The issue had split the Labor Party, and after Hughes and his supporters left the party, opposition to conscription became an article of faith within the Labor Party. Hence, when in October 1939 the Menzies government had introduced compulsory training for the militia, it had been opposed by the Labor Party. In June 1940 Curtin persuaded his party to support compulsory military training for home defence, and therefore on the outbreak of war with Japan, Curtin's government had approved the calling up of more soldiers to full-time militia service. During 1942 the militia—known as the Australian Military Forces, or AMF—formed the largest part of the army. Under the Defence Act, the militia was not permitted to serve outside of Australia. Because Papua and the Mandated Territory of New Guinea were Australian territories, the militia could serve there, but its units would not be permitted to serve beyond that area, such as in Dutch New Guinea, once MacArthur's forces began their counteroffensive. On the other hand, MacArthur's forces included conscripted American soldiers, and they were required to serve wherever they were ordered to do so.

After the outbreak of war with Japan it was not long before the leader of the Opposition, Arthur Fadden, and the former prime minister, Robert Menzies, were urging the government to change the Defence Act to allow the militia to serve overseas. But Curtin was likely to face fierce opposition to any such move from within his own party. Curtin's biographer John Edwards has argued that by April 1942 Curtin had decided that he would need to change the Defence Act. At the War Council on 28 April he had stated that the issue 'could not be decided on any other grounds than that of military necessity, and would be considered on that basis when the need arose'. According to Edwards, 'It would be helpful, though not essential, if the proposed amendment could be portrayed as a military necessity. MacArthur's endorsement would be useful.'[79] Curtin therefore asked Shedden to visit MacArthur in Brisbane to discuss the relationship of his operational plans to the use of the militia outside Australia.

A few days earlier, the War Cabinet had discussed an appreciation from the chiefs of staff warning that owing to dangerously depleted strengths in Australia, it was not possible to send further additional forces to New Guinea. MacArthur said that it was nothing to do with him but observed that 'there was one serious flaw in the Government's policy—the failure to amalgamate the AIF and the AMF by some formula which, while not giving any credit to the Opposition, would enable the Government to get out of what he felt would become an increasingly difficult position'. MacArthur 'hoped that the Prime Minister would find a way to act and would act quickly'.[80]

According to Shedden, after receiving MacArthur's advice, 'Curtin decided that he would seek an amendment of the Labour Party Platform to provide for service abroad by Militia Forces', and 'took the bold and risky decision that he would handle the amendment . . . as his personal responsibility'. Shedden wrote a detailed brief for Curtin in which he proposed expanding the area in which militiamen would be liable to serve to include all of the SWPA plus the area of the Solomon Islands that had originally been excluded from the SWPA. Shedden's brief formed the core of a confidential letter that Curtin wrote to the presidents of the state Labor parties.

The full Cabinet approved the approach on 23 November. Shedden sought to take some credit for this outcome, but John Edwards argues otherwise, claiming with some justification that Shedden had done no more than expected in his role as the top defence bureaucrat.[81]

Eventually, on 5 January 1943, the federal ALP conference approved Curtin's proposal by 24 votes to twelve. The full Cabinet approved it on 26 January, and later that day Shedden went to Parliament House to give some papers to Curtin, and found him 'lying on his couch looking extremely depressed. On enquiring as to how he felt, he said that the minority in Cabinet had set about him, like a pack of dogs, for taking on himself the responsibility for his action without consulting them. He said that this was all the thanks he got for taking the risks of avoiding a split in the Party.'[82] The *Defence (Citizen Military Forces) Act 1943* became law on 19 February 1943. The militia was to be permitted to serve beyond Australian territory up to the equator. Credit for achieving this outcome must go to Curtin, but the advantage was more political than military. The army invited members of militia units to volunteer for overseas service, and when the majority of a unit volunteered, that unit was declared to be part of the AIF. These units would be available as MacArthur's forces moved to a counteroffensive in 1943. But in fact, few militia units actually served beyond Australian territory.

On balance, Curtin had proved to be an effective war leader in the first year of the Pacific War. In October 1942, the US Minister to Australia, Nelson Johnson, observed: 'The year in Australia . . . has been dominated by one man, John Curtin . . . A clear and forceful speaker, John Curtin impresses one with his sincerity, innate honesty of purpose, and earnestness . . . John Curtin has done an admirable job.'[83] But the war still had more than two and a half years to run, and Australia's war leaders would face different challenges.

7

'The decisions are matters for the Australian government'

Curtin, Second World War, 1943–45

From early 1943 the Allies moved to a counteroffensive in the Pacific, and rather than responding to crises, as it had in 1942, the Australian government now had to manage the nation's role within Allied military campaigns. This was still a challenging task, as the decisions as to where and how Australia's forces were to be deployed were largely determined by the United States and Britain. The big question was how to reconcile Australia's national interest with the wider interest of the grand alliance.

Two fundamental strategic issues needed to be decided. The first was to determine the SWPA's mission; but this decision rested with the US Joint Chiefs, and only after he received his directive would MacArthur be able to decide where and how to use his forces. Blamey, as Commander Allied Land Forces, would have a keen interest in this decision. The second issue was for Curtin and his government to determine what forces to allocate to MacArthur's command. Theoretically this was a purely Australian matter, but MacArthur had an important stake in it and attempted to influence the decision. The following years, 1944 and 1945, would require similar decisions, further illustrating the problem of operating as part of an Allied coalition. In all this, the key decision-maker in Australia would not just be the prime minister, John Curtin, but a foreign general, Douglas MacArthur.

The SWPA's Mission for 1943

Planning the military operations for 1943 began in earnest in January 1943, well before the Australian and American troops had completed the bitter and exhausting campaign to defeat the Japanese on the north coast of Papua. Six months earlier, on 2 July 1942, the US Joint Chiefs had issued MacArthur and the commander of the Pacific Ocean Area, Admiral Chester Nimitz, with a directive to seize the main Japanese base at Rabaul on the island of New Britain. The Japanese had thwarted the Allied offensive when they had thrust into the southern Solomon Islands and Papua in July and August 1942. Now, in January 1943, as the Australians and Americans were successfully concluding those campaigns, the Joint Chiefs instructed MacArthur to submit detailed plans to carry out the 2 July directive. In the meantime, Roosevelt and Churchill, supported by their service chiefs, headed to Casablanca in Morocco to decide Allied strategic priorities for the coming year. Australia, along with other smaller allies, would not be represented.

Hurrying back to his Brisbane headquarters from New Guinea, MacArthur immediately began to push for more resources, pleading to the US Army Chief of Staff, General Marshall, on 10 January, that he had insufficient forces to begin an offensive. MacArthur sought to enlist Curtin's support. Not wanting to be sidelined by MacArthur, Blamey too had hurried back from New Guinea, and when he met Curtin and Shedden in Canberra on 14 January, the prime minister stated that until greater forces were available the only alternative was a 'holding strategy in the Pacific'.[1]

After this conference, Shedden flew to Brisbane to discuss the recent campaign and the developing plans with MacArthur. The American general said that he had informed the Joint Chiefs that to achieve the aims of his directive he would need more aircraft, ships and troops, and the only way to secure assistance was to arouse

American public opinion. Shedden suggested that if MacArthur would provide the facts and figures he would draft a cable for Curtin to send to Roosevelt. Curtin's cable would quote a press statement from MacArthur that the outstanding lesson of the recent campaign was airpower, and that if sufficient aircraft were provided they could strike the Japanese 'a mortal blow'.[2]

As agreed, on 19 January Curtin cabled Roosevelt and Churchill at Casablanca, quoting MacArthur's statement, and appealing for an additional 2000 aircraft for offensive action. A few days later in an Australia Day broadcast, Curtin appealed directly to the American people, describing Australia as the 'bulwark of civilisation south of the Equator'. The broadcast attracted some criticism, and one reporter wrote that 'the spectacle' of Curtin appealing to the American people 'was rather pathetic', but MacArthur told Curtin that the speech 'was magnificent measured by any standard of strategy, courage, patriotism or common-sense'.[3] He promised to radio Washington at once to support the prime minister's argument.

These representations had little influence in the Casablanca conference, where the US Chief of Naval Operations, Admiral Ernest King, was already arguing vigorously in favour of the Pacific War. On 29 January, Churchill informed the Australian government that although the Pacific was fifth on the list of Allied strategic priorities—after the Atlantic, Russia, the Mediterranean and the United Kingdom—the directive of 2 July 1942 to capture Rabaul remained unchanged. MacArthur was not pleased with the decision to give the Pacific fifth priority. On 2 February the Advisory War Council agreed that there would be no profit in challenging the Casablanca decision. Curtin promised, however, to ask MacArthur whether he needed additional forces.[4]

Faced with what appeared to be the intransigence of the Joint Chiefs, MacArthur now sought Curtin's further help, and he seized on the build-up of Japanese strength in the islands north-west of Australia to stress the need for adequate forces to ensure the defence of Australia. Conveniently overlooking that he had sent his chief of staff, Major General Sutherland, to Washington to obtain more forces for the New Guinea offensive, MacArthur told Curtin that he had sent Sutherland to obtain forces to defend Australia against a possible Japanese attack in 'from two to four months'. MacArthur had not been completely honest with Curtin; in January he had told Curtin that there was nothing to fear from the Japanese in the north-west, and Blamey assured Curtin that he was 'not disturbed regarding the possibility of heavy Japanese attacks in the immediate future'. But now MacArthur stirred up Curtin further by telling him that Roosevelt and Churchill's failure to reply to Curtin's appeal of 19 January was 'an astonishing development', and that he should approach them again.[5] On 18 March Curtin made renewed representations to Roosevelt and Churchill, with further cables in April.

While Curtin was making these requests, planning continued in Washington, and on 28 March the Joint Chiefs issued a new directive for offensive operations in the South and Southwest Pacific. Unable to supply all the forces that MacArthur would need to take Rabaul, the Joint Chiefs modified their aim to that of advancing through the Solomons and New Guinea without actually capturing Rabaul, and undertook to provide MacArthur with two more infantry divisions, 524 additional combat aircraft and 33 non-combat aircraft.

Although MacArthur had received approval for a limited offensive, he was still not satisfied. He advised Curtin that Bert Evatt, the Minister for External Affairs, who was about to depart for a visit to America and Britain, should seek to obtain aircraft to allow the RAAF to expand to 72 squadrons. At MacArthur's request, on 9 April Curtin released a statement urging that the war in the Pacific be considered as the second front (Russia being the first). Blamey's support was enlisted, and on Anzac Day (25 April) he broadcast to America, appealing for 'a reasonable allocation of force'.[6]

Early in May, Churchill and the British chiefs of staff arrived in Washington for the so-called Trident conference with Roosevelt and the US Joint Chiefs. By this time Evatt was in Washington, and he tried to persuade the conference to give higher priority to the Pacific. He had little success. Nonetheless, for other reasons, Churchill informed the press on 25 May that the war would be waged with equal force on the European and Pacific fronts. In truth, Australia had had little influence over Allied strategy, but MacArthur flattered Curtin by suggesting that his representations had played a key role. Evatt returned to Australia claiming that he too had been instrumental in changing Allied strategy and that he had succeeded in obtaining additional aircraft for the RAAF. The British chiefs accompanying Churchill were adamant that the change in strategy had been decided on 'military grounds' before Evatt arrived.[7] As for the additional aircraft, of the promised 474 only 132 were delivered, and those that were sent were types then being superseded.

Resources for the 1943 Campaigns

While MacArthur and Curtin were seeking to influence Allied strategy and to obtain additional Allied resources, they knew that the coming operations would rely heavily on the men and materiel made available by the Australian government. But it was clear that Australia could not maintain the army at its present strength while also providing MacArthur with the necessary food and other supplies to sustain his forces. The Australian government therefore needed to make some careful judgements about the balance of the nation's war effort.

On 8 February, Curtin asked MacArthur what Australian forces he would require to fulfil his directive. Possibly because he was still negotiating with Washington, MacArthur chose not to reply, but whatever the outcome might be, Curtin knew that it would pose a heavy burden on Australia. On 12 February he told Blamey that Australia had 'reached the maximum of her manpower, material and financial resources', and he asked Blamey to 'drop a few hints' to MacArthur about American extravagance. Blamey had little success with this effort, and eventually he suggested that Curtin approach MacArthur directly on the matter.[8]

In the meantime, on 13 April, once MacArthur had told him what tasks were in store for the Australians, Blamey reported to the War Cabinet that to provide the offensive force of three divisions, which MacArthur demanded, and to maintain home security, Australia would require nine infantry divisions, two armoured divisions, one armoured brigade and one army tank brigade. If further manpower could not be released from industry, 'then the force being prepared for offensive operations should be reduced by an infantry division'. In view of the improving strategic situation, Blamey considered that it was now 'a justifiable indeed an unavoidable risk' to reduce the forces in the areas remote from the enemy.[9]

Seeking an answer to this problem, the War Cabinet asked the Defence Committee (senior military and civilian defence officials) to determine what strengths of the three services could be maintained if 10,000 men per month were available. The Defence Committee reported on 6 May that it could only answer the question once it had 'an authoritative and comprehensive review of the existing strategical situation'.[10] This could only be provided by MacArthur. If Australia were to have a major role in the coming offensives then the services would need the necessary manpower. Some politicians and bureaucrats, however, saw Australia's most important duty as the supply of food and war equipment. But whatever alternatives were followed, if Australia's overall contribution to the war was not reduced there would be a further decline in civilian living standards. It is clear that the War Cabinet did not know quite what to do. The heart of the problem was that MacArthur wanted as many combat troops as possible, as well as supplies and war materiel for his US forces.

In an effort to resolve the impasse, towards the end of May, Shedden visited MacArthur in Brisbane and explained that the manpower situation had 'reached saturation point'. MacArthur, however, still wanted an offensive force of three AIF divisions: 'Anything less would be incompatible with Australia's status and destiny as a Pacific power and would not guarantee her the same voice in the Peace Councils, to which she is entitled.' He promised to present Curtin with a strategic appreciation that might make it possible to reduce the demand for local defence. In the meantime, Blamey told Curtin that if the situation continued it would 'virtually remove Australian forces from active operations and result in Australian personnel being employed to render service to the US Forces'. Shedden reiterated his request to MacArthur to indicate in his strategic appreciation that the improvement in the security of Australia might allow a 'relatively small reduction to be made to the great number of men in the land forces'. To do so would furnish 'Mr Curtin a remedy for some of his problems which at present otherwise appear insoluble'.[11]

MacArthur took his cue, and when he met the prime minister in Sydney on 7 June told him that 'the threat of invasion to Australia had been removed'. After outlining his plans for the offensive, MacArthur turned to the problem of balancing the war effort. He opposed Blamey's proposal that the Americans provide many of their own services, but he realised that Australia could not continue to supply troops, munitions, aircraft and food at the present level. He therefore suggested that Australia maintain its military effort until Rabaul was captured (not mentioning that there was no longer a plan to capture Rabaul). Then its military commitment could be reduced to a land and air expeditionary force, enabling resources to be devoted to food production. Three days after the conference, Curtin released a statement that he did 'not think the enemy can now invade this country'. There would now be less imperative to maintain large forces in Australia.[12]

Meanwhile, in June MacArthur's forces began a major offensive in New Guinea, which by September included the Australian amphibious landings at Lae and Finschhafen, and the advance into the Ramu Valley. It was an outstanding campaign by three, eventually five Australian divisions, but could this effort be sustained? The way was now clear to determine the balance of the war effort for the following year.

Balancing the War Effort

Curtin set the process in train when, at a meeting of the War Cabinet on 13 July, he said that the time had come to review the war effort and that the adjustments had to 'be governed by operational considerations determined by the strategical policy of' General MacArthur and 'by the physical capacity of the Commonwealth to complete the programmes within the requisite time'. For a start, he recommended that the navy be maintained at its existing strength. The army should provide three infantry divisions for offensive operations and 'adequate forces for defence of Australia and New Guinea and for relief of units in New Guinea'. The RAAF should be maintained 'at the strength authorised under the 72 squadron programme to the extent to which aircraft can be provided'. The War Cabinet accepted these recommendations and also decided that MacArthur should be asked to provide Americans to relieve Australians of some of the maintenance services and work projects they were carrying out on behalf of the US forces.[13]

By this time the government was in the midst of an election campaign, and in the election on 21 August the government was re-elected handsomely, winning 49 seats in the House of Representatives and a majority in the Senate. The UAP–Country Party won 23 seats and independents two. When the new government was sworn in on 21 September, the War Cabinet remained unchanged. Eddie Ward, after his unfounded and outrageous claims that the previous government had planned to withdraw behind a 'Brisbane Line', was replaced as Minister for Labour and National Service by E.J. (Jack) Holloway, but he was re-elected as a minister by Caucus and Curtin gave him the minor portfolios of Transport and External Territories. Neither Ward nor Holloway were in the War Cabinet. Following the election, the UAP–Country Party coalition dissolved. Hughes, leader of the UAP, briefly succeeded Fadden as leader of the Opposition, until he was replaced in both capacities by Menzies. By this time the Advisory War Council had lost much of it earlier importance, and later Menzies formally withdrew from the council, although some of his senior colleagues continued in a personal capacity.

Discussions over manpower issues had continued throughout the election campaign. For example, on 5 August Curtin asked MacArthur whether American personnel could take over some of their administrative tasks. MacArthur replied on 24 August that he would like to make his forces independent of civilian support, but this 'could be achieved only at considerable cost to the military effectiveness of my command'. If additional service and maintenance personnel were brought from America without an increase in shipping then fewer combat troops could be sent. The alternative would be for Australia to provide sufficient combat troops, but he understood that there was not sufficient surplus manpower in Australia to permit such an increase. Curtin merely commented that the provision of Australian resources was 'one of broad policy', to be considered 'on the basis of the principles governing the nature and extent of the Australian War Effort'.[14]

It was not until 21 September, four weeks after MacArthur's reply, that Curtin forwarded a copy to Blamey. On 27 September, Blamey informed Curtin of the continuing difficulties being experienced in restricting American demands. Meanwhile, various government committees had been trying to find a solution. These committees failed to agree, and Shedden put his own staff to work. On 30 September he presented a detailed review of the manpower situation, which along with reports from the various committees, was considered when the War Cabinet met in Canberra on 1 October 1943.[15] Blamey and the CGS, Lieutenant General Northcott, were present to give their views.

After a discussion lasting five and a half hours the War Cabinet agreed that by June 1944, 20,000 men should be released from the services, 10,000 men should be released from munitions and aircraft industries, and that the monthly intake into the services be fixed at 5000 men and women. But apart from stabilising the RAAF at its 'present strength' in Australia at 48 squadrons, there was no commitment to reducing substantially the forces fighting in the SWPA.[16] The War Cabinet affirmed two key principles:

(a) It is of vital importance to the future of Australia and her status at the peace table in regard to the settlement in the Pacific that her military effort should be concentrated as far as possible in the Pacific and that it should be on a scale to guarantee her an effective voice in the peace settlement.

(b) If necessary, the extent of this effort should be maintained at the expense of commitments in other theatres . . .

The official historian, Paul Hasluck, thought that the War Cabinet's claim that Australia needed to maintain forces to guarantee an effective voice in the peace settlement was 'a new and opportunistic principle', pointing out that until then Australia's war effort had been governed by the security of Australia and the limits on manpower. To the authors of the official history of the war economy, S.J. Butlin and C.B. Schedvin, it was apparent that 'the structure of command of the direct war effort was in disarray'. The War Cabinet was unable to balance the demands of the military for an increased role in offensive operations against those who saw Australia's most important duty as the supply of food and war equipment. Hasluck wrote that there was an 'absence of clear, firm, exact and prompt determinations on policy by those responsible for the higher direction of the war in Australia'. Butlin and Schedvin were even more critical. They perceived 'a lack of leadership from the Prime Minister and the War Cabinet . . . An important part of the problem which could not be readily resolved was MacArthur's domination of Curtin.'[17]

The problem was that MacArthur had advised Shedden and Curtin that Australia should provide a striking force of three divisions. Although Blamey knew that MacArthur was already making plans to reduce Australia's offensive role, he too believed that Australia should maintain a substantial military commitment, warning Curtin that 'any reduction in the strength of the striking force below three divisions [would] greatly weaken Australia's place in determining the future' and that such a reduction was 'most undesirable in the national interest'.[18]

Although Blamey agreed with MacArthur's assertion that Australia could not provide additional combat forces, he reminded Curtin on 5 October that if the Americans continued to send combat forces without maintenance personnel then Australia would have to disband further combat formations. He continued: 'The issue which has arisen is that General MacArthur has been asked to relieve us of a burden which is causing a reduction in our force, and in reply takes the view that not only should the burden continue to be borne but that it should be increased.' Since MacArthur was disinclined to respond to Curtin's request, Blamey advised the prime minister to take up the matter with the US government.[19]

By the end of October, Curtin was becoming agitated over the lack of positive response from the Americans, and on 1 November he wrote to MacArthur outlining the proposed structure for the services, pointing out that if US combat forces arrived without their own support units, this would aggravate Australia's already critical manpower position. MacArthur replied that he had read Curtin's letter 'with some anxiety', and in blunt language he criticised aspects of Curtin's plans, warning Curtin that his proposals, if implemented, 'could not fail to endanger the basic cooperation between our countries'. For once Curtin was not to be browbeaten, reminding MacArthur that the 'principles covered by the decisions communicated to you are, of course, matters for the Australian government'.[20]

Curtin had successfully challenged MacArthur on this issue, and indeed meeting Curtin in Brisbane on 30 November, MacArthur said 'that he accepted absolutely that it was for the Australian Government to decide the nature and extent of its war effort'. Soon after the conference, Curtin released a press statement stating that MacArthur had 'expressed his full agreement with the general principles laid down by the Government'. But in a broadcast Curtin showed that to maintain good relations he would play up to MacArthur's pride; he concluded by saying: 'I am indebted to General MacArthur for the high statesmanship and breadth of world vision he has contributed to the discussions. The complete integration of our concepts, which has been a source of such strength in the past, will continue to the end.' These last two sentences had been written by MacArthur himself; he had asked Curtin to add them to the statement.[21]

The War Cabinet's decisions on 1 October were fundamental to the balance of Australia's war effort for the remainder of the war. While the War Cabinet had not displayed a complete grasp of the problem and had not performed particularly well, it was nevertheless frustrated by the arrangement established the previous year whereby strategic matters were in the hands of General MacArthur. However much there might have been an air of expediency in the government's decision, we can now see that it was a major turning point in the history of Australian strategic and defence policy. In the First World War, Australia deployed forces overseas to help the Empire to win the war. Similarly, at the beginning of the Second World War, Australia sent forces overseas to help the imperial war effort in the European theatre. Forces were also deployed to Malaya, the Netherlands East Indies and New Guinea to help ensure the security of Australia, culminating in the Papuan and New Guinea campaigns of 1942 and 1943. After 1944, however, Australian forces were deployed for purely political purposes—to guarantee a voice in the peace settlement. This does not necessarily mean that these commitments did not in some way contribute to Australian security, but if Australian forces had conducted no more offensive operations after 1944 there would have been no change in the outcome of the war. Over the next 70 years, Australia would deploy forces to seven more wars for political purposes. This broader view underlines the importance of the decision of October 1943.

Securing Allied Agreement

Having decided on its strategic policy, the government needed to obtain concurrence from the British and US governments, and, as the first step, on 8 October Curtin cabled an outline of the decision to Churchill, seeking his reaction. Meanwhile, the government was waiting on further advice from MacArthur as to how he was planning to use the Australian forces. In turn, MacArthur was waiting on the outcome of a meeting of Churchill, Franklin D. Roosevelt and the Combined Chiefs of Staff in Cairo in late November. In the short term, however, it was clear that the Australian Army would have little offensive role in the coming operations. The army had deployed five divisions during the New Guinea offensives, and these were progressively withdrawn to Australia for rest and retraining. US forces would take over the SWPA offensive as it moved along the north coast of New Guinea.

By this time, Curtin and the Minister for External Affairs, Evatt, were becoming increasingly wary of American intentions, fearing that they wished either to seize bases or secure commercial advantages in the Pacific. On 27 September 1943, Blamey had told Curtin that the operations in New Britain would be by American forces 'to strengthen a claim to retain New Britain in the post war settlement'. In view of the later controversy over the 1944–45 Bougainville campaign, it is pertinent to note that on 22 November 1943 Curtin reminded MacArthur that Australia had a mandate from the League of Nations over Australian New Guinea and Bougainville, and that Australia 'therefore has a special interest in the employment of its own forces in the operations for the ejectment of the enemy from territory under its administration'.[22] To balance American influence, Curtin was anxious to see an increase in British influence in the area, and he intended proposing a plan for increased Commonwealth cooperation when he attended a conference of Commonwealth prime ministers in London in May 1944.

Curtin was deeply offended that Churchill had not replied to his cable outlining the decision of 1 October, and annoyed that Australia was excluded from the discussion about Pacific strategy in Cairo. On 15 December he learned that the Combined Chiefs had agreed to maintain offensives in the Pacific, but the details had not yet been decided. Reacting to this feeling of exclusion, in January Evatt met his New Zealand counterpart in Canberra and proposed a regional organisation to be called the South Seas Regional Commission. They saw a need to take a strong part in the administration of the island colonies and, in collaboration with other allies, to establish bases and major defence installations in the islands. The Anzac Pact, as it was called, upset the British and antagonised the Americans, but indicated a desire to take a more independent line.

Eventually, on 14 March 1944, more than three months after the conclusion of the Cairo conference, Churchill informed Curtin that the British were considering establishing a base in Sydney. MacArthur had already been told that he was to lead an advance towards the Philippines, and it was expected that Britain would despatch a fleet and eventually troops to the SWPA. MacArthur could now develop his plans, and on 17 March at a meeting in Canberra he outlined the proposed US strategy in the Pacific, noting that by the time British forces were available to take part, the Americans would have advanced beyond the Philippines. MacArthur said that if the boundaries of SWPA were changed he would threaten to resign, and 'it would be destructive at this stage of the campaign for the Governments concerned to attempt or even seriously consider so drastic and inadvisable a step'. MacArthur told Curtin that three AIF divisions and an American paratrooper division would spearhead his advance to the Philippines. This 'sagacious advice', as Shedden put it, would influence Curtin once he arrived in London.[23] But MacArthur had not been completely honest with Curtin, for his outline plan for the capture of the Philippines actually made no mention of Australian units.

On 5 April 1944, Curtin, Shedden and Blamey set sail from Sydney on the US naval transport SS *Lurline* to visit the United States and Britain. Curtin's primary aims were to win approval for his modifications to the Australian war effort, and to establish guidelines for Commonwealth cooperation. He was unlikely to get a sympathetic hearing from Churchill, who thought that Australia's intention to maintain three divisions for offensive operations 'was a very poor show'. His chiefs of staff felt bound to remind him that the Australians had 'carried out practically the whole of the fighting in New Guinea' and that the effort of the Australian Army was 'a very remarkable achievement'. Blamey had slightly different aims. Unlike Curtin, he was convinced that MacArthur was going to exclude the Australians from the coming operations, and he was therefore thinking of an Australian and British offensive from Darwin into the Netherlands East Indies. Such an offensive would complement British plans to establish a base in Australia.[24]

When the prime minister's party arrived in London on 29 April they learned that the British chiefs were indeed contemplating an advance from Darwin to Ambon and Borneo and on to Indochina (the so-called Middle Strategy). Curtin was initially happy to have British forces based in Australia, but was unwilling to change the command arrangements already established with MacArthur. As the CIGS, General Brooke, wrote in his diary: 'Curtin and MacArthur are determined to stand together, support each other, and allow no outside interference.' While Blamey argued strongly for the new campaign, which he wistfully imagined he might lead, Curtin concentrated on obtaining endorsement for the reallocation of Australia's war effort. Eventually, on 27 May, after a month of discussion, Churchill agreed to the reallocation and also that the British military mission, then arriving in Australia, be integrated with Australian staff for possible future operations. In the view of biographer John Edwards, Curtin's rejection of Churchill's idea of a Commonwealth force based in Australia advancing through the Netherlands East Indies, perhaps under Blamey's command and separate from MacArthur's command, 'was one of the most important decisions he made in the Pacific War'.[25] For his part, Churchill had shown no interest in Curtin's plans for Commonwealth cooperation.

Churchill agreed that since Australia was 'in a sphere of American strategic responsibility', Australia's war effort should be discussed in Washington. Therefore on 2 June, on his return journey, Curtin outlined his proposals to the Combined Chiefs of Staff in Washington. He explained that Australia would maintain six divisions for active operations. The RAN was to stay at its present strength; the RAAF was to be maintained at its present 54 squadrons; food for Britain (including India) was to be exported on the 1944 scale; and Australia was to review other aspects of the war effort to see if production could be increased. The Combined Chiefs immediately referred these proposals to MacArthur, who replied that he considered that Australia's war effort should be determined by Australia. MacArthur had, of course, previously discussed the proposals with Curtin. The Combined Chiefs therefore approved them. The question remains, however, whether Curtin really needed to seek Allied agreement to the shape and size of Australia's war effort when Australia had not been involved in the Cairo or any of the other Allied conferences. The episode illustrates Australia's lack of confidence in framing and pursuing its own strategic policy.

Curtin's visit to London also reveals his attitude to his role as war leader. He had no particular interest in the mechanics of war. Curtin, Shedden and Blamey left London on 29 May, a week before the D Day landings in Normandy. Blamey was disappointed at not seeing something of this great event, but Curtin had no similar ambitions. Indeed when, soon after, rockets started landing on London, Curtin said that he was glad he had got away when he did. His private secretary observed that if Curtin had been in London when the rockets began, the exit would have been rapid 'or the PM would have had a bad attack of neuritis'. Curtin declined to accompany the other prime ministers when they toured D Day preparations a week or so before leaving England. Instead, he visited RAAF bomber squadrons based in Lincolnshire and watched the aircraft roar down the runway bound for Europe. As the bombers neared the coast of France he sent them a signal: 'Good luck—Curtin.'[26] It was the closest he ever got to an operational theatre.

Australians for the Philippines

On 26 June, the day their ship arrived in Brisbane from the United States, Curtin and Shedden met MacArthur, who said he was disturbed to learn from Blamey that the AIF divisions would not be battle-worthy until after the Philippines campaign. Although he had originally contemplated using the AIF divisions in his advance to the Philippines, 'he did not now intend using them until later on, when he proposed to attack Borneo and the Netherlands East Indies'. MacArthur strongly opposed any plan that would affect the boundaries of his command, and stated that if any additional Australian or British forces became available they should be allotted to him. Curtin was concerned at MacArthur's statement that the Australian divisions would take time to become battle-worthy. He was anxious that Australian forces be involved in the Philippines, but told MacArthur that since they had been assigned to him, 'their use was a matter for decision by him'.[27]

In further talks with Shedden, MacArthur said that he had

already had discussions with Blamey, who had flown back from the United States earlier, and he was convinced that Blamey wanted to be commander-in-chief of the new British–Australian command. MacArthur said that Blamey's position as Commander of the Allied Land Forces 'had now become a fiction' and that he (MacArthur) 'intended to take personal charge of the operations against the Philippines'. Since the Australians might be withdrawn from his command, he was planning on using only American forces in future operations. MacArthur thought that Blamey was holding back the Australian troops for the new command as well as hoping to command all the Australian defence forces.[28] Through his overenthusiastic advocacy of the use of Commonwealth forces on a separate axis, Blamey had provided MacArthur with a ready-made excuse for not using Australian troops in the Philippines.

Worried by MacArthur's claim that Australian troops could not be ready for the Philippines, Curtin asked Blamey to confirm when his major formations could be ready for operations. Blamey replied that the 6th Division was 'available at short notice if necessary', the 7th Division would be available in November and the 9th Division in October.[29] On the face of it, there seemed no reason why all three divisions should not have been available for the first operations in the Philippines, scheduled for November.

MacArthur's intentions soon became clear when, on 12 July, he issued a directive that Australian forces were to assume 'responsibility for the continued neutralisation of the Japanese' in the Bougainville area by 1 October 1944, and in Australian New Guinea, including New Britain, by 1 November. In the advance to the Philippines, MacArthur contemplated employing one AIF division in November 1944 and another in January 1945. Blamey objected to the deployment of the AIF divisions separately rather than as a corps, but MacArthur would not budge. Then, when Blamey developed a plan to relieve the American divisions in the New Guinea–Bougainville area with a total of seven Australian brigades, MacArthur said such forces were 'totally inadequate'.[30] Instead, MacArthur directed Blamey to deploy a minimum of twelve brigades. To find the additional five brigades

Blamey was required to use the 6th Division, thus reducing his striking force to the 7th and 9th Divisions, and making it even less likely that the AIF could be used in the Philippines. Blamey questioned MacArthur's motives in this matter, believing that the American general was holding out the possibility of using the Australians in the Philippines so that they would not be used in the Middle Strategy, without ever intending to do so. But Curtin and Shedden's confidence in Blamey had declined and they would not support him.

In early September 1944, Churchill, Roosevelt and their chiefs of staff gathered in Quebec to consider future operations in the Pacific. Churchill offered the British Main Fleet and Roosevelt immediately accepted. Blamey's hopes for a separate British Commonwealth offensive were dashed. During the conference, the Combined Chiefs also agreed to an accelerated timetable by which MacArthur's forces would invade Leyte Island in the Philippines the following month, thereby decreasing the chances of Australian involvement in the campaign.

When Curtin and Shedden met MacArthur in Canberra on 30 September, MacArthur said that the Australian divisions would now be involved in two groups of operations: garrison duties in Bougainville, New Britain and New Guinea; and operations by the 7th and 9th Divisions in Borneo and Java, not in the Philippines. Curtin offered no comment, and thereby gave tacit approval to this employment of Australian troops.

This was MacArthur's last meeting with Curtin, and when he left Australia two weeks later he never returned. He landed with his troops on Leyte on 20 October and made his headquarters there. In the final event, no Australians (except for an airfield construction unit and a signals intelligence team) were employed in the Philippines, but it was not until February 1945 that MacArthur completely dismissed the possibility of their being used. Curtin had not been willing to apply pressure to MacArthur, even when he found that MacArthur's claim that the Australians were not ready was false. But as biographer John Edwards has argued, Curtin could not insist that MacArthur use Australian troops and was in no position to 'contest MacArthur's military judgement'. Furthermore, Edwards has claimed that:

> If Curtin might have been more trenchant, it would have been in reprimanding Blamey. The Australian commander-in-chief had sought a separate command within MacArthur's South West Pacific Area, against the wishes of his prime minister. He had intrigued with the British, falsely told MacArthur that the AIF would not be ready for the earlier Philippines's timetable and then attempted to insist that the AIF could not be used at all unless in a corps formation. Curtin was if anything a little too tolerant.'[31]

No doubt Blamey over-played his hand, and in this respect he and Curtin should have had a more frank discussion. The initiative for a British advance from Darwin had come from Britain and the outcome of the British proposals had not been decided before Curtin and Blamey left Britain. The evidence that Blamey had falsely stated that the AIF would not be ready came from MacArthur, who had his own motives, and Blamey might have had sound military reasons for insisting on the AIF being deployed as a corps. As we have seen, Blamey believed that MacArthur was sidelining the Australians and had no intention of using the Australian forces in the Philippines.

Reallocating Manpower

Work on implementing Australia's new war effort plan began as soon as Curtin and Shedden arrived in Canberra after their overseas visit, and on 5 July the War Cabinet instructed the Defence Committee to report on manpower requirements for the services. From Blamey's comments while overseas, Curtin understood that the army would be able to release 50,000 and eventually 90,000 men. However, the Defence Committee now recommended no net reduction in total enlistments. At the same time, the War Commitments Committee estimated a need for 78,602 men in high-priority industries by the end of 1944, with a shortfall of at least 39,000 men between labour requirements and supply.

Faced with this impasse, on 2 August Curtin directed Blamey to investigate a way of releasing 50,000 men from the army. Blamey replied that 50,000 would be a 'severe blow' and suggested 20,000 or 25,000.[32] The remainder could be released by the RAAF. The CAS, Air Vice-Marshal Jones, had to admit that a reduction in air force personnel would not greatly impair RAAF operations, and Curtin therefore directed the army to release 30,000 men and the RAAF 15,000. Of these, 20,000 were to be released by 31 December and 25,000 by 30 June 1945.

Over the next two months, Blamey linked strategic policy directly to the manpower problem, advising Curtin that further reductions would 'greatly reduce the status of Australia and our voice later in important matters of policy'. Blamey said that MacArthur had directed him to employ additional forces in New Guinea, but if he lost manpower he would have 'grave misgivings as to the maintenance of our offensive forces in the event of protracted operations in 1945'.[33]

When on 18 October the War Cabinet ordered the Defence Committee to report on a proposal to release a further 40,000 men from the services as soon as possible, Blamey again protested strongly. He pointed out that in the coming months all six divisions and one armoured brigade would be in action overseas. If he was ordered to reduce his force by 40,000 he would need to advise the government that it should 'inform General MacArthur that the Australian Army cannot be maintained at the strength allotted and that it will be necessary to reduce the expeditionary force from one Army corps of two divisions and essential services to one division. This will bring the Australian expeditionary forces to approximately the same dimensions as that of New Zealand.'[34]

Curtin replied that so far he had given no direction to release an additional 40,000. Blamey had won the argument, but Shedden believed that Blamey had been dishonest, recalling that while overseas Blamey had told the Combined Chiefs that 'the reduction to 6 divisions would progressively release some 90,000 men'.[35] Shedden thought that Curtin had given way because he was unwell, and indeed on 3 November Curtin was admitted to hospital with an apparent heart attack.

Air Vice-Marshal Jones's willingness to release 15,000 men was evidence that the RAAF strength was out of proportion to that of the navy and the army. In the SWPA, MacArthur had sidelined much of the RAAF, and many of its aircraft were unsuited to front-line operations. On 1 July 1944, however, there were approximately 14,000 RAAF personnel in the United Kingdom, of whom 12,400 were air crew. Yet there was no RAAF bomber group within Bomber Command where most Australians were operating, so Australia received little recognition. As the official historian, John Herington, observed, 'few Australians (except air gunners) who arrived [in England] after the launching of OVERLORD [6 June 1944] reached combat units, and some who had arrived earlier still lacked active employment at the end of the war'.[36]

The Australian government had no way of determining whether its forces in Europe were vitally necessary, but they certainly did not contribute to the government's declared aim of giving Australia status at the peace table in the Pacific. Curtin pressed Jones to reduce Australia's contribution to Bomber Command, but Jones claimed that to do so would result in heavier casualties among the remaining forces.[37] On 31 December 1944 there were 34,520 personnel in the navy, 411,321 in the army and 179,544 in the air force.

Command Appointments

One of the chief concerns of Australia's war leaders in the First World War was to ensure that Australians were given higher command appointments in the AIF. In the Second World War, after the death of General Squires in March 1940, there was never any doubt that the army would be commanded by Australians. The same could not be said for the other services. As we have seen, when the CNS, Admiral Colvin, resigned through ill health in February 1941 he was replaced by a British officer, Admiral Royle. Further, the commander of the Australian Naval Squadron, Rear Admiral John Crace, was an RN officer, although he had been born in Australia. At the end of his appointment in August 1942 he was succeeded by another RN officer, Rear Admiral Victor Crutchley, VC. The two senior Australian Navy captains, John Collins and Harold Farncomb, were considered for the appointment, but Royle claimed that while their records and performance had been 'excellent', they still did not have enough experience to command the squadron.[38]

When Royle's term was extended in mid-1943, MacArthur commented that if he had been consulted he would have urged that Collins be appointed CNS instead of granting an extension to Royle. Furthermore, when in early 1944 Admiral Crutchley's term of duty drew to a close, Royle believed that he should be replaced by another RN officer because the Australian contenders were still too junior. The Minister for the Navy, Norman Makin, agreed with Royle, but Curtin did not, and in February 1944 the War Cabinet appointed Collins to replace Crutchley with the rank of commodore. Shedden had advised the War Cabinet that Collins was 44 years old, while the RN officer Lord Mountbatten, when appointed Commander-in-Chief of Combined Operations in February 1942, with the rank of vice-admiral, was only 41.[39]

A successor for Royle was discussed throughout 1944, with the Admiralty vigorously opposing the appointment of Collins on the grounds of lack of experience. Although urged by Shedden that it was 'desirable that we should have Australians in the top position, if possible', Curtin went along with the Admiralty for the time being, but the argument became academic when Collins was badly wounded at Leyte. On 22 October 1944, Curtin told newsmen: 'News came this morning that Collins is wounded in action. How badly no one knows. It may mean the end of our dream of an Australian Navy under an Australian-born Admiral.' To Curtin this was a tragedy, and the government now sought a British officer. On 8 March 1945 the War Cabinet approved the appointment of Vice-Admiral Sir Louis Hamilton RN to succeed Royle as CNS.[40] Collins had to wait until February 1948 until he was appointed, aged 49, as CNS.

As described in the previous chapter, when Air Chief Marshal Sir Charles Burnett had reached the end of his term as CAS, the Minister for Air, Arthur Drakeford, had appointed Air Vice-Marshal George Jones as CAS. Jones was junior to Air Vice-Marshal William

Bostock, commander of RAAF Command, thus triggering a bitter dispute between the two men that was to continue for the rest of the war. Bostock was responsible for RAAF operations, while Jones was responsible for administration of the RAAF.[41]

In an attempt to resolve this damaging problem of divided command, on the advice of Blamey and MacArthur, in March 1943 Curtin decided to abolish the Air Board and to appoint an Air Officer Commanding of the RAAF. He sought to appoint Air Vice-Marshal Peter Drummond, then Deputy Air Officer Commander-in-Chief RAF Middle East. Drummond was an Australian who had served in the Australian Flying Corps in the First World War and had subsequently transferred to the RAF. Although Drummond indicated that he was happy to serve in Australia, the British Air Ministry refused to release him and suggested two other officers.[42]

Not knowing what to do, the government turned to MacArthur for advice. MacArthur claimed that the two proposed officers were 'too old', and the government accepted his advice to continue as before. Drakeford had reservations about MacArthur's role in a matter that he believed was entirely for the government to decide, but Curtin dismissed this complaint, pointing out that MacArthur had consulted him about changes to the commanders of the Allied naval, land and air forces, and he felt bound to consult MacArthur about the appointment of an officer who would be responsible for RAAF operations. Shedden observed that it seemed neither MacArthur nor his air commander, Kenney, wished to have a senior British air officer in the SWPA. And Kenney made his feelings clear: 'except for the feud [between Bostock and Jones] which sometimes was a nuisance, I liked the situation as it was'.[43]

The divided command continued to cause a problem, and when he visited London in May 1944, Curtin consulted Churchill and senior British officials. Two RAF officers were considered for the Australian appointment, Air Marshal Sir Keith Park, who was born in New Zealand and appeared most suitable, and Air Marshal Hugh Saunders, who was born in South Africa. On his return to Australia, Curtin presented his proposal to the War Cabinet, which decided to appoint Park, but MacArthur now told Curtin that because of the increased tempo of operations it 'was no longer necessary to proceed with the proposal'. Shedden pointed out to Curtin that MacArthur was not correct in his claim that the differences between Bostock and Jones were 'now quiet'; rather, the position was 'still unsatisfactory'. He thought that the Americans preferred 'the divided command arrangement, because they can play one side off against the other'. Despite these views, Curtin accepted MacArthur's advice. Shedden was most unhappy with this decision, and made his feelings known in a private memorandum to Curtin: 'Some day there will be an outcry about the relatively poor RAAF effort in the Southwest Pacific Area in relation to the resources allocated to the air effort . . . due to the set up under which it has also been necessary to send senior officers to Europe to get operational experience which should be provided in the Southwest Pacific Area.' As RAAF historian Alan Stephens has pointed out, by this stage the RAAF had four officers—Air Commodores Bladin, McCauley, Scherger and Hewitt—'who had performed with distinction in operational and staff posts', and could have been promoted; but the 'prime minister continued to avoid decisions'.[44]

A Role for the AIF

By October 1944 the Allies were closing the ring around Japan and it seemed likely that Australian forces would be excluded from the main offensives. The government thought it important that Australia maintain an active role in the operations, but its exact nature depended to a large extent on MacArthur. The negotiations with MacArthur over a role for the AIF divisions were to highlight the limitations in Australian strategic decision-making.

Responding to MacArthur's directive to relieve the American divisions in New Guinea, New Britain and Bougainville, Blamey ordered the First Army of four divisions to undertake this task and they began taking over in October. This left the 1st Australian Corps (7th and 9th AIF Divisions) at MacArthur's disposal. The RAAF was to support the Australian forces, while the RAN squadron operated under MacArthur's naval commander. The government had been unable to withdraw its commitment to the air forces in Britain, but arranged for its naval units operating under British command in the Indian Ocean to return to Australian waters.

Four months later, in February 1945, little had changed with regard to the Australians. Although American forces were engaged in large-scale operations in Luzon, the 1st Corps had been out of action for almost a year and Blamey observed that 'a feeling that we are being side-tracked is growing strong throughout the country'. Urged by Blamey and Shedden, on 15 February Curtin told MacArthur that there was 'considerable public criticism of the inactivity' of the Australian forces, and said that it was 'a matter of vital importance to the future of Australia and her status at the peace table . . . that her military effort should be concentrated as far as possible in the Pacific and that it should be on a scale to guarantee her an effective voice in the peace settlement'.[45]

Meanwhile, Blamey learned that MacArthur was planning to use the 6th, 7th and 9th Divisions to undertake operations in Borneo, culminating in an attack on Java. This would involve withdrawing the 6th Division from operations at Aitape in New Guinea. Blamey knew that the chief of staff of the US Army, General Marshall, had told MacArthur 'operations in Borneo would have little immediate effect on the war against Japan', and Blamey deferred any plans to use the 6th Division until they had been considered by the government.[46]

Eventually, on 5 March, MacArthur replied to Curtin saying that he would be using the 7th and 9th Divisions in North Borneo, and was leaving open the possibility of using the 6th Division in Java. On 13 and 14 March, Blamey visited MacArthur in Manila, where he pointed out that although American forces were being retained in the southern Philippines to clear out the Japanese, MacArthur was wishing to withdraw Australian forces from New Guinea. MacArthur argued that he intended to use the Philippines as a base for the invasion of Japan, but Blamey said that if the Australians were withdrawn from New Guinea they would need to return later to complete their task.

On Blamey's advice, Curtin withheld the 6th Division from MacArthur, thereby disrupting MacArthur's plans to capture Java. As MacArthur's biographer D. Clayton James noted, 'it was most fortunate for the lives of the soldiers of the Australian I Corps' that MacArthur did not get 'his way on the Java plan, for that two division invasion could have produced the most tragic blood-bath of the Pacific War'.[47] On 1 May a brigade of the 9th Division landed at Tarakan off the north-east coast of Borneo, and the remainder of the division landed at Brunei on 10 June. While the operations were successful, neither of them shortened the war.

Unnecessary Operations

Two other issues—the Australian First Army's role in New Guinea and Bougainville, and the Balikpapan operation—illustrate the government's difficulty in deciding its strategy in the last months of the war. The operations in New Guinea and Bougainville drew early criticism, but when MacArthur told Curtin in October 1944 that 'if he were doing the job himself, he wouldn't jeopardise a single Australian life in an offensive in these back areas', the prime minister took no further action.[48] Blamey has been criticised for conducting these campaigns, but the decision to conduct them, and any criticism for doing so, should rest with the government, although it must be admitted that Curtin was ill from November 1944 to February 1945.

By April 1945 the First Army's operations were being criticised in parliament and the press as wasting Australian lives. There were also claims that the forces were insufficiently equipped, and the Acting Minister for the Army, Senator James Fraser, had visited the operational area to check on possible equipment shortages. When, on 17 April, Curtin sought MacArthur's views, the general replied that local commanders had considerable freedom of action in the methods they employed. Blamey, however, advised Curtin that he had discussed the campaigns with MacArthur, who had allocated the necessary landing craft for the 6th Division's operations. 'It is therefore a proper claim that these operations meet with General MacArthur's approval.' Belatedly, in parliament on 24 April, Curtin said that the government accepted full responsibility for the operations, but two months earlier he had explained his approach to parliament:

> I make no pretence of being, in any way, a strategist in defence matters. I have a plain and simple rule to which I have adhered. It is that in all matters relating to the operational direction of the war, the sole responsibility shall rest upon the High Command. The duty of the Government consists in allocating to the High Command such forces as it seeks and such equipment as it calls for.[49]

According to Shedden, Curtin was 'somewhat concerned about the reservations which appeared to be indicated' in MacArthur's reply, and wanted to discuss the matter personally, but he again fell ill, and with Deputy Prime Minister Forde and Evatt overseas, the treasurer, Ben Chifley, became acting prime minister. On 7 May, Chifley asked Blamey to attend a War Cabinet meeting to give the government 'fuller information in regard to your plans for the future use of the Australian Forces'. The same day, Chifley wrote to MacArthur that he assumed that the 6th Division's operations met with his approval. Blamey took issue with the view that the operations should not have been undertaken, advising Chifley that 'Any commander, who is prepared to remain with superior forces, equipped to a degree greatly superior to that of the enemy, and who does not bring him to battle rapidly, is deserving of censure.' Replying on 20 May, MacArthur said that although the operations were 'unnecessary and wasteful of lives and resources', it was a matter for the Australian commanders.[50]

By this time, Blamey had serious doubts about the 7th Division's landing at Balikpapan, in south-east Borneo, ordered by MacArthur and scheduled for 1 July. On 16 May he advised the government that if the 7th Division were to land at Balikpapan then Australia would be committed to a 'very large garrison', and he recommended withdrawing the division from the operation.[51]

Chifley and the acting defence minister, Jack Beasley, immediately put Blamey's suggestion to MacArthur, who replied promptly that the Borneo campaign had been ordered by the Joint Chiefs of Staff. To withdraw the 7th Division 'would disorganise completely not only the immediate campaign but also the strategic plan of the Joint Chiefs of Staff'. If the Australian government contemplated withdrawing the division, MacArthur said he would make representations to Washington and London. MacArthur's blunt reply was deceptive. The Joint Chiefs had reluctantly agreed to the Balikpapan operation only because MacArthur had advised that not to carry it out would 'produce grave repercussions with the Australian government and people'.[52] Now the Australians were being told that it had to be carried out because the Joint Chiefs had ordered it. It is hard to see how cancelling the operation would have disorganised completely 'the strategic plan of the Joint Chiefs'.

Shedden received MacArthur's signal in Canberra in the morning of Sunday 20 May. As he recalled later, the ministers were 'scattered in various parts of the Commonwealth', but he consulted Curtin in hospital. In his 'last administrative act relating to the war', Curtin 'had no hesitation in approving the reply' Shedden had drafted. Shedden then read it to Chifley and Beasley by phone and despatched a signal to MacArthur that the government had 'no hesitation in agreeing to the use of the 7th Division as planned'.[53]

On 22 May, Blamey attended a War Cabinet meeting, chaired by Chifley, to consider Australian operations.[54] Questioned closely about the First Army's operations, Blamey said, 'MacArthur was in complete agreement with his plans for operations.' He did not consider the enemy forces were 'strategically impotent' as stated by MacArthur, since they were still operating as organised forces with adequate supplies. The War Cabinet minute did not formally approve Blamey's policy, but Shedden later told Chifley that 'so far as the general question of strategy is concerned it is considered that General Blamey had made a very sound case in justification of the operations which he has been carrying out'.[55]

The War Cabinet then turned to the proposed landing by the 7th Division at Balikpapan, and Blamey explained that he had not agreed with Balikpapan, which was 'a derelict Dutch oilfield'. Blamey said that five Australian divisions were on operations, and if the sixth were to be used there would be no 'flexibility' left. He wanted to be able to release from the army men who had been serving for four or five years. Beasley asked Blamey to consider the government's position; it did not want 'disharmony' with MacArthur, and it would be difficult for the government to 'pull out' of the operation. Blamey pointed out that, with the end of the war in Europe, Australia would have twice as many men on operations in proportion to its population as any other country and he feared some would be left on garrison duty in the Netherlands East Indies. Balikpapan was 'unimportant and should not be undertaken'. (Neither he nor the government had any idea, of course, that the war was to end quickly after the dropping of the atomic bombs on Japan in August.) Finally Shedden, who obviously had a stake in the decision made two days earlier, said Chifley had had no alternative but to send his approval to MacArthur, since to do otherwise would have meant repudiating the government's earlier commitment.

Chifley was deeply disturbed at MacArthur's letter of 20 May, which had stated that the government was in error in construing the provision of landing craft as his approval of the 6th Division's operation, but he did not know quite what to do. Eventually, on 21 July (after the death of Curtin on 5 July and when he had become prime minister), Chifley wrote to MacArthur and reminded him that as commander-in-chief he was responsible for the operation of the forces assigned to him. Australia's only right was to withhold forces, and the government had assumed that 'even within the limits of discretion allowed to subordinate commanders, their plans would be subject to your broad approval'. He regretted that the government was 'greatly embarrassed by your reply. It has publicly defended the wisdom of these operations.'[56] This was the strongest letter written by an Australian prime minister to MacArthur, but the general never deigned to reply.

The operations by the Australians in Borneo differed from those in New Guinea and Bougainville in at least one respect. The Borneo operations had been proposed by MacArthur and were conducted for strategic purposes of doubtful merit. By contrast, the New Guinea and Bougainville operations were not supported by MacArthur, but were conducted for Australian strategic and political purposes. The controversy over the operations was a telling commentary on the shortcomings of Australian strategic decision-making.

The controversy also says much about the key players. MacArthur put US national interests, as well as his own, ahead of Australia's. Curtin found it easier to accept MacArthur's advice than to challenge it, and as he became ill he lacked the drive to maintain a grip on Australian war strategy. Blamey wanted to advance Australia's interests, but was distrusted by MacArthur, Curtin and Shedden, who believed Blamey was advancing his own cause. Shedden, capable and clear-thinking, worked to articulate and promote the government's policy, but, like Curtin, deferred to MacArthur.

The events of 1944 and 1945 had required the Australian government to ask a number of important questions about the use of its forces. Once the direct threat to Australia was removed, and after the Americans took over the main offensive, what should have been the guiding principle for the employment of Australian forces? To what extent should the government have left the employment of the AIF in the hands of Douglas MacArthur? And what about the aircrews in Britain? While the government recognised that it needed to keep troops fighting in the Pacific, it ducked the harder questions. As a junior partner in a coalition war, the Australian government's options were limited, but there is no evidence that it worked hard to find alternatives.

Curtin has been accorded recognition, even by his opponents, as one of Australia's great prime ministers. He unified the Labor Party, rallied Australia in the dark days of 1942, and put aside his party's socialist aims in the pursuit of national unity. His most important contribution to national strategy was his concern to maintain national cohesion. Curtin, however, did not appear to have any overall strategic view of his own, and once MacArthur arrived was content to accept his approach. His major decisions, such as to rely on America, to demand the recall of the AIF and to change the conscription act, were urged on him by his political and military advisers, although the decisions were certainly in accord with his own opinions. Nonetheless, as biographer Lloyd Ross observed: 'It is safer for a country to have a Prime Minister like Curtin than an amateur strategist like some members of the Advisory War Council.'[57]

Curtin's remoteness from responsibility for military strategy is emphasised by the fact that he never visited a battle zone. During the critical fighting in New Guinea, Blamey suggested to Curtin that he might visit Port Moresby, but MacArthur advised against it and he never went. It is difficult to discover any reason why he did not visit New Guinea at a later stage. As far as can be determined, the only time he visited troops in an operational area was when he visited RAAF units in Britain in May 1944. While a prime minister should not seek to interfere with his field commanders, direct contact with his fighting troops reinforces his status as the leader who bears the ultimate responsibility for the success of a campaign. Such visits are important not only for the servicemen, but also for the political leader, who can see for himself the execution of his decisions. Personal contact of this kind is perhaps even more important if the prime minister has never seen battle.

Paul Hasluck has been accused of bias against Curtin for political reasons. Nonetheless, a close study of the documents on Australian strategic policy appears to justify his judgement 'that eventually Curtin, the whole man, will emerge as a greater figure than Curtin the Prime Minister in war-time. In the Prime Ministership he spent himself unreservedly and the labour hastened his end, but it was a time of frustration rather than mastery.'[58]

So what can we conclude about Curtin as war leader and defence minister? In some ways, after MacArthur arrived, Curtin took the easy way by handing over military decision-making to a general. Some might say that given the power of the United States, he had little option, but it is a dangerous practice for any political leader not to take a close interest in operational matters. This is not to suggest that Curtin failed. He was faced with a devilishly difficult situation in dealing with the Americans. In the main, his approach worked, but much could have been done better.

8

'We have not a minute more than three years'

Menzies, Korean War and Malayan Emergency, 1950–55

In mid-1950, less than five years after the end of the Second World War, the Australian Liberal–Country Party government committed military forces to operations in Malaya and Korea. But unlike in the world wars, there was no declaration of war and, once the relatively small forces had been committed, the Australian government was not closely involved in directing their operations. Deploying forces to these conflicts marked the beginning of overseas military deployments that would continue for more than quarter of a century. While the Malayan and Korean commitments were not particularly contentious, they were forerunners to Australia's more controversial involvement in the Vietnam War.

Australia's war leadership during the Malayan and Korean conflicts does not fit the model of the two world wars. The conflicts were part of a wider Cold War, which the prime minister, Robert Menzies, saw as being fought by the Soviet Union through proxies in Korea, Malaya and Indochina, as well as in regions further from Australia. At home, he believed that the Communist Party was acting on behalf of the Soviet Union. Menzies feared that the Cold War was on the brink of turning into a global war in which Europe and the Middle East would be the main theatres, and Australia would be required to deploy forces to the Middle East. Australia therefore needed to strengthen its defences and alliance arrangements, while dealing at home with the threat of subversion by the Communist Party. It is thus difficult to separate war leadership from the broader issues of defence and foreign policy. After the experience of the world wars, this was a new paradigm, but it was, in fact, a foreshadowing of the way war leadership would evolve in the decades to come.

The Cold War was underway well before the Menzies government came to power in December 1949. In January 1949 the Chinese People's Liberation Army captured Beijing, and on 1 October the communist leader, Mao Zedong, proclaimed the People's Republic of China. In August 1949 the North Atlantic Treaty Organization (NATO) was established and the Soviet Union successfully tested its first atomic bomb. In Malaya, the so-called Communist Terrorists were stepping up their activities. Everywhere, it seemed, the communists were on the march.

The Menzies Government

In terms of its war leadership, the Liberal–Country Party government was vastly more experienced than its predecessors at the beginning of the world wars. Menzies had been prime minister for the first two years of the Second World War, and although initially crushed by losing the prime ministership in 1941, he had then formed and built the Liberal Party, as well as refining his leadership style. Arthur Fadden, leader of the Country Party, deputy prime minister and treasurer; Eric Harrison, deputy leader of the Liberal Party, Minister for Defence and Minister for Post-war Reconstruction; Percy Spender, Minister for External Affairs; Richard Casey, Minister for Supply and Development; and Philip McBride, Minister for the Interior, had all been members of the Menzies War Cabinet.

In April 1950, Harrison went to London as resident minister and McBride became acting defence minister. When Harrison returned to Australia in May 1951 he succeeded McBride as Minister for the Interior, and McBride was formally appointed defence minister, retaining the portfolio until December 1958. McBride was a grazier from South Australia who had been a senator from 1937 to 1944 and then been elected to the House of Representatives in 1946. In 1940–41 he had been successively Assistant Minister for Commerce, Minister for the Army and Repatriation, and Minister for Supply and Development and for Munitions. Lieutenant General Sydney Rowell, CGS from April 1950 to December 1954, described McBride as 'a rather dour Scotsman without the charm and affability of Mr Menzies but withal a likeable personality . . . Of all the ministers with whom I had close association, he was by a long street the most dedicated and able administrator.' Menzies called McBride 'my constant friend throughout my life at Canberra'.[1] As in the Second World War, the Ministers for the Navy, Army and Air were responsible for the administration of their service but not for defence policy.

The military advisers were also experienced officers. Vice-Admiral John Collins had been CNS since 1948 and had a distinguished wartime record. As noted above, Rowell became CGS in April 1950, the first Duntroon graduate to reach this position. Although he had been controversially dismissed as Commander New Guinea Force by General Blamey in 1942 (see Chapter 6), he had later worked at the War Office in London before returning to Australia as Vice Chief of the General Staff (VCGS). Air Marshal George Jones he had been CAS since May 1942. He had continued serving after the war and, like the other chiefs, was instrumental in establishing the post-war forces. Because of his seniority Rowell became chairman of the Chiefs of Staff Committee.

Frederick Shedden, wartime secretary of the Department of Defence (also secretary of the War Cabinet and the Advisory War Council), was still in the same appointment. As there was no longer a War Cabinet or an Advisory War Council, and as the prime minister was no longer also the defence minister, Shedden had lost some influence. Menzies tended to look to his own departmental head, Allen Brown, as his principal adviser. Nonetheless, Shedden had still gained some extra power, because in 1948 he had managed to persuade the chiefs (Collins, Sturdee and Jones) to recommend that he be appointed chairman of the Defence Committee, which consisted of him and the three chiefs. Some military officers resented this appointment, but Rowell was unwilling to criticise it too strongly. Rowell thought strategy was best left to those 'who are trained in it, namely the Chiefs of Staff', but saw Shedden as a special case; Australia was 'not likely again to have someone of the calibre and background of Shedden to fill the post'.[2] Perhaps Rowell recalled Shedden fondly because Shedden had saved his career in 1942 when Blamey had wanted to reduce him to the rank of colonel. Shedden played a role in having Rowell appointed VCGS in January 1946 and recommended him as CGS in 1950.

The Minister for External Affairs and his department now had more influence than had been the case when Menzies had first been prime minister. The new Minister for External Affairs, Percy Spender, was intelligent, quick and ambitious to bring changes in External Affairs policy.[3] Under its previous minister, Bert Evatt, the department had grown, and in the late 1940s was led by its young progressive secretary, John Burton. The feud that had developed between External Affairs and Defence, as each struggled to dominate defence and foreign policy in the late 1940s, did not abate with the arrival of a new government. Burton complained to his new minister, Spender, that Defence could not move quickly enough to respond to a changing international situation and that External Affairs was not often informed of Defence activities.[4] Agreeing, Spender complained to Menzies about the unresponsiveness of the Defence organisation.

Spender also complained to the acting defence minister, McBride, about the lack of effective consultation between the departments, and referred to 'a serious geographical separation between the two Departments which is not easily overcome by sparing officers to make frequent visits'. Defence was still in Melbourne while External Affairs was in Canberra. When Burton took extended leave in April 1950, Alan Watt succeeded him as External Affairs secretary. Watt was an experienced career diplomat who had been first secretary at the

Australian Legation in Washington during the war and, more recently, ambassador in Moscow. Watt realised that 'positive efforts had to be made to remove this mutual distrust, and to create an atmosphere of confidence and co-operation between the two Departments'. It was not long before the Cabinet decided that the secretary of External Affairs or his representative should attend meetings of the Defence Committee when it discussed foreign policy issues.[5]

Deploying Forces to Malaya

The Cold War brought an immediate focus on defence and security. While there was no direct external threat to Australia, events suggested that the Soviet Union and its communist acolytes were seeking to dominate the world, both by military action and by fostering internal unrest. In February 1950 the Chinese Communist Party leader, Mao Zedong, and Joseph Stalin of the Soviet Union signed a Treaty of Friendship, Alliance and Mutual Assistance. The 'loss' of China, along with the explosion of the Soviet Union's first atomic bomb, generated intense concern in Washington, and in January 1950 President Harry S. Truman ordered the development of the hydrogen bomb. The Cold War was to dominate Australia's defence and security policies for the next four years.[6]

The government's first initiative was to introduce its promised legislation to ban the Communist Party. In presenting the bill to the House of Representatives on 27 April, Menzies said that Australia was

> not, except in a technical sense, at peace. The Soviet Union has perfected the technique of 'cold war', has accompanied it by the organisation of peace demonstrations designed not to promote true peace but to prevent or impair defence preparations in the democracies . . . We . . . have witnessed the most threatening events in Eastern Europe, in Germany, in East Asia and in South-east Asia.[7]

Banning the Communist Party was a key part in countering the Soviet Union's cold war. The bill passed the House of Representatives on 23 May, but after it was delayed in the Senate, Menzies had it put aside to be reintroduced later in the year.

The initial defence preoccupation was the future of the British Commonwealth Occupation Force (BCOF) in Japan. BOCF had been established soon after the end of the Second World War as part of the larger occupation force provided by the Americans, all under the Supreme Commander for the Allied Powers, General Douglas MacArthur. BCOF included infantry brigades from Australia, New Zealand, Britain and India, as well as two air force wings and shore-based naval personnel, although naval ships from the respective countries did not serve as part of BCOF. The commander-in-chief of BCOF was an Australian officer, the flamboyant and capable Lieutenant General Horace Robertson, who had been appointed in 1946, and was still there in 1950.[8]

The Commonwealth countries provided direction to Robertson through the Joint Chiefs of Staff in Australia, which consisted of the Australian chiefs of staff, supplemented by military representatives from the other countries, based in Australia. Gradually the other countries withdrew their forces from BCOF, which by the end of 1948 consisted primarily of just the understrength 3rd Battalion of the Royal Australian Regiment (3 RAR), and the RAAF's No. 77 (Fighter) Squadron. The Australian Regular Army, recently formed in 1947, had only three infantry battalions, including 3 RAR.[9] The occupation had achieved its aims, and in April 1950 the Australian Army began planning to withdraw its forces from Japan.

The government's first major defence decision concerned the deployment of forces to the British colony of Malaya, where an insurrection had begun in 1948.[10] The insurrection was undertaken by the Malayan Communist Party, whose members were drawn mainly from the Malayan Chinese population. The Australian chiefs of staff had already identified Malaya and Singapore as important to Australia's security. At the request of the British authorities, in July 1948 Prime Minister Chifley approved the despatch to Malaya of 140 submachine guns along with 67,000 rounds of ammunition for use by the Malay police. Australia also later sent radio equipment. But this was the limit of Australia's support; the government tended to see the insurrection as a colonial struggle, and headed off a request from Britain to send troops. Nonetheless, the government's concern about security in the region led to its agreement with Britain and New Zealand to take part in planning for possible operations in the ANZAM (Australia, New Zealand and Malaya) area against an outside threat.

The Malayan Emergency, as it became known, received little attention during 1949, but by April 1950, with the British becoming stretched, discussion appeared in the press about a possible Australian contribution. The Menzies government was concerned that the Malayan insurgency was part of a worldwide communist offensive, and in press conferences, Menzies and his defence minister, Harrison, suggested that Australia might seriously consider a request from Britain for military help. It was soon clear that the Labor Party would oppose such a move, with Labor's Clyde Cameron describing the government's supporters as a 'gang of bloody war-mongers', for seeking to send 'good Labour men [to] be shot in the defence of British capital'.[11]

On 21 April the British government formally asked Australia for aircraft to assist with their operations against the Communist Terrorists in Malaya. Earlier, New Zealand had advised that it wished to withdraw its flight of Dakota transport aircraft from Malaya and had suggested that Australia replace it. The Defence Committee, chaired by Shedden, considered the British request on 27 April, and on the advice of Air Marshal Jones, concluded that the RAAF could provide eight Dakotas for transport tasks and four Lincoln bombers. The committee passed this advice to the government.

When the Cabinet met on 2 May, the ministers were cautious, seeking more details as to how the aircraft would be used. The government wanted to discuss the situation in Malaya with the British Commissioner-General for Southeast Asia, Malcolm MacDonald, who was shortly to visit Australia accompanied by the British Air Officer Commanding Malaya, Air Vice-Marshal Francis Mellersh. During the subsequent discussions with the visitors, Menzies suggested that Australia might send a small group of military officers with experience in jungle warfare to investigate, report and perhaps advise on an appropriate response to the Malayan insurgency. Indicating his careful approach, Menzies ensured that the visitors also met the Opposition leader, Chifley, and his spokesman on external affairs, Bert Evatt. Although the Labor leaders opposed an Australian commitment, they had at least been kept informed. As the official historian, Peter Edwards, observed: 'In 1950 the newly elected Prime Minister was cautious and sensitive, consulting widely.'[12]

Concerned at the apparent delay, on 19 May Shedden wrote to McBride urging a rapid decision, arguing that 'He gives twice who gives quickly.' He added that there were 'important political and psychological advantages to be gained by prompt action', while practical assistance would open 'the way to the reasonableness of a request for information about the conduct of the campaign. If our aid is sought we are entitled to know about things.' During the Second World War, Shedden had struggled to ensure that Australia's voice was heard by British strategic policymakers and, knowing that Menzies shared this view, he did not want to let any opportunity slip. The Cabinet agreed to offer a squadron of Dakotas, but reserved the politically sensitive issue of sending the Lincoln bombers for later discussion. Menzies announced the deployment of the Dakotas in parliament on 31 May. A relatively minor commitment, it was both the first step in Australia's involvement in the Malayan Emergency, and more generally, the first step in basing Australian forces in the near region, which was to last well into the 21st century.[13]

The Middle East

For the moment, this Malayan commitment seemed a diversion from the main issue of long-term strategic planning. The previous year, British and Australian planners had begun considering what forces Australia might send to the Middle East in time of war. This was just precautionary planning, based on the possibility that in a general war the Soviet Union might strike in the Middle East. Although this proposal had not been approved by the Chifley Labor government, the Menzies government was likely to be more sympathetic, but remained to be convinced. In June 1950, the British CIGS, Field Marshal Sir William Slim, arrived in Australia to try to persuade the Australians of the importance of the Middle East, and on 15 June he attended a meeting of the Defence Committee. The committee concluded that in war Australia should accept responsibility for its home defence and also, in conjunction with Britain and New Zealand, for the overall direction and control of operations in the ANZAM area. Plans should be developed for two alternatives: deployment of the first army contingent and an air force task force to the Middle East, with a later force going to Malaya; or deployment of the first contingent to Malaya with a later force going to the Middle East. As in the world wars, Australia would need to raise a special volunteer force for service overseas. Slim reported to Britain that Shedden and the Australian chiefs had 'agreed that Australia's main contribution at the outset of war should be in the Middle East'.[14]

A few days later Slim attended a Council of Defence meeting in Canberra. Chaired by the prime minister, the council consisted of senior government ministers and the members of the Defence Committee. At Menzies' invitation, Shedden explained that while the Labor government had emphasised the Pacific, the Defence Department wanted 'to extend the matter to the Middle East'. Slim then outlined the Middle East's place in British strategy.

'But what about the Pacific?' interjected Spender.

'Nothing terrible can happen there,' replied Slim.

'Except to us,' said Harold Holt, Minister for Labour, National Service and Immigration.

'There is no fear that Australia will be in danger of invasion,' Slim assured them.

Slim seemed to persuade Menzies of the importance of the Middle East, even though Spender, Casey and Holt were against it. As Slim's biographer wrote: 'Though Menzies himself . . . had an acute sense of what was at stake in the Middle East, his colleagues and his country were by now firmly oriented towards the Pacific.' Like his minister, the secretary of External Affairs, Watt, also opposed the Middle

East commitment: 'I did not believe that any Australian government could convince public opinion, in another general war, of the virtue of sending Australian divisions to the Middle East or Europe while Britain diverted her own forces from these areas for the defence of Singapore and Malaya.'[15] The Council of Defence endorsed the Defence Committee's recommendations to develop alternative plans.

Outbreak of the Korean War

The impetus towards planning for the Middle East was suddenly interrupted by the news on 26 June 1950 that North Korea had invaded the Republic of Korea (South Korea). Although the attack came as a surprise, under the Chifley government with its activist external affairs minister, Bert Evatt, Australia had been involved for several years with the problems on the Korean Peninsula. Since the Second World War, Korea had been divided at the 38th parallel between the communist-dominated North, supported by the Soviet Union, and the non-communist South, supported by the United States.[16] In November 1947 the United Nations (UN) had established a Temporary Commission on Korea to assist Korea (which had formerly been a Japanese colony) towards independence. Australia was one of eight countries represented on the commission, which Soviet bloc countries refused to join. Australia and fellow commission member Canada declined to support an election in Korea as the population in the North would be unable to vote. Nonetheless, elections went ahead in May 1948, bringing the authoritarian non-communist President Syngman Rhee to power. He ruthlessly suppressed all opposition.

The United Nations then replaced the Temporary Commission with a commission charged with bringing about the reunification of Korea. Again Australia was involved, but was concerned that the United States was not taking a neutral position. During 1949, South Korea claimed that armed infiltrators were crossing the border from the North, and suggested that the United Nations send military observers to report on these incursions. After much discussion, in

March 1950 the United Nations asked the members of the commission to deploy military observers.

Australia agreed to deploy two observers, Major Stuart Peach and Squadron Leader Ronald Rankin, and they arrived in South Korea at the end of May 1950. They were the only UN observers to reach South Korea before the outbreak of the war, and along with the head of the commission's secretariat, a British official, they undertook a two-week inspection tour of the border, completing their report on 24 June. Thus when the North Koreans poured across the border the following day, they could report to the UN General Assembly that South Korea's forces were deployed in defensive positions, and that North Korea had invaded South Korea. On this evidence, the UN Security Council, which the Soviet Union was boycotting over a separate issue, voted to authorise the use of force to eject the North Koreans from the South. Some authors have claimed that South Korea was planning to attack the North, but the evidence of a North Korean invasion seems indisputable.[17]

Despite Australia's history of previous involvement, when the Cabinet met on 27 June to consider the implications for Australia, there was no thought of becoming further involved. Although Australia had previously been critical of the undemocratic, repressive regime in South Korea, the ministers saw the outbreak of war in Korea in Cold War terms—a communist country invading an allegedly democratic non-communist country. Nonetheless, the Cabinet members believed that the invasion was 'only one phase of Russian aggression and that Australia's primary objection [sic] in the matter of opposing Communism was located in Malaya'.[18] The government therefore decided to send the Lincoln bombers and a team of military advisers to Malaya.

However, with US forces in Korea and Japan, under the command of General MacArthur, hurrying to assist South Korea, pressure soon mounted for Australia to commit forces to operations on the Korean Peninsula.[19] On 28 June, the day the South Korean capital, Seoul, fell to the North Koreans, the Australian government agreed that two Australian ships in Far Eastern waters, the frigate HMAS *Shoalhaven* and the destroyer HMAS *Bataan*, could be included with British ships in evacuating British and American nationals from Korea. The next day, Britain announced that the US authorities could use its ships to support the Republic of Korea and, after a brief consultation, Menzies agreed that the Australian ships could also be made available.

Before long, General MacArthur began pressing to be allowed to use the RAAF's No. 77 (Fighter) Squadron, based in Japan, for operations over Korea, as its long-range Mustang ground-attack fighters would be useful for attacking the advancing North Koreans. On 29 June he asked Lieutenant General Robertson for permission to use the squadron. The appeal was made publicly, which put more pressure on the government, and when a cable arrived from Norman Makin, the Australian ambassador in Washington, suggesting that there was an opportunity to pursue an alliance with the United States, the government saw advantage in making the RAAF squadron available. After discussions between the Departments of Air, Defence and the Prime Minister, Menzies released a statement in the evening of 30 June approving the commitment of the squadron. As Menzies told the British high commissioner, it was essential that the communist 'probe . . . should be resisted . . . If the UN did not make a stand on Korea the damage to the prestige of the democracies would be incalculable.'[20]

The outbreak of the Korean War lent urgency to the government's intention to increase defence preparedness, but it was reluctant to overreact. At the Council of Defence meeting on 5 July, the government endorsed a new three-year defence program and announced the National Service scheme to begin early in 1951 (whereby young men underwent 176 days of compulsory military training after their eighteenth birthday and then served in the Citizen Military Forces (CMF) for five years), but resisted committing army units to Korea.[21] This was the last meeting of the Council of Defence, which was allowed to lapse and was later replaced by a standing committee of Cabinet, the Committee on Defence Preparations, of which Shedden and the chiefs of staff were not members. In view of the commitments to Korea, the government recalled parliament on

6 July, and, despite criticism from some Labor members that parliament had not been consulted, the parliament, including Labor, approved the government's actions, noting that they had been made in support of an appeal by the UN Security Council.

Three days later Menzies began an overseas visit to the United States, Britain and Canada to discuss defence cooperation, the dollar shortage and immigration. Meanwhile, as the North Koreans thrust south in the Korean Peninsula, questions were raised as to whether Australia should send troops. Meeting the British Cabinet and chiefs of staff in London on 17 July, Menzies rejected any suggestion that Australian troops be sent to Korea. Australia had insufficient soldiers, and in the event of a major war Australia would make its best contribution in the Middle East. The Australian Defence Committee agreed that troops should not be sent.[22] But before long, Defence received advice that MacArthur, now UN commander-in-chief in Korea, had asked Robertson for the use of 3 RAR, and Robertson advised the Australian chiefs that the allied position in Korea was deteriorating rapidly. The chiefs concluded that to refuse the request would have a detrimental effect on Australian–American relations, and on the afternoon of 26 July they recommended the commitment of 3 RAR, even though it was understrength and inadequately equipped. It was a poor commentary on Australian defence preparedness that Australia should struggle to provide a battalion when it had had six divisions (more than 40 battalions) in action in 1945. Shedden slipped a note into the safe-hand airmail (carried by airline crews) to McBride in Adelaide, advising him of the recommendation.

Around the same time, Alan Watt, the External Affairs secretary, learned that Britain was about to announce its commitment of ground forces. When he heard of this, Spender, at Moss Vale, southwest of Sydney, believed that Australia had to act quickly if it was not to look like it was meekly following Britain. Menzies was sailing from Britain to the United States and could not be consulted. After discussions with Watt, who had driven from Canberra, Spender telephoned the acting prime minister, Fadden, in Queensland, and McBride (who had not yet received Shedden's note), in Adelaide, and persuaded them to approve the deployment of the battalion. In persuading Fadden, Spender recalled that as members of the War Cabinet in 1941, in the absence of Menzies in London, they had approved the commitment of the AIF to Greece. Fadden announced the commitment a few hours later. Menzies was not pleased when he learned of the decision, but on arriving in New York and after being briefed by Australian officials who had boarded the ship, he emerged to state there were 'good reasons for offering some ground forces for Korea'. By the time he arrived in Washington, Menzies was basking in the approval from US President Truman. According to the official historian, Robert O'Neill, Australia had 'passed through one of its rare significant crises of choice in the conduct of relations with its two major allies'.[23]

Arthur Tange, soon to be secretary of External Affairs, but at this time a senior External Affairs official, who had accompanied Watt to Moss Vale to brief Spender,

> advocated, unsuccessfully, that we make a larger contribution. It was not that I saw any reason for Australian sacrifices to protect the Korean people, governed by a corrupt leader; nor did I see much evidence of spontaneous popular sympathy for this remote [person]. But our memberships of the UN Commission for the Unification of Korea, which Evatt had sponsored and where we were represented by the highly regarded James Plimsoll, gave us a moral as well as a practical duty to come to the aid of the South.[24]

This was never realistic, given that Australia had only one understrength battalion in Korea and the other two battalions in Australia were even less prepared. Australia would now have units from all three services in action on or near the Korean Peninsula. It is difficult to claim that the Australian battalion made a difference in Korea, but the British brigade, of which the battalion was part, played a significant role in the difficult days ahead.

Threat of War

The months following the commitment of Australian troops saw a transformation in Australia's approach to defence. Menzies arrived back in Australia on 23 August convinced that the international situation had become more precarious and that Australia had to respond. That day, Shedden advised McBride that the Soviet Union was seeking to promote communism by all means short of war and argued that 'to win the cold war is therefore the first defence priority and cold war policy must be related to military strength'. Events in Malaya, Indochina and especially Korea showed that the world had 'passed on to an intensified cold war with greater risks of it becoming a hot war overnight'. The possibility of a 'hot war' required 'an acceleration of preparedness for transition to a war footing'. Shedden emphasised the need to continue planning for cooperation with Britain and the United States, to finalise a peace treaty with Japan, to plan for defence production and supply, to organise for civil defence, and to review the work on the War Book (the document setting out actions to be taken on the outbreak of war) so as to coordinate national planning.[25]

The government's new approach was exemplified by its three-year defence program, whose budget was almost double that of the Chifley government. With the assistance of the National Service scheme the target for the part-time CMF was to be 50,000 personnel. The RAN was to build six anti-submarine frigates, to modernise three destroyers and to convert another five to anti-submarine frigates. The RAAF was to obtain 30 additional Vampire aircraft and expand the Citizen Air Force.[26]

Menzies followed these announcements with a series of broadcasts entitled 'A Defence Call to the Nation', on 20, 22 and 25 September and 1 October. Menzies called on Australians to prepare for the possibility of a third world war: 'If the evil day dawns on which the great world struggle begins, we must all be prepared to fight wherever it is essential that the enemy be met and overcome.' He described the need for a larger army and said that volunteer members of the Regular Army and the CMF would now have to undertake to serve overseas, because an army 'raised only for service in Australia would, in all probability, be raised for no service at all. It would be the equivalent of a wooden gun.'[27] For the first time since Federation, the government would be able to send units of the Regular Army overseas without seeking volunteers for a special force.

In his third broadcast, Menzies said that the government would set up a National Security Resources Board 'to examine our civil and military resources and needs, and to make such recommendations to the Government as may be necessary to produce some effective pre-war planning and priorities'. Menzies was to be its chairman and the other members were senior public servants, businessmen and a leading trade unionist.[28]

Between the third and fourth broadcasts, on 28 September Menzies reintroduced the bill to dissolve the Communist Party. As he did when he had first introduced the bill in April, Menzies declared that 'Australia is in a cold war', in that 'Australian lives are being lost in action', and also that there is a 'state of imminent danger of what people might call a hot war'.[29] Parliament passed the Communist Party Dissolution Act in October.

By this time the UN position in Korea had changed dramatically. North Korea's initial advance had pushed the South Korean Army into a pocket around the south-eastern port of Pusan (Busan). However, after a US corps mounted a daring amphibious landing at Inchon (Incheon), near Seoul, on 15 September, the UN forces, including the British brigade (and 3 RAR), drove the North Koreans back across the border between the two Koreas. By November the UN forces were approaching the Chinese border when suddenly the complexion of the war changed. Chinese forces poured into Korea and mounted a heavy and unexpected counteroffensive that bundled the UN forces southwards in disarray. The strategic situation was now more dangerous. If the United States attacked China, a wider war involving the Soviet Union might ensue. These events lent greater urgency to Australia's defence planning.

In January 1951, Menzies attended the Commonwealth Prime Ministers' Conference in London, where he learned that the British prime minister, Clement Attlee, had been working to persuade the Americans not to use an atomic bomb in Korea, and that the Western allies were likely to lose if a war developed with China.[30] In the Second World War, Menzies and Curtin had struggled to obtain a voice in Allied strategic decision-making, and in London in 1951, Menzies again faced this problem. The Korean War was ostensibly being fought by the United Nations, but in reality the United States was in charge. The Commonwealth prime ministers sought to develop a Commonwealth view, to be presented in the United Nations, but this proved difficult, with some countries such as India putting forward ceasefire proposals to be submitted to China without prior conditions.[31]

When the conference turned to the Middle East, Menzies reiterated that plans were to be developed for alternative deployments to either the Middle East or Malaya. Discussing higher military direction in war, the Australians stated that planning for the ANZAM region was being carried out by the Australian chiefs of staff with British and New Zealand representatives. They pointed out that during the Second World War, Australia had 'claimed the right of an effective voice in the Councils at the highest levels'. If, however, Australian forces went to the Middle East they would be assigned to a British commander as in the previous war.[32]

Menzies arrived home in mid-February to be confronted by a serious coal strike. About the same time, the US State Department's special negotiator, John Foster Dulles, arrived in Canberra for discussions with Spender over a draft tripartite treaty between the United States, Australia and New Zealand. Menzies was not involved, and to his surprise and satisfaction, Spender and Dulles initialled the draft treaty that eventually became the ANZUS Treaty.

As soon as Menzies reached Canberra, he began referring to the widespread belief that global war was inevitable, stating that while he did not share this view, the threat of war could not be ignored. The government, he said, would, therefore, be aiming to place Australia on a 'semi-war footing'. Shedden was feeding Menzies his view of the international situation. On 28 February, for example, he advised

Menzies that the main trend of Soviet policy since 1949 was the intensification of the Cold War, marked by 'aggression against South Korea' by North Korea and China, 'cold war operations in Indo-China and Malaya, and subversive activity and a war of nerves against Afghanistan, Persia [now Iran], Greece, Yugoslavia, and Western European countries'. Armaments needed to be built up 'as quickly as possible to meet any contingency that may arise in the immediate future . . . The public mind, which has habitually thought in terms of peace and war, must be educated to an understanding of the pattern of a prolonged twilight period which is neither one nor the other.'[33]

On 7 March, Menzies told parliament that the democracies had no more than three years to make defence preparations that alone could avert war. 'It is my solemn belief that we have not a minute more than three years at the best.' Menzies undertook to increase the strength of the services from 65,000 to a total mobilisation strength of 183,000 by the end of 1953, and to double direct defence expenditure in the next financial year.[34]

Meanwhile, on 9 March the High Court ruled that the Communist Party Dissolution Act was invalid under the Constitution, and Menzies asked the governor-general to approve a double dissolution of both houses of parliament with a general election to be held on 28 April. It is difficult to know whether Menzies deliberately over-emphasised the possibility of a global war to win the election or whether he genuinely believed in the likelihood of such a war. Either way, the Menzies government won the election and secured control of the Senate. Menzies would later initiate a referendum to ban the Communist Party, but the nation voted no.

Further Commitments

Between February and May 1951, Defence considered several requests from the United States to contribute additional forces to Korea. On 10 May the Defence Committee declined to recommend sending an additional battalion because the army was still well short of its target strength. Next day, Shedden advised Menzies that Australia could not afford to offend the United States 'as the main buttress of the defence of the democracies'. Because of Britain's extensive commitments in Europe, the Middle East and the Far East, it did not have the strength to help in the Pacific. A closer link with the United States was 'imperative', so that Australian forces could be deployed to the Middle East while reassuring the public that there was no 'risk to local security'. Although the Defence Committee had pointed out the military objections to extending Australian commitments in Korea, Shedden thought that 'the political considerations of Australian-American relations are very weighty and that we must keep with the Americans, short of imperilling the development of our military potential'.[35]

As this indicated, the prime issue was the extent to which Australia should plan on sending forces to the Middle East, and this was the subject of a Commonwealth Defence Ministers' conference held in London in June 1951. As expected, the British defence minister, Emanuel Shinwell, strongly supported by Field Marshal Slim, urged Australia to commit forces to the Middle East. McBride resisted, but on his return to Australia asked the Defence Committee for its views. The Defence Committee saw advantages in stationing token forces in the Middle East, but, because of manpower shortages, concluded that not even a single battalion could be provided before March 1953. It would only be possible to provide a fighter wing of two RAAF squadrons.[36]

Before the government could consider this advice, it received a further request from President Truman for more troops for Korea. The Defence Committee advised that there was no military necessity, while the provision of an extra battalion would severely disrupt the army's long-term development plan. By this time Casey had succeeded Spender as external affairs minister. (Spender had resigned to become Australian ambassador in Washington.) In Cabinet on 25 September, Casey defeated McBride, arguing the need to encourage the alliance with the United States, and the government decided to send a second infantry battalion to Korea. During that month the ANZUS Treaty was finally signed in Washington. Also that month, at a meeting in Hawaii, Admiral Collins concluded an agreement with the US Commander-in-Chief Pacific, Admiral Arthur Radford, providing for peacetime naval liaison, naval planning and provision for security of sea communications in the Pacific.[37]

Defence had its own victory over External Affairs, on 4 December 1951, when Cabinet, attended by Shedden and the service chiefs, agreed to commit army and air force contingents to the Middle East in time of war, and to maintain two RAAF fighter squadrons there in time of peace. Casey had argued that 'no matter how anxious we were to co-operate in the defence of the Middle East, public opinion simply would not allow the despatch of Australian troops to the Middle East if the present running sore in Malaya did not improve'. But he was unsuccessful. Rowell explained later that 'after three hours of heavy battling we succeeded in getting agreement on the Middle East as priority No 1'. Early in March 1952, Menzies announced that No. 78 (Fighter) Wing would be deployed to the Middle East. Malta would be the wing's home base, and it began to deploy there in July 1952.[38]

Although Australia had forces fighting in Korea and Malaya, and had just agreed to send forces to the Middle East, Menzies had not considered it necessary to form a War Cabinet as in the Second World War. As noted earlier, he had formed the National Security Resources Board in December 1950, but it consisted mainly of bureaucrats rather than ministers. In view of is claim that it needed to prepare for a major war within three years, and its expanding military commitments, the government needed to step up the purchase of military equipment. In response, on 20 August 1951 Menzies formed the Cabinet Committee on Defence Preparations to examine and approve the armed forces equipment program.[39] Menzies chaired the committee, which included the treasurer, Sir Arthur Fadden, the Minister for Defence, Philip McBride, the Minister for Defence Production, Eric Harrison, the Minister for National Development, Senator William Spooner, the Minister for Supply, Howard Beale, and the Minister for the Interior and Minister for Works and Housing, Wilfrid Kent Hughes. The service ministers attended when matters affecting their departments were being considered.

The committee first met on 23 August, but at this stage formal procedures had not been established, and the first formal meeting was held on 11 September.[40] With key senior ministers attending, the committee was able to approve the construction of defence facilities and the purchase of equipment. The committee continued to meet, although with decreasing frequency, until 1959. When approving equipment purchases the committee needed to consider the strategic and defence policy implications, but high policy issues were still referred to the full Cabinet.

Higher Command in Korea

The decision to deploy a second battalion to Korea brought a new focus on the higher command of the Commonwealth forces in Korea, complicated because the RAN's ships and the infantry battalion operated as part of British forces, which in turn were under the control of US commanders, and the RAAF squadron operated as part of a US force. In an effort to provide an element of control by the home governments, General Robertson, commander-in-chief of BCOF, was also appointed Commander-in-Chief British Commonwealth Forces Korea. He not only commanded the British Commonwealth administrative base in Japan, and had administrative responsibility for the Commonwealth forces in Korea, but was also required to interest himself 'in the operational tasks allotted to the United Kingdom, Australian, New Zealand and Canadian Forces'.[41] His higher direction came from the Joint Chiefs of Staff in Australia, which, as noted earlier, consisted of the Australian chiefs, augmented by military representatives located in Australia from the other Commonwealth countries. However, as the British were not willing to entrust their interests to an Australian officer, they appointed Air Vice-Marshal Cecil Bouchier as their representative at MacArthur's headquarters. Robertson would be succeeded in turn by Lieutenant General William Bridgeford in late 1951, and by Lieutenant General Henry Wells, a future Australian CGS, in 1953.

The Commonwealth's most important operational position was the commander of the 1st Commonwealth Division, which had been

Prime Minister Joseph Cook (right) beside Sir Ronald Munro Ferguson on the latter's arrival in Melbourne to take up his appointment as governor-general, 18 May 1914. The governor-general would play an influential role in the management of Australia's war effort. (State Library of Victoria)

Prime Minister Andrew Fisher (third on left) and his party during a visit to an army camp in his home state, Queensland, in late 1914. Fisher had become prime minister on 17 September 1914. His predecessor, Joseph Cook, had authorised the raising of the AIF, and Fisher supported it. (Poulsen Studios, State Library of Queensland)

Sir George Reid, Australian high commissioner to Britain, visiting the AIF at Mena, Egypt, in December 1914. With him are Lieutenant General Sir John Maxwell (centre), commander of the British troops in Egypt, and Major General William Bridges (right), commander of both the AIF and the 1st Australian Division. (C.E.W. Bean, AWM: G01600)

Major General James Gordon Legge on RMS *Mooltan* in May 1915. He was heading for the Middle East to take command of the 1st Australian Division after the death of General Bridges. (AWM: C01011)

Prime Minister Billy Hughes with the commander of the 1st Anzac Corps, Lieutenant General Sir William Birdwood, at Birdwood's headquarters, France, June 1916. (Bede George Donald Tongs, AWM: G01534B)

Andrew Fisher, Australian high commissioner (left), with Senator George Pearce, Australian Minister for Defence, in London in 1919. Pearce had gone to London to supervise the repatriation of Australian soldiers. Fisher was a former prime minister who had resigned in 1915 to take up his appointment in London. (J. Borwick, AWM: P02667.017)

Prime Minister Billy Hughes (centre) with the commander of the Australian Corps, Lieutenant General Sir John Monash (second on right), Picardy, France, 14 September 1918. On the left is Brigadier General Edwin Tivey, commander of the 8th Infantry Brigade, and on the right Thomas Marlowe, editor of the British *Daily Mail.* (AWM: EO 3851)

War Cabinet meeting, Melbourne, 1940. From the left, John McEwen (Minister for External Affairs), Sir Frederick Stewart (Minister for Supply), Geoffrey Street (Minister for the Army), Archie Cameron (Minister for Commerce and the Navy), Robert Menzies (prime minister and Minister for Defence Coordination), Frederick Shedden (secretary of the War Cabinet), Billy Hughes (attorney-general), Percy Spender (treasurer) and Senator Hattil Foll (Minister for the Interior). (Argus Newspaper Collection of Photographs, State Library of Victoria)

Prime Minister Robert Menzies with the Chief of the Air Staff, Air Marshal Sir Charles Burnett, visiting RAAF units at Archerfield, Brisbane, 1940.
(John Francis Jackson, AWM: P12424.009)

Prime Minister Robert Menzies with Frederick Shedden (left) and General Thomas Blamey (second on right), Tobruk, Libya, February 1941, during Menzies' visit to the Middle East.
(George Silk, AWM: 005836)

Advisory War Council meeting, Canberra, 19 November 1940. From the left, John Beasley, Norman Makin, Frank Forde (deputy leader of the Opposition), John Curtin (leader of the Opposition), Robert Menzies (prime minister and Minister for Defence Coordination), Billy Hughes (attorney-general and Minister for the Navy), Percy Spender (Minister for the Army), Arthur Fadden (treasurer) and Harold Holt (Minister for Labour and National Service). Forde, Curtin, Menzies, Hughes, Fadden and Holt were all, at one time, prime minister of Australia. As Minister for External Affairs in 1951 Spender negotiated the ANZUS Treaty. (Argus Newspaper Collection of Photographs, State Library of Victoria)

Lieutenant General Sir Thomas Blamey, commander of the 2nd AIF and 1st Australian Corps (left), with his chief operational staff officer, Brigadier Sydney Rowell, describing troop movements to the Minister for the Army, Percy Spender, during the minister's visit to the Middle East, 2 January 1941. Spender reported on this tour in the Advisory War Council on 5 February 1941. (George Silk, AWM: 004852)

Prime Minister Robert Menzies speaking at a press conference in London on 21 February 1941. Seated at the table on the far right is Frederick Shedden, secretary of the Australian Department of Defence. Menzies had come to London to seek reinforcements for Malaya. He had previously visited Australian troops in Libya, which is shown on his map.
(Records of Robert Menzies, National Library of Australia, MS 3939 box 342, series 9, folder 5)

Prime Minister John Curtin speaking at a Liberty War Loan rally in Martin Place, Sydney, on 18 February 1942. Seated behind him are (from the left) John Beasley (Minister for Supply and for Shipping), Alderman Stanley Crick (Lord Mayor of Sydney), Senator William Ashley (postmaster-general and Minister for Information), and Billy Hughes and Arthur Fadden (both former prime ministers and members of the Advisory War Council). The next day the War Cabinet demanded that the 1st Australian Corps return to Australia. (AWM: 042769)

General Douglas MacArthur, Commander-in-Chief Southwest Pacific Area, at the Advisory War Council, Canberra, 26 March 1942. On his left are the prime minister, John Curtin, the leader of the Country Party, Arthur Fadden, and the treasurer, Ben Chifley. MacArthur told Curtin, 'Mr Prime Minister, we two, you and I, will see this thing through together . . . You take care of the rear and I will handle the front.' (AWM: 042925)

From the left, the Minister for the Army, Frank Forde, General Douglas MacArthur and General Thomas Blamey, Commander-in-Chief Australian Military Forces, on their arrival at Port Moresby, New Guinea, on 12 October 1942. It was the first visit to New Guinea by Forde and MacArthur. (Clifford Bottomley, AWM: 013427)

Top left: Prime Minister John Curtin inspecting troops in Perth on 3 November 1942 before they marched through the city in support of the government's £100 million Austerity Loan campaign. This is one of the few occasions when Curtin was photographed with troops. (AWM: 028738)
Top right: Prime Minister John Curtin with Group Captain Hughie Edwards VC, DSO, DFC, an Australian serving with the RAF, at RAF Station Binbrook, Lincolnshire, May 1944—perhaps the only time Curtin visited Australian servicemen in an operational area. (AWM: SUK12677)

Commonwealth Prime Ministers' Conference, London, May 1944. From the left, W.L. Mackenzie King (Canada), Field Marshal Jan Smuts (South Africa), Winston Churchill (United Kingdom), Peter Fraser (New Zealand) and John Curtin (Australia). Curtin tried unsuccessfully to establish guidelines for Commonwealth cooperation, but rejected proposals for a Commonwealth force to be based in Australia. (John Curtin Prime Ministerial Library. Records of the Curtin Family. JCPML00376/77)

Prime Minister Robert Menzies, accompanied by Lieutenant General Sir Horace Robertson, Commander-in-Chief British Commonwealth Occupation Force, inspecting Australian troops at Kure, Japan, on 16 August 1950. The following month the troops deployed to Korea to begin operations as part of the UN force. (Claude Rudolph Holzheimer, AWM: 146505)

The Australian Minister for Air and the Navy, William McMahon, pointing during an inspection of the 28th Commonwealth Brigade, Korea, November 1952. With him (from the left) are Lieutenant General William Bridgeford, Commander-in-Chief British Commonwealth Forces Korea, and Major General Michael West, Commander of the British Commonwealth Division. (Philip Oliver Hobson, AWM: HOBJ3795)

Prime Minister Robert Menzies inspecting the RAAF's No. 77 Squadron at Butterworth air base, Malaya, in December 1959. In the background are the squadron's Sabre jet fighters. Menzies is accompanied by the commander of No. 78 Wing, Group Captain Glen Cooper. The Malayan Emergency formally ended six months later. (NAA: A1775, RGM197)

Prime Minister Harold Holt discussing operations with the commanding officer of the 1st Battalion of the Royal Australian Regiment, Lieutenant Colonel Alex Preece, at Bien Hoa, South Vietnam, 23 April 1966. With him are Lieutenant General Sir John Wilton, Chief of the General Staff (left), and Colonel David Jackson, Commander Australian Army Force Vietnam. (A. Preece, AWM: P01487.001)

Top left: Air Chief Marshal Sir Frederick Scherger (right) handing over to Lieutenant General Sir John Wilton as chairman of the Chiefs of Staff Committee, 18 May 1966. Between them are the Defence secretary, Sir Edwin Hicks, and the Minister for Defence, Allen Fairhall. (Jeffrey Graham Sebastian, AWM: CNB/66/25/3)

Top right: Lieutenant General Thomas Daly, Chief of the General Staff (right), with the Commander, 1st Australia Task Force, Brigadier David Jackson, at Nui Dat, South Vietnam, September 1966. (AWM: FOR/66/0780/VN)

The Minister for the Army, Malcolm Fraser, examining an M79 grenade launcher during a visit to a training unit near Da Nang, South Vietnam, in June 1966. With him (from the left) are the secretary of the Department of the Army, Bruce White, Major General Ken Mackay, Commander Australian Force Vietnam, a Montagnard leader and Captain Vin Murphy of the Australian Army Training Team. (Darrell Colin Ford, AWM: FOR/66/0543/VN)

The Minister for Defence, Allen Fairhall (left), examining an L5 105mm pack howitzer of 103 Field Battery during a visit to Nui Dat, South Vietnam, in November 1966. Fairhall was Minister for Defence from January 1966 to November 1969.
(Gabriell Carpay, AWM: P01404.004)

Prime Minister John Gorton greeting soldiers at the 1st Australian Task Force base at Nui Dat, South Vietnam, during his visit in June 1968. Gorton told the soldiers that the government and 90 per cent of the Australian people supported them.
(William Alexander Errington, AWM: ERR/68/064/VN)

Major General Robert Hay, Commander Australian Force Vietnam (centre), talks with Sir Henry Bland, secretary of the Department of Defence, soon after Bland arrived in Saigon for a three-day tour in South Vietnam in October 1969. General Sir John Wilton was annoyed that Bland discussed military matters with the US commander in Vietnam.
(Brian Edwin L'Estrange, AWM: LES/69/0685/VN)

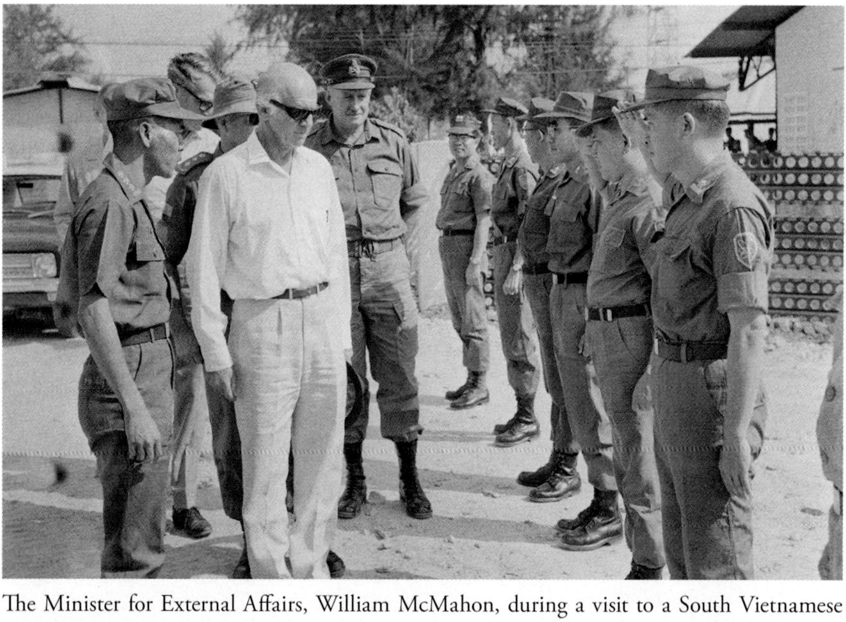

The Minister for External Affairs, William McMahon, during a visit to a South Vietnamese medical facility in Vung Tau, built as an Australian civil affairs project, April 1970. The Australian officer is Major General Colin Fraser, Commander Australian Force Vietnam. A year later Australian Army civic action became a political issue, resulting in McMahon replacing John Gorton as prime minister. Within a few months McMahon announced Australia's withdrawal from Vietnam. (John Geoffrey Fairley, AWM: FAI/70/0252/VN)

Newly appointed Australian Minister for Defence John Gorton holding a drink while speaking with soldiers during a visit to the 1st Australian Task Force, South Vietnam, in March 1971. Gorton had voted himself out of the position of prime minister earlier in the month. (Philip John Errington, AWM: PJE/71/0140/VN)

Prime Minister Bob Hawke greeting Captain Chris Ritchie, Commanding Officer of HMAS *Brisbane*, in Brisbane on 19 April 1991, after the ship returned from the Gulf War. On the right is Vice-Admiral Ian MacDougall, Chief of Naval Staff. (Fred Adler, AWM: P03654.081)

Return to Australia of the Defence Intelligence Organisation (DIO) team that had served at Riyadh, Saudi Arabia, during the Gulf War, March 1991. Third on the left is Major General John Baker, Director DIO, standing beside Senator Robert Ray, Minister for Defence. On the far right is General Peter Gration, Chief of the Defence Force. (AWM: P02446.001)

Australia's military chiefs and senior officials, who played key roles in planning the country's part in the invasion of Iraq, during the visit of the chairman of the US Joint Chiefs of Staff, General Richard B. Myers (who is seated second on right, and accompanied by three of his staff), in January 2004. Seated with Myers are (from the left) Vice-Admiral Russ Shalders, Vice Chief of the Defence Force; and General Peter Cosgrove, Chief of the Defence Force. The Australians in the back row are (from second on left) Shane Carmody, Deputy Secretary Strategic Policy; Ron Bonighton, Deputy Secretary Intelligence and Security; Air Marshal Angus Houston, Chief of Air Force; Vice-Admiral Chris Ritchie, Chief of Navy; and Lieutenant General Peter Leahy, Chief of Army. (Department of Defence, 2004_S025_049.jpg)

Prime Minister John Howard (second on right) and the Minister for Defence, Senator Robert Hill (second on left), during a visit to the Defence Signals Division during the Iraq War, 24 March 2003. With them are General Peter Cosgrove, Chief of the Defence Force, and Ric Smith, secretary of the Department of Defence.
(WO2 Gary Ramage, Department of Defence, JPAU24MAR03GR09.jpg)

Prime Minister John Howard with Brigadier Maurie McNarn during a visit to the headquarters of the Australian contingent in Qatar on 9 May 2003, soon after the end of the Iraq War. Howard was on a visit to thank the Australian forces for their effort during the war.
(JC, Department of Defence, 2004_S1157_02.jpg)

formed in July 1951 and brought together the 28th Commonwealth Brigade (including 3 RAR), the British 29th Brigade and the Canadian 25th Brigade, with support troops, including some from India and New Zealand. The commander of the division was a British officer, Major General James Cassels. When 1 RAR arrived in Korea in June 1952, joining with 3 RAR and two British battalions in the 28th Brigade, an Australian officer, Brigadier Thomas Daly, took command of the brigade. He was later succeeded by Brigadier John Wilton. Both Daly and Wilton were later to become CGS, with Wilton also being appointed chairman of the Chiefs of Staff Committee.[42]

Influencing the Conduct of the War

With these arrangements, Australia's political leaders had only a very limited capacity to influence Australian operations in Korea. Menzies did not visit Korea, although he visited Japan in August 1950 when he inspected 3 RAR soldiers about to depart for Korea, members of No. 77 Squadron (accompanied by Air Marshal Jones), and the ship's company of HMAS *Bataan*. There is no evidence that McBride visited Korea during the war, but the Minister for the Army, Josiah Francis, inspected conditions and equipment of Australian Army units when he visited Korea in December 1951 and January 1952. On his return he warned that Australia could expect to keep troops there for a considerable time. The Minister for Air and the Navy, William McMahon, visited Korea in November 1952. The Minister for External Affairs, Richard Casey, accompanied by Alan Watt, visited 3 RAR in August 1951, but when he lectured the soldiers on the RAAF's operations in Malaya, the troops became restive and Watt 'acted quickly to extricate him before the situation became worse'.[43]

The service chiefs also visited their forces in Korea: General Rowell in May 1952 and May 1953; Vice-Admiral Collins in August 1952; and the new CAS, Air Marshal Sir Donald Hardman, in April 1952. When Air Marshal Jones retired after ten years as CAS in January 1952, Menzies had appointed Hardman, an officer of the RAF, as

CAS. Menzies' decision caused resentment in the RAAF, but in fact Hardman would prove to be an outstanding CAS. On his return from Korea, Rowell provided an extensive report in Melbourne's *Argus* newspaper. Collins returned convinced that the war was justified: 'It is not a vain, purposeless, relatively insignificant backyard brawl,' he told reporters. 'It is a real war, one that had already helped to support and demonstrate the purposes and ideals of democracy.'[44] These visitors could not substantially influence the operations in Korea, but they returned better informed for when matters of high policy were discussed in Canberra.

It was much easier for politicians and service chiefs to visit their forces on operations than in earlier wars. Aircraft were available, and because Korea was a limited war there was no military threat while flying from Australia to Japan. The static nature of the war in Korea after mid-1951 reduced the danger of becoming embroiled in major operations. It is surprising then that neither Menzies nor McBride visited Korea to familiarise themselves with conditions there.

Negotiations towards an armistice began in mid-1951 and continued for two years. Australia was not directly involved, although the Australian ambassador in Washington, Spender, worked assiduously to find out what was being proposed. James Plimsoll, the Australian representative on the UN Commission for the Unification and Rehabilitation of Korea, maintained close relations with President Syngman Rhee. As the official historian, Robert O'Neill, observed, 'the initiative lay in United States hands and even the British made little impact on United Nations Command policy. It is not surprising, therefore, that Australia achieved no significant influence in the opening phase of negotiations.'[45]

One of the sticking points in negotiations was President Truman's insistence that UN Command would only accept the voluntary repatriation of prisoners of war. The Chinese were demanding forcible repatriation, obviously concerned that Chinese and North Korean prisoners might choose to stay in South Korea. On the other hand, with voluntary repatriation the communists might force prisoners held by them to say that they did not want to be repatriated. Menzies saw the danger of voluntary repatriation, and indeed argued that if the alternative was to continue the war, forcible repatriation should be accepted. To press his point, he could either exert diplomatic pressure on the United States, seek support from UN allies or, as a final step, threaten to withdraw the Australian forces. This radical move 'would have caused a major crisis in Australian-American relations while the ANZUS alliance was still at an early stage of development'. Menzies therefore chose to do nothing, and thus for the final year of the war the Australian forces in Korea were fighting to maintain the principle of voluntary repatriation while their government privately had major reservations about it.[46]

Eventually a compromise was reached over the repatriation of prisoners, but the negotiations took another year with the ceasefire taking effect on 27 July 1953. The Korean War is often described as the 'forgotten war', and many soldiers who fought there believed that they were not given adequate recognition. By comparison with the world wars, Australia's contribution was relatively small. Nonetheless, the soldiers had fought in a major war in which about half a million South Koreans and more than 33,000 Americans were killed, along with about 1.5 million Chinese and North Koreans. It was largely a ground war, and of the 339 Australians killed, 293 were from the battalions, which also had 1220 wounded and 23 taken prisoner. No. 77 Squadron lost 37 men killed while flying and seven taken prisoner. The squadron lost thirteen Mustangs and 46 Meteors, mostly to ground fire. As well as deploying frigates and destroyers on rotation, mainly involved in shore bombardment, the RAN also deployed the aircraft carrier HMAS *Sydney* for five months, with its aircraft conducting ground attacks over North Korea.

Robert O'Neill concluded that because the United States made the major decisions, 'Australia's influence on the conduct of the war was essentially of a minor nature'. More broadly, 'the Korean war helped set the course of Australia's foreign and defence polices for the following twenty years, if not longer'. During the war the United States, Australia and New Zealand signed the ANZUS Treaty, which was to remain a cornerstone of Australian strategic policy for the next 70 years. In terms of war leadership, the Australian government learned 'to manage a broader array of problems, many of which had widely differing priorities'. Although the Cabinet always played a key role, on 'several occasions urgent decisions were taken after consultations between the Prime Minister and the Ministers of External Affairs and Defence'. In all this, 'Menzies' authority was paramount'.[47] In the main, the Australian government reacted as issues developed, rather than trying to pursue an overall strategic policy.

Focus on South-East Asia

By mid-1952, a year before the armistice in Korea, the Australian government was gradually changing its strategic policy. In May and June 1952, Menzies, accompanied by his departmental head Brown, visited London, Washington and Ottawa to discuss defence and finance issues, and while they were away Casey delivered a speech in parliament in which he emphasised the strategic importance of South-East Asia to Australia; as O'Neill argued, this 'marked a turning point in Australian strategic policy'. In July, soon after they returned to Australia, Brown suggested to Menzies that plans be prepared to deploy forces to South-East Asia rather than to the Middle East, and Menzies asked McBride to prepare these plans. Menzies' overseas trip was generally disappointing in achieving defence arrangements with Britain and the United States, but he tried to put the best gloss on it by claiming, on his return, that Australia was better prepared to defend itself than ever before, and that the ANZUS pact was 'the greatest step' in Australia's history.[48]

Spender, who was working hard to cement the ANZUS pact, secured American agreement that the first meeting of the ANZUS Council be held in Hawaii in August 1952. The Australian delegation, headed by Casey and including Spender, Shedden, Watt and senior Australian Defence officials, hoped to initiate arrangements for detailed planning, but the Americans were reluctant. Dean Acheson, US Secretary of State, took a pragmatic stance and advised Truman that Australia and New Zealand 'suffered from a paucity of knowledge of what was going on and faulty appreciations of current situations. They felt remote, uninformed, and worried by the unknown. So Admiral Radford . . . and I decided that instead of starving the Australians and New Zealanders, we would give them indigestion.' Acheson wrote later: 'For two days we went over every situation in the world, political and military, with the utmost frankness and fullness. At the end they were very happy with political liaison through the council and military planning through the Commander in Chief Pacific.'[49] The important point was that the meeting had been held at all and, much to their annoyance, without British involvement or presence.

One development of note was Britain's successful explosion of an atomic bomb in the Montebello Islands off the coast of Western Australia in October 1952. Menzies had agreed to Britain's test without consulting or informing his Cabinet. In late November, at McBride's direction, the Defence Committee began preparing a paper entitled 'A Strategic Basis of Australian Defence Policy', which became the first of similar triennial papers prepared within Defence for the next 40 years. The report concluded that the threat of global war had receded but that the possibility of Australia being involved in 'cold war' or 'limited war' conflicts had increased, and greater priority had to be given to South-East Asia.[50]

Defence figured prominently when Menzies attended the next Prime Ministers' conference, held in London in June 1953, immediately after the coronation of Queen Elizabeth II. Churchill, Menzies and the New Zealand prime minister, Sidney Holland, held separate discussions on Pacific defence. Britain wanted to be part of ANZUS and doubted the utility of the ANZAM arrangements, but because the Americans were resisting any attempt to broaden the ANZUS pact, Churchill suggested a new Pacific pact that would include Britain and probably France. Menzies commented that Australia could not 'give up the substance for the shadow'. The British chiefs suggested, and Menzies agreed, that one of their number should visit Australia and New Zealand for further discussions. Menzies drew attention to the danger that would arise in the Far East following a likely armistice in Korea. In response, in late June, the British defence minister, Lord Alexander, advised Menzies that Britain proposed forming a Far East Strategic Reserve, to be located in Malaya. If Australia joined with Britain and New Zealand they could 'make an arrangement which would effectively safeguard our Commonwealth interests in the cold war'.[51]

Soon after the armistice in Korea on 27 July 1953, the Defence Committee generally endorsed the British proposals, but noted that it would take some time to withdraw Australian forces from Korea. In due course Australia could provide a destroyer for a full-time tour of duty, an aircraft carrier from time to time, an infantry battalion group, a bomber squadron and possibly a fighter squadron.[52] For many years Shedden and the Australian chiefs had sought to give top priority to the defence of the Middle East, but after the strategic review at the end of 1952 (which had concluded that the threat of global war had receded) they had refocused their attention on South-East Asia. They now had to persuade the British.

Between 24 August and 3 September, Australian, British and New Zealand planners considered various options for coordinating defence policy, but the crucial decisions were to be made when the CIGS, Field Marshal Sir John Harding, visited Australia in October. On 15 October 1953, the day Harding arrived, Britain exploded its first operational atomic bomb near Woomera in South Australia. The event added additional spice to attempts to improve Australian–British defence relations.

Shedden chaired the meetings in Melbourne between 19 and 21 October. Those taking part were Harding and Major General Arthur Shortt, head of the British Service Liaison Staff; the three New Zealand chiefs of staff; the three Australian chiefs (Rowell, Collins and Hardman); and Watt from External Affairs. The conference concentrated on the threat in South-East Asia, noting that the situation in Indochina was 'extremely brittle'. It was vitally important to maintain a presence in Malaya and to block any advance into that country. Australia's primary objective in the event of global war would therefore be the security of Malaya, and priority in planning would be given to the deployment of Australian land and air forces to the Malayan area. ANZAM would be preserved as a regional arrangement and in war a Commander-in-Chief ANZAM Region might be required. In the meantime, strategic direction would be exercised by the ANZAM chiefs of staff. Note was taken of possible contributions to the Far East Strategic Reserve. The Defence Committee's major success was to secure British agreement to continuing the ANZAM arrangement, and to downplay the Middle East.[53]

It was several months before the Australian government could consider all the conference's recommendations, and the decision to send a force to Malaya was delayed, but the conference marked a major change in Australian defence policy. It was the beginning of the strategic policy known as Forward Defence.

There were other indicators of change. The National Security Resources Board had failed as an economic planning body and ceased to exist about the end of 1953. Also, at midnight on 31 December 1953 the Defence Preparations Act expired. It signified that the government considered the immediate danger of war to have passed.[54]

The Cold War had dominated the Menzies' government's first four years. Forces had been deployed to Malaya, Korea and Malta. Plans had been developed for further deployments to the Middle East. The National Service scheme had been initiated and the defence program had been expanded. By the end of 1953, however, the focus was moving towards South-East Asia rather than global war, and the defence program was slowing down. In all these developments, Menzies remained the key decision-maker. As Arthur Tange, who had succeeded Watt as External Affairs secretary, recalled:

> Menzies was the pillar to whom we turned when crises demanded a prompt response. He was resident in Canberra and sought the advice of officials methodically, and of relevant Ministers when they were available to meet with him. When Parliament was sitting, these meetings occurred not in the Cabinet sub-committee but around Menzies' desk, often late at night. Generally the Ministers for Defence and External Affairs would be present along

> with the Secretaries of the Prime Minister's and External Affairs Departments, but seldom the Secretary of Defence or a Service Chief because of their isolation in Melbourne.[55]

Sydney Rowell, CGS from April 1950 to December 1954, found that Menzies

> did not want courtiers who would give easy answers. When he asked for advice he expected, and was entitled to receive, a frank answer, even if it ran counter to his own point of view . . . Quite apart from his great skill and penetrating brain in debate and conference he had a marvellous grasp of strategy and all its implications. This quality enabled him to take pure straight military advice at its true value and to see clearly the extent to which that advice had to be modified to meet the requirements of diplomacy, economics and other material matters.[56]

SEATO

South-East Asia had figured prominently in Australian defence planning from as early as 1923 with the beginning of the Singapore Strategy, and the 1949 ANZAM arrangements had reconfirmed its importance to Australia. But events in northern Indochina in 1954 were to give it greater significance. In March 1954, Viet Minh forces surrounded a French garrison at the small town of Dien Bien Phu and, as weeks passed, a crushing Viet Minh victory appeared increasingly probable. There was intense diplomatic activity as America debated whether to bomb the Viet Minh attackers or to assist the French in other ways. The US Secretary of State, John Foster Dulles, suggested that Australia join a 'united action' to fight communism in Indochina. The minutes of the Cabinet meeting on 19 April to discuss this request reveals some of the ministers' views, although they were not made public. The defence minister, Philip McBride, stated gloomily: 'If the US decides to put forces in we will have to come in, but things will go badly and then [the] US will be forced to use the atom bomb.'

The Minister for Commerce and Agriculture, John McEwen, took a realpolitik view: 'Is the final survival of Australia better served by war there or peace? I suspect war.' The postmaster-general, Larry Anthony, said that it was 'only the support of the US which will enable us to hold Australia . . . We have to stick with the US, even when it is wrong.' The Minister for the Interior, Wilfrid Kent Hughes, declared that 'Australia's security is in the greatest danger that it has ever been in'. Menzies summed up: 'We are being asked to participate in a forlorn hope . . . The US are not incapable of unreality . . . I do not believe that the US has thought this out . . . How can we justify a war which will fail, merely to keep with the US?' Australia therefore resisted the US pressure to go to war; but Menzies would have a different view in 1965. Although Britain and Australia opposed the use of American force, they were anxious to keep America involved in the region.[57] Eventually the Americans decided not to act. After the French garrison surrendered on 7 May 1954, representatives of the major powers assembled at Geneva to discuss the future of Indochina.

In January 1953 the United States, Britain, France, Australia and New Zealand had established a Five Power Staff Agency to discuss military issues. Whatever its limitations might have been, the agency did provide a forum for discussing the military response to the communist victory in Indochina, such as when General Rowell met other military officers in Washington in early June 1954. Rowell arrived back in Canberra on 23 June and next day, accompanied by Shedden, reported to the Cabinet. Briefed by Shedden, McBride said that the best that could be contemplated under a ceasefire, but 'not likely to be achieved', was a foothold in the Tonkin Delta, and the preservation of South Vietnam, Cambodia, Laos and Thailand. The ministers did 'not underestimate the importance of events in Indo-China to Australia'. Indeed, some thought again that Australia's 'destiny in the Pacific is so wrapped up with the United States that we should support them even if we believe that the course of action proposed by them is wrong'. In the end, however, the Cabinet agreed that Australia should try to restrain the United States from active military intervention. Effort should be put into a regional defensive arrangement to support the settlement in Indochina once it was agreed at Geneva.[58]

Under the ceasefire agreement, signed at Geneva on 21 July 1954, the Viet Minh remained in control of North Vietnam, the south came under a non-communist regime, and France agreed to withdraw from Vietnam, Cambodia and Laos. Nationwide elections would be held in the future. Concern about further communist expansion in South-East Asia accelerated discussions about a regional defensive pact involving the United States, Britain, France, Australia, New Zealand, the Philippines and Pakistan. The resultant body would be known as the South-East Asia Treaty Organisation (SEATO). Negotiations over the treaty began in Manila on 6 September, with Australia represented by Casey, and the treaty was signed on 8 September. Among its articles, the treaty stated that each country recognised that an attack against another would 'endanger its own peace and safety' and that joint action would be taken to meet the common danger.[59]

Far East Strategic Reserve

The signing of the SEATO Treaty confirmed the change in Australia's strategic priorities. The government had already announced that the RAAF's No. 78 Wing would be withdrawn from Malta when its period of service expired in December 1954. Then, before leaving for Manila, Casey stated that Australia was willing to accept a peacetime commitment to South-East Asia. But the government was still cautious. In October 1954, after a year of deliberation, Menzies advised Churchill that Australia agreed 'in principle' to establish a strategic reserve for possible action in South-East Asia, but wanted an assurance of support from the United States before it could make a firm commitment.[60] Britain kept up the pressure, and in December urged the early formation of the Far East Strategic Reserve. The issue was not resolved at Cabinet meetings held on 6 and 7 January 1955, but would be discussed at a Commonwealth Prime Ministers' Conference to be held in London between 31 January and 8 February.

The conference considered a wide range of defence issues, including the ANZAM defence machinery, ANZAM planning for the defence of Malaya, problems in mobilising the Australian services, and atomic testing facilities in Australia. Churchill chaired a meeting with the Australians and New Zealanders where they discussed priorities for planning in the Malayan area, the formation of the Commonwealth Strategic Reserve and the possibility of attaching Australian and New Zealand staff officers to British staff in Singapore. Australia did not formally announce the commitment of forces to Malaya, but Tange (who was present) noted that Australia 'agreed to start the process of putting forces in'. Menzies returned home via Washington, where he asked for an indication of American support in the case of an attack on Malaya.[61]

Menzies reported to Cabinet on 30 and 31 March 1955, when he told his colleagues that in Washington he had 'obtained general agreement that the United States would co-operate in the plans for the defence of Malaya'. On 1 April Menzies announced that Australia, along with Britain and New Zealand, would be establishing a Far East Strategic Reserve. Australia would contribute two destroyers or two frigates, an aircraft carrier on an annual visit, additional ships in an emergency, an infantry battalion with supporting arms, a fighter wing of two squadrons, a bomber wing of one squadron, and an airfield construction squadron. While this announcement finalised a commitment that had been discussed for eighteen months, it confirmed the new direction in Australian defence policy. The *Sydney Morning Herald* called it 'a historic decision . . . It sets the seal on the change-over in Australia's strategic outlook from the Middle East to the Far East; it is the most dramatic indication of the swing in Australian thinking from opposition to the commitment of armed forces overseas in peacetime.' The commitment was opposed by the Labor Party, with its leader, Bert Evatt, implying that the government's policy was 'militaristic swashbuckling'.[62]

Whether the Australians could be used against the Malayan insurgents had still not been resolved. Finally, on 15 June a meeting of ministers, attended by Shedden, Brown, Tange and the three chiefs, agreed that the strategic reserve's primary role was to 'provide a deterrent to, and be available at short notice to assist in countering, further communist aggression in South East Asia'. Its secondary role was to assist in maintaining the security of Malaya against the insurgents, and units could be used for this task as long as it did 'not prejudice' the reserve's readiness 'to perform its primary role'.[63]

It took some time before the RAAF units could be deployed to Malaya, but the advance party of 2 RAR sailed for Penang in September and the main body in October. The battalion began operations on 1 January 1956, having been delayed by the Australian federal election of 10 December, in which the Menzies government was returned comfortably.[64] After two years, 3 RAR relieved 2 RAR, and after a further two years 3 RAR was relieved by 1 RAR.

In some respects, the RAAF and army units in Malaya were out of sight and mind and received little attention from Australia. Casey visited in 1951 when, as mentioned earlier, he visited Korea. Perhaps this lack of attention reflected the fact that the deployed units consisted entirely of regular servicemen, not citizen soldiers and airmen as in the Second World War. Menzies did not visit Malaya during the height of the Emergency, but as part of a goodwill visit to Indonesia visited Malaya in December 1959 when the Emergency was winding down. Menzies inspected the RAAF's Canberra bomber squadron and two Sabre fighter squadrons at the Butterworth air base, the Lincoln bombers having returned to Australia. At Terendak Barracks at Malacca he inspected the soldiers of 1 RAR.

The decision to deploy 2 RAR to Malaya had been a slow, careful process and was only possible after the Korean armistice in July 1953 and the Australian battalions started to return to Australia, and even then it took a further two and a half years before 2 RAR arrived in Malaya. Once there, the battalion conducted demanding operations in difficult terrain, but against a low-level enemy. By the time the Emergency formally ended in July 1960, a third battalion was on rotation in Malaya. Battle casualties in the three battalions that had served there numbered seven killed in action. The effectiveness of the bombing campaign carried out by the Australian Lincoln bombers has been the subject of much criticism, as the bombers killed only 23 Communist Terrorists in 4000 sorties. But many years later Chin Peng, leader of the Malayan Communist Party, testified that the bombing raids severely disrupted life in the guerrilla camps in the jungle.[65] As the official historian, Peter Edwards, noted, 'the Malayan experience at least served to encourage the view that Western military intervention to oppose a communist-led insurgency in a former European colony in South-East Asia was not necessarily a doomed cause'.[66] The success of the intervention led the government and its supporters to believe that a similar intervention in Vietnam might also be successful. It was to prove a false lesson.

9

'Looking for a way in and not a way out'

Menzies, Confrontation and Vietnam, 1962–65

The commitment of Australian combat troops to the Vietnam War by the Menzies government in 1965 is one of the most controversial decisions in Australian history. In terms of preventing the Republic of Vietnam (South Vietnam) from being overrun by the communists, the war was a failure. Ten years later, North Vietnamese forces captured the southern capital of Saigon (now Ho Chi Minh City) and reunited the country as the Socialist Republic of Vietnam. It can be argued that the commitment by the United States and its allies gave the rest of South-East Asia a breathing space to deal with the communist threat. Nonetheless, more than 500 Australian servicemen were killed in the war, about 2400 were wounded, and many others suffered health issues, particularly post-traumatic stress disorder.[1] Protests against Australia's involvement, and particularly against conscription for the war, bitterly divided the country. In considering Australia's war leadership in the Vietnam War, two broad issues need to be examined: the decision to become involved, and the conduct of the war. This chapter considers the first issue, and the next two describe the second.

It is sometimes overlooked that between 1962 and 1965 the

Australian government committed combat forces to both Vietnam and Borneo. It was not, however, a case of suddenly going to war; rather, the forces were committed incrementally, with each commitment a response to a deteriorating strategic situation. In Vietnam, army trainers were deployed in 1962, then they were permitted to accompany South Vietnamese forces on operations, until finally an infantry battalion was deployed in 1965. In Malaya, an infantry battalion and support troops had served as part of the Commonwealth Far East Strategic Reserve since 1955. When Indonesia's Confrontation over the formation of the new nation of Malaysia began in 1963, Australians assisted the British and Malay security forces in dealing with Indonesian infiltrators on the Malay Peninsula, until in 1965 an infantry battalion and a Special Air Service (SAS) squadron were deployed to Borneo. Australian forces would operate in and around Borneo until the end of the Confrontation in 1966. In Vietnam, under the Holt government, Australia's commitment grew to include the training team, a three-battalion task force, warships, helicopters and an RAAF bomber squadron. This commitment was wound back in 1970 and ended in 1972. The deployments to Borneo and Vietnam were only possible because of the introduction of selective conscription—another contentious decision.

The Decision-makers

The government that committed forces to operations in 1962–65 was essentially the same one that had sent forces to Korea and Malaya more than a decade earlier, although it was now more experienced. Menzies, aged 67, was still prime minister in 1962, and his key ministers had held portfolios for most of the 1950s. The deputy prime minister, John McEwen, leader of the Country Party and Minister for Trade since 1956, had been a member of the War Cabinet in the Second World War. Harold Holt, deputy leader of the Liberal Party, had been treasurer since 1958; as Minister for Labour and National Service from 1949 to 1958 he had been responsible for the 1950s National Service scheme.[2]

The two ministries directly involved in committing Australian forces to war were External Affairs and Defence. The Minister for External Affairs in 1962 was Sir Garfield Barwick, a top Queens Counsel who had become attorney-general when elected to parliament in 1958, and held the External Affairs portfolio from 1961 to 1964, when he became Chief Justice of Australia.[3] The Minister for Defence was Athol Townley, a Tasmanian businessman who had served in the RAN in the Second World War and had been elected to parliament in 1949. A minister since 1951, he had been appointed defence minister in December 1958. An 'earthy and gregarious, but able politician', Townley 'was renowned for his fund of risqué stories which, on occasions, appeared to appeal to the prime minister'.[4] In December 1963, he was appointed ambassador to the United States, but died of illness within the month.

Townley was succeeded as defence minister by Paul Hasluck, but Hasluck held the appointment for only four months before succeeding Barwick as Minister for External Affairs in April 1964. Hasluck was well qualified for External Affairs. Born in 1905, he had been a diplomat from 1941 to 1947, had been a history lecturer at the University of Western Australia, had written the two home-front volumes of the Second World War official history, had been elected to parliament in 1949, and from 1951 to 1963 had been Minister for Territories including Papua New Guinea. He was succeeded in Defence by Shane Paltridge. A Western Australian senator elected in 1951, Paltridge had been a minister since 1955 and was a close confidant of Robert Menzies.[5]

Military advice was provided by the Chiefs of Staff Committee, headed by its chairman, Air Marshal Sir Frederick Scherger. In 1958, the government had appointed the retiring CGS, Lieutenant General Sir Henry Wells, as the first separate chairman of the Chiefs of Staff Committee. Previously one of the chiefs, usually the most senior, had held the position. The chairman had no command authority over the services, held the same rank as the service chiefs, and was responsible for putting the joint-service view to the minister. Wells was succeeded in 1959 by the retiring CNS, Vice-Admiral Sir Roy Dowling, and in turn in May 1961 he was succeeded by Scherger, who had been CAS for the previous four years.

Born in 1904, Scherger had graduated from the Royal Military College and then transferred to the RAAF. In the Second World War he held key command appointments—in Darwin at the time of the Japanese air raid in 1942, and as commander of No. 10 Operational Group in 1943–44, then the First Tactical Air Force in 1945. He had headed the Australian Joint Services Staff in Washington, before commanding RAF Air Headquarters in Malaya during the Emergency in 1953–54. Scherger therefore had experience not only as a senior commander but also in appointments dealing with strategy and higher policy. As CAS, he advocated the purchase of aircraft from the United States. He was the first chairman to give the position substantial influence, helping to resolve the important policy matters arising in the early 1960s. In 1965, he was promoted to the rank of air chief marshal, the first Australian airman to reach that rank, and continued as chairman until 1966. Sir Arthur Tange, secretary of the Department of External Affairs, thought that Scherger 'was a cut above many of his associates in the services in his grasp of issues'. To Vice-Admiral Sir Alan McNicoll, who served under him as CNS, Scherger was a good politician who 'tended to grow where he was planted'—he recommended to the government what he thought it wanted to hear. He was a great advocate of anything the Americans wanted to do.[6] This view would figure prominently in the decision to commit Australian forces to the Vietnam War.

The three service chiefs in 1962 were Vice-Admiral Sir Hastings (Arch) Harrington, Lieutenant General Sir Reginald Pollard and Air Marshal Sir Valston Hancock. All had distinguished wartime records. A graduate of the RAN College, Harrington had commanded the sloop HMAS *Yarra*, and later the destroyer HMAS *Quiberon* in the Second World War. Before being appointed CNS in 1962, he had commanded the Australian fleet. Pollard was a Duntroon graduate who, except for a short period commanding an infantry battalion, had spent most the Second World War in key staff appointments in combat formations. Like Scherger, Hancock was a graduate of Duntroon; he had commanded an RAAF wing in combat in the Southwest Pacific in 1945 and had commanded an air group in Malaya in 1957–59.[7] Harrington and Hancock retained their appointments into 1965, while Pollard was succeeded in January 1963 by Lieutenant General John Wilton.

Wilton would play a key role in the Vietnam War. When he graduated from Duntroon in 1930 he joined the British Army, no position being available in the Australian Army, and he saw minor action with an Indian mountain battery in Burma. After transferring back to the Australian Army, during the Second World War he served in the Middle East, New Guinea, the United States and Morotai in demanding staff appointments. He commanded the 28th Commonwealth Brigade in Korea in 1953–54, and headed the SEATO planning office in Bangkok from 1960 to 1962, which allowed him to observe closely the deteriorating situation in Laos, and the Western powers' growing focus on South Vietnam. Reserved, self-disciplined and tactful, he easily won the confidence of ministers. Wilton recalled that Menzies always liked to have the service chiefs present at Cabinet meetings when important defence and military matters were under discussion.[8]

While the chiefs of staff were concerned mainly with a military perspective, matters of wider strategic importance were usually considered by the Defence Committee. This committee included the chiefs and four civilians: the secretary of the Department of Defence, Edwin (Ted) Hicks, who was chairman; the secretary of External Affairs, Sir Arthur Tange; the secretary of the Treasury, Sir Roland Wilson; and the secretary of the Prime Minister's Department, Sir John Bunting. Ted Hicks, who had succeeded Shedden as secretary of Defence in 1956, had wide experience in service administration, having previously been secretary of the Department of Air. Admiral McNicoll thought that although Hicks was a 'brilliant chairman of committees', he had no broader view of what role Defence could take in advising the government on strategic issues or on the need to exercise stronger control of the services. According to the journalist John Farquharson, 'His genial, chubby-faced appearance belied the big, capable mind he brought to bear on all he undertook. Among colleagues he commanded respect as a "straight-down-the-centre man of innate honesty, never swayed by friendship or a useful argument that might not be valid".[9] The Defence Committee would bear an important responsibility in advising the government.

Crisis in Laos

The decisions in 1962 to deploy an army training team to Vietnam and an RAAF fighter squadron to Thailand were made against a background of several years of crisis. At the time, the government was seeking to ensure Australia's security through three alliance arrangements: ANZUS, in which the principal partner was the United States; ANZAM, which involved Britain in the security issues of South-East Asia; and SEATO, which included both the United States and Britain.

By 1959, SEATO's focus was on the small country of Laos, which under the Geneva Conference agreement was effectively partitioned between the northern areas, controlled by the communist Pathet Lao, supported by North Vietnam; and the southern and eastern areas under a right-wing government of Laos. In July 1959 fighting broke out between the Pathet Lao and the government forces, and in early September the Lao government appealed to the United Nations, claiming aggression from North Vietnam; it also considered appealing to SEATO should the United Nations be unable to assist. As a member of SEATO, Australia faced the prospect of committing forces, and on 22 September the Australian government informed Vice-Admiral Dowling, the Australian military adviser to SEATO, that if asked he could state that Australia would commit an infantry battalion, a squadron of RAAF fighters, air transport and two RAN destroyers.[10] The battalion would come from the 28th Commonwealth Brigade in Malaya. The crisis died down and none of the SEATO nations deployed forces to Laos. The Australian government never made public that it had agreed to deploy forces if necessary, but the decision showed how anxious the government was to ensure that the United States remained involved in the region.

When, in early March 1961, the Pathet Lao defeated the Royal

Lao Army and threatened Vientiane, the United States responded by deploying three aircraft carriers and 1000 marines into the Gulf of Thailand. On 27 March, the SEATO Council began meeting in Bangkok, with the United States keen to obtain a statement of SEATO's determination to take action. Menzies, attending the council, was instrumental in drafting a resolution that expressed concern over the Pathet Lao offensive but favoured a negotiated settlement. Vice-Admiral Dowling, however, 'indicated publicly, and indiscreetly, that Australia would respond favourably to a SEATO request and could place troops in Laos "within hours"'.[11]

In fact, on 29 March the Australian Cabinet secretly agreed that if called upon to act by SEATO or the United States, Australia would participate in military action in Laos. The External Affairs minister, Barwick, had argued that 'The United States would certainly resent any Australian failure to participate in a military intervention in Laos. Such a failure would have grave repercussions on general Australian-American relations.' The press statement by McEwen, who chaired the meeting in the absence of Menzies, 'gave no hint that a major decision in principle had been taken'.[12]

In an effort to encourage the Thais, during March the United States and Thailand jointly sponsored a SEATO air defence exercise in Thailand with participation from Australia and France, followed by a command-post exercise in which Thailand, the United States, Australia, New Zealand and Britain participated. Between 14 April and 7 May, Britain hosted a six-nation SEATO exercise in the South China Sea that culminated in an amphibious landing in North Borneo. More than 100 aircraft, 60 ships, 28,000 naval personnel and 6000 US, British and Australian troops took part.[13]

The conflict in Laos died down briefly, but towards the end of April the Pathet Lao resumed the offensive, threatening Vientiane and the royal capital, Luang Prabang. The United States considered supporting Laos with a military commitment, and on 1 May, the Australian Cabinet met to decide whether Australia should follow the United States' lead in agreeing to intervene, even though Britain would not be involved. The Cabinet agreed that Australia would accept its role under the SEATO plan, but decided to consult further with the United States and Britain. Thus, in both March and May 1961 the Australian government had decided that in the last resort it would 'provide military support for an intervention by SEATO, by the United States and some SEATO allies, or even by the United States alone'. The official historian, Peter Edwards, concluded that it was 'a major turning point in Australian policy'.[14]

When the SEATO military advisers met in Bangkok in early May, Australia, Britain and New Zealand declared that the 28th Commonwealth Brigade would be available. The United States offered two regimental combat teams, Thailand said that it would deploy forces along its own border, the Philippines said it would declare later, while France and Pakistan failed to make any declaration. The United States, Britain, Australia and New Zealand also made air and naval forces available.[15] The conference had barely concluded when, on 6 May, Pathet Lao forces overran Nam Tha, and some Royal Lao troops retreated into northern Thailand.

Committing Forces

Events in Laos now intersected with demands to assist the South Vietnam government, which had been fighting an increasingly assertive insurgency by communist guerrillas the Viet Cong, supported by North Vietnam. Already the United States had sent advisers, under its Military Assistance Command Vietnam (MACV), headed by General Paul Harkins, to assist the South Vietnamese forces. In November 1961, the Australian Army's Director of Military Intelligence, Colonel Stuart Graham, visited South Vietnam and reported that the war there had 'already reached a stage similar to that which had existed before Dien Bien Phu' (see Chapter 8).[16]

During November and December 1961, suggestions were heard in the United States that Australia could send experts in jungle and guerrilla warfare to assist South Vietnam, and on 16 February 1962 the Australian ambassador in Washington, Sir Howard Beale, reported that the United States could soon ask Australia to send expert trainers. Perhaps aware of this, Colonel F.P. (Ted) Serong, who had concluded two years as a counterinsurgency expert attached to the Burmese Army, suggested to the CGS, Lieutenant General Pollard, that Australia offer a training team of ten to fifteen officers to assist the Americans in South Vietnam. Asserting that he was Australia's premier counterinsurgency specialist, Serong offered to lead the team, which should, he said, 'take over one sector—the dirtiest they have, if they wish—and work that for them'. The army concluded that if asked it could make ten officers available. Meanwhile, on 31 March the president of South Vietnam, Ngo Dinh Diem, made a general appeal for assistance.[17]

The problems of Vietnam and Laos, and of Thailand, which was concerned about a communist incursion, were on the agenda when the ANZUS Council met in Canberra on 8 May. Barwick, the Queen's Counsel, cross-examined the US Secretary of State, Dean Rusk, about America's determination to stay in Vietnam. In response, Rusk referred to the need for other nations to help in Vietnam. On 15 May, the Cabinet discussed the crisis over Laos and Thailand, and Rusk's request for assistance. The ministers agreed to send 'a small contingent' to Thailand if requested by the Thais, and if the South Vietnamese government were to ask for army instructors Australia would agree to provide them. Admiral Harry Felt, US Commander-in-Chief Pacific, had visited Australia as part of the ANZUS Council meeting and in discussions with the Australian chiefs he had emphasised the need for 'a helping hand' in Vietnam more for political than military reasons. On 24 May the defence minister, Townley, announced that a group of 30 army officers and non-commissioned officers, later to be known as the Australian Army Training Team Vietnam (AATTV), would be sent to Vietnam, and four days later he announced that a squadron of RAAF Sabre jet fighters would be deployed to Ubon in Thailand, near the border with Laos.[18]

The logic of sending an RAAF fighter squadron to Thailand related to the fact that since 1958 two fighter squadrons had been based at Butterworth in Malaya as part of the Far East Strategic Reserve, whose main role was to deal with a possible attack by Communist China in

South-East Asia. As noted earlier, Australia had already taken part in SEATO air defence exercises in Thailand. On 31 May 1962, the first of the RAAF's eight F-86F Sabres reached Ubon. By this time, the Pathet Lao had announced a ceasefire, and the following month a coalition government assumed office in Laos, which was effectively neutralised. Nonetheless, as the RAAF official historian noted, the RAAF personnel deployed to Ubon 'had not the slightest doubt they were at war'.[19] On 20 June, there was concern that communist guerrillas were crossing the Mekong River (the border between Laos and Thailand), and the Australians were issued with weapons and live ammunition to defend the squadron area. The alert proved to be a false alarm, but the RAAF squadron continued to operate as a 'front-line' base. As for the AATTV, Pollard selected his friend Serong as its commander and, after pre-deployment training, it arrived in Saigon, Vietnam, in early August.

Strategic Policymaking

Australia's strategic policy was developed through an interaction between professional advisers and politicians, and at times it is difficult to know who was driving the policy discussions. The usual process was for a group of senior military planners, the Joint Planning Committee, to consider a strategic problem and propose a solution to be considered by the chiefs of staff. The chiefs' recommendations would then go to the Defence Committee, which in turn would prepare a report or proposal to be considered by the Cabinet. It is useful, therefore, to examine the views of the Defence Committee when in May 1962 they recommended that the RAAF squadron be deployed to Thailand, and the AATTV be sent to Vietnam.

In January 1962 the Defence Committee had prepared a new edition of the triennial paper 'A Strategic Basis of Australian Defence Policy'. In this paper, the committee argued that Australia's strategic position had deteriorated since the previous 1959 paper, and that Australia's security was best achieved by a 'forward defence strategy which involves the containment of enemy forces as far from our immediate environs as possible'. The key was to hold South-East Asia. As the paper put it:

> The immediate threat to Australia's interests and security stems from the mainland of South East Asia. Should Laos and South Vietnam become Communist, neutralist Cambodia would soon fall to Communist influence, and Thailand, facing pressure from surrounding States may not be able to maintain a pro-Western alignment and could fall to communism. If these States were lost to communism, the position of Malaya and Singapore would be precarious, as they could face an ever increasing external threat from the north and their large Chinese population would see their future as one associated with the policies of Communist China. These developments would destroy the forward defence posture upon which our present defence policy is based.

This report—with its resonance with the domino theory—had clear implications for the army, which had to be able to make 'a prompt, effective and sustained contribution to South East Asian defence in concert with our allies'. When it met on 19 July, the Cabinet deferred consideration of the report but largely approved the expenditure requested by the defence minister. Eventually the government approved £212.7 million for 1962–63, compared with £203.1 million for 1961–62. Each service benefited about equally, with the Army authorised to increase its strength from 21,000 to 22,500 by June 1963.[20] Whether the army could attract sufficient recruits was another matter.

With the strategic situation becoming more complicated, in January 1963 the Cabinet approved the establishment of a Foreign Affairs and Defence (FAD) Committee of senior ministers 'to keep a continuous interest in issues of national security'. Chaired by Menzies, it included the treasurer, Holt; the Ministers for Trade, McEwen; External Affairs, Barwick; Defence, Townley; and Territories, Hasluck; and later the Minister for Supply, Allen Fairhall. The ministers of the three services were not members of the committee, only attending when invited, and were often excluded even when matters were of specific concern to their portfolios.[21] Once the FAD Committee was established, it considered the reports and recommendations of the Defence Committee.

Confrontation

Despite concern about Vietnam during 1962, the greatest anxiety was over Indonesia. Australia had been forced to acquiesce in Indonesia's takeover of Dutch New Guinea that same year, but Indonesia's President Sukarno did not appear satisfied, complaining that the proposed formation of the Federation of Malaysia by the joining of Malaya, Singapore, Brunei, Sarawak and British North Borneo (Sabah) was a case of 'neo-colonialism'. Like Britain and Malaya, Australia viewed Sukarno's denunciation of Malaysia with great concern, fearing that it would have a destabilising effect on South-East Asia.

At the last minute, Brunei declined to join the federation and in December 1962 a revolt broke out in Brunei, which was put down by British troops flown in from Singapore. Britain suspected that Indonesia had encouraged the rebellion. Then on 20 January 1963, the Indonesian foreign minister announced a policy of confrontation (or *konfrontasi*) against Malaysia, and soon so-called volunteers (mainly Indonesian soldiers not in uniform) were undertaking indiscriminate raids into Sarawak and Sabah, trying to foment opposition to the formation of Malaysia, due to take place in September 1963.

Meeting on 5 March 1963, the Cabinet agreed to support the new state of Malaysia. Australian troops were not permitted to take part in internal security operations, but the new CGS, Lieutenant General Wilton, recommended that Australians already integrated in British units and headquarters deployed to Borneo should remain with them.[22] On 28 March the FAD Committee decided that the Australian forces presently stationed in Malaya should remain there.

When on 16 September 1963 Malaysia formally came into existence, Indonesia declared Malaysia to be illegal, and mobs attacked the British Embassy and the Malaysian Chancery in Jakarta. The British government asked Australia to make available its forces from the strategic reserve for counterinsurgency operations if needed, and the chiefs began a series of urgent meetings. On 24 September, they advised the Cabinet that the army could make available 3 RAR, which was already in Malaysia; and an SAS company or a company group from a Pentropic battalion. (Pentropic battalions were much larger than normal battalions, with five rather than four rifle companies.) There were disadvantages with all options. If 3 RAR were used it would not be available for any SEATO tasks that might be assigned to the 28th Commonwealth Brigade, and both the SAS and Pentropic companies were part of the first battle group earmarked for limited war tasks. Despite these reservations, the following day Menzies announced that if necessary Australia would provide military assistance to Malaysia to defend its 'territorial integrity'.[23]

The military chiefs continued to refine their views, so that by the time the Defence Committee met again on 9 November, the army had decided that it could no longer make the Pentropic company available, and that there were problems in providing air support for an SAS company.[24] Already Britain had deployed seven battalions to Sarawak, and in the following months Indonesia began sending regular troops on more substantial incursions into Malaysian territory. The discussions over Australia's commitment, and the continuing requirement to declare forces for SEATO plans, underlined the shortfall in the size of the army field force.

Australia was coming under mounting pressure to provide military support to the British in Malaysia. On 29 December, Indonesian forces raided a Malaysian police post in Sabah, killing nine Malaysians, and the Malaysian government asked the British Far East Command to make the Australian and New Zealand battalions in the 28th Brigade available for counterterrorist operations on the Malaysian–Thai border in order to release federation battalions to the operational reserve. Although Menzies declared on 16 January 1964 that there was 'no immediate need for further Australian assistance', on 23 January the Defence Committee recommended the use of

3 RAR.[25] On 28 January, the Cabinet approved the recommendation; 3 RAR deployed to the border on 20 February and remained there until a New Zealand battalion relieved it on 4 April.

Despite agreeing to the deployment of 3 RAR, the Defence Committee was reluctant to accede to a further request for assistance from Malaysia, advising the government during March that it 'would be wrong' to use forces 'for political purposes which were not sound militarily'. The Malaysians would not let the matter rest, and on 6 April they sought permission to use Australian forces to deal with Indonesian incursions on the mainland if the need arose. On 8 April, the Defence Committee recommended that the forces be made available, and the FAD Committee agreed the following day.[26]

The British prime minister, Sir Alec Douglas-Home, now cabled Menzies that the British and Malaysian security forces in Borneo were to be permitted to cross the Indonesian border in 'hot pursuit' for a distance of up to 3000 yards (2700 metres), and he raised the possibility of an Australian battalion or SAS troops being made available for operations in Borneo. The Defence Committee advised that while 3 RAR was 'a good, well-trained and well-equipped unit' and the SAS company was 'highly trained and permanently on seven days' notice to move', a decision to provide the SAS or a battalion should be taken only after it was considered 'that there was no further possibility of deterring the Indonesians by other means'. The committee recommended, however, that Australia reject Malaysia's requests for combat support. The government therefore declined to provide a battalion or the SAS at this stage, but agreed to send 7 Field Squadron, Royal Australian Engineers, to Borneo to build a strategically important road, and to provide two minesweepers, four helicopters and other air support to Malaysia. A little later it announced the deployment of 111 Light Anti-Aircraft Battery to Butterworth in case the Indonesians mounted an air attack on the air base. The FAD Committee accepted the Defence Committee's advice that there was no need 'at this stage' to provide combat troops for Borneo, but concluded that Australia should inform Britain it 'would participate militarily if overt aggression were to occur'.[27]

Expanding the Training Team

Meanwhile, developments in Vietnam were causing increasing concern. In early 1964 the only Australian troops in South Vietnam were the 30 officers and non-commissioned officers (NCOs) of the AATTV. The team had been involved primarily in training the South Vietnamese, although a few members had been attached to the Combined Studies Division—a counterinsurgency organisation run by the US Central Intelligence Agency (CIA). Colonel Serong had also become a counterinsurgency adviser to the Commander MACV, General Harkins. Towards the end of 1963, Global Serong, on his own initiative, began redeploying some of his team members, and by February 1964 two officers and eight NCOs were working with Special Forces teams on operations with South Vietnamese counter-insurgency forces. Wilton approved this deployment retrospectively on 3 March—a significant decision, as for the first time Australian troops would be involved in combat operations in Vietnam. The following month Captain Noel Delahunty was wounded in a battle for which he was awarded the Military Cross. Wilton thought that the government had been cautious initially to see 'how things worked out. I think when the Team was beginning to demonstrate its real value it became apparent that it could be more profitably used if the limitations were removed. I was certainly in favour of removing this limitation.'[28] It is unlikely that Wilton sought prior governmental approval for this implied change of role.

On 6 May the US government cabled the Australian government with a list of additional military forces that it might send to Vietnam. The Joint Planning Committee concluded that South Vietnam was 'a key strategic area in the defence of mainland South East Asia, and there would be serious consequences for the whole of South East Asia should it be lost', and therefore recommended an additional 30 NCOs for the AATTV, an army dental team, ten personnel to assist with driver training and maintenance, and a detachment of three Caribou transport aircraft and crew with a further three to be sent by October.[29] The Defence Committee endorsed this report, and the full Cabinet approved the recommendations on 29 May, noting that the employment of AATTV members in the field as advisers might result in casualties. For Serong and his team this latter conclusion seemed fatuous. Some team members had already been wounded, and Captain Delahunty's action had warranted a decoration for bravery. On 8 June, in general terms, the government announced the doubling of the AATTV and the sending of the Caribous.

Wilton now took a greater role in deciding Australia's commitment. Visiting Vietnam in late June, he had discussions with the new MACV commander, General William C. Westmoreland, and approved Serong's proposed deployment of the additional 30 AATTV members. Serong had already advised Army Headquarters that the dental team and the driving and maintenance personnel were not needed, and had suggested that they be replaced by an additional 23 advisers, bringing the team to 83 members. After Wilton had further discussions with 36-year-old Lieutenant General Nguyen Khanh, who had seized power in a coup in January, the ambassador, David Anderson, cabled Australia recommending that additional members be deployed to the AATTV. On 15 July the recently appointed defence minister, Shane Paltridge, approved the increase of the AATV to 83, the additional members being available for integration into US Special Forces teams 'on the understanding that such teams would not operate outside the borders of South Vietnam'.[30]

Wilton's visit to Vietnam and Singapore had given him insight into the strategic situation that was to prove valuable over the next few months, as events demanded frequent reports to the government. The first concerned the Gulf of Tonkin incident, when North Vietnamese gunboats allegedly attacked US ships between 2 and 4 August. The Defence Committee advised on 20 August that North Vietnam would be unlikely to force the issue to the point of risking open intervention by the United States. If the Viet Cong stepped up its insurgency in South Vietnam, the United States might ask Australia to contribute forces, but there was no need to expand Australia's forces further to meet any possible requests.[31]

By this time, however, there was an increasing threat in Malaysia. In June and July there had been cases of sabotage in Singapore, and on 17 August Indonesian guerrillas landed in the southern Malaysian state of Johore. In its report of 20 August, the Defence Committee observed that Australia faced the possibility of military operations in Vietnam, Malaysia and Papua New Guinea, where Indonesians might cross from their newly acquired province of West New Guinea. Australia did not have the military resources to deal with threats in all areas. On 2 September about 100 Indonesian paratroops landed in Johore and the Malaysian government declared a state of emergency. Indonesia and Malaysia were now close to war, with British planners considering sea and air strikes against Indonesian bases. Air Chief Marshal Scherger and Air Marshal Hancock advocated these attacks, although the government did not accept this advice.[32]

Towards Conscription

Six months earlier, in March 1964, at the direction of the army minister, Dr James (Jim) Forbes, Wilton had directed his staff to prepare a detailed paper on whether to introduce a selective national service scheme. The army paper rejected both large-scale and limited national service schemes, preferring to try to improve pay and conditions in an effort to attract sufficient officer cadets and recruits. The defence minister, Hasluck, was disappointed with this paper, and advised Hicks and Scherger that Cabinet was concerned about the disparity between the army's present strength and the figure of 33,000 that would be needed for the army to meet its commitments 'in the present situation'. Cabinet, he said, was 'looking for advice on the means of increasing rapidly to at least this figure of 33,000 and then proceeding on still further at a later stage'. He wanted the chiefs of staff to examine the army proposal.[33]

When the chiefs considered the army paper on 6 April, however, they endorsed the army's view that there was no need to introduce national service, as the strategic situation did not demand a substantially larger army at this stage. As the army had only four regular infantry battalions, this was a remarkably optimistic estimate, for if battalions were committed to each of Borneo, Vietnam and Papua

New Guinea (with one held in reserve) the army would not be able to relieve them once they had completed their tours of duty.[34]

Before the end of the month, Senator Shane Paltridge succeeded Hasluck as defence minister, Hasluck having become Minister for External Affairs. Aged 54, Paltridge was a Perth hotel-keeper and an experienced minister, having held various portfolios since 1955. He had served as a gunner at Tarakan in 1945. Hasluck remembered him fondly:

> His big merits as a politician were seen best in the Cabinet room and in the administration of his departments. He was a sturdy no-nonsense man in Cabinet . . . he could always be depended on for a clear and sound analysis of a problem and for a view that I can best describe as well-expressed commonsense . . .
>
> I found him a truthful, honest and courageous man . . . Menzies valued him highly and paid a great deal of respect to his opinions.[35]

It fell to Paltridge to take the chiefs' recommendations (with which he agreed) to Cabinet. He explained that the army proposed to expand the SAS company to a regiment and eventually to expand the Pacific Islands Regiment from one to three battalions. It was important to review the armed forces' pay and conditions, establish an emergency reserve (for former regular members) and introduce legislation to ensure that the CMF was available for overseas service.[36] The Cabinet accepted these recommendations, and in June the government announced its intention to improve service conditions and to change the legislation.

Although the army had presented an optimistic view about its capacity to meet a range of threats, on 27 May Wilton warned that while an army of 33,000 would be sufficient to meet the short-term requirements of both cold war and limited war contingencies, if recruiting rates did not improve, the target could not be reached before about 1980. This was 'completely unacceptable'. It was likely, he said, 'that Australia could be called upon to render substantial as opposed to token assistance' in South Vietnam, and while it was 'not possible to predict a date by which Australia might be committed, for example, to SEATO action in South Vietnam or Thailand', the probability of being committed to such action within the next two to four years was much greater than twelve months earlier, when the proposals for an increase were put to Cabinet.[37]

Following the Tonkin Gulf incident, on 3 September the Cabinet asked Defence to undertake a special study on manpower deficiencies, including the need for compulsory military training, and invited the defence minister to make the case for the immediate purchase of additional Caribou aircraft, helicopters and minesweepers.[38] After the Cabinet meeting External Affairs also sent out a message to all diplomatic posts emphasising Hasluck's view of the importance to Australia of the outcome of events in South Vietnam. It was in Australia's national interest to have a government in South Vietnam that would continue to fight the Viet Cong. Australia's 'second interest is to retain an active United States presence in South Viet Nam. Our third major interest is to prevent (not merely avoid) any failure in South-East Asia of such a kind as to lead to a collapse of will to resist in other countries.' It was a good summary of a policy that was to guide the Australian government over the next six months before the commitment of the battalion in April 1965.[39]

Responding to the Cabinet direction, on 30 September the army staff completed its new manpower paper, which indicated that for the first time Wilton thought the situation serious enough to justify the introduction of a selective national service scheme. The key factors were the 'accelerated deterioration in the strategic situation in South East Asia over recent months', and the 'serious shortfall' in the army's manpower 'against approved targets'. The army still maintained that it could 'meet with difficulty the initial planned overseas contributions in the event of limited war', but the provision of reinforcements would present a problem.[40]

Meanwhile, on 15 October the Defence Committee discussed its periodic 'Strategic Basis of Australian Defence Policy'. When the government had considered the previous strategic basis paper in July 1962, it had endorsed an increase in Defence spending and a moderate army expansion. Now, in its 1964 review, the Defence Committee concluded that the position in South Vietnam might be 'beyond recovery'. Australia should therefore seek to keep the United States committed to South-East Asia and to help maintain its alliances—ANZUS, ANZAM and SEATO. The loss of South Vietnam would have a domino effect on Laos, Burma and Cambodia, and would put pressure on Thailand. But the only 'direct threat to Australia and its territories' was from Indonesia, which in addition to its Confrontation with Malaysia, was expected to 'show an increasing interest in Papua/New Guinea'. Australia therefore needed to 'be prepared to respond immediately to situations which might arise at any time from Indonesia's expanding military capability and aggressive policy', as well as responding to requests for assistance in mainland South-East Asia 'such as to South Vietnam and Thailand'. The 'degree of national preparedness envisaged' in the review required 'increases to our present defence forces, their arms and equipment and their means of strategic and tactical mobility'.[41]

Before the Cabinet could consider this report there were further developments in Malaysia. On 28 October about 59 Indonesian guerrillas landed near Malacca on the Malay Peninsula, and next day a company of 3 RAR and 102 Field Battery, Royal Australian Artillery, helped round them up, with no Australian casualties. The Cabinet learned of 3 RAR's involvement later that day.[42] Australia's argument that its troops should not be employed in Borneo was now starting to wear thin.

In the face of this deteriorating situation, there were differing views about the need for national service. When Paltridge presented his submission to the Cabinet in early November, he pointed out that the navy and the air force had firmly rejected national service and that the army had only reluctantly concluded that a selective scheme was necessary. According to Paltridge's Cabinet submission, the army proposed an initial intake of 3000 per year rising to 6900 per year in the fourth year to allow it to reach 28,000 by June 1967 and 33,000 by December 1969. Paltridge advised against national service for the present, advocating one last effort to attract voluntary recruits.[43]

When the Cabinet met at 2.30 p.m. on 4 November, it dealt first with the strategic basis paper and substantially agreed with it, although it thought that it had given insufficient attention to the possibility of Australia having to act against Indonesian forces in Papua New Guinea without US assistance.[44] The Cabinet then turned to Paltridge's submission on manpower. At this point, with 'great daring', the army minister, Jim Forbes (who had been invited to the Cabinet), leaped into the argument and said: 'I have to make it clear, Mr Prime Minister, that I just can't agree with the Minister for Defence. We will not get the men and the Army can't perform its function in the time scale that the Cabinet is requiring it to unless we do get more men and there is only one way we can get them in that time scale and that is by selective conscription.' Forbes then explained the army's scheme. Menzies was more receptive than Forbes expected; he had with him a brief from his own department that advised that it was 'extremely unlikely we will get within coo-ee of the target by voluntary enlistment'. The brief argued that the target should be 55,000, rather than the 33,000 proposed by the army. Menzies then turned to Paltridge and said: 'I want you to get Wilton in and categorically assure you that he advises this scheme.' He refused to make a decision that evening, and directed Paltridge to come back with the advice the next day. Peter Howson, the Minister for Air, who was also present, saw that both Menzies and the treasurer, Holt, favoured national service. He thought Menzies wanted it for political reasons (to win the Senate election) and had twisted 'the military need to accord with the political need'.[45]

That night, Forbes told Wilton that the Cabinet was likely to introduce conscription and that the timeframes might need to be accelerated. At 7 a.m. next morning, Scherger telephoned Wilton that at the Cabinet meeting that day Paltridge would require him to state how a strength of 33,000 could be reached by the end of 1966. Wilton immediately conferred with his staff and amended his brief.[46]

In the Cabinet meeting at 10.30 a.m. that day, Wilton advised that a national service intake of 4200 in 1965 (beginning on 30 June 1965) rising to 6900 in subsequent years would allow the army to reach an effective strength of 33,000 by 31 December 1966. But he advised that the accelerated scheme was 'practicable' only if the government approved 'urgent action' on several issues: the 'highest priority' for the construction of accommodation; and speedy resolution of outstanding matters concerning conditions of service, particularly pensions, and conditions for short-service commissions. Accepting this advice, the Cabinet then approved the introduction of the selective National Service scheme. As Forbes recalled later, Paltridge had miscalculated Menzies' attitude:

> Nobody knew as well as he did the risks that were involved, given the fierce battles there had been over the issue in Australian history. I can remember, when the die was cast and the decision was finally taken, that he sat back in his chair and just looked around the table and said, 'There comes a time in the life of any government where it just has to make decisions it believes are in the best interests of the country even if they believe they are committing political suicide.'

Howson and William McMahon, Minister for Labour and National Service, dissented; Howson thought it was 'a terribly bad decision'.[47]

Defence Build-up

On 10 November, in a major speech in parliament, Menzies announced both the introduction of national service and the largest increase in defence expenditure since the Second World War.[48] In its review of May 1963, the government had forecast an expenditure of £816 million between mid-1965 and mid-1968; this was now increased to £1.22 billion. Two additional infantry battalions would be raised, the SAS Regiment would be doubled to four combat squadrons, and the Pacific Islands Regiment would be doubled to two battalions. Already the army had begun to receive or had ordered new equipment and more would now be purchased. While perhaps a future deployment to Vietnam was a consideration, the expansion was directed primarily towards Indonesia. The *Sydney Morning Herald*'s editorial of 11 November stated that the 'basic message to the nation of the Prime Minister's historic defence review last night was that there was "a real risk of war" with Indonesia. It is evident that the Government considers that this risk has suddenly and steeply increased.' Within days, and with the government's approval, Wilton reorganised the army and abandoned the Pentropic organisation. Rather than the two battalions announced by Menzies, with the introduction of national service the army would be able to raise four more regular infantry battalions on the new Tropical Warfare establishment (a new structure for the army, which included smaller battalions that were suitable for jungle warfare), bringing the total to eight.

Proposing a Battalion for Vietnam

The decision to expand the army to eight battalions came just in time to allow the possible deployment of a battalion to Vietnam. When Hasluck visited Washington in late November 1964, he learned that the United States was likely to take stronger action in Vietnam. Then, on 4 December, the US Assistant Secretary of State, William Bundy, in discussion with the Australian and New Zealand ambassadors, asked Australia to provide an additional 200 advisers. He also mentioned that if further action became necessary, the United States planned to deploy one army division and two battalions of marines to Vietnam, along with whatever troops Australia and New Zealand might be able to provide. Bundy sought responses from the two countries and suggested military staff discussions about the possibility of deploying forces. Responding to this, the Joint Planning Committee assessed that Australia could provide one infantry battalion, an SAS squadron, logistic support elements, about ten extra instructors, and naval ships to transport them. The committee cautiously warned, however, that 'before any decision could be taken on possible Australian participation in South Vietnam it would be essential to obtain a great deal of additional information from the United States'.[49]

Meanwhile, a few days later on 14 December US president Lyndon Johnson suggested to Menzies that Australia provide 200 extra advisers and various naval craft, but not combat troops at this stage. The next day the Defence Committee met to consider this request. The navy and air chiefs thought that Johnson's letter was a 'political exercise' and Australia 'should act cautiously'. As former External Affairs official Garry Woodard wrote, Scherger was 'the most gung-ho. He stated that Australia could not avoid making a contribution, since it must aid the Americans because it was in their confidence.' However, since Australia had committed all its forces it would only have a capacity to provide civil aid. The Defence Committee never prepared a report, and Woodard's account is based on notes taken by Sir Arthur Tange.[50]

Tange would later complain that the government avoided receiving advice from External Affairs experts, who might have had a contrary view. Historian Joan Beaumont was less sure, noting that 'Senior diplomats in Washington, who were responsible for managing the relationship with the United States in the critical days of the Vietnam commitment, showed few signs in 1964 to 1965 of being uneasy about Australian policy, or indeed the strategic assumptions that underpinned it.' Nevertheless, there was a note of caution in External Affairs' comments on the Washington cable: 'While military opinion might not regard it as impossible to defeat the Viet Cong (if external aid to them is reduced), it is not possible to be optimistic about the [South Vietnam] Government retaining the will and morale to continue with protracted fighting.' It is unclear whether this view was ever presented to the ministers.[51]

On 16 December the chiefs of staff met and, ignoring the Joint Planning Committee's warning and the reservations expressed in the Defence Committee meeting, they responded to what author Michael Sexton called Bundy's 'speculative' comment about perhaps providing combat troops at a later stage, rather than the more conservative request from Johnson. They therefore advised the government that the introduction of ground forces was 'the only way of achieving a solution to the South Vietnam problem', and that Australia was 'in a position to offer now, if required, an infantry battalion for combat operations in South Vietnam'. As Scherger was an air force officer,

Wilton, who had already visited Vietnam twice, played a key part in this decision. The Director of Military Intelligence, Colonel Olof (Zac) Isaksson, recalled Wilton asking him whether a commitment to Vietnam was sustainable. Isaksson was convinced that the war was winnable; 38 years later he still believed that 'given those circumstances again, my advice would be unchanged'.[52]

The following night the FAD Committee considered the chiefs' recommendations, and agreed, if necessary, 'to consider the contribution of an Australian battalion as suggested'. Australia replied to the United States that 'we might be able to make a contribution', and that this might be considered at 'the military staff level'. The acting secretary's notes of the meeting indicate that Menzies strongly supported the deployment of the battalion, and that the government was therefore psychologically committed to it. In Woodard's view, this was the crucial decision, even though the government later tried to imply that the matter was under discussion right through to the formal announcement on 29 April 1965. Thirty years later, 'Tange still seethed over what he considered Hasluck's worst transgression of good and proper governance', writing that 'I always remember his failure to ensure that Departmental opinion accompanied the chiefs of staff paper—of low quality—in late 1964 giving military judgements on what was essentially a strategic question—long recognised by all previous Cabinets as requiring an overlay of external political advice.' The official historian, Peter Edwards, summed up the government's decision-making: 'Policy debates and consultation were narrowed when they most needed to be broadened: in the mind of Menzies and the few to whom he entrusted crucial decisions and discussions, the complexities of the challenge were simplified. Menzies listened only to those who agreed with him, and excluded knowledgeable advisers who recommended caution.'[53]

Committing Troops to Borneo

The policy issues continued to mount. Although Sukarno's promise that 'before the cock crows in 1965' he would crush Malaysia was not fulfilled, British intelligence assessments showed that at the end of 1964 the Indonesians were building up their forces on the Sarawak border near the state capital, Kuching. In the midst of these concerns, on 2 January 1965 Menzies, having recently turned 70, departed from Sydney for a cruise across the Pacific to North America, leaving John McEwen as acting prime minister. On 15 January the British prime minister, Harold Wilson, informed McEwen that he had given permission for operations to be extended to 10,000 yards (around 9000 metres) across the border, and he mentioned the need for additional SAS troops and another battalion. McEwen's reply was non-committal: 'It seems to us that more and more, the two conflicts in Vietnam and against Indonesia are coming to form a part of a common pattern and a common thread.'[54]

The government received more information when Senator Paltridge visited Malaysia and Vietnam in late January and early February. On 21 January the Malaysian government asked Paltridge to seek Australia's approval to send SAS troops, 3 RAR and another battalion to Borneo. The chiefs recommended deploying an SAS squadron and 3 RAR but not another battalion. The Cabinet approved the deployment, which was announced publicly on 3 February. The first elements of 1 SAS squadron arrived in Brunei on 16 February, and the remainder of the squadron arrived later that month. By 23 March 3 RAR had arrived in Sarawak.[55] As this was primarily an army deployment, Wilton's advice had been crucial. While the political and strategic situation perhaps made the deployment to Borneo inevitable, he was much happier to recommend it now that he knew the army was on track to increase the number of its battalions.

Committing a Battalion to Vietnam

Events were now leading to the crucial decision to commit an infantry battalion to Vietnam. While Menzies and Hasluck were keen to do something about the deteriorating situation in Vietnam, they needed further information about what the Americans planned to do. Wilton, who would be responsible for the deployment, strongly believed in the need to commit forces to Vietnam. Interviewed in 1976, he recalled that 'we wanted to stop the spread of communism south, and despite criticisms of this hackneyed phrase, the domino theory, it was right. We did not want South Vietnam, Cambodia, Laos or subsequently Thailand to be Communist controlled. That is still my view.'[56] In addition, an operational commitment would provide good command experience for officers and NCOs at all levels, with a beneficial effect on the army's capability for future operations. Provided that the Australian government was clear about its purpose, a combat commitment to Vietnam was necessary. Thus, when in the previous December the chiefs had advised that Australia could provide a battalion, they had added that first there should be detailed military discussions with the United States about the feasibility of its plan to position troops, including Australian and New Zealand forces, in the northern provinces of South Vietnam.

Australia was now encouraging an escalation of American involvement in Vietnam rather than negotiations with North Vietnam. On 15 January an External Affairs paper raised the question of whether Australia could offer a battalion 'in order to obtain some forward momentum in American policy formulation'.[57] Three days later the FAD Committee decided to send seventeen more instructors to Vietnam, bringing the AATTV numbers to 100. On 27 January, when Senator Paltridge was arriving in Vietnam, yet another coup replaced the South Vietnamese government. While there, Paltridge announced the decision to increase the size of the AATTV. Wilton was not pleased. With the army facing what he called 'the very heavy burden of establishing and maintaining a special National Service training organisation', he needed every trained instructor possible. His advice in December that the army was 'not in a position to provide further combat advisers without seriously disrupting the introduction of the National Service scheme' had apparently been ignored.[58]

Despite the coup in South Vietnam, Australia was urging the United States to disregard the political instability in Saigon. The Americans finally acted, and on 13 February Johnson ordered an intense 30-day bombing campaign against North Vietnam known as Rolling Thunder. A week later, on 20 February the Americans notified that they had organised a military staff conference in Honolulu, to begin on 30 March. On 26 February Johnson approved the landing of 3500 marines at Da Nang, in northern South Vietnam, and two battalions of marines went ashore on 8 March.

The Australian government now began preparing for the Honolulu conference, where it would be represented by Air Chief Marshal Scherger. He would be accompanied by Brigadier Ken Mackay, the army's Director of Military Operations and Plans, to provide specialist army advice. On 25 March the Defence Committee endorsed a brief for the Australian delegation to Honolulu, directing that it should 'probe the military feasibility of the measures proposed and the results expected of them'. The brief hardly mentioned sending a battalion, but it must have been discussed, because that afternoon Wilton wrote to Scherger to remind him that 'we do not wish to contribute a larger ground force element than a battalion in the present circumstances', and that once deployed it would have to operate as part of a larger US force, drawing maximum logistic support from it. Undue haste should be avoided and staff would need to visit Saigon for discussions before details of the contribution could be finalised. Later that day the FAD Committee approved the Defence Committee's brief. Wilton clearly believed that the deployment would eventuate. A month earlier, on 25 February, he had warned the commanding officer of 1 RAR that his battalion might be required to deploy to Vietnam in May.[59]

On 30 March, Scherger and Mackay, along with Rear Admiral Sir Peter Phipps from New Zealand, gathered at Honolulu to meet the US Commander-in-Chief Pacific, Admiral Ulysses Sharp, and other senior US officials. Although Scherger was supposed to find out what the Americans planned to do in Vietnam, he went beyond his brief and offered a battalion. According to Edwards, 'Phipps reported that Scherger had seemed more anxious than Sharp to have Australia involved, that he made no secret of his intentions to recommend that Australia send a battalion, and that he expected Cabinet to agree.' It is clear that the army had encouraged this offer. Mackay recalled discussing with Scherger in detail why a battalion was the most appropriate force to send to Vietnam, and Bill Major, a senior army civilian official, observed that the army was very keen for Mackay to report favourably. Scherger was required to discuss the general concept of operations for the ground troops in Vietnam, but he found that the Americans had not thought through an overall strategy and he failed to press this issue. As Ian McNeill commented in the official history: 'If Australia were to have any say in how [the political] aim might be achieved before it committed its troops, this was the opportunity . . . Instead Scherger was given a preferred area of deployment for an Australian battalion and a role expressed blankly as "counter-insurgency" operations.'[60] Perhaps Scherger did not want to ask difficult questions.

On his return, Scherger reported to the Defence Committee, where Wilton questioned him about the meaning of the 'counter-insurgency' task. Patrick Shaw, acting secretary of External Affairs, also questioned the lack of clarity over the Australian role. He felt strongly that the 'job of winkling out Viet Cong terrorists and safeguarding hamlets and policing highways was a job for the Vietnamese and not for foreign troops'. Despite these concerns, the Defence Committee recommended committing a battalion.[61]

Before the government could consider this advice, news came that the US Secretary of State, Rusk, and William Bundy's deputy, Leonard Unger, had told the Australian representatives in Washington that Australia would soon be asked to provide a battalion. Unger formally requested that Australia and New Zealand provide a further 150 instructors. On 7 April the FAD Committee met to consider the Defence Committee's advice and this new request from the United States. Hasluck and McMahon wanted to defer a decision while they waited for further information about American plans. But the other ministers overruled them. Harold Holt said that 'whatever the final outcome of United States intervention in Vietnam', Australia had to give the maximum contribution possible. McEwen thought that reported comments from Admiral Sharp and Rusk were 'tantamount to a request' for a battalion. Menzies agreed: 'We would be prepared to put in a battalion and were looking for a way in and not a way out. With this approach the psychological effect on the United States would be phenomenally valuable, including in Australia's interest.' As Edwards concluded, 'The FAD Committee had thus decided clearly in favour of Scherger's enthusiasm against Hasluck's caution.' Australia

> would offer a battalion to assist in a strategy which was still being formulated . . .The offer would be made essentially because Menzies and his senior ministers believed that it was in Australia's own security interests, as well as in the interest of good Australian-American defence relations, to help the United States to keep South Vietnam out of communist hands.

The request for 150 instructors would be declined.[62]

The decision to deploy the battalion to Vietnam was taken by a handful of senior ministers. Sir Arthur Tange, who handed over to Sir James Plimsoll as secretary of External Affairs on 5 April 1965 but for some months had been 'mentally and physically disengaging from the department and its policy concerns', was adamant that the initiative to commit the battalion did not come from his department. 'What has never adequately been recognised is the extent to which cabinet ministers formed their own view as to what would be a desirable relationship with the United States and then took advice from the Chiefs of Staff Committee which of course excludes External Affairs.' Vice-Admiral Sir Alan McNicoll, who took over as CNS in February 1965, agreed with Tange that the 'initiative came from the political side', adding however that 'we had to pay our subscription to the club we belonged to'. Tange doubted the capacity of the service chiefs to make wise decisions about strategic issues. As we have seen, the chiefs strongly supported the Vietnam commitment, and Wilton had been a keen advocate. Scherger, who had committed Australia without assessing all the political and military issues, later commented: 'Our advice was based on the simple premise that if America was in and was anxious for us to go in, then we ought to go in, up to the extent of providing up to a brigade of troops, which is what we did eventually. If one expected America to do anything on our behalf, then we had to do something to show willingness to assist. It was never conceivable to us that America would lose—no way; but lose she did.'[63]

Announcement

Although the government had decided to commit a battalion to Vietnam, a number of matters needed to be resolved, including receiving a formal request from the United States. Arrangements also had to be made so that the South Vietnamese government would request the battalion, noting that some nationalist groups were reluctant to see the introduction of foreign troops. Although three months earlier, on 10 December, the South Vietnamese government had asked Peter Howson, then visiting Vietnam, for Australia to provide military assistance, since then there had been several coups. The Australian ambassador in Saigon, David Anderson, was in frequent discussion with the US ambassador, General Maxwell Taylor, and the new South Vietnamese prime minister, Phan Huy Quat.

Following the FAD Committee's decision, on 9 April Hasluck told the Australian ambassador in Washington, Keith Waller, to inform the Americans that Australia was willing to offer a combat battalion. Waller replied on 13 April that the Americans said 'it would be helpful if the Australian battalion could join the United States Marine forces in the Da Nang area'. After discussion with Rusk, Waller reported 'that it was the President's desire that Australia should supply a battalion for use in South Vietnam at a time and place to be fixed'.[64] A week later, Army Headquarters issued its formal order for the deployment of 1 RAR.

But where would it be operating? That question was answered during a series of discussions in Honolulu, Washington and Saigon between 20 and 26 April. It was eventually agreed that the Australian battalion should go to the Bien Hoa area near Saigon, that it would be involved in conventional combat operations, and that Quat should be approached to seek his approval. Quat accepted the Australian offer when Anderson met him in the morning of 28 April, and the following day cables from Saigon reported that at 9 p.m. Canberra time the South Vietnamese government would announce that, at South Vietnam's request, Australia had decided to send a battalion. The government was hurried into announcing its decision when a story appeared in the Sydney *Daily Telegraph* in the morning of 29 April revealing the commitment of the battalion. Since then there has been much speculation that the story was leaked to the press by William McMahon. At 8 p.m. on 29 April, one hour before the South Vietnamese announcement, Menzies rose to address the House of Representatives:

> The Australian Government is now in receipt of a request from the Government of South Vietnam for further military assistance. We have decided—and this has been after close consultation with the Government of the United States—to provide an infantry battalion for service to South Vietnam. We decided in principle some weeks ago that we would be willing to do this if we had the necessary request from the Government of South Vietnam and the necessary collaboration from the United States.

Menzies added that the 'takeover of South Vietnam would be a direct military threat to all the countries of South and South-East Asia. It must be seen as part of a threat by Communist China between the Indian and Pacific Oceans.' As Edwards commented, 'This was a gravely misleading interpretation of the policy-making that had led to the decision, and one that would distort the debate on Vietnam for the next decade.'[65]

In subsequent years, critics claimed that the Australian government pressured the South Vietnam government into requesting the battalion and had deceptively portrayed the commitment as responding to the South Vietnamese 'request'. This criticism is not valid, for the South Vietnamese had frequently sought support over the previous years, and Menzies indeed explained that the decision had been made in principle 'some weeks ago' and after 'close consultation' with the United States. He did not mention, however, that the decision had actually been made in principle on 17 December, more than three months earlier.

The government's senior ministers believed that the communist thrust in South-East Asia needed to be stopped and that the United States needed to be encouraged to commit forces to Vietnam. But they had failed to understand the true nature of the war in Vietnam, and in particular had not fully considered the fact that the South Vietnam government that Australia would be supporting was corrupt and unstable. The United States and Australia thought that somehow their military commitment would help create a stable government in Saigon. Australia's military advisers saw the war in purely military terms, and encouraged the government to commit forces to Vietnam. The Australian government's policy over the previous five years created a momentum towards a further commitment in Vietnam. In measured terms the official historian, Peter Edwards, concluded that 'the handling of the crucial decisions was less adept and less prudent than it should have been'. Other commentators would be far more critical of the government's decision-making.[66]

The Menzies government should have had a greater capacity for effective war leadership than any of its predecessors. Menzies himself was an experienced war leader. He had taken Australia into the Second World War and had approved the commitments to Greece, which turned into a disaster, and to Syria, which was more successful. He had committed forces to Korea, which had strengthened the US alliance, and to the Malayan Emergency, which was a successful campaign, even if Australia's role was relatively minor. His ministers were also experienced and capable, with two, McEwen and Holt, having served with him in the War Cabinet in the Second World War. With Menzies' blessing, McEwen had committed combat troops to Borneo in a campaign in which, remarkably, Australia maintained good relations with Indonesia.

The Menzies government had skilled advisers. The Australian diplomatic corps was much larger and more effective than in the past, and had talented officials such as Tange, Plimsoll, Waller and Shaw.

Australia had also developed its own intelligence gathering capacity and could call on intelligence sharing arrangements with allied countries. All the military advisers had had wartime experience and had held senior command and diplomatic positions overseas—both Scherger and Wilton had served in the United States.

Yet these political leaders and their advisers led Australia into a war in Vietnam, which, with the passing of time, seems difficult to justify. It needs to be remembered that it was a time of strategic uncertainty, with Indonesia seen as a major threat. The commitment to Vietnam consolidated the US alliance and secured South-East Asia from the communist threat. But there is no evidence of the government trying to pursue a more subtle approach to these problems. Menzies and his ministers were arrogant and overconfident in their own judgements. Edwards summed up the differences between the commitments to the Indonesian Confrontation and Vietnam:

> In the case of Confrontation . . . Menzies and his ministers did not simply respond to British pressures, but repeatedly challenged London's political and military strategies. Their response to requests for military intervention, especially for boots on the ground, was cautious, and balanced by vigorous and independent diplomacy in Asian capitals.
>
> On Vietnam, by contrast, Menzies and his closest advisers relied uncritically on American power and judgement. They pressed Australian troops on to the Americans, when Washington policymakers had no clear strategy and had only indicated a vague request for more advisers.
>
> In the case of Confrontation, policy was made by vigorous argument within the key departments (External Affairs, Defence and Prime Minister) and their respective ministers. In the case of Vietnam, Menzies sidelined many who advised caution and relied heavily on advisers who shared his assumptions.[67]

10

'All the way with LBJ'

Holt, Vietnam War, 1965–67

The Vietnam War divided Australian politics and society, with ever more vociferous protests about both conscription for the war and Australia's involvement in it. While the government's management of this important episode in Australian history is worthy of detailed study,[1] this chapter and the next concentrate more particularly on the government's handling of the actual military commitment. What was the mechanism by which the government ensured that its policies were followed on the battlefield? What were the strategic and military imperatives behind the expansion of the military commitment? Who were the key decision-makers? And what were the strategic and military considerations behind the eventual withdrawal?

Restrictions on 1 RAR's Role

Following the commitment of 1 RAR in April 1965, the first task—one that was substantially left to the CGS, Lieutenant General Wilton—was to ensure that the battalion was deployed in such a way as to meet the policies of the Australian government. As Wilton explained to the Defence secretary Sir Edwin Hicks, the Australian battalion would operate as part of a US force, and in no circumstances could it be given 'responsibility for a separate area as it is not large enough nor is it organised to handle such a situation'. When the Defence Committee met on 20 April, nine days before the public announcement, Sir James Plimsoll, secretary of External Affairs, questioned Wilton closely on this matter, and warned that:

> Australian troops should not be used on their own in exposed positions. If Australia's only battalion in Vietnam was completely lost, our presence there would be gone, quite apart from other considerations. The expression of this to the Americans would need to be handled carefully, and we must avoid any suggestion of mollycoddling our forces, but something could be said orally between the relevant Commanders.[2]

On the following weekend, Wilton reviewed the plans with Brigadier Ken Mackay, the Director of Military Operations and Plans, who had accompanied Scherger to Honolulu. Wilton directed Mackay to begin planning to send a full battalion group, including a battery of artillery and a troop of engineers, to Vietnam.[3] It was the first step in building the force beyond the initial battalion. The army's planning was kept secret until the evening of 29 April, when Menzies announced in parliament that 1 RAR would be deployed to Vietnam.

Three days later, Mackay and a small planning team arrived in Saigon, where General William Westmoreland, commander of MACV welcomed them. They learned that the Americans planned for 1 RAR to become the third battalion in the 173rd Airborne Brigade that was to defend the Bien Hoa air base near Saigon. They discussed 1 RAR's proposed roles and conducted a reconnaissance of Bien Hoa and Vung Tau, which would be the entry point for the battalion. By then the commander of the AATTV, Colonel David Jackson, had been appointed Commander Australian Army Force, Vietnam (AAFV) and together they agreed on a Military Working Arrangement with the Americans.[4]

Returning to Canberra, Mackay accompanied Wilton to the Defence Committee, which endorsed his report, approved draft directives for the Commander AAFV and the battalion commander, and approved the command arrangement whereby Westmoreland, not the South Vietnamese, would exercise operational control over the Australians. Wilton and Mackay also attended the meeting of the FAD Committee on 18 May that approved the Defence Committee's report. Mackay recalled that he and Wilton came under intense questioning about the security of 1 RAR's position at Bien Hoa. Menzies even asked about 'adequate fields of fire'.[5] Wilton issued his directive to Colonel Jackson on 27 May, and the main body of 1 RAR arrived in Vietnam in early June.

With 1 RAR preparing for operations Wilton flew to Saigon on 22 June to ensure there would be no problems integrating the battalion into an American brigade. Tactfully as possible, Wilton told the brigade commander that he could not 'treat an Australian battalion in the same way as he can an American battalion'.[6] Having resolved these command concerns, Wilton left Colonel Jackson to ensure the directives concerning the security of the Australians were followed and that 1 RAR's operations conformed to its agreed role.

Wilton had been back in Canberra less than two weeks before there was an apparent attempt to change 1 RAR's role. On 4 July, Jackson informed him that Westmoreland planned to form a general reserve based on the 173rd Brigade that could be deployed anywhere in Vietnam and he recommended the inclusion of 1 RAR. Wilton did not agree, explaining to the army minister, Jim Forbes, that 1 RAR's inclusion would involve it in 'a succession of hazardous operations which would inevitably result in heavy casualties'. Jackson (now promoted to brigadier) replied that Westmoreland wanted to conduct operations in a relatively near area and he thought 1 RAR should be permitted to take part, as it would allow the Australians to 'have the greatest impact' on the war. Wilton was unmoved; he considered that Jackson would not be able to watch over Australian national interests effectively and there was the possibility of higher casualties.[7]

The restrictions on the use of 1 RAR were still in force when Wilton visited Saigon at the beginning of September. After discussion with Westmoreland, Wilton agreed that 1 RAR should be permitted to operate anywhere in the III Corps area. (Vietnam was divided into four South Vietnamese corps areas, and III Corps, which included 173rd Brigade, covered all the south-central area of South Vietnam and surrounded, but did not include, Saigon.) Wilton then signalled Canberra, requesting the chairman of the Chiefs of Staff Committee, Air Chief Marshal Scherger, seek approval from the defence minister, Shane Paltridge. He explained that 1 RAR should now 'have a more active role. It is the best battalion in the theatre and its morale will suffer if it is not used to best effect in the mobile offensive role.' Securing the extension to 1 RAR's area of operations took longer than Wilton had hoped, mainly because Paltridge had fallen ill, and because of the need to get agreement from the Minister for External Affairs, Paul Hasluck. The postmaster-general, Alan Hulme, had taken over as acting defence minister. It was 1 October before Wilton signalled Jackson that 1 RAR was 'available for operations more distant from Bien Hoa'.[8] The importance of this episode lies in what it reveals about the attitude of the Australian government, and particularly of Wilton, who was determined to limit casualties and not expose Australian troops to capricious American operations.

Expanding Australia's Commitment

No sooner had 1 RAR arrived in Vietnam, than Wilton and his advisers began considering how the force could be built up to an independent task force. Meanwhile, information arrived that the US government might soon ask Australia to increase its force contribution. Setting out how Australia might respond, Wilton explained to Scherger on 20 July that the 'war in Vietnam is essentially an infantry war and the requirement for additional forces is basically for more infantry battalions. Other supporting arms such as artillery, APCs [armoured personnel carriers] and engineers are important but have a less vital part to play in the present situation.' However, the earliest that the uncommitted battalions (which were being built up with national servicemen) would be ready for operations would be February 1966. Wilton argued that 'we should plan now to build up our existing force to a Task Force of two infantry battalions plus the required scale of combat and logistic support units, together with a detachment of Army light aircraft and a detachment of RAAF Iroquois utility helicopters'. This was a timely assessment, because on 26 July, President Johnson asked Menzies for increased assistance in Vietnam, and in response the Defence Committee recommended increasing the force by an artillery battery and an engineer troop, with another infantry battalion to be made ready by February or March 1966.[9]

With these plans in mind, in early August Brigadier Mackay visited Saigon, where he learned that President Johnson was requesting additional Australian forces, and had asked what Australia had in mind. Johnson had approved the deployment of a further 125,000 US troops to Vietnam, and the Republic of Korea was expected to despatch a division. Anxious to reserve an area for an Australian task force, Mackay asked the Americans to 'Just put a ring around Phuoc Tuy Province. If we're going to come in with a force, this is the place I believe we ought to come in to.'[10]

For the moment, this was just prudent planning, as Wilton recognised that a force of two battalions could not yet be sustained. But clearly a larger force was being discussed, and when Wilton explained the problem of providing such a force to the defence minister, Paltridge toyed with the idea of increasing the national service intake beyond its current figure of 8400 per year. On 17 August, Paltridge met Scherger, Hicks, Forbes and Wilton to discuss the proposal, but Wilton argued that it would have implications for all three services and Paltridge decided not to press it further. Later that day the FAD Committee agreed to send an additional 350 troops to Vietnam, enabling the battalion to be reinforced with a battery of artillery and a troop of engineers to form a battalion group, but directed that the army not undertake any further planning to deploy a task force.[11]

The army ceased planning for a two-battalion task force for the remainder of the year. On 29 November, however, the US Secretary of Defense, Robert McNamara, told the Australian ambassador in Saigon that a request for a second battalion would be made shortly. On 7 December, Hicks advised the acting defence minister, Hulme, that 'if an additional Australian contribution in Vietnam is judged to be the most effective Australian contribution, then it would seem that nothing short of a task force of at least two battalions with appropriate supporting units (say a total of 3,500 men) would meet the requirement'.[12]

Brigadier Mackay visited Vietnam between 14 and 20 December 1965, when he was specifically directed 'not to give any indication that Australia would be prepared to supply additional units for service in Vietnam at this stage'. Nonetheless, the possibility was raised. Three alternative areas were offered: the Phan Rang area in central South Vietnam, the Mekong Delta, and Phuoc Tuy Province. According to Mackay, the Americans were 'very keen to have our forces in Phuoc Tuy'. Considering the geography of the province, he thought 'it would be relatively easy to put our force, small as it was, between say 100,000 people in Phuoc Tuy and the VC [Viet Cong] who were out in the bush . . . if we with a national force could sit in the centre of things here we could play an important role in the liberation and defeat of the VC'.[13]

While Mackay was still in Saigon, on 18 December the Minister for External Affairs, Hasluck, who was also visiting Saigon, cabled Canberra that the latest South Vietnamese prime minister, Nguyen Cao Ky, had made 'almost a request' for additional army and air force assistance. The head of the Australian Defence staff in Washington, Major General Charles Long, followed this with advice from Westmoreland that he envisaged an Anzac brigade with two Australian and one New Zealand battalions plus supporting arms and services, logistic support units and an SAS squadron. Moving quickly, on 4 January Hicks sent Hulme two papers—one prepared by Scherger in consultation with the military chiefs, the other by Hicks's staff—outlining the forces that could be sent to Vietnam. The Cabinet considered them on 5 January; although it took no decision, it permitted the chiefs to prepare a formal proposal.[14]

The Holt Government

Before the chiefs could submit this proposal there was a major change in the government. On 19 January, Paltridge, who had been fighting cancer for several months, resigned as defence minister, and two days later he died. Then on 20 January Menzies, now aged 71, announced his retirement, and on 26 January 1966, Harold Holt, Menzies' deputy, was sworn in as prime minister. In forming his new ministry, Holt appointed McMahon as treasurer, with Leslie Bury taking over McMahon's previous portfolio as Minister for Labour and National Service. The Minister for Supply, Allen Fairhall, become defence minister, while McEwen and Hasluck retained their portfolios. The FAD Committee would consist of Holt, McEwen, McMahon, Fairhall, Hulme (who had attended the committee as acting defence minister) and Senator John Gorton, who as well as being Minister for Education and Science, represented Defence and External Affairs in the Senate.

Although he had been a member of the FAD Committee since its inception in 1963, Holt had no special expertise in defence or external affairs. He was, however, an experienced politician. A Melbourne lawyer, he had been elected to the House of Representatives in 1935 at the age of 27, and was Minister for Labour and National Service in 1940–41. He returned to that portfolio on the election of the Menzies government in 1949, and became treasurer in 1958. The historian Ian Hancock wrote that Holt's

> achievements as a senior minister in the postwar Menzies governments were considerable, he contributed to the nation's standing overseas and he helped his own party achieve a permanence lacking in its earlier manifestations. Overshadowed by Menzies, he had attributes which made him an admirable deputy and, in less turbulent times, a good leader: integrity, a willingness to listen, a sense of what was possible, and a team spirit which made him the least likely of his colleagues to undermine or gossip about the others.[15]

Holt brought a different approach to international affairs, concentrating on establishing relations in South-East Asia. Even more than Menzies, he was determined to assist the United States in Vietnam.

The new Minister for Defence, Allen Fairhall, aged 57, was an electrical engineer and businessman who had established a commercial radio station in his home town, Newcastle. For the previous four years he had been Minister for Supply and, according to journalist Don Whitington, had run the department 'more efficiently than it had been run for nearly a generation'. Tough, natural, shrewd and without pretensions, Fairhall was a man of ability and courage. Journalist Ray Aitchison wrote that he 'had always been the most discreet and close-mouthed of ministers'. Fairhall was fiercely anti-communist and provided firm, unwavering support for the commitment in Vietnam.[16]

A junior appointment, although one with future ramifications, was that of Malcolm Fraser as Minister for the Army. The previous minister, Forbes, had been appointed Minister for Health. An Oxford-educated grazier from western Victoria, Fraser was tall, aloof, patrician and ambitious. Although he was only 35, he had been in parliament for ten years. He had been chairman of the government members' defence committee and had visited Vietnam. Wilton found Fraser 'young, inexperienced and, rightly, unsure of himself, but obviously ambitious and keen to make his mark and at the same time avoid making errors'. Wilton assessed him as 'a bit of a loner, and rather suspicious and unable to trust people completely'.[17] Fraser made an immediate mark by demanding to see background files before signing documents and by seeking advice from more junior members of the department. He was the first minister actively to challenge the CGS on military matters. As army minister he was not a member of the FAD Committee.

A Two-battalion Task Force

Following the Cabinet decision on 5 January to permit planning, the Joint Planning Committee prepared a detailed report on what forces could be made available for Vietnam. The committee stated that the ground war was 'essentially an infantry war with brigade sized forces securing major bases throughout the country'. At this stage 4 RAR was still on operations in Borneo, and the committee considered that while Indonesia was 'unlikely to step up confrontation . . . the possibility of limited war cannot be excluded'. Both 5 and 6 RAR would be ready for operations by May–June 1966, but 3 RAR, which had returned from operations in Borneo, and 7 RAR, which had recently been formed, would not be ready until September 1966; 1 RAR was still in Vietnam and 2 RAR would not be ready for operations until October 1966. The final battalion, 8 RAR, which was being raised, would not be ready until March 1967. Planning needed to be based on 'the possibility that the operations may have to be sustained for an indefinite period'. That is, at this stage only a two-battalion task force could be maintained.[18]

The Defence Committee endorsed this report on 10 February 1966. Wilton was adamant that if further forces were requested for service in South Vietnam, it would not be practical 'to meet such a request in a situation short of a defence emergency'. Scherger noted that a brigade was 'the optimum unit which operates alone' in Vietnam. If Australia did not deploy 'one national force incorporating all Australian units in the theatre', it risked the loss of national identity, the loss of valuable experience, especially in command appointments, the 'repetition of the problems which General Monash had in World War I and General Blamey in World War II of getting national units together under national command', and 'subjection to tactical doctrine to which we may not subscribe'. A national force would preserve 'national identity', provide essential military experience particularly in command and, because it would use Australian tactical doctrine, provide a force that was militarily more effective.[19]

These issues went to the heart of the problem of a small country operating in a larger coalition, and were brought home just a few days later when the Americans sought to use 1 RAR in operations close to the Cambodian border. Jackson objected and 1 RAR was withdrawn. Wilton agreed with Jackson's action and advised Hicks that this was 'the first occasion on which it has been necessary for Brigadier Jackson to exercise his responsibility, laid down in his directive for the safety and well-being of AAFV'.[20]

Having permitted the Joint Planning Committee to study the problem, clearly the government was considering expanding the force. After a visit to Canberra by Denis Healey, the British defence minister, who intimated that Britain would continue to have a role in South-East Asia, the Holt Cabinet decided on 15 February that 'it would in principle like to make an offer' of increased military involvement in Vietnam. A few days later US vice president Hubert Humphrey visited Australia and gave a qualified optimistic assessment of the situation in Vietnam.[21]

The Cabinet considered the Defence Committee's report on 2 March, and approved the deployment of a task force of two infantry battalions, an SAS squadron, combat and logistic support units, and eight RAAF Iroquois helicopters. The total contribution of about 4500 would include national servicemen. Much of the initiative for expanding the force had come directly from Wilton, who saw sound military reasons for it. As he said later, 'When we sent our first battalion up, it was the most we could do in terms of the size of the force. We'd always, I think, known in the backs of our minds that when our manpower and other resources permitted this would have to be increased.' But Wilton had been pushing on an open door. Holt was keen to support the Americans, as the Cabinet minute made clear: 'The prime consideration for Australia is the continued commitment of the United States to the defence of South East Asia, and thus to play what the United States will recognise as a full part in the defence of South Vietnam.'[22] Holt announced the increase on 8 March, a day after receiving a formal request from the South Vietnamese prime minister, Nguyen Cao Ky.

Selecting Phuoc Tuy Province

On 12 March, just four days after Holt announced the deployment of the task force, Wilton departed for Saigon for meetings with Westmoreland and the head of the Vietnamese Joint Chiefs of Staff, General Cao Van Vien. In preparing his brief, Wilton had discussed his proposals with Fraser, explaining the advantages of finding a separate 'piece of geography' for the Australian task force.[23]

In Saigon, Wilton and Westmoreland agreed that on all matters concerning the Australian forces, Westmoreland would deal directly with the Commander, Australia Force Vietnam (COMAFV), who would be an officer of major general rank. Brigadier Mackay was shortly to be promoted to fill this position. The US commanding general of II Field Force (the US corps-level formation covering the same area as the South Vietnamese III Corps) would exercise operational control of the 1st Australian Task Force (1 ATF), which would be located in Phuoc Tuy Province. The Logistic Support Group would be at nearby Vung Tau. There would be four tasks for 1 ATF: to secure and dominate its assigned area in Phuoc Tuy Province; to secure the highway linking Vung Tau and Saigon when required; to conduct other operations in the province; and to conduct operations in the III Corps Tactical Zone and in the adjacent province of Binh Tuy (in the II Corps Tactical Zone) as agreed between Westmoreland and COMAFV. Thus Australia placed clear limits on 1 ATF's operations.

The key decision was the allocation of Phuoc Tuy Province to 1 ATF. As Wilton recalled, the choice was between Phuoc Tuy and Bien Hoa. Although for military reasons 1 ATF had to be under US operational control, 'I wanted to have as much independence within the force limitations as I could so I could keep a closer eye on it.' He thought that 'our two-battalion task force was worth any US three-battalion brigade', and that placing it in the province gave 'us the best opportunity to make the most impact nationally—which is always an important consideration in a war like this'. But the most important reason concerned the safety of the force. Vung Tau was on a nearby and isolated peninsula, so 1 ATF could be evacuated or reinforced by Australian national resources should the situation in the province deteriorate. As Wilton explained, 'if the war went really bad and some frightful disaster was impending, we could look after ourselves'. Considering all these reasons, Wilton said, 'all right, we'll go to Phuoc Tuy Province'.[24]

Wilton's decision to locate 1 ATF in Phuoc Tuy Province has not been seriously questioned, but the decision to base 1 ATF specifically at Nui Dat in the centre of the province has been criticised. Brigadier Jackson, who had been nominated to command 1 ATF, later explained that he selected Nui Dat because it was located between the enemy's main force bases and the areas of most dense civilian population. The base had to be capable of being held by a minimum force but also had to provide for a small airfield, a task force maintenance area, tactically located unit base areas and sufficient room to fight should the base come under heavy attack. It needed to be close enough to the Vung Tau–Baria (Ba Ria) area to avoid diverting forces to protect supply lines or alternatively to allow maintenance by air.[25]

Wilton's successor as CGS, Sir Thomas Daly, thought 'with the advantage of hindsight' that 'it would have been a better proposition to develop Vung Tau as the Task Force base', arguing that it was 'unwise to set up two permanent bases'.[26] Wilton rejected this argument. He wanted the troops based away from a populated area. Placing the base in the centre of the province posed a continuing threat to Viet Cong operations. And importantly, if the troops had been at Vung Tau the American high command might have wished to deploy them away from the province on the sort of deep operations that, from the beginning, he had wanted to avoid. Wilton was determined not to risk the lives of Australians in more adventurous American operations, and he wanted to ensure that 1 ATF had the best possible opportunity to conduct operations according to Australian tactical doctrine.

Wilton concluded his visit to Vietnam on 17 March, when he signed a Military Working Arrangement with Westmoreland, and on 23 March the chiefs of staff endorsed these arrangements. Wilton's visit in March 1966 was the most important by any military chief during the Vietnam War and, according to Malcolm Fraser, it was carried out 'brilliantly'. Indeed, Fraser thought that Wilton was 'an extraordinarily able soldier and diplomat'.[27] Whatever the judgement about selecting the base at Nui Dat, Wilton's decision established 1 ATF in Phuoc Tuy Province and set guidelines for its employment that were to continue for the remainder of the war. It was a clear reflection of the Australian government's policy of minimising the chances of excessive casualties.

Wilton's visit also established the command arrangements. The decision to appoint the COMAFV, who reported to the Chiefs of

Staff Committee through its chairman, set a precedent for appointing Australian national commanders with joint-service responsibilities in future conflicts. The chiefs had already recommended the deployment of a naval destroyer and an RAAF bomber squadron, and although the government had yet to approve these additional forces, the chiefs were looking ahead to a force with larger RAN and RAAF components. Fairhall approved the COMAFV's directive on 11 May.[28]

Military Advisers

By mid-1966 there had been considerable changes to the government's military advisers. In February 1965, Vice-Admiral Alan McNicoll had taken over as CNS. Aged 56, he had entered the Naval College at Jervis Bay at the age of thirteen and had been awarded the George Medal as a lieutenant commander with the RN in the Mediterranean in 1941. As deputy secretary (military) in the Department of Defence in 1958–59 he had gained valuable experience in Defence issues, but as CNS he found himself concerned more with naval matters than with wider strategic questions. 'A man of culture and refined literary tastes', he had a reputation as a well-informed, hardworking and skilled administrator, but his greatest challenge was to restore the morale of the navy after the inquiry into the sinking of HMAS *Voyager* off the coast of New South Wales after a collision with HMAS *Melbourne* during a training exercise in February 1964.[29]

In June 1965, Air Marshal Alister Murdoch, 53, became the next CAS. He had begun his service at Duntroon in 1929 before transferring as an air cadet to the RAAF in 1931. In the Second World War he had served in the RAF in the Atlantic and the Middle East, and with the RAAF in the Southwest Pacific. According to the RAAF historian Alan Stephens, his flying experience had been 'thin' but his staff work at senior levels was 'outstandingly efficient' and 'brilliant'. Like McNicoll, he had been deputy secretary (military) in the Department of Defence. Initially the Minister for Air, Peter Howson, was not satisfied with Murdoch, complaining that he did not keep him informed and did not pay enough attention to detail, but eventually he arranged for his appointment to be extended beyond four years, and considered that Murdoch could have been chairman of the Chiefs of Staff Committee. A later chairman, Admiral Sir Victor Smith, thought that Murdoch was 'a very able contributor' to the Chiefs of Staff Committee, even if the CGS thought 'he was a pain in the neck' in the committee.[30]

The government had been considering a successor to Scherger as chairman of the Chiefs of Staff Committee since November 1965. Although it had been assumed that Wilton would receive the appointment, McNicoll was lobbying hard. Hicks advised the acting defence minister, Hulme, that he should not consider Murdoch as he was from the same service as Scherger and was the junior chief by age and tenure of appointment. On the other hand, both Wilton and McNicoll were competent, although the latter was 'more intelligent'. Armed with this advice, Hulme then discussed the appointment with the three service ministers and interviewed the three contenders.[31]

On 29 November, Hicks again wrote to Hulme, this time strongly supporting McNicoll. He thought that McNicoll's service experience better fitted him for the appointment. McNicoll, he asserted, would be more objective when dealing with the claims of the other services. Perhaps thinking of Wilton's alleged lack of charisma, Hicks considered that 'publicly and internationally', McNicoll 'would be the more impressive appointee'. Hicks regarded McNicoll as

> having the better policy mind and the greater acuity of mind; being better fitted in his intellectual processes to analyse the difficult problems which appear to be likely to develop in the future and discuss them logically and objectively with both military and civilian officers at all levels; and possessed of the greater capacity to express his views clearly and concisely.[32]

It is difficult to judge how much Hicks was influenced by Menzies' preference for McNicoll, but Wilton was certainly more inclined than McNicoll to challenge the structure of the defence department and the role of the chairman of the Chiefs of Staff Committee.

On 10 December the FAD Committee met to consider Scherger's replacement; but after an hour's debate the ministers could not decide between McNicoll and Wilton. While both Menzies and Hulme supported McNicoll, Paltridge, who was absent, probably preferred Wilton. Menzies therefore decided to defer the decision until the New Year, when Paltridge might be able to participate in the discussion. The head of the British Defence Liaison Staff, Air Vice-Marshal Peter Philpott, reported to London that Scherger had told him 'general Service opinion seems to be increasingly tending to back McNicoll'. He noted that Menzies supported McNicoll, but added presciently that if Menzies were to retire, the field would 'be wide open once again'.[33]

Philpott was right. By the end of January, Holt had succeeded Menzies, and Fairhall had become defence minister following the death of Paltridge. Hicks wasted no time in advising Fairhall that McNicoll would be the 'better appointee', but he put the case with less vehemence than previously, explaining that both Wilton and McNicoll were 'excellent officers and any decision must be a marginal one'. Years later, Fairhall claimed that he preferred Wilton as he had been Paltridge's choice, and he did not like the way Lady McNicoll had tried to influence him at various social functions. The Cabinet considered the appointment on 15 March, and Wilton's appointment went through unanimously.[34]

Wilton was succeeded as CGS by Lieutenant General Thomas Daly, aged 53.[35] After graduating from Duntroon in 1933, Daly had served in the Middle East, in the Southwest Pacific, where he had commanded a battalion in action, and in Korea, where he had commanded a brigade. He had been commander of both the Northern and Eastern Commands as well as adjutant-general. Urbane, dignified and charming, although sharing few confidences, he was fiercely loyal to the army, putting its interests before his own. Fairhall, Wilton, McNicoll, Daly and Murdoch were to remain in office for the crucial period of the Vietnam War.

Holt Visits the Troops

Soon after becoming prime minister, Holt decided that a visit to the forces in the region was his first priority, and he directed Wilton, as the incoming chairman of the Chiefs of Staff Committee, to accompany him as military adviser. They arrived in Saigon on 22 April, and over the next two days met senior members of the Vietnamese government, Westmoreland, the staff of Headquarters AAFV, the Commanding General II Field Force, the commander of the Vietnamese III Corps, and the officers and men of the 1 RAR battalion group at Bien Hoa. They visited Vung Tau to see the RAAF Caribou flight and members of the AATTV resting there, and then flew over Phuoc Tuy Province to Bien Hoa, where they visited various hospitals and met the Australian surgical team. On 25 April they returned to 1 RAR for an Anzac Day service. The political journalist Wallace Brown commented that nobody in attendance doubted Holt's 'sincerity, his political savvy, his showmanship and his bravery, when deliberately conspicuous as a potential sniper target in sparkling white safari suit, he stood on a dais at Bien Hoa airport and addressed 1 RAR while in the background Viet Cong mortar bombs were exploding along the heavily guarded perimeter'.[36]

Next stop was at Ubon in north-east Thailand to visit the squadron of RAAF Sabres. Then it was on to Bangkok for discussions with the Thai prime minister and his senior ministers. On 27 April Holt and his party arrived at Kuala Lumpur for meetings with senior Malaysian officials, including the prime minister, Tunku Abdul Rahman, and then flew down to Terendak army camp to inspect the 28th Commonwealth Brigade. They returned north to see the RAAF staff at the Butterworth air base. By the morning of 29 April they were in Singapore to visit the British naval base and the Australian minesweepers, *Curlew*, *Gull*, *Hawk* and *Snipe*, that had been patrolling the sea frontier between Malaysia and Indonesia.[37]

Flying to Kuching in Sarawak, they visited the headquarters of 2 SAS Squadron, where Major Jim Hughes described how his men had been operating across the border since January. At the headquarters of 4 RAR at Bau, the commanding officer, Lieutenant Colonel

David Thomson, explained that his recently arrived battalion had not yet operated in Indonesian territory.[38] It was an illuminating visit, but knowledge of Australia's secret cross-border operations was kept from the press and remained secret for another twenty years.

Back in Canberra on 1 May, Holt reflected that it was 'all an eye opener to him and very educational'. Wilton thought that the visit was of 'great value' to Holt 'when it came to making political decisions on military matters . . . the troops were glad to see him and he enjoyed himself once he became acclimatised to the heat and other conditions'.[39] The experience immediately proved valuable. During April, the British commander in Borneo, Major General George Lea, had warned Lieutenant Colonel Thomson that he intended to use 4 RAR to mount a cordon and search operation in the Bau district. Under his directive, Thomson was not permitted to use his battalion for internal security operations. When Thomson queried whether the operation was directly related to external infiltration, Lea replied that the Chinese had been coming and going from Indonesia and that they could jeopardise military operations in the Bau district.[40] The Defence Committee recommended that 4 RAR be permitted to take part in the operation, but on 18 May the Cabinet rejected it as Australia might be seen to be taking 'political sides' within Sarawak. Both Holt and Wilton had been informed by their recent visit to 4 RAR. In one of his first actions as chairman of the Chiefs of Staff Committee, Wilton directed his successor, Lieutenant General Daly, to inform the Australian commander in Singapore that the government had made no final decision and that he was to obtain further information about the proposed operation.[41] In the end Lea postponed the operation.

That the government needed to consider the actions of a single battalion reveals the way the political aspects of Australia's military operations had changed over the years. In the First World War the British government had committed the 1st Australian Division to the Gallipoli campaign without consulting Australia. In the Second World War the Australian government had approved the commitments to campaigns in Greece and Syria, but had not tried to manage the employment and conduct of their forces once they were committed. As we saw in Chapter 7, the government approved Blamey's campaigns in Bougainville and New Guinea in 1945 months after they had begun.

All the Way

Continuing his involvement with international affairs, on 27 June Holt headed overseas for visits to Washington and London. In Washington he made his famous speech in which he stated that Australia would be 'all the way with LBJ'. Although Holt was criticised for apparently giving the United States a 'blank cheque', his comment was extremely well received in Washington.[42] While intended more as a rhetorical flourish, the statement summed up the fact that Australia would make its largest increases to its Vietnam commitment with Holt as prime minister.

In deciding what forces Australia could send to Vietnam, one of the most important considerations was the need to assist Britain during Indonesia's Confrontation with Malaysia. By mid-1966, however, it was clear that the Confrontation was drawing to a close. The previous October, military forces in Indonesia, led by General Suharto, had mounted a coup, and while Sukarno was still president, he had lost much of his power. By March 1966 Suharto was in firm control. After negotiations, the peace treaty between Malaysia and Indonesia was ratified in Jakarta on 11 August. By the end of August, the only Australian Army unit remaining in Borneo was the engineer squadron. A total of seven Australian soldiers were killed on operations during the Confrontation.

Australia was still committed to maintaining a battalion in the 28th Commonwealth Brigade, but the end of the Confrontation gave the Australian chiefs more flexibility in considering reinforcements or even additional forces for Vietnam. Indeed, the CNS, Vice-Admiral McNicoll, suggested that the four Australian minesweepers operating out of Singapore be deployed to Vietnamese waters; but Fairhall was 'adamant that no such proposals shall be considered before

December'.[43] The government was planning an election in November and did not want to think about force expansion before then.

Fairhall was, however, receptive to arguments for moderate increases. On 1 August, Wilton advised Fairhall that the Viet Cong was building up its forces in Phuoc Tuy Province, and that 1 ATF was preparing to meet the threat. In the second week of August the COMAFV, Major General Mackay, visited Canberra for the annual CGS exercise at Duntroon. Wilton took Mackay to see Fairhall, and followed up with a formal request to increase the force by 69 personnel (to a strength of 4623), arguing that this was a 'marginal adjustment to an existing force commitment rather than an increase in our force commitment in the operational sense'. On 17 August, Wilton advised Fairhall that that morning the Nui Dat base had come under 'extensive enemy mortar fire'. Next day, D Company 6 RAR fought an intense battle with several Viet Cong battalions in the Long Tan rubber plantation east of the base. Seventeen Australians were killed.[44] Although Viet Cong casualties were in the hundreds (the Australians found 245 bodies) and the outcome was a great victory for the task force, the Australians had come close to disaster. Westmoreland arranged for President Johnson to send a letter of appreciation to the prime minister. With this background, it was difficult for Fairhall to deny the additional personnel requested by Wilton, and he approved them on 13 September.

On 21 and 22 October, President Johnson visited Australia. Aware that Holt's statement that Australia would be 'all the way with LBJ' had drawn criticism, during a parliamentary luncheon Johnson said that he would 'like every Aussie who stands there in the rice paddies on this warm summer day to know that America—and LBJ—is with Australia all the way'.[45] Johnson then journeyed onwards to Manila for a meeting of the heads of government of the seven nations involved in the Vietnam War. The Australian delegation included Holt, Hasluck, Fairhall, Wilton, Bunting, the Australian ambassadors to the United States, Vietnam and the Philippines, and other senior government officials. Before the conference, the chiefs of staff had prepared a military brief explaining 'that at this stage only a non-committal reply could be given to any suggestion about deploying additional Australian forces to Vietnam'.[46]

In the November federal election, the Liberal–Country Party coalition government was returned with a huge majority, seemingly justifying the government's Vietnam policy. As the official historian, Peter Edwards, commented, 'The Election result, and especially Holt's personal reaction to it, locked him and his Government into unequivocal support for the Vietnam commitment and conscription, leaving no room to manoeuvre.' Within the government and bureaucracy, however, there was concern about Holt's capacity to handle international affairs. According to Hasluck, Holt needed 'nursing', and there 'was a tacit understanding between Plimsoll (External Affairs), Bunting (Prime Minister's Department), Hicks (Defence Department) and myself that we gave him as much of this nursing as we could'.[47] But it would be hard to control Holt after his election victory.

By this time most members of the Defence Committee had visited Vietnam, and they began preparing their arguments for expanding the force there. Air Marshal Murdoch had visited in August, shortly before the Long Tan battle, and Daly visited in September. McNicoll, still keen to have the navy involved, visited in mid-October, and Hicks accompanied Fairhall to Vietnam after the Manila conference.

Wilton had already been to Vietnam twice during the year, but in early December he visited again as he wanted to see how the COMAFV and 1 ATF were settling into their tasks.[48] Mackay told Wilton that he needed an additional 940 soldiers to meet deficiencies in the 1 ATF units, to provide for a Civil Affairs Unit, and to allow for soldiers absent through battle casualties, sickness, and rest and recreation. Westmoreland added that any increase in the force would be welcome. Mackay claimed later that he also told Wilton he had grave doubts about the outcome of the war: the South Vietnamese were chronically inefficient; corruption and graft were rife; there were no outstanding Vietnamese military or civilian leaders; and there seemed to be no will to win. Apparently Wilton disagreed with Mackay's assessment, as he took no action.[49]

While Wilton had been absent, Holt, buoyed by his electoral victory, had bypassed Fairhall and asked Hicks to prepare recommendations for expanding the force in Vietnam. The Defence Committee, meeting on 13 December with Wilton back from Vietnam, noted that although the military situation had improved, 'defeat of the military aggression from North Vietnam, and of the Viet Cong, is unlikely to be achieved for some considerable time'. The committee considered that 'the rate of progress in defeating aggression from North Vietnam and of pacification is directly related to the size of Allied forces available'. It recommended deployment of the 940 soldiers requested by Mackay, HMAS *Hobart* (a new American-built guided-missile destroyer), a navy clearance diving team of six personnel, and an RAAF squadron of eight Canberra bombers—in all, a further 1700 personnel. The committee rejected a proposal to send another battalion, as it would 'produce training, equipment and movement problems'.[50] Australia was still maintaining one battalion in Malaysia, and if 1 ATF were to be built up to three battalions the army would need to expand from eight to nine battalions to allow for a sensible rotation.

Next day, Wilton gave the Cabinet a verbal report on his recent visit to Vietnam. The Cabinet approved the Defence Committee's recommendations, although apparently Holt was keen to deploy another battalion and needed 'considerable persuasion to change his mind'. Senator John Gorton, Minister for Education and Science, opposed the increase; as he told Holt, 'if decisions on our force levels are *not* going to effect the United States' decision one way or the other, I believe that instead of spending the money envisaged on Defence we should spend it on developing and strengthening Australia itself'.[51] It was a hint of an approach that would appear when Gorton became prime minister a year later.

Despite this additional commitment, during 1967 the government came under intense pressure from the United States to increase it further. Pressure also came from the COMAFV, Major General Douglas (Tim) Vincent, who had succeeded Mackay at the beginning of the year. 1 ATF was finding it extremely difficult to operate with only two combat battalions, as it had permanently to devote at least two companies to the defence of Nui Dat, and by January 1967 Westmoreland was pressing for a third Australian battalion. The following month, Hicks advised the government that a third battalion would 'almost double the operational capability of the Force. The present Task Force is doing an effective and worthwhile job but it could do it more quickly if a third battalion could be made available.'[52] But as there were considerable resource implications in deploying another battalion, the government needed to consider carefully whether it wished to increase the commitment.

There was, however, an alternative approach. While visiting Vietnam, Daly had suggested deploying a tank squadron. Vincent was thinking along the same lines, and on 22 June he sent Wilton a detailed report, arguing that tanks could operate successfully in Vietnam and that they would increase 1 ATF's capacity to destroy the enemy. Vincent added that as well as another battalion, he needed additional helicopter pilots and other support troops, including engineers.[53]

The pressure from the Australian commanders in Vietnam was matched by even greater pressure from President Johnson, who on 15 July sent a message to Holt that there was 'a clear need for us to consider additional effort'. Four days later he said that he would be sending his top advisers, Clark Clifford and General Maxwell Taylor, to Australia, noting that 'General Westmoreland feels substantial additional need for external help'.[54]

On 27 July the Defence Committee considered a report from the chiefs on additions to the force in Vietnam. The chiefs assessed that the army could deploy a tank squadron, additional engineers and small numbers of supporting troops, while the RAN and the RAAF could jointly increase the size of their helicopter contribution. The chiefs saw problems, however, with deploying a third battalion, as to do so would require an increase in the army's manpower ceiling. For the moment the Defence Committee merely noted the paper.[55]

The next day the FAD Committee discussed the government's approach to the forthcoming visit of Clifford and Taylor.[56] Wilton, who was present, explained that any US request to redeploy Australian forces from Phuoc Tuy Province 'should be resisted strongly'.[57]

Australia had made progress there and had established a national identity. If 1 ATF were to be deployed elsewhere, its casualties would be higher. Indeed, the Americans were not making progress because they were moving their troops around the country and were not building up rapport with local forces and the population. Wilton noted that when the Viet Cong suffered a tactical reverse in the north of South Vietnam they merely withdrew across the border into North Vietnam. He therefore considered that the 'proper operation' was to send ground troops into North Vietnam. If this was not done, the war would be 'just a stalemate. Without a change in policy this will go on for years.' He also said that the allies should send troops to interdict the Ho Chi Minh Trail through Laos and Cambodia. He saw no end in sight during the year. For success against regular guerrilla troops the allies would need a ten to one majority.

In response to a question from Holt as to whether Australia could meet America's request for another battalion, Wilton replied that there were still insufficient battalions to provide complete relief for those that were there. It would be necessary to raise another battalion, but this would increase the proportion of national servicemen in Vietnam. Looking beyond five years, the extra expenditure on the army would affect the development of the navy and the air force. The ministers seemed to be surprised by this reply, with Hasluck asking why the chiefs had left the provision of an additional battalion out of their priorities. Wilton replied that they preferred to deploy tanks, but he admitted that the battalion would certainly improve the effectiveness of the task force and, if directed, it could be deployed by October at the earliest.[58]

The chiefs' views about priorities were confirmed when they met on 2 August. At one stage, Fairhall sent for Daly and asked him for an unequivocal answer as to whether tanks would be effective. 'Yes,' replied Daly, 'in the close support role', and Fairhall agreed to recommend their deployment to Cabinet. The members of the Defence Committee were then invited to the FAD Committee on 25 August to consider the deployment of forces to Vietnam, but the ministers were still uncertain about how far to go.[59]

The decision to send an additional battalion to Vietnam was made essentially on political grounds. On 6 September, Bunting set out the arguments for Holt before the next FAD Committee meeting: 'The time to respond in Vietnam in the interest of the American alliance appears to be now. This would mean sending the battalion since it is the battalion and not, e.g., a tank squadron, which is the test of our adherence to the Vietnam issue and to the United States.' Later that day the FAD Committee approved the addition of a tank squadron, a joint RAAF/RAN helicopter contribution, additional engineers and other support troops. It also approved in principle the deployment of a third battalion, with an announcement to be made at a later stage.[60]

The announcement was delayed while the treasurer, William McMahon, tried to secure better financial terms for the purchase of 24 new F-111 aircraft during a visit to Washington. When McMahon and the Australian ambassador, Keith Waller, met Johnson on 3 October, Waller commented that he could not remember 'stronger pressure being brought to bear', for Australia to increase its commitment. In response, Holt told Waller to tell Johnson privately that Australia had decided the send a third battalion, a tank squadron and other elements, bringing the total Australian contribution to more than 8000 personnel. Holt explained that this would bring Australia 'to the full stretch of our present and planned military capacity'. The government informed the South Vietnam government in confidence on 14 October, and Holt announced the increases in parliament on 17 October.[61]

Australia had made a major commitment—the largest since the Second World War—but ironically it had a dampening effect on Clark Clifford, who succeed Robert McNamara as US Secretary of Defense before the end of the year. In 1969 he was to comment that although the Australians had been willing to send 300,000 troops overseas in the Second World War, they were 'reluctant to send more than 7,000 to Vietnam', and this suggested that 'perhaps the Americans had exaggerated the danger of a communist victory in Vietnam'. As Edwards concluded, Holt, 'renowned at the time and in Australian memory as a champion of the Vietnam commitment, had in fact helped initiate a crucial turning point in American policy on Vietnam'.[62]

Holt might have claimed that Australia was 'all the way' with the United States, but in fact Australia was applying a strategy that a journalist later described as being 'ruthlessly cynical'. Australia was finely calibrating how much military support it needed to commit to gain approval from the United States, while ensuring that the commitment was not too burdensome, and that casualties were limited. It was a strategy Australia had applied since 1950 and one that would be pursued for the next 60 years.

Australia's military commanders, however, were more focused on military outcomes than on political recognition, although they knew that a superior military performance would win greater approval. Thus, while the government was sensitive to requests for additional troops from the United States, much of the initiative had come from the army commanders in Vietnam and from Generals Wilton and Daly, who were keen to provide the most potent force possible in Phuoc Tuy Province. In October 1968, after the tanks had been in action for about six months, Daly advised Fairhall that according to the task force commander, the tanks had proven to be 'an asset of considerable value'. Westmoreland certainly recognised Wilton's role in arguing strongly for the force expansion, and hurried to congratulate him on his 'success in achieving this augmentation'.[63]

This would be the last increase to Australia's Vietnam commitment. On 17 December 1967 Holt drowned near Portsea in Victoria. The deputy prime minister and leader of the Country Party, John McEwen, became prime minister until the Parliamentary Liberal Party met on 9 January 1968 and elected Senator John Gorton, then Minister for Education and Science, as the new prime minister. Holt would have struggled to increase Australia's commitment further because the army in particular had reached its limit, but in any case Gorton would bring a new approach, and the United States would now move towards limiting, and indeed reducing, its commitment.

11

'I'm certainly no trained strategist'

Gorton and McMahon, Vietnam War, 1968–72

The five years from the beginning of 1968 to the end of 1972 would see Australian soldiers fighting several intense battles, but would also see a gradual winding down of the Vietnam commitment. As prime minister for more than three years of this period, John Gorton would shoulder the burden of managing Australia's conduct of and withdrawal from the Vietnam War. Born in 1911, and educated at Oxford University, Gorton was a farmer from Victoria who had served as a fighter pilot in the Second World War, and had suffered severe facial injuries in a crash landing on an Indonesian island in 1942. Elected as a senator in 1949, he had been navy minister from 1958 to 1963 before becoming Minister for Education and Science. He joined the Cabinet in 1966. McMahon and Hasluck were more senior in the Liberal Party, but the Country Party leader, McEwen, refused to remain in the coalition if McMahon became prime minister, and Hasluck was thought to be too dour to counter the new charismatic Labor leader, Gough Whitlam. Gorton's colleagues hoped that his relaxed manner would be more appealing on television.

Before he was elected prime minister, Gorton and his wife, Bettina, had spent the previous weekend at the Wiltons' house at Batehaven on the New South Wales south coast. The Wiltons and the Gortons had been friends since the late 1950s, when John Wilton had been commandant at Duntroon. It would have been strange if Gorton had not discussed the Vietnam War with Wilton while at Batehaven, for as a prospective prime minister he had been refocusing his mind from the more narrow concerns of his education portfolio to broader issues. In a television interview in the evening of Sunday 7 January he said that 'aggression must be stopped anywhere it takes place', and after he was sworn in on 10 January he vowed to go to Vietnam as soon as possible.[1]

The Gorton Government

Gorton's elevation brought changes to the government, the most important, with regard to the war, being the appointment of the former army minister, Malcolm Fraser, to succeed him as Minister for Education and Science; within two years Fraser would be defence minister. Another significant appointment was that of Lenox Hewitt as secretary of the Prime Minister's Department, sidelining Sir John Bunting, who became secretary of the Cabinet Office (which Gorton had split from the Prime Minister's Department). Supported by Hewitt, Gorton was to have a different approach to defence issues from that of Holt and Fairhall, who continued as defence minister.

Another change, announced before Holt's death, was the appointment of Sir Henry Bland as secretary of the Department of Defence, succeeding Hicks, who became Australian high commissioner in New Zealand. Bland, aged 58, came to Defence with vast experience of governmental administration. He held senior positions in the Directorate General of Manpower during the Second World War, and then in the Department of Postwar Reconstruction, before becoming secretary of the Department of Labour and National Service in 1952, working firstly under Harold Holt, and then under William McMahon. When appointing Bland to Defence, Holt had remarked that he was 'a man of whom I still stand in awe'.[2] But he had no experience of defence and had never served in the armed forces.

The Australian newspaper observed that Sir Henry was as 'charming socially as the next man', but was 'a hard-as-nails scrapper in the clinches; he rules with an iron fist when necessary and talks in the same manner'. Fairhall and Bland worked well together, Bland describing Fairhall as 'one of the more honest politicians I have ever come across'. Wilton soon found Bland to be a 'hard worker with a great capacity for getting things done—provided it was something he wanted done'. They were to fight over many issues, but somehow retained respect for each other, Wilton describing their personal relationship as 'friendly and close'. In Lieutenant General Daly's opinion, Bland could be 'as tough as old boots or he could charm the green piece out of a gate post'.[3]

Viet Cong Offensive

Two immediate strategic problems for the Gorton government were the Vietnam War and Britain's withdrawal from 'east of Suez', that is, the withdrawal of British forces from Malaysia and Singapore. Early in January, Britain announced that its withdrawal would be more rapid than earlier advised, and on 11 January the Cabinet discussed the implications for regional security. Next day Wilton and Bland joined the FAD Committee to meet a British delegation, and the committee asked the delegation to convey Australia's 'dismay and anxiety' back to London. Wilton and Bland returned to the FAD Committee on 25 January for further discussions about Britain's withdrawal. The ministers on the committee presumably expected the Vietnam War to end fairly soon, for they wanted 'to discover what U.S. policy towards South East Asia will be after Vietnam'; but in the short term they thought that Australia should 'continue to maintain in Malaysia and Singapore a military contribution of the order of existing operational force levels'.[4]

Less than a week later the Viet Cong Tet Offensive 'shattered the credibility of the optimistic official assessments of the war'. While the ferocity and magnitude of the attacks was surprising, in fact the offensive had been expected before or during the Vietnamese New Year

(Tet), due to begin on 27 January. Australian forces would become deeply involved in repulsing the offensive, with policy implications that reverberated in Canberra. When in mid-January the Commander II Field Force, Lieutenant General Frederick Weyand, warned the COMAFV, Major General Vincent, that he might need to use 1 ATF outside Phuoc Tuy, Vincent replied that he did not want the Australians committed once the situation had deteriorated. He therefore approved the operation, which was within his directive, believing that if he sought permission it might not arrive before it was too late.[5]

There were, however, political problems with 1 ATF's deployment. In July 1967 the then Minister for the Army, Malcolm Fraser, had stated that the Australians were going to stay in Phuoc Tuy, and as recently as a week before this latest deployment he had commented that if the Australians 'were moved out of the province and other forces took our place, the continuity of our program would . . . be interrupted'. On 8 February he was forced to explain the apparent change of policy: 'When I returned from Vietnam last July I should have made it clear that further-ranging operations were envisaged as the security situation in Phuoc Tuy Province improves . . . if we continue to disrupt [the enemy's] operations outside Phuoc Tuy we will at the same time be adding to the security of the province'.[6]

By that time the strategic situation had changed considerably. Major General Arthur MacDonald succeeded Vincent as COMAFV at midnight on 30 January, and in the early hours of 31 January the Viet Cong began their anticipated offensive in Saigon. While 2 and 7 RAR engaged in frequent contacts across the approaches to Saigon in Long Khanh and Bien Hoa provinces, within Phuoc Tuy, 3 RAR resisted attempts by the Viet Cong to take over the main towns. On 8 February, MacDonald signalled Wilton that Westmoreland expected further attacks on Saigon and wanted to deploy 3 RAR from Phuoc Tuy to join the other two battalions in Bien Hoa. There was no time to bring the matter to the Chiefs of Staff Committee, so Wilton spoke to Gorton in the 'early hours' and approved the deployment. As it happened, Westmoreland did not require the battalion, but Wilton reminded MacDonald 'there are many important political implications' and that in future he needed to secure approval from Canberra before approving deployments out of Phuoc Tuy.[7]

Wilton was right about the government's sensitivity. On 2 February, without consulting the Cabinet, Gorton announced that Australia would not commit further troops to Vietnam. When the FAD Committee met on 12 March, the ministers discussed a possible response if the United States asked for more troops. They concluded that they needed more information and directed Wilton to go to Vietnam to provide a 'personal assessment of the overall situation'. As a result, Wilton spent five days meeting all the key officers and visiting most of the Australian forces in Vietnam. It is not known what he reported to Fairhall, but his view was likely to have been similar to that of MacDonald, who reported on 10 March that very little damage had been done in Phuoc Tuy Province.[8]

Both Daly and MacDonald were changing their minds about the war. When MacDonald had visited Vietnam in September 1967 he had thought that the war was being won, but following Tet he lost confidence in American intelligence assessments and began to doubt the outcome. He discussed these views with Wilton during his visit in March, and perhaps with Daly, and by the time he finished his tour in February 1969 he believed that the Department of Defence and the government were trying to work out how to get out. There was less action in this regard than he thought. Vice-Admiral McNicoll visited Saigon during the Tet Offensive and he accompanied MacDonald when he visited 1 ATF on operations in Bien Hoa Province. Like MacDonald he was shocked by the extent to which the Americans had been caught unawares, and impressed by the futility of trying to intercept the Viet Cong in the jungle. He claimed that when he returned to Australia, neither the chiefs of staff nor the Department of External Affairs gave him an opportunity to comment on what he had learned. He thought that Wilton took it upon himself to run the Vietnam War and did not consult the chiefs very much on it. Daly later claimed that he knew that while the allies were not losing the war they were not winning it either; he made his views known to the government, but it was a 'political-foreign affairs matter', not a military one.[9]

Rethinking Policy

The Viet Cong offensive brought a fundamental change in the war. Although the Americans and South Vietnamese had major victories across the country, the result was 'two months of policy paralysis in Washington, culminating in an announcement by Lyndon Johnson on 31 March that he would stop the bombing of most of North Vietnam and withdraw from the 1968 presidential election'. Gorton was not informed in advance of either decision, causing him and his advisers great concern that US resolve was weakening. Astonishingly, in view of its losses, North Vietnam initiated another offensive in May, and again the Americans wanted to deploy two Australian battalions into Bien Hoa Province. MacDonald sought permission from Wilton, who concurred without consulting the chiefs of staff. The deployment led to Coral and Balmoral—two of the largest battles fought by Australians during the war.[10]

Back in Australia, the Defence Committee began to consider Australia's military presence in Malaysia and Singapore following Britain's withdrawal. Clearly the changing strategic environment demanded a new assessment, but this was causing much frustration. Peter Howson (the former Minister for Air who had been dumped by Gorton) wrote in his diary on 10 May after discussion with Wilton and Air Marshal Murdoch that they were

> having a pretty unhappy time in the Defence Committee at present. These newcomers, like Gorton and Bland, come in with a lot of ideas, but they haven't done any homework . . . the three Chiefs of Staff and the chairman have decided on their own to have a complete revision of the strategic basis, really now completely out of date, and try to get their own ideas straight, not brooking any interference from Bland and Hewitt.[11]

These comments give a hint of a broader problem. The political machinery for directing and determining defence and strategic policy had been weakened; Gorton took a personal role in policymaking and tended to disregard the FAD Committee, which sat less frequently.

Writing of the value of the committee in 1970, Bland commented that 'Many observers would wish the practice [of using the committee] resumed.'[12]

In May 1968 Gorton visited the United States and met President Johnson, who said that there would be no withdrawal from Vietnam while he was in office. Gorton was more interested in ensuring that the United States remain committed to the region in general if they left Vietnam, and he seemed reassured on this point. With regard to Vietnam, Gorton's biographer Ian Hancock commented that Gorton 'did not share his predecessor's commitment to a war which seemed to be heading nowhere'.[13]

In early June, Gorton visited South-East Asia, and in Vietnam he went out of his way to meet the soldiers, who greeted him enthusiastically. Addressing a gathering at the task force base on 8 June, he told the soldiers that they 'were doing a magnificent job for our own country . . . [and] the results will be felt in our own country for decades to come'. After making disparaging comments about public protests in Australia, he said, 'your Government is behind you and ninety per cent of the Australian people are behind you in what you are trying to do'.[14] He also visited the field hospital at Vung Tau and the RAAF units based there. He and his wife, Bettina, who accompanied him, even went for a swim in the sea at Vung Tau.

At a press conference in Saigon on 9 June, a journalist asked Gorton for his assessment of the military situation in Vietnam. Gorton replied that he did not

> believe I'm competent to make a military assessment, I'm not a military man. We get assessments given to us by our military advisers and I'm certainly no trained strategist nor a trained tactician, but there is one thing I do believe is quite certain, and that is the spirit and morale of our Australian troops here is as high as I have ever seen in any body of troops anywhere.

Questioned as to whether he had 'offered, or been asked, for any more Australian troops for Vietnam', Gorton replied no to both questions.[15]

While Gorton was in Vietnam, Hasluck and Fairhall led Australia's delegation to five-power talks at Kuala Lumpur. When the Cabinet met in September it agreed to keep forces in the Malaysia area until 1971, but deferred major decisions about them until it had considered a new review of the strategic basis of defence policy.[16]

A military victory in Vietnam now seemed more remote than ever. The pause to US bombing of North Vietnam had been followed by the beginning of peace talks in Paris, but there had been little progress. In August 1968 there were anti-war protests and riots in Chicago during the Democratic Party's national convention, while in Australia there were some anti-war and anti-conscription demonstrations. Militarily, the Americans and their allies were continuing to prosecute the land campaign with full energy, but they had one eye on political developments in the United States.

The election of Richard Nixon as US president in November 1968 changed the American approach to the war, as the new president set a course for eventual withdrawal, committed to seeking 'peace with honour'. What this meant for Australia was hard to discern: indeed, Gorton said that Nixon's intentions were 'imponderable'. Gorton had his first meeting with President Nixon when he visited Washington in May 1969. It was during this visit that Gorton, while promising to support the United States in 'resisting aggression', declared that Australia 'will go a Waltzing Matilda with you'.[17] Ironically, in following the United States, Australia would not send more troops to Vietnam, but would follow with a withdrawal.

Nixon was already pointing the United States towards eventual withdrawal from Vietnam, announcing in June that 25,000 American troops would be withdrawn. Gorton was given little warning of Nixon's announcement and in a television interview said that it would be 'militarily ridiculous' to withdraw part of the task force, which was a self-contained force.[18] General Creighton Abrams, who had taken over from Westmoreland as the US commander in Vietnam, was charged with implementing the Nixon administration's Vietnamization policy to decrease US involvement in Vietnam by increasing the role of South Vietnamese troops until they could assume full responsibility for the fighting. The change in American policy was highlighted when Nixon visited Guam in July 1969 and enunciated what was later called the Guam doctrine. Nixon stated that each allied nation was expected to look after its own security, although the United States would act as a nuclear umbrella when requested.

Towards Withdrawal

The initiative for planning for Australia's withdrawal came from the military; indeed, the implications had first been considered by the newly formed Joint Staff in the Defence Department in November 1968. The Joint Planning Committee produced a report in May 1969 and updated it in August 1969. The Defence Committee considered the latter report on 11 September 1969, when the deputy CGS, Major General Stuart Graham, representing the CGS, took the lead and argued strongly that 1 ATF constituted a balanced force and should not be reduced by one battalion. If a reduction was ordered the whole task force should be withdrawn. Other members of the committee pointed out that 1 ATF had been built up progressively and the public was aware of this. Further, perhaps a South Vietnamese battalion or a US battalion could replace an Australian battalion. Graham remained unmoved. The problem was how to deal with Gorton's television interviews in which he had emphasised that 1 ATF was a self-contained force and to withdraw parts of it would be 'quite ridiculous'. This made it 'difficult to bring about a suitably graduated Australian participation in the overall reduction programme'.[19]

Despite his earlier comments, on 21 September Gorton urgently asked the chiefs for their views on a possible withdrawal. In the absence of the other chiefs, Wilton (now promoted to general) and Daly jointly advised that a 'premature reduction or withdrawal of our forces would cause further pressures on the US to withdraw their forces in the minimum time without regard to the "criteria" and "principles"' already expounded by President Nixon. It was 'therefore in Australia's strategic interest to maintain all our present forces in

Vietnam' unless an agreement was reached with Hanoi for a mutual withdrawal, or a stage was reached in a US withdrawal plan where 1 ATF could be completely withdrawn by agreement with the United States and South Vietnam. However, 'Under present circumstances and failing an agreement with Hanoi for mutual withdrawal, we could not withdraw the Australian Task Force and its supporting units from Vietnam in progressive stages without endangering the safety of the Force.'[20] The key to Australia's decision-making was to determine the United States' plans.

Australia was soon in the midst of an election campaign, and on 25 October 1969 the Gorton government was re-elected with a severely reduced majority. Earlier, in February 1969, Paul Hasluck had been appointed governor-general. His successor in External Affairs, Gordon Freeth, was defeated in the October election, and William McMahon became Minister for External Affairs. In addition, Fairhall had retired from politics before the election because of ill health, and after the election 39-year-old Malcolm Fraser was appointed defence minister; he did not assume his new appointment until 12 November.

In the meantime, Gorton dealt directly with Wilton, who had returned from yet another visit to Vietnam where he had discussions with General Abrams. Wilton reported to Gorton that Abrams had a plan for withdrawal but no timetable for it. Abrams had said that he hoped the Australian force would not be prematurely reduced or withdrawn. Wilton had replied that Australia 'had no plans to do so at present and that our decisions are dependent on US decisions and that it was essential that we be kept informed and consulted before decisions are made'. Wilton had stressed to Abrams the need for 'realistic assessments of the progress of Vietnamization and Pacification and said that some of the reports [he] had seen were over optimistic and inaccurate'. Wilton advised Gorton that it would be a further 12–18 months before the South Vietnamese would be in a position to accept further responsibility.[21]

Over the next few weeks, and particularly following an optimistic speech by President Nixon on 3 November about the success of

Vietnamization, the COMAFV, General MacDonald, made strenuous efforts to find out the plans for the US withdrawal, and as these became available, Wilton passed them to Gorton and Fraser. But as he warned Fraser, 'on no account should we let Washington know we have this information unless or until we know that General Abrams has been authorised by Washington to give it to us'. Armed with this information, on 1 December the Chiefs of Staff Committee met to consider a possible withdrawal from Vietnam. If the government decided to reduce the task force 'for political reasons', the chiefs now admitted that it could be reduced to two battalions if a US battalion were available to be placed under Australian operational control if necessary. The Defence Committee endorsed this view and passed it to the Cabinet on 9 December.[22]

It was this Cabinet meeting that led to Gorton's cable to Nixon of 13 December seeking his 'long-term thinking' so that Australian withdrawals could be based on joint Australian–American planning. Wilton had agreed that the cable would state: 'The Military advice relating to our Army task force is that any adjustment could call for co-ordinated Australian/United States Military planning.' The final text, as approved by Gorton, read: 'As to our Army Task Force our military advice is that all our ground force units should, if possible, be withdrawn as one unit though it is possible this might be avoided if there were co-ordinated Australian/United States planning.' Wilton thought that this paragraph made it look as though the chiefs had recommended withdrawal.

On the night of Saturday 12 December, Gorton discussed the matter with Bland and the Secretary of External Affairs, Sir James Plimsoll. He then telephoned Fraser, who promised to bring Wilton's views to the prime minister. Later that night Gorton telephoned Wilton, who pointed out that the proposed text applied only if the government had decided for political reasons to reduce the force. Gorton argued that the text was 'a logical interpretation of the military advice in the event of a government decision for political reasons to withdraw or reduce the Task Force under present circumstances'. Gorton asked Wilton to confirm that this was the military advice.

Wilton did so and the cable was sent as Gorton wished. One suspects that Wilton was not happy, as he made a detailed three-page note of the matter for file.[23]

Daly was not happy either. Interviewed in 1975, he explained that in giving his initial advice he had thought that a large-scale American withdrawal would tip the scales in favour of the North Vietnamese and therefore increase the risk to Australia's forces. Hence Australia should either maintain a three-battalion task force, or withdraw the whole force. He subsequently changed that advice to a 'phased withdrawal'. When asked whether this was 'under political pressure' or 'your own judgement', Daly replied that 'it might have been both . . . I altered my advice because subsequent Intelligence information indicated that the immediate threat wasn't as great as I had previously assessed it to be.' As the official history put it: 'The military chiefs were overruled.'[24]

Nixon's reply to Gorton's cable, sent on 14 December, was not encouraging, but it did raise the possibility that increased Australian economic aid might offset a reduced troop strength. Gorton spoke to Nixon by phone but the details of the conversation were not released. According to Howson, McMahon told him that he, Gorton and McEwen spent most of 14 December 'deciding on a new policy for Vietnam'. On 15 December, Nixon announced further troop reductions. Next day Gorton stated that when the military situation in Vietnam allowed the Americans to make another substantial withdrawal then, 'in consultation with the Government of the Republic of Vietnam, some Australian units will be included in the numbers scheduled for such a withdrawal'. As official historian Peter Edwards commented: 'It was the beginning of the end of the Vietnam commitment, but all too obviously it was an immediate reaction to an American announcement, not the first phase of a carefully considered Australian defence strategy.'[25]

Planning the Withdrawal

Fraser moved quickly to take the initiative. On 18 December he wrote to Wilton and asked for 'various possibilities' to be canvassed by the

Chiefs of Staff and Defence committees. He was not convinced that the withdrawal of one battalion, even with the proviso of an American battalion being made available, was 'the only appropriate solution or indeed whether . . . it is relevant'. For planning purposes, Fraser suggested that the chiefs should be considering a much lower level of threat in Phuoc Tuy Province. More effort should be put into training the South Vietnamese in the province, and as 'we develop a training role there should be a lesser requirement for our forces to continue in their current roles'.[26] The course was set for the withdrawal of one battalion before the end of 1970.

On 9 January 1970, Daly produced a thirteen-page brief on a possible reduction of 1 ATF and the development of training schemes for the Army of the Republic of Vietnam (ARVN), and the Defence Committee considered the brief on 29 January. As Fraser had already said that he did not envisage the first battalion being withdrawn before July or August, the committee recommended that 2 RAR relieve 6 RAR in May and that 8 RAR not be replaced in November. The committee agreed that the establishment of a training complex in Phuoc Tuy Province would contribute to the Vietnamization process, but it was preferable that it be for South Vietnamese Regional and Popular Forces rather than for the ARVN.[27]

More probing and demanding than his predecessor, Fraser was not happy with this advice. In particular he was concerned that the chiefs still apparently wanted assurance that a US battalion would be available if things turned bad in Phuoc Tuy. He did 'not adequately understand why it was safe for a two-battalion force to enter Phuoc Tuy for the first time [i.e. in 1966] while additional support is now necessary in an area that should be much safer than it was then'. Wilton quickly called the chiefs together to rework their advice. They remained cautious about maintaining security in the province, pointing out that if one battalion were withdrawn, 1 ATF's capacity to operate away from Nui Dat would be reduced by about half. Unless additional ARVN or US forces were deployed into the province, the enemy would 'have more freedom of manoeuvre'. In summary, they advised that 'provided there is no change in the enemy threat and level of activity and provided the US withdrawal proceeds with due regard to the president's criteria, a two-battalion task force can still perform a worthwhile mission without undue risk'. On 17 March the Cabinet agreed with the Defence Committee's plans, with the announcement to be made in April. First, however, Fraser would visit Saigon to inform the South Vietnamese and to explore arrangements to train ARVN instructors in Phuoc Tuy.[28]

The government's belated decision to withdraw one battalion from Vietnam raises questions as to whether the graduated withdrawal and the stepping up of the training of the South Vietnamese should at least have been considered much earlier. Abrams had issued his new directive with its emphasis on Vietnamization by April 1969, and this should have been the time for Australia to begin considering its own Vietnamization program. The failure to do so resulted in the government being caught unprepared when Nixon announced the first US withdrawal in June 1969. The chiefs then insisted on answering the questions from the government in an unequivocal manner. Thus, when on 21 September 1969 Gorton asked for their views on a possible withdrawal, Wilton and Daly argued strenuously against it. Apparently Wilton and Daly made no effort to explore alternative approaches, such as stepping up the training and advisory function within Phuoc Tuy, and they did not do so until prodded by Fraser in January 1970. This late decision was to cause problems with the implementation of Australia's training assistance later in the year.

The official historian, Peter Edwards, has argued that while the decisions concerning Australia's commitment to Vietnam were 'ill-advised in hindsight', they were 'at least understandable in the context of their times, especially in the mid-1960s'. Edwards is more critical of the Gorton government in the period from mid-1968 to late 1969, noting that when at the end of 1969 it raised the question of withdrawal with Nixon, the latter hinted that economic aid might balance the withdrawal of troops. As Edwards put it,

> The hint was not pursued. If the Government in 1968–69 had developed a coherent strategy, including the withdrawal of troops,

> especially conscripts, from Vietnam, it would probably have spared Australia from much of the tension and division associated with the Moratorium protests, which did not begin until 1970 . . . The failure even to address the possibility of such an approach in 1968–69 deserves more criticism than does the original commitment of 1965.[29]

Fraser, who became defence minister in November 1969, and who therefore cannot be held responsible for the policy in 1968 and 1969, did not agree with this criticism. He thought that the government had not received clear signals from Washington. Further, he claimed that he had no need to encourage the chiefs to agree to the piecemeal withdrawal of the task force in 1970—they had read the political wind for themselves.[30] Still, by mid-1969 it was obvious to all that the United States was withdrawing and that this would eventually put pressure on Australia to do likewise. By then the defence officials were already preparing plans for withdrawal in the more unlikely event of a sudden ceasefire arrangement. Wilton responded precisely to the government's wishes, but he might have served Australia even better had he presented the government with a wider range of options in mid- to late 1969. Whether Gorton and Fairhall would have listened is another matter, but he may well have found an ally in the government had he sought one.

During the decisive period from August to December 1969, Bland's tense relationship with the chiefs did not help matters. Bland thought that Wilton kept matters concerning Vietnam strictly under his own control. For their part, Wilton and the chiefs were antagonised by Bland's abrasive personality and were critical of his lack of specialist knowledge. Admiral McNicoll thought that he 'despised all uniformed characters'. Bland criticised the 'calibre, orientation and lack of continuity of the Service members', and claimed that defence administration was 'too important to be left to generals'. While Bland did not consider himself to be responsible for military operations, he was surprised that Wilton failed to take an independent Australian line in considering either broad strategic options or the operations in

Vietnam. He thought Wilton was 'pedestrian in many respects', and was 'never really critical of what was going on on the American side'. In October 1969, Bland visited Abrams in Saigon and came away very unhappy with the solution being pursued. On his return he reported his views to Fairhall. Soon, however, Wilton came to see him 'quite upset' that Bland had taken it upon himself to speak to Abrams. Wilton said that it was 'quite improper—I am the one who deals with Abrams'. Bland claimed that Air Marshal Murdoch sympathised with his views but was never willing to bring the matter to a head in the Chiefs of Staff Committee. In the absence of any strong direction being given to the fighting in Vietnam, Bland thought that the best approach was to minimise casualties, a view shared by Fairhall and Gorton.[31]

Fraser as Defence Minister

The ambitious and activist Malcolm Fraser wanted to take firm control of his department and its policies. In this, he was helped by the new Defence secretary, the abrasive and impatient Sir Arthur Tange, who in March 1970 took over from Bland, who had resigned because of his wife's illness. A former secretary of External Affairs, Tange had been Australia's high commissioner in India from 1965 to 1970. A later chief of the Defence Force Staff, General Sir Arthur MacDonald, found Tange to be 'a man of remarkably strong character and a very high degree of ability, not to be underestimated in any respect at all'.[32]

Fraser's approach was set on his first day as defence minister, when he gave the services urgent deadlines to prepare their requirements for the new five-year Defence rolling program.[33] He followed this by meeting with the new service ministers—Jim Killen (Navy), a young Andrew Peacock (Army) and Senator Tom Drake-Brockman (Air)—to make it clear that he would be determining Defence policy. Then, as described earlier, he took the initiative in planning for the withdrawal from Vietnam.

Fraser was playing a delicate game. On the one hand he wanted planning to take account of the changing strategic situation, including the inevitable US withdrawal from Vietnam. On the other hand, by 1970 the war had become increasingly unpopular—indeed, large moratorium demonstrations were held in May and September of that year—and he believed that it was important to argue the case for the war strongly and at every opportunity. He was sensitive to criticism of both Australia's commitment to and conduct of the war.

The government's sensitivity about the conduct of operations was reflected in its concern about casualties. Successive COMAFVs later stated that they never received any political direction to limit casualties, but as one of them commented, there was a general understanding that the loss of lives needed to be balanced carefully against military gains. The COMAFVs did not exercise operational control over 1 ATF, but one COMAFV, MacDonald, observed that if an operational mistake were made that caused large numbers of casualties, he would not be able to hide from this responsibility.[34]

A particular example occurred in February 1970, when 8 RAR returned to the Long Hai hills, near Dat Do. The operation proceeded well until two mine incidents caused nine deaths and wounded sixteen, triggering a signal from Daly to the COMAFV, Major General Robert Hay, stating that he was 'most distressed and concerned at casualties', and that he was 'at a loss to understand 1 ATF undertaking operations in an area in which they have already been costly and of doubtful value'. Hay replied that until these incidents 8 RAR had achieved significant results for minimal casualties and that the operation was having a considerable effect on the enemy.[35]

In March 1970, soon after taking over from Hay, Major General Colin Fraser called on the Commander II Field Force, Lieutenant General Julian Ewell, who asked him directly whether he was under orders to limit Australian casualties. Fraser replied that he had been given no such direction, but that his own view was that in any projected operation casualties could only be justified if there was a sound military purpose offering prospects of substantial benefits from the operation.[36]

Back in Australia, Malcolm Fraser was continuing his active approach. On 10 March he delivered a major statement to parliament in which he emphasised Australia's regional obligations but also recognised the need for a more flexible defence capability. A week later, as described earlier, the Cabinet approved his submission to withdraw one battalion at the end of the year, and agreed that he should visit Saigon to inform the South Vietnamese and to explore arrangements to train ARVN instructors. The key decisions concerning Australia's graduated withdrawal would therefore be made during this visit. Accompanied by Wilton and other senior civilian and military officials, Fraser arrived in Saigon on 31 March and immediately launched into discussions with senior Australian, US and Vietnamese officers. The Vietnamese said they would have preferred Australia to postpone its force reduction until 1971.[37] Fraser departed for the United States on 3 April, where he successfully renegotiated the arrangement to purchase the 24 F-111 bombers.

Wilton remained in Vietnam to discuss training assistance with senior Vietnamese officers. These important discussions set the shape of Australia's training assistance in Phuoc Tuy Province for the remainder of the war. Mobile training teams would be established to train the Territorial Force units scattered across Phuoc Tuy and to accompany them on operations. Australia would also establish and staff a training complex (eventually called the Jungle Warfare Training Centre) at Nui Dat, in the area to be vacated by 8 RAR later in the year. On 22 April 1970, Gorton finally announced that a battalion would be withdrawn and not replaced at the end of the year, and added that Australia would provide a number of mobile advisory and training teams to train local forces in Phuoc Tuy.[38]

Fraser kept up the pressure. On 30 April he directed the National Intelligence Committee to produce monthly assessments, and next day he asked Wilton to arrange for COMAFV to send expanded operational reports with a description of the past month's operations 'set in the context of our longer term objectives; an estimate of the extent to which these objectives are being achieved, and the effect of our operations on security generally in the province'. In fact, Wilton had already asked COMAFV to provide a covering letter to his monthly reports, giving 'a brief rundown of the general military and pacification situations in the province as he saw them'.[39] But Fraser's reasonable questions could well have been asked a year earlier.

By this stage Wilton was turning his mind to the situation after the withdrawal of 8 RAR in November. Hoping for further progress with pacification and in the effectiveness of the 18th ARVN Division and provincial units, he envisaged that it might be possible to hand over responsibility for 1 ATF's area of operations to the 18th ARVN Division before the end of 1971, leaving 1 ATF at Nui Dat as a reserve force. This would, as he put it, 'set the stage for the complete withdrawal of 1 ATF from Phuoc Tuy Province when this is decided by the Government'. He asked General Fraser for a comprehensive review of the military situation. In his reply, Fraser concluded that '1ATF should continue responsibility for the security of Phuoc Tuy Province until the end of 1971', but he thought a progressive withdrawal could begin in August 1971.[40]

Planning for the withdrawal took place in the context of the broader strategic picture. Britain's intention had become clearer when on 31 July its defence minister, Lord Carrington, had met an ad hoc committee of the Australian Cabinet in Canberra. Wilton and Tange were present to hear him explain that Britain hoped to have five frigates or destroyers in the South-East Asia region, a battalion group, four long-range patrol aircraft, a flight of helicopters, and other aircraft to rotate in and out of the area.[41] Detailed planning continued that would lead to the Five Power Defence Arrangements.

On 25 August 1970 the Cabinet met to consider Wilton's replacement when he retired in November. There were two contenders—Daly and Vice-Admiral Sir Victor Smith. Air Marshal Colin Hannah, who had succeeded Murdoch as CAS in January, had not been in office long enough and, as Tange advised Fraser, there were no suitable officers available in the RAAF to succeed Hannah as CAS. Daly and Smith were almost the same age, 57. Daly had been a general since 1959 and CGS since May 1966. Smith had been an admiral since 1962, when he had commanded the Australian Fleet, and CNS since April 1968. Neither had had a joint-service appointment, although Daly had been a member of the Joint Planning Committee in the

1950s. A graduate of the RAN College, Smith had specialised in naval aviation and had served in the Atlantic, the Normandy invasion and the Pacific in the Second World War. Bland thought Smith was 'one of the nicest blokes I've ever dealt with in my life—very honest', but he was not impressed with any of the contenders: 'There were very few top brass who left an indelible impression on me.'[42]

Daly had already advised that he did not wish to be appointed, but the army minister, Andrew Peacock, sought permission to argue his case in the Cabinet. Fraser's view was decisive: 'Tom's old and tired and in any case I have enough fights on my hands without having to fight Tom all the time.' The navy minister, Jim Killen, strongly supported Smith, advising that he was 'keenly attuned to a great variety of very sensitive political and defence factors'. Killen had been 'profoundly impressed with his sweep of understanding of [Defence] problems and also by his willingness to listen to argument and to appraise that argument with complete intellectual honesty'. Smith was appointed and would take over from Wilton in November 1970, when he would be promoted to admiral.[43]

Meanwhile, Wilton set the Joint Staff to work on further planning for the withdrawal from Vietnam, with clear instructions that it was to recommend against withdrawing another battalion before the end of 1971. The External Affairs representative on the Joint Planning Committee urged it to take account of the likelihood that the United States would announce both a change in the role of its forces and further withdrawals. External Affairs suggested 'that it was not good enough to present ministers with the bald statement that for military reasons no Australian withdrawal should take place before the end of 1971'. When ministers were 'coming to a political decision' it would be best if Defence 'listed the military consequences of alternative courses of action. Ministers would thus know what any particular decision entailed in the way of military risks and restrictions on operational and other activities.'[44]

Such an attitude might have been helpful when the chiefs were advising the government about the viability of withdrawal a year earlier. When they met on 15 October, Daly was in the chair as Wilton was attending a SEATO meeting in Hawaii. The chiefs reaffirmed their view that there were 'strong military reasons' why there should not be significant reductions to 1 ATF before the end of 1971, and recommended that the government review the situation again in May 1971. But if, 'for reasons of policy, the government wished to make a decision now' the chiefs set out a three-stage plan for a phased withdrawal. The Defence Committee accepted the recommendations on 28 October, except it advised that the government would need to review the situation no later than February 1971.[45]

Meanwhile, the prospect of a force reduction was causing concern in Vietnam. In October 1970 the Commander 1 ATF, Brigadier Bill Henderson, commented publicly that the withdrawal of a battalion would mean that his men would have to work harder. Gorton, Fraser and Peacock were all forced to release explanatory statements, with Fraser explaining that 1 ATF would be conducting operations on a reduced scale. Unfortunately, in early November Henderson told a journalist that the withdrawal had not altered Australia's role 'one little bit'. His comments therefore raised questions as to whether the South Vietnamese forces had the capability to make up for the shortfall in 1 ATF's ability to conduct operations. After an exchange of signals with General Fraser, Wilton gave Malcolm Fraser a statement that he could use in dealing with further controversy. This stated that the workload of the individual soldiers would not be increased, as the reduced level of enemy activity in the area meant that 1 ATF would be required to conduct fewer operations. This was only partly true—the operations were fewer, but of longer duration.[46]

The Civic Action Affair

The politics of the withdrawal continued to cause problems, exemplified by the Civic Action affair, which resulted in Gorton's resignation as prime minister. It related more to political problems within the government, and particularly Malcolm Fraser's relations with Gorton, than to the actual conduct of the war, although it was triggered by it. In an effort to make the Vietnamese more self-sufficient, in the latter half of 1970 the activities of the army's Civil Affairs Unit, known as 'civic action', were reduced, and officers were becoming sensitive to 'over-involvement' in Vietnamese affairs. Yet as General Fraser observed, despite the political attractiveness of civic action, until the end of 1970 he received no directive about government priorities in this matter. When Daly visited in December 1970, he advised Fraser that the government was likely to order further withdrawals and that it would be unwise to undertake civic action commitments that could not be protected.[47] In February 1971, Fraser issued a directive outlining the options for the conduct of civic action during the expected reduction of the force in the following year. An Australian Broadcasting Commission (ABC) journalist obtained a copy of this directive and filed a story on the run-down of civic action, while on 22 February the *Canberra Times* ran a story alleging that the government was anxious about the changes to civic action policy.

Already, Malcolm Fraser had become concerned by the first story and on 19 February the chairman of the chiefs, Admiral Smith, sent a 'Flash' signal to Saigon seeking information on civic action. General Fraser was absent from Saigon, and in his absence his chief of staff, Colonel John Salmon, reported to Canberra that while there was some basis for the ABC story, it had been misconstrued and misinterpreted. Salmon was playing for time until General Fraser returned, but the idea developed in Defence that the army was withholding information.[48]

During the following week Defence Minister Fraser appeared to defuse the issue, but an article by Alan Ramsey in the *Sunday Australian* on 28 February accused the army of failing to keep the Department of Defence informed and of mismanagement in a range of other matters. With the army minister, Peacock, in hospital in Melbourne about to undergo an operation, Daly took the unusual step of inviting two journalists to visit him later that day. Before he could meet the journalists, however, Gorton asked him to call on him. When they met at about 4 p.m., Gorton expressed his concern that a senior person in Defence had given journalists briefings that were critical of both the army and Daly. In fact, Tange believed that Fraser had briefed 'selected media, making clear his disapproval of Army actions in Vietnam over civic action'. After explaining to Gorton what had happened with civic action, Daly added that in his 'experience there was usually a political motive behind such a campaign', noting that 'it would not be the first time that one of the Services had been attacked through the Press as a means of discrediting the Government or one of its Ministers'.[49]

On the following day an article (which Tange described as an 'outrageously inaccurate report') appeared in the Sydney *Daily Telegraph* alleging that Mr Fraser had ordered the Joint Intelligence Organisation to report on army operations in Vietnam and offering further criticism of the army. Daly's refutation of the Sunday article, which appeared that morning, received less attention. Nonetheless, at the Chiefs of Staff Committee meeting during the morning, Fraser indicated his displeasure at Daly's approach to the press. Daly said nothing, but the CAS, Air Marshal Sir Colin Hannah, inquired of the minister, 'and what is the Army supposed to say when kicked? Roll over on its back like a puppy and say "tickle my tummy"?' Already that day, after consulting Tange, Fraser had issued a statement denying the involvement of the Joint Intelligence Organisation.[50]

Wednesday 3 March brought another article criticising the army, this time from Peter Samuel in the *Bulletin* magazine. Daly persuaded Fraser to issue a further press release refuting *The Bulletin*'s allegations and indicating that the army was operating in Vietnam in accordance with government policy. If Daly thought the matter was over, his expectations were shattered the next morning with an article by Alan Ramsey in *The Australian* claiming that in his discussions with Gorton, Daly had accused Fraser of disloyalty to Peacock. That morning Daly met Gorton, who promptly issued a statement denying the allegations.[51]

The incident now moved firmly from a departmental matter to a political one concerning Fraser and Gorton. Ramsey had earlier given Gorton the opportunity of commenting on his article before publication, and he related Gorton's failure to comment in another article on Friday 5 March. Both Gorton and Daly issued statements that the story about disloyalty was untrue. Nonetheless, Fraser accused Gorton of disloyalty to him as defence minister and on Monday 8 March resigned as minister. Fraser explained his reasons in the House of Representatives on 9 March, and at a Liberal Party meeting on 10 March Gorton, on his own casting vote, was defeated as prime minister. He was succeeded by William McMahon and Gorton took Fraser's job as defence minister.[52]

Tange saw it as the outcome of Fraser's legitimate efforts to assert his authority as defence minister over a service department that was used to operating with little reference to the Department of Defence. On the one hand was the 'inherited attitude of servicemen to politicians' and on the other hand was a politician who sought to exert his power 'to implement what he regarded validly as a matter of high policy . . . Chuck into that a touch of a degree of vanity and a touch of abrasiveness, and a suspicion of whether truth was or was not being told and you get a witch's brew that was poisonous.' Tange observed that until Fraser became defence minister, 'The Vietnam show was really run by Army and the Defence Department's attitude was to act as an adding machine for the three services' budgets and the Defence Minister's job was to get them through a reluctant cabinet.' Fraser wanted to overthrow these attitudes and he 'exerted his power far more than his predecessors including Fairhall'. Tange thought that 'Defence lost a strong and purposeful leader, better in these respects than any Coalition Minister for Defence up to the time of my retirement in 1979, and possibly better than any predecessor.'[53]

Final Withdrawal

On 25 January, more than a month before the Civic Action affair, Fraser had told the defence chiefs that the Americans were expected to announce further withdrawals and that the government wanted to forestall the Americans by announcing a withdrawal of 1000 Australian troops. To meet this figure, the chiefs recommended withdrawing the tank squadron, the RAAF Canberra bomber squadron, some Caribou aircraft, and RAN helicopter pilots and clearance divers. Fraser took this recommendation to the Cabinet on 15 February, which endorsed it and agreed to a phased withdrawal beginning in May. There would be no announcement until Fraser could go to Vietnam to consult with the South Vietnamese and the Americans.[54] However, the decision was leaked to the press.

The Civic Action affair then intervened and it was left to Gorton, now the defence minister, to visit Vietnam in mid-March to explain the withdrawal to the South Vietnamese and the Americans. General Abrams advised him that Americans troops could no longer assist 1 ATF as they had in the past, and the Australians would need to rely more on the South Vietnamese. On 30 March, in his first major statement as prime minister, McMahon announced that the Australian force would be progressively reduced to about 6000 men, from its previous peak of about 8000 in 1968–70, and that the reduction would take four to six months beginning in May.[55]

To meet a political imperative, 1 ATF would therefore not only need to operate with only two battalions rather than three (as had been the case since the previous November), but also without tank support. The importance of tanks in providing fire support when attacking enemy bunker systems was demonstrated in battles in June and August 1971. In September, after the tanks were withdrawn, a company from 4 RAR was almost overrun in a savage battle in which five Australians were killed and 30 wounded. As the official history commented: 'Few soldiers would have been convinced by a statement prepared for the Army Minister, which argued that the recent withdrawal of the tank squadron "had no bearing on this particular operation".'[56]

In June, the Defence Committee recommended that all the forces except the AATTV be withdrawn progressively between February and August 1972. But on 26 July, in the light of President Nixon's proposed visit to Beijing, the Cabinet reviewed the situation and agreed that the battalions should be withdrawn in October–November 1971. On 18 August, McMahon announced that the withdrawal would begin in October and most of the Australian combat elements would be home by Christmas. McMahon explained that the government's decision was a 'mark of the success which has attended our policies and actions in Vietnam over the years'. The response from the Opposition leader, Gough Whitlam, was scathing: '"There is only one reason and one reason only why Australia is getting out. We are getting out because the US is getting out.' McMahon's biographer Patrick Mullins, however, thought that 'it was surely to McMahon's credit that he was extricating Australia from a conflict that had taken tremendous toll, caused extraordinary upheaval, and appeared to be a near failure in attaining its strategic goals'.[57]

All the combat units withdrew before the end of the year, and most of the AATTV withdrew during 1972. By the time the Whitlam Labor government was elected in December 1972, just 128 members of the AATTV were in Vietnam and they were winding down their activities. Whitlam recalled these last few soldiers immediately. The widely accepted view that Whitlam withdrew Australia from Vietnam is not true. Of the 50,000 Australian service personnel who served in Vietnam between 1962 and 1972, 519 were killed and about 2400 were wounded.

Ultimately, the higher direction of the Australian forces in Vietnam rested with the government, not its civilian and military advisers. Official historian Peter Edwards has shown that Prime Minister Menzies, his deputy John McEwen, and other senior ministers, Harold Holt, Paul Hasluck and Shane Paltridge, played the key roles in deciding to deploy 1 RAR to Vietnam in 1965. But they and their successors were less interested in the finer details of whether the Australian troops were actually achieving their purpose. It is true that service ministers, and particularly the Minister for the Army, were sensitive to administrative or disciplinary bungles that might reflect badly on their administration. In retrospect, however, Wilton considered that the government interfered very little in the operations of the force.[58]

Allen Fairhall, Minister for Defence from January 1966 to November 1969, was a competent administrator who took an interest in the technical side of military acquisitions. He was also a strong supporter and advocate of Australia's commitment to Vietnam. But he does not appear to have challenged the chiefs by asking them to consider alternatives in Vietnam, and despite later claims that Prime Minister Gorton perhaps favoured a withdrawal, there was no directive from him in this regard. As defence minister, Malcolm Fraser took a more activist approach. As mentioned, in December 1969 he directed the chiefs to come up with options for the withdrawal of forces, and in May 1970 he directed the COMAFV to expand his monthly reports to allow him to assess the extent to which objectives were being achieved. Eliot Cohen, in *Supreme Command: Soldiers, Statesmen, and Leadership in Wartime*, argues that 'the best civilian leaders are those who meddle and ask tough questions of their military subordinates'.[59] It seems that perhaps Australian war leadership in the Vietnam War did not have enough of this meddling.

12

'Australia had vital interests at stake'

Hawke, Gulf War, 1990–91

In December 1990, almost twenty years after Australia withdrew from Vietnam, the Australian government once again committed forces to war. Like the commitment to the Vietnam War, it was a controversial decision, but unlike in Australia's previous wars, the short Gulf War, fought from 16 January to 28 February 1991, would result in no Australian casualties. Nonetheless, although Australia played only a minor part in the war, it was a milestone in Australian defence and foreign policy.[1] It marked a change in the mindset of the Australian government and public which, following the Vietnam War, had seemed unwilling to countenance another overseas military expedition. Furthermore, it began a military involvement in the Gulf region that would stretch beyond three decades and involve Australia in the contentious war in Iraq (2003–09) and the extended conflict in Afghanistan (2001–2021). Australia's war leadership in these wars had evolved since the earlier conflicts, but some of the same issues remained. Australia was not directly threatened, and Australia's political leaders needed to balance the national interest against the cost in lives, treasure and reputation. In making these decisions, leaders would have at their disposal a military force that had evolved into a new, more responsive and capable entity, the Australian Defence Force (ADF).

The Hawke Government

The challenge of committing Australia to the Gulf War fell to Bob Hawke and his Labor government. By 1990, Hawke had been prime minister for seven years, and his government was capable and experienced. After studying at the University of Western Australia and Oxford University, he had worked his way up in the Australian Council of Trade Unions, becoming its president in 1969. He was also president of the Australian Labor Party (ALP) from 1973 to 1978. He entered the federal parliament in 1980 and became Opposition leader shortly before the ALP won the election in 1983. Aged 60 in 1990, Hawke was a charismatic political leader, a clever negotiator and a strong supporter of the US alliance.

The key ministers in deciding to go to the Gulf War were the Minister for Foreign Affairs, Senator Gareth Evans; and the Minister for Defence, Senator Robert Ray. Approaching his 46th birthday, Evans was a former academic and barrister from Melbourne who had held several portfolios before becoming foreign minister in 1988. A liberal multilateralist by instinct, he was a 'pragmatic idealist', keen to support UN peacekeeping.[2] Ray had succeeded Kim Beazley as defence minister in April 1990. Whereas Beazley had relished the technical side of Defence, and had a longstanding interest in strategy and international relations, Ray had no similar interest or expertise. Aged 42, he was a former teacher and taxi-driver, but as the chief 'numbers man' of the right wing of the Victorian party, he was a shrewd political operator. As Minister for Immigration he had avoided the press (unlike Evans, who delighted in such engagements) and he continued to do so in Defence. Ray preferred to leave the management of Defence to the experts while he dealt with the political side, but he was not afraid to challenge the military, nor to assert his authority. Defence, always a demanding portfolio, was now even more complex, as the departments of the Navy, Army and Air had been absorbed into the Department of Defence in 1973, and the positions of the service ministers had been abolished.

Hawke could not have committed Australia to its involvement in the Middle East without the agreement of Cabinet, and in this he worked well with Evans and Ray. He was also supported by the 42-year-old Minister for Transport and Communications and Leader of the House, Kim Beazley, who had been an effective defence minister from 1984 to 1990. Another key minister was the treasurer and deputy prime minister, Paul Keating. All these ministers were from the right wing of the party and supported the US alliance, but there were also ministers from the left wing who were far more wary.

Military Advisers

In the two decades since the withdrawal from Vietnam there had been substantial changes to Australia's military and to the institutions that might provide military advice. The three services had been brought together as the Australian Defence Force (ADF) with the establishment of many tri-service, or joint-service, units. The chairman of the Chiefs of Staff Committee, the principal military adviser in the Vietnam War, had been replaced by the Chief of the Defence Force (CDF), who commanded the ADF from ADF Headquarters. The CDF, General Peter Gration, had held the position since 1987. Born in 1932, he had graduated from Duntroon into the Royal Australian Engineers, and had served in Malaya during the Emergency, in Papua New Guinea, and in South Vietnam. He had been CGS before his promotion to full general as CDF. As CDF, Gration had a quick mind, an outstanding grasp of detail and a fierce determination to implement his own ideas when he was convinced they were right. There was no hint that he was merely the chairman of a committee of equals—he was clearly the commander—but nonetheless he relied on the service chiefs as his specialist advisers.

The three chiefs of staff were no longer just the senior officers of their service boards; they commanded their services. The CNS, Vice-Admiral Mike Hudson, who had held his appointment since 1985, was due to retire in March 1991. He often stood in for Gration when he was absent overseas. The CGS, Lieutenant General John Coates, would play only a minor role in the Gulf War, as few army personnel were involved. The CAS, Air Marshal Ray Funnell, had previously been Vice Chief of the Defence Force (VCDF). Quick to move with the times, he had encouraged the study of airpower doctrine. The chiefs provided their advice to the CDF through the Chiefs of Staff Committee.

The defence department was run by what was known as the diarchy. Gration commanded the military side; the secretary, Tony Ayers, ran the civilian side, and they were jointly responsible for the administration of the ADF. Appointed to Defence in August 1988, Ayers had spent 35 years as a public servant, but never in Defence. With a quick sense of humour and a willingness to consult with the CDF, he was determined to bring efficiency to the department.

Gration's headquarters staff included the VCDF, Vice-Admiral Alan Beaumont; the Assistant CDF (Operations) (ACOPS), Rear Admiral Rod Taylor; and the director of the Defence Intelligence Organisation, Major General John Baker, who was effectively Gration's chief intelligence officer.[3] By the time of the Gulf crisis, most of the policy decisions were taken by the so-called Augmented Chiefs of Staff Committee, which was chaired by the CDF and included the secretary, the civilian deputy secretaries and other key officers. Between 20 August 1990 and 28 February 1991, the Augmented Chiefs of Staff Committee met on almost 60 occasions to discuss the Gulf operation.

Another major change to the ADF was the formation of joint operational commands—Maritime, Land and Air Commands—which reported directly to the CDF for operations. Based in Sydney and commanded by Rear Admiral Ken Doolan, Maritime Command would be the crucial command for the Gulf War. Doolan was responsible both to the CNS for raising, training and sustaining naval units, and to the CDF for the conduct of operations. When Doolan formed a naval task group, such as in the Gulf War, its chain of command ran back through him to the CDF. This meant that the service chiefs had no direct responsibility for operations, but they still retained a powerful influence through their membership of the Chiefs of Staff Committee.

These command arrangements were substantially different from those in the Vietnam War, when advice was provided by the Defence Committee, based on military input from the Chiefs of Staff Committee. In the Gulf War, the CDF and the secretary were the government's principal advisers. Furthermore, as mentioned, the CDF directly commanded operations through designated joint force commanders. This gave the government greater control of the ADF's operations. Nonetheless, the challenge of operating within a coalition force dominated by the United States still remained.

Invasion of Kuwait

The Gulf War was caused primarily by the ruthless president of Iraq, Saddam Hussein. Between 1980 and 1988 Iraq had fought a costly and exhausting war with Iran. Neighbouring Kuwait lent Iraq billions of dollars, but after the war Kuwait asked for it to be repaid. Iraq was unable to pay and had longstanding grievances against Kuwait. Saddam therefore sought to resolve his problems; on 2 August 1990 Iraq invaded Kuwait and quickly took over the country.

At that time, two key government decision-makers were absent from Australia. The prime minister, Hawke, was in Vanuatu for a meeting of the South Pacific Forum; and the foreign minister, Evans, was visiting India.[4] Immediately, their respective departments began considering Australia's response, and that morning the attorney-general and acting foreign minister, Michael Duffy, issued a press statement condemning the Iraqi invasion and calling for the immediate withdrawal of all Iraqi forces.

Later in the day, at a press conference in New Delhi, Evans declared that Iraq's action was an 'outright violation' of the UN Charter, and that Australia condemned it 'absolutely outright and unreservedly'. Evans admitted that Australia's condemnation might threaten Australian trade, 'but that won't alter the nature of our initial policy response. When you are dealing with fundamental questions of war and peace and human rights . . . one can't let those considerations be dominant'.[5]

Security Council Resolutions

Already the United States was taking swift action, and US President George H.W. Bush sought an emergency meeting of the UN Security Council. In the early hours of 2 August (New York time), the council passed Resolution 660, condemning Iraq's invasion and demanding its immediate and unconditional withdrawal.

Within hours of the UN resolution, American warships were heading towards the Gulf. Next morning at a press conference, Bush announced that he had frozen Iraqi and Kuwaiti assets in the United States, and that he had been in touch with governments around the world urging that they too condemn the 'Iraqi aggression'. Late in the morning of 2 August (Washington time), Australia's ambassador in Washington, Michael Cook, advised Canberra that the United States 'had asked a number of countries to freeze Iraqi and Kuwaiti assets' and that Australia 'was one of the first to be approached'. Australian officials were cautious about immediately applying sanctions, conscious of the effect on Australian trade.[6] Nonetheless, the Australian government advised Washington that it was willing to consider the US request.

After examining the military options, Bush decided to deploy forces to Saudi Arabia to deter an Iraqi attack (Operation Desert Shield); to mount a concerted diplomatic campaign to gain support around the world for UN resolutions against Iraq, and for military and financial support for allies; and to establish a multinational naval force to enforce sanctions against Iraq. Meanwhile, in Canberra both the Department of Foreign Affairs and Trade (DFAT) and the defence department had been monitoring the cables, and by the morning of Monday 6 August they knew that the United States was sponsoring another UN Security Council resolution to apply sanctions against Iraq. The Cabinet met at 6.15 p.m. that evening, and 40 minutes later

Duffy announced that the government had decided to impose sanctions on Iraq, including an embargo on oil imports from Iraq and Kuwait, the freezing of any Iraqi assets in Australia, and an embargo on the sale of defence-related equipment to Iraq.[7] It was a relatively straightforward decision. As most countries were likely to impose sanctions, Australia had no option but to conform if it was to remain in step with its allies.

Next morning came confirmation that the UN Security Council had passed Resolution 661 declaring its determination to bring the invasion and occupation of Kuwait to an end and to restore Kuwait's sovereignty. The resolution imposed mandatory economic sanctions on Iraq. In what one author described as 'a dazzling display of personal diplomacy', President Bush had rallied international opinion against Iraq and had gained widespread support for the application of sanctions. Later that day, Duffy announced that Australia fully supported the sanctions. He acknowledged that applying these sanctions, particularly the cessation of wheat exports, would have 'serious implications for Australia', but the government believed that Australia and the international community had 'a duty to respond in this way to Iraq's invasion of Kuwait'.[8]

Multinational Naval Force

The next problem was enforcing the sanctions, and with this in mind the United States immediately began putting together a multinational naval force. The United States was not inclined to seek further UN authorisation, believing that Article 51 of the UN Charter, which affirms 'the inherent right of individual and collective self-defence', was sufficient authority. Not all Security Council members agreed with this assessment, so for the moment the United States planned to form the multinational force outside the UN framework.

Initially, the ADF's senior commanders had not expected that Australia would be involved militarily in the Gulf. However, on 7 August a cable arrived from the head of the Australian Defence Liaison Staff in Washington, Rear Admiral A.M. (Gerry) Carwardine, reporting that the United States was putting together a multinational naval force. Carwardine had come across this news by accident. While a senior US Navy officer had stated that 'there were no US plans to seek allied military assistance', Carwardine concluded that the United States was indeed considering a multinational force and that it was in Australia's interests to be involved.[9]

The Australian government's decision to join the sanctions regime had been relatively easy. Carwardine's cable, however, presented it with a new challenge. While Britain already had a destroyer in the Gulf and because of its long commitment there would probably cooperate with the Americans, it was not clear whether other countries would be joining the multinational naval force, especially since it had not yet been authorised by the United Nations.

A Labor Government's Dilemma

The Australian government faced a dilemma. The ALP had a long tradition of resisting the deployment of forces overseas. In the First World War the party had supported the raising of a voluntary expeditionary force, but its opposition to conscription for overseas service had split the party. After the outbreak of the Second World War, the ALP only reluctantly accepted the deployment of an expeditionary force overseas. When the Menzies government committed troops to Malaya in 1955 it was criticised by the ALP Opposition leader, Bert Evatt. Led by Arthur Calwell, the party's opposition to the commitment of combat troops to Vietnam in 1965 was even more vociferous. In view of the communist victory in South Vietnam, many Australians thought Calwell had been right. By the 1980s, some of those who had demonstrated against the Vietnam War, including the foreign minister, Evans, and the defence minister, Ray, were now members of the government. As recently as 1984, the Party Platform had declared that a Labor government would 'not commit Australian forces overseas except where there is a clear and imminent threat to Australia'.[10]

The ALP, however, had always advocated international collective security. The party had supported the League of Nations, and Evatt had played a major role in helping to form the United Nations. Years later, reflecting on the ALP's history, Gareth Evans believed that 'the Hawke and Keating governments were in the great Labor tradition—intensely nationalistic in our determination to find and articulate a distinctive Australian place in the world; intensely internationalist in our willingness to work through multilateral institutions and processes in finding solution to problems'.[11] In Evans's view, the Iraqi invasion of Kuwait was a clear example of the sort of crisis that should be solved by the international community working together.

There was another consideration. The US alliance had been a cornerstone of Australia's foreign and defence policy since the signing of the ANZUS Treaty in 1951. However, the Western alliance, of which Australia was a member, was broader. Australia was not a member of NATO, but there were other connections, such as the UKUSA agreement (for the sharing of intelligence among the United States, Britain, Canada, Australia and New Zealand). As a member of the Western alliance, Australia needed to be seen to be playing its part.

During the Second World War, the Labor Party had embraced the US alliance. Now, Hawke, Evans and Ray, as well as the former defence minister, Beazley, understood the importance of maintaining the alliance, and were strong supporters of it. Evans welcomed the fact that the alliance gave Australia a voice in Washington that might not otherwise have been available to a relatively small nation. The defence minister, Ray, knew the benefits, particularly in the area of access to US intelligence and technology.

Hawke prided himself on his close relationship with President Bush, and was friends with the previous Secretary of State, George Schultz. He later explained his reaction to the Iraqi invasion: 'From the very beginning of the crisis in the Gulf I believed that Australia had vital interests at stake. Of course, oil was important, for if Saddam Hussein was allowed to gobble up Kuwait he would be eyeing off Saudi Arabia next, and the security and price of oil would be in jeopardy. More important however, I was appalled by the thought that such a blatant act of aggression should be allowed to stand.'[12]

Hawke's reference to vital interests was important. Certainly, the

Australian economy would be damaged by an increase in oil prices, but Hawke and his ministers were committed to collective security and were anxious to see the United Nations play an effective role in dealing with a clear case of aggression. The most telling factor, however, was the imperative to support the United States and more broadly the Western alliance. This was the true vital interest for Australia. But what could Australia provide?

Committing Naval Forces

Even before the arrival of Carwardine's cable, on 6 August the CDF, General Gration, had directed the ACOPS, Rear Admiral Taylor, to begin considering military options. Taylor's staff developed two possibilities: a short-term deployment for three months or less of two frigates and one replenishment ship; or a deployment for longer than three months of one frigate, to be rotated every three months, and a replenishment ship, to be rotated in due course with tankers from other navies. Gration passed these options to Ray on 7 August.[13]

Meanwhile, the Office of National Assessments advised the government that Washington seemed determined to force Iraq to back down, if necessary applying a naval blockade to make the UN sanctions fully effective. Key ministers now seriously began considering sending ships to the Gulf. Senator Ray, who was visiting Townsville, said that there had been no request for Australia to take part in an economic blockade, but the most likely option for Australian involvement was naval. He added, however, that 'the US is our ally: if it were a United Nations [force] I couldn't imagine Cabinet saying no, but I'll leave that to them'.[14]

Next morning news arrived from Washington that the US Navy was informally asking the NATO countries, as well as Australia and Japan, what forces they might be able to make available to the multinational force, should a request be made. Carwardine reported that National Security Council staff in the White House had commented favourably on Australia's action in immediately announcing comprehensive sanctions, and 'an early agreement to contribute [forces] would mean a lot more here than our coming in late at the tail of a large field'.[15]

The last comment was a telling point. If other countries were to join the multinational force there would be great advantage to Australia (in its relations with the United States) if it were to commit forces as early as possible. There was an echo here of Australia's early decision to send an infantry battalion to South Korea in July 1950 following the North Korean invasion, when Australia's action was praised by the United States. About midday, Taylor phoned Admiral Doolan in Sydney to say that Hawke had asked the size of the naval force that could be deployed, how soon it could be provided, and how long it could be sustained. Ten minutes later Doolan replied that the navy could provide one supply ship, two frigates and one guided missile destroyer, that they could sail early in the week beginning 13 August, that they would be on task in the Gulf 22 days later, and that they could be deployed for three months, with the effort sustainable until mid-1991. Meanwhile, Taylor's staff were preparing a Cabinet submission.[16] General Gration was not present as he was visiting military units in Perth.

At lunchtime on Thursday 9 August, Hawke met his deputy and treasurer, Paul Keating, and the acting foreign minister, Michael Duffy, to discuss Washington's request. During the two-hour meeting Hawke phoned Ray, who was visiting northern Queensland, Evans in Dacca (Dhaka, Bangladesh) and the Senate leader and Minister for Industry and Commerce, John Button, in Melbourne. According to one journalist, Hawke 'was steeled in his resolve by a gung-ho treasurer. Mr Keating is reported to have vigorously endorsed the moves to teach a lesson to "that turd" Saddam Hussein.' Keating subsequently denied that he had used these words and had 'behaved as some kind of adventurer . . . nothing could be further from the truth . . . my approach to Australia's involvement was cautious and considered'. When the meeting ended, the five ministers had agreed to commit three Australian warships to the US naval blockade, although as Hawke recalled, Button had 'been unhappy' with the decision.[17] The idea of deploying the destroyer had been dropped.

Hawke's view had been decisive, although he had certainly discussed the options with Ray and Evans. 'In directing Australia's role,' he said, 'I knew I had in them colleagues whose judgment could be trusted on every aspect of the crisis. This group remained the key decision-making body throughout the months which followed.' Evans believed that based on the earlier Cabinet meeting, Hawke was confident that its members would support the decisions made by the smaller group of ministers.[18] At this stage, however, the United States had still not formally asked Australia for a commitment.

Hawke now cabled Washington that Australia was 'prepared to receive and would expect to react positively to an invitation to join a multinational task force'. Australia expected to provide up to two frigates and an oiler for up to three months, but needed to clarify command arrangements and have a clear statement of the task force's purpose. Australia expected the force to include a number of Western European countries and Canada. 'Canadian participation, while not a condition of our acceptance, is most important to us.'[19]

In an effort to resolve this last matter, Hawke telephoned his Canadian counterpart, Brian Mulroney, who reported that while he had not received a request from the United States, NATO might choose to deploy forces, including Canadians, to Turkey. Hawke and Mulroney agreed that 'neither party' would take any action to deploy forces without consulting the other.[20]

Hawke was sufficiently encouraged by Mulroney to continue with his plans to commit the ships. But if Hawke approved the deployment, Admiral Doolan would have only a very short time to prepare his forces. To give him as much warning as possible, Gration therefore issued a secret warning order, directing Doolan to prepare ships for the mission in the Gulf.[21]

At 7.15 a.m. on Friday 10 August, Hawke spoke by phone to President Bush for half an hour and they agreed that Australia should provide the ships. Bush wrote later that 'without equivocation', Hawke 'said he was solidly behind us and offered to send warships but he wanted Canada to commit as well'. After speaking with Bush, Hawke met his senior ministers to confirm Australia's involvement. Ray recalled that Hawke was keen to make the announcement that morning to set an example to Canada and other nations. The ministers agreed that Australia should provide vessels to the multinational naval force to support Security Council sanctions against Iraq.[22]

At 10.30 a.m., at a press conference, flanked by Ray and the VCDF, Vice-Admiral Beaumont (Gration was still in Perth), Hawke announced that HMAS *Adelaide* and HMAS *Darwin* would depart for the Gulf on Monday 13 August, accompanied by the supply ship HMAS *Success*. Hawke explained that the primary purpose of the multinational force was 'to enforce the blockade of Iraq and Kuwait and . . . to protect the exports from other oil producing countries and to protect other trade in the Gulf'. He acknowledged that 'the deployment may involve significant risks . . . but we have profound faith in the equipment and the training of our men in their capacity to meet any situation [with] which they will be confronted'. Questioned as to whether it would have been better to have waited for the United Nations before committing the ships, Hawke replied that one could 'always find a reason and an excuse for not playing a responsible role in a threatening situation . . . but I believe that the gravity of the situation is such that it warranted this action at this time by Australia'. It would have been preferable for the operation to be under a UN flag, and he said that might yet happen.[23]

And so, eight days after Iraq's invasion of Kuwait, Australia had committed a naval task group to possible warlike operations. The decision—perhaps the most important foreign and defence policy decision in two decades—had been made so quickly that there had been little public discussion before it was announced. Across Australia there was widespread support for the decision, but there was also considerable criticism in some quarters and some demonstrations. Hawke argued his case in parliament on 21 August, and on 25 August, fifteen days after he had announced the commitment, the UN Security Council authorised maritime forces to apply the sanctions against Iraq.

Despatching the Ships

Prime responsibility for the deployment of the ships rested with the Maritime Commander, Rear Admiral Doolan, while Commodore Don Chalmers, the Commodore Flotillas in Maritime Command, would command the task group from one of the ships. After a remarkably rapid preparation, in the morning of Monday 13 August, HMAS *Adelaide* and HMAS *Darwin* set sail from Sydney. Hawke (along with other ministers, as well as Gration and the CNS, Hudson) was present to farewell the ships, telling the men that they were leaving 'on an extremely important mission'.[24]

With the ships sailing towards the Gulf, Commodore Rob Walls from the Navy Office and several other officers flew to the Gulf to discuss Australia's role in the Maritime Interception Force, and to establish a logistic support base in the Oman capital, Muscat. One crucial issue to be decided was the rules of engagement, to ensure that the ships operated in accordance with the government's policy. The rules were eventually agreed after discussions involving Senators Ray and Evans, Gration, senior Defence officials, Commodore Walls in the Gulf, and the prime minister's defence and foreign affairs adviser, Hugh White. Dr Paul Dibb, Deputy Secretary Strategic and Intelligence in the defence department, who had been closely involved, recalled that 'it was a painful, incremental process to have the cabinet submissions accepted by all concerned parties'.[25]

The naval task group entered the Gulf of Oman on 6 September and began operations on 11 September as part of the Maritime Interception Force. During three months of operations, the multinational forces identified and interrogated more than 400 merchant ships and there were more than 500 boardings. In total, nineteen merchant ships were diverted to other ports and eleven had initially refused to stop. Ten incidents involved the firing of warning shots, with the RAN involved in five cases.[26]

Managing the Commitment

While the RAN task group conducted interception operations, the government was preoccupied with a range of issues: securing the release of hostages held in Iraq; assessing the terrorist threat; considering whether to expand the military commitment; and deciding how to react if the United Nations authorised the use of force to expel Iraq from Kuwait. If the government responded positively to the latter situation, it would be the first commitment of Australian forces to war since Menzies had sent an infantry battalion to South Vietnam in 1965.

The government had sent forces to the Gulf for purely political and diplomatic reasons. Whether Australia deployed forces or not would make no difference to the eventual outcome, and the government needed to judge the extent of Australia's commitment against this calculus. As with the initial decision to apply sanctions, the dominant figure was the prime minister, Hawke, who received strong support from his key ministers, Evans and Ray. They were acutely sensitive to the views of the Left-faction members of their party, who generally opposed the commitment, and they needed to balance these views against their belief that it was in Australia's interest to support the United States and more broadly the United Nations.

Hawke was also aware that his own leadership was under attack. His government had been re-elected in March 1990, and the treasurer, Keating, had taken on the additional role of deputy prime minister. But, as the respected political correspondent Paul Kelly observed, after its electoral victory 'the Hawke government collapsed . . . due to public disenchantment, a protracted recession and a leadership struggle'.[27] Opinion polls were showing that the Coalition was ahead of Labor, and Keating had begun a campaign to overthrow Hawke, believing that the latter had gone back on a promise to stand down in favour of his 'legitimate successor'. These domestic political considerations influenced Hawke's decision-making during this period.

The first major decision was whether to relieve the ships of the first task group. On 3 September, Admiral Doolan warned the frigate *Sydney* and the destroyer *Brisbane* to prepare to replace *Darwin* and

Adelaide at the end of their three-month deployment; the tanker *Westralia* would replace *Success* at a later date. In parliament on 11 September, Ray announced that plans were 'being developed to replace the current task group when its rotation is completed'.[28]

It was not long before the government came under pressure to deploy more forces to the Middle East. On 3 October the shadow foreign minister, Senator Robert Hill, visited Washington, where he was told that the United States would welcome an Australian presence 'on the ground', meaning either troops or aircraft, especially a squadron of F/A-18 fighters, or better still, a squadron of F-111 bombers, to be based in Saudi Arabia.[29]

Shortly afterwards, Ray and Evans visited Washington for their annual ministerial meeting with their US counterparts, the Secretary of Defense, Dick Cheney; and the Secretary of State, James Baker. General Gration, who accompanied Ray, had discussions with General Colin Powell, chairman of the US Joint Chiefs, about the possibility of deploying RF-111 reconnaissance aircraft to assess bomb damage. The United States was careful to avoid making a direct request for further military support, and assured the Australians that no 'premature' military action was planned against Iraq.[30]

Although the US government had not directly requested further Australian support, Defence and DFAT were already examining seven broad options. The most attractive was to provide several RF-111 reconnaissance aircraft, and some senior air force officers, including the CAS, Air Marshal Ray Funnell, were keen for the aircraft to be deployed. Gration told Ray that he generally agreed but the options needed further study. The Defence secretary, Tony Ayers, finely tuned to political sensitivities, was less enthusiastic about the F-111s.[31] In the event, with the exception of some minor deployments later, the government did not approve an expansion of the commitment.

Prospect of Hostilities

While the government was reluctant to increase the force commitment, it was facing pressure to decide how to react if the United

Nations authorised the use of force to drive Iraq out of Kuwait. Some of the pressure came from the defence department, which realised that preparatory action was necessary. For example, Commodore Chalmers had been suggesting to Admiral Doolan that he needed an expansion to his area of operations if he was to continue operating effectively. This view received more support when Admiral Hudson visited the Gulf region in late October. Chalmers told him that Australia was now the only country not operating its naval vessels inside the Persian Gulf on a regular basis. Chalmers believed that there was an urgent need to familiarise his team with the Gulf so that they could be well settled in if they were committed to combat operations there. In Bahrain, Vice-Admiral Henry Mauz, commander of the US naval forces in the Gulf region, wanted to know what Australia's reaction might be in the event of hostilities, as this would affect his contingency planning. Hudson replied that it was a matter for the Australian government to decide.[32]

On his return to Australia, Hudson argued strongly for RAN ships to be permitted to enter the Persian Gulf. By this time President Bush had concluded that he must do whatever was necessary to liberate Kuwait, and on 8 November he announced that he was reinforcing the forces that had been deployed for Operation Desert Shield. The next step was to secure an appropriate Security Council resolution.[33] Then on 13 November the Australian liaison officer on the US headquarters ship, USS *Blue Ridge*, reported that Admiral Mauz was anxious to know whether the RAN ships would be able to operate in the Persian Gulf.

On 14 November, Gration submitted options for expanding Australia's involvement in the Gulf to Hawke, Ray and Evans. Gration pointed out that the Americans had a shortage of anti-air warfare ships in the Persian Gulf, but if the Australian ships were to be employed in this role they would need to deploy into the Persian Gulf early enough to be integrated into the US force and become familiar with its operations.[34]

With this advice, Hawke, Ray and Evans met on 15 November to consider the future of Australia's involvement. They agreed that if they permitted the Australian ships to enter the Persian Gulf to exercise with the Americans there would be 'a very strong presumption' that Australia had committed them to a possible war. There was no need to make this decision before *Darwin* and *Adelaide* left the Gulf on 3 December, and the United States was 'likely to have UN Security Council cover for a war by then'. Next day President Bush spoke by telephone to Hawke, who told Bush that he agreed with his hopes for a peaceful resolution, but if that did not prove possible he hoped that Bush would consult him. Bush said that he would do his 'level best to ensure that you are in the loop'.[35]

Australia's future commitment was therefore still being discussed when on 19 November Gration visited the Middle East for discussions with US, Saudi, British and Canadian commanders. On 24 November he met up with Ray, and together they visited the Australian ships before departing for Australia on 27 November. It had been important for Gration to familiarise himself with the region, to meet the principal commanders, and to see at first hand the conditions under which the ships were operating. He found that the Australian frigates had a high level of interoperability with the US ships and had won the confidence of the US carrier battle group. Admiral Mauz advised Gration that he was keen to continue the relationship if hostilities began. Operations in the Gulf of Oman were declining in importance, and if Australia were to continue to play a useful role its ships needed to move into the Persian Gulf. For political reasons, however, the government needed to link its decision with an appropriate UN Security Council resolution. Ray and Gration discussed these issues as they flew back to Australia and, as Vice-Admiral Beaumont observed, 'the minister returned convinced of the need to firm up an Australian position'.[36]

The Government's Decision

Following President Bush's announcement that he was sending additional forces to the Gulf, the United States had worked assiduously to gain support for its proposed Security Council resolution authorising the use of force to eject Iraq from Kuwait. On 29 November the Security Council passed Resolution 678, which authorised member states 'to use all necessary means to uphold and implement' the previous resolutions and 'to restore international peace and security in the region'. Baker made it clear that the United States believed that 'necessary means' was synonymous with force.[37]

The Australian government had been following these developments closely, and after discussing Australia's response with his advisers, Hawke believed that 'Australia should indicate as soon as practicable that we would be prepared to commit our forces in the Gulf to operations under Resolution 678, and to take steps now to ensure that they could make an effective contribution if and when war came.' He decided the government should authorise the Australian ships to move into the Persian Gulf, 'to operate and exercise with US ships and other allied ships with which they would have to fight'.[38]

At 10 a.m. on 29 November, Hawke met Ray, Evans, Keating and Button to agree on the position to be put to Cabinet. They all knew that they 'were contemplating the first commitment of Australian forces to combat since the Vietnam War'. Hawke's international adviser, Hugh White, had pointed out that there were 'important advantages in tying our response as directly as possible to the UN resolution . . . It would be preferable to be able to say that we had not received a US request. So it's best to move before we get one.' The events at the meeting were to generate controversy after Hawke wrote in his memoirs that both Keating and Button had

> grave reservations. Button who had been unhappy about our initial decision to deploy ships to enforce sanctions, was opposed but he volunteered that he would say nothing about his opposition publicly. Paul Keating was opposed on the grounds that we did not owe the US such support. 'What has the US done for us?' he asked. I was quick to point out, as was Gareth, that we were acting to back the UN, not the US. At this Keating subsided into acquiescence.[39]

When Hawke published this account in October 1994, Keating, by then prime minister, accused Hawke of 'lying' about his reported comments. Rather, Keating claimed that he had wanted to 'finish off' Saddam Hussein. Hawke responded that it was 'a matter of common knowledge' that he was in charge of Australia's commitment to the Gulf and that 'if there was any criticism at the time it was not of lack of leadership, but that I was running the show'. Defending himself in parliament, Keating claimed that in the context of concerns about 'a number of trade related matters', it was Button who had used the words, 'What has the United States done for us?' Keating stated that Hawke's recollection was 'biased and jaundiced . . . we all now know that he is entirely wrong'.[40]

Whatever was said in the meeting on 29 November 1990, the result was that the ministers agreed that the three ships should be committed to operations in the Persian Gulf. Next day news arrived that the Security Council had passed Resolution 678. Press speculation followed about Australia's likely reaction, although as one journalist noted, 'The meeting in Mr Hawke's office was extraordinarily hush-hush. Only a couple of staff were there, and no bureaucrats. Mr Hawke is particularly paranoid about leaks after details got out of discussions in his office at an early stage of the Iraq crisis.' Nonetheless, over the following days Australia's likely reaction became clearer. In an interview on 30 November, Hawke would not rule out increasing Australia's forces in the Middle East, but he indicated that Australia had no intention of committing ground forces.[41]

Hawke knew that the main criticism would come from the left wing of his own party, and on 3 December, along with Evans and Ray, he met the leaders of the Right, Centre Left and Left factions. The Right was firmly behind the government, the Centre Left agreed to support the plan only if Hawke guaranteed in parliament that no more Australians would be committed to the Gulf, and the Left split into two views, one similar to that of the Centre Left and the other represented by the former minister Stewart West, who completely opposed the commitment. That afternoon the Cabinet formally agreed to make the naval task group available for operations in the

Gulf under allied command, and also to send another two medical teams to the Gulf. However, to meet the demands of the Centre Left and Left factions, the Cabinet stated that 'it was not anticipated that Australia would make any other contribution of naval, air or ground forces to operations'.[42]

The following afternoon in the House of Representatives, Hawke formally announced that the government was prepared to make a naval task force available to serve with allied forces in operations authorised by UN Security Council Resolution 678, and if conflict occurred the ships would be available to participate. The task group was therefore permitted to enter the Persian Gulf to exercise and operate with allied naval forces in preparation for that role. The Australian ships would remain under Australian national command, but would operate principally with US, British and Canadian units under US 'operational control'.

Hawke went on to announce the deployment of another two medical teams, totalling 20 people, to join the two teams already serving in US hospital ships in the Gulf. He said that the number of ships committed to the Gulf would remain unchanged. 'This is a significant commitment which is proportionate to the interest we have at stake and to our national resources. It is also a practical commitment.' Should conflict break out, the role of the ships would be to help defend against the threat from Iraqi aircraft. It was a 'hazardous role'. Hawke concluded: 'Should it come to conflict, Australians may be involved in combat for the first time in 20 years—albeit in very different circumstances. It is a heavy responsibility, but I and my Government will not shirk the exercise of that responsibility.'[43]

As with the original decision to send the ships, Hawke had judged the mood of the Australian public accurately. A poll of 1000 voters conducted for the *Age* newspaper on 5 and 6 December found that 80 per cent supported the use of Australian ships in military action to drive Iraq out of Kuwait should this be necessary.[44]

Although Hawke and his ministers had deliberated long and hard over their decision to approve Australia's involvement in a possible war, there was never any doubt that they would do so. The problem was to manage their critics in the party, and this was best achieved by waiting for the passing of the necessary Security Council resolution. Hawke assessed that there was little more to be gained politically and diplomatically by increasing Australia's military commitment.

Preparing for War

War was probably inevitable once the UN Security Council had passed Resolution 678. Saddam Hussein had no intention of withdrawing from Kuwait by the deadline of 15 January (16 January Kuwait time) as it would be an unbearable loss of face in the Arab world, while President Bush and his advisers believed that nothing short of armed force would compel Saddam to comply. War was the only way that this impasse could be resolved. It did not seem that certain at the time, however, especially when, on 30 November, Bush suggested direct talks with Iraq, offering to send his Secretary of State, James Baker, to Baghdad. Bush's offer caused much consternation to his advisers and allies, who initially feared that he was weakening in his resolve. But Bush knew that he needed to persuade the US public, the American allies in the UN and pro-Western Arab nations that all options had been exhausted.[45] The negotiations eventually failed.

The Australian government kept abreast of these developments. An important issue was to ensure that it received advance warning about the coalition offensive so that it could formally approve participation by the Australian ships. On 8 January, Michael Cook in Washington reported to Hawke that the US National Security Advisor, Brent Scowcroft, had assured him that the president would phone 'you before 15 January . . . The President would need no persuading; he valued highly Australia's unfailing help and support, and your particular part in it.'[46] Evans was not completely confident about the promise of advance warning, and with this in mind early in January he headed overseas.

In Washington on 13 January, Scowcroft assured Evans that Australia would be given advance notice of the military offensive.

Regarding the coalition's 'politico-military objectives', Scowcroft stated that the withdrawal of Iraq from Kuwait would 'be the bulk of it', although the allies would need to put in place arrangements to eliminate Saddam's weapons of mass destruction.[47] It was clear that the Americans had no intention of capturing Baghdad or of overthrowing Saddam's regime.

The next day Evans sought assurances from the US Secretary of State, Baker, that the United States would give the Australian government sufficient warning of the beginning of the offensive to enable it to approve Australia's participation. After what Evans described as a 'slightly sharp' discussion, Baker eventually conceded that 'if you want one or two hours notice—through a political rather than a military channel we can handle that'. Baker recalled that he 'reacted poorly' to Evans' insistence on receiving 'advance notice of the attack . . . We have 500,000 men and women on the ground. I will not risk their security by premature notification.'[48]

America's reluctance to warn Australia was partly through concern 'that a leak might alert the Iraqis and cost some of the pilots their lives'. However, the Australian government received early warning from an Australian intelligence officer working in the Australian Embassy in the Saudi capital, Riyadh.[49] At 9 p.m. in the evening of 16 January, Captain Chris Ritchie on HMAS *Brisbane* was informed that the offensive would begin in the next five or six hours. When Commodore Chris Oxenbould (who had succeeded Chalmers as commander of the RAN task group) received information 'that coalition action would commence shortly' he immediately signalled Admiral Doolan in Sydney, who informed Gration early in the morning of 17 January (Canberra time).

Information came from another source. In Riyadh the Australian ambassador, Alexander McGoldrick, had been concerned that 'great and powerful friends' like the United States and Britain were 'not always as helpful as one might reasonably expect them to be in a crisis', so he had worked closely with the New Zealand and Canadian ambassadors. The latter received advance warning from the commander of the Canadian Air Force contingent and advised McGoldrick at

11 p.m. that the attack would begin at 3 a.m. McGoldrick immediately informed Canberra by secure telephone. It was just after 7 a.m. in Canberra.[50] Ray telephoned this news to Hawke.

Baker's promise that President Bush would warn Hawke of the impending attack with 'one or two hours notice' was honoured only in the most technical sense. Canberra was eight hours ahead of the Gulf, and hence when Bush telephoned Hawke at 9.48 a.m. (Canberra time) to tell him 'that the first actions would start within an hour' it was 1.48 a.m. in the Gulf. According to Hawke, they 'exchanged a few words of encouragement and hope'.[51] By this time, operations had already begun. The other promise, that Cook would be told in advance so that he could warn Hawke, was not fulfilled. Evans had been right to suspect that the US administration would be loath to give Australia much early warning of the attack.

Hawke immediately contacted his key ministers—Ray, Evans (who was overseas), Keating, Button, Neal Blewett (Minister for Trade Negotiations) and Duffy. Then, soon after 10 a.m., Hawke telephoned Gration and also signed a pre-prepared letter, authorising Gration to implement the contingency directive and rules of engagement. Oxenbould received the authorisation nine minutes before the first Iraqi defences were attacked.[52]

At midday on 17 January, Gration, accompanied by Rear Admiral Taylor, briefed Hawke, who then called a press conference. Hawke announced that the Australian task group was 'now with other members of the United Nations co-operating in armed action to fulfil the United Nations resolutions'. He advised that he had decided to recall parliament on 21 January, when he would report on the efforts that had led to this commitment. He explained that the government's decision had been based on 'five grave considerations': 'the right of every independent nation not to be invaded'; 'the commanding moral authority of the United Nations'; that the 'world alliance' had acted 'only at the end of a process without precedent in history' of seeking peaceful means to resolve the conflict; that the decision had 'a clear and achievable goal—to end this aggression, as a necessary step towards establishing the conditions for peace and stability in the

Middle East'; and finally 'to further the great quest for a new world order of peace, security and freedom'.[53]

When the war began, American and British aircraft began bombing Iraq, while American ships launched cruise missiles at Iraqi cities. *Brisbane* and *Sydney* helped provide the protective screen around the American aircraft carriers *Midway* and *Ranger*. As the bombing campaign continued, the coalition ships sailed north up the Persian Gulf, where they became more vulnerable to Iraqi air attacks and to the sea mines the Iraqis had released into the Gulf. While no Iraqi aircraft actually attacked the coalition ships, it was a tense time, made worse when on 18 February two large American warships were damaged by Iraqi mines

Over the next several days, following Hawke's announcement, opposition demonstrations were held in the Australian capital cities. During a meeting of the federal Parliamentary Labor Party in the morning of 21 January, at least eight Left-faction backbenchers opposed outright Australia's involvement in the war. Hawke, however, knew that he had the support of most Australians. A poll taken between 18 and 20 January for the *Australian* newspaper revealed that 60 per cent of adults favoured Australia having ships in the Gulf region, while 75 per cent favoured military action against Iraq.[54]

Parliament was recalled in the afternoon of 21 January, and Hawke began by proposing a motion that the House: reaffirm its support for the role of the United Nations in its actions 'to end the aggression against Kuwait'; affirm its support for Australia's response; and express 'full confidence in, and support for, Australian forces' in the Gulf. Hawke declared that the government believed 'most fervently—that the cause which our forces now serve does embody nothing less than our highest aspirations and interests and that we have committed our forces only as a last resort'.[55]

He explained that there were three main reasons for Australia's involvement in the Gulf War. First, Australia was seeking to establish conditions for peace and stability in the Middle East, and there could be no peace while Iraq remained in occupation of Kuwait. Second, Australia was seeking 'to prevent the catastrophic distortion and disruption of the international economy that would result from Saddam Hussein being placed to pursue his goal of domination of the world oil market'. The third reason, beyond even these vital interests, was that Australia was seeking 'to achieve the promise of a more free, more peaceful and more prosperous world order in which the goals of the Charter of the United Nations can at last be fulfilled'. He continued that it seemed that each generation had 'to learn anew the same hard truth . . . that peace with justice is not given free of charge, but sometimes demands a high and terrible price'.[56]

The leader of the Opposition, Dr John Hewson, supported Hawke's motion. The Opposition leader in the Senate, Senator Robert Hill, also supported Hawke's motion, although he added, quite reasonably in view of the vote of the US Congress, that the debate should have taken place before deciding to send forces. The Democrats leader, Senator Janet Powell, claimed that the war need never have happened as sanctions would have driven Saddam out of Kuwait. Evans countered that sanctions would have taken too long for them to create the 'massive hurt' necessary to bring a change in Iraq's policy. Considering Saddam's obdurate response to further sanctions in the 1990s, this was undoubtedly true. Evans declared that war was 'always a hateful business', but 'sometimes wars have to be fought because the consequences of not fighting them are worse, postponing the destruction to another time and guaranteeing that it will occur on a greater and more horrifying scale when it does'.[57]

Managing Information

With the war underway, the next priority was the management of information—a new facet of Australian war leadership. On the eve of war the government had established a Gulf Media Centre in Parliament House, but it still fell to Defence to keep track of information about activities in the Gulf. Each morning at 2 a.m. the Director-General of Public Information, Brigadier Adrian d'Hagé, would come into Russell Offices, in Canberra, where the Department of Defence and ADF Headquarters are based, to watch on CNN television the morning news briefings by Pete Williams, his Pentagon counterpart. He would check other reports from the United States and from Riyadh, and then at 7 a.m. would attend the morning briefings in the Defence Intelligence Organisation (DIO).[58] By the beginning of the work day he would be fully aware of what information had been released around the world and what was known by DIO.

Major General Baker, director of DIO, was also aware of the need to be ahead of the media. He would arrive at work at about 4 a.m., have a session with the Office of National Assessments (ONA) at about 5.30 a.m., then be briefed by his own Gulf Crisis Analysis Group, and by 9 a.m. would be ready to brief Hawke. The briefings took place in the Crisis Coordination Centre.[59]

Ray, who was in constant touch with the ADF Command Centre via a secure telephone, left the day-to-day management of the ADF's commitment to the Defence chiefs, and generally he and his staff did not cut across the chain of command. The only instance of bypassing the chain of command came soon after the outbreak of the air war, when ABC radio ran an unconfirmed story of a collision between an Australian frigate and a US warship. One of Ray's staff telephoned Maritime Headquarters when they believed they had not received a rapid enough reply from Headquarters ADF. The story was false and the ABC's managing director, David Hill, admitted that the ABC had been wrong to run the story. About the same time, the ABC and its subsidiary, Radio Australia, refused to send messages from families to sailors in the Gulf because the messages would 'give overt support for the Government's political-military endeavour'. The ABC gave way after Ray publicly threatened to cut its funding and the Minister for Transport and Communications, Kim Beazley, privately threatened to use a clause in the ABC Act to direct it to comply. Ray was widely criticised for his threat, but there was little public sympathy for the ABC on this issue; as the *Australian* newspaper noted, the sailors had not been asked whether they agreed with the government, but 'the ABC was content effectively to punish them, by withholding a service'.[60]

General Gration believed that it was nationally important that the activities of the Australian task group be reported fully, but there were several difficulties. First, Senator Ray had not changed his earlier directive that there be only limited access on a short-term basis. Second, senior naval officers were reluctant to allow the media aboard, due to problems of space and danger should an enemy attack eventuate. Third, the media themselves were having difficulties coordinating their arrangements. Several of the newspaper and television organisations were in receivership and could not afford to keep their journalists on stand-by in the Gulf. On 28 January a newspaper reporter and two television crew joined an Australian ship in the Gulf, but as the television journalist who was supposed to accompany them had been sent to Israel, the television crew lacked direction and in early February asked to go ashore.

The media continued to be unhappy about the amount of information being released on the operations in the Gulf, and when the Gulf Media Centre in Parliament House closed in mid-February, journalists claimed that it had not been of much value. The problem was that the Australian ships were doing little independently, and Australian officials did not believe that it was their role to give a detailed description of operations carried out by coalition partners, especially when that information might have been provided because of Australia's alliance status.

End of the War

On 24 February the coalition ground forces, mainly American and British troops, but with units from France, Kuwait, Saudi Arabia and Syria, launched the ground attack. The war was swift and ruthless, as American and British tanks thrust though the desert, liberated Kuwait, and surrounded many Iraqi units. Iraq surrendered and the ceasefire came into effect on 28 February.

At precisely 4 p.m. on 28 February—8 a.m. Iraq time—Hawke strode into a press conference in Parliament House to announce that the Gulf War was over. He explained that on his instructions, General Gration had directed the Australian task group in the Gulf to suspend hostilities. He continued: 'we rejoice that the war has been won quickly and with so few casualties to our own forces'. But he also knew 'that the end of the war was not the end of the crisis. Much remains to be done to bring stability to the Gulf, and to bring a wider, durable peace to the Middle East.' Next morning Hawke spoke to President Bush by phone to congratulate him on 'the magnificent victory'.[61]

Australia's war leadership had been purposeful and efficient. Although there was no War Cabinet or Foreign Affairs and Defence Committee, Hawke's small group of key ministers acted in a similar fashion, conscious that their decisions ultimately had to be approved by the Cabinet. Hawke had taken firm control, even though, interestingly, the first initiative had come from Rear Admiral Carwardine. Aware of the doubts and potential opposition of his own Left-faction members, Hawke was careful to lay out the reasons for the first commitment and the consequent decision to join the war.

Once the decision had been made, the defence minister, Ray, did not interfere in the conduct of ADF operations or in the detailed work of ADF Headquarters. At the same time, he did not ignore these details; he kept himself well informed and made his wishes known. His prime concern was with the political presentation of what Defence was doing or planned to do. He consulted closely with Hawke and Evans, and put the Defence view strongly in Cabinet.

Except for Carwardine's initiative, the government's military advisers were not involved in deciding whether to go to the Gulf. Their role was to provide the government with alternatives and then to meet the challenge of deploying the forces. Gration and his senior staff were highly experienced, forward thinking, sensitive to political requirements and determined not to interfere in the conduct of operations. After more than three years as CDF, Gration had a clear understanding of his role as the government's principal military adviser. The new command arrangements in the ADF made it more responsive to the government.

Given Australia's membership of the Western alliance and the fact that the UN endorsed the sanctions and the eventual use of military force, Australia's involvement seemed justified. What was not fully anticipated was that it would draw Australia into a continuing commitment in the Middle East, which in the end would have damaging consequences. Critics claim that the subsequent sanctions against Iraq resulted in further deaths and suffering in Iraq, but that situation would have continued even if the Gulf War had not been fought, and Saddam would still have continued his occupation of Kuwait.

13

'It is right, it is lawful and it's in Australia's national interest'

Howard, Afghanistan and Iraq Commitments, 2001–03

On the afternoon of 12 September 2001, the day after the terrorist attacks on the World Trade Center in New York and the Pentagon in Washington, Australian prime minister John Howard addressed the press on the front lawn of the residence of the Australian ambassador in Washington. In a few words, without consulting his colleagues or seeking approval from the Cabinet, he committed Australia to war: 'We haven't been requested to provide any military assistance but obviously if we were asked to help, we would.' A decade later he recalled that 'there are occasions when a national leader should be pre-emptive'. But, he added, he knew that the Australian public, his own party and the leader of the Opposition, Kim Beazley, would support him. He admitted that if he had not been in Washington he would not have come to the same conclusion so quickly. 'Being on the spot had a powerful effect on me.' Nonetheless, he was sure that even if he had not been in Washington his decision would have been the same.[1] So, with these few words, Howard set Australia on a course for two decades of war, first in Afghanistan and then in Iraq.

There are several difficulties with telling the story of Australia's war leadership in the Afghanistan and Iraq conflicts. The first is their length. With a three-year break (2002–05), Australian troops served in Afghanistan from 2001 to 2021. Australia's commitment to Iraq was similarly long, from the invasion in 2003 to the formal withdrawal in 2009, with further operations against the so-called Islamic State until 2020. A full examination of Australia's role in these wars would therefore require a complete book. The second problem is that the documentary evidence, particularly official records, is not yet available to allow the depth of discussion necessary to do justice to the subject.[2] Furthermore, the issues are complex, requiring an examination of the broader context of world affairs and the role of intelligence in supporting government decisions. Therefore, to round out the story of Australia's war leadership over 90 years, this chapter is restricted to a discussion of Australia's decisions to take part in the Afghanistan War in 2001 and the invasion of Iraq in 2003, drawing on publicly available information

Continuing Gulf Commitment

Although it is possible to pinpoint the exact dates on which the government formally committed forces to the Afghanistan and Iraq wars, in fact, like the commitment to Vietnam, Australia's military involvement in the Middle East had grown over the previous dozen years to a point that made it difficult to avoid continuing once the Americans sought further assistance.

The previous chapter described how Australia committed a naval task force to the allied coalition to eject Iraq from Kuwait. On 3 April 1991, a month after the end of the war, the UN Security Council passed Resolution 687, which set out what Iraq needed to do before sanctions were lifted. Having deployed only a modest naval force to the war, the Australian government could not resist a request from the United States to allow the oiler HMAS *Westralia* to remain in the Persian Gulf as part of the Maritime Interception Force (MIF), enforcing the sanctions against Iraq. When *Westralia* returned to Australia it was replaced by the frigate HMAS *Darwin*. Continuing the commitment, four Australian warships served in the Red Sea between 1991 and 1993. By 1996 an Australian ship was back in the Persian Gulf.[3]

Under Security Council Resolution 687, Iraq was supposed to destroy all its weapons of mass destruction (WMD). These included chemical, biological and possibly nuclear weapons, as well as the means of delivering them, such as long-range rockets. The UN Commission on Iraq (UNSCOM) was formed to inspect and destroy Iraq's WMD, and Australia provided some of the weapons inspectors. Indeed, between 1991 and 1999 about 135 ADF officers, NCOs and civilian Australian officials took part in the weapons inspection program. As well as this commitment, in 1991 Australia deployed a team of medical personnel and engineers to provide humanitarian relief to displaced Kurds in northern Iraq.

The Liberal–National Party Coalition, led by John Howard, which came to power in 1996, inherited the Middle East involvement. The following year, Australia provided the chairman of UNSCOM. The Iraq president, Saddam Hussein, continued to hinder the work of UNSCOM, and in October 1997 he banned all UNSCOM inspections. By January 1998 US president Bill Clinton had decided to take military action, and he asked Australia to contribute to a coalition force. The Howard government, with bipartisan support, agreed and offered a Special Air Service (SAS) squadron and two Boeing 707 tanker aircraft. It was clear evidence that the Howard government was receptive to US requests, and saw vital interests at stake in the Middle East.

These forces were duly deployed to Kuwait as part of Operation Pollard, but the UN secretary general struck a deal with Saddam and the planned strike on Iraq did not proceed. Although the SAS and aircraft returned home after three months, an ADF liaison officer remained in Kuwait with the Coalition Joint Task Force, and provided Australia with forewarning of future US operations. The UNSCOM inspections resumed, but when Saddam again hindered their activities, in December 1998 the United States and Britain conducted a four-day bombing campaign against Iraqi targets, known as Operation Desert Fox. Australia was not involved.

In view of Saddam's intransigence, the United States then asked Australia to deploy a frigate to the MIF. In March 1999 Australia announced the deployment of a frigate to the region for the first time in three years, thus reviving Australia's role in the MIF—one that was to become important after the terrorist attacks of 11 September 2001. Australia had been drawn back into the Middle East with a stake in seeing Saddam Hussein stripped of his WMD. Iraq ceased cooperating with UNSCOM in May 1999 and UNSCOM dissolved in December 1999.

The Howard Government

The Howard government had come to power with a policy of revitalising the US alliance, which it alleged had been weakened under the Keating government. The main focus of the US–Australia relationship was the Asia-Pacific region, and this was underlined by the Asian financial crisis of mid-1997, which severely undermined the economies of Indonesia, South Korea and Thailand. The crisis in Indonesia led to rioting and eventually, in May 1998, to the resignation of President Suharto. He was succeeded by his vice president, B.J. Habibie, who agreed to allow the people of East Timor to vote on independence or autonomy.

The Australian government's emphasis on the region had already been demonstrated in December 1997, when it contributed to a New Zealand–led Truce Monitoring Group in Bougainville to monitor the truce between the Papua New Guinea government and the rebels in Bougainville. The following April, Australia took over leadership of the renamed Peace Monitoring Group. This commitment, known as Operation Bel Isi, was to continue for another five years.[4]

Meanwhile, the East Timorese had voted for independence, leading to indiscriminate violence by Indonesian-backed militia. In response, in September 1999 Australia led and provided the largest component of a military mission to East Timor, known as the International Force East Timor (INTERFET), to restore peace and to enable the country to begin its path towards independence.[5]

The commitment to East Timor had a fundamental effect on Howard and his government. A Sydney solicitor born in 1939, Howard had entered the federal parliament in 1974, and by 1977 was treasurer in the Fraser government until its demise in 1983. Elected leader of the Opposition in 1985, he lost the 1987 election and two years later the leadership. Regaining the leadership in 1995, he won the 1996 election. Socially conservative and an advocate of free-market economics, Howard initially had no particular interest or expertise in international affairs, although by instinct he strongly supported the US alliance.[6] Indeed, the government's initiative in trying to resolve the Bougainville crisis rested more on the work of activist foreign minister Alexander Downer, who had been Opposition leader before Howard became leader for the second time. Downer had been a diplomat for six years, and had been executive director of the Australian Chamber of Commerce before being elected to parliament, aged 33, from a South Australian electorate in 1984. But a prime minister cannot escape international and defence affairs, and the commitments to Bougainville, the Persian Gulf in 1998 and East Timor in 1999 soon had Howard relishing these issues and gaining confidence in his handling of them. The Howard government was re-elected in October 1998, and thus by September 2001 Howard had been prime minister for five and a half years.

Howard was supported by the National Security Committee of Cabinet, which apart from him included the deputy prime minister and leader of the National Party, John Anderson; the treasurer, Peter Costello; the foreign minister, Downer; the defence minister, Peter Reith; the attorney-general, Daryl Williams; and the Minister for Immigration, Philip Ruddock. The defence minister is always important, but since the election of the Howard government in March 1996 there had been three ministers—Ian McLachlan, John Moore and Peter Reith. For all three it was their last portfolio before leaving politics. Appointed in January 2001, Reith would resign from parliament in the November 2001 election, to be succeeded by Senator Robert Hill. An Adelaide lawyer from the moderate wing of the Liberal Party, Hill had been Minister for the Environment and was Leader of the Government in the Senate.

The National Security Committee was advised by the Secretaries Committee on National Security, which consisted of the secretaries of all the departments represented on the National Security Committee as well as the Chief of the Defence Force (CDF). The secretary of the Department of the Prime Minister and Cabinet, Max Moore-Wilton, played a key role, supported by defence, security and international staff in his department. There were now more mechanisms for interdepartmental coordination, such as the Strategic Policy Coordination Group, with representatives from Prime Minister and Cabinet, Foreign Affairs, and Defence, the latter represented by the Vice Chief of the Defence Force (VCDF) and the Deputy Secretary Strategic Policy.[7]

Military Advisers

The government's principal military adviser was the CDF, Admiral Chris Barrie, who had held the position since July 1998. He had worked closely with Howard and the government during the INTERFET deployment in 1999 and was therefore experienced in balancing strategic and political issues. Since the Gulf War, the chiefs of staff had changed their title to chief of their service, and in 2001 the three chiefs were Vice-Admiral David Shackleton, Lieutenant General Peter Cosgrove and Air Marshal Angus Houston. Aged 54, Cosgrove was a decorated Vietnam veteran who had commanded an infantry battalion, a brigade and the 1st Division, as well as being the successful and widely acclaimed commander of INTERFET. Houston had long experience in joint plans and operations, having previously been head of Strategic Command Division. The latter appointment, held by Air Vice-Marshal Alan Titheridge in 2001, was the key officer in ADF Headquarters in supporting the CDF in his command of operations. Another important appointment was that of Commander Australian Theatre, held by Rear Admiral Chris Ritchie, and located in Sydney. This position had been established in 1996 to command Australian forces on operations.[8]

In providing military advice to the government and also in exercising his command of deployed ADF units, the CDF was supported by the Strategic Command Group, which he chaired. It included the secretary of Defence, Dr Allan Hawke; the VCDF; the chiefs of the services; the Deputy Secretary Strategic Policy; the heads of Strategic Command and International Policy Divisions; and the Director of the Defence Intelligence Organisation. Invited members included the Commander Australian Theatre, the Support Commander Australia, the Head of Public Affairs, and staff from the defence minister's office. The inclusion of Hawke and his senior subordinates was a reminder that the Defence secretary also had a key role in advising the government. The Defence command structure was far more sophisticated than in the past. It was better suited to producing military options when the government was planning to send forces overseas, and to deploying and commanding ADF forces on operations once ordered by the government. But the big questions were whether Defence was able to provide advice to the government about the wisdom of committing forces to operations, and whether the government would even welcome such advice.

Deploying Forces to Afghanistan

As noted earlier, Howard had not sought advice from any of his ministerial colleagues or advisers before deciding to support the United States with military forces in September 2001. In Washington, Howard learned that the United States believed that the Islamic terrorist group al-Qaeda, led by Osama bin Laden, was responsible for the attacks, and was based in Afghanistan, protected by the ruling Taliban government. It was clear that the United States was planning a strike against the al-Qaeda bases in Afghanistan. Flying home, initially on Air Force Two (the US vice president's plane) for the flight from Washington to Hawaii, Howard spoke to Downer by phone, and the foreign minister first raised the idea of invoking the ANZUS Treaty. As journalist Karen Middleton wrote: 'This was how many decisions were taken throughout the tenure of the Howard government, especially on security—Howard and Downer deciding together, and then getting Cabinet's endorsement.'[9]

Back in Canberra on 14 September, Howard told his Cabinet that the Americans were going to strike in Afghanistan and Cabinet endorsed the invoking of the ANZUS Treaty, in which the parties would 'act to meet the common danger'. Later in the day Howard told the press that the decision had been based on the belief that the attacks had been initiated and coordinated from outside the United States, and the action had been taken to 'demonstrate our steadfast commitment to work with the United States in combating international terrorism'.[10]

Before finally committing forces, however, Howard wanted a clear request from US president George W. Bush. As Australia was approaching a federal election, to be held on 10 November, Howard wanted to be able to say that Australian forces had been deployed at the request of the United States. Because other countries were starting to join the coalition against al-Qaeda, the United States was reluctant to single out Australia. Eventually, the US State Department issued a generic request to its allies, and on 28 September Bush phoned Howard. According to Middleton, Bush said: 'John, our two militaries are talking. We'll leave it to them.'[11] That same day the UN Security Council passed Resolution 1373, recognising the right of UN member countries to combat 'by all means' the threats to international security posed by terrorism. The United States and Australia took this as permission to undertake military operations.

Meanwhile, the Department of Defence was considering what forces it could provide, guided by Howard's view that 'Australia's mission should be deliberately specific: to go in and help demolish al-Qaeda, dismantle the Taliban government which was supporting it, and then get out.' Defence was assisted by information gained by the CDF, Admiral Barrie, when he visited Washington in late September to meet the incoming chairman of the US Joint Chiefs of Staff, General Richard Myers, as well as the commander-in-chief of US Central Command (CENTCOM), General Tommy Franks.[12] Franks would be commanding the US campaign in Afghanistan as well as other operations in the Persian Gulf.

On 4 October, two days after Cabinet had formally endorsed the deployment of Australian forces, Howard announced the commitment at a press conference. The forces would include an SAS squadron and two Boeing 707 aircraft for air-to-air refuelling. The frigate HMAS *Anzac*, which was already in the Persian Gulf, would extend its tour. Howard explained that the previous day the US ambassador to Australia, Tom Schieffer, had shown him a large dossier based on intelligence information, which he had read over 45 minutes and had returned to Schieffer: 'it amounted to a very compelling case in support of the allegations concerning bin Laden and his terrorist organisation that have been made by the United States and others'.[13] There was widespread public support for Howard's decision.

In making his announcement, Howard had added that the Australian forces would be under a separate identifiable national commander. Brigadier Ken Gillespie, who had recently completed his tour as commander of a brigade in East Timor, was selected to lead the Australian contingent. Aged 49, Gillespie was an officer of the Royal Australian Engineers who had earlier served in Namibia and had also commanded the joint intelligence centre in Headquarters Australian Theatre. His first task was to go to CENTCOM Headquarters in Tampa, Florida, and find a way Australia could play a role in the 'war against terror'.[14] In fact, the US operations had begun in Afghanistan on 7 October, about a week before Gillespie arrived at Tampa. Gillespie soon found that in Tampa there were two levels to the coalition against terrorism: the first consisted of the United States and Britain, while all the other coalition partners were on a second level. He set about trying to increase Australia's influence.

The next task was to find a country in the Middle East that would be willing to provide a base for the SAS when they deployed into Afghanistan. This task was given to the Chief of the Air Force, Air Marshal Angus Houston, who with great skill and diplomacy secured the agreement of Kuwait. It proved to be a fortunate choice, because CENTCOM had set up a forward headquarters there to command operations in the Middle East and Afghanistan.

On 22 October, the defence minister, Peter Reith, and the leader of the Opposition, Kim Beazley, farewelled the SAS advance party in

Perth. Three days later Howard announced the deployment of additional forces. At the same time, Howard set out the arguments for supporting the Australian commitment. He stated that the al-Qaeda network responsible for the terrorist attacks on 11 September was based in Afghanistan, where the Taliban government had given it safe haven. The terrorist attacks had been directed not just at the United States, but at all Western countries, and 22 Australians had died in New York. The United Nations, the European Union and NATO had all supported the United States; indeed NATO had declared that the attack on the United States could be considered an attack on the entire nineteen-nation alliance. 'Whilst the destruction of the al-Qaeda network must be our first priority,' said Howard, 'the long-term aim of this campaign is to demonstrate that organised international, state-sanctioned terrorism will not be tolerated by the world community.'[15]

Before the end of the year, the Australian forces deployed on what became Operation Slipper had grown to about 1300 ADF personnel and included a Special Forces Task Group, which was deployed to Afghanistan, two RAAF Boeing 707 air-to-air refuelling aircraft, based in Kyrgyzstan to support coalition air operations, two frigates and an amphibious ship supporting the war against terrorism in the Persian Gulf, up to three RAAF C-130 Hercules transport aircraft to move personnel and equipment, two RAAF AP-3C Orion maritime patrol aircraft based in the Persian Gulf region to conduct surveillance operations, and four F/A-18 Hornet strike aircraft, based at Diego Garcia in the Indian Ocean to provide back-up for the Americans. Gillespie moved to Kuwait with his headquarters to command the ADF units in the Persian Gulf–Afghanistan area.

The main body of the Australian SAS squadron left Perth in late November and arrived in Afghanistan on 10 December, the same day Gillespie arrived in Kuwait. Australian operations began a week later. In the accepted jargon, as commander of the Australian contingent Gillespie had authority to issue a 'red card' to the Americans if any of Australia's intended operations were contrary to Australian rules of engagement or national interest, and hence to veto the use of

Australians in those operations. The Australian Special Forces operated in Afghanistan for almost twelve months, with rotations of three SAS squadrons. They were involved in several major battles and had one fatality.[16]

The initiative to commit forces had come directly from Howard, based purely on his instinct while in Washington. The government's Defence advisers reacted quickly not only to deploy forces at short notice, but also to gain a privileged place in the US command structure. In considering the decision to go to Afghanistan, the CDF, Admiral Barrie, reflected later that there had been 'a clear exit strategy. Success was defined as the destruction of al-Qaeda terrorist training camps in Afghanistan and significantly reducing its presence in the country. This success we achieved quite quickly, but then the priorities and complications presented by the invasion of Iraq meant we took our eyes of this ball too early.'[17] The decision to go to Afghanistan was supported by the Opposition and generally by the Australian public. Indeed, the Howard government won the federal election on 10 November. After the election Robert Hill was appointed defence minister. The next decision, to take part in the invasion of Iraq in 2003, was to prove to be far more contentious.

Planning for the Iraq War

Within days of the terrorist attacks on 11 September 2001, information began to appear that as well as striking at al-Qaeda in Afghanistan, the United States was also planning to invade Iraq.[18] On 30 September the *New York Times* reported that the United States had amassed military forces across the Middle East theatre 'with Iraq and Afghanistan at its heart'. A few days later *Newsweek* magazine claimed that the Pentagon's Defense Policy Board had decided Iraq should be targeted quickly after Afghanistan. Later that month the US ambassador to the United Nations warned that the United States would take action against states other than Afghanistan. These indications culminated in the president's State of the Union address on 29 January 2002, when Bush included North Korea, Iran and Iraq in an 'axis of evil', and vowed not to 'stand by, as peril draws closer and closer'.[19]

The United States had been concerned about Iraq since the first Gulf War. Between 1991 and 1999, UNSCOM's weapons inspectors had tried to locate and destroy Iraq's WMD, but as we have seen in 1999 UNSCOM had been forced to leave Iraq. Saddam Hussein continued to pose a threat to stability in the Middle East, and many of President Bush's senior advisers, especially his vice president, Dick Cheney, and his defense secretary, Donald Rumsfeld, were determined that Saddam should be overthrown and replaced by a democratic government. The Australian ambassador in Washington, Michael Thawley, was aware of this attitude, and on the day of the 11 September terrorist attacks told Howard that as a result, 'Iraq would be back on the agenda for the Americans.'[20]

Early warning that the United States was starting to plan a war with Iraq came from Brigadier Gillespie in Kuwait, where he had been given privileged access to the US headquarters. Gillespie immediately reported this information to Canberra. On 10 December Admiral Barrie warned the National Security Committee of Cabinet 'that the United States may be contemplating counter-terrorism-related military operations outside Afghanistan, and may wish to have ADF assets participate in such activity'. The committee agreed that the ADF would not contribute to such operations unless 'a specific request was made' and was then agreed to by the committee. Then, in early 2002, US Defense Secretary Rumsfeld and his deputy, Paul Wolfowitz, raised with Thawley the possibility of Australia participating in the planning for the Iraq operation. With these indications, the ADF's planners in Strategic Command Division started thinking about what this development would mean for the ADF. According to one account, alerted through the SAS's connections with US Special Forces, by mid-May 2002 Australia's Special Operations Command was starting to plan for an operation in Iraq.[21]

The Australian government was already giving some indication of its thinking. The journalist Karen Middleton wrote that in mid-April at a Queensland Liberal Council meeting in Brisbane, Howard had told his federal ministers 'with a heavy heart, that a military operation in Iraq was likely'. In the second week of June, Howard visited Washington again. Speaking to journalists, he was non-committal about a possible involvement in further operations, but he added that if any approaches were made to Australia, 'we'd consider them in the circumstances, at the time, if they occur'. Bush responded that he had told Howard 'there are no war plans on my desk'. As Middleton commented: 'He may have been keeping them in a drawer because they were certainly being drafted.'[22]

In his memoirs, Howard wrote:

> President Bush and I were careful to avoid specifics about Australian troop commitments to a possible invasion of Iraq. He knew that close discussions were under way between the US military and their Australian counterparts. He was entitled to assume on the basis of that, and also the tenor of our discussion, that if the military option was chosen by the United States then, in all likelihood, Australia would join. But he knew that I had not made any commitment to this effect and that for understandable political and other reasons I would keep my options open until the time when a final decision was needed.

Howard left Washington believing that Bush's efforts to resolve the problem with Saddam Hussein through diplomacy would ultimately fail, 'and that, in the end, he would take military action against Iraq'.[23] As Howard admitted, he had given Bush the strong impression that Australia would take part in the Iraq operations.

The first public hint of Australian involvement came on 18 June, when the defence minister, Hill, delivered a major speech at the Australian Defence College. Referring to the implications of the terrorist attacks of 11 September, Hill stated:

> Commentators are talking about the emergence of a new US doctrine, one which some suggest emphasises pre-emption over diplomacy and deterrence.

> This applies in particular when stakes are raised—as they are in Iraq—by the frightening possibility of terrorists gaining access to weapons of mass destruction.
>
> The United States is clearly no longer going to allow problems to fester and threats to remain unresolved. The need to act swiftly and firmly before threats become attacks is perhaps the clearest lesson of 11 September, and is one that is clearly driving US policy and strategy. It is a position which we share, in principle.[24]

Hill had given a clear indication that if the United States was planning military action against Iraq, Australia would at least consider supporting the Americans.

Australian officers serving in or near US headquarters were gaining further insight into American thinking. When Gillespie had moved from Tampa to Kuwait the previous December, an Australian liaison officer had remained at Tampa. He now received 'overtures' from senior CENTCOM officers about a possible Australian contribution. Brigadier Gary Bornholt, who had taken over from Gillespie as the Australian commander in Kuwait, reported similar information to the head of Strategic Command Division, Air Vice-Marshal Alan Titheridge. In a minute to the CDF, Admiral Barrie, and to the defence minister, Hill, Titheridge advised that it would be critical for Australia to be admitted to 'US planning compartments . . . if Australia was to remain aware of the developing US campaign plan'. He also forecast that the government would receive an invitation to deploy an Australian planning team to Tampa.[25]

Brigadier Gillespie was due to take over from Titheridge in August, so when the US invitation arrived, Admiral Barrie ordered both of them to go to Tampa. Gillespie was promoted to major general, and the two officers departed in a hurry on 28 June. Once they arrived, the 'Americans made it clear to Titheridge and Gillespie that they were planning an Iraq operation and wanted to bring Australia in as a "trusted friend"'.[26]

As well as the appointment of Gillespie to take over from Titheridge, who was retiring, in mid-2002, there were other changes among the ADF's senior commanders. Admiral Barrie retired after four years as CDF and was succeeded by General Cosgrove, whose position as Chief of Army was taken by his deputy, the newly promoted Lieutenant General Peter Leahy. Vice-Admiral Chris Ritchie succeeded Shackleton as Chief of Navy, while Ritchie's position as Commander Australian Theatre was taken by Rear Admiral Mark Bonser, who had previously been Director-General of Coastwatch in the Australian Customs Service. Vice-Admiral Russ Shalders took over as VCDF, and Cosgrove appointed him as his designated deputy so that he would act as CDF in his absence. Admiral Barrie recalled that when he retired in early July 2002, 'no special evidence existed to make an invasion of Iraq essential, which became one topic of conversation during my final call with the Prime Minister'.[27] One can only speculate whether Barrie would have continued with such advice if he had continued as CDF.

Cosgrove's first task as CDF was to travel to Tampa for discussions with the Commander US Special Operations Command, Major General Charles Holland, and the commander-in-chief of CENTCOM, General Franks. Cosgrove informed Franks that he intended to withdraw Australia's SAS contingent from Afghanistan. Acting on advice from his liaison officers, Australia's Special Forces commander, Brigadier Duncan Lewis, believed that the Americans would like Australian Special Forces troops to take part in the Iraq operation. To achieve this, however, the SAS squadron in Afghanistan would need to be withdrawn in time to allow the troops to regroup and refresh. The defence minister, Hill, has denied that the SAS was withdrawn from Afghanistan 'in preparation for pending operations in Iraq. In truth, both the government and I were concerned with avoiding mission creep. The advice of the defence leadership was that the task for which our special forces were sent had been achieved.'[28] This might be true, but the SAS could only take part in the Iraq invasion if they were withdrawn from Afghanistan.

The government was well aware of these planning initiatives, and Hill later admitted that the Cabinet 'had been party to decisions over some time to support the ADF being prepared in the event that

Cabinet made a decision to commit Australian forces to combat'. He expected the ADF sensibly to begin planning for various scenarios, but 'some preparations such as entering the US planning process, did require my political imprimatur'. Howard has emphasised that the key body in deciding these sort of issues was the National Security Committee of Cabinet, which, as well as its usual ministers, included, 'except on very rare occasions', the CDF, the secretaries of Defence, Foreign Affairs, and the Prime Minister's Department, the Director-General of Security and the Director-General of the Office of National Assessments. 'From the view of operational decision-making I cannot emphasise too much how valuable it was to have these senior advisers present.' According to the journalist Tony Wright, on 27 July the National Security Committee met and 'concluded that if the US was preparing to take action against Iraq, then Australia better be in on the ground floor'.[29] Although the government continued to deny that it had made any decision, this crucial meeting had fixed on a course of action that made the outcome almost inevitable.

Hence, with the approval of the government, in August Cosgrove sent a planning team to Tampa, led by Brigadier Maurie McNarn, the senior operations and planning officer in Strategic Command Division. A former Signals Corps officer, McNarn had served as a UN observer in Israel and Lebanon in 1986–87. McNarn was 'issued with two sets of instructions—one written and one verbal. The written instructions were not to commit Australia to anything. The verbal instructions were completely different. He was told to do everything necessary to make sure Australia was in a position to deploy, if—or when—a decision was made.'[30]

During the INTERFET operation in East Timor in 1999, the CDF, Admiral Barrie, had bypassed the Commander Australian Theatre and placed Cosgrove, the commander of INTERFET, directly under his command, appreciating that as the government's principal military adviser he needed to keep a close watch on operations. As CDF, Cosgrove decided to take similar action, especially because if information leaked out that the ADF was planning for operations in Iraq this would cause political problems for the government.[31] Brigadier McNarn was therefore instructed to report directly to the CDF through the head of Strategic Command Division, Major General Gillespie. Recognising Gillespie's new responsibility, his division was renamed Strategic Operations Division.

Planning for the operations took place in Strategic Operations Division, advised by the work of McNarn's team in Tampa. The planners considered a range of options, which then needed to be approved by the government, conscious that 'Howard's preferred form of military intervention was always quick and clean—in at the pointy end and then out fast.' The problem was that knowledge of the planning for the possible operation, codenamed Plan Bastille, was restricted to a very small number of key senior commanders and their staffs. As a result, the units that were likely to be involved were unable to undertake their own detailed planning.[32] This was to cause severe problems in the area of logistics.

In initiating the planning process, on 30 August Cosgrove reminded his staff that there had 'been no formal US request for an Australian contribution to US operations to effect regime change in Iraq' and that the government had not made any decision 'to commit the ADF to operations'. The 'critical immediate task' was to 'confirm the viability of strategic options' that the government had agreed should be developed. As the Australian Army's historian, Albert Palazzo, noted, there was no 'mention of what Australia actually hoped to accomplish in Iraq'. Australia had therefore

> removed itself from any role in the war's strategic decision making process, or in the selection of its political aim. As a minor coalition partner this was probably inevitable. That the Government's only option was to follow the US lead can be inferred by the equanimity with which Cosgrove, and one assumes the Prime Minister, accepted the Bush Administration's intent to impose regime change on Iraq.[33]

The Australian Government's Preparations

In the second half of 2002 the government started laying the groundwork for the case to support the war against Iraq, and by September, Australian newspapers were beginning to speculate on Australia's possible involvement. On 8 September, President Bush telephoned Howard to discuss the situation in Iraq, and in a subsequent press interview Howard said that Bush had not made up his mind to attack Iraq. But at the same time, the US Deputy Secretary of State, Richard Armitage, told reporters that if the US took military action 'we'd want to be involved with our Australian allies'. The *Sydney Morning Herald* also discussed some of the US military planning, noting that all versions of the US battle plan called for the early capture of Basra.[34]

On 11 September, one year after the terrorist attack, Howard addressed the National Press Club, and the following day in another address a journalist asked him to comment on a speech by President Bush in which he had appeared to stress the importance of regime change in Iraq. In reply, Howard seemed to accept the idea of regime change, stating that the most important thing was to remove the threat posed by Iraq's possession of WMD. 'It's hard to conceive that you could have a total dismantling of those weapons and a full enforcement of the UN resolutions without the regime changing. But the main issue . . . the main objective is to remove the threat.' At about the same time, Major General John Vines, commander of the US and coalition forces in Afghanistan, said that if he were involved in any attack on Iraq he would do everything in his power to ensure that the Australian SAS were present. On 15 September, Senator Hill confirmed that Australia might support a US-led attack on Iraq even if it did not have backing from the United Nations. In Parliament on 17 September, in a ministerial statement, the foreign minister, Downer, said that Australia could no longer leave the threat posed by Iraq and its WMD 'unattended'.[35]

Australia received a sharp and tragic appreciation of the nature of the threat from Islamic terrorists on 12 October, when they bombed two nightclubs on the Indonesian island of Bali, resulting in the deaths of 88 Australians, 38 Indonesians, 23 Britons and people of more than twenty other nationalities. More than 200 people were killed and a similar number injured. Australia hurried to provide support to the Indonesian authorities. The incident had a profound effect on Australia's political leaders, such that any suggestion that Iraq might be harbouring Islamic terrorists was likely to make them more willing to accept the need to invade Iraq. As Howard wrote later, 'The Bali attack was a reminder that the war against terrorism had to go on in an uncompromising fashion. Any other course of action would be folly.'[36]

By this stage the forces to take part in the possible operations were beginning to be identified, although this planning was kept secret. Eventually the Australian force, to be known as Task Force 633, would consist of five components. The first would be a national headquarters to be located alongside CENTCOM Headquarters, which had moved to Qatar. The second would consist of the frigates *Anzac* and *Darwin*, which were already operating in the Persian Gulf as part of Operation Slipper (the war against terrorism, including operations in Afghanistan), as well as the amphibious ship HMAS *Kanimbla* with an RAN clearance diving team. The third component would consist of RAAF AP-3C Orion maritime patrol aircraft already operating in the Persian Gulf as part of Operation Slipper. The fourth would be a Special Forces Task Group with an SAS squadron, a large 90-strong platoon of commandos, engineers and three Chinook helicopters. And the fifth component would be an RAAF air wing with fourteen F/A-18 Hornet strike aircraft and three C-130 Hercules transport aircraft.

What forces might be deployed had been the subject of considerable discussion both among the senior ADF officers and with the government. There were at least two crucial issues. The first was a strong suggestion from the Americans that Australia provide a cavalry reconnaissance group, but there was not enough time for it to be prepared for operations. In truth, Australia's cavalry forces were not prepared for high-level war. The second issue was the decision to deploy the F/A-18 Hornet dual-role strike aircraft, the first time these aircraft had been deployed on operations. The forces to be sent to the

Gulf were not selected to meet a strategic objective, but rather were guided by what was available, what could be deployed within the required timeframe, what could survive on the modern battlefield, and 'lastly and perhaps most importantly, what force elements would the United States appreciate'. The government capped the numbers to be deployed at 2058, to minimise the possibility of casualties, but this caused considerable, and potentially dangerous, shortfalls in logistics. The Defence leaders were unwilling to press the government to lift the cap.[37]

The decision to include the Australian SAS had been made early, which permitted the SAS to send planning officers to Tampa, and allowed the SAS planners to select an area of operations in western Iraq with the task of preventing the Iraqis from launching Scud missiles from this area towards Israel. The SAS were therefore able to make an important contribution to the coming campaign, while operating in an area where they were unlikely to face heavy casualties.[38]

Even though the government had been careful not to commit forces to the US operation, the ADF needed to complete some essential planning to be able to take part if they were ordered, and one crucial issue was to secure bases for its forces. In September, Air Marshal Houston, accompanied by Brigadier McNarn, visited all the Gulf countries and Jordan, seeking permission to base the Australian forces. Houston returned to the Gulf in late December to finalise the arrangements. Eventually, Australian forces would be based across the region. The Orion aircraft would be in the United Arab Emirates (UAE), the navy would have logistics bases in Bahrain and the UAE, the Hornets and Hercules aircraft would be based in Qatar, and the Special Forces would be based in Jordan.[39] McNarn would be transferred from his planning role at Tampa to become the Australian National Commander with his headquarters in Qatar.

By December 2002, McNarn and his staff were arriving in the Gulf region, and the frigates and the Orion aircraft were also operating there. But the other forces had not yet been deployed. General Cosgrove was advising the government, however, that if it ultimately wanted to commit forces to operations, they would need to be deployed early enough to allow them to become acclimatised and integrated with the Americans before the operations began. If the forces were deployed to the Gulf, the government would be able to delay its decision to take part in the war until the last minute. Furthermore, if Australia decided to join the United States in the invasion of Iraq and took part from the very first day, then Australia could withdraw its forces as soon as the invasion had been completed. An early involvement would win much more credit with the United States.

On 20 November, Howard announced that the SAS squadron in Afghanistan would be returning to Australia at the end of the month and would not be replaced. Further, he announced that ADF officers had 'had contingency discussions with the United States as a matter of prudent military planning' and that the ADF had 'made appropriate contingent arrangements' in case it was necessary to contribute 'to a new theatre such as Iraq'. Howard said that the Australian government had strongly endorsed the recent UN Security Council Resolution on Iraq, which called for a comprehensive program of weapons inspection and reinforced the demand of the international community that Iraq eliminate its WMD. He declared: 'It is now up to Iraq. It can choose to co-operate fully with the weapons inspectors and remove its WMD capabilities. This would deliver a peaceful outcome and offers the best chance to avoid armed conflict. Iraq should fully understand that if it does not meet its clearly understood international obligations, it must face the consequences.' Howard added that if the government were 'to decide to commit Australian military forces to action involving Iraq, there would be a full Parliamentary debate on that decision'.[40]

The decision to withdraw from Afghanistan corresponded with the arrival of a new Defence secretary, the experienced diplomat Ric Smith, who had previously served in Defence and had been ambassador in both China and Indonesia. Smith recalled that the government had not yet decided to go to war in Iraq. Nonetheless, 'the ADF leadership was concerned with being well positioned so that if the government made a decision to commit to conflict, we would not be caught with our forces unprepared or in long transit. The government accepted this view.'[41]

As Smith indicated, his and the CDF's concern was to provide the government with the optimum plan to achieve its aims. But this approach begs the question of whether the government's senior advisers ever presented a considered assessment of the wisdom of joining the US operation. The political scientist Judith Betts has argued that Howard had instituted arrangements that tended to preclude receiving such advice. Howard established a Cabinet Policy Unit that provided him 'with advice independent of the bureaucracy and ensured that Cabinet business reflected political rather than bureaucratic priorities'. The major decisions were made in the National Security Committee, which never 'considered an integrated Cabinet submission examining the merits of going to war in Iraq'. Betts concluded that there were two possible explanations for the senior advisers failing to provide an examination of the 'merits of going to war in Iraq': either the 'bureaucracy had been cowed into compliance', or the policy advisers actually agreed with Howard and saw Australia's participation as the price to pay to maintain the alliance'.[42]

Smith explained later that the

> message from ministers by that time was that they did not want strategic advice from the Defence Department. This reflected a conviction that ministers knew the issues and would take the decision for or against the war . . . Ministers were not seeking advice from the department on whether we should go to war as distinct from how we should go to war.

Secretaries of other departments had the same view. Ashton Calvert from Foreign Affairs thought that the government 'did not need advice on what they should do because they had, in effect, made up their minds'. Peter Shergold from the Department of the Prime Minister and Cabinet thought that 'ministers felt it was their responsibility to decide whether or not Australia entered the war . . . the advice they wanted from the policy departments and intelligence agencies was about the conduct of the war and capabilities, not the decision to go to war'.[43]

In the morning of 10 January 2003, the National Security Committee met to discuss various matters including the situation regarding Iraq's WMD, and later that afternoon Howard addressed a press conference to describe the outcome of the meeting. He explained that the government had not decided to be involved in military action, 'indeed no decision has yet been taken by the United States or other countries involved', but if Australia did make a commitment 'our men and women are entitled to the opportunity of that preparation' that would ensure their 'safety and their capacity to execute their obligations in a very professional way'. Hence, over the following weeks there would 'be some forward deployment of assets and personnel'. The forces involved might include Special Forces with appropriate support, an additional naval vessel (two already being in the Gulf), and a squadron of fourteen F/A-18 fighters. The AP-3C Orions, which had been deployed for the war against terror, would continue on that task.[44]

This was the signal for the ADF to start deploying forces to the Middle East. On 22 January the governor-general, the prime minister, the Minister for Defence, the CDF, the Chief of Navy and the leader of the Opposition, Simon Crean, who had replaced Beazley after the election, farewelled HMAS *Kanimbla* at Garden Island, Sydney. Howard told the sailors that they were going to the Persian Gulf 'as part of the existing multinational interception force but it may be' that they would be 'involved in wider operations'. Crean wished the navy men and women 'God speed and a safe and speedy return', but added that he did not 'believe that you should be going. I don't think that there should be a deployment of troops to Iraq ahead of the United Nations determining it.'[45]

This was followed on 24 January by a farewell ceremony at Campbell Barracks, Swanbourne, in Perth, for the SAS squadron of the Special Forces Task Group; on 7 February at RAAF Base, Richmond, in Sydney, for three C-130 aircraft; on 8 February at RAAF Base Tindal, Northern Territory, for the F/A-18 aircraft; on 11 February at RAAF Base Townsville for the C47 Chinooks of the 5th Aviation Regiment; and on 14 February at Holsworthy army base,

Sydney, for members of the engineer Incident Response Regiment, the commandos and the logistic elements of the Special Forces Task Group; and at HMAS *Waterhen* on Sydney Harbour for the RAN clearance diving team. Thus by mid-February the complete force of about 2000 personnel had been deployed, or were on their way to the Middle East.

Countdown to War

On 4 February 2003, Howard delivered a long and detailed statement to parliament in which he explained why the government had 'authorised the forward positioning of elements' of the ADF in the Persian Gulf. He argued that Iraq had failed to give up its WMD and at some time in the future would use them to dominate the region. He pointed out that the UN Security Council had given Saddam one last opportunity to fulfil the commitments he made in 1991 and he had failed to fulfil them. Furthermore, Australia was a close ally of the United States and the alliance 'has been and will remain an important element in the government's decision making process' on Iraq. He concluded that no decision had yet been made to go to war, and although the 'natural instinct was to recoil from it . . . the realities of the world in which we now live do not permit us that luxury'.[46] The following day the US Secretary of State, Colin Powell, addressed the United Nations and presented evidence, allegedly based on intelligence sources, that Saddam Hussein was hiding his WMD.

Soon afterwards, Bush invited Howard to visit him in Washington to discuss the situation, and when they met on 10 February, Bush said that he counted Australia as part of the 'coalition of the willing'. Howard went on to London, where he met the British prime minister, Tony Blair, and the head of the British Secret Intelligence Service (MI6), who showed him the most recent British intelligence assessments about Iraq's WMD. Howard found it 'quite compelling'. While Howard was away, on 15 February 600,000 people across Australia demonstrated against the prospect of going to war. By one account, around the world at least 10 million people demonstrated against the proposed invasion of Iraq. Back in Australia, on 13 March Howard addressed the National Press Club, making the case for military operations against Iraq in great detail. He said that he based his conclusions on British and US intelligence sources. Howard emphasised the threat from Saddam's WMD, rather than the imperatives of supporting the US alliance.[47]

As in the first Gulf War, the management of information would play a major role in the coming operations. Therefore, on 21 February Brigadier Mike Hannan, Director-General of Military Public Affairs, gave the first of a continuing series of media briefings on the operations of the ADF in the Gulf. He announced that the forces had previously been deployed as part of Operation Slipper in the war against terrorism, including the enforcement of sanctions against Iraq. But the troops deployed in preparation for a possible war with Iraq were now part of Operation Bastille. Hannan gave further briefings on 27 February and 6 March. On 10 March, Brigadier McNarn in Qatar was interviewed on Channel Nine television and emphasised that 'the Government's made absolutely no commitment and I'm under tight constraints on any activities we do. We are ready for whatever the Government call upon us to do.' He was adamant that none of his troops had been or were operating in Iraq.[48]

McNarn reported directly to Cosgrove, or in his absence to Gillespie, bypassing the Commander Australian Theatre, Admiral Bonser. This ensured that once operations began Cosgrove would have the most up-to-date information, and that if necessary he could react quickly to ensure that the operations were in accordance with government policy. Palazzo wrote that due to the CDF's 'intent to manage issues that had parliamentary or media implications—and almost everything fell within this mandate—Cosgrove effectively became the deployment's decision-maker for virtually everything'.[49]

On 8 March the chief UN arms inspector, Hans Blix, said that Iraq had speeded up compliance with demands for its disarmament but called for a 'sober judgement' of the value of its cooperation.[50] The next day the United States and Britain tabled an ultimatum in the United Nations giving Saddam Hussein until 17 March to disarm or face war. But the United States and Britain were having great difficulty raising support in the Security Council for their new resolution calling for the disarmament of Iraq (in addition to Resolution 1441, which required Iraq to support inspections by UN teams under threat of further action), and the Americans delayed the date for the initiation of operations.

On Sunday 16 March the US president met the leaders of Britain, Spain and Portugal at an American air base on the Portuguese Azores Islands, and that evening (7.30 a.m. 17 March Canberra time) the leaders issued a statement that if Saddam refused to cooperate fully with the United Nations he would bring 'on himself the serious consequences foreseen in UNSCR 1441 and previous resolutions'. In amplification, Bush added that the following day would be a 'moment of truth for the world'.[51] Shortly after the press conference, Bush telephoned Howard, who then called a Cabinet meeting for that evening.

When the Cabinet met at 8 p.m. on 17 March, Howard briefed the ministers on his discussions with Bush and Blair. General Cosgrove and the Chief of Air Force, Air Marshal Houston, then gave a briefing on operational matters if military action was authorised. However, the Cabinet did not, at this stage, formally agree to the use of Australian troops in the war.[52]

At 6 a.m. the following morning Howard received a telephone call from the US president, who explained that the United States, Britain and Spain had decided not to put their resolution to the UN Security Council. As Howard described it in an interview on ABC radio an hour or so later, the president 'asked whether Australia would be part of the coalition of the willing if it became necessary to finally use force against Iraq to enforce Iraq's obligations under previously passed Security Council resolutions. I indicated that Cabinet would meet again this morning . . . at 8.30 to formally consider that request'.[53]

When the National Security Committee met at 8.30 a.m. the ministers approved Australia's commitment to operations and authorised Cosgrove, who was present, to take the necessary action. Cosgrove returned to Russell Offices, convened the Strategic Command Group to check if the officers had any last-minute concerns, and then issued the order to begin operations. At 10 a.m. Howard called a press conference to announce, in slightly convoluted language, that the government had authorised the CDF 'to place the Australian forces already deployed in the Gulf region as part of any US-led coalition operation that may take place in the future directed in accordance with existing authority under United Nations resolutions to disarm Iraq'. A journalist put it in more straightforward language: 'Howard has ordered Australian troops to join the expected United States-led invasion of Iraq, effectively declaring Australia at war.' Howard said that he was 'very comfortable' with being the first prime minister to order the invasion of a country that had not committed a clear and present military threat to another country.[54]

Meanwhile, at 8 p.m. on Monday 17 March in Washington (midday Tuesday 18 March Canberra time), President Bush delivered an 'address to the nation' from the Oval Office at the White House, saying that 'Saddam Hussein and his sons must leave Iraq within 48 hours. Their refusal to do so will result in military conflict, commenced at a time of our choosing.' Two hours later in parliament Howard formally announced Australia's commitment and asked the House to 'endorse' the government's decision to commit the ADF to the Gulf region 'to enforce Iraq's compliance with its international obligations under successive resolutions of the United Nations Security Council'.[55] The debate about the government's decision continued until 9 p.m., resumed for most of the following day with numerous speakers arguing for and against Howard's motion, and ended at 4.40 p.m. on 20 March when the House voted 80 votes to 63 to support the government's decision.

War Begins

Earlier, in the morning of 20 March 2003, Howard gave a press conference and announced that Australian 'forces have started combat and combat support operations'. In the evening of 20 March, Howard addressed the nation and announced that the government had 'decided to commit Australian forces to action to disarm

Iraq because we believe it is right, it is lawful and it's in Australia's national interest'. He then repeated many of the arguments he had been emphasising for the past three months. The following evening Howard invited the CDF, VCDF and service chiefs and their wives to dinner at the Lodge to thank them for their assistance. Howard thought that these 'five men were a deeply impressive group', and he felt a 'special bond' with them.[56]

After the war there was considerable public debate about when the SAS went into action, with claims that the SAS had started operations before the 48-hour deadline set by President Bush, and before Howard committed Australian troops to war in his press conference at 10 a.m. on 18 March. It is true that the SAS patrols moved from Jordan to their positions along the Saudi–Iraq border during the nights of 16 and 17 March. However, the SAS did not cross the Iraq border until about 9 p.m. (Iraq time) on 19 March.[57] At that time it was 4 a.m., 20 March in Canberra, at least 36 hours after Howard had formally announced the commitment of troops in parliament. It was also 1 p.m. in the afternoon of 19 March in Washington when the SAS crossed the border. Bush's ultimatum to Saddam to leave Iraq within 48 hours was due to expire at 8 p.m. on 19 March (Washington time). The Australian SAS had begun operations some seven hours before that time. Bush and Howard have argued that since Saddam had already rejected Bush's ultimatum to leave Iraq it was permissible to begin operations, and that Bush had warned that military operations would begin 'at a time of our choosing'.

Within an hour of crossing the border, the SAS were involved in a short fire-fight with Iraqi troops, possibly the first contact of the Iraq War. As the coalition Special Forces deployed into western Iraq, American and British aircraft bombed Iraqi Army positions. Meanwhile, British troops seized the southern city of Basra, while American divisions with tanks advanced north towards Baghdad. HMAS *Anzac* provided naval gunfire support for the British amphibious operations. American, Australian and British Special Forces continued to take control of Iraq's western desert. On 23 March, Australian F/A-18 Hornets began flying strike missions against Iraqi positions. On several occasions Brigadier McNarn used his 'red card' to prevent the conduct of missions that were not in accordance with Australian government policy.[58] Baghdad was captured on 9 April and President Bush declared the combat operations over on 1 May. Most Australian combat forces returned to Australia, leaving smaller forces in the Middle East. Australia had had no combat deaths.

And what of the WMD that Iraq was supposed to have, which were one of the main justifications for the war? After the war the Iraq Survey Group (run by the United States, but including Australians) found that Iraq had no WMD. UNSCOM, which had worked hard to eliminate Iraq's WMD during the 1990s, actually had been very effective before Saddam stopped the inspectors from interfering. Saddam had pretended that he possessed WMD to maintain his prestige. The decision proved to be a fatal mistake for him and his regime. As for the US claim about evidence of Iraq's WMD, some scholars believe that this was merely '"a cover story" that the United States created and sold to its own people as well as the people of other countries'. It was 'misdirection from the start'. In Australia some researchers have claimed that the intelligence reports on Iraq's WMD were used as an excuse for decisions that had already been made for alliance reasons [59]

The end of the invasion did not end the fighting. The US-led coalition soon found itself fighting a savage insurgency throughout Iraq. As the situation deteriorated, in 2005 Howard agreed to send troops to Iraq, although they went to a relatively safe area. The Labor government, led by Prime Minister Kevin Rudd, elected in November 2007, had vowed to withdraw Australian combat and training units from Iraq, and the withdrawal began in June 2008. By the time the last combat and training soldiers departed in July 2009, about 20,000 ADF personnel had served in and around Iraq over a six-year period.

The tragedy for Iraq was an ongoing bloody insurgency, an unstable government, and the general misery of its citizens. All this was compounded by the rise of the so-called Islamic State, straddling the border with Syria. The United States was saddled with a major military commitment and the loss of prestige.

Modern War Leadership

Australian war leadership had evolved substantially since the First World War. The issues were now more complex; but one issue remained constant, namely, the need to make decisions in the context of alliance politics. In one respect, the government, assisted by the ADF leadership, managed the commitment to the invasion of Iraq quite brilliantly. The government wanted a commitment that would cement the alliance with the United States yet not result in a heavy burden or casualties. By virtue of its established connections and reputation, the ADF was able to take part in the early US planning. This enabled the ADF to determine what forces it could send, and importantly where they could operate. The ADF persuaded the government that if the forces were pre-positioned in the Gulf region they would be able to take part in the initial invasion, thereby winning the gratitude of the United States, and also be able to withdraw as soon as the invasion had achieved its initial aims. Palazzo summed it up: 'It was sufficient for the United States that an Australian commitment was present in Iraq. What this commitment did, how it was organised, what capabilities it possessed and how large it was were all secondary to the vital requirement of it just being there . . . Howard and Cosgrove understood the nuances of the US political/military interface and in this case were able to achieve an important political goal that was far in excess of the resources they were required to expend.'[60]

Modern governments are now required to explain or at least be seen to be trying to explain their actions.[61] From the beginning, Howard, playing the media well, did not rule out eventual involvement in any operations decided upon by the United States, and as it became clear that the United States might invade Iraq, he talked about the possibility that Australia might be involved. This became even more likely when on 10 January 2003 he announced the pre-positioning of forces to the Middle East, and on 4 February when he argued the case in detail in parliament. He undertook to allow the decision to be debated in parliament, and indeed it was debated on 18, 19 and 20 March. However, the National Security Committee decided to commit Australian forces on the morning of 18 March, before the parliamentary debate began. Furthermore, by the time the parliament voted on Howard's motion and approved it in the afternoon of 20 March, Australian forces were already in action.

Beyond this public presentation, once the National Security Committee approved the involvement of Australian military officers in the US planning process on 27 July 2002, resulting in the subsequent integration of Australian forces within the US operational plans, it would have been difficult for Australia not to be involved. With regard to his involvement in US planning, Brigadier McNarn commented that 'the consequences of not going would have been serious for the alliance . . . The only one the Americans will turn on faster than an enemy is an ally who creates an expectation and then pulls out.'[62] Thus while Howard spoke frequently about the possibility of taking part in the invasion, he and his government were highly secretive about what they ultimately intended to do. In the past, war preparations were kept secret so as not to give forewarning to the enemy; in Australia's case they were kept secret so as not to alarm the Australian public, which would need to carry the burden of the decision. The proposition that the Howard government managed the commitment effectively does not necessarily lead to the conclusion that it was wise.

The most contentious issue was that Howard had built his case for involvement in the Iraq War on the claim that Saddam had WMD, which might find their way into the hands of terrorists. When, after the war, the Americans found that there were no Iraqi WMD, questions were asked about the reliability of the intelligence assessments that Howard had accepted. In June 2003 the parliamentary committee on the key intelligence agencies, chaired by David Jull, MP, inquired into the intelligence on Iraq provided to Australia's intelligence services. When it reported in March 2004, the committee declared that the intelligence agencies had not been put under political pressure. They found that the DIO assessment was more accurate than that of the ONA. Indeed, right up to the war, DIO 'assessed that there were no nuclear weapons, no evidence of construction of chemical or biological weapons, no intelligence on the location of WMD, and no reliable intelligence that Saddam had delegated authority to use chemical or biological weapons in the event of war'. By contrast, the ONA's assessments changed unexplainably between 12 and 13 September at the request of the Department of Foreign Affairs, and was the basis of the government's speeches. The Jull committee thought that this was, at least unconsciously, a case of the ONA responding to 'policy running strong'. Furthermore, the prime minister's statements were more strongly worded than most of the judgements from the Australian intelligence community.[63] The key conclusion of the Jull report is significant:

> the case made by the government was that Iraq possessed WMD in large quantities and posed a grave and unacceptable threat to the region and the world, particularly as there was a danger that Iraq's WMD might be passed to terrorist organisations. This is not the picture that emerges from an examination of all the assessments provided to the Committee by Australia's two analytical agencies.[64]

However, Howard had managed the release of the report carefully in order to minimise its impact.

A further inquiry conducted by Philip Flood, former secretary of Foreign Affairs, delivered in July 2004, largely confirmed the views of the Jull inquiry. Flood found that most mistakes were made by the US and British agencies that shared information with Australia, and that the Australian agencies failed to analyse the information on Iraq's WMD rigorously enough to establish its bona fides. In response, Howard rejected 'the proposition that we took this country to war based on a lie. That has never been the situation. There were assessments made, with the fullness of time those assessments have not so far been matched, but they were honest assessments arrived at without political pressure.'[65]

The massive inquiry conducted in Britain by Sir John Chilcot and completed in July 2016 concluded that the severity of the threat posed by Iraq's WMD was presented with a certainty that was not justified and, despite explicit warnings, the consequences of the invasion were underestimated. While most of the conclusions related to Britain, the matter of the intelligence on WMD had relevance to Australia, which was shown to have gone to war on faulty intelligence. Howard later accepted that the intelligence assessments 'were flawed', but was still adamant that he made the right decision to go to war.[66]

Beyond the question of WMD is the more general question as to whether the government and its advisers ever conducted a detailed analysis of the likely longer term outcome of the war in Iraq. Such an assessment would have required a sophisticated understanding of the dynamics of the societies in the Middle East. Rather, Australia seems to have accepted the American desire to topple Saddam as a worthy enterprise without looking into what would happen in Iraq and the region. Howard accepts that there is some merit in the claim that the Pentagon had 'skimped on the number of troops committed to Iraq', especially for the 'stabilisation of Iraq after Saddam had gone'. In fact, the whole post-war phase was handled in a disastrous manner, and Australian planners had expressed their concern about this before the invasion. Historian and former diplomat Garry Woodard compared the decisions to go to war in Vietnam and Iraq and found parallels, including: 'the dominance of the Prime Minster, decisions made in secret by a small group of ministers obedient to him, minds closed against area expertise, preference for party political advantage over bipartisanship, and willing subservience to and some credulity about an ally, the United States'. The strategy expert Professor Hugh White concluded: 'History seems likely to judge the decision to support the invasion as a muddled attempt to strengthen the US alliance and one that was taken without deep consideration of the purposes and motives of our allies, the costs and risks of the enterprise, or the consequences for our allies and for ourselves.'[67]

There is, however, a more cynical conclusion. If Australia had not joined the war, the resulting disaster in Iraq and the Middle East, the extreme financial burden imposed on the United States, and the loss of its reputation and authority, would have been the same.[68] By joining the war, Australia did not affect this outcome, but gained status within the US alliance, with its continuing access to US intelligence, technology and perhaps even trade. In return, Australia was seen as a willing supporter of the United States in whatever venture it might have. As Palazzo concluded, 'Australia went to war in Iraq in order to improve its alliance with the United States, its great power protector. In doing so, it chained its future to a power that, at the time, was on the cusp of an unseen decline—a decline that it is becoming increasingly difficult to deny.'[69]

In terms of management, Australia's war leadership had been highly effective. Both initial campaigns in Afghanistan and Iraq were successful, with the loss of only one ADF person to enemy action. As a measure of success, the Howard government was re-elected in 2005. But the following years would see Australian forces return to both war theatres, where success would become more elusive. The commitment of a nation to war is likely to have unexpected and unwanted consequences.

Conclusion

For a century, Australia's leaders have been engaged in the war game. And just as a game has rules, there are rules for effectively playing the war leadership game. The first rule is to acknowledge that the war leader's most important decision is whether to commit the nation to war. In his book *The Commanders*, about decision-making during the 1991 Gulf War, the decorated American journalist Bob Woodward wrote: 'The decision to go to war is one that defines a nation, both to the world and, perhaps more importantly, to itself. There is no more serious business for a national government, no more accurate measure of national leadership.'[1] In the First World War and to a certain extent in the Second World War, this decision was taken out of the hands of the Australian government. In the midst of the Second World War, the Menzies government had to decide whether to approve the campaign in Greece. But the decisions to commit forces to the subsequent wars, from Korea to Iraq, became increasingly controversial, raising questions about the process, and whether legislation should be introduced to ensure that these decisions are taken by the parliament rather than the executive government. What is clear is that going to war is likely to lead to unintended consequences.

The second rule for war leaders is to determine the level and nature of the commitment. In the First World War this decision was actually taken before the formal outbreak of the war. The Menzies government was more cautious about this in 1939. The decisions in the Vietnam War were made incrementally. But during all the wars from Korea to Iraq the Australian government tried to keep the commitment as small as possible while reaping the benefits of being seen to support the alliances with Britain and the United States.

The third rule is to acknowledge that war leaders are not the source of all wisdom. Obviously, expert military advice is important, but so too is the advice of senior ministers, with their specific responsibilities. In the First World War the Cabinet was relatively small and the Australian prime minister did not establish a War Cabinet. By contrast, at the beginning of the Second World War Menzies established a War Cabinet to which the service chiefs were regularly invited. The Advisory War Council, formed for political reasons, became a source of further advice. Curtin's Prime Minister's War Conference was formed because of the special position of General Douglas MacArthur. When Menzies formed the National Security Resources Board in 1950 and the Cabinet Committee on Defence Preparations in 1951, he was building on the Second World War experience. More importantly, in 1963 he established the Foreign Affairs and Defence (FAD) Committee of Cabinet in the lead-up to the Vietnam War. Unfortunately, Gorton disregarded the FAD Committee, to the detriment of good policymaking. Hawke did not have a formal committee, but used an informal group of ministers. The Howard government had the National Security Committee of Cabinet.

Governments have always established formal structures for the provision of military advice. In the First World War these structures included the Defence Council, which was rarely used, and the Naval and Military boards. In the Second World War through to the Vietnam War, advice was provided by the Defence Committee (generally the service chiefs and senior public servants) and the Chiefs of Staff Committee. By the time of the Gulf War in 1991, military advice had been focused more closely in the person of the CDF, although he was advised by the Augmented Chiefs of Staff Committee. This arrangement continued to evolve, and by 2001 the National Security Committee was advised by the Secretaries Committee on National Security, although the CDF still had the prime role as military adviser.

The important role of advisers leads to the fourth rule for war leaders, namely the imperative to select military commanders in whom the government has confidence. These include not only the service chiefs, who become the government's principal military advisers, but also the commanders of the forces deployed overseas, who are responsible for ensuring that the forces are employed in accordance with the government's policy. In the First World War General Birdwood, an officer of the British Indian Army, selected himself to command the AIF, although Prime Minister Hughes was involved in the later decision to retain Monash as commander of the Australian Corps. In the Second World War the government selected several British officers as service chiefs, but made a major decision in appointing Blamey to command the 2nd AIF. From 1942 to 1945 the government's principal military adviser was an American general, Douglas MacArthur. In the Vietnam War the government gave much consideration to the appointment of the chairman of the Chiefs of Staff Committee, but was not closely involved in selecting the successive Commanders Australian Force Vietnam. In later wars the commanders in the field were largely selected by the service chiefs and approved by the defence ministers. In the Gulf War, Admiral Doolan commanded the naval force by virtue of his role as Maritime Commander.

The fifth rule is ensure that the operations are conducted in accordance with the government's policy. There is one view that the government should give the military its orders and allow it to carry them out. But there is another view that the political leaders need to take a more 'hands-on' approach. In 1918, Prime Minister Billy Hughes intervened to ensure that troops were given leave or rest from operations. In 1945 the Acting Minister for the Army, Senator James Fraser, visited the operational areas in New Guinea and Bougainville to check on possible equipment shortages. In Vietnam, the government largely left the conduct of operations in the hands of the military commanders until Malcolm Fraser, as defence minister, took a more active approach. It is, of course, the field commander's prime responsibility to ensure that operations are in accordance with Australia's best interests. For that reason Blamey fought, with the government's support, to withdraw his troops from Tobruk, and on Blamey's advice the Curtin government stopped the 6th Division taking part in the invasion of Java. Wilton was keenly aware of this responsibility during the Vietnam War. In the invasion of Iraq, Brigadier McNarn prevented the RAAF Hornets from conducting certain missions that were not in accordance with government policy. A fundamental of effective war leadership is to ensure that the government's wishes are followed on the battlefield.

The sixth rule is the necessity of trying to gain access to allied strategic decision-making. It took until 1918 before Hughes fully appreciated this requirement. Menzies and Curtin struggled with this issue in the Second World War, and it persisted in the later wars. In the invasion of Iraq, the Australians detected that the plans for the subsequent post-invasion phase were deficient, but were unable to change them. The lesson for Australia is to remain constantly vigilant, and a prime task for war leaders is to manage Australia's role in the alliance.

This leads to the seventh rule, the need to ensure that the country has its own intelligence-gathering capacity. A fundamental requirement for good decision-making is information and intelligence. In the First World War, Australia had little ability to make its own judgements about the world situation. In the Second World War, Australia started to develop its own diplomatic services and appointed representatives to several countries, including Japan and the United States. Australia also started to establish its own strategic intelligence gathering capabilities, but these were limited. In the Vietnam War, the government was not made aware of, or ignored, US reports indicating that the allies were unlikely to prevent a communist victory. Before the Iraq War in 2003 Australia's intelligence agencies made assessments that appeared at variance with those of their allies. So the lesson is not just the need to have effective diplomatic and intelligence agencies, but also for the government to listen to them. The Australian Defence official Rod Barton, who was at the coalface of intelligence collection in Iraq, wrote: 'One thing my intelligence career has taught me is that, with a few exceptions, politicians only take professional advice when it supports their policies, and even then, only pick the bits that suit them.'[2]

The eighth rule is to accept that it will be necessary to deal with the political arena. An effective war leader has to manage the politics successfully. Hughes split his own party over conscription, believing that it was necessary to achieve the government's war aims. With the assistance of John Curtin, Menzies introduced the Advisory War Council, which largely nullified the threat from the Opposition, but he nonetheless failed to manage the politics of his own party in 1941. It is just as important to deal with the politics within the party as to deal with the Opposition. Hawke understood this as he sought to deal with his party critics in the Gulf War. Howard managed the Coalition's politicians superbly and gave the Opposition little capacity to manoeuvre in the lead-up to the invasion of Iraq.

The ninth rule is the need to manage the media. Hughes did this through the ruthless use of regulations to ban newspapers. Menzies appointed a Director-General of Information, but Curtin ran up against the restrictions General MacArthur imposed on the release of information. Hawke and Howard gave much attention to the management of media during the Gulf War and the invasion of Iraq.

The tenth rule is to accept that war leadership will always take place in an environment of uncertainty. Intelligence assessments can usually determine an enemy's or potential enemy's capabilities, but they are less certain about actual intentions. The Australian government spent much effort from September 1939 to late 1941 trying to discern Japan's intentions. Many of the government's decisions about force deployment in the 1950s and the first half of 1960s were made against the uncertainty of how the strategic situation was going to evolve in South-East Asia.

It is all very well to develop lists of rules. It is another thing to ensure that prime ministers even think about these issues before they are presented with the situation. Field Marshal Sir William Robertson, the CIGS from 1916 until he was forced to resign after a dispute with Prime Minister David Lloyd George in February 1918, commented that in 'all trades and professions the man who aims at taking the lead knows that he must first learn the business he purposes to follow . . . Only in the business of war—the most difficult of all—is no special training or study demanded from those charged with, and paid for, its management.'[3]

If a National Security Committee of Cabinet exists in peacetime and, with the military advisers present, deals frequently with security and defence issues, its members are likely to develop some understanding of problems likely to be faced in a deteriorating strategic situation. It would be even better if the political leaders had some understanding of how their predecessors handled these issues in the past. Australia's experience of war leadership over more than a century provides a resource and a guide for developing an understanding of how the nation and its leaders might face future challenges.

Many of the lessons drawn from the past century are still relevant today. The failure of the United States in Iraq, brought out in Thomas Ricks' book *Fiasco*, should lead to at least two vital conclusions: that the US process for going to war was deeply flawed and Australia would be wise to treat any US plan for war with deep suspicion; and Australia should not smugly assume that it might not engage in the same faulty process in the future. It is hoped that this study of Australian war leadership can contribute to further understanding of the importance of a most vital aspect in national affairs.

Endnotes

Introduction

1 Quoted in Heinl, *Dictionary of Military and Naval Quotations*, p. 343.

2 Ibid., p. 344.

3 In his 1963 book *The War Game: Studies of the New Civilian Militarists* the distinguished sociologist Irving Horowitz used the term 'war game' in a different context. Published at the height of the Cold War, the book focuses on the US government's civilian advisers, who were doing calculations on how to fight a nuclear war. As Horowitz wrote (p. 11), these advisers 'inhabit a world of nightmarish intellectual "play", while ridiculing the "ossification" of American military posture'.

4 Catton, *Grant Takes Command*, p. 177.

5 Sheffield, 'The challenges of high command in the twentieth century', p. 2.

6 Connor, Stanley and Yule, *The War at Home*, p. 117.

7 Rowell, *Full Circle*, p. 196.

Chapter 1: 'To our last man and our last shilling'

1 Numerous articles discuss this issue; for a more recent discussion, see Beaumont, '"Unitedly we have fought"'.

2 Scott, *Australia During the War*, p. 6.

3 Murdoch, *Sir Joe*, pp. 13, 16. For Cook's life, see Murdoch, *Sir Joe*, and F.K. Crowley, 'Cook, Sir Joseph (1860–1947)', *ADB*, vol. 8, 1981.

4 Bean, *The Story of Anzac*, p. 20, quoted in Connor, Stanley and Yule, *The War at Home*, p. 84; Hyslop, *Australian Naval Administration*, p. 45; Marchant, 'Millen, Edward Davis (1860–1923)', pp. 18–22; see also Stevens, *In All Respects Ready*, p. 14.

5 Hyslop, 'Trumble, Thomas (1872–1954)', *ADB*, vol. 12, 1990; quoted in Scott, *Australia During the War*, p. 201; see also 'Report upon the Department of Defence 1914–1917', AWM 51, Ex Confidential documents [120].

6 For a short biography of Creswell, see Webster, 'Vice-Admiral Sir William Creswell'; Stevens, *In All Respects Ready*, p. 18. For the establishment and role of the Naval Board, see Hyslop, *Australian Naval Administration*, ch. 2, and Andrews, *The Department of Defence*, p. 48.

7 Hyslop, *Australian Naval Administration*, p. 49.

8 For the establishment of the Military Board, see Wood, *Chiefs of the Australian Army*, ch. 4. For Hutton's views and activities, see Stockings, *Britannia's Shield*, and Mordike, *An Army for a Nation*.

9 For White's career, see Derham, *The Silence Ruse*, and Bean, *Two Men I Knew*. For an incisive study of White, see Hazlehurst, *Ten Journeys to Cameron's Farm*.

10 Hyslop, 'The Council of Defence 1905–1939'; *Commonwealth Gazette*, no. 1 of 1905, with 1912 amendment, NAA: B197, 1851/2/18.

11 J.R. Poynter, 'Munro Ferguson, Sir Ronald Craufurd (1860–1934)', *ADB*, vol. 10, 1986.

12 Newton, *Hell-bent*, pp. 84–85; Scott, *Australia During the War*, p. 7.

13 Newton, *Hell-bent*, p. 115; Scott, *Australia During the War*, p. 8.

14 'Premier attacked', *Sydney Morning Herald*, 3 August 1914; Bean, *Two Men I Knew*, p. 92, quoted in Derham, *The Silence Ruse*, p. 204; Newton, *Hell-bent*, pp. 119–22; 'Position in Australia', *Brisbane Courier*, 3 August 1914, p. 7.

15 Scott, *Australia During the War*, p. 22; Meaney, *Australia and World Crisis*, p. 7.

16 For the White Australia policy and the defence of Australia, see Cochrane, *Best We Forget*, and Meaney, *The Search for Security in the Pacific*, ch. 5.

17 Parkin and Lee, *Great White Fleet to Coral Sea*.

18 For Hughes's early career, see Fitzhardinge, *That Fiery Particle*.

19 For biographies of Fisher, see Bastian, *Andrew Fisher*, and Day, *Andrew Fisher*.

20 For Pearce's biographies, see Heydon, *Quiet Decision*, and Connor, *Anzac and Empire*. Pearce's autobiography is *Carpenter to Cabinet*.

21 Newton, *Hell-bent*, p. 31.

22 Mordike, *An Army for a Nation*, pp. 240–41.

23 Bean, *Two Men I Knew*, p. 89.

24 Mordike, *An Army for a Nation*, pp. 244–45; Newton, 'Choosing war, and choosing war aims', p. 18, quoted in Wood, *Chiefs of the Australian Army*, p. 168.

25 Scott, *Australia During the War*, pp. 201–2.

26 Newton, *Hell-bent*, p. 165. See the footnote on this page for evidence that other accounts of which ministers were present are wrong.

27 'Naval officers consulted', *Mercury* (Hobart), 5 August 1914, p. 5; Bou and Dennis, *The Australian Imperial Force*, p. 5.

28 Newton, *Hell-bent*, p. 167; Scott, *Australia During the War*, p. 11; Bean, *The Story of Anzac*, pp. 28–29.

29 Newton, *Hell-bent*, pp. 168, 253–54.

30 For Australia's reaction to the declaration of war, see Mansfield, '"Unbounded enthusiasm"'; Andrews, *The Anzac Illusion*, p. 45; Moses, 'Gallipoli or other people's wars revisited'.

31 For Bridges' career, see Coulthard-Clark, *A Heritage of Spirit*.

32 Ibid., p. 118. For Bridges' recommendation, see letter, Bridges to Millen, 8 August 1914, NAA: B539, 95/1/34; Bean, *The Story of Anzac*, p. 31.

33 Coulthard-Clark, 'Major-General Sir William Throsby Bridges', p. 17; letter, White to Hutton, 4 July 1915, Hutton Papers, British Library, 50089.

34 For Legge's career, see Coulthard-Clark, *No Australian Need Apply*.

35 Stevenson, *The War with Germany*, p. 33. For the raising of the force, see Mallett, 'The preparation and deployment of the Australian Naval and Military Expeditionary Force'.

36 See Overlack, 'German commerce warfare planning for the Australian Station', and many other articles by this author.

37 For an examination of this issue, see McGinley, 'Divergent paths'.

38 For a description of the campaign, see MacKenzie, *The Australians at Rabaul*, and Stevenson, *Australia's First Campaign*.
39 'Australia at the front', *Argus*, 31 August 1914, p. 81; Scott, *Australia During the War*, pp. 212, 225–56.
40 Greenwood and Grimshaw, *Documents on Australian International Affairs*, pp. 566–67; Scott, *Australia During the War*, p. 22. For an examination of the statement, see Oliver, '"Our last man and our last shilling"'.
41 Meaney, 'The first high commissioners', pp. 45–46.
42 Quoted in Day, *Andrew Fisher*, p. 296.
43 Scott, *Australia During the War*, pp. 53–54.
44 Day, *Andrew Fisher*, p. 298.
45 Connor, *Anzac and Empire*, pp. 47–48; Bean, *The Story of Anzac*, pp. 87–93.
46 Meaney, *Australia and World Crisis*, p. 76.
47 Stevens, *In All Respects Ready*, p. 85.
48 Meaney, *Australia and World Crisis*, pp. 79–81.
49 Connor, *Anzac and Empire*, p. 52; CGS Diary of Events; also cable Australian Government to High Commissioner's Office, 3 December 1914, NAA: B539, 112/2/241.
50 Connor, *Anzac and Empire*, p. 61.
51 Bastian, *Andrew Fisher*, p. 278; Meaney, *Australia and World Crisis*, pp. 39–41.
52 Verney, 'The army high command', p. 187; 'Report upon the Department of Defence 1914–1917', AWM 51, Ex Confidential documents [120]; Hyslop, 'The Council of Defence 1905–1939'.
53 Connor, *Anzac and Empire*, p. 61; Bastian, *Andrew Fisher*, p. 283; Meaney, *Australia and World Crisis*, pp. 94–96.
54 'Statement in parliament', *Argus*, 30 April 1915, p. 7; Scott, *Australia During the War*, p. 287; 'Report upon the Department of Defence 1914–1917', AWM 51, Ex Confidential documents [120]. The account in the *Argus* of 8 May 1915 is reproduced in Crowley, *Modern Australia in Documents*, p. 234.
55 Letter, Pearce to Birdwood, 11 September 1915, Birdwood Papers, 214/2; 'Report upon the Department of Defence 1914–1917', AWM 51, Ex Confidential documents [120].
56 Chris Clark, 'Irving, Godfrey George Howy (1876–1937)', *ADB*, vol. 9, 1983; letter, Munro Ferguson to Birdwood, 1 December 1915, Birdwood Papers, 215/1.
57 A.J. Hill, 'Dodds, Thomas Henry (1873–1943)', *ADB*, vol. 8, 1981.
58 Letter, Munro Ferguson to Birdwood, 4 August 1915, Birdwood Papers, 215/1; letter, Hamilton to Kitchener, 27 May 1915, TNA, 30/57/61; Coulthard-Clark, *No Australian Need Apply*, pp. 98–102.
59 Coulthard-Clark, *No Australian Need Apply*, pp. 110–11.
60 Day, *Andrew Fisher*, pp. 331–32; Michael McKernan, 'Introduction', in Murdoch, *The Gallipoli Letter*, pp. 16–17; Younger, *Keith Murdoch*, pp. 56–57.
61 Robson, *The First A.I.F.*, pp. 50–51, 64; Bastian, *Andrew Fisher*, p. 283.
62 See Crawley, *Climax at Gallipoli*.
63 Quoted in Andrews, *The Anzac Illusion*, p. 57; Murdoch, *The Gallipoli Letter*, p. 40.

64 Robertson, *Anzac and Empire*, p. 159; letter, Munro Ferguson to Birdwood, 24 September 1915, Birdwood Papers, 215/1.

Chapter 2: 'I'm an Attorney-General not a Major General'

1 Robertson, *Anzac and Empire*, p. 168.

2 Letter, Munro Ferguson to Birdwood, 9 November 1915, Birdwood Papers, 215/1.

3 Letters, Pearce to Birdwood, 16 November 1915, Birdwood Papers, 214/2; Munro Ferguson to Birdwood, 9 November 1915, Birdwood Papers, 215/1; Andrews, *The Anzac Illusion*, p. 58; Hughes, *Policies and Potentates*, pp. 155–56; Newton, 'Choosing war, and choosing war aims', p. 22.

4 'Report upon the Department of Defence 1914–1917', AWM 51, Ex Confidential documents [120]; Pugsley, 'At the Empire's call', p. 234; Robson, *The First A.I.F.*, pp. 72–76.

5 Letter, Irving to Secretary, Department of Defence, 1 February 1916, NAA: B539, 264/1/128.

6 Letters, Birdwood to Munro Ferguson, 23 January 1916, to Pearce, 29 January 1916, Birdwood Papers, 215/2, 214/3.

7 Bean, *The A.I.F. in France 1916*, p. 45; cable, Pearce to Birdwood, 4 February 1916, Birdwood Papers, 214/2.

8 Letter, Birdwood to Pearce, 24 March 1916, Birdwood Papers, 214/3.

9 Warren Perry, 'Foster, Hubert John (1855–1919)', *ADB*, vol. 8, 1981; letters, Munro Ferguson to Birdwood, 21 February 1916, 7 March 1916, Birdwood Papers, 215/1; Bean, *The A.I.F. in France 1916*, p. 38 (footnote).

10 Letters, Munro Ferguson to Birdwood, 26 July 1916, 5 September 1916, Birdwood Papers, 215/1.

11 Bean, *The A.I.F. in France 1916*, p. 151.

12 Fitzhardinge, *The Little Digger*, pp. 103, 114–15.

13 Letters, Robertson to Murray, 7 March 1916, Murray to Robertson, 9 March 1916, Robertson Papers, I/14/4, I/14/115; Hankey, *The Supreme Command*, vol. 2, p. 501; Hughes, *Policies and Potentates*, p. 158; letter, Robertson to Murray, 14 March 1916, AWM 45, bundle 32, and Robertson Papers, I/14/16; Bean, *The A.I.F. in France 1916*, p. 67; letter, Pearce to War Office, 31 March 1916, NAA: B539, 264/1/224.

14 Bean, *The A.I.F. in France 1916*, pp. 156, 686; letters, Hughes to Robertson, 12 April 1916, Haig to Robertson, 16 April 1916, Robertson Papers, I/35/51–53; Haig Diary, 16 April 1916.

15 Minutes of conferences and associated correspondence, AWM: 3DRL 606.

16 Letter, Birdwood to Munro Ferguson, 3 May 1916, Birdwood Papers, 215/2.

17 Cables, Pearce to War Office, 6 May 1916, War Office to Defence, Melbourne, 8 May 1916, NAA: B539, 265/1/224.

18 Haig Diary, 31 May, 1 June 1916; letters, Hughes to Haig, 16 June 1916, Haig to Hughes, 25 June 1916, AWM 45, bundle 31. See also Kiggell Papers, v/22.

19 Letters, Haig to Kiggell, 23 June 1916, Haig to War Office, 25 June 12916, AWM 45, bundle 31; Hughes, *The Splendid Adventure*, p. 76.

20 Bean Diary, 1 June 1916, 44/39–49; Bean, *The A.I.F. in France 1916*, p. 471; Fitzhardinge, *The Little Digger*, pp. 119–20; letter, Fisher to Pearce, 6 June 1916, Pearce Papers.

21 Geoffrey Serle, 'Murdoch, Sir Keith Arthur (1885–1952)', *ADB*, vol. 10, 1986; Gilbert, *Winston S. Churchill*, companion vol. III, part 2, p. 1519.

22 Letter, Hughes to Pearce, 24 May 1916, Pearce Papers.

23 Spartalis, *The Diplomatic Battles of Billy Hughes*, p. 16.

24 Robertson, *Anzac and Empire*, p. 232. This book has a useful chapter on the conduct and outcome of the commission.

25 Haig Diary, 14 August 1916; letter, Birdwood to Pearce, 14 August 1916, Birdwood Papers, 214/3; Carlyon, *The Great War*, p. 256; Robson, *The First A.I.F.*, pp. 84–85; Fitzhardinge, *The Little Digger*, pp. 182–83.

26 Meaney, *Australia and World Crisis*, p. 178.

27 Fitzhardinge, *The Little Digger*, p. 235.

28 Quoted in Spartalis, *The Diplomatic Battles of Billy Hughes*, pp. 46–47; Fitzhardinge, *The Little Digger*, p. 251; Andrews, *The Anzac Illusion*, pp. 190, 135; Newton, 'Choosing war, and choosing war aims', p. 22.

29 'Report upon the Department of Defence 1914–1917', AWM 51, Ex Confidential documents [120]; letter, Munro Ferguson to Birdwood, 11 July 1917, Birdwood Papers, 215/1.

30 Bean, *The A.I.F. in France 1917*, pp. 15–16; Connor, *Anzac and Empire*, p. 103.

31 Connor, *Anzac and Empire*, p. 109.

32 Letter, Birdwood to Pearce, 30 November 1916, Birdwood Papers, 214/3; letter, Birdwood to Munro Ferguson, 31 December 1916, Pearce Papers, and Birdwood Papers, 215/2; Hobbs Diary, 14 December 1916.

33 Letter, Birdwood to Munro Ferguson, 31 December 1916, Pearce Papers.

34 Cable, Pearce to Birdwood, 20 January 1917, Pearce Papers; letter, Legge to Trumble, 23 January 1917, AWM: 3DRL 606.

35 Letters, Birdwood to Pearce, 24 January 1917, to Munro Ferguson, 29 January 1917, McCay to Birdwood, 26 January 1917, Moore to Birdwood, 3 February 1916, Pearce to Birdwood, 2 February 1917, Birdwood Papers, 214/3, 212/9, 212/5, 214/2.

36 Letters, Legge to Birdwood, 16 February 1917, Birdwood Papers, 212/7; Bean Diary, 16 February 1917, 70/3–8, 20 February 1917, 70/82/86; letter, Murdoch to Birdwood, 12 February 1917, Birdwood Papers, 214/5.

37 No 4 Command Depot held wounded and sick men recovering before joining their units. It is likely that unrest was caused by the lack of adequate accommodation and other facilities during the severe winter of 1916–17. As GOC of the AIF Depots, Moore was responsible for the Wareham depot.

38 Letter, Birdwood to Pearce, 11 March 1917, Birdwood Papers, 214/3; Bean Diary, 28 April 1917, 77/13; letters, Birdwood to Pearce, 11 March 1917, 2 April 1917, to Munro Ferguson, 4 April 1917, to Anderson, 1 April 1917, Birdwood Papers, 214/3, 214/4, 215/3, 217/3.

Chapter 3: 'We shall have to humour them'

1 The Nationalist Party was formed formally on 13 June 1917, the day before the first session of the new parliament (Fitzhardinge, *The Little Digger*, p. 265).
2 Letter, Munro Ferguson to Birdwood, 16 January 1917, Birdwood Papers, 215/1.
3 Letters, Munro Ferguson to Birdwood, 5 February 1917, 4 June 1917, 24 June 1917, Birdwood Papers, 215/1.
4 Letter, Munro Ferguson to Pearce, 24 June 1917, Pearce Papers.
5 Cables, Murdoch to Hughes, 11 July 1917, AWM: Murdoch Papers, folder 2; Governor-General to Colonial Secretary, 30 July 1917, AWM 45, bundle 31; Pearce to Birdwood, 4 August 1917, Birdwood Papers, 217/5.
6 Letter, Army Council to Colonial Office, 6 August 1917; cable, Colonial Secretary to Governor-General, 11 August 1917, AWM 45, bundle 27; cable, Hughes to Colonial Office, 25 August 1917, AWM 45, bundle 31.
7 Cables, Colonial Secretary to Governor-General, 12 September 1917, AWM 45, bundle 31; Pearce to Birdwood, 20 September 1917, Birdwood Papers, 214/2; Pearce to Hughes, 24 September 1917, Pearce Papers.
8 Letter, Murdoch to Hughes, 30 August 1917, AWM: Murdoch Papers, folder 2; Haig Diary, 29 August 1917; letter, Murdoch to Hughes c. May–June 1918, Hughes Papers, series 19, folder 1.
9 Cable, Hughes to Colonial Secretary, 26 September 1917; letter, Army Council to Haig, 5 October 1917, AWM 45, bundle 31.
10 Haig Diary, 29 August, 15, 17 September 1917; Bean Diary, 11 October 1917, 90/21, referring to an incident while the Corps HQ was at Hazebrouck.
11 Letter, Monash to his wife, 18 October 1917, NLA: Monash Papers, MS 1884, box 128, folder 947.
12 Letters, Haig to War Office, 19 October 1917, Birdwood to Kiggell, 27 October 1917, AWM 45, bundle 31.
13 Letters, Long to Lloyd George, 31 October 1917, Lloyd George to Long, 1 November 1917, Amery to Lloyd George, 11 July 1918, Lloyd George Papers, F/32/4/103–104.
14 Ibid.; War Cabinet 261, 31 October 1917, and 262, 9 November 1917, 13 November 1917, TNA: CAB 23/4.
15 Blake, *The Private Papers of Douglas Haig*, p. 266; cables, Colonial Secretary to Governor-General, 13 November 1917, Hughes to Colonial Secretary, 24 November 1917, AWM 45, bundle 31.
16 Robson, *The First A.I.F.*, pp. 141, 167.
17 Connor, *Anzac and Empire*, p. 111.
18 Cable, Hughes to Murdoch, 31 March 1918, AWM: Murdoch Papers, folder 1.
19 Cables, Murdoch to Hughes, 1, 2, 7 April 1918, AWM: Murdoch Papers, folder 1.
20 Cables, Murdoch to Hughes, 15, 18 April, 8 May 1918, AWM: Murdoch Papers, folder 1.
21 Blake, *The Private Papers of Douglas Haig*, p. 290.
22 Bean Diary, 16 May 1918, 11/3; letter, Pearce to Munro Ferguson, 16 May 1918, Novar Papers; 'Rough notes upon the Australian Army changes', NLA: Murdoch Papers, MS 2823, folder 34.

23 Cables, Murdoch to Hughes, 20 May 1918, Murdoch to Watt, 21 May 1918, AWM: Murdoch Papers, folder 2; cable, Watt to Hughes, 24 May 1918, Hughes Papers, series 23, folder 1; Fitzhardinge, *The Little Digger*, p. 338.

24 Carlyon, *The Great War*, pp. 624–65.

25 Serle, *John Monash*, p. 328; letter, Murdoch to Birdwood, 3 June 1918, Birdwood Papers, 214/5; letters, Murdoch to Monash, 6 June 1918, Monash to Birdwood, 11 June 1918, not sent, AWM: Monash Papers, box 92; letter, Birdwood to Munro Ferguson, 10 July 1918, AWM: Novar Papers; letter, Rawlinson to Birdwood, 27 June 1918, Birdwood Papers, 212/8; letter, Monash to his wife, 31 May 1918, NLA: Monash Papers, MS 1884, box 129, folder 949; letter, Bean to Hughes, 10 June 1918, Hughes Papers, series 23, folder 1.

26 Hobbs Diary, 14 June 1918; Bean Diary, 15 June 1918, 114/99, 111/32; letters, Hobbs to Birdwood, 21 June 1918, Birdwood Papers, 212/7; Hobbs to Pearce, 27 June 1918, Hobbs Papers, 56A/A6, quoted in Coombes, *The Lionheart*, p. 261; Monash to Pearce, 21 June 1918, NLA: Monash Papers, MS 1884, box 129, folder 949.

27 Bean Diary, 16 June 1918, 115/1; Rosenthal Diary, 20 June 1918.

28 Letter, Monash to Hughes, 2 June 1918, AWM: Monash Papers, box 92; letters, Birdwood to Hughes, 8, 21 June 1918, Birdwood Papers, 213/5; letter, Birdwood to Munro Ferguson, 10 July 1918, Novar Papers; letter, Murdoch to McCay, 22 June 1918, NLA: Murdoch Papers, MS 2823, folder 42.

29 'Minutes of Imperial War Cabinet 16', Minute 7, 13 June 1918; Hughes Papers, series 2, folder 8; Brown, *Robert Laird Borden*, pp. 137–38.

30 'Minutes of Imperial War Cabinet 19', Minute 8, 20 June 1918, Hughes Papers, series 23, folder 8; Spartalis, *The Diplomatic Battles of Billy Hughes*, pp. 72, 73; Hughes, *The Splendid Adventure*, pp. 63–64, 72.

31 Bean's notes of interview with Hughes, 1926, AWM: 3DRL 606.

32 Meaney, *Australia and World Crisis*, p. 268.

33 Hankey, *The Supreme Command*, p. 818; War Cabinet unnumbered meeting, 16 July 1918, TNA: CAB 23/11; War Cabinet unnumbered meeting, 31 August 1918, TNA: CAB 23/17.31.

34 Bean, *The A.I.F. in France: May 1918–The Armistice*, pp. 487, 485.

35 Hobbs Diary, 2 July 1918; letter, Bruche to Bazley, 11 January 1959, AWM 42, box 6 Bruche; letter, Monash to Birdwood, 2 July 1918, AWM: Monash Papers, box 92; letter, Birdwood to Pearce, 8 July 1918, Birdwood Papers, 214/4; letter, Murdoch to Bean, 21 July 1918, AWM: 3 DRL 6673, item 195; Bean Diary, 2 July 1918 in Burness, *The Western Front Diaries*, p. 511.

36 Serle, *John Monash*, p. 326; Bean, *The A.I.F. in France: May 1918–the Armistice*, p. 334.

37 Letter, Murdoch to Bean, 12 July 1918, NLA: Murdoch Papers, MS 2823, folder 34.

38 Letter, Wilson to Hughes, 27 July 1918, Hughes Papers, series 23, folder 2; cable, Hughes to Acting Prime Minister, 1 August 1918, and letter, Hughes to Birdwood, 12 August 1918, Pearce Papers.

39 Letters, Birdwood to Hughes, 15, 24 August 1918, Lt Gen. Lawrence to Birdwood, 24 August 1918, Pearce Papers; Pearce to Munro Ferguson, 16 November 1918,

quoted in Connor, *Anzac and Empire*, p. 122.

40 Letter, Harrington to Edmonds, 15 December 1932, Bean Papers, AWM: 3DRL 7953, 34; Bean, *The A.I.F. in France: May 1918–The Armistice*, p. 878.

41 Ibid.; Fitzhardinge, *The Little Digger*, p. 341; Scott, *Australia During the War*, p. 745; Hughes outlined these steps in an interview with Bean in 1935 or 1936, Bean Papers, AWM: 3 DRL 606; W.M. Hughes, 'Aussies barred', *Reveille*, 30 April 1930.

42 Hughes, 'Aussies barred'; Bean, *The A.I.F. in France: May 1918–The Armistice*, pp. 878, 879; Fitzhardinge, *The Little Digger*, pp. 340–41; see also Bean Diary, 17 September 1918, 116/124.

43 Serle, *John Monash*, p. 360; Pedersen, *Monash as Military Commander*, p. 278; Bean, *The A.I.F. in France: May 1918–The Armistice*, p. 896.

44 Pedersen, *Monash as Military Commander*, p. 278; Bean, *The A.I.F. in France: May 1918–The Armistice*, pp. 878, 879.

45 Bean, *The A.I.F. in France: May 1918–The Armistice*, pp. 1048–49; Bean Diary, 31 October 1918; letter, Hughes to Monash, 22 October 1918, AWM: Monash Papers, box 89; Haig Diary, 25 October 1918; Bean Diary, 13 October 1918 in Burness, *The Western Front Diaries*, p. 614.

46 Fitzhardinge, *The Little Digger*, pp. 354, 355.

47 Andrews, *The Anzac Illusion*, p. 203.

48 Meaney, *Australia and World Crisis*, pp. 299–300.

49 Letter, Birdwood to Munro Ferguson, 28 October 1918, Novar Papers.

50 Fitzhardinge, *The Little Digger*, p. 396.

51 Hudson, *Billy Hughes in Paris*; see also Bridge, *William Hughes*. For a recent analysis of Hughes at Versailles, see Cuffe, 'Plans for peace'.

52 Connor, *Anzac and Empire*, p. 124.

53 Ibid.

54 Robertson, *Anzac and Empire*, p. 228.

Chapter 4: 'A disposition to treat Australia as a colony'

1 Spender, *Politics and a Man*, p. 40.

2 For Menzies' early career, see Martin, *Robert Menzies*, vol. 1.

3 For a defence of the appeasement policy, see Bridge, 'Appeasement and after'; Bramston, *Robert Menzies*, pp. 61–63. For the most thorough examination of the appeasement policy, with the conclusion that Menzies and his colleagues failed to appreciate the Nazi threat, see Waters, *Australia and Appeasement*.

4 Hasluck, *The Government and the People, 1939–1941*, p. 115.

5 For a biography of Shedden, see Horner, *Defence Supremo*.

6 *Sydney Morning Herald*, 16 September 1939, p. 15; minutes of the Cabinet Meeting, Melbourne, 26 September 1939, NAA: A2697/XR1, vol. 2.

7 For a discussion of the Singapore Strategy, see Horner, *High Command*, ch. 1; Collins interview, 9 October 1978.

8 For a biography of Lavarack, see Lodge, *Rival General*.

9 For the RAAF's inter-war problems, see Coulthard-Clark, *The Third Brother*.

10 Cable, Menzies to Chamberlain, 24 June 1939, *DAFP*, vol. II, p. 139.

11 Cable, Menzies to Bruce, 5 September 1939, *DAFP*, vol. II, p. 232.

12 Cable, Secretary of State for Dominion Affairs to UK High Commissioner to Australia, 8 September 1939, *DAFP*, vol. II, pp. 249–52.
13 'Observations and recommendations of chiefs of staff', attached to Cabinet Agendum 6/1939, 11 September 1939, NAA: A2671, 6/1939.
14 Ibid.
15 Letter, Menzies to Bruce, 11 September 1939, *DAFP*, vol. II, p. 257; cable, UK High Commissioner to Dominions Secretary, 11 September 1939, *DAFP*, vol. II, p. 258; Bramston, *Robert Menzies*, p. 77; Department of Defence, 'Review of the international situation', 24 September 1939, NAA: A2671, 15/1939.
16 For a biography of Blamey, see Horner, *Blamey*.
17 Gill, *Royal Australian Navy, 1939–1942*, pp. 74–76.
18 Gillison, *Royal Australian Air Force, 1939–1942*, p. 58; War Cabinet Agendum 11/1939, NAA: A2671, 11/1939; War Cabinet Agendum 16/1939, NAA: A2671, 16/1939.
19 Cable, Dominions Secretary to Menzies, 26 September 1942, *DAFP*, vol. II, pp. 284–86; Gillison, *Royal Australian Air Force, 1939–1942*, pp. 60, 63.
20 McCarthy, 'The defence of Australia and the Empire Air Training Scheme'; see also McCarthy, *Australia and Imperial Defence, 1918–1939*.
21 See McCarthy, 'The defence of Australia and the Empire Air Training Scheme'; Gillison, *Royal Australian Air Force, 1939–1942*, pp. 77, 78; and Williams, *These Are Facts*, ch. 19.
22 Cables, Casey to Menzies, 5 November 1939, Northcott to Squires, 6 November 1939, NAA: A2671, 34/1939.
23 Defence Committee Minutes, 13 November 1939, NAA: A2671, 34/1939.
24 Cable, Menzies to Casey, 14 November 1939, *DAFP*, vol. II, pp. 405–406; War Cabinet Minutes 76 and 77, 15, 16 November 1939, Canberra, NAA: A2671, 34/1939.
25 Cables, Casey to Menzies, 17 November 1939, NAA: A816/1, 52/302/135; Record of Decisions of Full Cabinet, Canberra, 20 November 1939, NAA: A5954/46, 803/1.
26 Bridge, 'Casey, Menzies, and the politics of Australia's participation in the European war', p. 85; cable, Menzies to Casey, 21 November 1939, NAA: A816/1, 52/302/135.
27 Cable, UK High Commissioner to Dominions Office, 23 November 1939, *DAFP*, vol. II, pp. 431–44.
28 Minutes of Meeting with Dominions Ministers, 20 November 1939, TNA: ADM 1/11062; cable, Casey to Menzies, 23 November 1939, *DAFP*, vol. II, pp. 428–30.
29 Statement by the Prime Minister, House of Representatives, 29 November 1939, NAA: A816/1, 52/302/135.
30 Cables, Casey to Menzies, 29 November 1939, Menzies to Casey, 1 December 1939, *DAFP*, vol. II, pp. 439–41.
31 For Australia's pre-war intelligence, see Horner, 'Australian estimates of the Japanese threat'.
32 War Cabinet Agendum 46/1939, NAA: A2671XR, 34/1939; Butlin, *War Economy 1939–1942*, p. 125; Edwards, 'Menzies and the imperial connection', p. 198.

33 Hazlehurst, *Ten Journeys to Cameron's Farm*, p. 175; Bean, *Two Men I Knew*, p. 206.
34 Letters, White to Blamey, 13 December 1939, Blamey to Squires, 18 December 1939, Squires to Blamey, 22 December 1939, Blamey to Squires, 27 December 1939, AWM 63, 157/500/200; letters, Bean to Street, 3, 23 November 1939, NAA: A5954, 260/2.
35 Letter, Menzies to Street, 5 December 1939, NAA: A5954, 260/2, War Cabinet Agendum 37/1940, 12 February 1940, and cables, Menzies to Dominions Office, 9 March 1940, Dominions Office to Menzies, 26 March 1940, NAA: A2671, 37/1940; memorandum, Street to Blamey, 19 April 1940, AWM 63, 157/500/200.
36 Dedman, 'Defence policy decisions before Pearl Harbour', pp. 337–38.
37 Cables, Dominions Secretary to Commonwealth Government, 15, 17 May 1940, Commonwealth Government to Dominions Secretary, 17, 19 May 1940, *DAFP*, vol. II, pp. 301, 307, 308, 309.
38 Cable, Menzies to Colonial Secretary, 13 June 1940, NAA: CP 292/6, 68b.
39 Spender, *Politics and a Man*, p. 53; Records of Decision of Full Cabinet, Melbourne, 13 June 1940; cable, Menzies to Colonial Secretary, 13 June 1940, NAA: A5954, 583/1; Gill, *Royal Australian Navy, 1939–1942*, p. 250; cable, Dominions Secretary to Menzies, 13 June 1940, *DAFP*, vol. III, pp. 429–30.
40 Edwards, *John Curtin's War*, vol. I, pp. 174–76.
41 War Cabinet Minute 345, Melbourne, 18 June 1940, and cable, Dominions Secretary to Menzies, 19 June 1940, *DAFP*, vol. III, pp. 451–53, 458–61.
42 Interview with W.M. Hughes, 20 February 1944, AWM: Gavin Long Notes, no. 45.
43 Hazlehurst, *Ten Journeys to Cameron's Farm*, pp. 144, 183; War Cabinet Minute 296, Melbourne, 4 June 1940, NAA: A2671, 96/97 1940; Bean, *Two Men I Knew*, pp. 215, 217.
44 Edwards, *John Curtin's War*, vol. I, p. 179; cable, Dominions Secretary to Commonwealth Government, 28 June 1940, *DAFP*, vol. III, pp. 517, 518.
45 War Cabinet Minute 394, Melbourne, 3 July 1940, *DAFP*, vol. IV, pp. 8, 9.
46 Cable, Churchill to Menzies, 11 August 1940, *DAFP*, vol. IV, pp. 84–86.
47 Report by the Australian Chiefs of Staff, 23 August 1940, NAA: A2671, 186/1940.
48 Menzies, *Afternoon Light*, p. 18; for a thorough account of the tragedy, see Hazlehurst, *Ten Journeys to Cameron's Farm*.
49 Hasluck, *The Government and the People, 1939–1941*, p. 244.
50 Rowell, 'General Sturdee and the Australian Army'.
51 Cable, Dominion Secretary to Menzies, 18 September 1940, and War Cabinet Minute 523, Melbourne, 23 September 1940, NAA: A2671, 186/1940.
52 Hasluck, *The Government and the People, 1939–1941*, p. 266; Spender, *Politics and a Man*, p. 74.
53 Letter, Curtin to Menzies, 22 October 1940, in Weller, *Caucus Minutes 1901–1949*, p. 248.
54 There are numerous biographies and other studies of Curtin, the most useful being Day, *John Curtin*, and Edwards, *John Curtin's War*, vols I and II.

55 Cables, Dominions Secretary to UK High Commissioner, 22 September 1940, Menzies to Churchill, 29 September 1940, Churchill to Menzies, 2 October 1940, NAA: A1608, F41/1/7.
56 War Cabinet Minute 543, Melbourne, 1 October 1940, NAA: A2671, 186/1940, Supp. 1.
57 War Cabinet Minute 601, Melbourne, 31 October 1940, NAA: A2671, 239/1940.
58 Report of Singapore Defence Conference—Review by Chiefs of Staff, 16 November 1940, NAA: A2671/1, 254/1940.
59 Advisory War Council Minute 39, Canberra, 25 November 1940, NAA: A5954/46, 812/1; War Cabinet Minute 632, Canberra, 26 November 1940, NAA: A5954/46, 804/2; cable, Commonwealth Government to Dominion Secretary, 1 December 1940, NAA: A2671, 254/1940; Advisory War Council Minute 57, Canberra, 2 December 1940, NAA: A5954/46, 812/1; cable, Menzies to Bruce, 3 December 1940, NAA: A2680, 10/1940; cable, Churchill to Menzies, 23 December 1940, NAA: A2671, 254/1940.
60 Advisory War Council Minute 79, Melbourne, 8 January 1941, NAA: A5954/46, 812/1.
61 Hasluck, *The Government and the People, 1939–1941*, p. 298.

Chapter 5: 'Australia's very existence is at stake'

1 Spender, *Politics and a Man*, pp. 79–80.
2 Letters, Blamey to Minister for the Army, 16 August 1940, AWM 113, MH 1/81; also AWM 54, 425/11/17; Blamey to Menzies, 17 August 1940, AWM: 3DRL 6643, 1/2a(i).
3 The relevant cables are in NAA: A5954, 260/5.
4 Letters, Menzies to Blamey, 22 October 1940; Blamey to Menzies, 23 October 1940, NAA: A2671, 186/1940; Menzies to Spender, 11 November 1940, Spender Papers, NLA: MS 4875, box 1.
5 Letter, Blamey to Sturdee, 16 November 1940, AWM 113, MH 1/81; see also AWM: 3DRL 6643, 1/5a.
6 'Summary of the AIF's first year abroad', AWM 54, 492/4/57; 'Notes by BGS [brigadier general staff] for military history', 25 January 1941, AWM: 3DRL 6643, 2/67.
7 Spender, *Politics and a Man*, p. 85.
8 Shedden Manuscript, book 3, ch. 25, p. 1, NAA: A5954/1, 766/19.
9 Menzies, *Afternoon Light*, p. 27; Martin and Hardy, *Dark and Hurrying Days*, p. 51; Long, *Greece, Crete and Syria*, p. 8.
10 Martin and Hardy, *Dark and Hurrying Days*, pp. 51–52; Menzies, *Afternoon Light*, p. 28.
11 Churchill, *The Second World War*, vol. II, p. 59; Martin and Hardy, *Dark and Hurrying Days*, p. 53; Menzies, *Afternoon Light*, pp. 26, 33.
12 Letter, Blamey to Spender, 12 March 1942, AWM 54, 534/2/19; Rowell, *Full Circle*, p. 61; Comments by Freyberg on Long's Narrative, AWM: Gavin Long Correspondence, Freyberg.
13 Interview, Menzies to Chester Wilmot, 2 December 1948, Wilmot Papers;

Martin and Hardy, *Dark and Hurrying Days*, p. 64.

14 Parkinson, *Blood, Toil*, p. 186.

15 Interview, Menzies to Chester Wilmot, 2 December, Wilmot Papers; Parkinson, *Blood, Toil*, p. 196.

16 Cable, Dominions Office to High Commissioner in Australia, 25 February 1941, TNA: PREM 3 63/11.

17 Cable, Menzies to Fadden, 25 February 1941, *DAFP*, vol. IV, pp. 452–53; Edwards, *John Curtin's War*, vol. I, p. 228.

18 War Cabinet Minute, 838, Sydney, 26 February 1941, NAA: A5954, 805/1; Spender, *Politics and a Man*, pp. 87–99.

19 Cable, Fadden to Menzies, 26 February 1941, NAA: CP 290/9 bundle 1 (11).

20 Cruickshank, *Greece*, p. 108; Parkinson, *Blood, Toil*, p. 198.

21 Parkinson, *Blood, Toil*, pp. 205–206.

22 Churchill to Eden, 7 March 1941, Churchill, *The Second World War*, vol. III, pp. 92–93.

23 Cable, Fadden to Menzies, 6 March 1941, NAA: CP 290/9, bundle 1 (1); minute, F.S. Yule to Mr Rowan, 7 July 1942, TNA: PREM 3 288/7; Parkinson, *Blood, Toil*, p. 209.

24 Cable, Menzies to Fadden, 8 March 1941, NAA: PREM 3 63/11.

25 Letter, Blamey to Menzies, 5 March 1941, NAA: MP729/7, 2/421/26, and AWM: 3DRL 6643, 1/2a (v); cables, Blamey to Spender, 8, 9/10 March 1941, AWM: 3DRL 6643, 1/2a(v).

26 Letter, Blamey to Spender, 12 March 1941, AWM 54, 534/2/19; see also AWM: 3DRL 6643, 1/2a(vi).

27 Letter, Blamey to Sturdee, 14 March 1941, AWM: 3DRL 6643, 1/2a(vi).

28 Cable, Fadden to Menzies, 10 March 1941, *DAFP*, vol. IV, pp. 486–88.

29 Cables, Menzies to Fadden, 14 March 1941, NAA: CP 290/9, bundle 1 (13), Churchill to Fadden, 30 March 1941, TNA: PREM 3 63/13.

30 Cables, Fadden to Menzies, 27 March 1941, NAA: CP 290/9, bundle 1 (11), Menzies to Fadden, 29 March 1941, NAA: CP 290/9, bundle 1 (13); Advisory War Council Minute 564, Canberra, 11 November 1941, NAA: A2684, 365.

31 Memorandum, Churchill to First Lord and First Sea Lord, 22 November 1941, Churchill, *The Second World War*, vol. II, p. 614; cable, Dominions Secretary to UK High Commissioner, for Prime Minister, 29 December 1940, NAA: A1608, Y/27/1/1; Burrell interview, 1 February 1979.

32 Advisory War Council Minute 119, Melbourne, 5 February 1941, NAA: A5954, 812/1.

33 Cables, Dominions Secretary to Prime Minister of Australia, 7 February 1941, Latham to Department of External Affairs, 8 February 1941, NAA: A816, 19/304/426. For the development of Australian signals intelligence in 1940 and 1941, see Ball and Horner, *Breaking the Codes*, ch. 4.

34 War Cabinet Minute 790, Sydney, 12 February 1941, NAA: A5954, 805/1; cable, Fadden to Dominions Secretary, *DAFP*, vol. IV, pp. 382–84.

35 Advisory War Council Minute 145, Sydney, 13 February 1941, NAA: A5954/46, 812/1; *Canberra Times*, 14 February 1941, p. 1.

36 Hasluck, *The Government and the People, 1939–1941*, p. 315, fn 6.
37 Combined Far Eastern Appreciation of Australian Chiefs of Staff, 13 February 1941, NAA: A2671, 64/1941.
38 War Cabinet Minute 802, Sydney, 14 February 1941, NAA: A5954/46, 805/1; Hamill, 'The imperial commitment', p. 147.
39 Cable, Naval Attaché to CNS, 7 February 1941, received 8 February, NAA: MP1185/8, 1877/10/29 and NAA: A1608, Y27/1/1.
40 UK War Cabinet, COSC, Aide-Memoire for Meeting with Prime Minister of Australia, 25 February 1941, NAA: A5954, 625/7; cable, Naval Attaché to CNS, 7 February 1941, NAA: A3300, 123 and NAA: A1608, Y27/1/1; cable, Watt to Department of External Affairs, 12 February 1941, received 13 February, NAA: A2671, 64/1941.
41 Fadden, *They Called Me Artie*, p. 54; cable, Commonwealth Government to Dominions Office, 15 February 1941, TNA: PREM 3 63/13.
42 Cable, Naval Attaché to CNS, 21 February 1941, NAA: A1608, Y27/1/1; quoted in Edwards, *John Curtin's War*, vol. I, p. 224.
43 War Cabinet Minute 909, Sydney, 22 March 1941, NAA: A5954, 805/2.
44 AHQ Operation Instruction No. 12, 24 February 1941, AWM 54, 243/6/42.
45 Quoted in Day, *The Great Betrayal*, p. 116.
46 *The Argus*, 18 March 1941, p. 5.
47 'Report of U.S.–British staff conversations, Washington ABC-1', 27 March 1941, NAA: A5954, 567/1; War Cabinet Minute 1073, Sydney, 15 May 1941, NAA: A2671, 135/1941; cable, Commonwealth Government to Dominions Office, 23 May 1941, NAA: A5954, 567/1.
48 Quoted in Stirling, *Lord Bruce*, p. 180; cable, Menzies to Fadden, 5 March 1941, CP290/9, bundle 1, 2nd series.
49 Shedden Manuscript, book 3, ch. 26, p. 1; 'Memorandum by the Prime Minister of Australia', Paper, no. 7A, 29 March 1941, Reply by the Chiefs of Staff (COS (41) 230 Final), 11 April 1941, NAA: A5954, 625/4.
50 Memo, Shedden to Menzies, 14 April 1941, NAA: A5954, 625/4.
51 Note by Shedden, NAA: A5954, 626/4.
52 Dilks, *The Diaries of Sir Alexander Cadogan*, p. 375; cable, Commonwealth Government to Dominions Office, 5 May 1941, NAA: A5954, 62/75.
53 Kennedy, *The Business of War*, p. 115; Hankey, diary entry, 1 May 1941, quoted in Roskill, *Hankey*, vol. III, p. 501.
54 Day, *Menzies & Churchill*, p. 150; Martin, *Robert Menzies*, vol. 1, pp. 354–55.
55 Cable, Menzies to Churchill, 29 May 1941, NAA: A1608, J41/1/3; letter, Blamey to Menzies, AWM: 3DRL 6643, 6A.
56 Advisory War Council Minute 373, Melbourne, 12 June 1941, NAA: A2682, vol. 2; War Cabinet Minute 1136, Melbourne, 10 June 1941, NAA: A2673, vol. 7.
57 Cable, Dominions Secretary to Menzies, 5 July 1941, NAA: A816, 19/304/428.
58 Gill, *Royal Australian Navy, 1939–1942*, p. 418.
59 Cables, Menzies to Blamey, 21 June 1941, Blamey to Menzies, 23 June 1941, AWM: 3DRL 6643, 2A2.

60 Hetherington, *Blamey*, pp. 177, 178; Maughan, *Tobruk and El Alamein*, p. 709; letter, Blamey to Auchinleck, 18 July 1941, and signal, Blamey to Menzies, 18 July 1951, AWM: 3DRL 6643, 33.1e.
61 Cable, Churchill to Lyttelton, 18 September 1941, TNA: PREM 3, 63/2; Minutes of Commanders-in-Chief Meeting, 3 September 1941, TNA: CAB 106/722; letters, Spender to Menzies, 30 July 1941, Menzies to Spender, 6 August 1941, NAA: A2671, 197/1941.
62 Cable, Menzies to Dominions Secretary, 9 August 1941, TNA: PREM 3, 63/2; Spender, *Politics and a Man*, p. 140; cable, Dominions Secretary to Australian Government, 9 August 1941, TNA: PREM 3, 63/2.
63 Cables, Fadden to Churchill, 5 September 1941, Churchill to Auchinleck, 6 September 1941, TNA: PREM 3, 63/2.
64 Letter, Blamey to Spender, 8 September 1951, AWM: 3DRL 6643, 1/2a (ix); quoted in Hetherington, *Blamey*, p. 183.
65 Cables, Churchill to Fadden, 11 September 1941, Fadden to Churchill, 15 September 1941, Lyttelton to Churchill, 17 September 1941, TNA: PREM 3/63/2; Horner, *Blamey*, p. 244.
66 Letter, Blamey to Auchinleck, 2 October 1941, AWM 63, 157/500/20; Carlyon, *I Remember Blamey*, p. 68.
67 Cables, Churchill to Fadden, 29 September 1941, received 30 September, Fadden to Churchill, 4 October 1941, Churchill to Curtin, 13 October 1941, Curtin to Churchill, 16 October 1941, Churchill to Auchinleck, 17 October 1941, TNA: PREM 3, 63/2; Maughan, *Tobruk and El Alamein*, p. 401.
68 Minute, Churchill to Cranborne, 6 September 1941, TNA: PREM 4, 50/5.
69 Shedden Manuscript, book 3, ch. 41, pp. 1, 3.

Chapter 6: 'This is a new war'

1 Fadden, *They Called Me Artie*, p. 80; Menzies, *Afternoon Light*, p. 130; Spender, *Politics and a Man*, p. 146; Calwell, *Be Just and Fear Not*, p. 48.
2 Memo, Hawkins (for Secretary Navy) to Shedden, 8 December 1941, NAA: A5954, 581/10.
3 War Cabinet Minute 1557, Melbourne, 8 December 1941, NAA: A5954, 807/1; letters, Shedden to Curtin, Curtin to Shedden, 8 December 1941, NAA: A5954, 555/10.
4 Hasluck, *The Government and the People, 1942–45*, p. 5; Penglase and Horner, *When the War Came to Australia*, p. 57.
5 War Cabinet Minutes 1558, 1569, Melbourne, 9, 11 December 1941, NAA: A5954, 807/1.
6 Shedden Manuscript, book 4, ch. 8, p. 1; 'Defence of Australia and adjacent areas—appreciation by Australian chiefs of staff—December 1941', NAA: A2671, 14/301/227.
7 'Chiefs of staff appreciation', 15 December 1941, NAA: A2671, 14/301/227.
8 Cable, Bennett to Sturdee, 17 December 1941, AWM 553/2/3.
9 Advisory War Council Minute 623, Canberra, 23 December 1941; cable, Curtin to Roosevelt, 23 December 1941, NAA: A5954, 535/1.
10 Cable, Bowden to Evatt, 11.51 pm, 23 December 1941, NAA: A5954, 571/4.

11 Cable, Churchill to Curtin, 25 December 1941, quoted in Churchill, *The Second World War*, vol. III, pp. 592–93.
12 Cable, Churchill to Curtin, 29 December 1941, TNA: PREM 4, 50/15.
13 Report by the Australian Chiefs of Staff, 29 December 1941, NAA: A2671, 445/1941.
14 Signal, Bennett to Sturdee, 19 January 1942, AWM 553/2/3; signals, Bennett to Sturdee, 20, 21, 23 January 1942, Bennett to Forde, 20, 22 January 1942, and cable, Bowden to Curtin, quoted in draft cable, Curtin to Churchill, 23 January 1942, NAA: A816, 31/301/136; cable, Curtin to Churchill, 21 January 1942, *DAFP*, vol. V, p. 450.
15 Wurth, *The Battle for Australia*, pp. 2, 117, 126–29.
16 War Cabinet Minutes 1741, 1742, Melbourne, 23 January 1942, NAA: A2673, vol. X.
17 Cables, Page to Curtin, 22 January 1942, Curtin to Churchill, 23 January 1942, NAA: A5954, 571/4.
18 Cable, Churchill to Curtin, 25 January 1942, TNA: PREM 3, 150/3; Churchill, *The Second World War*, vol. IV, pp. 81, 82; Brooke, 'Notes on my life', 19–23 January 1942, Alanbrooke Papers, 3/A/V.
19 Cable, Churchill to Curtin, 20 February 1942, TNA: PREM 3, 63/4; Churchill, *The Second World War*, vol. IV, p. 145.
20 Menzies, *Afternoon Light*, p. 52.
21 Edwards, *John Curtin's War*, vol. I, p. 404.
22 Advisory War Council Minute 644, Canberra, 5 January 1942, NAA: A5954, 813/2.
23 Letter, Lavarack to Sturdee, 6 February 1942, AWM 54, 541/1/4; Berryman Diary, AWM.
24 Paper by the Chief of the General Staff on Future Employment of AIF, 15 February 1942, and letter, Sturdee to Curtin, 15 February 1942, AWM 54, 541/1/4; cable, Wavell to Curtin and Sturdee, NAA: A816, 52/302/142.
25 B.J.F. Wright (Sturdee's military assistant), interview, 12 October 1978; Rowell, 'General Sturdee and the Australian Army', p. 9; teleprinter, Wilson to Shedden, 16 February 1942, NAA: A5954, 573/2.
26 Ross, *John Curtin*, p. 260; cable, Curtin to Churchill, 17 February 1942, NAA: A816, 52/302/112.
27 *The Herald* (Melbourne), 17 February 1942, p. 3, 18 February 1942, pp. 3, 9.
28 Colonel J.P. Buckley (Sturdee's son-in-law), interview, 20 August 1974; Dedman, 'The return of the AIF from the Middle East', p. 159; War Cabinet Minute 1896, Sydney, 18 February 1942, NAA: A816, 52/302/112; Advisory War Council Minute 770, Sydney, 18 February 1942, NAA: A5954, 813/2, and Quealy notebook, NAA: A9240/1, 1, vol. 2.
29 Cables, Page to Curtin, 18 February 1942, NAA: A816, 52/302/142; Curtin to Page, 18 February 1942, NAA: A816, 52/302/142.
30 Advisory War Council Minute 777, Sydney, 19 February 1942, NAA: A5954/46, 813/2; Spender, *Politics and a Man*, pp. 148–49.
31 Cables, Curtin to Page, 19 February 1942, Page to Curtin, 19 February 1942, Curtin to Page, 20 February 1942, NAA: A816, 52/302/142.

32 Cable, Churchill to Curtin, 20 February 1942, NAA: A816, 52/302/142; cable, Churchill to Roosevelt, 20 February 1942, TNA: PREM 3 63/4; cable, Casey to Curtin, 20 February 1942, NAA: A816, 52/302/142; cable, Roosevelt to Curtin, 21 February 1942, NAA: A5954, 573/2.

33 War Cabinet Minute 1915, Canberra, 21 February 1942, NAA: A5954/46, 807/2; cable, Curtin to Churchill, 2 February 1942, TNA: PREM 3 63/4.

34 Cable, Cross to Dominions Office, 21 February 1942, TNA: PREM 3 63/4; cable, Churchill to Curtin, 22 February 1942, NAA: A816, 52/302/142.

35 Cable, Curtin to Dominions Secretary, 23 February 1942, *DAFP*, vol. IV, p. 366; Edwards, *John Curtin's War*, vol. I, p. 424; cable, Curtin to Churchill, 23 February 1942, NAA: A816, 52/302/142.

36 Connell and Roberts, *Wavell: Supreme Commander*, p. 196.

37 Signal, Combined Chiefs of Staff to ABDA Command, 22 February 1942, Great Britain Cabinet Office, *Principal War Telegrams and Memoranda, 1940–1943, Far East*.

38 Milner, *Victory in Papua*, p. 13.

39 Forde interview with E.D. and A. Potts, Brisbane, 19 December 1973, copy in MMMA.

40 Advisory War Council Minute 869 Canberra, 26 March 1942, NAA: A5954, 813/2; MacArthur, *Reminiscences*, p. 151.

41 Minutes of Prime Minister's War Conference, Melbourne, 8 April 1942, NAA: A5954/46, 813/2.

42 Letter, Curtin to MacArthur, 10 April 1942, NAA: A5954, 1598/5.

43 For signals intelligence in Australia in the Second World War, see Horner, *High Command*, Drea, *MacArthur's Ultra*, Fahey, *Australia's First Spies*, and Bou, *MacArthur's Secret Bureau*.

44 Plan A, 24 April 1942, AWM: 3DRL 6643, 43.5, pt 1.

45 Combined Operational Intelligence Centre Minute, 11 April 1942, NAA: MP1587, 218, SRS 575, 'Magic summary', 18 April 1942, NARA: RG 457; minutes of Prime Minister's War Conference, Melbourne, 23 April 1942, NAA: A5954, 1/1; Hasluck, *The Government and the People, 1942–1945*, p. 162.

46 Minutes of Prime Minister's War Conference, Melbourne, 20 April 1942, NAA: A5954, 1/1; cable, Curtin to Evatt, 17 April 1942, NAA: A5954, box 474.

47 Minutes of Prime Minister's War Conference, Melbourne, 11 May 1942, NAA: A5954, 1/1; letter, MacArthur to Curtin, 12 May 1942, MMMA, RG 4, box 1B; Advisory War Council Minute 938, Canberra, 13 May 1942, NAA: A2670, Agendum No. 228/1942; letter, MacArthur to Curtin, 18 May 1942, MMMA, RG 4, box 1B.

48 Minutes of Prime Minister's War Conference, Melbourne, 1 June 1942, NAA: A5954, 1/1.

49 Peter Edwards, 'From Curtin to Beazley: Labor leaders and the American alliance', public lecture at JCPML, 8 October 2001.

50 Stephens, *The Royal Australian Air Force*, p. 118; minutes of Prime Minister's War Conference, Melbourne, 2 June 1942, NAA: A5954, 1/1.

51 Minutes of Prime Minister's War Conference, Melbourne, 11 June 1942, NAA: A5954, 1/1.

52 Advisory War Council Minute 967, 17 June 1942, NAA: A5954/46, 814/1.

53 'Invasion plans frustrated for present', *Canberra Times*, 11 May 1942, p. 1; Layton, *"And I Was There"*, p. 419; quoted in Wurth, *The Battle for Australia*, p. 320; for reports of many of these briefings, see Lloyd and Hall, *Backroom Briefings*.

54 Morton, *Strategy and Command*, pp. 297–98; minutes of Prime Minister's War Conference, Canberra, 17 July 1942, NAA: A5954, 1/1; quoted in Edwards, *John Curtin's War*, vol. II, pp. 92–93.

55 See Edwards, 'Curtin, Macarthur and the "surrender of sovereignty"'; Long, *The Six Years War*, p. 181; Edwards, *John Curtin's War*, vol. II, p. 28; Edwards, *Curtin's Gift*, p. 65; Edwards, *John Curtin's War*, vol. II, p. 57.

56 Edwards, *John Curtin's War*, vol. II, p. 18; quoted in *The Bulletin*, 8 April 1942, p. 6.

57 'Our mistakes in war', *The Age*, 6 August 1942, p. 2; Fitzhardinge, *The Little Digger*, p. 659; statement attached to Advisory War Council Minute 1013, Melbourne, 6 August 1942, NAA: A5954/46, 814/1.

58 Minutes of Prime Minister's War Conference, Melbourne, 10 August 1942, NAA: A5954, 1/1; Advisory War Council Minute 1030, Melbourne, 13 August 1942, NAA: A5954/46, 814/1.

59 Rowell, *Full Circle*, p. 104; Jones, *From Private to Air Marshal*, pp. 99–100.

60 Minutes of Prime Minister's War Conference, Brisbane, 17 and 18 August 1942, NAA: A5954, 1/1.

61 Advisory War Council Minute 1044, Canberra, 27 August 1942, NAA: A5954, 814/1; Shedden notebook, NAA: A5954/2, 214/1; Quealy notebook, NAA: A9240/1, set 1, vol. 4.

62 Notes for Prime Minister's secret session speech, 3 September 1942, NAA: A5954, 611/4.

63 'Stirring call to nation for austerity', *The Argus*, 4 September 1942, pp. 1, 3.

64 Advisory War Council Minute 1052, Canberra, 9 September 1942, NAA: A5954, 814/1; Shedden notebook, NAA: A5954/2, 214/1.

65 'No need to visit N Guinea, says PM', *The Argus*, 11 September 1942, p. 3; Broadcasts by C-in-C, AWM: 3DRL 6643, 2/136.61; 'Tough men, tough task', *The Argus*, 16 September 1942, p. 2.

66 F.T. Smith Reports, 11 September 1942; Kenney, *General Kenney Reports*, p. 94.

67 'General Bennett: transfer to New Guinea unlikely', *The Age*, 17 September 1942, p. 6.

68 Advisory War Council Minute 1067, Canberra, 17 September 1942, NAA: A5954, 814/1; Shedden notebook, NAA: A5954, 214/1; Quealy notebook, NAA: A9240/1, set 1, vol. 4.

69 Ibid.; letter, Forde to author, 28 October 1974; F.T. Smith Reports, 17 September 1942.

70 'Note of Secraphone conversation between the Prime Minister and the Commander-in-Chief Southwest Pacific Area—17/9/1942', NAA: A5954, 266/1.

71 Edwards, *John Curtin's War*, vol. II, pp. 107–108; Paull, *Retreat from Kokoda*, p. 247; Hetherington, *Blamey*, pp. 240, 239, 241–42.

72 National Institute of Defence Studies, *Japanese Army Operations in the South Pacific Area*; Horner, *Crisis of Command*; F.T. Smith Reports, 21 September 1942.
73 Advisory War Council Minute 1074, Canberra, 24 September 1942, NAA: A5954, 814/2; Shedden notebook, NAA: A5954, 214/1; Quealy notebook, NAA: A9240/1, set 1, vol. 4.
74 Colonel D.H. Dwyer, 'Blamey: a personal memoir', *Sydney Morning Herald*, 6 December 1972; F.T. Smith Reports, 3 October 1942.
75 Advisory War Council Minute 1080, Canberra, 1 October 1942, NAA: A5954, 814/2; Shedden's minutes, NAA: A5954/2, 214/1.
76 Horner, *Blamey*; for Rowell's account, see Rowell, *Full Circle*.
77 *The Bulletin*, 7 October 1942, p. 22; F.T. Smith Reports, 3 October 1942; letter, Blamey to Curtin, 4 October 1942, AWM: 3DRL 6643, 2/43.631.
78 Letter, Blamey to Curtin, 8 October 1942, AWM: 3DRL 6643, 2/23.81; letter, MacArthur to Curtin, 10 October 1942, MMMA: RG 4, box 1B; Horner, *Blamey*, p. 341.
79 Edwards, *John Curtin's War*, vol. II, pp. 136, 141.
80 War Cabinet Minute 248, Canberra, 14 October 1942, NAA: A2673, vol. XII; 'Notes of Discussions with Commander-in-Chief . . . 20–26 October 1942', NAA: A5954, 2/7.
81 Shedden Manuscript, book 4, ch. 33, pp. 8, 9; letters, Shedden to Curtin, 21 November 1942, Curtin to presidents of state Labor parties, 27 November 1942, NAA: A5954, 1937/1; Edwards, *John Curtin's War*, vol. II, p. 142.
82 For a detailed account of Curtin's efforts to win the support of the ALP state branches, see Edwards, *John Curtin's War*, vol. II, pp. 143–65; Shedden Manuscript, book 4, ch. 33, pp. 8, 9.
83 Quoted in Ross, *John Curtin*, p. 294.

Chapter 7: 'The decisions are matters for the Australian government'

1 Minutes of Prime Minister's War Conference, Canberra, 14 January 1943, NAA: A5954, 1/1.
2 'Notes of Discussion with Commander-in-Chief . . . 16–20 January 1943', NAA: A5954, 2/1.
3 Broadcast by Prime Minister, 26 January 1943, message by Dickson Brown to *News Chronicle*, quoted in teleprinter message, Deputy Chief Publicity Censor to Chief Publicity Censor, 27 January 1943, and message, MacArthur to Curtin, 27 January 1943, all in NAA: A5954, 611/5.
4 Miller, *Cartwheel*, p. 10; Advisory War Council Minutes 1129, 11321, 1132, Canberra, 2 February 1943, NAA: A2682, vol. VI.
5 Notes of secraphone conversation, 16 March 1943, NAA: A5954, 524/6; minutes of Prime Minister's War Conference, Canberra, 17 March 1943, NAA: A5954, 4/8; teleprinter message, MacArthur to Curtin, 17 March 1943, NAA: A5954, 289/6.
6 Prime Minister's press release, 8 April 1943, NAA: A5954, 2037/2; broadcast by Blamey, 25 April 1943, AWM: 3DRL 6643, 2/136.61.
7 Memorandum, CAS to Churchill, 24 May 1943, quoted in Bell, *Unequal Allies*, p. 85.

8 Letter, Curtin to MacArthur, 8 February 1943, NAA: A5954, 575/2; minutes of Prime Minister's War Conference, Canberra, 12 February 1943, NAA: A5954, 4/6; letter, Blamey to Forde, 10 May 1943, NAA: A5954, 291/6.

9 War Cabinet Agendum 106/1943, Supplement 1, 13 April 1943, NAA: A2671, 106/1943.

10 War Cabinet Minute 2810, Melbourne, 30 April 1943, NAA: A5954, 809/1; Recommendations of Defence Committee, 6 May 1943, NAA: A2671, 106/1943.

11 'Notes of Discussions with Commander-in-Chief . . . 25 to 31st May 1943', and attached memorandum, 30 May 1943, NAA: A5954, 2/3; letter, Blamey to Curtin, 2 June 1943, NAA: A5954, 306/3; letter, Shedden to MacArthur, 4 June 1943, NARA: RG 316, box 71.

12 Minutes of Prime Minister's War Conference, Sydney, 7 June 1943, NAA: A5954, 2/5; 'Strategical situation in Southwest Pacific Area—Prime Minister's statement of 10th June', Advisory War Council Minute 1204, 16 June 1943, NAA: A5954, 815/1.

13 War Cabinet Agendum 311/1943, 10 July 1943, and War Cabinet Minute 2968, Melbourne, 13 July 1943, NAA: A5954, 311/1943.

14 Letters, Curtin to MacArthur, 5 August 1943, MacArthur to Curtin, 24 August 1943, Curtin to MacArthur, 3 September 1943, NAA: A5954, 306/3.

15 Letter, Curtin to Blamey, 21 September 1943, NAA: A5954, 306/3; minutes of Prime Minister's War Conference, Canberra, 27 September 1943, NAA: A5954, 4/2; report, 'A review of the nature, extent, and balance of the war effort in the light of the manpower position', signed by Curtin, 30 September 1943, NAA: A2680, 35/1943.

16 War Cabinet Minute 3065, Canberra, 1 October 1943, NAA: A5954, 809/2.

17 Hasluck, *The Government and the People 1942–1945*, pp. 301–302, 29; Butlin and Schedvin, *War Economy 1942–1945*, pp. 382, 393.

18 Letter, Blamey to Forde and Curtin, 12 July 1943, NAA: A816, 31/301/274.

19 Letter, Blamey to Curtin, 5 October 1943, NAA: A5954, 306/3.

20 Letters, Curtin to MacArthur, 1 November 1943, MacArthur to Curtin, 6 November 1943, Curtin to MacArthur, 13 November 1943, NAA: CP 290/16, bundle 1.

21 'Notes of discussion with the commander-in-chief . . . 29th November to 1st December 1943', NAA: A5954, 2/6; statement by the Prime Minister, 3 December 1943; letter, Shedden to Curtin, 1 December 1943, NAA: A5954, 306/2. The statement is reproduced in MacArthur, *Reminiscences*, p. 183.

22 Minutes of Prime Minister's War Conference, Canberra, 27 September 1943, NAA: A5954, 4/2; letter, Curtin to MacArthur, 22 November 1943, AWM: 3DRL 6643, 2/5.1.

23 'Notes of Discussion with Commander-in-Chief . . . 17 March 1944', NAA: A5954, 3/8; letter, Shedden to Curtin, 10 March 1944, MMMA: RG 4.

24 Memoranda, Churchill to Ismay, 16 April 1944, Chiefs of Staff to Churchill, 1 May 1944, TNA: PREM 3 68/8; for Blamey's aims, see Horner, *Blamey*, ch. 19.

25 Brooke, entry, 18 May 1944, Alanbrooke Diary 5/8, Alanbrooke Papers; Edwards, *John Curtin's War*, vol. II, p. 324.

26 D.H. Dwyer, 'Interlude with Blamey', unpublished manuscript, copy held by author; Shedden Diary, NAA: A5954, 16/2; Day, *John Curtin*, pp. 546–47.
27 'Notes of Discussions with Commander-in-Chief . . . 26 and 27 June 1944', NAA: A5954, 3/10.
28 'Notes of Discussions with Commander-in-Chief . . . 27 June 1944', NAA: A5954, 3/10.
29 Letter, Blamey to Curtin, 11 July 1944, AWM: 3DRL 6643, 2/23.11.
30 Letter, MacArthur to Blamey, 12 July 1944, AWM: 3DRL 6643, 2/ 23.11; 'Notes of an interview with General MacArthur', 1 August 1944, TNA: CAB 127/33.
31 Edwards, *John Curtin's War*, vol. II, pp. 366–67.
32 'Notes of conference between the Prime Minister and the Commander-in-Chief, Australian Military Forces', Melbourne, 2 August 1944, NAA: A2680, 17/1944 part 1.
33 Letters, Blamey to Curtin, 11 August 1944, 15 September 1944, AWM: 3DRL 6643, 2/23.1.
34 Letter, Blamey to Curtin, 27 October 1944, AWM: 3DRL 6643, 2/23.1.
35 Shedden Manuscript, book 4, ch. 48, p. 4.
36 Herington, *Air Power Over Europe 1944–1945*, p. 285.
37 Jones interview, 24 January 1979.
38 Memorandum, Royle to Minister, 17 January 1942, NAA: A2671, 95/1942; for a biography of Collins, see Macdougall, *Collins of the* Sydney.
39 Minutes of Prime Minister's War Conference, Sydney, 7 June 1943, NAA: A5954, 2/5; memorandum, Royle to Makin, 13 December 1943, with appended note, Makin to Curtin, no date, letter, Shedden to Makin, 8 February 1944, and notes on War Cabinet Agendum 29/1944, 21 January 1944, NAA: A2671, 29/1944.
40 Letter, A.V. Alexander, First Lord of the Admiralty, to Curtin, 26 May 1944, and memorandum, Shedden to Curtin, 31 July 1944, NAA: A5954, 509/2; Lloyd Ross, 'I'm too tired to live', *Sun-Herald* (Sydney), 17 August 1958; War Cabinet Minute 4085, Canberra, 8 March 1945, NAA: A2671, 329/1944.
41 For a detailed study of the RAAF command scandal, see Ashworth, *How Not to Run an Airforce!*
42 War Cabinet Agendum 107/1943, 16 March 1943, and cable, Curtin to Bruce, 17 April 1943, NAA: A816, 31/301/196A; cables, Bruce to Curtin, 20, 22, 29 April 1943, NAA: A816, 31/301/300A.
43 'Notes of Discussions with Commander-in-Chief . . . 25–31 May 1943', NAA: A5954, 2/3; letters, Drakeford to Curtin, 25 June 1943, Curtin to Drakeford, 17 July 1943, NAA: A816, 31/301/300A; Shedden Manuscript, book 4, ch. 25, p. 15; Kenney, *General Kenney Reports*, p. 30.
44 Letter, Curtin to Churchill, 24 May 1944, TNA, PREM 3, 63/13; War Cabinet Minute 3693, Melbourne, 4 August 1944, NAA: A816, 31/301/196A; 'Notes of discussion with the commander-in-chief . . . 30 September 1944', NAA: A5954, 3/11; memoranda, Shedden to Curtin, 30 October 1944, 4 November 1944, with Shedden's notes on the first memorandum, NAA: A5954, 238/2; Stephens, *The Royal Australian Air Force*, p. 122.

45 Letter, Blamey to Berryman, AWM: 3DRL 6643, 2/43.68; letter, Curtin to MacArthur, AWM: 3DRL 6643, 2/23.11.
46 Letter, Berryman to Blamey, 10 February 1945, AWM: Berryman Papers, PR84/370.
47 James, *The Years of MacArthur*, vol. II, pp. 716–17.
48 Letter, Gairdner to Ismay, 30 May 1945, TNA: WO 216/137.
49 Letter, Blamey to Curtin, 19 April 1945, AWM: 3DRL 6643, 23.11; *CPD*, H of R, 1 February 1945.
50 Letters, Chifley to Blamey, 7 May 1945, Blamey to Chifley, 18 May 1945, AWM: 3DRL 6643, 2/23.11; letter, MacArthur to Chifley, 20 May 1945, NARA: RG200, Sutherland Papers, Correspondence with Australian Government.
51 Letter, Blamey to Fraser, 16 May 1945, AWM: 3DRL 6643, 2/ 23.11.
52 Letter, MacArthur to Chifley, 20 May 1945, NAA: A5954, 570/2; signal, MacArthur to Marshall, 12 April 1945, NARA: RG 218, CCS 381, Pacific Ocean Area (6-10-43) Sec 11.
53 Signal, Shedden to MacArthur, 21 July 1945, NAA: A5954, 1133/2; teleprinter message, Chifley to MacArthur, 20 May 1945, NAA: A5954, 570/2.
54 The following paragraphs are based on: War Cabinet Minute 4194, Canberra, 22 May 1945, NAA: A5954, 811/1; Shedden notebook, NAA: A5954, 733/2; Quealy notebook, NAA: A92401/1, set 1, vol. 9.
55 Notes on War Cabinet Agendum No. 209/1945, 22 May 1945, NAA: A5954, 570/3.
56 Letter, Chifley to MacArthur, 21 July 1945, NARA: RG200, Correspondence with Australian Government.
57 Ross, *John Curtin*, p. 293.
58 Sir Paul Hasluck, review of Norman E. Lee, *John Curtin: Saviour of Australia*, in *The Age*, 1 October 1983.

Chapter 8: 'We have not a minute more than three years'

1 Rowell, *Full Circle*, p. 198; Menzies, *The Measure of the Years*, p. 35.
2 Defence Committee Minute, 24 June 1948, NAA: A5954, 1490/6; Rowell, *Full Circle*, pp. 194–95.
3 For Spender's achievements as External Affairs Minister, see Lowe, *Australian Between Empires*.
4 Brief for Minister, 24 January 1950, NAA: A1068/7, DL47/3/3.
5 Letter, Spender to McBride, 17 April 1950, NAA: A1068/7, DI47/33; Watt, *Australian Diplomat*, p. 191.
6 For Menzies' approach to the Cold War, see Lowe, *Menzies and the 'Great World Struggle'*, and Lee, *Search for Security*.
7 *CPD*, H of R, 27 April 1950, pp. 1996–97.
8 For Australia's involvement in BCOF, see Wood, *The Forgotten Force*; for a biography of Robertson, see Grey, *Australian Brass*.
9 For the establishment and role of JCOSA, see Horner, *High Command*, ch. 18; for the formation of the Royal Australian Regiment, see Horner, *Duty First*, ch. 3.
10 The following account is based on Edwards, *Crises and Commitments*, ch. 6.
11 Quoted in Edwards, *Crises and Commitments*, p. 89.

12 Edwards, *Crises and Commitments*, pp. 94, 378.

13 Letter, Shedden to McBride, 19 May 1950, NAA: A5954, 2293/5. At time of writing in 2021, an Australian infantry rifle company was still rotating through the RAAF air base at Butterworth in Malaysia.

14 Minute by Defence Committee, 15 June 1950, NAA: A5954, 1627/2; cable, Slim to Chiefs of Staff, 22 June 1950, TNA: WO 216/600.

15 Handwritten minutes of Council of Defence Meeting, 21 June 1950, NAA: A9786/2, 11. The formal minutes are in NAA: A9787/2, 113. See also Lowe, 'Menzies, memory and Britain in the 1950s', p. 116; Lewin, *Slim*, pp. 275–76; Watt, *Australian Diplomat*, p. 173.

16 This and the next two paragraphs are based on Londey et.al, *The Long Search for Peace*, ch. 6.

17 Ibid., p. 151.

18 Cabinet Minute, quoted in O'Neill, *Australia in the Korean War 1950–53*, vol. I, p. 48.

19 This section is based on ibid., ch. 4.

20 Quoted in Martin, *Robert Menzies*, vol. 2, p. 154.

21 Minutes of Council of Defence, 5 July 1950, NAA: A9787/2, 113.

22 O'Neill, *Australia in the Korean War 1950–53*, vol. 1, pp. 65–66.

23 Ibid., pp. 73, 80, 76.

24 Edwards, *Arthur Tange*, p. 57; Tange, *Defence Policy-Making*, p. 4. The text of the quote states 'people' rather than 'person', but this is probably a typographical error.

25 Letter, Shedden to McBride, 23 August 1950, NAA: A5954, 1557/8.

26 Ibid.; letter, McBride to Ministers of Navy, Army, Air and Supply, 19 September 1950, NAA: A5954, 1642/2.

27 'A defence call to the nation', broadcasts by the Prime Minister, 20, 22 and 25 September and 1 October 1950, NAA: A5954, 828/2.

28 Statement by the Prime Minister, 8 December 1950, NAA: A5954, 1879/1; for a discussion of the National Security Resources Board, see Lee, 'The national security planning and defence preparations of the Menzies government'.

29 Quoted in Martin, *Robert Menzies*, vol. 2, p. 171.

30 Martin, 'Mr Menzies' anticommunism', p. 55.

31 O'Neill, *Australia in the Korean War 1950–53*, vol. 1, pp. 172–78.

32 Cables, Menzies to Fadden, 9 and 7 January 1951, NAA: A5954, 1873/11.

33 'A semi-war footing', *Sydney Morning Heral*d, 15 February 1951, p. 1; letter, Shedden to McBride, 12 March 1951, which refers to an earlier memo of 28 February 1950, NAA: A5954, 1557/7.

34 'Three years—no more', *Sydney Morning Herald*, 8 March 1951, p. 1; 'Mr Menzies repeats "prepare now" warning', *The Age*, 8 March 1951, p. 1

35 Letter, Shedden to Menzies, 11 May 1951, NAA: A5954, 864/6.

36 For cables describing the discussions, see NAA: A5954, 1799/1; Cabinet submission, 31 July 1951, NAA: A5954, 2384/1.

37 O'Neill, *Australia in the Korean War 1950–53*, vol. 1, p. 251; Frame, *Pacific Partners*, p. 86.

38 Quoted in Millar, *Australian Foreign Minister*, p. 59; letter, Rowell to VCIGS, 23 January 1952, TNA: WO 216/479; Stephens, *Going Solo*, pp. 203–204.

39 Letter, Bunting to McBride, 31 August 1951, NAA: A816, 11/301/787. The formation of a Cabinet committee was not unusual; at that time the Cabinet had a series of committees, including the Cabinet Committee on Conditions of Defence Forces.

40 For the committee's procedures and decisions, see NAA: A816, 11/301/785 and 11/301/787, and A4933, Volumes 6, 7 and 9. For a summary of its decisions, see NAA: A5954, 1366/1.

41 Grey, *The Commonwealth Armies and the Korean War*, p. 110.

42 For Wilton in Korea, see Horner, 'Australian higher command in the Korean War'.

43 'Minister on future of Korea', *The Advertiser* (Adelaide), 11 January 1952, p. 3; for the dates of these visits, see the captions on the photographs held by the Australian War Memorial. See also O'Neill, *Australia in the Korean War 1950–53*, vol. II, p. 175.

44 Stephens, *Going Solo*, p. 7; Sydney Rowell, 'It's back to trench warfare in Korea', *The Argus*, 22 May 1952, p. 2; quoted in Macdougall, *Collins of the* Sydney, p. 470.

45 O'Neill, *Australia in the Korean War 1950–53*, vol. 1, pp. 245.

46 Ibid., pp. 288–89.

47 Ibid., pp. 402–404, 407–408.

48 Ibid., pp. 288, 333–34; 'Menzies reports on mission', *Daily Telegraph* (Sydney), 16 July 1952.

49 Acheson, *Present at the Creation*, p. 689.

50 Martin, *Robert Menzies*, vol. 2, pp. 222–23; Department of Defence, 'Key elements in the triennial reviews of strategic guidance since 1945', April 1986.

51 Letters, Watt to Casey, 3 June 1953, Watt to External Affairs, 10 June 1953, NAA: A5954, 1680/7; letter, Alexander to Menzies, 29 June 1953, NAA: A5954, 1464/1; for British planning leading to the FESR, see Umetsu, 'The origins of the British Commonwealth Strategic Reserve'.

52 Minute by Defence Committee, 13 August 1953, NAA: A5954, 1464/1.

53 Report of discussions etc., Melbourne, 19–21 October 1953, NAA: A5954, 1561/3.

54 'Defence Act to expire', *The Herald* (Melbourne), 29 December 1953.

55 Tange, *Defence Policy-making*, p. 8.

56 Rowell, *Full Circle*, p. 197.

57 Handwritten Cabinet notebook, quoted in 'Once more dear friends', *Sydney Morning Herald*, 5 February 2005, smh.com.au/national/once-more-dear-friends-20050205-gdkmw8.html, accessed 24 June 2021; Edwards, *Crises and Commitments*, p. 131.

58 'Note on origins of the Five Power Agency', 23 July 1954, NAA: A5954, 2306/4; 'The political objective in the defence of South East Asia', 23 June 1954; Cabinet Minute, 24 June 1954, NAA: A5954, 2297/7.

59 Defence Committee Minutes, 29 July 1954, NAA: A5954, 1428/2; Edwards, *Crises and Commitments*, p. 153; 'The Manila Conference, 1954, report on defence aspects', 17 September 1954, NAA: A5954, 1428/3.

60 Stephens, *Going Solo*, p. 207; Pemberton, *All the Way*, p. 51; letter, Menzies to Churchill, 12 October 1954, TNA: DEFE 13/218; for a history of SEATO, see Buszynski, *SEATO*.
61 Letter, Tange to Menzies, 8 February 1955, NAA: A5954, 1563/2; Edwards, *Crises and Commitments*, p. 168.
62 Edwards, *Crises and Commitments*, p. 168; 'Statement by the Prime Minister', 1 April 1955, NAA: A5954, 828/1; 'A historic decision', *Sydney Morning Herald*, 2 April 1955; Edwards, *Crises and Commitments*, p. 169.
63 Cabinet Minute, 15 June 1955, NAA: A5954, 1467/9.
64 Edwards, *Crises and Commitments*, p. 180; Dennis and Grey, *Emergency and Confrontation*, p. 93.
65 Chin Peng, *My Side of History*, pp. 321–22, and author's discussion with Chin Peng, 3 February 1998. For a comprehensive discussion, see Lax, *Malayan Emergency and Indonesian Confrontation*, ch 13.
66 Edwards, *Crises and Commitments*, p. 377.

Chapter 9: 'Looking for a way in and not a way out'

1 For a detailed examination of the medical and psychological legacies of the Vietnam War, see Yule, *The Long Shadow*.
2 For a biography of McEwen, see Golding, *Black Jack McEwen*; for a biography of Holt, see Frame, *The Life and Death of Harold Holt*.
3 For Barwick's biography, see Marr, *Barwick*.
4 Rayner, *Scherger*, p. 145.
5 For Hasluck's autobiography, see *Mucking About*; see also Beaumont, 'Paul Hasluck: the diplomat as minister'; B.K. De Garis, 'Paltridge, Sir Shane Dunne (1910–1966)', *ADB*, vol. 15, 2000.
6 Tange interview, 4 March 1986; McNicoll interview, 6 March 1986; for biographies of Scherger, see Rayner, *Scherger*; Rayner, 'Air Chief Marshal Sir Frederick Scherger'; Garrisson, 'Air Chief Marshal Sir Frederick Scherger'.
7 For Hancock's autobiography, see Hancock, *Challenge*.
8 Wilton Transcript, pp. 121–22. For a biography of Wilton, see Horner, *Strategic Command*.
9 McNicoll interview, 6 March 1986; John Farquharson, 'Hicks, Sir Edwin William (Ted) (1910–1984)', *ADB*, vol. 17, 2007.
10 Edwards, *Crises and Commitments*, p. 215. This book—the official history, written with full access to government records—is the key source for the events leading to the Vietnam commitment.
11 Pemberton, *All the Way*, p. 124.
12 Edwards, *Crises and Commitments*, p. 220.
13 SEATO press release, 27 April 1961, NAA: A6059/2, 65/441/125.
14 Edwards, *Crises and Commitments*, pp. 223, 227.
15 Report by the Australian Military Adviser, May 1962, CCOSC files, box 10, file 245; Defence Committee Minute, 14 June 1962, CCOSC files, box 9A, file 228.
16 McNeill, *To Long Tan*, p. 24.
17 Letter, Serong to CGS, 20 February 1962, NAA: A6840/1, 1; Edwards, *Crises and Commitments*, pp. 235–36.

18 Edwards, *Crises and Commitments*, pp. 240–43.

19 Coulthard-Clark, *The RAAF in Vietnam*, pp. 9–11.

20 'Strategic basis of Australian defence policy', 26 January 1962, and Cabinet Minute, Decision No. 344 (M), 19 July 1962, NAA: A1945, 83/2/8; 'Progress report on achievement of approved objective as at 31 December 1962', CCOSC files, box 9, file 239.

21 Edwards, *Crises and Commitments*, p. 254; Horner, *Australian Higher Command in the Vietnam War*, p. 7.

22 Cabinet Minute, Decision No. 675, 5 March 1963, NAA: A1945, 832/8; note on file, and minute, Wilton to DMO&P, 5 March 1963, AWM 121, 213/A/1, also quoted in Dennis and Grey, *Emergency and Confrontation*, p. 315.

23 Letter, Hicks to Defence Minister, 24 September 1963, NAA: A1945, 245/3/4; 'Initial views of the Chiefs of Staff Committee', 24 September 1963, AWM 121, 31/A/2; Edwards, *Crises and Commitments*, p. 269.

24 Defence Committee Minutes, 9 November 1963, NAA: A1945, 245/3/4, and AWM 121, 31/A/2.

25 Edwards, *Crises and Commitments*, p. 287; Defence Committee Minute, 23 January 1964, AWM 121, 211/A/3.

26 Quoted in Dee, 'In Australia's own interests'; cable, Kuala Lumpur to Canberra, 6 April 1964; Defence Committee Minute, 9 April 1964; and minute by Secretary, FAD Committee, 10 April 1964, AWM 121, 211/A/3.

27 Defence Committee Minute, 13 April 1964, AWM 121, 211/A/3; Edwards, *Crises and Commitments*, pp. 290–91.

28 McNeill, *The Team*, p. 77; Wilton interview, Army Historical Programme.

29 Report by the Defence Committee, 21 May 1964, NAA: A1945, 248/4/85.

30 AATTV Commander's Diary, 23 June 1964, AWM 95, 1/2/25; cable, Anderson to Department of External Affairs, 25 June 1964, NAA: A1945, 248/4/85; Edwards, *Crises and Commitments*, p. 291; letter, Hicks to Defence Minister, 8 July 1964, and Paltridge's marginal note giving approval, 15 July 1964, NAA: A1945, 248/4/85.

31 Defence Committee Minute, 20 August 1964, CCOSC files, box 11, file 310, part 2.

32 Dennis and Grey, *Emergency and Confrontation*, p. 229.

33 Army paper dated 19 March attached to COSC Minute, 6 April 1964, CCOSC files, box 14, file 476; letter, Hasluck to Secretary and CCOSC, 23 March 1964, AWM 121, 28/C/1.

34 COSC Minute, 6 April 1964, CCOSC files, box 14, file 476.

35 Hasluck, *The Chance of Politics*, pp. 99–104.

36 'Summary of conclusions and recommendations by Minister for Defence', 19 May 1964, CCOSC files, box 14, file 476.

37 Letter, Wilton to Army Minister, 27 May 1964, AWM 121, 28/C/1.

38 Cabinet Minute, Foreign Affairs and Defence Committee, Decision No. 451 (FAD), 3 September 1964, CCOSC files, box 11, file 310, part 2. I have used the word 'manpower' as was the practice in the 1960s, rather than now preferred term 'human resources'.

39 Quoted in Pemberton, *All the Way*, p. 212.

40 Military Board minute 2 October 1964, and attached paper, 'Review of army manpower—September 1964', *Military Board Proceedings*, vol. 4, 1964.

41 Defence Committee Minute, 15 October 1964, NAA: A1945/42, 83/2/9.

42 Horner, *Duty First*, p. 157; Edwards, *Crises and Commitments*, p. 485, fn 82; Denis and Grey, *Emergency and Confrontation*, pp. 226–27.

43 Cabinet submission, 'Service Manpower Review', November 1964, CCOSC files, box 15, file 499. It is not dated but an accompanying minute from Hicks to Paltridge is dated 3 November 1964.

44 Cabinet Minute, Decision No. 592, 4 November 1964, CCOSC files, box 15, file 499.

45 Notes on Cabinet Submission No. 521, 3 November 1964, A4940/1, C162 part 2; Forbes interview, 21 February 2003; Howson and Aitkin, *The Howson Diaries*, p. 121; see also, Howson interview, 25 March 2003.

46 'Background to the introduction of selective service', AWM 101, 7.

47 'Notes on professional military advice to be given to cabinet', attached to letter, Wilton to Bunting, 6 November 1964, NAA: A4940/1, C162 part 2; Forbes interview, 21 February 2003; Howson and Aitkin, *The Howson Diaries*, p. 121.

48 'Defence review', ministerial statement by Sir Robert Menzies, *CPD*, H of R, 10 November 1964.

49 Edwards, *Crises and Commitments*, p. 337; McNeill, *To Long Tan*, p. 53; Sexton, *War for the Asking*, p. 57; Report by the Joint Planning Committee, 11 December 1964, NAA: A1945, 248/4/100.

50 Woodard, *Asian Alternatives*, pp. 194–95, 203.

51 Ibid., p. 203; Beaumont, 'Paul Hasluck', p. 149; 'Department of External Affairs comments on Washington telegrams numbers 3305 and 3414', 16 December 1964, NAA: A1838, 696/8/4 part 6.

52 Sexton, *War for the Asking*, p. 63; COSC minute, 16 December 1964, NAA: A1945, 248/4/100; Isaksson interview, 15 July 2002; Isaksson, *Encounters in Asia*, p. 54.

53 Cabinet Minute, Decision No. 659 (FAD), 17 December 1964, NAA: A1945, 248/4/100; cable, Menzies to Johnson, 19 December 1964, NAA: A1945, 71/1/131; Notes of FAD Committee, 17 December 1964, NAA: A4940/1, C3811; Woodard, *Asian Alternatives*, pp. 197, 206; Edwards, *Australia and the Vietnam War*, p. 285; for further discussion, see Woodard, 'Australia's war in Vietnam: debate without end'.

54 Cables, Wilson to McEwen, 15 January 1965, McEwen to Wilson, 19 January 1965, AWM 121, 211/A/6.

55 Edwards, *Crises and Commitments*, p. 343; Cabinet submission, 26 January 1965, AWM 121, 211/A/6; For an account of the SAS's operations in Borneo, see Horner, *SAS: Phantoms of War*; for 3 RAR's operations, see Horner, *Duty First*, ch. 7.

56 Wilton interview, Army Historical Programme.

57 Edwards, *Crises and Commitments*, p. 339.

58 Minute, CGS 7/1965, 'The impracticability of increasing the Australian Army

Training Team in South Vietnam', 29 January 1965, AWM 121, 161/A/1; JPC minute, 11 December 1964, and COSC minute, 16 December 1964, NAA: A1945/39, 248/4/100.

59 Defence Committee Minute, 25 March 1965, NAA: A1945/37, 71/1/131; minute, Wilton to Scherger, 25 March 1965, CCOSC files, box 16, file 513; Edwards, *Crises and Commitments*, p. 358; McNeill, *To Long Tan*, pp. 73–74; Breen, *First to Fight*, p. 13.

60 Edwards, *Crises and Commitments*, pp. 358–60; Edwards, *Australia and the Vietnam War*, p. 113; Mackay interview, 10 October 1985; K.W. Major (First Assistant Secretary, Department of the Army) interview, 7 April 1986; McNeill, *To Long Tan*, p. 64.

61 Minute, Shaw to G.A. Jockel, 6 April 1965, NAA: A1838, TS3014/2/1 part 7; Defence Committee Minute, 5 April 1965, NAA: A1945, 71/1/31.

62 Edwards, *Crises and Commitments*, pp, 360–62.

63 Edwards, *Arthur Tange*, p. 154; Tange interview, 4 March 1986; McNicoll interview, 6 March 1986; Rayner, *Scherger*, pp. 153–54.

64 Sexton, *War for the Asking*, pp. 148–49.

65 Pemberton, *All the Way*, p. 294; Edwards, *Crises and Commitments*, pp. 370–72; Edwards, *Australia and the Vietnam War*, p. 118; Edwards, *A Nation at War*, p. 28.

66 Edwards, *Crises and Commitments*, p. 386.

67 Peter Edwards, 'The foreign and defence polices of Robert Menzies: 50 years on', *The Strategist*, 28 January 2016.

Chapter 10: 'All the way with LBJ'

1 For a detailed and authoritative account, see Edwards, *A Nation at War*.

2 Letter, Wilton to Hicks, 15 April 1965, and Defence Committee Minute, 20 April 1965, both in CCOSC files, box 16, file 513; note for file re Defence Committee Minute 21/1965, M, 22 April 1965, NAA: A1838, TS 696/8/4 part 8.

3 Letter, A.M. Morris (External Affairs representative on JPC) to Jockel, 27 April 1965, NAA: A1838, TS 696/8/4 part 8.

4 Report, Mackay to CGS, 'Report by the Leader of Planning Team Visit to Saigon', 11 May 1965, NAA: A1945, 248/4/114.

5 Defence Committee Minute, 13 May 1965, AWM 121, 161/A/4; Cabinet Minute, Decision No. 975 (FAD), 18 May 1965, NAA: A1945/43, 248/4/116; Mackay interview, 7 April 1986; letter, McMahon to Paltridge, 23 June 1965, NAA: A1945/39, 248/4/19.

6 Wilton interview, Army Historical Programme.

7 Signal, Jackson to Wilton, 4 July 1965; letter, Wilton to Army Minister, 6 July 1965; signal, Jackson to Wilton, 4 July 1965; letter, Wilton to Army Minister, 6 July 1965; signal, Wilton to Jackson, 9 July, all in AWM 121, 161/A/4.

8 Signals, Wilton to Hassett, 3 September 1965, NAA: A1945/42, 248/4/128; Mackay to Wilton, 13 September 1965, AWM 121, 161/A/5; McNeill, *To Long Tan*, p. 121.

9 Letter, Wilton to Scherger, 20 July 1965, and attached paper, 'An assessment of the Army's ability to expand its force in Vietnam', AWM 121, 161/A/4; Edwards, *A Nation at War*, pp 56–57.

10 Letter, Wilton to Forbes, 19 August 1965, AWM 121, 161.A/1; Mackay interview, Army Historical Programme; McNeill, *To Long Tan*, pp. 182–84.

11 Letter, Hicks to CGS, 18 August 1965, AWM 121, 161/A/5.

12 Report by the Joint Planning Committee, 7 February 1966; letter, Wilton to Hicks, 12 August 1965, and handwritten notes by Scherger, 17 August 1965, all in CCOSC files, box 16, file 313, part 2; Edwards, *A Nation at War*, p. 57; letter, Hicks to CGS, 18 August 1965, AWM 121, 161/A/5; Report by the Joint Planning Committee, 7 February 1966, CCOSC files, box 16, file 513, part 3; letter, Hicks to Acting Defence Minister, 7 December 1965, NAA: A1945, 248/4/138.

13 Minute, Hicks to Wilton, 16 December 1965, AWM 121, 161/A/5; Jackson interview, Army Historical Programme; Mackay interview, Army Historical Programme.

14 Edwards, *A Nation at War*, p. 86; cable, Washington to Canberra, 23 December 1965, NAA: A1945, 248/4/138. The papers are in NAA: A1945, 248/4/138 and 248/4/145; Cabinet Minute No. 1467, Melbourne, 5 January 1966, NAA: A1945, 248/4/138.

15 For a biography of Holt, see Frame, *The Life and Death of Harold Holt*; I.R. Hancock, 'Holt, Harold Edward (1908–1967)', *ADB*, vol. 14, 1996.

16 Whitington, *Fifteen Years of the Liberals*, p. 85; Aitchison, *From Bob to Bungles*, pp. 9–10.

17 Wilton Diary; Wilton Transcript, p. 116.

18 'Report by the Joint Planning Committee at a meeting on 7th February 1966', CCOSC files, box 16, file 513, part 3.

19 Minute by the Defence Committee, 10 February 1966, NAA: A1945, 248/4/145; 'South Vietnam—Australian Military Assistance', prepared by Scherger, 10 February 1966, CCOSC files, box 16, file 513, part 3.

20 'South Vietnam—Australian Military Assistance', a paper prepared by Scherger, 10 February 1966, CCOSC files, box 16, file 513, part 3; letter, Wilton to Hicks, 18 February 1966, NAA: A1945, 248/4/145.

21 Edwards, *A Nation at War*, p. 91.

22 Cabinet Minute, Decision No. 60, 2 March 1966, NAA: A1945, 248/4/145; Wilton interview, Army Historical Programme; Holt quoted in Edwards, *A Nation at War*, p. 94.

23 Fraser interview, 18 November 2002.

24 Wilton interview, Army Historical Programme.

25 Brig O.D. Jackson, CGS Exercise 1971, 'Presentation Operation Hardihood—Deployment of 1 ATF to Nui Dat' (held by author); for a discussion of the selection of Nui Dat, see Horner, 'Why was 5 RAR stationed at Nuit Dat?'.

26 Daly interview, Army Historical Programme.

27 Westmoreland Diary, 17 March 1966; COSC minute, 23 March 1966, CCOSC files, box 25, file 1910; Fraser interview, 18 November 2002; Fraser, *Dangerous Allies*, p. 143.

28 COSC minute, 4 May 1966, NAA: A1945/42, 248/4/158.
29 Sam Lipski, 'The view from Russell Hill', *The Bulletin*, 18 December 1965; Trengove, *John Grey Gorton*, p. 141; McNicoll interview, 6 March 1986; Frame, *Where Fate Calls*, p. 150.
30 Stephens, *Going Solo*, p. 321; Sam Lipski, 'The view from Russell Hill', *The Bulletin*, 18 December 1965; Howson and Aitkin, *The Howson Diaries*, pp. 159, 168, 232–33, 277, 455; Smith interview, 6 November 1985; letter, Sir Thomas Daly to author, 10 February 1986.
31 Frame, *Where Fate Calls*, p. 150; letter, Hicks to Hulme, 10 November 1965, NAA: A1945, 65/7/1.
32 Letter, Hicks to Hulme, 29 November 1965, NAA: A1945, 65/7/1.
33 Cabinet Minute, Decision No. 1456 (FAD), 10 December 1965, NAA: A1945, 65/7/1; Howson and Aitkin, *The Howson Diaries*, p. 193; cable, Philpott to Secretary, COSC, London, 22 December 1965, TNA: DEFE 11/637.
34 Letter, Hicks to Fairhall, 9 February 1966, NAA: A1945, 65/7/1; Fairhall interview, 21 March 2002; Cabinet Minute, Decision No. 75, 15 March 1966, NAA: A1945, 65/7/1; Howson and Aitkin, *The Howson Diaries*, p. 211.
35 For a biography of Daly, see Grey, *A Soldier's Soldier*.
36 The detailed itinerary is in NAA: A1945, 292/2/394 part 2; Wilton Diary; quoted in Frame, *The Life and Death of Harold Holt*, p. 179.
37 Grey, *Up Top*, p. 55; Reports of Proceedings for the ships in AWM 95, 98/2, 96/2, 126/2, 136/3, 315/3.
38 2 SAS Squadron's operations are described in Horner, *SAS: Phantoms of War*, ch. 10; Avery, *Our Secret War*, p. 93.
39 Wilton Diary.
40 Cable, Australian High Commissioner to External Affairs, 10 April 1966, AWM 121, 211/A/7. The official history, Dennis and Grey, *Emergency and Confrontation*, p. 297, claims erroneously that this incident took place in June.
41 Defence Committee report, 12 May 1965; Cabinet Minute, Decision No. 267, 18 May 1966; letter, Wilton to Daly, 20 May 1966, NAA: A1945, 248/5/14.
42 Edwards, *A Nation at War*, pp. 112–13.
43 Grey, *Up Top*, p. 78. See also letter, Blakers (Acting Secretary) to Defence Minister, 16 August 1966, and Minister's note of 30 August 1966, NAA: A1945, 248/4/159.
44 Letters, Wilton to Minister, 1 August 1966, Wilton to Acting Secretary, 5 September 1966, Fairhall's note of 13 September on Acting Secretary to Minister, 7 September 1966, and letter, Wilton to Minister, 17 August 1966, all in NAA: A1945, 248/4/159. There are several published accounts of the Long Tan battle; for the standard and authoritative account, see McNeill, *To Long Tan*.
45 Edwards, *A Nation at War*, pp. 114–15.
46 COSC minute, 12 October 1966, NAA: A1945, 71/1/172.
47 Edwards, *A Nation at War*, pp. 139, 140.
48 Itinerary for visit of Lieutenant General Wilton, AWM 98, R875/2/110.
49 Mackay interview, 10 October 1985.

50 Defence Committee Minutes, 13 December 1966, CCOSC files, box 18, file, part 3, Proposals for Further Contribution to Vietnam Force.
51 Cabinet Minute, 14 December 1966, NAA: A5840 XM1, vol. 1; Edwards, *A Nation at War*, p. 141; letter, Gorton to Holt, 16 December 1966, quoted in Frame, *The Life and Death of Harold Holt*, p. 189.
52 Cable, Australian Ambassador, Saigon, to Secretary, Department of External Affairs, 28 January 1967, AWM 121, 161/G/1; letter, Hicks to Minister for Defence, 20 April 1967, NAA: A1946, 1967/1176 part 1.
53 Daly interview, Army Historical Programme; letter, Vincent to Wilton, 22 June 1967, Vincent Papers, and NAA: A1946, 1967/1176 part 1.
54 Edwards, *A Nation at War*, p. 150.
55 Defence Committee Minute, 27 July 1967, CCOSC files, box 29, file 19320(2).
56 Cabinet Minute, Decision No. 499 (FAD), 28 July 1967, NAA: A5840 XM1, vol. 2.
57 The following comments are from 'Clark Clifford talks, July 1967, Main points from ministerial/official preliminary discussions', NAA: A4940/1, C1473, part 3.
58 'Clark Clifford talks, July 1967, Main points from ministerial/official preliminary discussions', NAA: A4940/1, C1473 part 3.
59 Daly interview, 26 November 1985; Cabinet Minute, Decision No. 656 (FAD), 25 August 1967, NAA: A5840 XM1, vol. 3.
60 Letter, Bunting to Holt, 6 September 1967, NAA: A4940/1, C1473 part 3; Cabinet Minute, Decision No. 563 (FAD), 6 September 1967, NAA: A5840 XM1, vol. 2.
61 Edwards, *A Nation at War*, pp. 154–55.
62 Ibid., p. 156.
63 Letter, Daly to Minister for the Army, 28 October 1968 (to be passed to the Minister for Defence), NAA: A6835/1, 1; signal, Westmoreland to Wilton, 20 October 1967, CCOSC Files, box 34, file Signals between CCOSC and COMAFV.

Chapter 11: 'I'm certainly no trained strategist'

1 'Australia: As the PM sees it', *Daily Mirror*, 10 January 1968.
2 Alan Ramsey, 'Has he come to bury integration—or to kill it?' *The Australian*, 9 December 1967, p. 9.
3 Ibid.; Bland interview, 29 April 1986; Wilton Diary; Daly interview, 26 November 1985.
4 Cabinet Minute, Decision No. 4, 11 January 1968, NAA: A5871/1, vol. 1; 'Foreign Affairs and Defence Committee' (list of those present, 12 January 1968), NAA: A5875/1, vol. 2. Edwards, *A Nation at War*, p. 194 states erroneously that this meeting took place on 12 February; cable, Thomson to Commonwealth Office, 12 January 1968, TNA: PREM 13/2081; Cabinet Minute, Decision No. 12 (FAD), 25 January 1968, NAA: A5871/1, vol. 1.
5 Edwards, *A Nation at War*, p. 196; HQ AFV Monthly Report, January 1968, AWM 98, R723/1/13, vol. 3; Vincent interview, Army Historical Programme, 1971; Vincent address, 27 November 1985, in the possession of the author.

6 *Canberra Times*, 24 July 1967, 13 February 1968; see also letter, Fraser to Prime Minister, 2 February 1968. NAA: A1209, 1967/7130 part 3.
7 Latham interview, 11 January 1983. The numerous signals to and from COMAFV and CCOSC are in CCOSC files, boxes 32 and 34.
8 Edwards, *A Nation at War*, p. 196; Cabinet Minute, Decision No. 70 (FAD), 12 March 1968, NAA: A5872, vol. 1; signal, CCOSC to COMAFV, 11 and 13 March 1968, CCOSC files, box 32, Chiefs Of Staff Signal File, Outwards to COMAFV from No. 140–202; letter, MacDonald to Daly, 10 March 1968, AWM 98, CGS to COMAFV, Period 1 Jan 67 to 28 Feb 70.
9 MacDonald interview, 13 December 1985; McNicoll interview, 6 March 1986; Daly interview, 26 November 1985.
10 Edwards, *A Nation at War*, p. 193; signals, COMAFV to and from CCOSC, 10 May 1968, CCOSC files, box 34, file, Signals from COMAFV to CCOSC, Inwards No. 1220; for a description of these battles, see McNeill and Ekins, *On the Offensive*.
11 Howson and Aitkin, *The Howson Diaries*, p. 424.
12 Reid, *The Gorton Experiment*, p. 45; Bland, *Some Aspects of Defence Administration*, p. 16.
13 Hancock, *John Gorton*, pp. 177–78.
14 McNeill and Ekins, *On the Offensive*, pp. 402–404.
15 Transcript of press conference given by the Prime Minister, Mr John Gorton, 9 June 1968, pmtranscripts.pmc.gov.au/release/transcript-1875, accessed 5 April 2021.
16 Cabinet Minute, Decision No. 543, CCOSC files, box 21, file 1117, part II.
17 'Gorton, Nixon to discuss defence', *Daily Telegraph*, 5 December 1968; Hancock, *John Gorton*, p. 225.
18 Edwards, *A Nation at War*, pp. 203–204.
19 Minute, Dovers to DJOP and DJP, 6 November 1968, AWM 122, 68/3016; Defence Committee Minute, 11 September 1969, and minute, Blakers to Secretary, Department of Defence, 10 September 1969, CCOSC Files, box 26, file 1858, part 1.
20 Letter, Wilton and Daly to Defence Minister, 22 September 1969, CCOSC Files, box 26, file 1858, part 1.
21 'Points for P.M.—Vietnam visit', CCOSC files, box 26, file 1857.
22 Letter, Wilton to Fraser, 18 November 1969, CCOSC files, box 26, file 1857; COSC Minute, 1 December 1969, and Defence Committee Minute, 5 December 1969, CCOSC files, box 26, file 1858, part 1.
23 Note for file by CCOSC, 17 December 1969, CCOSC files, box 26, file 1858, part 1.
24 Daly interview, Army Historical Programme; Ekins, *Fighting to the Finish*, p. 412.
25 Edwards, *A Nation at War*, p. 241.
26 Letter, Fraser to Wilton, 18 December 1969, CCOSC Files, box 26, file 1858, part 1.
27 Signal, COMAFV to CCOSC, 12 January 1970, AWM 122, 53; letter, Daly to Wilton, 9 January 1970, and Defence Committee Minute, 29 January 1970, CCOSC files, box 26, file 1858, part II.

28 Letters, Fraser to Wilton, 9 March 1970, Wilton to Fraser, 11 March 1970, and COSC minute, 11 March 1970, CCOSC files, box 26, file 1858, part II; Cabinet Minute, Decision No. 218, 17 March 1970, NAA: A5869/1, vol. 9.
29 Edwards, *Crises and Commitments*, p. 380; Edwards, *A Nation at War*, pp. 348–49.
30 Fraser interview, 18 November 2002.
31 Bland interview, 29 April 1986; McNicoll interview, 6 March 1986; for a record of Bland's interview with Abrams, see report attached to letter, Hay to Wilton, 15 October 1969, AWM: AAAGV, Hay DO letters.
32 Alan Ramsey, 'The real reasons Sir Henry resigned', *The Australian*, 19 November 1969, p. 4; MacDonald interview, 13 December 1985.
33 For Fraser's role as Defence Minister, see Ayres, *Malcolm Fraser*, ch. 9.
34 Vincent interview, Army Historical Programme, 1971; Hay interview, 5 November 1985; MacDonald interview, 13 December 1985.
35 Signal, Daly to COMAFV, 28 February 1970, NAA: A6836/1, 5 and AWM 98, NN COM AFV 1/1/67-28 Feb 70; signal, Hay to CGS and CCOSC, 1 March 1970, NAA: A6836/1, 5; AWM 98 NN COMAFV-CGS 1/3/70-3/71 and CCOSC files, box 34, file Incoming signals for CCOSC 1970.
36 Letter, Major General C.A.E. Fraser to author, 10 August 1985.
37 Letter, Fraser to Gorton, 2 April 1970, CCOSC files, box 26, file 1858, part II.V.
38 Letters, Wilton to Vien and Abrams, 5 April 1970; Vien and Abrams to Wilton, 6 April 1970, NAA: A7123/2, 1856; McNeill, *The Team*, p. 443.
39 Letters, Fraser to Secretary, Department of Defence, CCOSC and Director JIO, 30 April 1970, and Fraser to Wilton, 1 May 1970, AWM 121, 4/B/6 part III; signal, Wilton to COMAFV, 13 April 1970, CCOSC files, box 32, file Outgoing signals COSAFV 261 to COSAFV 466.
40 'Notes on future of 1 ATF', 27 July 1970, CCOSC files, box 26, file 1858, part II; signal, COMAFV to Wilton, 24 September 1970, AWM 122, 69/2000.
41 Cabinet Minute, Decision No. 575 (ad hoc), 31 July 1970, NAA: A5873/1, vol. 2.
42 Letter, Tange to Fraser, undated, but probably August 1970, NAA: A1946/25, 68/1138; Bland interview, 29 April 1986; for Smith's career, see Smith, *A Few Memories of Sir Victor Smith*.
43 Carey and McCrea, *Peacock*, p. 80; letter, Killen to Fraser, 29 July 1970, NAA: A1946, 68/1138; Cabinet Minute, Decision No. 607, 25 August 1970, NAA: A1945, 68/1138.
44 Minute, Acting FAS Division I (H.D. Anderson) to Acting Secretary, 27 October 1970, NAA: A1838, 696/8/4/11 part II.
45 COSC Minute, 15 October 1970, and Defence Committee Minute, 28 October 1970, both in CCOSC files, box 27, file 1858, part IV.
46 Frost, *Australia's War in Vietnam*, p. 145; letter, Wilton to Minister, 16 November 1970, CCOSC files, box 27, file 1858, part IV; for a description of these operations, see Ekins, *Fighting to the Finish*.
47 Fraser interview, 10 August 1986; Daly interview, 26 November 1985.
48 Salmon interview, 28 July 1986.

49 This account is based largely on Sir Thomas Daly, 'The Fraser affair—February 1971', unpublished paper lent to author. (For a similar account, see Grey, *A Soldier's Soldier*, ch. 7.) Tange, *Defence Policy-making*, p. 32; Edwards, *Arthur Tange*, p. 188.
50 Tange, *Defence Policy-making*. 32; Sir Thomas Daly, 'The Fraser affair—February 1971', lent to author; Hancock, *John Gorton*, p. 317.
51 Sir Thomas Daly, 'The Fraser affair—February 1971', lent to author.
52 Hancock, *John Gorton*, pp. 319–21.
53 Tange interview, 4 March 1986; Tange, *Defence Policy-making*, p. 33.
54 Edwards, *A Nation at War*, p. 293; Ekins, *Fighting to the Finish*, pp. 535–36.
55 Ekins, *Fighting to the Finish*, pp. 537; Edwards, *A Nation at War*, p. 297.
56 Ekins, *Fighting to the Finish*, p. 621.
57 Mullins, *Tiberius with a Telephone*, p. 453.
58 Wilton interview, Army Historical Programme.
59 Letters, Fraser to Wilton, 1 May 1970, Wilton to COMAFV, 4 May 1970, AWM 98, R723/1/13, vol. 6; dust jacket of Cohen, *Supreme Command*.

Chapter 12: 'Australia had vital interests at stake'

1 For a detailed study of Australia in the Gulf War, see Horner, *Australia and the 'New World Order'*, and Horner, *The Gulf Commitment*.
2 Scott, *Gareth Evans*, pp. 218, 222.
3 The Joint Intelligence Organisation changed its name to Defence Intelligence Organisation on 1 January 1991.
4 Cable, New Delhi to Canberra, 3 August 1990, NAA: M3571/1, 86.
5 Cables, Canberra to Washington, 3 August 1990, SPC-A: Op Damask records, box 7.
6 US Department of Defense, *Conduct of the Persian Gulf War*, p. 30; Bush and Scowcroft, *A World Transformed*, p. 315; cable, Washington to Canberra, 2 August 1990, SPC-A: Op Damask records, box 27; minute, Michael Thawley, DFAT, to Duffy, 3 August 1990, NAA: M3571/1, 86.
7 Cohen and Gatti, *In the Eye of the Storm*, p. 187; cable, 6 August 1990, New York to Canberra, NAA: M3128/2, box 11, 114; Cabinet Minute No. 14261, Canberra, 6 August 1990, NAA: M3588/1, 14100-14299; news release, 'Australian sanctions against Iraq', 6 August 1990, NAA: M3571/1, 86.
8 Cable, New York to Canberra, 6 August 1990, NAA: M3128/2, box 11, 114; Hilsman, *George Bush vs Saddam Hussein*, p. 47; statement, 'Australian sanctions against Iraq', 7 August 1990, NAA: M3128/2, box 11, 114.
9 Report, R Adm K.A. Doolan, 'Report of the Maritime Commander to the Chief of the Defence Force and the Chief of the Naval Staff on Operation Damask', 17 September 1991, SPC-A: Op Damask records, box 6; cable, Washington to Canberra, 6 August 1990, NAA: M3571/1, 87; Carwardine interview, 6 March 2007.
10 *Australian Labor Party Platform . . . 1984*, p. 88.
11 Evans, 'The Labor tradition: a view from the 1990s', pp. 13, 15–16.
12 Hawke, *The Hawke Memoirs*, pp. 511–12.
13 Lecture notes, 'Input from ACOPS (R Adm R. Taylor) to VCDF presentation

to JSSC', 17 May 1991, provided to author by R Adm R.G. Taylor, 3 June 1991; handwritten note by Gration dated 7 August on minute, Taylor to Gration, 6 August 1990, Defence: A6721, OPS93/9814/1.

14 'Aussies await the call', *Melbourne Sun*, 10 August 1990, p. 2; minute, Allan Gyngell to Hawke, 8 August 1990, NAA: M3571/1, 87; Robert Hadlee and Bryan Boswell, 'US sends troops to Gulf blockade', *The Australian*, 9 August 1990, p. 1.

15 Cable, Washington to Canberra, 8 August 1990, NAA: M3571/1, 88, and Defence: A6721, OPS93/9814/1.

16 Lt Cdr J. Straczek, 'The history of Operation Damask', unpublished manuscript, p. 4, SPC-A: Op Damask records, box 25; Taylor, interview, 3 June 1991.

17 Mark Baker, 'The imperious Hawke style', *The Age*, 7 September 1990, p. 13; see also Paul Grigson, 'How we begged to go to the Gulf', *Sydney Morning Herald*, 1 September 1990; letter to the editor, P.J. Keating. 'Far from the truth', *Sydney Morning Herald*, 4 September 1990; Ian McPhedran, 'The war cry grows dim with memory', *Canberra Times*, 15 October 1994, p. 14; Hawke, *The Hawke Memoirs*, p. 517.

18 Hawke, *The Hawke Memoirs*, p. 512; transcript of interview in cable, Canberra to Baghdad, 13 August 1990, SPC-A: Op Damask records, box 22.

19 Cable, Canberra to Washington, 9 August 1990, NAA: M3128/2, box 11, 114.

20 'Summary of telephone conversation between Prime Minister and Mr Mulrony [sic]', 9 August 1990, NAA: M3571/1, 88.

21 Signal, HQADF to MCAUST, 091236Z August 1990, Defence: A6721, OPS93/9814/1.

22 Handwritten notes of Hawke's conversation with Bush, 7.15 a.m., 10 August 1991, NAA: M3571/1, 89; Alan Ramsey, 'President Bob rolls over for a tickle', *Sydney Morning Herald*, 11 August 1990, p. 25; Ray interview, 19 June 1991; lecture notes, 'Input from ACOPS (R Adm R. Taylor) to VCDF presentation to JSSC', 17 May 1991, provided to author by R Adm R.G. Taylor, 3 June 1991.

23 Transcript of news conference, Parliament House, 10 August 1990, NAA: A1274, B90/00313.

24 Transcript of speech, in cable, Canberra to Baghdad, 13 August 1990, SPC-A: Op Damask records, box 22.

25 Dibb interview, 20 December 1991.

26 Defence press release no. 203/90, 21 December 1990.

27 Kelly, *The End of Certainty*, p. 615.

28 Straczek, 'The history of Operation Damask', p. 18; COSC Minute No. 110/1990, 6 September 1990, Defence: A6721, N90/28571/1; Diary of Events, Operation Damask, 6 September 1990, Defence: A6721, OPS93/9814/2; *CPD*, Senate, 11 September 1990, p. 2229.

29 Cable, Washington to Canberra, 3 October 1990, NAA: M3128/2, 120.

30 Carwardine interview, 6 March 2007; Brief, Chronology, Australian Task Group, SPC-A: Op Damask records, box 14.

31 Draft ministerial brief, DFAT to Evans, 9 November 1990, with Defence comments, Defence: A6721, OPS93/9814/5; COSC Minute No. 133/1990, 8 October 1990, Defence: A6721, N90/31729/1; minute, Gration to Ray,

10 November 1990, Defence: A6721, OPS93/9814/5; Domney interview, 22 May 1991.

32 Report, Cdre D.B. Chalmers, 'Operation Damask—CTG 627.4 Overview First Deployment', n.d., SPC-A: Op Damask records, box 7; Report, R Adm K.A. Doolan, 'Report of the Maritime Commander to the Chief of the Defence Force and the Chief of the Naval Staff on Operation Damask', 17 September 1991, SPC-A: Op Damask records, box 6; cable, Washington to Canberra, 6 August 1990, NAA: M3571/1, 87, pp. 2–4; Chalmers interview, 26 November 1991; minute, Hudson to Gration, 1 November 1990, Defence: A6721, N90/34540/1.

33 *CPD*, Senate, 6 November 1990, p. 3473; Jeremy Thompson, 'Australia could join US Gulf attack: Evans', *Canberra Times*, 7 November 1990, p. 2; Bush and Scowcroft, *A World Transformed*, p. 382.

34 Minute, Gration to Ray, 14 November 1990, NAA: M3128/2, 109.

35 Note, Meeting, PM, Ray and Evans, 15 November 1990; and handwritten notes, Bush—PM, 16 November 1990, NAA: M3571/1, 108.

36 *CPD*, Senate, 4 December 1990, p. 4907, 21 January 1991, p. 30, 22 January 1991, p. 38; presentation to Joint SOSP, V Adm A. Beaumont, 'Decision making during the Gulf crisis', SPC-A: Op Damask records, box 7.

37 Freedman and Karsh, *The Gulf Conflict*, p. 234.

38 Hawke, *The Hawke Memoirs*, p. 517.

39 Hawke, *The Hawke Memoirs*, pp. 517; memo, White to Hawke, 29 November 1990, NAA: M3571/1, 110; Hawke, *The Hawke Memoirs*, pp. 517–18.

40 Transcript, interview with Bob Hawke, '1130 news', Network Ten, 12 October 1994, NAA: M3128/9, 1650; *CPD*, H of R, 13 October 1994, pp. 1997–99.

41 Michelle Grattan, 'Canberra expects our ships to do their duty', *The Age*, 3 December 1990, p. 13; Paul Grigson, 'Cabinet to decide Australia's commitment', *Sydney Morning Herald*, 1 December 1990, p. 19; Mark Metherell, 'No troops to Gulf war, says Hawke', *The Age*, 1 December 1990, p. 4.

42 Jeremy Thompson, 'PM gets tougher new role for ships', *Canberra Times*, 4 December 1990, p. 1; Cabinet Minute 14712, Canberra, 3 December 1990, NAA: M3128/2, 101.

43 *CPD*, H of R, 4 December 1990, pp. 4322–24.

44 Denis Muller, 'Poll finds wide support for our ships to fight', *The Age*, 8 December 1990, p. 6.

45 Bush and Scowcroft, *A World Transformed*, p. 382; Freedman and Karsh, *The Gulf Conflict*, p. 235.

46 Cable, Washington (Cook) to Canberra (Hawke), 8 January 1991, NAA: M3128/2, 101 and NAA: M3571/1, 117.

47 Cable, Washington to Canberra, 13 January 1991, NAA: M3128/2, 101.

48 The account of the interview is based on cables, New York to Canberra, 14 January 1991, NAA: M312/2, 101; Baker with Defrank, *The Politics of Diplomacy*, pp. 377–78.

49 Bush and Scowcroft, *A World Transformed*, pp. 448–49; cable, Langlands (Riyadh) to Baker, Director DIO, (Canberra), 14 January 1991, NAA: M3571/1, 119.

50 McGoldrick, *A Memoir of Arabia*, 'The Gulf War', pp. 9, 15–16.

51 Roy Eccleston 'PM orders RAN ships into "fight for peace"', *The Australian*, 18 January 1991, p. 1; Hawke, *The Hawke Memoirs*, p. 521.
52 Transcript of news conference, Parliament House, 17 January 1991, NAA: M3571/1, 140; letter, Hawke to Gration, 17 January 1991, NAA: M3571/1, 122; Diary of Events, Operation Damask, 17 January 1991, Defence: A6721, OPS93/9814/6.
53 Statement by the Prime Minister, The Gulf, 17 January 1991, NAA: M3571/1, 125.
54 Louise Dodson, 'Caucus pushes Hawke to crank up peace rhetoric', *Financial Review*, 22 January 1991, p. 4; 'Most support Gulf role', *The Australian*, 22 January 1991, pp. 1–2.
55 *CPD*, H of R, 21 January 1991, pp. 2–3.
56 Ibid., pp. 4–5.
57 Ibid., pp. 8, 13, 19.
58 d'Hagé interview, 20 November 1991.
59 Baker interview, 26 June 1991; Bobbi Mahlab, 'Daily briefings keep PM in touch with war', *Sunday Mail*, 27 January 1991, p. 8.
60 Ray interview, 19 June 1991; Ross Peake and Leon Gettler, 'Agreement reached on Gulf messages', *The Age*, 24 January 1991, p. 3; Inglis, *Whose ABC?*, p. 226; Beazley interview, 23 May 2007; 'The ABC's political endeavour', *The Australian*, 24 January 1991, p. 10; Leon Gettler, 'Ray threatens ABC failure to provide a message link', *The Age*, 23 January 1991, p. 7.
61 'The prime minister's speech', *Canberra Times*, 1 March 1991, p. 2; letter, Hawke to Gration, 28 February 1991, Defence: CDF DO File 1988–94; memo, 'Record of phone call—Prime Minister and President Bush, 1 March 1991', NAA: M3571, 135.

Chapter 13: 'It is right, it is lawful and it's in Australia's national interest'

1 Quoted in Middleton, *An Unwinnable War*, p. 29; Michael Gordon, 'Howard: Why I went to war', *Sydney Morning Herald*, 10 September 2011.
2 The wars are the subject of a major official history project managed by the Australian War Memorial, due to be completed (or at least drafted) by the end of 2022.
3 Australia's continuing commitment to the Gulf region is described in Horner and Connor, *The Good International Citizen*, chs 16–19.
4 For a history of Operation Bel Isi, see Breen, *The Good Neighbour*.
5 For a useful study of the INTERFET operation, see Blaxland (ed.), *East Timor Intervention*.
6 White, 'Defence policy', pp. 220–21; White, 'Mr Howard goes to Washington'; Wesley, 'Managing the region', p. 209.
7 Weller, Scott and Stevens, *From Postbox to Powerhouse*, pp. 135–38; Department of Defence, *The War in Iraq*, p. 9.
8 For Cosgrove's career, see his memoirs, *My Story*; for the development of the ADF command structure for joint operations, see Horner, *Strategy and Command*, ch. 14.
9 Middleton, *An Unwinnable War*, p. 38.

10 Ibid., p. 36.
11 Ibid., p. 42.
12 Ibid., p. 38; Barrie, 'A Chief of Defence Force's perspective', p. 54.
13 Transcript of Press Conference, 4 October, 2001, parlinfo.aph.gov.au/parlInfo/search/display/display.w3p;query=Id:"media/pressrel/IV256", accessed 24 April 2021.
14 Middleton, *An Unwinnable War*, p. 56.
15 Transcript of Prime Minister's address to Australian Defence Association, 25 October 2001, pmtranscripts.pmc.gov.au/release/transcript-12374, accessed 20 April 2021.
16 For the SAS operations in Afghanistan in 2001–02, see McPhedran, *The Amazing SAS*.
17 Barrie, 'A Chief of Defence Force's perspective', pp. 60–61.
18 For an account of the early planning, see Woodward, *Plan of Attack*.
19 'Large U.S. Force is assembling as Bush decides how to strike', *New York Times*, 30 September 2001, p. 8; Michael Hirsh and Roy Gutman, 'Powell in the middle', *Newsweek*, 2 October 2001, p. 55; Richard Beston, 'Iraq accuses US of trying to settle old scores', *The Times* (London), 10 October 2001, p. 12; The President's State of the Union Address, 29 January 2002. www.whitehouse.gov/newsrelease/2002/01/20020129, downloaded 3 June 2003, now at georgew-bush-whitehouse.archives.gov/news/releases/2002/01/20020129-11.html.
20 Middleton, *An Unwinnable War*, p. 10; for a description of Australia's role in UNSCOM, see Horner and Connor, *The Good International Citizen*, chs 17, 18, 19.
21 Palazzo, 'The Australian Army and the war in Iraq', pp. 46–47; Cabinet Minute, National Security Committee, JH01/0337/NS, 10 December 2001, NAA: A14370, JH2001/337; Howard. *Lazarus Rising*, p. 425; Macklin, *Warrior Elite*, p. 247.
22 Middleton, *An Unwinnable War*, pp. 107, 110.
23 Howard, *Lazarus Rising*, pp. 431–32. Howard states that he visited Washington in July 2002; in fact, he visited 8–13 June 2002.
24 Senator the Hon. Robert Hill, 'Beyond the White Paper: strategic directions for Defence', Canberra, 18 June 2002, www.defense-aerospace.com/article-view/verbatim/16056/mod%3A-australia-approves-first-strike-doctrine.html.
25 Palazzo, 'The Australian Army and the war in Iraq', pp. 49–50.
26 Middleton, *An Unwinnable War*, p. 111.
27 Barrie, 'A Chief of Defence Force's perspective', p. 58.
28 Palazzo, 'The Australian Army and the war in Iraq', pp. 51, 156; Hill, 'A minister's perspective', p. 24.
29 Hill, 'A minister's perspective', p. 27; Howard, 'The army and national interest', pp. 25–26; Tony Wright, 'The road to Iraq', *The Bulletin*, 8 April 2003.
30 Middleton, *An Unwinnable War*, p. 114.
31 Cosgrove, *My Story*, pp. 365–66.
32 Middleton, *An Unwinnable War*, p. 113; Palazzo, 'The Australian Army and the war in Iraq', pp. 62, 66, 67.
33 Palazzo, 'The Australian Army and the war in Iraq', pp. 175–76.

34 Fia Cummings, ‘Howard urges Bush to hold fire’, *Sydney Morning Herald*, 9 September 200; Marian Wilkinson and Mark Metherell, ‘Bush will call on Australian troops’, *Sydney Morning Herald*, 9 September 2002; Paul McGeough, ‘A rumour of war’, *Sydney Morning Herald*, 9 September 2002.

35 Transcript of address to National Press Club, 11 September 2002; pmtranscripts.pmc.gov.au/release/transcript-12900, accessed 26 April 2021. Transcript of press conference, 12 September 2002, pmtranscripts.pmc.gov.au/release/transcript-12486, accessed 26 April 2021; Craig Skehan, ‘We’d love to have SAS for Iraq attack, says US general’, *Sydney Morning Herald*, 12 September 2002; Tom Allard, ‘US need not go it alone, says Hill’, *Sydney Morning Herald*, 16 September 2002; *CPD*, H of R, 17 September 2002, p. 6379.

36 Howard, *Lazarus Rising*, p. 411.

37 Palazzo, ‘The Australian Army and the war in Iraq’, pp. 156–64; Cosgrove, *My Story*, p. 363; Palazzo, ‘The Australian Army and the war in Iraq’, p. 174; Palazzo, ‘Deploy, sustain, return’.

38 For the SAS’s early planning, see McPhedran, *The Amazing SAS*, ch. 20.

39 Middleton, *An Unwinnable War*, p. 115.

40 Address by the Prime Minister to the Committee for Economic Development of Australia, Sydney, 20 November 2002, pmtranscripts.pmc.gov.au/release/transcript-12934, accessed 27 April 2021.

41 Smith, ‘A departmental secretary’s perspective’, p. 34.

42 Betts and Phythian, *The Iraq War and Democratic Governance*, pp. 60, 63, 66.

43 Kelly, *The March of Patriots*, pp. 261, 260, 262.

44 Transcript of the Prime Minister’s press conference, 10 January 2003, parlinfo.aph.gov.au/parlInfo/search/display/display.w3p;query=Id%3A”media%2Fpressrel%2FB3A86”22, accessed 27 April 2021.

45 Transcript of the Prime Minister’s address, 23 January 2003; Simon Crean, ‘Transcript—HMAS Kanimbla Farewell Ceremony—23 January 2003’, library.fes.de/aussies/2003/0103/20003443.html, accessed 27 April 2021.

46 ‘Howard’s statement to parliament on Iraq’, *CPD*, H of R, 4 February 2003, pp. 10642–50.

47 ‘President Bush meets with Prime Minister Howard of Australia’, Oval Office, 10 February 2003, georgewbush-whitehouse.archives.gov/news/releases/2003/02/20030210-10.html, accessed 27 April 2021; Howard, *Lazarus Rising*, p. 439; transcript of address to National Press Club, 13 March 2003, parlinfo.aph.gov.au/parlInfo/search/display/display.w3p;query=Id:”media/pressrel/PDS86”22, accessed 27 April 2021; for the Australian demonstrations, see Neil Mercer, Sean Nicolls, Ellen Connolly and Valerie Lawson, ‘Sydney protests the Iraq War’, *Sydney Morning Herald*, 17 February 2019, and Viney, ‘With one voice, one heartbeat’.

48 Defence media releases, 21 February, 10 March 2003 (held by author)

49 Palazzo, ‘The Australian Army and the war in Iraq’, p. 192.

50 For Blix’s experiences, see Blix, *Disarming Iraq*.

51 Summit communiqué, 17 March 2003; ‘Monday “moment of truth” for Saddam, says Bush’, *Sydney Morning Herald*, 17 March 2003.

52 ‘Cabinet briefing ends after hearing from defence chiefs’, *Sydney Morning Herald*, 18 March 2003.

53 Transcript of Howard's interview with Catherine McGrath, ABC *AM*, 18 March 2003, pmtranscripts.pmc.gov.au/release/transcript-20735.

54 'Australia commits troops to war', *Sydney Morning Herald*, 18 March 2003; Palazzo, 'The Australian Army and the war in Iraq', p. 216; Cosgrove, *My Story*, p. 368; transcript of Howard's press conference, 18 March 2003, https://www.smh.com.au/world/middle-east/transcript-of-howards-press-conference-20030318-gdgg5r.html, accessed 29 October 2021; Mark Riley, 'Australian troops get ready for invasion as PM sticks to his guns', *Sydney Morning Herald*, 18 March 2003.

55 Address to the nation by President George W. Bush, 17 March 2003, www.govinfo.gov/content/pkg/PPP-2003-book1/pdf/PPP-2003-book1-doc-pg277.pdf; *CPD*, H of R, 18 March 2003, p. 12505.

56 Transcript of press conference, 20 March 2003, https://parlinfo.aph.gov.au/parlInfo/search/display/display.w3p;query=Id%3A%22media%2Fpressrel%-2FLWU86%22, accessed 29 October 2021; transcript of the Prime Minister's address, 20 March 2003, parlinfo.aph.gov.au/parlInfo/search/display/display.w3p;query=Id:"media/pressrel/RZU86"22, accessed 29 October 2003; Howard, *Lazarus Rising*, p. 448.

57 Palazzo, 'The Australian Army and the war in Iraq', pp. 219–20.

58 Sheridan, *The Partnership*, p. 71.

59 For the experiences of Australians in the Iraq Survey Group, see Barton, *The Life of a Spy*, and Robinson, *Meeting Saddam's Men*; Woods et al., *The Saddam Tapes*; Palazzo, 'Iraq and the politics of alliance relationships', p. 237; Cotton, 'After the flood: foreign policy and the management of intelligence', p. 137.

60 Palazzo, 'The Australia Army and the war in Iraq', p. 524.

61 For an analysis of how Howard made the case for war, see McDonald and Merefield, 'How was Howard's war possible?'.

62 Middleton, *An Unwinnable War*, p. 114.

63 Transcript of ABC *PM* report, 1 March 2004, www.abc.net.au/pm/content/2004/s1056536.htm, accessed 4 May 2021.

64 Quoted in Betts and Phythian, *The Iraq War and Democratic Governance*, p. 148; for Betts's argument, see ch. 5.

65 Transcript of ABC *PM* report, 22 July 2004, www.abc.net.au/pm/content/2004/s1159802.htm, accessed 4 May 2021; Garry Woodard, 'We now know about going to war in Iraq', Nautilus Institute, 22 November 2007, nautilus.org/apsnet/we-now-know-about-going-to-war-in-iraq.

66 The Iraq Inquiry, public statement by Sir John Chilcot, 6 July 2016, iraqinquiry.org.uk/the-inquiry/sir-john-chilcots-public-statement, accessed 7 July 2017; Michael Gordon, 'Howard, why I went to war', *Sydney Morning Herald*, 10 September 2011; for a good discussion of this issue, see Garry Woodard, 'We now know about going to war in Iraq', Nautilus Institute, 22 November 2007, nautilus.org/apsnet/we-now-know-about-going-to-war-in-iraq, and Cotton, 'After the flood: foreign policy and the management of intelligence'.

67 Howard, *Lazarus Rising*, p. 448, quoted in Graham Dobell, 'What Vietnam and Iraq should teach Canberra', *The Strategist*, 25 March 2013; White, 'Security, defence and terrorism', p. 180.

68 According to one calculation, the cost of US involvement in Iraq was more than double that of the Korean War and a third more than the Vietnam War (Betts and Phythian, *The Iraq War and Democratic Governance*, p. 4).
69 Palazzo, 'Iraq and the politics of alliance relationships', p. 245.

Conclusion

1 Woodward, *The Commanders*, p. 34.
2 Barton, *The Life of a Spy*, 285.
3 Quoted in Tsouras, *Warriors' Words*, p. 77.

Bibliography

Books

Acheson, D., *Present at the Creation: My Years at the State Department*, Hamish Hamilton, London, 1969

Aitchison, R., *From Bob to Bungles and Now to Billy: People in Politics, 1966–71*, Sun Books, Melbourne, 1971

Andrews, E.M., *The Anzac Illusion: Anglo-Australian Relations during World War I*, Cambridge University Press, Melbourne, 1993

—— *The Australian Centenary History of Defence*, vol. V, *The Department of Defence Force*, Oxford University Press, Melbourne, 2001

Ashworth, N., *How Not to Run an Airforce! The Higher Command of the Royal Australian Air Force during the Second Word War*, vol. 1, *Narrative*, Air Power Studies Centre, Canberra, 2000

Australian Labor Party Platform, Constitution and Rules as Approved by the 36th National Conference, Canberra, 1984, Australian Labor Party, Canberra, 1984

Avery, B., *Our Secret War: The 4th Battalion the Royal Australian Regiment, Defending Malaysia against Indonesian Confrontation, 1965–1967*, Slouch Hat Publications, Melbourne, 2001

Ayres, P., *Malcolm Fraser: A Biography*, William Heinemann, Melbourne, 1987

Baker, J.A. III, with Defrank, Thomas M., *The Politics of Diplomacy: Resolution, War and Peace 1989–1992*, G.P. Putnam's Sons, New York, 1995

Ball, D., and D. Horner, *Breaking the Codes: Australia's KGB network, 1944–1950*, Allen & Unwin, Sydney, 1998

Barton, R., *The Life of a Spy: An Education in Truth, Lies and Power*, Black Inc., Melbourne, 2021

Bastian, P., *Andrew Fisher: An Underestimated Man*, UNSW Press, Sydney, 2009

Bean, C.E.W., *The Official History of Australia in the War of 1914–1918*, vol. I, *The Story of Anzac*, 10th edn, Angus & Robertson, Sydney, 1940

—— *The Official History of Australia in the War of 1914–1918*, vol. III, *The A.I.F. in France: 1916*, 2nd edn, Angus & Robertson, Sydney, 1934

—— *The Official History of Australia in the War of 1914–1918*, vol. IV, *The A.I.F. in France: 1917*, 1st edn, Angus & Robertson, Sydney, 1933

—— *The Official History of Australia in the War of 1914–1918*, vol. VI, *The A.I.F. in France: May 1918—The Armistice*, 1st edn, Angus & Robertson, Sydney, 1942

—— *Two Men I Knew: William Bridges and Brudenell White, Founders of the A.I.F.*, Angus & Robertson, Sydney, 1957

Bell, I., *Australian Army Mobilisation in 1914*, Australian Army History Unit Occasional Paper Series, no. 2, Canberra, 2017

Bell, R., *Unequal Allies: Australian–American Relations and the Pacific War*, Melbourne University Press, Melbourne, 1977

Betts, J., and M. Phythian, *The Iraq War and Democratic Governance: Britain and Australia Go to War*, Palgrave Macmillan, Melbourne, 2020

Birdwood, Field Marshal Lord, *Khaki and Gown: An Autobiography*, Ward, Lock & Co., London, 1941

Blake, R. (ed.), *The Private Papers of Douglas Haig, 1914–1919*, Eyre & Spottiswoode, London, 1952

Bland, H., *Some Aspects of Defence Administration in Australia*, 21st Roy Milne Memorial Lecture, Australian Institute of International Affairs, Perth, 1970

Blaxland, J. (ed.), *East Timor Intervention: A Retrospective on INTERFET*, Melbourne University Press, Melbourne, 2015

Blix, H., *Disarming Iraq*, Pantheon Books, New York, 2004

Bou, J., *MacArthur's Secret Bureau: The Story of the Central Bureau, General MacArthur's Signals Intelligence Organisation*, Australian Military History Publications, Sydney, 2012

——, and P. Dennis, with P. Dalgleish, *The Australian Imperial Force: The Centenary History of Australia and the Great War*, vol. 5, Oxford University Press, Melbourne, 2016

——, B. Breen, D. Horner, G. Pratten and M. de Vogel, *The Limits of Peacekeeping: Australian Missions in Africa and the Americas, 1992–2005*, Cambridge University Press, Melbourne, 2019

Bramston, T., *Robert Menzies: The Art of Politics*, Scribe, Melbourne, 2019

Breen, B., *First to Fight: Australian Diggers, N.Z. Kiwis and U.S. Paratroopers in Vietnam 1965–66*, Allen & Unwin, Sydney, 1988

—— *The Good Neighbour: Australian Peace Support Operations in the Pacific Islands, 1980–2006*, Cambridge University Press, Melbourne, 2006

Bridge, C., *William Hughes Australia: Makers of the Modern World*, Haus Histories, London, 2011

Brown, R.C., *Robert Laird Borden: A Biography*, vol. II, *1914–1937*, Macmillan, Toronto, 1980

Burness, P. (ed.), *The Western Front Diaries of Charles Bean*, NewSouth, Sydney, 2018

Bush, G. and B. Scowcroft, *A World Transformed*, Vintage, New York, 1999

Buszynski, L., *SEATO: The Failure of an Alliance Strategy*, Singapore University Press, Singapore, 1983

Butlin, S.J., *War Economy 1939–1942*, Australian War Memorial, Canberra, 1955

—— and C.B. Schedvin, *War Economy 1942–1945*, Australian War Memorial, Canberra, 1977

Calwell, A.A., *Be Just and Fear Not*, Lloyd O'Neill, Melbourne, 1972

Carey, J., and T. McCrae, *Peacock M.P.*, Rigby, Adelaide, 1982

Carlyon, L., *The Great War*, Macmillan, Sydney, 2006

Carlyon, N., *I Remember Blamey*, Macmillan, Melbourne, 1980

Catton, B., *Grant Takes Command: The Vital Years of the American Civil War*, J.M. Dent & Sons, London, 1970

Chadwick, J., *Sword and Baton: Senior Australian Army Officers from Federation to 2001*, vol. 1, *1900–1939*, Big Sky Publishing, Sydney, 2017

Chandler, A.D. (ed.), *The Papers of Dwight David Eisenhower: The War Years*, vol. 1, Johns Hopkins Press, Baltimore, 1970
Chin Peng, *My Side of History*, Media Masters, Singapore, 2003
Churchill, W.S., *The Second World War*, vol. II, *Their Finest Hour*, Cassell, London, 1949
—— *The Second World War*, vol. III, *The Grand Alliance*, Cassell, London, 1950
—— *The Second World War*, vol. IV, *The Hinge of Fate*, Cassell, London, 1951
Cochrane, P., *Best We Forget: The War for White Australia, 1914–18*, Text Publishing, Melbourne, 2018
Cohen, E., *Supreme Command: Soldiers, Statesmen, and Leadership in Wartime*, The Free Press, New York, 2002
Cohen, R., and C. Gatti, *In the Eye of the Storm: The Life of General H. Norman Schwarzkopf*, Bloomsbury, London, 1991
Connell, J., and M. Roberts, *Wavell: Supreme Commander, 1941–1943*, Collins, London, 1969
Connor, J., *Anzac and Empire: George Foster Pearce and the Foundations of Australian Defence*, Cambridge University Press, Melbourne, 2011
——, P. Stanley and P. Yule, *The War at Home: The Centenary History of Australia and the Great War*, vol. 4, Oxford University Press, Melbourne, 2015
Coombes, D., *The Lionheart: A Life of Lieutenant-General Sir Talbot Hobbs*, Australian Military History Publications, Sydney, 2007
Cosgrove, General P., *My Story*, HarperCollins, Sydney, 2010
Coulthard-Clark, C.D., *A Heritage of Spirit*, Melbourne University Press, Melbourne, 1979
—— *No Australian Need Apply: The Troubled Career of Lieutenant-General Gordon Legge*, Allen & Unwin, Sydney, 1988
—— *The Third Brother: The Royal Australian Air Force, 1921–39*, Allen & Unwin, Sydney, 1991
—— *The RAAF in Vietnam: Australian Air Involvement in the Vietnam War 1962–1975*, Allen & Unwin, Sydney, 1995
Crawley, R., *Climax at Gallipoli: The Failure of the August Offensive*, University of Oklahoma Press, Norman, OK, 2014
Crowley, F.K., *Modern Australia in Documents*, vol. 1, *1901–1939*, Wren, Melbourne, 1973
Cruickshank, C., *Greece, 1940–1941*, Davis-Poynter, London, 1976
Day, D., *The Great Betrayal: Britain, Australia and the Onset of the Pacific War, 1939–42*, Angus & Robertson, Sydney, 1988
—— *Menzies and Churchill at War: A revealing account of the 1941 struggle for power*, Simon & Schuster, Sydney, 2001
—— *John Curtin: A Life*, HarperCollins, Sydney, 2006
—— *Andrew Fisher: Prime Minister of Australia*, Fourth Estate, Sydney, 2008
Dennis, P., and J. Grey, *Emergency and Confrontation: Australian Military Operations in Malaya and Borneo, 1950–1966*, Allen & Unwin, Sydney, 1996
Department of Defence, *The War in Iraq: ADF Operations in the Middle East in 2003*, Department of Defence, Canberra, 2004
Derham, R., *The Silence Ruse: Escape from Gallipoli*, Cliffe Books, Melbourne, 1998
Dilks, D. (ed.), *The Diaries of Sir Alexander Cadogan, 1938–1945*, Cassell, London, 1971

Drea, E.J., *MacArthur's Ultra: Codebreaking and the War against Japan, 1942–1945*, University Press of Kansas, Lawrence, KA, 1992

Dyer, G., *War*, Guild Publishing, London, 1985

Edwards, C., *Bruce of Melbourne: Man of Two Worlds*, Heinemann, London, 1965

Edwards, J., *Curtin's Gift: Reinterpreting Australia's Greatest Prime Minister*, Allen & Unwin, Sydney, 2005

—— *John Curtin's War*, vol. I, *The Coming of War in the Pacific, and Reinventing Australia*, Viking, Melbourne, 2017

—— *John Curtin's War*, vol. II, *Triumph and Decline*, Viking, Melbourne, 2018

Edwards, P., *A Nation at War: Australian Politics, Society and Diplomacy during the Vietnam War 1965–1975*, Allen & Unwin in association with the Australian War Memorial, Canberra, 1997

—— *Arthur Tange: Last of the Mandarins*, Allen & Unwin, Sydney, 2006

—— *Australia and the Vietnam War*, NewSouth, Sydney, 2014

—— with G. Pemberton, *Crises and Commitments: The Politics and Diplomacy of Australia's Involvement in Southeast Asian Conflicts 1948–1965*, Allen & Unwin in association with the Australian War Memorial, Sydney, 1992

Ekins, A. with I. McNeill, *Fighting to the Finish: The Australian Army and the Vietnam War 1968–1975*, Allen & Unwin in association with the Australian War Memorial, Sydney, 2012

Fadden, A., *They Called Me Artie*, Jacaranda Press, Brisbane, 1969

Fahey, J., *Australia's First Spies: The Remarkable Story of Australia's Intelligence Operations, 1901–45*, Allen & Unwin, Sydney, 2018

Fathi, R., *Our Corner of the Somme: Australia at Villers-Bretonneux*, Cambridge University Press, Melbourne, 2019

Fitzhardinge, L.F., *That Fiery Particle, 1862–1914: William Morris Hughes, a political biography*, vol. 1, Angus & Robertson, Sydney, 1964

—— *The Little Digger, 1914–1952: William Morris Hughes, a political biography*, vol. 2, Angus & Robertson, Sydney, 1979

Frame, T., *Pacific Partners: A History of Australian–American Naval Relations*, Hodder & Stoughton, Sydney, 1992

—— *Where Fate Calls: The HMAS* Voyager *Tragedy*, Hodder & Stoughton, Sydney, 1992

—— *The Life and Death of Harold Holt*, Allen & Unwin, Sydney, 2005

Fraser, M., with D. Roberts, *Dangerous Allies*, Melbourne University Press, 2014

Freedman, L., and E. Karsh, *The Gulf Conflict*, Faber & Faber, London, 1995

Frost, F., *Australia's War in Vietnam*, Allen & Unwin, Sydney, 1987

Frühling, S. (ed.), *A History of Australian Strategic Policy*, Defence Publishing Service, Canberra, 2009

Gilbert, M., *Winston S. Churchill*, companion vol. III, part 2, *May 1915–December 1916*, Heinemann, London, 1972

Gill, G.H., *Royal Australian Navy, 1939–1942*, Australian War Memorial, Canberra, 1957

Gillison, D., *Royal Australian Air Force, 1939–1942*, Australian War Memorial, Canberra, 1962

Golding, P.S., *Black Jack McEwen: Political Gladiator*, Melbourne University Press, Melbourne, 1996

Great Britain Cabinet Office, *Principal War Telegrams and Memoranda, 1940–1943, Far East*, KTO Press, Nendeln, Liechtenstein, 1976

Greenwood, G., and C. Grimshaw (eds), *Documents on Australian International Affairs 1901–1918*, Nelson, Melbourne, 1977

Grey, J., *The Commonwealth Armies and the Korean War: An Alliance Study*, Manchester University Press, Manchester, 1988

—— *Australian Brass: The Career of Lieutenant-General Sir Horace Robertson*, Cambridge University Press, Melbourne, 1992

—— *Up Top: The Royal Australian Navy and Southeast Asian conflicts, 1955–1972*, Allen & Unwin, Sydney, 1998

—— *A Soldier's Soldier: A Biography of Lieutenant-General Sir Thomas Daly*, Cambridge University Press, Melbourne, 2013

Hancock, I., *John Gorton: He did it his way*, Hodder, Sydney, 2002

Hancock, V., *Challenge*, Access Press, Perth, 1990

Hankey, Lord, *The Supreme Command, 1914–1918*, vol. 2, George Allen & Unwin, London, 1960

Hasluck, P., *The Government and the People, 1939–1941*, Australian War Memorial, Canberra, 1952

—— *The Government and the People, 1942–1945*, Australian War Memorial, Canberra, 1970

—— *Mucking About: An Autobiography*, University of Western Australia Press, Perth, 1994

—— *The Chance of Politics*, Text Publishing, Melbourne, 1997

Hawke, R., *The Hawke Memoirs*, William Heinemann, Melbourne, 1994

Hazlehurst, C. *Ten Journeys to Cameron's Farm: An Australian tragedy*, ANU E Press, Canberra, 2013

Heinl, R.D. Jr, *Dictionary of Military and Naval Quotations*, United States Naval Institute, Annapolis, MD, 1966

Herington, J., *Air Power over Europe 1944–1945*, Australian War Memorial, Canberra, 1963

Hetherington, J., *Blamey: Controversial Soldier*, Australian War Memorial, Canberra, 1973

Heydon, P., *Quiet Decision: A Study of George Foster Pearce*, Melbourne University Press, Melbourne, 1965

Hill, A.J., *Chauvel of the Light Horse*, Melbourne University Press, Melbourne, 1978

Hilsman, R., *George Bush vs. Saddam Hussein: Military Success! Political Failure?*, Lyford Books, Novato, CA, 1992

Horowitz, I.L., *The War Game: Studies of the New Civilian Militarists*, Ballantine Books, New York, 1963

Horner, D., *Crisis of Command: Australian Generalship and the Japanese Threat, 1941–1943*, Australian National University Press, Canberra, 1978

—— *High Command: Australia and Allied Strategy, 1939–1945*, George Allen & Unwin, Sydney, in association with the Australian War Memorial, Canberra, 1982

—— *Australian Higher Command in the Vietnam War*, Canberra Papers on Strategy and Defence no. 40, Strategic and Defence Studies Centre, Australian National University, Canberra, 1986

—— (ed.) *Duty First: The Royal Australian Regiment in War and Peace*, Allen & Unwin, Sydney, 1990
—— *The Gulf Commitment: The Australian Defence Force's First War*, Melbourne University Press, Melbourne, 1992
—— *The Gunners: A History of Australian Artillery*, Allen & Unwin, Sydney, 1995
—— *Inside the War Cabinet: Directing Australia's War Effort 1939–45*, Allen & Unwin, Sydney, 1996
—— *Blamey: The Commander-in-Chief*, Allen & Unwin, Sydney, 1998
—— *Defence Supremo: Sir Frederick Shedden and the Making of Australian Defence Policy*, Allen & Unwin, Sydney, 2000
—— *The Australian Centenary History of Defence*, vol. 4, *Making the Australian Defence Force*, Oxford University Press, Melbourne, 2001
—— *SAS: Phantoms of War: A History of the Australian Special Air Service*, Allen & Unwin, Sydney, 2002
—— *Strategic Command: General Sir John Wilton and Australia's Asian Wars*, Oxford University Press, Melbourne, 2005
—— *Australia and the 'New World Order': From Peacekeeping to Peace Enforcement, 1988–1991*, Cambridge University Press, Melbourne, 2011
—— *Strategy and Command: Issues in Australia's Twentieth Century Wars*, Cambridge University Press, Melbourne, 2021
—— and J. Connor, *The Good International Citizen: Australian Peacekeeping in Asia, Africa and Europe: 1991–1993*, Cambridge University Press, Melbourne, 2014
Howard, J., *Lazarus Rising: A Personal and Political Autobiography*, HarperCollins, Sydney, 2010
Howson, P., and D. Aitkin (eds), *The Howson Diaries: The Life of Politics*, Viking, Melbourne, 1984
Hudson, W.J., *Billy Hughes in Paris: The Birth of Australian Diplomacy*, Nelson, Melbourne, 1978
Hughes, W.M., *The Splendid Adventure*, Ernest Benn, London, 1929
—— *Policies and Potentates*, Angus & Robertson, Sydney, 1950
Huntington, S., *The Soldier and the State*, Belknap Press, New York, 1957
Hyslop, R., *Australian Naval Administration 1900–1939*, Hawthorn Press, Melbourne, 1973
Inglis, K.S., *Whose ABC? The Australian Broadcasting Corporation, 1983–2002*, Black Inc., Melbourne, 2006
Isaksson, O.H., *Encounters with Asia: A Soldier's Story*, Centre for the Study of Australia–Asia Relations, Griffith University, Brisbane, 1997
James, D.C., *The Years of MacArthur*, vol. II, *1941–1945*, Houghton Mifflin, Boston, MA, 1975
Jones, G., *From Private to Air Marshal*, Greenhouse Publications, Melbourne, 1988
Jose, A.W., *The Royal Australian Navy 1914–1918*, Angus & Robertson, Sydney, 1937
Kelly, P., *The End of Certainty: The Story of the 1980s*, Allen & Unwin, Sydney, 1992
—— *The March of Patriots: The Struggle for Modern Australia*, Melbourne University Press, Melbourne, 2009
Kenney, G.C., *General Kenney Reports*, Duell, Sloan and Pearce, New York, 1949

Kennedy, J., *The Business of War*, Hutchinson, London, 1957

Lax, M., *Malayan Emergency and Indonesian Confrontation*, Big Sky Publishing, Sydney, 2021

Layton, E.T., *"And I Was There": Pearl Harbor and Midway—Breaking the Secrets*, William Morrow, New York, 1985

Lee, D., *Search for Security: The Political Economy of Australia's Postwar Foreign and Defence Policy*, Allen & Unwin, in association with the Department of International Relations, Research School of Pacific and Asian Studies, Australian National University, Canberra, 1995

Lewin, R., *Slim, the Standardbearer: A biography of Field Marshal the Viscount Slim*, Cooper, London, 1976

Lloyd, C., and R. Hall (eds), *Backroom Briefings: John Curtin's War*, National Library of Australia, Canberra, 1997

Lodge, B., *Lavarack: Rival General*, Allen & Unwin, Sydney, 1998

Londey, P., R. Crawley and D. Horner, *The Long Search for Peace: Observer Mission and Beyond, 1947–2006*, Cambridge University Press, Melbourne, 2020

Long, G., *Greece, Crete and Syria*, Australian War Memorial, Canberra, 1953

—— *The Final Campaigns*, Australian War Memorial, Canberra, 1963

—— *The Six Years War: A Concise History of Australia in the 1939–45 War*, Australian War Memorial and Australian Government Publishing Service, Canberra, 1973

Lowe, D., *Menzies and the 'Great World Struggle': Australia's Cold War 1948–1954*, UNSW Press, Sydney, 1999

—— *Australian Between Empires: The Life of Percy Spender*, Routledge, London, 2010

MacArthur, D., *Reminiscences*, McGraw-Hill, New York, 1964

McCarthy, D., *South-West Pacific Area—First Year: Kokoda to Wau*, Australian War Memorial, Canberra, 1959

McCarthy, J., *Australia and Imperial Defence 1918–1939: A Study in Air and Sea Power*, University of Queensland Press, Brisbane, 1976

Macdougall, A.K., *Collins of the* Sydney*: A Life of Vice-Admiral Sir John Collins, KBE, CB, RAN*, Clarion Editions, Mudgee, 2018

McGoldrick, A., *A Memoir of Arabia*, privately published, Canberra, 2010

MacKenzie, S.S., *The Australians at Rabaul*, Angus & Robertson, Sydney, 1927

Macklin, R., *Warrior Elite: Australia's Special Forces, Z Force to the SAS, Intelligence Operations to Cyberwarfare*, Hachette, Sydney, 2015

McNeill, I., *The Team: Australian Army advisers in Vietnam, 1962–1972*, Australian War Memorial, Canberra, 1984

—— *To Long Tan: The Australian Army in the Vietnam War 1950–1966*, Allen & Unwin in association with the Australian War Memorial, Sydney, 1993

——, and A. Ekins, *On the Offensive: The Australian Army in the Vietnam War January 1967–June 1968*, Allen & Unwin in association with the Australian War Memorial, Sydney, 2003

McPhedran, I., *The Amazing SAS: The Inside Story of Australia's Special Forces*, HarperCollins, Sydney, 2005

Marolda, E.J., and R.J. Schneller, *Shield and Sword: The United States Navy and the Persian Gulf War*, Naval Historical Center, Washington DC, 1998

Marr, D., *Barwick*, George Allen & Unwin, Sydney, 1980

Martin, A.W., *Robert Menzies: A Life*, vol. 1, *1894–1943*, Melbourne University Press, Melbourne, 1993

—— *Robert Menzies: A Life*, vol. 2, *1944–1978*, Melbourne University Press, Melbourne, 1999

—— and Hardy, P. (eds), *Dark and Hurrying Days: Menzies' 1941 Diary*, National Library of Australia, Canberra, 1993

Maughan, B., *Tobruk and El Alamein*, Australian War Memorial, Canberra, 1968

Meaney, N., *The Search for Security in the Pacific, 1901–1914*, Sydney University Press, Sydney, 1976

—— *Australia and World Crisis, 1914–1923*, Sydney University Press, Sydney, 2009

Menzies, R.G., *Afternoon Light*, Cassell, Melbourne, 1967

—— *The Measure of the Years*, Cassell, Melbourne, 1970

Middleton, K., *An Unwinnable War: Australia in Afghanistan*, Melbourne University Press, Melbourne, 2011

Millar, T.B., *Australia's Defence*, 2nd edn, Melbourne University Press, Melbourne, 1969

—— (ed.), *Australian Foreign Minister: The Diaries of R.G. Casey 1951–1960*, Collins, London, 1972

Miller, J. Jr, *Cartwheel: The Reduction of Rabaul*, Office of the Chief of Military History, Washington DC, 1959

Milner, S., *Victory in Papua*, Office of the Chief of Military History, Washington DC, 1957

Mordike, J., *An Army for a Nation*, Allen & Unwin, Sydney, 1992

—— *We Should Do This Thing Quietly: Japan and the Great Deception in Australian Defence Policy 1911–1914*, Aerospace Centre, Canberra, 2002

Morton, L., *Strategy and Command: The First Two Years*, Office of the Chief of Military History, Washington DC, 1953

Mullins, P., *Tiberius with a Telephone: The Life and Stories of William McMahon*, Scribe, Melbourne, 2018

Murdoch, J., *Sir Joe: A Political Biography of Sir Joseph Cook*, Minerva Press, London, 1996

Murdoch, K., *The Gallipoli Letter*, with an introduction by M. McKernan, Allen & Unwin, Sydney, 2010

National Institute for Defense Studies, *Japanese Army Operations in the South Pacific Area: New Britain and Papua Campaigns, 1942–43*, trans. S. Bullard, Australian War Memorial, Canberra, 2007

Newton, D., *Hell-bent: Australia's Leap into the Great War*, Scribe, Melbourne, 2014

Oliver, B. (ed.), *1914: Mobilising for the Great War*, Big Sky Publishing, Sydney, 2016

O'Neill, R., *Australia in the Korean War 1950–53*, vol. I, *Strategy and Diplomacy*, Australian War Memorial and Australian Government Publishing Service, Canberra, 1981

—— *Australia in the Korean War 1950–53*, vol. II, *Combat Operations*, Australian War Memorial and Australian Government Publishing Service, Canberra, 1985

Parkin, R., and D. Lee, *Great White Fleet to Coral Sea: Naval Strategy and the Development of Australia–United States Relations, 1900–1945*, Department of Foreign Affairs and Trade, Canberra, 2008

Parkinson, R., *Blood, Toil, Tears and Sweat*, Hart-Davis, McGibbon, London, 1973
Paull, R., *Retreat from Kokoda*, Heinemann, Melbourne, 1958
Pearce, G.F., *Carpenter to Cabinet: Thirty-seven Years of Parliament*, Hutchinson & Co., London, 1951
Pedersen, P., *Monash as Military Commander*, Melbourne University Press, Melbourne, 1985
Pemberton, G., *All the Way: Australia's Road to Vietnam*, Allen & Unwin, Sydney, 1987
Penglase, J., and D. Horner, *When the War Came to Australia: Memories of the Second World War*, Allen & Unwin, Sydney, 1992
Phelps, J., *Australian Code Breakers: Our Top Secret War with the Kaiser's Reich*, HarperCollins, Sydney, 2020
Rayner, H., *Scherger*, Australian War Memorial, Canberra, 1984
Reid, A., *The Gorton Experiment*, Shakespeare Head, Sydney, 1971
Roberts, A., *Leadership in War: Lessons from Those Who Made History*, Allen Lane, London, 2019
Robertson, J., *Anzac and Empire: The Tragedy and Glory of Gallipoli*, Hamlyn, Melbourne, 1990
Robinson, A., *Meeting Saddam's Men: Looking for Iraq's Weapons of Mass Destruction*, Big Sky Publishing, Sydney, 2019
Robson, L.L., *The First A.I.F.: A Study of its Recruitment, 1914–1918*, Melbourne University Press, Melbourne, 1970
Roskill, S., *Hankey: Man of Secrets*, vol. III, Collins, London, 1974
Ross, L., *John Curtin: A Biography*, Macmillan Melbourne, 1977
Rowell, S.F., *Full Circle*, Melbourne University Press, Melbourne, 1974
Scott. E., *Official History of Australia in the War of 1914–1918*, vol. XI, *Australia during the War*, Angus & Robertson, Sydney, 1938
Scott, K., *Gareth Evans*, Allen & Unwin, Sydney, 1999
Serle, G., *John Monash: A Biography*, Melbourne University Press, Melbourne, 1982
Sexton, M., *War for the Asking: Australia's Vietnam Secrets*, Penguin, Melbourne, 1981
Sheffield, G., and G. Till (eds), *The Challenges of High Command: The British Experience*, Palgrave Macmillan, London, 2003
Sheridan, G., *The Partnership: The Inside Story of the US–Australian Alliance under Howard and Bush*, UNSW Press, Sydney, 2006
Smith, V., *A Few Memories of Sir Victor Smith,* Australian Naval Institute, Canberra, 1992
Spartalis, P., *The Diplomatic Battles of Billy Hughes*, Hale & Iremonger, Sydney, 1983
Spender, P.C., *Politics and a Man*, Collins, Sydney, 1972
Stephens, A., *Going Solo: The Royal Australian Air Force, 1946–1971*, Australian Government Publishing Service, Canberra, 1995
—— *The Royal Australian Air Force*, Oxford University Press, Melbourne, 2001
Stevens, D., *In All Respects Ready: Australia's Navy in World War One*, Oxford University Press, Melbourne, 2014
Stevenson, R., *The War with Germany: The Centenary History of Australia and the Great War*, Oxford University Press, Melbourne, 2015
—— *Australia's First Campaign: The Capture of German New Guinea, 1914*, Army History Unit, Canberra, 2021

Stockings, C., *The Making and Breaking of the Post-Federation Australian Army, 1901–09*, Land Warfare Studies Centre, Canberra, 2007
—— *Britannia's Shield: Lieutenant-General Sir Edward Hutton and Late-Victorian Imperial Defence*, Cambridge University Press, Melbourne, 2015
Tange, A., *Defence Policy-making: A Close-up View, 1950–1980, a Personal Memoir*, ed. Peter Edwards, Strategic and Defence Studies Centre, Canberra Papers on Strategy and Defence, no. 169, Australian National University E Press, Canberra, 2008
Tennant, K., *Evatt: Politics and Justice*, Angus & Robertson, Sydney, 1970
Trengove, A., *John Grey Gorton: An Informal Biography*, Cassell, Melbourne, 1969
Tsouras, P.G., *Warriors' Words: A Quotation Book: From Sesostris III to Schwarzkopf, 1871 BC to AD 1991*, Arms & Armour, London, 1992
US Department of Defense, *Conduct of the Persian Gulf War*, Final Report to Congress, Washington DC, April 1992
Waters, C., *Australia and Appeasement: Imperial Foreign Policy and the Origins of World War II*, I.B. Taurus, London, 2012
Watt, A., *Australian Diplomat: Memoirs of Sir Alan Watt*, Angus & Robertson, Sydney, 1972
Weller, P. (ed.), *Caucus Minutes 1901–1949*, Melbourne University Press, Melbourne, 1975
——, J. Scott and B. Stevens, *From Postbox to Powerhouse: A Centenary History of the Department of the Prime Minister and Cabinet*, Allen & Unwin, Sydney, 2011
Whitington, D., *Fifteen Years of the Liberals*, Lansdowne, Melbourne, 1964
Wood, J., *The Forgotten Force: The Australian Military Contribution to the Occupation of Japan, 1945–1952*, Allen & Unwin, Sydney, 1998
—— *Chiefs of the Australian Army: Higher Command of the Australian Military Forces 1901–1914*, Australian Military History Publications, Sydney, 2006
Woodard, G., *Asian Alternatives: Australia's Vietnam Decision and Lessons on Going to War*, Melbourne University Publishing, Melbourne, 2004
Woodward, B., *The Commanders*, Simon & Schuster, New York, 1991
—— *Plan of Attack*, Simon & Schuster, New York, 2004
Woods, K.M., D.D. Palkki and M.E. Stout (eds), *The Saddam Tapes: The Inner Workings of a Tyrant's Regime, 1978–2001*, Cambridge University Press, Cambridge, 2011
Wurth, B., *The Battle for Australia: A Nation and its Leader under Siege*, Macmillan, Sydney, 2013
Younger, R.M., *Keith Murdoch: Founder of a Media Empire*, HarperCollins, Sydney, 2003
Yule, P., *The Long Shadow: Australia's Vietnam Veterans since the War*, NewSouth and the Australian War Memorial, Sydney, 2020

Unpublished monographs

Palazzo, A., 'Deploy, sustain, return', Army Land Warfare Studies Centre, Canberra, 2008
—— 'The Australian Army and the war in Iraq, 2002–2003', Directorate of Research and Analysis, 2011, redacted version released in 2017, smh.com.au/interactive/2017/iraq-dossier, accessed 28 February 2017, see apo.org.au/node/74411

Straczek, J., 'The History of Operation Damask', prepared in Maritime Headquarters and held by Sea Power Centre—Australia

Articles, Book Chapters, etc.

Andrews, E.M., 'Managing the war: The Department of Defence, 1914–1919', in P. Dennis and J. Grey (eds), *1918: Defining Victory*, Army History Unit, Canberra, 1999

Barrie, C., 'A Chief of Defence Force's perspective', in J. Blaxland, M. Fielding and T. Gellerfy (eds), *Niche Wars: Australia in Afghanistan and Iraq, 2011–2014*, Australian National University Press, Canberra, 2020

Beaumont, J., 'Paul Hasluck: The diplomat as minister', in J. Beaumont, C. Waters, D. Lowe and G. Woodard (eds), *Ministers, Mandarins and Diplomats: Australian Foreign Policy Making 1941–1969*, Melbourne University Press, Melbourne, 2003

—— '"Unitedly we have fought": Imperial loyalty and the Australian war effort', *International Affairs*, vol. 90, no. 2, 2014, pp. 397–412

Bridge, C., 'Casey, Menzies and the politics of Australia's participation in the European war, October 1939 to January 1940', *Flinders Journal of History and Politics*, vol. 11, 1985, pp. 79–90

—— 'Appeasement and after: Towards a re-assessment of the Lyons and Menzies governments' defence and foreign policies, 1939–1941', *Australian Journal of Politics and History*, vol. 51, no. 3, 2005, pp. 372–79

Buckley, J.P., 'Sir Frederick Shedden, defence strategist, administrator and public servant', *Defence Force Journal*, January–February 1985, pp. 21–49

Cotton, J., 'After the flood: Foreign policy and the management of intelligence', in J. Cotton and J. Ravenhill (eds), *Trading on Security: Australia in World Affairs 2001–2005*, Oxford University Press, Melbourne, 2007, pp. 329–51

Coulthard-Clark, C., 'Major-General Sir William Throsby Bridges: Australia's first field commander', in D.M. Horner (ed.), *The Commanders: Australian Military Leadership in the Twentieth Century*, George Allen & Unwin, Sydney, 1984

Cuffe, H., 'Plans for peace, fear of war: Defending Australia in 1918', in C. Holbrook and K. Reeves (eds), *The Great War: Aftermath and Commemoration*, UNSW Press, Sydney, 2019, pp. 79–88

Dedman, J.J., 'The return of the AIF from the Middle East', *Australian Journal of Politics and History*, vol. XXI, no. 2, August 1967, pp. 151–64

—— 'Defence policy decisions before Pearl Harbour', *Australian Journal of Politics and History*, vol. XIII, no. 3, December 1967, pp. 331–45

Department of Defence, 'Key elements in the Triennial Reviews of Strategic Guidance since 1945', April 1986

Edwards, P., 'Menzies and the imperial connection, 1939–41', in C. Hazelhurst (ed.), *Australian Conservatism: Essays in Twentieth Century Political History*, ANU Press, Canberra, 1979, pp. 193–212

—— 'Curtin, MacArthur and the "surrender of sovereignty": A historiographical assessment', *Australian Journal of International Affairs*, vol. 55, no. 2, 2001, pp. 175–85

Evans, G., 'The Labor tradition: A view from the 1990s', in D. Lee and C. Waters (eds), *Evatt to Evans: The Labor Tradition in Australian Foreign Policy*, Allen & Unwin, Sydney, 1997, pp. 11–22

Fadden, A., 'Forty days and forty nights: Memoir of a war-time prime minister', *Australian Outlook*, vol. 27, no. 1, April 1973, pp. 3–11

Garrisson, A.D., 'Air Chief Marshal Sir Frederick Scherger, KBE, CB, DSO, AFC. 1904–1984', *Journal of the Royal United Services Institute of Australia*, vol. 6, no. 2, 1984, pp. 2–4

Hill, R., 'A minister's perspective', in J. Blaxland, M. Fielding and T. Gellerfy (eds), *Niche Wars: Australia in Afghanistan and Iraq, 2011–2014*, Australian National University Press, Canberra, 2020, pp. 21–30

Horner, D., 'Australian estimates of the Japanese threat, 1905–1941', in P. Towle (ed.), *Estimating Foreign Military Power*, Croom Helm, London, 1982, pp. 139–71

—— 'Australian higher command in the Korean War: The experience of Brigadier John Wilton', in J. Blaxland, M. Kelly and L. Brewin Higgins (eds), *In from the Cold: Reflections on Australia's Korean War*, ANU Press, Canberra, 2020, pp. 165–82

—— 'Why was 5 RAR stationed at Nui Dat?', in R. Boxall and R. O'Neill (eds), *Vietnam Vanguard: The 5th Battalion's Approach to Counter-insurgency, 1966*, ANU Press, Canberra, 2020, pp. 21–44

Howard, J., 'The army and the national interest', in T. Frame and A. Palazzo (eds), *On Ops: Lessons and Challenges for the Australian Army since East Timor*, UNSW Press, Sydney, 2016, pp. 18–32

Hyslop, R., 'The Council of Defence 1905–1939', *Canberra Historical Journal*, no. 27, March 1991, pp. 40–46

Lee, D., 'The national security planning and defence preparations of the Menzies government, 1950–1953', *War & Society*, vol. 10, no. 2, October 1992, pp. 119–38

Lowe, D., 'Menzies, memory and Britain in the 1950s', in K. Darian-Smith (ed.), *Working Papers in Australian Studies Nos 88–96*, Sir Robert Menzies Centre for Australian Studies, London, 1994

McCarthy, J.M., 'The defence of Australia and the Empire Air Training Scheme: 1939–1942', *Australian Journal of Politics and History*, vol. XX, no. 3, December 1974, pp. 326–34

McDonald, M. and M. Merefield, 'How was Howard's war possible? Winning the war position over Iraq', *Australian Journal of International Affairs*, vol. 64, no. 2, 2010, pp. 186–204

McGinley, G., 'Divergent paths: problems of command and strategy in Anglo-Australasian naval operations in the Asia-Pacific (August–November 1914)', in D. Stevens and J. Reeve (eds), *Southern Trident: Strategy, History and the Rise of Australian Naval Power*, Allen & Unwin, Sydney, 2001, pp. 242–61

Maclean, P., 'An almost universal scheme of national service in Australia in the 1950s', *Australian Journal of Politics and History*, vol. 52, no. 3, 2006, pp. 378–97

Mallett, R., 'The preparation and deployment of the Australian naval and military expeditionary force', in P. Dennis and J. Grey (eds), *Battles Near and Far: A Century of Overseas Deployment*, Army History Unit, Canberra, 2005, pp. 21–32

Mansfield, G., '"Unbounded enthusiasm": Australian historians and the outbreak of the Great War', *Australian Journal of Politics and History*, vol. 53, no. 3, 2007, pp. 360–74

Marchant, S., 'Millen, Edward Davis (1860–1923)', in A. Millar (ed.), *The Biographical*

Dictionary of the Australian Senate, vol. 1, Melbourne University Press. Melbourne, 2000, pp. 18–22

Martin, A.W., 'Mr Menzies' anticommunism', *Quadrant*, vol. 40, no. 5, May 1996, pp. 47–56

Meaney, N., 'The first high commissioners: George Reid and Andrew Fisher', in C. Bridge, F. Bongiorno and D. Lee (eds), *The High Commissioners: Australia's Representatives in the United Kingdom, 1910–2010*, Department of Foreign Affairs and Trade, Canberra, 2010, pp. 36–55

Moses, J.A., 'Gallipoli or other people's wars revisited: Sundry reflections on ANZAC: Review article', *Australian Journal of Politics and History*, vol. 57, no. 3, 2011, pp. 434–42

Newton, D., 'Choosing war, and choosing war aims: British and Australian decision-making, 1914–1918', in P. Stanley (ed.), *Why Did Australia Go to the Great War?* Occasional Papers Series, no. 8, University of New South Wales, Canberra, 2018, pp. 17–24

Oliver, B., '"Our last man and our last shilling": The Australian Labor Party's approach to war in 1914', in B. Oliver (ed.), *1914: Mobilising for the Great War*, Big Sky Publishing, Sydney, 2016, pp. 38–55

Overlack, P., 'German commerce warfare planning for the Australian Station 1900–1914', *War & Society*, vol. 14, no. 1, May 1996, pp. 17–48

Palazzo, A., 'Iraq and the politics of alliance relationships', in T. Frame (ed.), *Trials and Transformations, 2001–2004: The Howard Government*, vol. III, UNSW Press, Sydney, 2019, pp. 235–47

Pugsley, C., 'At the Empire's call: New Zealand Expeditionary Force planning, 1901–1918', in J.A. Moses and C. Pugsley (eds), *The German Empire and Britain's Pacific Dominions, 1871–1919: Essays on the Role of Australia and New Zealand in World Politics in the Age of Imperialism*, Regina Books, Claremont, California, 2000, pp. 221–38

Rayner, H., 'Air Chief Marshal Sir Frederick Scherger: Chairman, Chiefs of Staff Committee', in D.M. Horner (ed.), *The Commanders: Australian Military Leadership in the Twentieth Century*, George Allen & Unwin, Sydney, 1984, pp. 298–315

Rowell, S., 'General Sturdee and the Australian Army', *Australian Army Journal*, August 1966, pp. 279–86

Sheffield, G., 'The challenges of high command in the twentieth century', in G. Sheffield and G. Till (eds), *The Challenges of High Command: The British Experience*, Palgrave Macmillan, London, 2003, pp. 1–12

Smith, R., 'A departmental secretary's perspective', in J. Blaxland, M. Fielding and T. Gellerfy (eds), *Niche Wars: Australia in Afghanistan and Iraq, 2011–2014*, Australian National University Press, Canberra, 2020

Stevens, D., '"Defend the north": Commander Thring, Captain Hughes-Onslow and the beginnings of Australian naval strategic thought', in D. Stevens and J. Reeve (eds), *Southern Trident: Strategy, History and the Rise of Australian Naval Power*, Allen & Unwin, Sydney, 2001, pp. 225–41

Umetsu, H., 'The origins of the British Commonwealth Strategic Reserve: The UK proposal to revitalise ANZAM and the increased Australian defence commitment

to Malaya', *Australian Journal of Politics and History*, vol. 50, no. 4, 2004, pp. 509–25
Viney, Hannah, 'With one voice, one heartbeat', *Wartime*, no 97, Spring 2021, pp. 58–62.
Webster, S.D., 'Vice-Admiral Sir William Creswell: Member of the Australian Naval Board, 1911–1919', in D.M. Horner (ed.), *The Commanders: Australian military leadership in the twentieth century*, George Allen & Unwin, Sydney, 1984, pp. 44–59
Wesley, M., 'Managing the region: The coalition approach', in T. Frame (ed.), *Back from the Brink, 1997–2001: The Howard Government*, vol. II, UNSW Press, Sydney, 2018, pp. 199–210
White, H., 'Mr Howard goes to Washington: The U.S. and Australia in the Age of Terror', *Comparative Connections*, vol. 5, no. 2, July 2003, cc.pacforum.org/2003/07/mr-howard-goes-washington-u-s-australia-age-terror
—— 'Security, defence and terrorism', in J. Cotton and J. Ravenhill (eds), *Trading on Alliance Security: Australia in World Affairs 2001–2005*, Oxford University Press, Melbourne, 2007, pp. 173–91
—— 'Defence policy: The making of a reputation', in T. Frame (ed.), *Back from the Brink, 1997–2001: The Howard Government*, vol. II, UNSW Press, Sydney, 2018, pp. 136–42
Woodard, G., 'Australia's war in Vietnam: Debate without end', *Australian Journal of International Affairs*, vol. 71, no. 2, 2017, pp. 216–30

Archival Records

Archival records held in government and private archives are indicated in the footnotes by the name of the archive in abbreviated or short form and, when appropriate, the record series.

AWM: Australian War Memorial, Canberra
CCOSC: Records of the Chairman Chiefs of Staff Committee held at Defence Archives, Queanbeyan, but not accessioned into an archival series
Defence: Department of Defence Archives, Queanbeyan, New South Wales
MMMA: MacArthur Memorial Military Archives, Norfolk, Virginia
NAA: National Archives of Australia
NARA: National Archives and Records Administration, Washington DC
SPC-A: Sea Power Centre–Australia, Canberra
TNA: The National Archives, Kew, UK

Private Papers

Alanbrooke Papers: Papers of Field Marshal Viscount Alanbrooke, Liddell Hart Centre for Military Archives, King's College London
Bean Diary and Papers: Papers of C.E.W. Bean, AWM, PR00283
Berryman Diary: Diary of Lieutenant General Sir Frank Berryman, AWM, PR 84
Birdwood Papers: Papers of Field Marshal Lord Birdwood, AWM, 3DRL 3376
F.T. Smith Reports: Reports of Confidential Press Conferences given by Curtin, 1942–45, NLA, MS 4675
Haig Diary, Diary of Field Marshal Viscount Haig, National Library of Scotland

Hobbs Diary: Papers of Lieutenant General Sir Talbot Hobbs, AWM, PR 82/153
Hughes Papers, Papers of Rt Hon. W.M. Hughes, NLA, MS 1538
Kiggell Papers, Papers of Lieutenant General Sir Launcelot Kiggell, Liddell Hart Centre for Military Archives, King's College London
Lloyd George Papers, Papers of Earl Lloyd George, House of Lords Records Office, London
Long, Gavin, Notebooks, diaries and correspondence, AWM, PR88/072
Monash Papers: Papers of General Sir John Monash, AWM, 3DRL 2316
Monash Papers: Papers of General Sir John Monash, NLA, MS 1884
Murdoch Papers: Papers of Keith Arthur Murdoch, AWM, 3DRL 2925
Murdoch Papers: Papers of Keith Arthur Murdoch, NLA, MS 2823
Novar Papers: Papers of Lord Novar, AWM, 3DRL 2574
Pearce Papers: Papers of Sir George Pearce, AWM, 3DRL 2222
Robertson Papers, Papers of Field Marshal Sir William Robertson, Liddell Hart Centre for Military Archives, London
Rosenthal Diary: Papers of Major General Sir Charles Rosenthal, AWM, PR90/12
Shedden Manuscript: unpublished manuscript of 'The history of Australian defence policy' held across numerous files in NAA: A5954; consolidated copy held by author
Spender Papers: Papers of Sir Percy Spender, NLA, MS 4875
Vincent Papers: Papers of Major General D. Vincent (held privately)
Westmoreland Diary: Diary of General William C. Westmoreland, US Army Center of Military History
Wilmot Papers: Papers of Chester Wilmot, Liddell Hart Centre for Military Archives, King's College London
Wilton Diary: Diary of General Sir John Wilton, Wilton Papers, Australian Defence Force Academy Library, Canberra
Wilton Transcript: Transcript of interviews with General Sir John Wilton, August 1978–January 1980, held by author

Interviews

Baker, Major General J.S., with author, 22 May 1991
Beazley, the Hon. Kim, with author, 23 May 2007
Bland, Sir Henry, with author, 29 April 1986
Buckley, Colonel J.P., with author, 20 August 1974
Burrell, Vice-Admiral Sir Henry, with author, 1 February 1979
Carwardine, Rear Admiral A.M. (Gerry), with author, 6 March 2007
Chalmers, Commodore D.B., with author, 21 October, 26 November 1991
Collins, Vice-Admiral Sir John, with author, 9 October 1978
Daly, Lieutenant General Sir Thomas, interview for Army Historical Programme, 22 November 1974, 4 June 1975, AWM 107
Daly, Lieutenant General Sir Thomas, with author, 26 November 1985
d'Hagé, Brigadier A.S., with author, 20 November 1991
Dibb, Professor P., with author, 20 December 1991
Domney, M.F., with author, 22 May 1991

Fairhall, the Hon. Sir Allen, with author, 21 March 2002
Forbes, the Hon. Dr James, with author, 21 February 2003
Fraser, Major General C.A.E., with author, 10 August 1986
Fraser, the Rt Hon. Malcolm, with author, 18 November 2002
Hay, Major General R.A., with author, 5 November 1985
Howson, the Hon. Peter, with author, 25 March 2003
Isaksson, Brigadier O.H., with author, 15 July 2002
Jackson, Brigadier O.D., interview for Army Historical Programme, 9 March 1972, AWM 107
Jones, Air Marshal Sir George, with author, 24 January 1979
Latham, Group Captain J.S., with I.G. McNeill, 11 January 1983
MacDonald, General Sir Arthur, with author, 13 December 1985
Mackay, Major General K., interview for Army Historical Programme, 8 March 1972, AWM 107
Mackay, Major General K., with author, 10 October 1985
McNicoll, Vice-Admiral Sir Alan, with author, 6 March 1986
Major, K.W., with author, 7 April 1986
Ray, Senator R.F., with author, 19 June 1991
Salmon, Brigadier J.R., with author, 28 July 1986
Smith, Admiral Sir Victor, with author, 6 November 1985
Tange, Sir Arthur, with author, 4 March 1986, 10 April 1986
Taylor, Rear Admiral R.G., with author, 3 June 1991
Vincent, Major General D., interview for Army Historical Programme, 20 March 1971, AWM 107
Wilton, General Sir John, interview for Army Historical Programme, 9, 13, 14 September 1976, AWM 107
Woolrych, Rear Admiral G.J.H., with author, 19 March 2003
Wright, B.J.F., with author, 12 October 1978

Theses

Hamill, I., 'The imperial commitment: the Singapore Strategy in the defence of Australia and New Zealand 1939–1945', MA thesis, Australian National University, 1974
Moreen, D., 'In Australia's own interests: Australian foreign policy during Confrontation 1963–1966', PhD thesis, University of New England, 2000
Verney, G., 'The army high command and Australian defence policy, 1901–1918', PhD thesis, University of Sydney, 1985

Index

Abrams, Gen Creighton 306, 308, 309, 314, 323
Acheson, Dean 230, 231
Advisory War Council 391, 394
  Curtin 141–4, 150, 151, 154, 155, 158, 160, 163, 164, 167, 169, 172, 176
  Menzies 107–10, 112, 122, 124–7, 208, 394
Afghanistan War 6, 326, 356, 357, 362–6, 376, 389
Air Board 196
Aitchison, Ray 281
al-Qaeda 362, 363, 365, 366
Alexander, Joe 161
Alexander, Lord 232
Allen, Maj Gen Arthur 167
Amery, Leo 64
Anderson, David 12, 255, 270
Anderson, John 360
Anderson, Brig Gen Robert (Mac) 49, 51, 55, 57, 59
Andrews, Eric 22, 41, 53
Anthony, HL (Larry) 235
Anzac Pact 186
ANZAM region 212, 214, 222, 231, 233, 234, 237, 245, 259
ANZUS Council 230, 248, 259
ANZUS Treaty 222, 224, 229–31, 245, 334, 362, 363
Armitage, Richard 373
Ashmead-Bartlett, Ellis 32, 36, 37, 40
Asquith, Herbert 36–7, 47, 53
atomic bomb tests 231, 234
Attlee, Clement 222
Auchinleck, FM Claude 134, 135, 136
Augmented Chiefs of Staff Committee 329, 391
Australian and New Zealand Army Corps (ANZAC) 30
  1st Anzac Corps 45, 61, 63, 65
  2nd Anzac Corps 45, 61, 63, 64, 65
Australian Army Force Vietnam (AAFV) 275, 282, 289
Australian Army Training Team Vietnam (AATTV) 248, 249, 254–6, 266, 323
Australian Corps 45–7, 50, 60–5, 76–8
Australian Defence Force (ADF) 327, 328, 354, 367, 376, 385
Australian Imperial Force (1st AIF)
  1st Division 31, 33, 34, 44, 45, 50
  2nd Division 34, 44, 45, 50, 60
  3rd Division 44, 49, 51, 54, 63, 69
  4th Division 44, 45, 50, 55, 60, 63, 64, 69
  5th Division 43, 45, 50, 55, 70
  6th Division 54, 61
  'Australianisation' of command and staff 34
  British authority over 30–1, 37, 392
  command of 45–50, 66–75, 392
  expansion under Hughes 42–5
  formation 23–31
  leave for troops 76, 392
  light horse brigades 54
  Monash in command 68–78, 392
Australian Imperial Force (2nd AIF)
  1st Australian Corps 197, 198
  6th Division 91, 93–7, 111, 114, 122, 148, 152, 153, 155, 166, 190, 191, 198, 199, 202
  7th Division 100, 103–5, 108, 117, 130, 132, 147, 148, 151, 152, 153, 155, 163, 190, 191, 197, 198, 200
  8th Division 100, 105, 109, 126–8, 144, 149
  9th Division 130, 134, 135, 136, 155, 160, 190, 191, 197, 198
  Anzac Corps 122
  Blamey in command 98, 112–22, 132–6, 392
  excessive pay allegations 93

Australian Imperial Force (2nd AIF) *continued*
  maintaining integrity of 113–15
  sending overseas 93–9
  training 101, 112
Australian involvement in wars 1–2
Australian Military Forces (AMF) 171–3
Australian Naval and Military Expeditionary Force 24
Australian War Cabinet (WWII) 391
  Curtin 140–3, 146, 148, 150–5, 163, 178–84, 192–7, 200, 202
  Menzies 86–106, 109, 119–22, 126–9, 132, 136, 207, 208, 272
Ayers, AJ (Tony) 329, 341

Baker, James 341, 344, 347, 348, 349
Baker, Gen John 329, 352
Barrie, Adm Chris 361, 363, 366, 367, 369, 370
Barton Rod 393
Barwick, Garfield 242, 246, 248, 250
Beale, Howard 225, 247
Bean, Charles 11, 16, 23, 36, 46, 57, 68, 70, 71, 74, 78, 98, 102
Beasley, John (Jack) 107, 125, 140, 141, 151, 167, 201, 202
Beaumont, Adm Alan 329, 338, 343
Beaumont, Joan 263
Beazley, Kim 327, 328, 334, 352, 364, 378
Ben Gurion, David 3
Bennett, Lt Gen H Gordon 144, 167
Betts, Judith 377
Bin Laden, Osama 362, 364
Birdwood, Gen William 30, 34–5, 42–51, 55–77, 82–3, 98, 392
Bladin, AVM Francis 197
Blair, Tony 379, 381
Blamey, Gen Thomas 91, 98, 103, 112–22, 132–6, 154–203, 392
  AIF command 98, 112–22, 132–6, 190, 282, 392
  New Guinea and Bougainville campaigns 186, 199, 203, 291
  Second World War 91, 98, 103, 112–22, 132–6, 154–203, 208, 209
  visiting US and Britain 187–9
Bland, Henry 300–1, 304, 305, 309, 313, 314, 318
Blewett, Neil 349
Blix, Hans 380
Bonaparte, Napoleon 3
Bonar Law, Andrew 37
Bonser, R Adm Mark 370, 380
Borden, Robert 61, 71–2
Borneo 198–203, 241, 259, 264–5, 272, 281
Bornholt, Brig Gary 369
Bosnia 4
Bostock, AVM William 109, 159–60, 195–7
Boucher, R Adm Maitland 90, 94
Bouchier, AVM Cecil 226
Bougainville 203, 290, 359, 360
  Peace Monitoring Group 359
  Second World War 186, 190, 191, 197, 199, 392
Bowden, Vivian 145, 146
Bridgeford, Lt Gen William 226
Bridges, Maj Gen William 13, 19, 22–4, 28, 30–3, 44
British Army Council 30, 51, 54, 62, 63
British Commonwealth Occupation Force (BCOF) 211, 226
British War Cabinet 3, 49, 97, 115, 117, 119–22, 130–1, 133, 137
Brooke, Gen Alan 147, 188
Brooke-Popham, ACM Robert 126
Brown, Allen 208, 237
Brown, Wallace 289
Bruce, Stanley 89, 90
Bruche, Maj Gen Julius 74
Brunei 251
Bullecourt 60, 61, 64, 73
Bundy, William 262, 263, 268
Bunting, John 244, 292, 293, 297, 300
Burma 147–52
Burnett, ACM Charles 92, 124, 138, 142, 149, 159, 195
Burnett, Capt Joseph 109
Burrell, V Adm Henry 124, 127, 128
Burton, John 209
Bury, Les 280
Bush, George HW 331, 332, 334, 337, 342, 343, 347, 349, 354
Bush, George W 363, 366, 368, 373, 379, 381–3
Butlin, SJ 183
Button, John 336, 344, 349

Cabinet Committee on Defence Preparations 225, 391
Cabinet Policy Unit 377
Cadogan, Alexander 129, 131
Calvert, Ashton 377

Calwell, Arthur 141, 166, 333
Cameron, Archie 103, 106
Cameron, Clyde 212
Carlyon, Les 69
Carrington, Lord 317
Carwardine, R Adm AM (Gerry) 332–3, 354
Casablanca conference 176
Casey, Richard 86–7, 207, 214, 224, 227
  Second World War 86–7, 93–6, 103, 124, 132, 144
  South-East Asia 230, 236
Cassels, FM James 227
Central Bureau 156
Chalmers, V Adm Don 339, 342, 348
Chamberlain, Neville 85, 94, 103
Chauvel, Gen Harry 34, 43, 54
Cheney, Dick 341, 367
Chief of the Defence Force (CDF) 328–30, 361, 363, 370, 391
Chiefs of Staff Committee 328–30, 391
  Korean War 227
  Second World War 163, 208
  Vietnam War 242–4, 269, 287, 289, 309, 328, 392
Chifley, JB (Ben) 140, 200, 201, 202, 211, 213
Chilcot, John 387
Chin Peng 239
China, People's Republic of 207, 210, 222
Churchill, Jack 49
Churchill, Winston 3, 4, 11, 49, 103–52
  books about 3
  Curtin and 144–52, 170, 175–8, 185–8
  First World War 11, 29
  Menzies and 113–22, 130–2
  Pacific defence policy 231, 236, 237
  Second World War 3, 96, 103–22, 130–8, 144 52, 170, 175 8, 185 8, 191, 196
Citizen Military Forces (CMF) 19, 21, 171–3, 217, 220
Clemenceau, Georges 1, 3
Clifford, Clark 295, 297
Clinton, Bill 358
Coates, Lt Gen John 329
Cohen, Eliot 3, 325
Cold War 206–7, 210, 216, 221–3, 233
Coles, Arthur 169
Collins, V Adm John 88, 195, 208, 209, 224, 227, 228
Colonial Office 30, 67
Colvin, Adm Ragnar 88, 90, 91, 100, 101, 124, 133, 194
Commander, Australia Force Vietnam (COMAFV) 284–6, 292–4, 302, 309, 315, 316, 325, 392
Committee of Imperial Defence 93, 94
Commonwealth Prime Ministers' Conference 186, 221, 236
communism 206–7, 210–11, 234, 240, 248, 266
Communist Party of Australia 206, 207, 210, 221
  attempts to ban 210, 221, 223
compulsory military training 33, 93, 171, 217, 258
compulsory service, Deakin 17, 18
Connor, John 82
conscription
  Curtin 171–3
  First World War 36, 37, 39, 51–4, 65–6, 171
  Fisher opposing 28, 37
  Hughes 39, 51–4, 65–6, 171, 394
  National Service scheme 220, 233, 241, 261
  referenda 39, 52–4, 65–6
  Second World War 171–3
  Vietnam War 240, 256–61
Cook, Joseph 4, 10–26, 53, 59, 66, 71, 74, 75
  conscription debate 52
  defence minister 4
  deputy prime minister 53, 59, 66, 74, 79
  navy minister 53, 66
  prime minister 4 10–11, 15–17, 20–1, 25–6
Cook, Michael 331, 347, 349
Coral Sea, Battle of 160
Coronel, Battle of 29
Cosgrove, Gen Peter 361, 370, 372, 375, 380, 381, 385
Costello, Peter 360
Coulthard-Clark, Chris 23
Council of Defence 14, 31, 217
Cox, E Harold 150, 161
Cox, Gen (Herbert) Vaughan 55
Crace, V Adm John 194
Cranborne, Lord 123, 135, 137
Crean, Simon 378
Creswell, V Adm William 12–13, 15, 16, 19, 21, 29, 31
Cross, Ronald 152

Crutchley, Adm Victor 194, 195
Currie, Gen Arthur 63, 68, 71
Curtin, John 3, 93, 106–8, 112, 124–8, 136–205, 222, 391–3
Advisory War Council 107–8, 112, 124–6, 141, 391, 394
books about 3
prime minister 136, 137, 140–205
relationship with MacArthur 155, 161, 168, 178, 191, 203, 391
Second World War 93, 106–8, 112, 124–8, 136–205, 222, 391–3
visiting US and Britain 187–9, 196

D Day landings 189
Daly, Lt Gen Thomas 227, 285, 317–21
Korean War 227
Vietnam War 285, 288, 290, 293–8, 301, 303, 307, 310, 317–21
Dardanelles Army 42
Dardanelles Commission 50
Darwin bombing 148, 151
Day, David 28, 131
De Gaule, Charles 3
Deakin, Alfred 11, 17, 18
Dedman, John 99, 141, 150
Defence (Citizen Military Forces) Act 1943 172
Defence Committee 391
Indonesian Confrontation 251–6
Korean War 218, 224
Malayan Emergency 209, 212, 214–15
Second World War 94, 131, 179, 192, 193
Vietnam War 244, 249, 254, 255, 258, 263, 268, 275, 282, 293–5, 304, 319, 330
Defence Intelligence Organisation (DIO) 352, 362, 386
Delahunty, Maj Noel 254, 255
Derby, Lord 65
D'Este, Carlo 3
d'Hagé, Brig Adrian 351
Dibb, Paul 339
Diem, Ngo Dinh 248
Dill, FM John 116, 118, 120, 121
Dodds, Maj Gen Thomas 33–5, 43, 44, 55, 59, 60
Doolan, R Adm Ken 329, 336, 337, 339, 340, 342, 348, 392
Douglas-Home, Alec 253
Dowling V Adm Roy 242, 246
Downer, Alexander 360, 362, 373
Drake-Brockman, Tom 314
Drakeford, Arthur 140, 159, 169, 195, 196
Drummond, AM Peter 196
Duffy, Michael 330, 332, 336, 349
Dulles, John Foster 222, 234
Durnford, V Adm John 133, 142

East Timor 359–61, 371
INTERFET operation 359, 361, 371
Eden, Anthony 94, 116, 120, 122
Edwards, John 103, 119, 147, 162, 168, 172, 188, 191
Edwards, Peter 97, 159, 213, 239, 264, 267, 269, 271–3, 293, 297, 310, 312, 324
Eisenhower, Dwight 3
Empire Air Training Scheme 92, 95, 98
Evans, Gareth 327, 328, 330, 333–51, 354
Evatt, HV (Bert) 140–52, 237, 334
Korean War 215
Malayan Emergency 209, 213, 333
opposing Far East Strategic Reserve 237
Second World War 140, 141, 145–7, 151, 152, 158, 177, 178, 186, 200
United Nations 334
Ewell, Lt Gen Julian 315

Fadden, Arthur 104, 106, 112, 118–29, 140, 172
acting prime minister 118, 119
Advisory War Council 107, 122, 124–9, 141, 151, 181
Cabinet Committee on Defence Preparations 225
deputy prime minister 112, 207, 218
Korean War 218, 219
prime minister 133, 135, 136
Second World War 104, 106, 112, 118–29, 133–41, 151, 172
treasurer 106, 225
War Cabinet 104, 106, 129
Fairbairn, James 87, 92, 104
Fairhall, Allen 250, 280–1, 288, 291–308, 313, 314, 322, 324
Far East Strategic Reserve 232, 233, 236–9, 241, 248
Farncombe, R Adm Harold 195
Farquarson, John 244
Felt, Adm Harry 248
Ferdinand, Archduke Franz 10

Ferguson, Ronald Munro *see* Munro Ferguson, Ronald
Fiddes, George 63
First World War 1, 5, 6, 9–83, 390
  AIF *see* Australian Imperial Force (1st AIF)
  armistice 78–80
  Australia automatically at war 9
  Cook government 10–26
  cost to Australia 81
  decision-makers 10–15
  Expeditionary Forces 20–32, 36
  Fisher government 26–38
  Hughes government 39–83
  imperative to support Britain 16–20
  lack of consultation by Britain 29, 30, 32, 41, 67
  preliminary measures 15–16
  universal training scheme 18, 19, 24, 27
Fisher, Andrew 11, 18–20, 26–38, 40, 47–50
  attitude to war 27
  high commissioner 37, 47–50, 53, 62
  opposing conscription 28, 37
  prime minister 26–38
Five Power Staff Agency 235
Flanders 58, 61, 63, 72, 73
Flood, Philip 387
Foll, Hattil (Harry) 87, 119
Forbes, James (Jim) 256, 260, 261, 276, 278, 281
Forde, Francis (Frank) 107, 140, 141, 146, 150, 154, 166, 169, 200
Foreign Affairs and Defence (FAD) Committee 250–3, 264–70, 278, 280, 287, 288, 295, 297, 303, 304, 391
Forrest, John 66
Forward Defence policy 233
Foster, Brig Gen Hubert 44, 46, 51, 54, 60, 61
Francis, Josiah 227
Franks, Gen Tommy 363, 370
Fraser, Maj Gen Colin 315, 317, 320
Fraser, James 199, 392
Fraser, Malcolm 281, 283, 285, 300, 302, 308, 309, 313–25, 392
Fraser, Peter 125
Free Traders 17
Freeth, Gordon 308
Freyberg, Lt Gen Bernard 117
Funnell, AM Ray 329, 341

Gallipoli 6, 32–7, 40–3, 102, 290
Gellibrand, Maj Gen John 69, 74
Gill, George Hermon 134
Gillespie, Lt Gen Ken 364, 365, 367, 369, 372, 380
Glasgow, Maj Gen William 69
Goble, AVM Stanley 88, 89, 90, 92, 94
Godley, Gen Alexander 20, 30, 42, 43, 45, 61
Gordon, Maj Gen Joseph 13, 14, 20
Gorton, Bettina 299, 305
Gorton, John 4, 5, 280, 294, 298–322, 391
  Civil Action affair 319–22
  Nixon and 306–10
  Vietnam War 280, 294, 298–322, 325
  visiting troops in Vietnam 305–6
Gough, Gen Hubert 61
Graham, Maj Gen Stuart 307
Grant, Gen Ulysses 3
Gration, Gen Peter 328, 329, 335–43, 348, 349, 352–4
Greek campaign 115–23, 132, 133, 290, 390
Griffiths, Brig Gen Thomas 59
Guam doctrine 307
Gulf War 6, 326–55, 390, 392, 394
  Hawke government 327–55, 394
  information management 351–3, 380
  military advisers 328–30
  naval force 332–9
  UN Security Council resolution 338, 343–7
Gullett, Henry 87, 100, 104

Habibie, President BJ 359
Haig, Gen Douglas 46–51, 56, 61–5, 68, 71, 73, 75, 77, 105
Haining, Gen Robert 118
Hamilton, Adm Louis 195
Hamilton, Gen Ian 37
Hancock, Ian 280, 305
Hancock, AM Valston 243–4, 256
Hankey, Maurice 3, 86
Hannah, AM Colin 317, 321
Hannan, Brig Michael 380
Harding FM John 232
Hardman, ACM Donald 227–8
Harkins, Gen Paul 247, 254
Harrington, VA Hastings (Arch) 243, 244
Harrison, Eric 166, 207–8, 225
Hasluck, Paul 242, 256–70, 299, 308
  defence minister 242, 256
  external affairs minister 242, 250, 257, 277, 279

Hasluck, Paul *continued*
governor-general 308
Second World War historian 85, 104, 106, 110, 126, 183, 204, 242
Vietnam War 256–8, 262, 264–70, 277, 279, 280, 292, 293, 296, 306, 324
Hawke, Allan 362
Hawke, Bob 327–55, 362, 391, 394
Hay, Maj Gen Robert 315
Healey, Denis 283
Henderson, Maj Gen William 319
Herington, John 194
Hewitt, AVM JE (Joe) 197
Hewitt, Lennox 300, 304
Hewson, John 351
Hicks, Edwin (Ted) 244, 256, 274, 278, 279, 287, 288, 293, 295
Hill, Alec 33
Hill, David 352
Hill, Robert 341, 351, 360, 366, 368–70, 373
Hindenburg Line 60, 73, 77, 78
Hitler, Adolf 3, 85, 90
HMAS *Adelaide* 108, 338, 339, 341, 343
HMAS *Anzac* 364, 374, 383
HMAS *Australia* 25, 29, 108
HMAS *Brisbane* 340, 348, 350
HMAS *Darwin* 338, 339, 340, 343, 357, 374
HMAS *Hobart* 294
HMAS *Kanimbla* 374, 378
HMAS *Melbourne* 28, 286
HMAS *Perth* 89, 153
HMAS *Success* 338, 341
HMAS *Sydney* 28, 112, 229, 340, 350
HMAS *Voyager* 286
HMAS *Waterhen* 379
HMAS *Westralia* 341, 357
HMS *Prince of Wales* 138, 142
HMS *Repulse* 138, 142
Hobbs, Lt Gen JJ Talbot 55, 70, 73, 74, 78
Holland, Maj Gen Charles 370
Holland, Sidney 231
Holloway, EJ (Jack) 181
Holman, William 36
Holmes, Maj Gen William 24, 25, 43, 55, 69
Holt, Harold 214, 241, 250, 280, 288–98, 300, 324
FAD Committee 250
National Service scheme 241
prime minister 280, 283, 288–98
Vietnam War 241, 268, 272, 279–81, 288–98, 324
visiting troops in Vietnam 289–91
visiting US and UK 291–8
Houston, ACM Angus 361, 364, 375
Howard, John 356–89, 391, 394
Afghanistan War 356, 357, 362–6, 376, 389
government 359–61
Iraq War 356–9, 362, 376–89
Howse, Maj Gen Neville 68
Howson, Peter 260, 270, 286, 304, 310
Hudson, Adm Michael 328–9, 339, 342
Hudson, WJ (Bill) 80
Hughes, Maj Gen James (Jim) 289
Hughes, William (Billy) 5, 18, 20, 27, 31, 37–83, 392
Advisory War Council 141, 151, 163–4, 167, 181
AIF command and 45–58, 392
attorney-general 27, 31, 38, 86, 94, 106
conscription 37, 39, 51–4, 65–6, 394
expanding AIF 42–5
First World War 39–83, 116, 392, 393
navy minister 101–2, 106
prime minister 38–83
Second World War 86, 94, 101–2, 106, 119, 141, 151, 163–4, 167
War Cabinet 106, 119
Hulme, Alan 277, 278, 280, 287
Humphrey, Hubert 283
Huntington, Samuel 2
Hussein, Saddam 330, 334, 336, 345, 347, 351, 355, 358, 359, 367, 368, 379–84, 388
Hutton, Lt Gen Edward 13, 14, 23, 24

Imperial Defence Scheme 10
Imperial War Cabinet 61, 64–7, 71–3, 76, 78–9
Indochina 102, 108, 206, 220, 223, 234–6
Indonesia
Bali nightclub bombing 373–4
Confrontation 6, 241, 251–3, 259, 264, 273, 291
East Timor independence 359–61
Industrial Workers of the World 52, 57, 66
information management 351–3, 380, 394
Inspector-General of Commonwealth Military Forces 13, 14
intelligence gathering 156–7, 160, 393

International Force East Timor (INTERFET) 359, 361, 371
Iraq War 6, 326, 356–9, 362, 366–90, 393, 395
  Australian withdrawal 384
  Howard government 356–9, 366–89
  inquiries into 386–7
  leadership 385–9
  planning and preparations 366–82
  Rudd government 384
  start of 382–4
  Task Force 633 374
  weapons of mass destruction (WMD) 358, 367, 373, 376–80, 384–8
Irvine, William 16, 21
Irving, Maj Gen Godfrey 33, 42, 43, 44
Isaksson, Brig Olaf (Zac) 264

Jackson, Brig David 275, 276, 277, 282, 284
James, D Clayton 199
Japan 17, 19, 27–9, 80, 88–91, 100–4, 108–12, 123–205
  commencement of hostilities against 142
  First World War 17, 19, 22, 27, 41, 51, 81
  peace treaty 220
  Second World War 88–91, 100–4, 108–12, 123–205
Jensen, Jens 53
Johnson, Lyndon 3, 262–3, 266, 278, 292, 295, 297, 305
Johnson, Nelson 173
Joint Planning Committee 249, 254, 262–3, 281, 282, 307, 317, 318
Jones, AM George 159–60, 163, 193–7, 208, 209, 212, 227
Jull, David 386
Jull inquiry 386–7

Keating, Paul 328, 336, 340, 344, 345, 349, 359
Kelly, Paul 340
Kennedy Regiment 21
Kenney, Gen George 160, 166, 168, 196
Kent Hughes, Wilfrid 225, 235
Khanh, Gen Nguyen 255
Killen, James 314, 318
King, Adm Ernest 176
King George V 32
Kirkpatrick, Gen George 13
Kitchener, FM Lord 19, 26, 30, 42, 45, 46
Kokoda Trail 6, 162–71
Korean War 6, 206, 215–23, 226–32, 336, 390
Kuwait 330–53
Ky, AVM Nguyen Cao 279, 283

Laos 235, 236, 244, 245–8, 266
Latham, John 125
Lavarack, Lt Gen John 88, 149
Layton, R Adm Edwin 160, 161
Lea, Lt Gen George 290
League of Nations 80, 186, 333
Leahy, Lt Gen Peter 370
Legge, Lt Gen J Gordon 13, 24, 31, 33–4, 37, 43, 44, 48, 55–8, 60, 83
Lewis, Maj Gen Duncan 370
Liberty War Loan 150
Lincoln, Abraham 3
Lloyd George, David 36, 53, 63, 64, 67, 72, 73, 78–80, 131, 394
Long, Maj Gen Charles 279
Long, Gavin 161
Long, Walter 63, 64
Lyons, Joseph 85
Lyttelton, Oliver 136

Macandie, George 13, 15, 16, 21
MacArthur, Gen Douglas 153–204, 211, 217, 391, 392, 394
  Curtin's relationship with 155, 161, 168, 178, 191, 203, 391
  defence of Australia 156–62
  Korean War 217, 218
  Second World War 153–204, 392
MacDonald, Gen Arthur 302, 303, 304, 309, 314, 315
MacDonald, Malcolm 212
Mackay, Lt Gen Iven 114
Mackay, Maj Gen Ken 267–8, 275–9, 284, 292, 294
Major, KW (Bill) 268
Makin, Norman 107, 140, 141, 195, 217
Malaya/Malaysia
  ANZAM area 212, 214, 222, 231, 233, 234, 237
  Emergency 6, 206, 210–14, 220, 225, 238–9, 333
  Far East Strategic Reserve 232, 233, 236–9, 241, 248
  Federation of Malaysia 251
  Indonesian Confrontation 6, 241, 251–3, 259, 264, 273, 291

Malaya/Malaysia *continued*
  Second World War 102–5, 109, 110, 125–32, 137, 144–8, 185
Malta 225, 233, 236
Mao Zedong 207, 210
Maritime Interception Force (MIF) 357, 359
Marshall, Gen George 3, 158, 175
Martin, Alan 131
Massey, William (Bill) 28
Mauz, Adm Henry 342, 343
McBride, Philip 104, 106, 207–9, 213, 218, 220, 224–8, 234
  Cabinet Committee on Defence Preparations 225, 231
  Korean War 218, 227, 228
  Second World War 104, 106
  South-East Asia 230, 234, 235
McCarthy, John 92
McCauley, AM John 197
McCay, Lt Gen James 34, 43, 50, 55–7, 70
McColl, James 21
McEwen, John 106, 119, 141, 151, 235, 241, 246, 298, 299
  Second World War 106, 119, 141, 151
  South-East Asia 235, 241, 246
  Vietnam 250, 265, 268, 272, 280, 298, 310, 324
McGoldrick, Alexander 348–9
McLachlan, Ian 360
McLeay, George 87
McMahon, William 227, 261, 268, 280, 299, 300
  external affairs minister 308
  prime minister 322–5
  Vietnam War 261, 268, 271, 280, 297, 308, 310, 322–5
McNamara, Robert 278, 297
McNarn, Maj Gen Maurie 371, 372, 375, 380, 384, 386, 392
McNeill, Ian 268
McNicoll, V Adm Alan 243, 244, 269, 286–8, 291, 303, 313
McNicoll, Ruth 288
Meaney, Neville 17, 29, 79
Mellersh, AVM Francis 212
Menzies, Robert 84–139, 141, 172, 206–80, 324, 390, 392
  Advisory War Council 107, 109, 141, 151, 181, 394
  Cold War 206–7, 210, 221–3, 233
  Communist Party dissolution 210, 221, 223
  defence expenditure 261
  government in 1950 207–10
  Indonesian Confrontation 252, 265, 273
  Korean War 217–30
  London visits 129–32, 230
  Malayan Emergency 206, 210–13, 333
  Minister for Defence Coordination 87, 103, 133, 135
  National Security Resources Board 221, 225
  Pacific defence policy 230–9
  prime minister 84–139
  resignation as PM 133
  retirement 280
  Second World War 84–139, 141, 151, 172, 181, 207, 222, 390, 393
  Southeast Asia 230–73
  Vietnam War 240, 260–80, 287, 288, 324, 340
Messines 60, 61
Middle East 213, 222–5, 232
  Afghanistan War 6, 326, 356, 357
  continuing commitment 357–9
  Gulf War 6, 326–55
  Iraq War 6, 326, 256–9
  Second World War 94–9, 103, 105, 108, 112–14, 130, 132
Middleton, Karen 362, 367–8
Midway, Battle of 160, 161
military advisers 286–9, 328–30, 361–2
Military Board 13–14, 33, 60, 154
Millen, Edward 10–12, 15, 16, 21, 22, 26, 80
Milner, Lord 73
Monash, Gen John 26, 30, 34, 43, 49, 63, 68–80, 91, 282, 392
Montebello Islands, atomic bomb 231
Moore, John 360
Moore, Maj Gen Newton 56, 57
Moore-Wilton, Max 361
Morshead, Lt Gen Leslie 130, 134
Mountbatten, Adm of Fleet Louis 195
Mullins, Patrick 324
Mulroney, Brian 337
Munro Ferguson, Ronald 11, 14–16, 21, 28, 31, 33, 34, 37, 41, 44, 60, 61, 75
Murdoch, AM Alister 286–8, 293, 304, 314
Murdoch, Keith 35–7, 40, 49, 57, 61, 62, 64, 67–71, 74–5, 82
Murray, Gen Archibald 45, 54
Myers, Gen Richard 363

National Security Committee of Cabinet 360–1, 367, 371, 377, 378, 381, 385, 391, 395
National Security Resources Board 221, 225, 233, 391
National Service scheme 220, 233, 241, 261
Naval Board of Administration 12–13, 15
Nelson, Adm Horatio 3
Netherlands East Indies 104, 110, 126, 138, 148, 149, 185, 187, 202
New Guinea *see* Papua New Guinea
Newton, Douglas 21, 41
Nimitz, Adm Chester 160, 175
Nixon, Richard 306–12, 323
North Atlantic Treaty Organization (NATO) 207, 335, 337, 365
Northcott, Lt Gen John 93–4, 104, 105, 109, 163, 164, 165, 169, 182

Office of National Assessments (ONA) 352, 386, 387
O'Neill, Robert 219, 228, 230
Operation Bastille 380
Operation Bel Isi 359
Operation Desert Fox 358
Operation Desert Shield 331, 342
Operation Slipper 374, 380
Oxenbould, R Adm Chris 348, 349

Pacific War Council 146, 151, 158
Page, Earle 85, 137, 138, 146, 148, 150, 151
Palazzo, Albert 372, 380, 385, 389
Paltridge, Shane 242, 255, 257, 259, 261, 265–80, 288, 324
Papagos, FM Alexandros 120
Papua New Guinea
  Australian territories 171
  First World War 22, 24–5, 28–9, 80
  Kokoda Trail 6, 162–71
  Peace Monitoring Group 359
  Second World War 126, 143, 146, 153–71, 175–7, 180, 185, 186, 190, 193, 197, 203, 290, 392
  truce with Bougainville 359
  unnecessary operations 199–205
Paris Peace Conference 79, 80
Park, ACM Keith 196–7
Passchendaele 63, 64, 72
Patey, Adm George 15, 25, 29
Peach, Col Stuart 216
Peacock, Andrew 314, 318, 319, 320
Pearce, George 12, 19–20, 27–61, 66, 70, 71, 75, 80–3
Petherbridge, Brig Gen Samuel 12, 28
Philippines 153, 156, 186, 187, 189–92, 198
Philpott, AVM Peter 288
Phipps, R Adm Peter 267
Plan Bastille 372
Plimsoll, James 219, 228, 269, 272, 275, 293, 309
Plumer, Gen Herbert 64, 71
Pollard, Lt Gen Reginald 243, 244, 248, 249
Powell, Gen Colin 341, 379
Powell, Janet 351
Prime Minister's War Conference 156–61, 391
Pugsley, Christopher 42

Quat, Phan Huy 270
Queen Elizabeth II 231

Radford, Adm Arthur 224, 231
Rahman, Tunku Abdul 289
Ramsey, Alan 320, 321
Rankin, Wg Cdr Ronald 216
Rawlinson, Gen Henry 70, 71, 77, 78
Ray, Robert 327, 328, 333–45, 349, 352, 353
Reid, George 37
Reith, Peter 360, 364
Rhee, Syngman 215, 228
Ricks, Thomas 395
Ritchie, V Adm Chris 348, 361, 370
Roberts, Andrew 3
Robertson, Lt Gen Horace 211, 217, 218, 226
Robertson, John 83
Robertson, FM William 45, 46, 54, 394
Rommel, FM Erwin 130
Roosevelt, Franklin 133, 144, 145, 148, 153, 175, 176, 177, 185, 191
Rosenthal, Maj Gen Charles 69, 71, 74
Ross, Lloyd 204
Rourke, Brig Henry 169
Rowell, Lt Gen Sydney 5, 105, 114, 166–70, 208, 209, 225, 227, 235
  Indochina 235
  Korea 225, 227
  Second World War 105, 114, 116, 150, 163, 166–70
Royal Air Force (RAF) 92, 100, 197
  Empire Air Training Scheme 92, 95, 98

Royal Australian Air Force (RAAF) 89, 90, 92
  Afghanistan 365
  command 159–60, 195–7, 227–8
  expansion 177
  Gulf War 341
  Iraq War 374, 378, 393
  Korean War 217, 226–9
  Malaya 211, 212, 227, 238, 248
  Middle East 224, 225
  National Service scheme 220
  No 77 (Fighter) Squadron 211, 217, 227, 229
  No 78 (Fighter) Wing 225, 236
  Pacific War (WWII) 100, 142, 181, 188, 193–7
  Thailand 248–9
Royal Australian Navy (RAN) 12, 18–19, 29, 188
  establishment 18–19, 27
  Gulf War 338–42
  Iraq War 374, 378
  Korean War 226, 229
  National Service scheme 220
  release of Australian ships 91
  reserve 25
Royal Australian Regiment (RAR)
  1 RAR 227, 238, 267, 274–7, 282, 289, 324
  2 RAR 238, 282, 311
  3 RAR 211, 218, 221, 227, 238, 252–3, 259, 265, 282, 302
  4 RAR 281, 289, 290
  5 RAR 282
  6 RAR 282, 292, 311
  7 RAR 282, 302
  8 RAR 282, 311, 315, 317
  Malaya 211, 218, 227, 238, 252
  Vietnam 265, 270, 274–7, 281–2, 289, 290, 302, 311
Royal Military College, Duntroon 60, 243, 300
Royle, Adm Guy 133–4, 142, 145, 149, 159, 194, 195
Rudd, Kevin 384
Ruddock, Philip 360
Rumsfeld, Donald 367
Rusk, Dean 248, 268, 270

Salmon, Brig John 320
Samuel, Peter 321
Saunders, ACM Hugh 196
Schedvin, CB (Boris) 183
Scherger, ACM Frederick 197, 242, 243, 256, 260, 263, 267–79, 287–8
  Vietnam War 260, 263, 267–9, 275–9, 282, 287–8
Schieffer, Tom 364
Schultz, George 334
Scott, Ernest 27
Scowcroft, Lt Gen Brent 347–8
Scullin, James 107
Second World War 6, 84–205, 390
  AIF *see* Australian Imperial Force (2nd AIF)
  conscription 171–3
  Curtin government 136–205
  Europe 6, 115–23
  Fadden government 133
  key decisions 91–3
  Menzies government 84–139, 207, 390
  Middle East 94–9, 103, 105, 108, 112–14, 130, 132, 222
  Pacific War 2, 6, 89–90, 100, 123–205
  'Phoney War' 98
  unnecessary operations 199–205
Secretaries Committee on National Security 361, 391
Sellheim, Maj Gen Victor 4, 21, 33, 43, 47, 49
September 11 terrorist attacks 356, 359, 365, 367–9
Serle, Geoffrey 70, 77
Serong, Brig FP (Ted) 248, 254, 255
Sexton, Michael 263
Shackleton V Adm David 361, 370
Shalders, V Adm Russ 370
Sharp, Adm Ulysses 267, 268
Shaw, Patrick 268, 272
Shedden, Frederick 86–9, 208–9, 217, 222–5
  Advisory War Council 107, 110, 119, 141, 155, 208
  ANZUS Council 230
  Defence Committee 209, 212, 214, 232
  Defence secretary 86, 208
  Korean War 218, 220, 223
  Malayan Emergency 213
  Middle East 223–5, 232
  Prime Minister's War Conference 156, 158, 159
  Second World War 86–9, 101, 107, 110–19, 130, 131, 138–48, 155–9, 175–6, 179, 182, 187–209
  Southeast Asia 232, 235, 237

visiting US and Britain 187–9
War Cabinet 86–9, 119, 140–3, 146, 148, 183, 192, 208, 213
Sheffield, Gary 3
Shergold, Peter 377
Shinwell, Emanuel 224
Shortt, Maj Gen Arthur 232
signals intelligence 156–7, 160
Sinclair-MacLagan, Maj Gen Ewen 69, 74
Singapore 94–6, 100, 104, 109, 110, 125, 128, 130, 137, 147–9
Singapore Strategy 88, 105, 234
Sinn Fein 66
Slim, FM William 214, 224
Smith, Richard (Ric) 376–7
Smith, Adm Victor 287, 317–18, 320
Smyth, Maj Gen Nevill 55, 69
Solomon Islands 153, 158, 161, 162, 165, 172, 177
Somme offensive 48, 50
South-East Asia 230–73, 394
South-East Asia Treaty Organisation (SEATO) 236, 244–7, 252, 259, 319
South Seas Regional Commission 186
Southwest Pacific Area (SWPA) 154, 159, 161, 172–8, 182, 185, 187, 194
Soviet Union 206, 207, 210, 213, 220–3
Spartalis, Peter 53
Special Air Service (SAS)
Afghanistan War 364, 365, 366, 370
Iraq War 358, 374, 375, 378, 383
Vietnam War 241, 252, 265, 289
Spee, Adm Maximilian von 25, 29
Spender, Percy 84, 100, 106, 107, 112–15
Advisory War Council 107, 113, 124, 141, 151
ANZUS Council 230
Australian ambassador in Washington 224, 228, 230
external affairs minister 207, 209, 214
Korean War 218–19, 222
Second World War 84, 100, 106, 107, 112–15, 121, 124, 135, 141, 151, 169
Spooner, William 225
Squires, Lt Gen Ernest 88, 90, 94, 98, 194
Stalin, Joseph 3, 210
Stephens, Alan 159, 197, 286
Stewart, Frederick 87
Storey, John 110
Strategic Command Division 361, 367, 369, 371, 372
Strategic Command Group 362, 381
Strategic Operations Division 372
Strategic Policy Coordination Group 361
Street, Geoffrey 87, 98, 104, 112
Sturdee, Lt Gen Vernon 104–5, 113–15, 121, 142, 145, 149–50, 163, 209
Suharto, President 291, 359
Sukarno, President 251, 264, 291
Supreme War Council 74
Sutherland, Lt Gen Richard 158, 166, 176–7
Swift, Jonathan 1

Taliban government 362, 363, 365
Tange, Arthur 219, 233, 237, 243, 244, 263, 264, 269, 272, 314, 317, 320–2
Taylor, Gen Maxwell 270, 295
Taylor, V Adm Rod 329, 335, 336, 349
terrorism 363–74
al-Qaeda 362–6
Bali nightclub bombing 373–4
coalition against 364
Communist Terrorists (Malaya) 207, 212, 239
Iraq hostages 340
Operation Slipper 374, 380
September 11 attacks 356, 359, 365, 367–9
Thailand 235, 245–9, 266
Thatcher, Margaret 3
Thawley, Michael 367
Thomson, Brig David 289–90
Till, Geoffrey 3
Titheridge, AVM Alan 361, 369
Tobruk 115, 119, 130, 134–7, 392
Townley, Athol 242, 250
Trading with the Enemy Bill 27
Tropical Force 28–9
Truman, Harry 210, 219, 224, 228, 230
Trumble, Thomas 12, 56

Unger, Leonard 268
United Nations 334
Afghanistan 363, 365
Commission on Iraq (UNSCOM) 358, 359, 367, 384
Iraq 330–2, 338, 340, 343–50, 357, 358, 376, 379–84
Korea 215–16, 222, 228
Security Council 218, 331–2, 338, 343–7, 376, 379–82
Universal Service League 36

universal training scheme 18, 19, 24, 27
US Central Command (CENTCOM) 363, 364, 369, 370, 374
US Civil War 3
US Joint Chiefs of Staff 161, 162, 174, 175, 177, 201, 363
US Navy Fleet Radio Unit Melbourne (FRUMEL) 156–7

Vien, Gen Cao Van 283
Vietnam War 3, 6, 206, 240, 254–325, 390, 392
  1 ATF 284–5, 292–6, 302, 307–9, 317, 319, 323
  Australian Army Force (AAFV) 275, 282, 289
  Australian Army Training Team (AATTV) 248, 249, 254–6, 266, 323
  Australian commitment 265–70, 277–83
  Calwell opposing 333
  Civil Action affair 319–23
  conscription 240, 256–61
  Gorton government 298–322, 325
  Holt government 241, 268, 272, 279–98
  Honolulu conference 267
  McMahon government 322–5
  Menzies government 240–79, 324
  military advisers 286–8
  Military Assistance Command Vietnam (MACV) 247
  Phuoc Tuy Province 283–6, 292, 295, 311
  protests 240
  Rolling Thunder campaign 267
  Tonkin Gulf incident 255, 258
  Tropical Warfare establishment 262
  Viet Cong Tet Offensive 301–3
  withdrawal 307–25
Vietnamization 306, 308, 309, 311, 312
Vincent, Maj Gen Douglas (Tim) 294, 295, 302
Vines, Maj Gen John 373
volunteerism 28

Walker, Lt Gen Harold 34, 69
Waller, Keith 270, 272, 297
Walls, V Adm Rob 339
Walpole, Horace 1, 7
War Book 220
War Census 36, 46
war leadership 2–7
  Australian 4–7, 80–1, 390–5
  books on 3
  civil–military tension 5
  modern 385–9
War Office 20, 24, 31, 46, 47, 49, 54, 62, 64, 86
War Precautions Act 27, 39, 52
Ward, EJ (Eddie) 181
warfare as game 1
Watson, JC (Chris) 32, 36
Watt, Alan 209–10, 214–15, 218, 219, 227, 230, 233
Watt, William 66, 67, 69, 75
Wavell, Gen Archibald 113–21, 134, 149, 150, 152
Wells, Lt Gen Henry 226, 242
West, Stewart 345
Western Desert 111, 114, 115, 118
Western Front 66–8, 72, 95
Westmoreland, Gen William 255, 275–6, 283–5, 289, 292–5, 302, 306
Weyand, Gen Frederick 302
Whiskard, Geoffrey 95
White Australia policy 17, 41, 80
White, Gen Cyril Brudenell 14, 16, 20–3, 70–5, 101–5
  First World War 16, 20–3, 42, 43, 56, 57, 63, 64, 68, 70–5
  Second World War 98, 101–2
White, Hugh 339, 344, 388
Whitington, Don 281
Whitlam, Gough 299, 324
Williams, Daryl 360
Williams, Pete 352
Williams, AM Richard 88, 89
Wilson, Harold 265
Wilson, Gen Henry 73, 75, 76, 78
Wilson, Roland 244
Wilson, Woodrow 79, 80
Wilton, Gen John 227, 244, 251, 254–7, 273–8, 281–318
  Indonesian Confrontation 251, 254–5
  Vietnam 256, 257, 260, 264, 267, 269, 273–8, 281–318, 392
Wolfowitz, Paul 367
Woodard, Garry 263, 264, 388
Woodward, Bob 390
Woomera, atomic bomb 231
Wright, Tony 371